NETWARE® 3.11/3.12:
Network Administrator

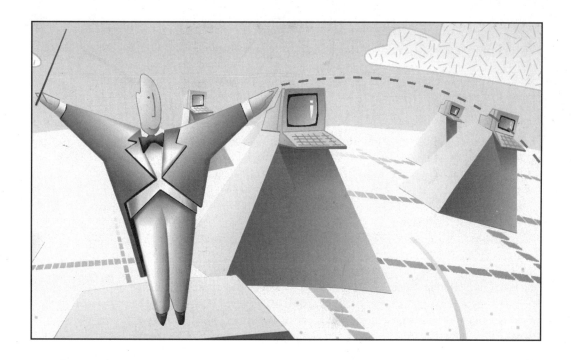

Ted L. Simpson

A DIVISION OF COURSE TECHNOLOGY
ONE MAIN STREET, CAMBRIDGE, MA 02142

an International Thomson Publishing company I(T)P®

Cambridge • Albany • Bonn • Boston • Cincinnati • London • Madrid • Melbourne • Mexico City
New York • Paris • San Francisco • Singapore • Tokyo • Toronto • Washington

NetWare 3.11/3.12: Network Administrator is published by CTI.

Managing Editor	Mac Mendelsohn
Product Manager	Karla Mitchell
Production Editor	Christine Spillett
Cover Designer	John Gamache

© 1995 by CTI.
A Division of Course Technology—I(T)P®
For more information contact:
Course Technology
One Main Street
Cambridge, MA 02142

International Thomson Publishing Europe
Berkshire House 168-173
High Holborn
London WCIV 7AA
England

International Thomson Publishing GmbH
Königswinterer Strasse 418
53227 Bonn
Germany

Thomas Nelson Australia
102 Dodds Street
South Melbourne, 3205
Victoria, Australia

International Thomson Publishing Asia
211 Henderson Road
#05-10 Henderson Building
Singapore 0315

Nelson Canada
1120 Birchmount Road
Scarborough, Ontario
Canada M1K 5G4

International Thomson Publishing
Hirakawacho Kyowa Building, 3F
2-2-1 Hirakawacho
Chiyoda-ku, Tokyo 102
Japan

International Thomson Editores
Campos Eliseos 385, Piso 7
Col. Polanco
11560 Mexico D.F. Mexico

Trademarks

Disclaimer

Course Technology reserves the right to revise this publication and make changes from time to time in its content without notice.
1-56527-282-X
Printed in the United States of America
10 9 8 7 6 5 4

PREFACE

This *NetWare v3.11/3.12: Network Administrator* book will provide you with an in-depth study of networks based on Novell's NetWare v3.1x local area network operating system. One of the primary goals of this book is providing you with the knowledge and skills you need to pass the Novell Certified NetWare Administrator exam upon completion of the course. The knowledge and skills presented in this book, along with the CNA designation, will put you in a position to take advantage of the many opportunities taking place in the rapidly growing and changing field of local area networks. Each chapter in the book contains a detailed explanation of networking concepts and techniques and examples containing numerous screen shots and diagrams that easily allow you to learn the NetWare commands and utilities. Starting with basic networking concepts, the chapters progressively build on your knowledge of networking, showing you how to implement and manage a network system based on NetWare v3.1x. In addition, each chapter includes a command summary, key terms list, and review questions to help you study for the CNA exam. One of the unique features of this book is the comprehensive set of exercises, case studies, and continuing problems included at the end of each chapter. The continuing problems give you a feel for using NetWare in the "real world" by allowing you to apply the techniques and utilities learned in each chapter to build a network system for a simulated organization. Because these projects progressively build on each other, by the last chapter you will have the experience of creating a complete, working, network system that will help you implement and maintain networks on the job.

NetWare Versions

Since its introduction in the early 1980s, NetWare has gone through three major revisions starting with NetWare v2.x in 1986, NetWare v3.1 in 1990, and NetWare v4.1 in 1994. While this book uses NetWare v3.12 for all screen shots and examples, the similarity between v3.11 and v3.12 allow the material to be easily adapted using the notes and comments which have been included in the chapters where there are significant differences between the two versions. The biggest difference between NetWare v3.11 and v3.12 is in the installation process and the new menu system found in v3.12. Chapter 5 contains information on installing either v3.11 and v3.12 on both the file server and workstation computers. However, chapter 13 covers only the new NetWare v3.12

menu system so if you will be working on a NetWare v3.11 file server you will need to either obtain the new menu software from Novell, or refer to the NetWare v3.11 reference materials to implement the older menu system.

Although NetWare v4.1 is a significantly different environment, the concepts covered in chapters 1 through 3 along with the login script commands and menu system described in chapters 12 and 13 can be applied to both v3.1x and v4.1. In addition, both NetWare v3.1x and v4.1 have similar console commands and NetWare loadable modules allowing the material covered in the last two chapters to be relevant for NetWare v4.1 as well as v3.1x. As a result, much of what you will be learning from this book and course can be applied to the new NetWare v4.1 operating system.

Text and Graphic Conventions

In addition to the normal text discussions, each chapter in this book contains one or more of the following icons representing notes, trends, and factoids:

The note icons are used to present additional helpful material related to the subject being described.

The factoid icons provide relevant information intended to provide you with additional insight into the development or use of certain concepts or commands.

The trend icons are intended to provide you with relevant information about future directions in the computer industry. Trends can help you to see the current and future value of the concepts and techniques you are learning in the chapter.

Exercises

Hands-on exercises at the end of each chapter provide you with the opportunity to practice using various commands and techniques presented in the chapter. Each hands-on exercise is intended to stand alone allowing you to do just the exercises that will help you the most. Case study exercises allow you to apply certain commands, concepts, and techniques learned in the chapter to solving a problem in a simulated business or organization. The Superior Technical College problems included at the end of each chapter contain a continuing project that puts you in the position of a newly hired NetWare technician setting up a Novell NetWare system under the direction of a NetWare administrator for the college campus. Each chapter's step-by-step problems will walk you through the tasks required to achieve a particular network goal. By the end of the book you will have implemented a working network system for the college thereby gaining the experience of applying NetWare to an actual job environment.

To perform your chapter exercises and problems, your instructor will assign you to a file server and provide you with a user name, password, student reference number, and home directory. The reference number is needed to separate the users, groups, and other objects you create on your assigned file server from those of other students. Your user name has been granted the ability to create and manage other users and groups without having access to the entire file server in order to prevent mistakes made by you or other students from affecting the work of others. The home directory is your work area on your assigned file server where you have been given all rights to create and manage files and directories for exercises and case studies. In addition to your home directory, you will also be assigned a directory in which you are to create your Superior Technical College files and directories. Your instructor will provide you with information regarding your user name and the names and locations of your directories.

Supplements

Instructor's Manual

The Instructor's Manual is written by the author and is quality-assurance tested. It includes:

■ Answers and solutions to all the Questions, Exercises, and Case Problems.

■ A 3.5-inch disk containing solutions to all the Questions, Exercises, and Case Problems.

■ Transparency Masters of key concepts.

Test Bank   The Test Bank contains 50 questions per tutorial in true/false, multiple choice, and fill-in-the-blank formats, plus two essay questions. Each question has been quality-assurance tested by students to achieve clarity and accuracy.

Electronic Test Bank   The Electronic Test Bank allows instructors to edit individual test questions, select questions individually or at random, and print out scrambled versions of the same test to any supported printer.

File Server Setup Disk

See the inside front or inside back cover for details on how to obtain a copy of this disk. The setup program is used to establish student accounts and work areas along with uploading a copy of the Student Work disk to the file server. One of the students first assignments is to copy the contents of the Student Work disk onto a blank disk for use in the exercises.

Student Work Disk

In order to do the exercises and problems at the end of each chapter, you will need a copy of the Student Work disk. See the inside front or inside back cover for details on how to obtain a copy of this disk. This disk contains sample files and applications which you will be using in your Superior Technical College project. The Student Work disk also contains a self study testing system to help you test your Novell NetWare knowledge and aid you in studying for tests including the Novell CNA test. In addition to the study program, you will probably want to obtain a copy of Novell's CNA Evaluation disk. This disk will help you determine your level of NetWare knowledge prior to taking the actual CNA exam.

Other Resources

In addition to this book, CTI offers the following books for students of Novell NetWare:

Hands-On NetWare 3.11/3.12

The *Hands-On NetWare v3.11/3.12* book provides a project oriented approach to learning NetWare v3.11/3.12 by actually setting up a network system. Each chapter in this book describes how a network administrator uses NetWare commands and utilities to progressively implement each step of the network system. Problems at the end of the chapter allow the student to apply the same NetWare commands and utilities to setting up a similar network in a different setting.

Hands-On NetWare v4.1

The *Hands-On NetWare v4.1* book provides a project oriented approach to learning NetWare v4.1 by actually setting up a network system. Each chapter in this book describes how a network administrator uses NetWare commands and utilities to progressively implement each step of the network system. Problems at the end of the chapter allow the student to apply the same NetWare commands and utilities to setting up a similar network in a different setting.

Novell NetWare v4.1: Network Administrator

The *Novell NetWare v4.1: Network Administrator* book is organized in the same manner as this book but contains complete coverage of the NetWare v4.1 system and utilities, including the new Network Directory Services (NDS).

Acknowledgments

Creating a book of this magnitude is an incredibly complex process with many people involved in editing, artwork, reviewing, testing, and coordinating changes. For the last year I have never been far from a computer spending time nearly every day researching and writing. While I have spent a great many hours writing the book, it would have never been completed without the help of many others. I especially owe many thanks to my editor Robert Epp, whose vision and technical advice has helped to shape and polish this book into a valuable product. The credit for making this book so useful goes to the CTI staff, especially Kim Crowley and Karla Mitchell, who have had the difficult job of coordinating all the tasks and maintaining the schedule despite deadlines that slipped by too often. Thanks is also due to the excellent reviewers including Behrouz Forouzan (De Anza College), Pam McGlasson (San Mateo College), and Norman Hahn (Thomas Nelson Community College) who added important comments and suggestions that I have incorporated into the finished book. I feel very fortunate to have had Jeffrey Andrews and William Fletcher from the Systems Group, Inc. perform the complex and detailed job of testing the exercises and verifying the technical content of the materials.

I want to thank my wife Mary whose loving and patient help enabled me to complete this project. In addition, any success this book achieves is ultimately due to my parents, William and Rosemarie, who have made many sacrifices to provide a stable and motivating environment for learning and growing. I would also like to acknowledge Phil Soltis, Bert Richard, Tom Lemler, and Lois Eichman at Wisconsin Indianhead Technical College for maintaining our school as a leader in the area of Novell Education. A special thank you is due to Gary Clark, K. C. Sue, Joe Rostowsky, and Wayne Larsen of Novell's Education department for their support in bringing Novell education to the college. Finally, I would like to dedicate this book to the Computer Information System students at WITC, and other colleges, who are taking on the challenge of becoming computer networking professionals. I hope this text and its exercises will help prepare you to succeed in your goals.

TABLE OF CONTENTS

NOVELL NETWARE 3.11/3.12: NETWORK ADMINISTRATOR

READ THIS BEFORE YOU BEGIN

To the Student

To use this book, you must have a Student Work Disk. See the inside front or inside back cover for details on how to obtain a copy of the Student Work Disk. Since most of the hands-on exercises in this book require access to a file server, your workstation will need to be connected to a network and your instructor will provide you with a valid username on your assigned file server.

To the Instructor

Setting up the classroom file server. To complete the exercises and projects in this book, your students will need to access a classroom file server. Providing student access to the classroom file server involves creating a username and two directories for each student along with copying some sample files and uploading the Student Work Disk. To help you perform the file server setup process, Course Technology, Inc. has provided a special File Server Setup Disk. See the inside front or inside back cover for details on how to obtain copies of the Student Work Disk and the File Server Setup Disk. To setup your classroom file server, follow the instructions in the README file located on the File Server Setup Disk. Complete file server setup instructions are also included at the beginning of your Instructor's Manual.

README File. The README.TXT file located on the File Server Setup Disk provides additional notes on performing the file server setup process. You can view the README.TXT file using any word processor or text editor.

System Requirements

The minimum software and hardware requirements for each network lab computer are as follows:

- A 286 or higher processor with a minimum of 1 MB RAM (386 recommended)
- VGA monitor
- A network card cabled to the classroom file server
- A hard disk drive with 10 MB free is highly recommended
- NetWare client software necessary to log in to the file server
- DOS v5.0 or higher (if the computer has a hard drive, DOS should be installed on the hard drive)
- At least one high density disk drive

The minimum file server hardware requirements are as follow:

- A 386 or higher computer system with a minimum of 8 MB RAM
- A volume with at least 4 MB free for each student's directories
- At least 60 MB disk space for the SYS volume, sample files and print queues

NETWORKING BASICS

The decade of the 1980s brought about a major change in the way data has traditionally been processed, moving from centralized processing on mini and mainframe computers to decentralized or distributed personalized applications and productivity tools running on desktop and notebook-sized microcomputers. Along with the rapid development of microcomputer hardware and application software has come the ability to connect these devices and applications together in order to share resources and communicate among users. In this chapter you will learn about the role that you will play as a network administrator in this exciting area and specifically how Novell's NetWare system can be used to meet the requirements and challenges you will face when integrating microcomputers into a community that can share resources as well as allow diverse systems to communicate and exchange data.

AFTER READING THIS CHAPTER AND COMPLETING THE EXERCISES YOU WILL BE ABLE TO:

- DESCRIBE THE RESPONSIBILITIES OF A CERTIFIED NETWARE ADMINISTRATOR.

- IDENTIFY AND DESCRIBE THE HARDWARE AND SOFTWARE COMPONENTS THAT MAKE UP A LOCAL AREA NETWORK.

- DEVELOP A RECOMMENDATION FOR THE IMPLEMENTATION OF A LOCAL AREA NETWORK SYSTEM.

CNA RESPONSIBILITIES

The microcomputer networking field is an exciting arena with new developments occurring on an almost daily basis. As a Certified NetWare Administrator (CNA) your job will be to provide the knowledge necessary to direct your organization's networking services and support in order to meet the workgroup-oriented processing needs of microcomputer users. As briefly mentioned in the introduction to this book, the Certified NetWare Administrator (CNA) program was developed by Novell in 1992 to help define the role of network administrators in a NetWare environment by providing a standard of knowledge and performance that organizations can use to help ensure the quality of network administration and support. Becoming a CNA involves demonstrating your knowledge and ability with microcomputers and NetWare local area networks by passing a certification exam at a Novell-authorized testing center. In Appendix A you will find more information on Novell's CNA program and how to register for the CNA exam as well as how to obtain a CNA self-evaluation test disk that you can use to help determine your readiness to take the test.

To develop the CNA program, Novell researched the job duties of thousands of NetWare network administrators around the world in order to determine the common tasks that need to be performed by network administrators on a regular basis. The sections that follow summarize Novell's research and will provide you insight into the typical duties you will be performing as a network administrator as well as an overview of the NetWare knowledge and skills you will need in order to achieve your goal of becoming a Certified NetWare Administrator.

UNDERSTANDING NETWARE COMPONENTS AND COMMANDS

One of the fundamentals a NetWare administrator needs is a solid foundation in the components that make up a NetWare network and how they interoperate. When a problem—such as the message "File server not found"—occurs on a workstation attached to the network, the network administrator must be able to troubleshoot the network and isolate the cause of the error by drawing upon his or her knowledge of the network components.

Just as a mechanic must learn how to use the tools necessary to maintain and repair an automobile, a CNA will need to know how to use the many NetWare commands and utilities to be able to apply the correct tool needed to perform network maintenance and repair tasks such as creating users, granting access rights, listing directory information, and working with printers. Starting with this chapter and continuing throughout the book, you will be learning how to use the commands and utilities that are essential tools that CNAs use daily.

SUPPORTING CLIENT WORKSTATION ENVIRONMENTS

The majority of computers attached to NetWare networks today run either the DOS or Windows operating system, and therefore, as a CNA, you will need to know how to install and configure the client software used to attach DOS or Windows workstations to the network and establish communications. With the rapid advances in microcomputer technology that require organizations to add new computers and replace existing ones each year, one of your main CNA tasks will be to install and update client software regularly.

In addition to the DOS and Windows workstations, your organization might also need to provide network support for Apple Macintosh and Unix-based computers. While Novell does not currently require a CNA to install client software on Macintosh and Unix operating systems, you will need to be able to identify how the NetWare software components allow Unix and Macintosh computers to attach to a NetWare network.

DESIGNING A WORKABLE DIRECTORY STRUCTURE

A network directory structure defines the way in which the data storage of your file server(s) is organized. You might already be aware of how a good directory structure on your workstation's local hard disk makes it easier to run applications and access files. On a file server, a good directory structure becomes even more important because many users share the same storage device. As a result, one of the most important tasks a CNA must undertake when installing a new file server is planning and implementing an efficient directory structure to support the processing needs of the users. In this book you will learn the essential NetWare directory components as well as the design techniques that will help you create and maintain a workable network directory structure.

ESTABLISHING AND MAINTAINING NETWORK USERS AND SECURITY

NetWare has a very sophisticated security system that allows the network administrator to provide users with the access they need to certain information while at the same time protecting special information from unauthorized access. To implement this security system, as a CNA you will need to create a user account for each person who will access the network and then assign the appropriate security restrictions such as passwords and other limitations that you feel are necessary to protect user accounts from unauthorized access. In addition, in order to access files on the network, users need to be given access rights to the directories and files they will be using by assigning these rights to groups or individual users. In Chapters 7 and 8, you will learn how to use NetWare utilities and commands to create users and groups as well as assign the necessary rights to access the network file system. Because organizational structures continually change, an ongoing task you will have as a CNA is to add and delete users as well as modify the rights assigned to users and groups.

SETTING UP AND MAINTAINING NETWORK PRINTING

Perhaps one of the most complex and demanding tasks of a network administrator is creating and maintaining the network printing environment. Network printing has become an increasingly important issue on networks with sophisticated applications such as desktop publishing and WYSIWYG (what you see is what you get) word processors and spreadsheets. These applications require expensive high-resolution laser and ink-jet printers that are often shared in order to justify their cost. As a CNA, you will find that you need to continue to upgrade your network printing environment in order to support faster and more sophisticated printers and applications as they become available. In this book you will learn how to use the NetWare printing components and tools that allow you to install and maintain a network printing environment that will meet the network printing needs of your users.

LOADING AND UPDATING APPLICATION SOFTWARE

An ongoing and important job of the network administrator is installing and upgrading application software packages that run on the client workstations. Whenever possible you will want to install applications on the file server so they can be shared and centrally maintained. However, some applications will not run from a file server, or will run much more efficiently when installed on the workstation's local hard drive. As a CNA, you will need to be familiar with installing and configuring many different application software packages as well as how to support these packages on either the file server or local workstations. An ongoing job of the CNA is to obtain and install software upgrades as well as respond to user questions and problems. As a result, CNAs often find that they need to be "jacks of all trades" as well as have the strong interpersonal skills sometimes required to work with frustrated or angry users.

Another responsibility of the network administrator is policing copyright licenses of application software to be sure your organization always has enough licenses to cover the number of users that are running the applications. This task can be very important because your company can be exposed to a lawsuit and fined if it is found in violation of copyright laws. To make the CNA's responsibility easier, some companies provide software that will count the number of users that are currently using a software package and not allow more users than the number you have identified according to your software licenses.

CREATING AN AUTOMATED USER ENVIRONMENT

Providing users with an easy-to-use system that prompts them to enter their username whenever they boot their workstation and then presents them with a simple menu containing their applications is another important task you will have as a network administrator. In order that CNAs can set up and maintain an easy-to-use network environment, Novell requires them to know how to use NetWare utilities to create and maintain login script files as well as NetWare menus. In Chapters 11 and 12, you will learn how to use NetWare login scripts and menus to create a user-friendly network environment that will allow users on your network to log into their assigned file server easily and immediately bring up menus that allow them to select and run their software applications.

DEVELOPING AND IMPLEMENTING A BACKUP AND RECOVERY SYSTEM

Information is the life blood of an organization, and as a CNA you will be the guardian of the information stored on the local area network system. One of the worst nightmares a CNA can have is a file server crashing with the loss of all the network information stored on its hard drives. To prevent this catastrophe and allow you to sleep easier, you will need to be sure your file server environment is as reliable as possible and that you have a good backup system that you feel confident can be used to restore all the programs and data on your server in the event of a major system failure. In this chapter you will learn about the fail safe measures that can be implemented on NetWare file servers and how you can develop system specifications that will provide you with a reliable and fault-tolerant system. No matter how reliable or fault-tolerant a system is, however, you still need to be prepared for a worst case scenario, such as your building being destroyed or the equipment being damaged by an electrical failure or lightning. In Chapter 15 you will learn how to plan for disasters by implementing a backup and recovery system using the NetWare Storage Management System and utilities.

MANAGING THE FILE SERVER AND MONITOR NETWORK PERFORMANCE

A NetWare file server has its own operating system and console commands that allow a network administrator to control the server environment as well as run special software called **NetWare Loadable Modules (NLMs)** in order to perform certain tasks or add new services. As a result, a CNA will need to spend some time each week at the file server console using console commands and utilities to monitor server activity as well as adding new services and modifying or configuring existing ones.

Network performance can sometimes falter with the addition of users to the network, large printing loads, and the ever-increasing demands by the high-speed workstations needed for graphics applications. As a CNA, you will regularly need to monitor your network system as well as the file server in order to detect performance bottlenecks or problems and then determine if additional hardware or configuration changes are necessary. In Chapter 16, you will learn about several common network problems that are caused by insufficient hardware as well as how to configure your server and workstations to help improve performance and avoid problems.

SUPPORTING NETWORK COMMUNICATIONS

In addition to allowing users to share resources on a file server, an important use of a local area network is communication among users as well as access to a mini or mainframe computer. One of the most common and rapidly growing segments of local area network communications is electronic mail and "suites" of office applications. As a CNA, you will be expected to help implement, maintain, and administer an electronic mail or suite of applications in your organization. Novell has also provided NetWare with a built-in message delivery system called the Message Handling Services (MHS). In Chapter 14, you will learn how to install MHS on a file server as well as perform the functions necessary to administer an electronic mail system that allows network users to send and receive messages and files.

NETWORKING SYSTEMS

The job responsibilities described in the previous section show that the network administrator has one of the most exciting, challenging, and important jobs in an organization's information systems department. However, it can also be one of the most frustrating jobs due to the rapid changes in the field and the need to be involved with many different responsibilities ranging from application software and operating systems to hardware and cable systems. Therefore, in order to prepare to be a successful CNA, you will need to build a strong understanding of the basic components that make up the network system. This background will act as a foundation upon which you can build the skills you will need in order to become a CNA and perform your job responsibilities. In this section you will learn about the basic components that make up a local area network (LAN) system as well as some of the different options you will need to consider.

Before getting into the components that make up a local area network, you need to understand what a LAN is and how it differs from traditional mini or mainframe computers. A **local area network** or **LAN** is a high-speed communication system consisting of cables and cards (hardware) along with instructions (software) that provides a means for different types of computers to communicate and share resources over short distances such as within a building or room. One of the major differences between a LAN and a mini computer system is that, with a mini computer, all the processing is done by the mini computer running the programs. The workstations are simply used as input and output devices for entering data and displaying results. This type of processing is called **centralized processing** because all the processing is done by the "central" mini computer.

Because a LAN is basically a high-speed communication system, the processing is performed by programs running on the workstations rather than on a central host computer. The LAN is primarily used to allow the workstations to have access to shared data files and other hardware devices such as printers, which are necessary to perform the processing requests. This type of processing is referred to as distributed processing because the processing is distributed to each of the workstations.

LAN ADVANTAGES

While distributed processing can be performed by standalone computers without the use of a network, a LAN offers many advantages that make distributed processing a strong competitor of traditional centralized mini and mainframe computer systems.

As a network administrator, you need to be aware of the six following LAN advantages in order to help you prepare a recommendation for a network system.

Cost Savings

In order to justify implementing a network system to the accounting staff of a company, you will probably need to show them that the system will save money for the organization. The most direct cost savings a LAN will provide involves sharing expensive computer hardware such as disk drives, CD-ROMs, printers, and communication devices such as modems. For example, assume your company needs to install an application package that requires 75 Mbytes of disk space along with access to a high-resolution laser printer on ten different computers. The simple spreadsheets in Figure 1-1 compare the cost of implementing this system on standalone computers versus sharing the application software package and laser printer on a network server.

Figure 1-1

Network cost savings

Standalone Computers

Component	Qty	Cost	Value
Disk Space	10 × 75 Mbytes	$1.50 per Mbytes	$1,125.00
Printers	10	$1,500.00	$15,000.00
Total			$16,125.00

Network Savings

Component	Qty	Cost	Value
Disk Space	75 Mbytes	$1.50 per Mbytes	$112.50
Printers	2	$1,500.00	$3,000.00
Total			$3,112.50

Time Savings

A less tangible, but perhaps even more important advantage of networks is the time saved by providing users with access to shared data and communication capability. Without a LAN, users have to resort to what is commonly called "sneaker net" where shared files are copied onto a floppy disk and physically transferred to another user's computer workstation by being carried on foot and copied to another hard drive.

Another time savings advantage of LANs is that they allow the network administrator to install and maintain a software package in one location (on the server) rather than installing the package many times on each workstation and then having to spend additional time going to each workstation in order to configure the software or install an upgrade.

Centralized Data

Without a network, certain critical and often-used data files, such as customer and inventory files, might need to be duplicated on several workstations, resulting in redundant data storage and the inherent difficulty of keeping all files current. Storing database files on the network file server allows the information to be kept current while also enabling many users to have access to it. The ability to have shared access to centralized database files allows the LAN to provide a competitive alternative to centralized processing on a mini or mainframe computer.

In addition to providing shared access to centralized data files, a network file server used for centralized data storage facilitates regular backups and establishing a disaster recovery system. Data stored on workstations is rarely backed up, making it very difficult for users to recover lost data in the event of a workstation crash or physical damage to the building or equipment. On the other hand, keeping all of an organization's critical data on the network file server allows you to make a backup each night and store weekly backups off-site to provide recovery in the event of damage to the building. Disaster recovery is also greatly simplified and restoring the software and data onto a new file server can allow the organization to get up and running again very quickly. In contrast, the alternative entails finding and restoring software and data to individual workstations.

Security

At first glance, centralizing company data on a network file server might appear to cause more security problems than it solves. In the case of NetWare file servers, however, data can be made more secure on the server than data stored on local workstations. The reason is that NetWare provides many security features, such as restricting access to certain network directories to certain users and then requiring users to identify themselves by using a password. In addition, user accounts can be limited to accessing the system only during the normal working day from a specific workstation, making it difficult for an intruder to gain access to the system by logging in with another user's name and password after normal office hours. Compare those security advantages to the alternative of storing data on a local workstation, where anyone with a little knowledge of DOS and physical access to the office can sit down at the computer and access the applications and data, and the benefits of using NetWare to centralize sensitive data are clear.

Fault Tolerance

When data is stored on standalone workstations there is an increased probability for data loss due to operator error, software bugs, computer viruses, or hardware failure on the workstation. Data stored on the network can be placed on file server computers that are specially designed and configured to provide protection against loss of data due to software or hardware problems on the workstation. For example, with a NetWare file server, the data stored on disk drives can be synchronized through a process called mirroring in order to prevent a failure of one drive from making the data inaccessible.

Communication

Because a LAN provides high-speed communication system computers, workgroup-oriented applications such as electronic mail and scheduling are facilitating major changes in the way offices are managed. Electronic mail applications allow users to send messages and files around the office quickly and efficiently. Many users feel electronic mail is quicker and more effective than voice mail messages and many times solves the problem of playing "phone tag" with people who are hard to reach.

Scheduling applications can save time by allowing managers to check the schedules of people and facilities quickly in order to find a free time to schedule meetings.

 Network communication systems are rapidly incorporating support for new applications that utilize both video and voice data. Video conferencing and the integration of computers with telephone systems are just beginning to become popular in office environments and could see widespread use in the near future.

Additional advantages and conveniences of local area networks are too numerous to include in this chapter. Examining the major advantages, however, makes it clear why the use of LANs has been growing at such a fast pace and why the need for certified network professionals has become so important to the industry.

NETWORK COMPONENTS

As defined previously, a LAN is basically a communication system that allows computers of different types to communicate and share data. As a CNA, you need to become familiar with the hardware and software components that make up the network in order to select and maintain a network system that will meet the communication needs of your organization. This chapter introduces you to a network system's hardware and software components and explains why Novell's NetWare is the most common type of network system in use today. Chapters 2 and 3 will give you an in-depth view of the network cable system as well as the microcomputer hardware components and options you will need to know in order to select and maintain computers on the network.

Hardware Components

Hardware components are the most obvious parts of a network system to identify because they can be easily seen. In this section you will take a tour of the hardware components that make up a typical network system, as shown in the sample network in Figure 1-2, on the following page, and gain an understanding of how they work together to create a communication system.

The file server. The first stop on our tour of the network is the file server computer. Many who are familiar with mini and mainframe computers tend to think of the file server in terms of network control. In a LAN, however, a **network file server** computer is actually a servant of the network, responding to the requests of workstations for access to the files and software stored on its disk system. With the exception of its disk system and typically large memory capacity, a file server computer need be no different from any of the other client computers on the network. Some file servers are **nondedicated**, meaning that they can function as a user's workstation in addition to providing access to shared areas of the disk system. The file server in the sample network is dedicated in order to provide better performance and eliminate the possibility of a user shutting down or rebooting the file server computer while other users are still accessing it. Most network administrators keep the file server computer in a separate room that can be secured in order to prevent unauthorized access to the file server computer's hardware and software.

Figure 1-2

Sample network
hardware components

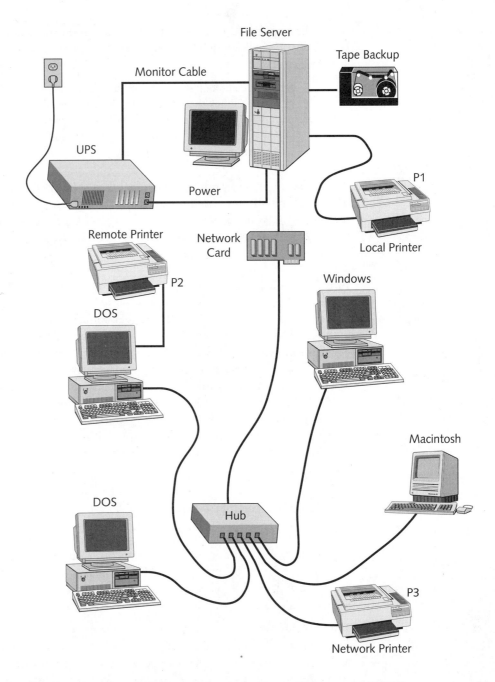

The sample network file server shown in Figure 1-2 is an 80486DX computer with 24 Mbytes of memory and two high-capacity 1.2-Gbyte (one billion bytes) disk drives. The two disk drives are automatically synchronized so that if one drive fails, the file server can continue to provide information services using the data from the other drive. Like the other network computers, a file server contains a network card that attaches it to the cable system allowing communication with other workstations.

Cable system.   A network's **cable system** is the highway through which information travels from one computer to another. Just as getting onto a highway requires obeying certain traffic laws, so sending information down the network requires each computer to follow a set of access rules. Just as "gridlock" can slow down or stop traffic on a high-way, a network can also experience bottlenecks when the amount of information on the network exceeds the transmission capacity of the cable system. One of the responsibilities you will have as a CNA is to monitor the network cable system for errors or performance bottlenecks. In Chapter 2 you will learn about the different types of cable systems and access methods that are commonly used in LANs along with some of the advantages and disadvantages of each system.

The cable system in the sample network consists of twisted-pair wire similar to the wire that connects your telephone's handset to its base unit. The term **twisted pair** reflects the fact that the wire strands are twisted around each other, as shown in Figure 1-3, in order to reduce interference between wires. In the sample network, twisted-pair wiring runs from each computer in the network to a central connection box called a **hub** or **concentrator**, allowing all computers equal access to the network system. This type of network design is referred to as a **star network** topology, because all cables radiate out from the hub.

Figure 1-3

Cable types

Twisted-Pair Wire

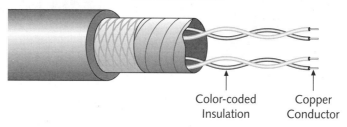

Color-coded Insulation   Copper Conductor

Coaxial Cable

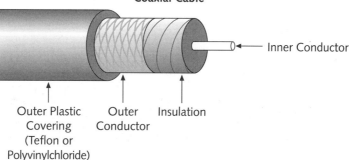

Inner Conductor

Outer Plastic Covering (Teflon or Polyvinylchloride)   Outer Conductor   Insulation

Another popular type of cable shown in Figure 1-3 is **coaxial cable**, which is similar to the cable used to connect a television to the local cable system. A popular coaxial cable network called Ethernet connects computers together with the cable running from one computer to the next as shown in Figure 1-4 on the following page. This type of network is sometimes configured as a **linear bus** because all computers are attached to the same cable or bus line.

Trend

Linear bus networks are gradually being replaced by star networks in many organizations because star networks are easier to troubleshoot. A broken wire in a star network configuration affects only one workstation. In a linear bus network, in contrast, all computers on the cable segment fail when the cable is disconnected or broken anywhere in the network.

Figure 1-4

Coaxial cable network

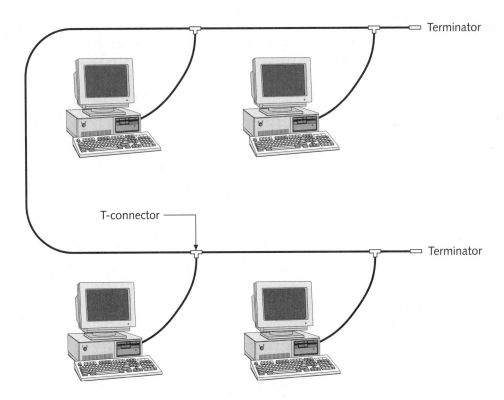

Uninterruptible power supply. The box next to the file server computer in Figure 1-2 is the **uninterruptible power supply (UPS)**. The UPS contains batteries that will be used to supply temporary power to the file server if the local power system fails. The UPS is a very important piece of equipment for the file server computer in that it will prevent the loss of data on the file server in the event of a power outage or brownout.

As a CNA, you should not consider running a file server computer without first obtaining a UPS, because a power outage that occurs while many users are accessing the server is likely to result in lost data. Power interruptions caused by not having a UPS unit attached to the file server can even make it necessary to restore the disk volume from a backup tape in order to restart the file server.

The UPS in the sample network contains an optional monitor cable that connects to a port on the file server computer allowing the file server to know when the UPS is using battery power. This is an important feature in the event of a longer power outage, it allows the file server to close all files and take itself off line automatically before the power stored in the UPS batteries is exhausted.

Tape backup. The tape backup system in the sample network consists of a 1.2-Gbyte cartridge tape drive and uses Novell's Storage Management System (SMS) software to backup all data on the file server automatically every night. At 1:00 A.M. each weekday morning the tape software starts up and copies all data to the tape cartridge. The network administrator then places this tape in the organization's fireproof vault for safe storage. A rotation system utilizing several tapes allows each backup to be kept for at least one week. Friday's backups are then stored off site. In Chapter 15 you will learn more about developing a backup and recovery system for your file server environment.

LAN card. A **network interface card (NIC)** is installed in each computer attached to the network including the file server. The NIC allows the computer to be attached to the network cable system and is responsible for the transmission and reception of data packets on the network. A packet consists of 1500 to 4200 bytes of formatted data that is framed with control bits identifying the address of the computer it is being sent to. Each NIC has a unique address or serial number when it is manufactured. The NIC listens to the network and accepts any packets that contain its address. It then notifies the computer that a packet has been received, and if no errors are detected in the packet, it is sent to the operating system software for processing. When transmitting data, the operating system will send a block of data to the NIC, which then waits for the network cable to become available. When no other computers are using the cable system, the NIC transmits the packet bit by bit.

Client workstation. Generally each computer that is attached to the network for the purpose of running user applications is referred to as a **client** workstation. Because it is at the client workstations that the actual processing for applications run by users is performed, placing more memory or a faster processor on the file server computer does not directly affect the speed of programs used by client workstations. For example, if your client workstation is an old XT-based computer with an 8086 microprocessor chip, attaching it to network with a high-performance Pentium-based file server will not improve the ability of the XT computer to run large programs. The processing power of the client workstations often equals or exceeds the speed of the file server computer. For example, in the sample network, the file server contains a medium-speed 80486 processor with lots of memory and disk space with a black and white monitor. The Windows-based workstations contain high-speed Pentium processors with 8 Mbytes of memory, 500 Mbytes of disk storage, and fast high-resolution color monitors. Because most of the files and software will be kept on the network file server, the client workstations can focus on processing speed and graphics resolution rather than high-capacity disk storage.

 On most networks, the file server computer should be specialized to provide high-speed disk access, whereas the client workstations will require fast processors and high-resolution graphics.

Network printers. As mentioned in the discussion of LAN benefits, sharing printers on the network is often an important advantage of implementing a LAN. Each client workstation can send output to any printer by first directing the printed output to the file server to be stored in a special directory called a print queue. After a workstation has completed its printing, the file server will direct the printout to the selected printer via the print server software. Printers can be attached and shared on the network in three different ways: as local printers, as remote printers, and as directly attached printers.

Notice that printer P1 in the sample network shown in Figure 1-2 is attached to the file server computer. This makes it a local network printer because it is attached to the file server's local printer port. Local printers have the advantage of being high speed and reducing network traffic, but have the disadvantage of limiting the locations in which the printers can be placed.

Printer P2 in the sample network is attached to a user's workstation. It is controlled by the print server, which allows users on any client workstation to send output through the file server to printer P2. Printer P2 is referred to as a remote printer because it is not directly attached to a printer port of the file server. Remote printers have the advantage of being located anywhere on the network where there is a workstation. Performance problems, as well as software conflicts for the workstation's user, can occur, however, when large print jobs are processed.

The third network printer shown in Figure 1-2, P3, has its own network card and is attached directly to the network cable system. This direct connection offers the benefits of independence from a workstation with no loss of speed associated with a remote printer. Today most network administrators attach their high-speed printers directly to the network cable system to obtain the highest possible levels of performance.

Software Components

As with any computer system, the software components of the network are perhaps the most difficult to understand because they are not physical objects. In our sample network configuration, the network software components can be broken into three major categories: card drivers, protocol stacks the network operating system, and client support. Figure 1-5 shows how these software components are combined in the sample network to allow workstations and file servers to communicate on the network. In this section you will learn what role each of these software components plays in implementing a local area network.

Card drivers. As described previously, each file server and client workstation must have a network interface card (NIC) to allow it to be attached to the cable system and to communicate on the network. Driver software contains the instructions that allow the processor on the computer to control card functions and interface with the application software. Periodically, new versions of driver software are released by card manufacturers in order to fix bugs or provide compatibility with new applications. As a result, one of the responsibilities of a network administrator involves updating application and system software. In Chapter 16, you will learn how you can make this task more efficient by implementing the automatic software update utilities built into the NetWare operating system. In the sample network configuration, the NE2000 driver program is used to control the network interface cards and provide an interface with the DOS or Windows operating system software.

Protocol stack. The **protocol stack** is the software used to format the requests and information packets that are transmitted on the network. The protocol you use will depend upon your file server and client workstations. One of the most common protocols on NetWare networks is the Internetwork Packet eXchange (IPX) protocol because it is the default system used with the NetWare operating system. However, NetWare networks will support other protocols, such as the LocalTalk protocol used with Macintosh computers or the TCP/IP (Transport Control Protocol/Internet Protocol) commonly used with the Unix operating system.

 The IPX protocol used by NetWare was first developed by the Xerox company in the late 1970s and later adopted by Novell for use in its networking products.

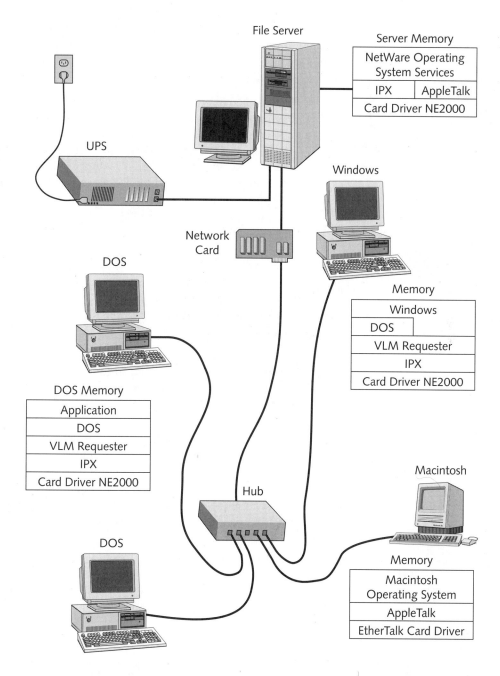

Figure 1-5

Network software
components

Network operating system.   The **network operating system (NOS)** is the system software that controls the file server in order to provide services to the client workstations. While most of the NetWare operating system resides on the file server computer, the client workstations also require a requester program, such as the VLM requester shown in Figure 1-5, to format and direct requests for network services to the file server for processing. In Chapter 5 you will learn the steps for installing NetWare on both the file server and client workstations.

Novell's NetWare network operating system was specifically designed to control the file server computer as well as provide a server environment to support file sharing and other network services. Because it does not require a general purpose operating system such as DOS or Unix to control the hardware of the file server computer, NetWare is much more efficient than many competing network operating system products because it allows a NetWare file server computer to provide faster support with fewer hardware requirements.

There have been several versions of the NetWare operating system prior to NetWare v3.12. Earlier versions include ELS NetWare, NetWare v2.1x and v2.2. ELS NetWare was a very limited version of NetWare intended for small networks consisting of fewer than 10 users. It ran in nondedicated mode, which allowed the file server computer to function as a user workstation as well. The NetWare v2.2 operating system was a much more powerful system that could be run either dedicated or nondedicated and could support up to 100 workstations.

The file server in the sample network runs Novell's NetWare v3.12 network operating system using both the IPX protocol to communicate with the DOS workstations and the AppleTalk protocol to communicate with Apple Macintosh computers. This allows both DOS and Macintosh computers to access the NetWare file server and share data and other resources.

The ability to provide faster support for clients will become even more important as file servers are increasingly used to store large documents, images, and multimedia files.

Client software. Client computers require their own operating systems such as DOS, Windows 95, or Macintosh to support the running of applications and control of local devices. In addition, client workstations need to have driver software to control the network interface card along with requester and protocol software programs to format and send requests for network file and print services to the file server. The requester program works closely with DOS to provide access to network services. The sample network in Figure 1-5 illustrates DOS computers using VLM requesters to send IPX-formatted requests via the NE2000 driver through the cable system to the NetWare file server. The Macintosh computer in the same figure can simultaneously use the AppleTalk protocol to send requests to the file server via the EtherTalk driver using the same cable. The ability to support different types of client operating systems is one of the strengths of the NetWare file server.

TYPES OF NETWORK OPERATING SYSTEMS

Since Novell first introduced the NetWare operating system in 1983, several other competitors have appeared on the market offering alternative network operating systems. While other network operating systems offer cost savings or fill special needs, networks using NetWare still far outnumber any other network operating systems in use today. Depending upon their design, network operating systems can be defined as either server centric or peer-to-peer. NetWare is a **server centric** (also called client server) operating system because its operation depends upon the existence of a dedicated file server computer. **Peer-to-peer** network operating systems, on the other hand, allow workstations to communicate and share data with each other without the need of a dedicated file server computer. In this section you will learn about the features found in both peer-to-peer and client server network operating systems and how they compare to the NetWare operating system.

Peer-to-Peer

In peer-to-peer networks, each computer can be both a file server and client workstation, allowing any computer to share its printer and files with other users on the network. The main advantage of peer-to-peer network operating systems is the ability to implement low-cost networks by saving the expense of dedicating a computer as a file server. In addition, peer-to-peer systems allow users in workgroups to share data files and communicate with each other easily. In theory this reduces the load on the network administrator by placing more responsibility for data sharing in the hands of the users. However, large peer-to-peer networks can be very difficult to administer because shared data can exist in several locations, making it more difficult to retrieve, secure, and back up. For example, if a workstation containing data needed by other users fails to boot its system or shuts down unexpectedly, other users can lose data or will not be able to access the information they need. In this section you will learn about several peer-to-peer network operating systems as well as some of their advantages and disadvantages when compared to Novell NetWare.

LANtastic.   LANtastic is a DOS-based peer-to-peer network operating system that is produced by Artisoft Corporation. LANtastic is a great network system for sharing files and communicating among DOS-based computers and is very popular for small networks in which all computers are attached to the same cable system. The primary advantages of LANtastic are low cost and ease of installation, making it a great choice for networks consisting of less than 10 workstations. Unfortunately, the major drawback of LANtastic as a peer-to-peer network operating system is that it requires the use of DOS, thereby reducing the performance and reliability of the server computers due to the memory limitations of the DOS operating system, which was not designed to support high-demand peer-to-peer network servers.

Personal NetWare.   Because of the popularity of peer-to-peer networks as well as the demand for users in workgroups to be able to share files without requiring them to be placed on a file server, Novell first introduced the NetWare Lite peer-to-peer operating system in 1992. Because of its slow speed and incompatibility with the client server NetWare environment, the NetWare Lite product was re-released as Personal NetWare in 1993. By using the same card drivers, protocol, and DOS requester, Personal NetWare is compatible with traditional NetWare file servers and allows workstations to access both the NetWare file server as well as other client workstations. The major disadvantage of the Personal NetWare product is that it is not as efficient as LANtastic in providing peer-to-peer connections.

Windows for Workgroups and Windows 95.   The most rapidly growing peer-to-peer operating systems are Microsoft's Windows for Workgroups v3.11 and Windows 95. With the wide acceptance of the Windows environment on most new computers today, using WFW or Windows 95 to share files and printers eliminates the need to obtain and integrate another network operating system into the network as well as providing a number of icon-oriented network services such as mail and scheduling built into each workstation. Windows 95 also integrates easily into NetWare networks by allowing Windows users to access NetWare servers in addition to shared resources on other Windows stations. The major disadvantage of Windows 95 as a peer-to-peer network operating system is the need to have computers with a minimum of 6 Mbytes of RAM and 80486 processors in order to provide satisfactory performance.

Windows NT. Windows NT represents a more powerful "big brother" of the Windows family of operating systems. Windows NT is a leading-edge operating system designed to support the advanced capabilities of Pentium and multiprocessor-based computers. It provides additional levels of reliability, protection, and security not available in the Windows 95 product. When used in peer-to-peer networks, the Windows NT operating system is intended to be used on very powerful workstations with at least 16 Mbytes of RAM. They usually require the advanced features of Windows NT in order to support complex applications for technical, engineering, and scientific users.

Server Centric

Server Centric networks are also referred to as client server networks because file server computers running specialized software are used to provide services to client workstation computers rather than the workstations sharing data among themselves. As a result, client server-based networks, such as those using NetWare, provide the advantages of centralized data storage, reliability, and high performance that are not currently attainable with peer-to-peer networks. One reason for the increased performance and reliability of client server networks such as NetWare is that the server computer's hardware can be specialized to perform the function of file sharing by providing multiple high-speed disk channels along with a large memory capacity for file caching. In Chapter 3 you will learn about many of the hardware options available that allow you to increase the performance and reliability of your file server computers. The rest of this section compares the client server-based network operating systems currently available.

NetWare v3.1x. NetWare v3.1x is a 32-bit dedicated network operating system that is highly specialized to provide a variety of services to client workstations. One of the big advantages of the NetWare v3 system over previous versions of NetWare is its ability to load and unload programs called NetWare Loadable Modules (NLM) in order to provide hardware drivers and additional services to the operating system. In many cases, NLMs can allow the network administrator to configure the network operating system without needing to shut down the server.

A drawback of NetWare v3.1x is that it is a server-centric operating system. A user must log into each file server in order to access any of its services. For example, if there are three NetWare v3.1x servers on your network, a user who needs files on the first server, software on the second server, and printers on the third server needs to log in three times, once for each server. This process makes installing and maintaining multiple server networks difficult because the network administrator needs to maintain user accounts for each user on all file servers the user accesses.

NetWare v4.0. NetWare v4.0 was Novell's first attempt to create a network-oriented file server environment, called the network global database (NDS), that would allow a user to log into the network rather than to each file server as required in NetWare v3.1x. Unfortunately, NetWare v4.0 was never widely implemented due to the scope of the changes it introduced, along with some problems with the initial release. In addition to the network global database, NetWare v4.0 introduced such innovative features as increased security, graphical utilities, and enhanced file and printing services.

NetWare v4.1. NetWare v4.1 is the latest release of NetWare. It contains corrections and enhancements to the NDS system that make the new product readily adaptable by the large firm that needs to support multiple file servers in multiple locations.

The many improvements added to NetWare v4.1 combined with the increased need for large multiserver networks in industry, are causing many organizations to plan the conversion of their NetWare v3.1x file servers to NetWare v4.1. The scope of the changes between these two versions of NetWare requires much training and planning on the part of the network administrator before the conversion process from an existing v3.1x network to v4.1 can take place.

Banyon Vines. One of the major strengths of the Banyon Vines network is its "streettalk" protocol, which allows users to log in once to a multi-server network and then be able to access any file server to which they have been granted access rights. Unlike NetWare v4.1, Vines does not use the industry X.500 standard for implementing a network global database. Despite this disadvantage, the Vines network operating system, which has been in existence several years prior to the release of NetWare v4.1, has obtained a respectable share of the client server network operating system market. This is due to the fact that it offered several of the advantages only recently introduced in NetWare v4.1. In many ways, Banyon forced Novell to move to a network-based file server environment or face losing many of its large multiserver customers.

Windows NT Server. The Windows NT Server client server operating system provides client workstations with centralized and highly fault-tolerant high-speed access to data. The advantages of Windows NT are that it provides centralized management of multiple servers through the familiar Windows environment, that it supports access to TCP/IP and NetWare file servers as well as mainframe computers, and that it can be used as an application server with several software applications from Microsoft and third-party vendors.

THE NETWARE FILE SERVER

As explained earlier in this chapter, the main function of a file server computer in a client server-based network is to provide file and printer services to client workstations. As a result, the file server computer in a client server-oriented environment can be enhanced with specialized hardware and software to improve performance, security, and reliability over what can be expected from a peer-to-peer network operating system. Although Microsoft Windows NT and Banyon Vines offer client server network operating systems, Novell NetWare is still by far the major player in the client server network field, offering server-based software that is designed from the ground up to make the maximum use of the file server computer's hardware. It does this by implementing features described in the following section.

Performance Features

The performance of a file server is determined by how fast it can respond to requests for data from client workstations. Therefore the major factors that affect the server's performance are its ability to keep frequently used information in memory, the speed of its disk system, and, if the first two are adequate, the speed of its processor unit. NetWare is the best-performing network operating system in the industry because it was designed to be a file server and therefore does not contain some of the additional overhead associated with general purpose operating systems such as DOS, Unix, or Windows NT. Some of the performance features of NetWare include file caching, directory caching, and elevator seeking.

File caching. **File caching** is the process by which NetWare increases the speed of response to requests for disk information. It does this by keeping the most frequently accessed disk blocks in memory. Because the computer's memory is approximately 100 times faster than the disk system, retrieving a block of data from the file cache greatly improves the performance of the server. As a general rule, at least 50% of the computer's memory should be allocated to file caching, resulting in over 70% of the data requests being handled from the computer's memory rather than directly read from the disk.

Directory caching. directory caching is the process of keeping the directory entry table and file allocation table for each disk volume in the memory of the computer. Like file caching, directory caching greatly increases the performance of the server by allowing it to find file names 100 times faster than when the directory information is read directly from disk. In addition to directory caching, NetWare also uses a process called **directory hashing** to create a binary index system that improves file lookup time by as much as 30%.

Figure 1-6 illustrates how requests from two different workstations to run the WP.EXE program would be handled by NetWare's caching system. In step 1, the server initially loads the directory cache and file allocation tables (FAT) with directory information from the disk volume and then builds the hash table. In step 2, the first request arrives from workstation A for the file WP.EXE. The server looks up the WP.EXE file in the hash table and then uses the directory table and FAT to identify the necessary disk blocks. Because the cache buffers are empty, the server reads the necessary disk blocks into the cache and then sends the WP.EXE file to workstation A. In step 3, a second request, from workstation B, is received for the WP.EXE program file. This time, after looking up the filename in the hash table, the server finds that the needed disk blocks are contained in the cache buffers. The server then immediately responds to the request by sending the data directly to workstation B from the file cache, thereby saving the time required to read the WP.EXE file from disk.

Figure 1-6

Cache memory

Step 1. Loading directory and FAT buffers

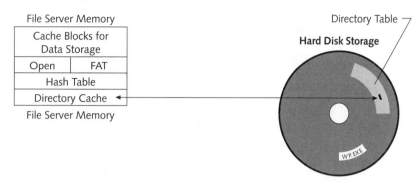

Step 2. First request for WP.EXE file from disk

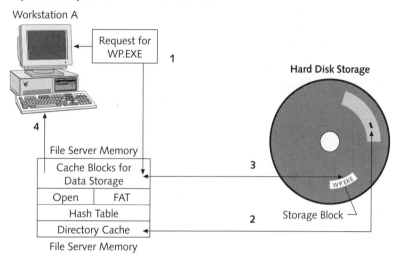

Step 3. Second request for WP.EXE from Cache

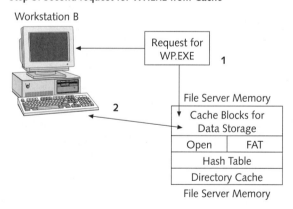

Elevator seeking.   Because the NetWare file server environment is multi-tasking, at any given time it might be responding to several data requests from different client workstations. **Elevator seeking** is the process of minimizing the amount of disk drive head movement by accessing the information in the sequence of the head movement rather than in the order in which the requests were received. Elevator seeking gets its name from the way an elevator works when picking up people on different floors. Imagine that an elevator is at the top of a 10-story building when someone on floor 2 pushes the down button. As the elevator passes the eighth floor, another person on floor 5 also pushes the down button. The elevator will then stop at floor 5 first and then floor 2 even though the person on floor 2 pushed the down button first.

Fault tolerance.   **Fault tolerance** can be defined as the ability of a system to continue to operate satisfactorily in the event of errors or other problems. The NetWare file server environment was designed with three levels of fault tolerance in its disk system in order to continue server operations in the event of physical errors on the disk drives or controller cards.

A hard disk's directory information is extremely important in enabling the server to locate information on the disk system. Because of this, NetWare's first level of fault tolerance is provided by second copies of the directory entry table and file allocation table on different locations of the disk drive. If a storage block in one of the tables is damaged, NetWare automatically switches to the duplicate table to retrieve the requested directory information. The faulty sector is then listed in the disk's bad block table, and the data contained in the bad sector is stored in another disk location.

As a disk drive ages, certain recording sectors of the disk's surface can become unreliable. To make sure that data written to the disk is stored in a good storage sector, NetWare implements a read-after-write verification process. If data cannot be reliably written to a disk sector after three attempts, NetWare implements the second level of fault tolerance, referred to as "hot fix." **Hot fix** involves redirecting bad and unreliable disk storage sectors to a redirection area location elsewhere on the disk surface. When a new disk drive is first formatted by NetWare, a certain percentage of the disk capacity (2 % by default) is reserved for the hot fix redirection area, allowing the disk drive to continue normal operation despite bad sectors that might develop on the disk surface. Step 1 in Figure 1-7 illustrates the file server attempting to write a data buffer to disk block 201 and receiving a disk error when the data is read back using the read-after-write verification process. In step 2, the data in the cache memory buffer is written to the redirection area and block 201 of the disk is remapped by the file server to point to the block in the redirection area. As mentioned previously, one of the responsibilities of a CNA is to monitor the file server in order to determine how many blocks have been redirected and thereby help determine when the disk drive should be replaced. In Chapter 15, you will learn how to use the NetWare MONITOR utility to track the condition of the redirection area and determine when a disk drive should be replaced.

Figure 1-7

Using hot fix

Step 1. Data written to a bad disk block

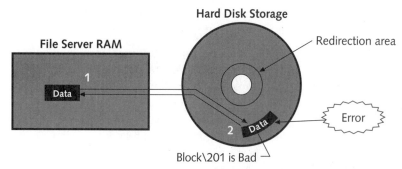

Step 2. Hot fix redirection area utilized

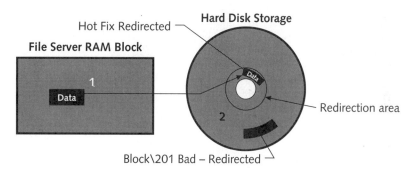

The third level of fault tolerance is the continued operation of the file server in spite of a complete failure of the disk system. NetWare provides two methods to protect a file server from major failures of the disk storage system. The first method, called **mirroring**, involves attaching two drives to the same disk controller card and then mirroring the drives in order to synchronize the data on both disks. After the disks have been mirrored, NetWare automatically keeps the information updated on both drives so that, in the event of a failure of one of the disk drives, the server will be able to continue normal operation using the second drive. The network administrator can then replace the defective drive at a time that is convenient, and NetWare will resynchronize the data on the new drive without requiring the network administrator to restore any information from the backup tape. Figure 1-8 illustrates the use of disk mirroring to protect your server against failure of a disk drive. Disk mirroring works well, but requires each block to be written twice by the controller card, which can decrease the performance of the file server. In addition, with disk mirroring, a failure of the controller card will make data on both drives unusable.

Figure 1-8

Disk mirroring

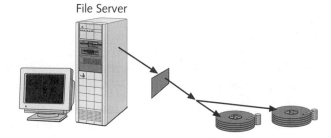

With **disk duplexing** Novell has provided a way for NetWare to provide fault tolerance for both the disk drive and controller card. Disk duplexing uses two disk drives, as illustrated in Figure 1-9.

Disk duplexing also increases performance over disk mirroring in that one disk write operation can be used to write data to both disk drives. An additional advantage of disk duplexing over a single disk drive is that it actually increases a file server's performance. Both controllers are requested to find data and then the information from whichever drive is closest to the data location is read first. In a sense, implementing disk duplexing is like doubling the number of disk heads and thereby increasing disk-read performance.

Figure 1-9

Disk duplexing

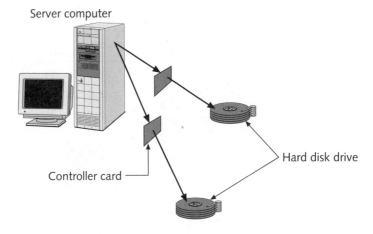

Server computer

Hard disk drive

Controller card

Novell's NetWare v4.1 provides a fourth level of fault tolerance called server duplexing, which allows two file servers on the network to be duplicated. This prevents a crash of one file server from affecting the operation of the network. This feature is important in implementing "mission critical" applications on LANs, which appeals to organizations that cannot afford any interruption in network services.

Security.   Preventing unauthorized access to information on the file server is one of the important responsibilities of a network administrator. To help you in this area the NetWare file server provides two security levels that can be used to create an environment that will meet the security needs of your organization's users and data.

Login security is NetWare's first security level. It requires all users of the file server to provide a valid username and optional password before being allowed access to the file server. As a network administrator you can assign usernames and passwords for each of your network users, thereby controlling use of the file server. To provide additional protection for passwords, NetWare allows you to require users to have passwords of at least five characters and to force users to change their passwords within a specified time limit. In addition, the optional intruder protection system will lock out a user's account if someone exceeds the number of login attempts you have set.

File system security allows you to assign privileges, called **trustee rights**, to NetWare users in order to allow them to perform certain functions within the directory structure of the file server. When a user account is first created, the user has no rights to the file server's data until you provide the new user with specific rights or make him or her a member of a group that has been granted rights to use certain functions of your file system. Figure 1-10 provides a list of rights that can be assigned to users in order to allow them access to directories and files in the NetWare file system.

Figure 1-10

Access rights

Right	What It Allows
(F) File scan	View file names in a directory listing
(R) Read	Open and read information from a file
(C) Create	Create subdirectories and new files
(W) Write	Write information into an existing file
(E) Erase	Erase existing subdirectories and files
(M) Modify	Change a filename and attributes
(A) Access control	Grant rights to other users for the directory or files in the directory
(S) Supervisory	All rights; cannot be blocked or revoked in any of the subdirectories

Users must be assigned trustee rights to a directory or file before they will be able to access it.

Client support. Because a NetWare file server runs its own network operating system, it is not dependent on a specific type of client environment (unlike peer-to-peer networks) and can support many types of workstations. As a result, implementing a NetWare file server can allow you to integrate diverse computing environments, making it possible for Apple Macintosh users to share files with DOS- and Windows-based computers. In some organizations, NetWare has provided a means for engineering departments using Unix-based computers for **computer aided design** (CAD) software to make the design files available to DOS-based computers that control the machines that actually cut out the parts that were engineered.

Combining computer aided design applications with process control and business applications is referred to as computer integrated manufacturing (CIM). The network-based implementation of CIM is a rapidly growing speciality that many network administrators working in manufacturing organizations will need to master.

SELECTING A NETWORK

Selecting a network system for an organization involves three steps. The first step is deciding on the type of network operating system to use, second is determining the cable system that will best support the needs of the network, and third is specifying any computer hardware that will be needed to implement file servers and attach workstations to the network. In this section you will learn about the criteria you should consider when developing a recommendation for a network operating system. In Chapters 2 and 3 you will learn about cable configurations and computer hardware options that you will need to know when recommending and implementing a new network or maintaining an existing system.

DEFINING NETWORK NEEDS

Before recommending or justifying a network operating system, you first need to analyze the processing needs of the organization and determine how they will be supported by the network. The processing needs of an organization that affect the type of network operating system to be selected include: number of users, diversity of workstations, type of applications to be supported, and the need for centralized data.

Network Size

An important consideration in determining whether to use a peer-to-peer or client server network operating system is the number of workstations that will be attached to the network. As a general rule, the fewer users, the more likely a peer-to-peer network will meet the needs of the organization. In addition to the size of the current network, you also need to look at the future growth of the organization and how this will affect the network system. If you can see that the organization will expand in the next few years to include more users requiring heavy-duty file and printer sharing in order to support such applications as desktop publishing and computer aided design, you might want to recommend using a network operating system that can be easily expanded to provide a dedicated file server, which will provide the advantages of a client server environment. For example, a Personal NetWare peer-to-peer network can easily be expanded to a client server network by the addition of a NetWare file server.

Client Workstations

The types of client workstations that will be attached to the network is another factor to consider in determining the type of network operating system to be selected. Peer-to-peer networks are best used in networks in which all the attached clients are running the same type of operating system. For example, if all workstations will run Windows, the Windows 95 system could be an attractive alternative provided it meets the other processing needs of the network. If the client workstations are running a combination of DOS and Windows, then LANtastic, Personal NetWare, or a client server operating system such as NetWare v3.1 might be the best choice depending upon the organization's other processing needs.

Network Use

Certain common uses of networks, such as printer sharing and electronic mail routing, have small disk storage needs and can run nicely on peer-to-peer networks. For example, if an organization plans to use its network to support workgroup-oriented software such as e-mail and scheduling with some sharing of files and printers within small workgroups, a peer-to-peer operating system that supports its workstation operating systems might be the best choice.

If an organization will be running applications that require fast access to large network data files such as desktop publishing, document imaging, and multimedia presentation packages, the speed and file storage capability of a client server network such as NetWare should be selected in order to provide reliable, high-speed access to large disk systems consisting of gigabytes of data storage.

Networks are also used to run shared applications on the file server. This makes the file server an "application server," able to share some of the processing with the client workstations. The Windows NT environment provides a good platform for serving applications because the operating system is designed to support application development.

 Database software such as Microsoft SQL server is designed to run on a file server in order to perform certain database functions for the workstations, thereby reducing the load on the network and workstation. Sharing applications among computers will become an increasingly important function of LANs in the future.

Centralized Storage

Another important consideration in selecting a network operating system is the need for the network to contain centralized storage for files and documents. If an organization's employees use word processors and spreadsheet programs to access common documents and files, a client server network system will provide them with consistent and reliable shared storage areas that can be routinely backed up in order to provide for disaster recovery.

Client server environments are also the best choice when users in an organization need access to large centralized databases containing inventory and customer information. These database files should be placed on a dedicated file server using NetWare in order to take advantage of the speed associated with file caching and the assurance of high reliability and fault tolerance that can be gained by mirroring or duplexing the disk drives.

SELECTING A NETWORK OPERATING SYSTEM

The flowchart shown in Figure 1-11 illustrates the manner in which the network processing needs of an organization can be used to help select a network operating system. As shown in the flowchart, the number of user workstations to be attached to the network is the first consideration. If there are fewer than 15 workstations, a peer-to-peer system will probably be the best network alternative unless several of these workstations will be working with large files that need to be shared on the network, such as those used by departments running computer aided design applications. The type of peer-to-peer network will depend on the type of operating systems used by client workstations.

Figure 1-11

Selecting a network operating system

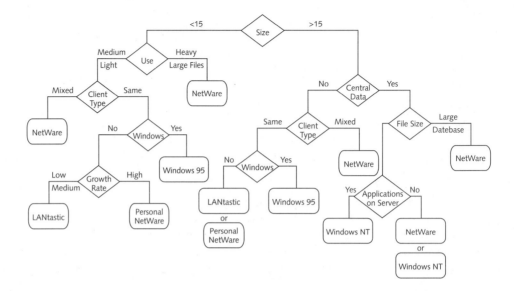

When the number of users exceeds 15, the need for centralized data typically becomes an important factor in choosing between a client server and peer-to-peer system. If the network will be mostly used for sharing printers and personal communication, you will need to consider the operating systems that the client workstations will be running. If client workstations will be running different types of operating systems, NetWare is usually the best operating system choice because it can be configured to support communications and file sharing between different client operating environments.

When centralized data storage is a major function of the network, a client server system such as NetWare or Windows NT will be the best choice because it provides a secure and efficient platform that helps ensure that data will be available at all times. When large database or multimedia files that are critical to an organization's operation need to be accessed from a centralized file server, either NetWare v3.12 or v4.1 will generally be the best choice, depending upon the number of file servers. In most situations in which performance, security, and reliability are a must, NetWare is probably the best choice, because it has been used extensively for many years and its performance and compatibility with many applications has been well established. Other client server environments, such as Windows NT, are newer to the marketplace and should be considered and researched carefully to determine their performance and compatibility in the proposed network environment.

Today, many network administrators are gaining the best of both peer-to-peer and client server networks by implementing networks consisting of combinations of network operating systems. For example, a NetWare client server network can include clients running Windows 95 or Windows for Workgroups as well as Window NT used to provide access to certain client server applications running on the NT server machine. As these operating systems gain popularity, CNAs will be increasingly needed to implement network systems using a combination of compatible products in order to provide the services needed by the organization's LAN users.

CHAPTER SUMMARY

Network administration is an exciting field with a great future, and a Novell CNA will be in a position to grow with the industry. As a CNA, your responsibilities will include such activities as supporting client workstation applications, designing and maintaining the network directory structures, establishing network users and security, setting up and maintaining the network printing environment, managing the file server console, maintaining a user-friendly environment, implementing a fail safe backup and recovery system, and supporting network communications.

Networks are becoming widespread in many organizations because they provide such advantages as cost savings by allowing users to share expensive hardware and software, time savings by making it easier for users to work together, shared access to database and document files, a more secure environment to protect sensitive data from unauthorized access, a more reliable storage system to prevent loss of data and time, and a communication system that can be used for electronic mail and scheduling applications as well as providing access to mini and mainframe systems.

In order to succeed as a network administrator, you will need a good understanding of the hardware and software components that make up a network system and how they interoperate. The basic hardware components of a network consist of the file server, cable system, network cards, the UPS, client workstations, and shared printers. Printers can be added to the network by attaching them to a local printer port on the file server, attaching them remotely to a client workstation, or attaching them directly to the network cable. The software components of a network consist of the card driver program, which is responsible for directly controlling the network interface card; the protocol stack, which performs the formatting of the data transmitted between computers; the DOS requester program, which provides an interface between applications and the network; and the network operating system, which runs on the file server computer and provides the shared network services.

Network operating systems can be classified into two types: peer-to-peer and client server. Peer-to-peer operating systems do not require a dedicated file server but instead are able to share data among the client workstations. Generally peer-to-peer operating systems such as LANtastic, Personal NetWare, Windows for Workgroups and Windows 95 are best implemented for smaller workgroups that do not require frequent access to centralized data files. Because client server operating systems such as NetWare have dedicated file servers, they can be more efficient and reliable platforms for storage of centralized files.

Novell designed the NetWare network operating system specifically as a file server operating system, with performance features such as high-volume file caching, directory caching and hashing, and elevator seeking. In addition to its high performance, NetWare includes such fault-tolerant features as hot fix, disk mirroring, and disk duplexing along with security features that allow the network administrator to protect data from unauthorized access.

When selecting an operating system for your network, you need to consider such factors as the number of users and workstations, the type of operating systems and applications that will be used by the client workstations, and the need for high-speed centralized data storage. In almost all cases in which a client server network is needed, NetWare equals or exceeds the capabilities of other systems such as Windows NT and

Banyon Vines. Because each type of operating system has certain strengths, however, many organizations must be able to integrate combinations of network operating systems and workstations in order to meet their network processing needs.

KEY TERMS

cable system

centralized processing

client workstation

client server

coaxial cable

computer aided design (CAD)

concentrator

directory hashing

disk duplexing

distributed processing

elevator seeking

fault tolerance

file caching

file system security

hub

linear bus

local area network (LAN)

login security

mirroring

network file server

network interface card (NIC)

netware loadable module (NLM)

network operating system (NOS)

non-dedicated

peer-to-peer

protocol stack

star network topology

twisted-pair wire

uninterruptible power system (UPS)

REVIEW QUESTIONS

For questions 1–8, identify the CNA responsibility under which each of the following tasks belongs.

1. _____ Deciding where to place the quality-control database in order to allow shared access by several users throughout an organization.

2. _Setting up and Maintaining Network Printing_ Making a new printer available to the users in the sales department.

3. _Setting up and Maintaining Network Printing_ Making it possible for the users in the sales department to select the new sales printer easily from their menu.

4. _Establishing & Maintaining Network Users & Security_ Determining why certain workstations cannot log into the new file server.

5. _Loading and Updating Application Software_ Providing computers in the sales department the ability to run the new PowerPoint presentation software.

6. _Managing the file Server & Monitoring Network Performance_ Determine how much memory the file server computer is using for file caching.

7. _Developing & Implementing a backup & Recovery system_ Get a good night's sleep.

8. _Supporting Network Communications_ Add users to the electronic mail system.

9. A LAN supports ___centralized_____ processing by allowing microcomputers to access centralized data and resources.

10. List two advantages of using a LAN for centralized data storage:
Duplicating on several workstations
Regular Backups

11. Identify two areas in which a LAN can be used to save personnel time:
Shared data & communication
Install & maintain a software package in one location.

12. In many networks, sharing ___expensive   hardware_____ will provide the most direct cost savings.

13. List four network hardware components:
The file server
Cable System
Uninterruptible Power Supply (UPS)
Network Interface Card (NIC)

14. ___Twisted Pair_____ network cable is similar to the wire used to connect your telephone to the phone system.

15. In a ___Linear   Bush_____ network, all computers are attached to the same cable segment.

16. List three ways a printer can be attached to the network:
To the File Server
To the User's Workstation
Directly to the network cable system

17. The ___Card Drivers_____ software component controls communications on the network cable.

18. The ___Protocol   Stack_____ software component formats the information being transmitted between computers.

19. The ___Network   Operating   System__ software component provides access to shared files and other resources.

20. The ___Card Drivers_____ software component interfaces the network to DOS.

21. A network system that allows client computers to share files among themselves is called ___Peer - to - Peer_____.

22. A ___Server   Centric   (Client Server)___network system requires a file server computer.

23. List two advantages of peer-to-peer network systems:
Each computer can be a file server & client workstation
Implement low-cost networks

24. List two advantages of client server network systems:
Centralized data storage
Reliability & High Performance

EXERCISES

Exercise 1-1: Recording Network Information

1. So that you can perform the exercises and project assignments in this book, your instructor has assigned you to a file server and provided you with a username, student reference number, and home directory. In the space below, record your network information:

   File Server Name: CTS_HOST

   Username: 50 Admin

   Student Reference number: _____

   Home Directory Location:

       Volume name: SYS

       Home directory name and path: F:\50 Admin

2. Your instructor will take your class on a tour of the computer network. Use information presented during the tour to fill in the following information.

   Network File Server Information

Name	Operating System	Memory (MB)	Disk Capacity	Cable Type	NIC	UPS
CTS-Host	V3.12	V6		Tw Pc CAT5	S.M.C.	

   Network Printer Information

Printer Name/Type	Location	Attachment Method

Your Client Workstation

Operating System	Protocol	LAN Driver Name	Cable	Ram Memory
Win95				64 k

Exercise 1-2: Accessing the Network

In this exercise you will learn about the two levels of NetWare security by first logging into the file server with your assigned username and then using a NetWare command to determine what rights you have in the network file system.

1. Boot your workstation.

2. Try changing to drive F: and record the message in the space below:

    Invalid drive specification

3. Perform the commands necessary to load the client software as described by your instructor. In the space below, record any commands you need to enter in order to load the software necessary to attach your workstation:

    _____

    _____

    _____

    _____

4. Change to drive F: and, in the space below, record why you now have access to the F: drive:

    _____

5. Type the command **LOGIN server_name\username** and press **[Enter]**. (*Be sure* to include the backslash between the file server's name and your name.) In the space below, record the login message you receive:

    _____

Exercise 1-3: Determining Your Rights

The NetWare WHOAMI command is useful to determine information about your current session with the file server. In this exercise you will be using the NetWare WHOAMI command line utility to learn more about your username and current login session. If you are not already logged in to your assigned file server, follow the instructions in Exercise 2 to log in using your assigned username.

1. When used without any options, the WHOAMI command will reveal certain information about your current session on the file server. After successfully logging in and obtaining a DOS prompt, type the command **WHOAMI** and press **[Enter]**. Record the information obtained from the WHOAMI command below:

    Your username: _____

    The file server you are attached to: _____

The version of NetWare installed on your file server: _✓ 3.12_

The time and date you logged in: _Tuesday Sept. 15, 1998, 9:00 am_

2. In this chapter we discussed the concept of NetWare providing login and file system security. Your username is an example of login security. Later in this exercise you will assign a password to your username to prevent other people from using it to login. Another major part of NetWare security involves your rights to access files and directories. In the table below, record the seven access rights and their corresponding action as defined in this chapter.

Access right	Action that can be performed if you have this right
S	Supervisor
R	Read from File
W	Write to File
C	Create Subdirectories & Files
E	Erase
M	Modify
F	Scan for Files
A	Access Control

3. To determine the access rights assigned to your username, type the command **WHOAMI /R** and press **[Enter]**. Each directory in which you have rights assigned to your username or one of the groups you belong to will be displayed. In the table below, record the directory path along with your access rights in each directory in which you have more than Read and File scan rights.

Directory Path	Rights
SYS: MAIL / 35000001	RWCEMF
SYS: Example / Sales / Survey	RWCE F
SYS: 50 ADMIN	SRWCEMFA
SYS: 50STC	SRWCEMFA

4. You can assign a password to provide more security for your username. Be sure to assign a password you can remember or you will suffer the embarrassment of having to ask your instructor or lab supervisor to reassign a new password for you. To assign a password for your username, type the command **SETPASS** and press **[Enter]**. The SETPASS program will ask you to enter your password, but will not display it on the screen. After you enter your password, the system will ask you to verify it by entering it a second time.

5. To log out of the file server, type **LOGOUT** and press **[Enter]**. In the space below, record the logout information you receive. Try using the LOGIN command to log in using your newly assigned password.

Exercise 1-4: Creating Your Student Work Disk

In this assignment you will copy your student work files and chapter study system from the file server onto a formatted high-density disk. You will use this disk to do assignments in later chapters. The disk also contains a study system that will help you review and test your knowledge of each chapter.

1. Log into the file server using your assigned ##ADMIN username.

2. Type the following command to change to the directory containing the student work disk files: **CD SYS:SOFTWARE.STC\WORKDISK** and press **[Enter]**

3. Insert a formatted disk into a floppy disk drive.

4. The CHKDIR command will report the amount of space used in a directory and all its subdirectories. To determine the amount of space needed for the student work disk, type the command **CHKDIR** and press the **[Enter]**. Record the CHKDIR information below:

   Maximum 600,000 K   In Use 32,620   Available 567,380

5. The NetWare NCOPY command is similar in function and syntax to the DOS XCOPY command. For copying files between network directories, however, the NCOPY is more efficient and reliable. In this step you will practice using the NCOPY command to copy all files and subdirectories from SOFTWARE.STC\WORKDISK onto your student work disk. To copy all files with one NCOPY command, type the command shown below. The /S option is used to copy all subdirectories, and the /V option verifies that the files have been copied correctly.

   If your formatted disk is in drive A:, type:
   F:\SOFTWARE.STC\WORKDISK>NCOPY *.* A:\ /S /V
   and press **[Enter]**.

   If your formatted disk is in drive B:, type:
   F:\SOFTWARE.STC\WORKDISK>NCOPY *.* B:\ /S /V
   and press **[Enter]**.

Exercise 1-5: Run the Study System

In this exercise you will test your student work disk along with your knowledge of Chapter 1 by reviewing the study program as described below.

1. Change the default DOS prompt to the drive containing your student work disk.

2. Type the command **STUDY** and press **[Enter]**. Type your name and press **[Enter]**.

3. Use the arrow keys to highlight your course and press **[Enter]**.

4. Use the arrow keys to highlight Network Basics and press **[Enter]**.

5. The program will start in **study mode**. In this mode it will inform you when you make an invalid choice, give the page number of your reference material, and let you try the question again. To change to **test mode**, use the **[Tab]** to select the **Option Setting** option and press **[Enter]**. You can then change from study mode to test mode and then return to the question screen. Use the Tab key to select your desired answer and press **[Enter]**.

6. When you have completed the test, use the print function to print your results.

EXERCISES

Case 1-1: Selecting a Network Operating System

The PC Solutions company is a small manufacturer of specialized computer devices to aid the handicapped. In the last year, the company has grown quickly and it now has five computers in the business department that need to share access to accounting files, word processing documents, and printers. Currently the customer and inventory files are kept on one computer, but this might change in the future if more order-entry staff are needed. Currently all the computers except one are running DOS, with one workstation using Windows to run a desktop publishing program used to create the company's catalog and flyers.

1.   Given the above information, use the flowchart in Figure 1-11 to help you select the best network operating system for the PC Solutions company. In the space below, diagram your path through the decision tree and write a brief paragraph justifying your selection.

_____

2.   Assume the PC Solutions company has two additional workstations that are used for computer aided design (CAD) applications and run the Unix operating system. If the CAD users also want to be able to use the network to perform applications such as sharing files and sending electronic mail, what network operating system would you choose and why?

_____

Case 1-2: Selecting a Network Operating System for ACME

The ACME company is planning to downsize its quality-control system from a minicomputer to a LAN. Part of this system involves collecting information such as quantities produced and inspection results from the shop floor and saving them in a central database. Product defects from returned goods will also be coded and stored in a separate database. These database files are expected to become quite large and it is critical that the collection process not be interrupted during daily operations. Other computers in the office will then have access to this data to be used in spreadsheet and database software in order to produce reports and analyze production problems.

Given the above information, use the flowchart in Figure 1-11 to help select the best network operating system for the ACME company. In the space below, diagram your path through the decision tree and write a brief paragraph justifying your selection.

_____

Case 1-3: Selecting a Network for the Court House

The county court house would like to set up a network to connect 20 users in the social services department in order to allow them to implement electronic mail and group scheduling applications while sharing access to two laser printers. The department secretary, Terry, is familiar with advanced features of the word processing package and often does final editing of the documents created by the social workers. As a result, social workers will need to pass documents periodically to Terry's computer so she can finalize them for printing.

Given the above information, use the flowchart in Figure 1-11 to help select the best network operating system for the county court house social services department. In the space below, diagram your path through the decision tree and write a brief paragraph justifying your selection.

SUPERIOR TECHNICAL COLLEGE PROBLEMS

Congratulations! You have just been hired by Superior Technical College (STC) as a computer lab technician for its major campus. The college campus where you are located contains a main computer lab with two rooms with 25 computers each, 2 computers in the student services department, a computer for each of the two faculty administrative assistants, and 3 computers in the faculty workroom. Your job is to implement and manage the microcomputer network at the college campus as well as to help students and faculty with computer problems. Dave Johnson, whose office is in the administration building, is the head of Computer Information Systems for the college. He will be your direct supervisor in implementing the campus network. An organizational chart for Superior Technical College is shown in Figure 1-11.

Figure 1-12

Organizational chart for Superior Technical College

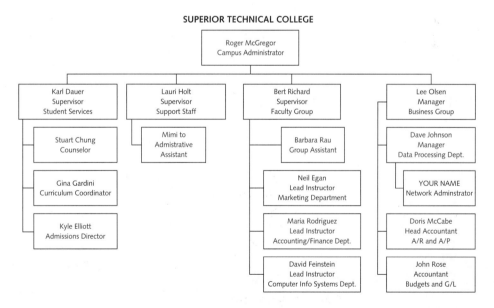

In your first meeting after being hired, Dave explained his plan for the campus network. The network at the campus will be used both by the computer lab, to store software for student access, and by the administration and faculty. He wants you to take security measures to ensure that students cannot access or damage the faculty or administrative data. In addition, Dave wants administrative and faculty data to be backed up daily, with weekly backups of student files and software. To meet the printing needs of the campus, Dave would like five laser printers to be placed on the network. The computer lab is to have for each room one shared laser printer per room. In addition, one shared laser printer is to be used by the faculty, one for student service use, and one for faculty secretaries.

Dave explained that word processing, database, and spreadsheet software is currently installed separately on each computer in the lab. This software has become quite a problem to maintain due to students' changing the configurations and frequent software updates. The faculty have pointed out that it is very important for student learning that software configurations remain the same on all computers. The faculty want to have their computers on the network so they can access the laser printers, work with the same software the students use, and be able to allow the students to access files they create without having to copy them to floppy disks.

Dave explained that the student services department has recently obtained a network version of a recruitment system. This system will allow student service staff to keep track of students who have inquired about programs being offered at the college and follow up on their registration status. Faculty members have also expressed an interest in being able to access this recruitment data to help follow up on potential students for their programs. In addition to the recruitment system, the student services department uses a word processing program to draft letters and memos, and has an aptitude testing program that it uses to help students select a career path. Currently, the testing software is on a standalone computer. However, this computer is sometimes in use and the student services department would like students to be able to take the tests on another machine.

Finally, administrative assistants are responsible for preparing reports and typing for faculty. Currently the faculty members often bring disks to the administrative assistants with rough drafts of their documents to be formatted and printed. Dave hopes this process can be improved with the network system. Because of busy schedules, it is often difficult for faculty members to respond to requests made by other staff. Dave would like you to consider whether or not a network could be used to help this communication problem.

Project 1-1: Comparing Network Operating Systems

Dave Johnson would like you to write a recommendation listing the benefits that can be derived from implementing a network at the STC campus. This proposal should list benefits in the following categories: hardware, sharing data, software, and communications. In addition, Dave would like you to compare and contrast the advantages and disadvantages of using client server versus peer-to-peer network operating systems and make a recommendation as to which type of system you think would be most suitable. Dave said he would carefully consider your recommendation in making his purchasing decision.

see page 28

Project 1-2: Taking a Network Test Drive

Dave suggested that you visit Tammie, a CNA at a local computer supply store, and have her show you how her system operates. Dave believes seeing another NetWare system in operation will help give you ideas on how to setup the campus network. Tammie was happy to oblige and after lunch she had you sit down at a computer station to see how the network is organized. Because Ode Wiggerts was not in her office, Tammie decided to use her computer for the demonstration. Tammie explained that she uses the first three letters of the first and last name for each user's login name because it makes a standardized name that is easy for her to remember.

1. To log in as Ode Wiggerts, first use the LOGOUT command to log out of the file server and then type the command **LOGIN ODEWIG** and press **[Enter].** In the space below, list all options under Ode's main menu: ① Word Processing ② Spreadsheet ③ Printer Options ④ Network Options ⑤ Logout ⑥ Exit to DOS prompt

2. Try the various network and DOS menu options and use the Esc key to return back to the main menu after each submenu. In the space below, list the options in the Network and DOS submenus.

   Network submenu:

   ① Change Password ② Drive mappings ③ View print jobs ④ Send a Message

   DOS submenu:

   M:\F

3. Next, use the printer option of the network menu to direct output to the network laser printer.

4. Now try the word processing option to create a small document that contains your name and date, along with a description of today's weather, including temperature, sky, and precipitation in a format similar to the one shown below:

   Date:

   Created by:

   Today's weather conditions:

   Wind:

   Temperature:

   Sky:

   Precipitation:

   Comments:

5. Print the document. The output will be redirected to the network printer.

6. Save the document on drive L: using your initials as the filename. Tammie explained that drive L: is mapped to a shared work area on the file server used by the student services department.

7. For a demonstration of shared files, use the word processing program to call up a document created by another student. Make a modification to the comments on the document and add your name to the Created By list.

8. Save the document.

9. Select the Message function from the network submenu. Notice how the menu system prompts for the message and username. Try sending a message to ODEWIG. Because multiple students can be logged in as ODEWIG, your message will be sent to each ODEWIG user who is currently logged in to the server.

10. Now use the Exit to DOS option to exit the menu system. Go to the L: drive and use the DIR command to obtain a disk directory. Try using the NetWare NDIR command to obtain another directory listing. In the space below, record any additional information from the NDIR command:

    Flags & owner

11. Next, use the DEL command to delete a file from drive L:. In the space below, record the message you received.

    Access Denied

12. Enter the RIGHTS command and record the effective rights in Ode's directory.

    RWFC

13. Using this information, explain why the delete command in step 11 did not work.

    We don't have the rights.

14. Use the LOGOUT command and record the logout information in the space below:

    _ODEWIG logged out from server CTS_Host connection 13_
    Login Time: Tues Sept 15, 1998, 9:57 am
    Logout Time: Tues Sept 15, 1988. 10:10 am.

NETWORK DESIGN

An important responsibility of a CNA is understanding the hardware and software components that make up a local area network. This knowledge will allow you to recommend and implement network systems as well as troubleshoot problems on the network. In Chapter 1 you were introduced to the hardware and software components that make up a LAN along with the criteria you should use to select a network operating system that will meet the processing needs of an organization. Another important decision you need to make when recommending and implementing a LAN is the type of cable system and the types of network interface cards that will be used to send information from computer to computer. As a CNA, you will probably be the main source of network information for your organization. As a result, you will want to have a good background in how computers use LANs to communicate, as well as what options and standards are currently available to accomplish the communication needs of your network system. In this chapter you will learn about how data is transmitted between computers and about the hardware and software options that are available when making a network recommendation.

AFTER READING THIS CHAPTER AND COMPLETING THE EXERCISES YOU WILL BE ABLE TO:

- DESCRIBE THE PROCESS OF TRANSMITTING DATA ON A NETWARE NETWORK.

- IDENTIFY AND DESCRIBE THE HARDWARE AND SOFTWARE THAT CONNECT COMPUTERS TO THE NETWARE LAN.

- APPLY YOUR KNOWLEDGE OF LAN SYSTEMS TO DEVELOP A RECOMMENDATION FOR A NETWORK SYSTEM.

LAN COMMUNICATION

Computers communicate over LANs by sending blocks of data, called **packets**. Each packet contains the information to be transmitted, along with control information used by the receiving computer to identify and process the data contained in the packet. The reliable transmission of data packets over a network is a complex and technical task performed by the hardware and software, but the concepts can be broken down into basic steps or modules that are reasonably easy to understand.

For LAN communication to occur, it is first necessary to have standards that will allow products from different manufacturers to be able to work together. The term **interoperability** refers to the ability of different computers and applications to communicate and share resources on a network. Today, several organizations help to set and control recognized standards that help provide worldwide interoperability. Because many products you will need to implement your network system depend on standards developed by these organizations, you should be familiar with the basic functions of these organizations. The two major organizations that play a role in LAN standards are the **International Standards Organization (ISO)**, which works on LAN communication software models, and the **Institute of Electrical and Electronic Engineers (IEEE)**, which works on physical cable and access method standards. In this chapter you will learn about the LAN standards maintained by these institutions and how they affect the network products you will be working with as a CNA.

OSI MODEL

In order to recommend and implement a LAN successfully, you first need a good understanding of the components that make up a network system and how they function together. Just as breaking a complex program into separate modules helps you to write a computer program, breaking the LAN communication process into separate logical tasks or modules makes it easier to understand and work with. To help develop standardized network system implementations, the ISO introduced a seven-layer model in 1980 known as the **open systems interconnect (OSI) model**. This seven-layer model acts as a blueprint to help network designers and developers build reliable network systems that can interoperate. As a CNA, you need to know the basic levels and functions of the OSI model in order to understand the LAN communication process and be better able to select and configure network hardware and software components. In addition to helping you implement and maintain network systems, a good understanding of the basic principles of network communication provided by the OSI model will be important to help you troubleshoot and identify network problems.

As shown in Figure 2-1, the seven layers of the OSI model start at the application software level and work down to the physical hardware. The layers allow network software to be implemented in structured modules, providing the network administrator with more flexibility in designing and configuring network systems.

Figure 2-1

OSI model

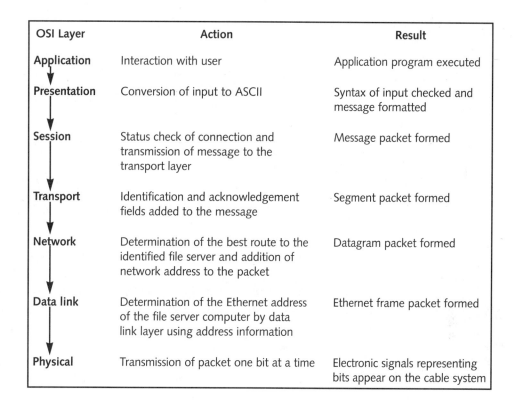

OSI Layer	Action	Result
Application	Interaction with user	Application program executed
Presentation	Conversion of input to ASCII	Syntax of input checked and message formatted
Session	Status check of connection and transmission of message to the transport layer	Message packet formed
Transport	Identification and acknowledgement fields added to the message	Segment packet formed
Network	Determination of the best route to the identified file server and addition of network address to the packet	Datagram packet formed
Data link	Determination of the Ethernet address of the file server computer by data link layer using address information	Ethernet frame packet formed
Physical	Transmission of packet one bit at a time	Electronic signals representing bits appear on the cable system

A simple phrase to help you remember the OSI layers, from the application layer to the physical layer: "All people seem to need data processing."

The **application layer** is where a request for network services—such as a word processing program you want to use to access a shared document stored on the file server—is initiated. Starting with the application layer, each layer is responsible for performing certain network processing and control operations and then passing the data packet on to the next lower layer. Each layer in the OSI model communicates with its peer layer on the receiving computer by going through the lower layers. For example, the transport layer on one computer will include control information in the network packet that can be used by the transport layer on the receiving computer to acknowledge receipt of the packet. At the bottom of the OSI model, the physical layer consists of the network cards and cables that actually carry the signals, representing ones and zeros, of the data packet from one machine to another.

Learning the purpose of each OSI level and how it is applied to the communication process is an important part of developing an understanding of network communication components that will help you design and maintain a network system. The paragraphs that follow briefly describe the function of each of the OSI layers. The OSI functions are compared to the process of sending a letter via the postal system. The comparison relates the functions of the OSI layers to a communication task with which you are familiar.

Application layer

The application layer consists of software that interacts with the users and allows them to perform their tasks without being involved with the complexity of the computer or network systems. Examples of application software include word processors, spreadsheets, and other software products used in offices. The function of the application layer is analogous to using a word processor to compose and print a letter you want to send. The word processor represents the application program you use to format and type the letter.

Presentation layer

The purpose of the **presentation layer** is to organize the data in machine-readable form. The desktop operating system of your computer is the software component that is directly involved in taking input from devices and converting it into a format the machine can process. The resulting block of information created by the presentation layer is referred to as a **message packet**. The information in the message packet is then transmitted to the presentation layer on the receiving computer for processing.

 Presentation layer software can also be used to compress information in order to save space and transmission time. For increased security, the presentation layer can also be used to encrypt the data using a password or key in order to make it difficult for an intruder to capture and access the information. Banking companies often use special encryption software to secure electronic fund transfers.

The presentation layer can be compared to the mechanics of the word processor that allow your keystrokes to be printed. The resulting piece of paper containing your formatted letter, which you next place in an in-box on your assistant's desk, is the equivalent of a message packet.

Session layer

The purpose of the **session layer** is to initiate and maintain a communication session with the network system. The session layer allows you to log into the file server by providing the server with a valid username and password. Upon successful completion of the login, you are granted access to certain resources of the server.

The job of the session layer can be compared to your company's mail delivery schedule that has been arranged with the local post office. In order to use the mail service, your organization initially contacts the post office and sets up an address along with a schedule for delivery and pickup services. This process corresponds to the session layer initiating a login session with a NetWare file server.

Transport layer

The primary function of the **transport layer** is the reliable delivery of information packets from the source to the destination. This is accomplished by the transport layer on the sending computer, which provides proper address information, and by the transport layer on the receiving computer, which sends an acknowledgement of each packet successfully received from the network. The transport layer creates a packet, called a **segment**, by surrounding the message packet with the necessary acknowledgement and identification fields. The segment packet is then sent to the network layer to complete its addressing requirements.

The transport layer on some multi-tasking computers can also be used to place parts of several message packets from different applications into each segment. The process of placing pieces of multiple message packets into one segment is called **multi-plexing**. Multi-plexing can save communication costs by allowing one cable connection to carry information from several applications simultaneously.

The function of the transport layer can be related to the task performed by your assistant removing the letter from the in-box, checking to be sure it contains all the necessary address information, and then determining the type of service needed for your letter. If this is a very urgent letter, your assistant will probably use an overnight delivery service. If the message contains information that you must be certain is received, the letter can be sent by registered mail, requiring the receiver to acknowledge delivery. After the type of service is determined, your assistant fills out any necessary forms and places the letter in the appropriate envelope.

Network layer

The **network layer** provides the information necessary to route packets through the proper network paths in order to arrive at the destination address. In order to route packets to a destination computer efficiently, the network layer uses **network addresses**, which identify each group of computers on your network system. The network layer then creates a **datagram** packet by encapsulating the information in the segment packet with the necessary packet routing information. The datagram packet is then sent to the data link layer for delivery.

When designing a NetWare network system, you will need to establish a network address for each cable system used in your network.

In postal delivery, a ZIP code is necessary to route a letter through the system. The ZIP code identifies the destination post office location. In a similar way, the network address is used to identify the destination location in a network. The network layers' task is comparable to looking up the correct ZIP code for the destination city and then correctly placing the ZIP code on the envelope along with the name and street address of the receiver. After the ZIP code information has been added to the letter, the envelope can be taken to the post office for delivery.

Data link

The **data link layer** is the delivery system of the computer network and is responsible for using the destination address to send the packet through the requested network cable system. Using the information provided by the network layer, the data link layer creates a packet, called a **frame**, that encapsulates the datagram packet with control information including the source and destination addresses.

In our example, once the letter is placed in the mailbox, it is up to the postal system to deliver the letter. A postal employee determines to which post office the letter gets sent, based on the ZIP code and address information. The letter is then placed in a delivery truck to be taken to that post office.

Physical layer

The **physical layer** comprises the network cable system and connectors that are responsible for sending the data frame packet out as a series of bits. (Bits consist of electronic signals representing ones and zeros.)

In the postal system example, the physical level consists of aircraft, trucks, and trains that physically deliver the letter to the designated post office.

SENDING A MESSAGE

Now that you have a better idea of the purpose and function of each OSI layer, you can apply that knowledge to understand how NetWare sends a message between two network users. Assume you want to use the computer network to send a message asking a friend to meet you for lunch.

On a NetWare network, all messages are first received by the file server and then distributed to the users in much the same way the post office receives mail and then distributes it to individual mailboxes. The following steps explain how the OSI model enables NetWare to send a message from one user to another. Figure 2-2 on the following page summarizes the steps.

To send the message from your computer, you start by running the NetWare SESSION utility and identifying the user to whom you want to send a message. You enter the message ("Can you meet me for lunch at Sam's?"), and press [Enter]. NetWare's SESSION program works with the DOS presentation layer to convert the input to the proper ASCII format needed to form a message packet. The formatted message packet is then combined with the recipient's username and passed to the session layer.

In a NetWare workstation, the session layer sets up and maintains a connection between DOS and the NetWare operating system. A session is originally established when you boot your computer and run the NetWare software that attaches it to the file server. When the session is established, the session layer maintains your workstation's connection to the network by responding to requests from the file server. When the session layer receives the message packet, it checks the status of the network connection, adds any necessary control information needed by the NetWare software, and then sends the message to the transport layer.

Figure 2-2

Sending a message

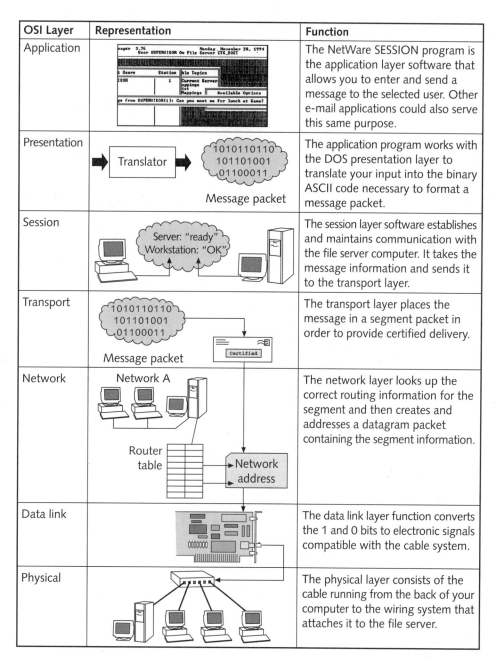

OSI Layer	Representation	Function
Application		The NetWare SESSION program is the application layer software that allows you to enter and send a message to the selected user. Other e-mail applications could also serve this same purpose.
Presentation	Translator → 1010110110 101101001 01100011 — Message packet	The application program works with the DOS presentation layer to translate your input into the binary ASCII code necessary to format a message packet.
Session	Server: "ready" Workstation: "OK"	The session layer software establishes and maintains communication with the file server computer. It takes the message information and sends it to the transport layer.
Transport	1010110110 101101001 01100011 — Message packet Certified	The transport layer places the message in a segment packet in order to provide certified delivery.
Network	Network A Router table → Network address	The network layer looks up the correct routing information for the segment and then creates and addresses a datagram packet containing the segment information.
Data link		The data link layer function converts the 1 and 0 bits to electronic signals compatible with the cable system.
Physical		The physical layer consists of the cable running from the back of your computer to the wiring system that attaches it to the file server.

One of the major functions of the transport layer is to guarantee the delivery of the message packet to your friend's computer. It does this by placing control information in the packet in much the same way you would fill out identifying information if you were sending a registered letter through the postal system. The control information uniquely identifies the packet and tells the receiving computer how to return an acknowledgement. The new packet containing the transport control information is called a **segment**. The segment heading information will be processed by the transport layer on your friend's computer in order to acknowledge that the segment packet has been received successfully. After adding its control information, the transport layer next passes the segment packet to the network layer.

The network layer in the computer is responsible for determining the correct route for sending the packet. In a NetWare network, each cable system is assigned a unique network address similar in purpose to the ZIP codes used by the postal system. The network address allows the packets to be routed quickly and efficiently to the cable system containing the destination computer. The network layer in each computer keeps a table—similar to a ZIP code reference book—that contains the correct network address of all NetWare file servers. In this example, the network layer looks up the address of your friend's file server and then creates a packet, called a **datagram**, by encapsulating the segment information with control information including the network address of your friend's file server.

The data link layer is responsible for delivering the datagram by first creating a unique **data frame** packet for the network cable system. The data link layer encapsulates the datagram packet received from the network layer with heading information, including the addresses for the destination and source computers along with error-checking codes. The data link layer then sends the data frame to the network card for transmission, working closely with the network card to ensure the data frame is transmitted successfully. If an error occurs during transmission, the data frame is sent again. After several unsuccessful attempts, the data link layer will report an error back to the network layer, indicating that the packet could not be delivered. This will usually result in an "Error sending on network" message, giving the user the option to either retry or abort.

The physical layer of a computer network consists of hardware devices such as network interface cards, connectors, and cable systems that are responsible for transmitting the message bit by bit across the network system. The task of transmitting the frame can be compared to the job of a telegraph operator. Just as the telegraph operator must wait for the line to become available and then translate the characters in a message into dots and dashes, so the physical layer must wait for the cable to be available and then use the network card to transmit the frame by encoding the binary digits into the correct electronic signals.

 The standards controlling access on the physical network, as well as the electronic signals used, are controlled by the IEEE organization. The standards used on different network systems will be discussed later in this chapter.

RECEIVING A MESSAGE

A packet of data that is received from the network goes up the OSI stack, reversing the steps used in transmission, starting with the physical layer and proceeding to the application layer. The following steps describe the process.

The frame of information transmitted by the network interface card is sent by the physical layer throughout the network—all network cards read the address contained in the data frame. When the network card in the specified file server recognizes its address, it reads the data frame and passes the bits of data to the data link layer. In the mail delivery example, this is comparable to unloading the letter at the destination post office.

The data link layer then uses the error-checking codes to perform a **cyclic redundancy check (CRC)**. In a CRC check, a mathematical algorithm compares bits received to the CRC code contained in the frame packet. If the calculated CRC matches the CRC contained in data frame, the frame is assumed to be valid and the datagram packet is unpacked and passed to the network layer. If the CRCs do not match, the frame is considered bad, which causes an error to be logged with the file server.

Next, the network layer on the file server checks the information contained in the datagram's heading. After confirming that the packet does not need to be sent to another server, it unpacks the segment packet and sends it to the transport layer. The transport layer then checks the control information contained in the segment packet heading, extracts the message packet and, depending on the control information, creates and sends an acknowledgement packet segment to your computer. The analogy of this process is the recipient of a registered letter signing to confirm that the letter was received. The transport layer on the sending computer is then informed that the packet has been successfully delivered. The transport layer extracts the message information and passes it to the correct NetWare session layer.

The NetWare server presentation and application layers next process the message information and retransmit the message to your friend's computer, where it is received and displayed on the bottom of the screen. After reading the message, your friend can use the [Ctrl][Enter] key combination to remove the message from the screen and continue with the current application.

NETWORK COMPONENTS

You can apply your knowledge of how information flows from one computer to another to understanding the components and product options available at each level of the OSI model. Knowledge of the common network components and product options will allow you to make good decisions in selecting, maintaining, and troubleshooting network systems. In this section you will learn about the network components that make up each layer of the OSI model, what product options are commonly used today, and some trends that might affect network products in the near future.

PHYSICAL LAYER COMPONENTS

The physical layer components of a network system consist of the hardware that sends electrical signals from computer to computer. A CNA will not normally be required to install cables between computers, but because you will probably be involved in decisions relating to the selection of network hardware, you do need to be familiar with the different options available for connecting computers. Understanding the network cable system will also enable you to isolate network problems that result from a faulty cable component.

The two aspects of the physical network system are the **media**, the transmission systems used to send electronic signals, and the **topology**, the physical geometry of the network wiring. In this section you will learn about some common network media and topologies and their advantages and disadvantages.

Network media

The **network media** consist of the communication systems that are used to transmit and receive bits of information. Most network media used today are in the form of cables or wires that run to each computer in the network. These types of media are often referred to as **bounded media** because the signals are contained in or "bounded" by a wire. Another medium type, which is much less common in LANs, involves beaming signals between computers with radio and light waves. These types of transmission media are referred to as **unbounded**. While unbounded media are generally used in wide area networks (WANs) and involve satellite and microwave links over hundreds or thousands of miles, certain specialized types of unbounded media, such as infrared, are gaining acceptance for specialized network applications.

There are three major factors that you should consider when selecting a medium for your network system: bandwidth, resistance to electromagnetic interference, and cost. The **bandwidth** of a network medium is a measure of the medium's capacity in terms of the number of bits per second that can be transmitted. A general rule is that the higher the bandwidth, the more traffic and higher speed the network medium can support.

Electromagnetic interference (EMI) refers to the susceptibility of a medium to interference from outside electrical or magnetic fields. Networks that operate in the vicinity of high levels of electrical and magnetic fields, such as those given off by power plants or large pieces of electrical equipment, will need to install a medium with a high EMI resistance that can carry the network signals reliably without interference.

The cost of installation is another factor in selecting a medium. If more than one medium meets the bandwidth and EMI specifications of an organization, the final factor will depend on the cost of installing the system. Some media types—such as fiber optics—are relatively expensive to install and maintain when compared to other media types, so even though fiber has a very high bandwidth and virtually no EMI problems, it is not a common medium in most LANs.

The following sections describe some of the most common network medium options and compare these systems in terms of bandwidth, EMI, and cost to help you select the best medium for a network system.

Twisted-pair wire

Twisted-pair cable is probably the most common form of bounded medium in use on LANs today. Twisted-pair cable can be unshielded or shielded and consists of pairs of single-strand wire twisted together, as shown in Figure 2-3 on the following page.

Twisting the wires together reduces the possibility of a signal in one wire affecting a signal in another wire. Normally if two wires run side by side, the electrical signal in one wire will create a magnetic field that can induce a small current in the nearby wire. This causes "noise" and results in errors on the network. Twisting the wires eliminates this noise by canceling out the magnetic field. Fifty or more pairs of twisted wire can be put together in one large cable, referred to as a **bundled pair**.

Figure 2-3

Twisted-pair cable

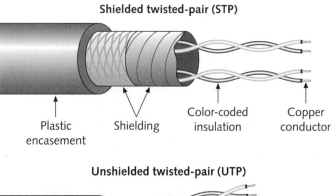

Shielded twisted-pair (STP)

Plastic encasement   Shielding   Color-coded insulation   Copper conductor

Unshielded twisted-pair (UTP)

Plastic encasement   Color-coded insulation   Copper wire conductor

One problem of **unshielded twisted-pair (UTP)** cable is that external electrical voltages and magnetic fields can create noise inside the wire. The noise, or EMI, is unwanted current that can result when the twisted-pair wire lies close to a fluorescent light fixture or an electrical motor. To reduce EMI, **shielded twisted-pair (STP)** cables are surrounded by a metal foil that acts as a barrier to ground out the interference. For STP cable to work, it is important to connect the cable ground to the building's grounding system properly. Unfortunately, the shield of STP cable changes the electrical characteristics of the wire, reducing the distance and speed at which the network's signal can be transmitted.

Figure 2-4

Connectors for twisted-pair wire

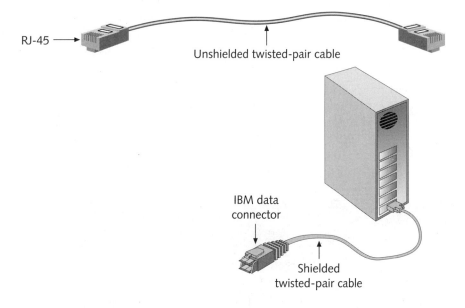

RJ-45

Unshielded twisted-pair cable

IBM data connector

Shielded twisted-pair cable

Two types of connectors can be used on the ends of twisted-pair cable, RJ-45 plugs and IBM data connectors, shown in Figure 2-4. RJ-45 plugs are similar to the modular RJ-11 plugs commonly used to connect telephones to wall jacks and are generally preferred for unshielded cable because of their low cost and ease of installation. The data connector was engineered by IBM to be a universal connector for use with STP cables. Although the data connector is rather large and difficult to install, it provides a very reliable connection for high-speed signals and has the advantage of being able to connect cables together without need for special cable connectors.

In general, UTP media are more common, less expensive, and more readily available than other bounded media. In addition to being shielded or unshielded, twisted-pair wire is available in different varieties that affect the speed at which signals can be sent over the cable. (Signal speed is measured in millions of bits per second or **Mbps**.) Figure 2-5 lists the common types of twisted-pair cable, their associated transmission speeds, and typical usage.

Figure 2-5

Twisted-pair wire types

Wire Type	Speed Range	Typical Usage
1 and 2	Up to 4 Mbps	Voice and low-speed data
3	Up to 16 Mbps	Data
4	Up to 20 Mbps	Data
5	Up to 100 Mbps	High-speed data

Companies that install twisted-pair wire will normally provide you with the correct type of wire for your networking needs. If you are evaluating the existing wiring of a building for use in your network, however, you should first have the cable evaluated by a wire expert to determine if it will support the required network speeds.

The major disadvantages of twisted-pair cable, especially UTP, are its sensitivity to EMI and increased susceptibility to wire tapping by intruders. Wire tapping involves using special equipment, called a sniffer, to detect the signals on the cable by sensing the electrical fields. A wire tapper can also physically splice into the cable in order to access all network signals. You should consider using STP cable or some other medium that is more secure and less vulnerable to EMI if your organization is concerned about the possibility of security violations due to wire tapping or if it needs to run network cable in the vicinity of electrical motors or generators.

Coaxial cable. **Coaxial cable**, commonly referred to as "coax," is made of two conductors (diagrammed in Figure 2-6). The name *coaxial* is derived from the fact that the two conductors in the cable share the same axis. At the center of the cable is a fairly stiff wire encased in insulating plastic. The plastic is surrounded by the second conductor, which is a wire mesh tube that also serves as a shield. A strong insulating plastic tube forms the cable's outer covering.

Figure 2-6

Coaxial cable

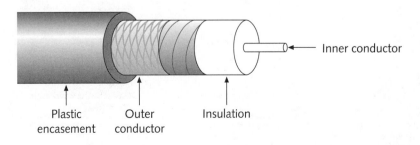

Plastic encasement   Outer conductor   Insulation   Inner conductor

Figure 2-7

Coaxial cable types

Cable Type	Resistance	Typical Usage
RG-8	50 ohms	Thick Ethernet networks
RG-58	50 ohms	Thin Ethernet networks
RG-59	75 ohms	Cable TV and IBM broadband networks
RG-62	93 ohms	ARCnet networks

Coaxial cable is available in a variety of types and thicknesses for different purposes. Figure 2-7 lists the varieties of coaxial cables, their electrical resistance, and their typical use. Generally, thicker cable is used to carry signals longer distances, but is more expensive and less flexible. When compared to twisted-pair, coaxial cable supports higher data rates and is less susceptible to EMI and wire tapping. On the other hand, coaxial cable is generally more expensive, harder to install, and more susceptible to damage due to linking. In the past, many networks were wired with coaxial cable. Improvements in twisted-pair wire's bandwidth, however, along with its flexibility and lower cost, are causing most organizations to select UTP as a medium over coaxial cable for new network installations.

Fiber optic cable. As shown in Figure 2-8, **fiber optic cable** looks similar to coaxial cable. It consists of light-conducting glass or plastic fibers at the center of a thick tube of protective cladding surrounded by a tough outer sheath. One or more fibers can be bounded in the center of the fiber optic cable. Pulses of light are transmitted through the cable by either lasers or light-emitting diodes and received by photo detectors at the far end. Fiber optic cables are much lighter and smaller than either coaxial or twisted-pair cables, and can support significantly higher data rates, from 100 million bits per second to over 2 billion bits per second. Because light signals do not attenuate (lose strength) over distances as quickly as electric signals, fiber optic cables can be used to carry high-speed signals over long distances. In addition, fiber optic transmission is not susceptible to EMI and is very difficult to tap. The principal disadvantages of fiber optic cable are its relatively high cost, lack of mature standards, and difficulty of locating trained technicians to install and troubleshoot it.

Figure 2-8

Fiber optic cable

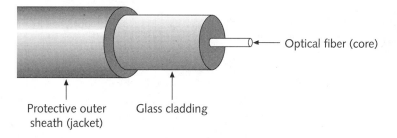

Optical fiber (core)

Protective outer
sheath (jacket)   Glass cladding

Fiber optic cable is used primarily to connect computers that require high-speed access to large data files or in situations where there is a need for maximum protection from EMI or wire tapping. One common use of fiber optic cable is in connecting several high-volume file servers or mini computers to form a backbone network, as shown in Figure 2-9. A **backbone network** is a cable system used primarily to connect a host computer to file servers, each of which can have its own local network. Fiber makes a good backbone network because it allows the file servers to be spread out over long distances and still provides a high-speed communication system that is safe from EMI or differences in grounding between buildings.

Figure 2-9

Backbone network

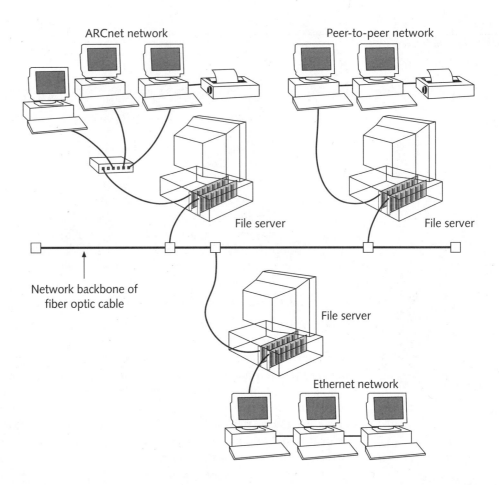

Infrared. **Infrared** is a wireless medium that is based on infrared light from light-emitting diodes (LEDs). Infrared signals can be detected by direct line-of-sight receivers or by indirect receivers capturing signals reflected off walls or ceilings. Infrared signals, however, are not capable of penetrating walls or other opaque objects and are diluted by strong light sources. These limitations make infrared most useful for small, open indoor environments such as a classroom or a small office area with cubicles.

Infrared transmission systems are very cost efficient and capable of high bandwidths similar to those found in fiber optic cables. As a result, an infrared medium can be a good way of connecting wireless LANs when computers are all located within a single room or office. Infrared eliminates the need for cables and allows computers to be easily moved as long as they can always be pointed toward the infrared transmitter/receiver, normally located near the ceiling (see Figure 2-10).

Although the high frequency of infrared waves can accommodate high data transfer rates, advances in infrared technology have been slow due primarily to its limitations in connecting computers separated by walls. Growth of infrared media is expected to accelerate as other radio frequencies become increasingly congested. A large pool of potential infrared installations exists in the networking of classroom computers and limited home or small business applications.

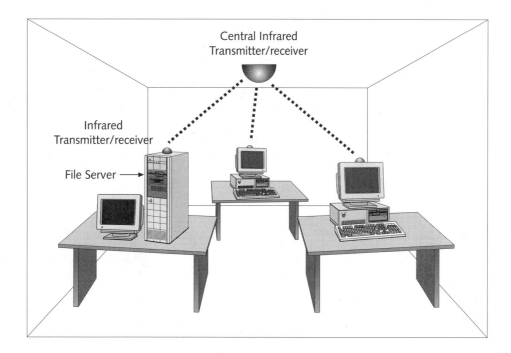

Figure 2-10

Infrared wireless network

Comparing network media

Figure 2-11 summarizes the various network media in terms of cost, ease of installation, transmission capacity, and immunity to EMI and tapping. The cost comparisons are based on costs of media and/or other required hardware. The numbers given for maximum transmission capacity might be deceiving because they are based on the current use of the signaling technology and not on the media's raw bandwidth potential. In the case study exercises at the end of this chapter you will have an opportunity to apply this information to selecting cable systems.

Figure 2-11

Media summary

Medium	Cost	Installation	Capacity	Immunity from EMI and Tapping
Unshielded twisted-pair wire	Low	Simple	1–100 Mbps	Low
Shielded twisted-pair wire	Moderate	Simple to moderate	1–100 Mbps	Moderate
Coaxial cable	Moderate	Simple	10–1000 Mbps	Moderate
Fiber optic cable	Moderate to high	Difficult	100–2000 Mbps	Very high
Infrared	Moderate	Simple	10–100 Mbps	Subject to interference from strong light sources

Network topologies

An important aspect of a network system using bounded media is the method chosen to connect the networked computers. The physical geometry or cable layout used to connect computers in a LAN is called a network **topology**. As a CNA, you will need to be familiar with the topology of your network in order to attach new computers or isolate network problems to a faulty segment of the cable. As shown in Figure 2-12, linear bus, ring, and star are the three major topologies used today to connect computers in a LAN. In this chapter section you will learn about each of these topologies and how they affect network systems in terms of cost, reliability, and expandability.

Figure 2-12

Topologies

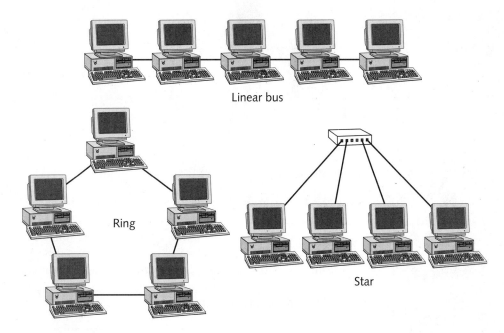

Linear bus

Ring

Star

Star topology.   The **star topology** derives its name from the fact that all cables on the network radiate out from a central hub. The hub is a device that connects the network cables together and passes the signals from one cable to the next. The type of hub you need will depend on the access system used by the network cards (described in the section on data link components). Although star topologies entail higher costs due to the amount of wire needed, they are generally more reliable and easier to troubleshoot than other topologies. Because each cable in a star topology is a separate component, the failure of one cable does not affect the operation of the rest of the network. Troubleshooting for star topologies is easy because a network cable problem can be quickly isolated to the cable "run," on which a network device is experiencing errors. Another advantage of the star topology is the ease of adding or removing devices on the network without affecting the operation of other computers—by using unallocated access ports on the hub you simply plug or unplug cables.

The star topology is rapidly becoming the most popular way to wire computers together due to its exceptional flexibility and reliability.

Today star networks are usually wired with a **patch panel**, as shown in Figure 2-13. In a patch panel system, a wire runs from each potential computer location in the building through a drop cable to a central patch panel. A **patch cable** is then used to connect a device in any given location to the hub. A patch panel system makes it easy to move a computer to another location as well as connect or disconnect computers from the network for troubleshooting purposes.

Figure 2-13

Patch panel system

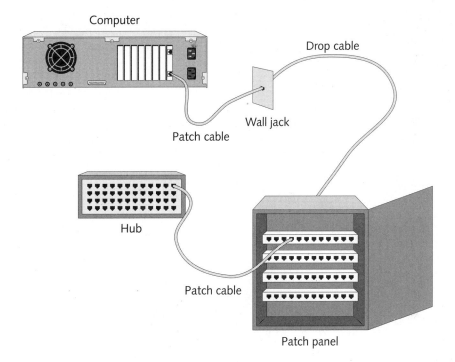

Generally star topologies are implemented with twisted-pair wire rather than coaxial cable because of lower cable cost combined with the increased flexibility and smaller size of twisted-pair cable. RJ-45 connectors on twisted-pair cable allow easy connection of computers to wall outlets and between hubs and patch panels.

Linear bus topology. The **linear bus topology** connects computers together in series by running a cable from one computer to the next. The method of attaching the computers to the "bus" depends on the network card and cable system. When coaxial cable is used, each computer is usually attached to the bus cable by means of a T-connector, as shown in Figure 2-14. When twisted-pair cable is used, each network card usually contains two RJ-45 female connectors that allow twisted-pair cable to be run from one computer to the next.

Figure 2-14

T-Connectors and
terminators

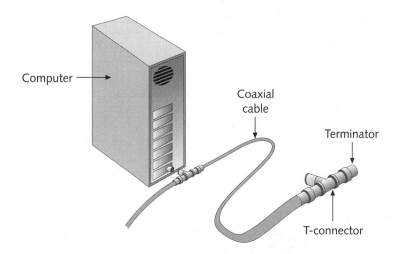

Each end of a linear bus network requires some sort of terminator or "wire-wrap" plug in order to prevent echo signals from interfering with communication signals. The resistance and size of coaxial cable is an important factor and depends on the requirements of the network cards (described in the section on data link components).

The primary advantages of a linear bus topology are the reduced amount of cable needed and the ease of wiring computers that are clustered together in locations such as a classroom or a computer lab. The two biggest disadvantages of a bus network are adding or removing computers and troubleshooting. Adding or removing a computer from a bus network often involves interrupting communication on the network segment. Troubleshooting the network is difficult because when the failure of a cable component causes a network error, it often disrupts communications on the entire network segment and requires the use of special test equipment to locate the faulty network component. Because of these disadvantages, linear bus networks are generally limited to smaller applications or are used in situations where linking computers together is a particularly cost-effective solution.

Ring topology. A **ring topology** is similar to a linear bus topology with the single difference being that the ends of the cable are connected instead of terminated. As a result, signals on the ring topology travel around the network in one direction until they return to the device from which they originated. In a ring topology, each computer in the ring receives signals and then retransmits them to the next computer in the ring. Because the signals are regenerated at each device along the network, a ring topology allows its network signals to traverse longer distances as long as there is another computer located within the distance limit of each network card's transmitter.

The disadvantage of a ring topology is the extra cable needed to complete the ring's circle when computers are spread out in a serial fashion. In addition, the ring has the same disadvantage as the linear bus in terms of interrupting network transmissions in order to add or remove workstations. An advantage of the ring topology over the linear bus topology is that rings are often easier to troubleshoot. Because each computer on the ring receives and then retransmits a signal, it is possible for the troubleshooter to use software that quickly determines which computer is not receiving the signal. The damaged cable component can then be isolated to the cable segment between the computer that does not receive the signal and its "upstream" neighbor.

Repeaters. Network cable systems consist of one or more cable lengths, called **segments**, that have termination points on each end. **Repeaters** are hardware devices that allow you to link network segments together. A repeater receives signals from one network segment and then retransmits them on to the next segments. The hub of a star network topology, for example, can act as a repeater, receiving a signal from one computer cable and broadcasting it on the other cables. Each computer in a ring topology acts as a repeater, receiving the signal from the "upstream" computer and retransmitting it to the next computer on the ring. Repeaters are also used to connect two linear bus segments together. (See Figure 2-18.) This use of repeaters increases the fault tolerance of a linear bus network because a bad connector or cable on one segment does not prevent computers on other segments from communicating. As a CNA, you should be aware of the role of repeaters on your network for easy maintenance and troubleshooting of network problems.

Comparing topologies

Figure 2-15 compares each of the three popular network topologies in terms of their wiring needs, ease of expansion, fault tolerance, and troubleshooting. The type of topology and cable system you select is closely linked to the types of network cards that will be supported on the network. The next section describes the major types of network cards commonly used today, along with the topologies needed to support them.

Figure 2-15

Topology comparisons

Topology	Wiring	Expansion	Fault Tolerance	Troubleshooting
Star	Requires the greatest amount of wire because a cable must be led from each computer to a central hub	Easy to expand by using a patch panel to plug new computers into the hub	Highly fault-tolerant because a bad cable or connector will affect only one computer	Easiest to troubleshoot by removing suspect computers from the network
Linear bus	Usually requires the least amount of cable because the cable is connected from one computer to the next	Difficult to expand unless a connector exists at the location of the new computer	Poor fault tolerance because a bad connector or cable will disrupt the entire network segment	Bus networks are the most difficult to troubleshoot because all computers can be affected by one problem
Ring	Wiring requirements are more than those of a linear bus due to the need to connect the cable ends, but are less than those of a star	Difficult to expand due to the need to break the ring in order to insert a new computer	Poor fault tolerance because a bad connector or cable will disrupt the entire network segment	With proper software, rings can be fairly easy to troubleshoot because software can identify which computer cannot receive the signal

DATA LINK LAYER COMPONENTS

As mentioned in the previous section, the data link components actually control the way signals are transmitted and received on the network cable system. As a result, the components you select for the data link level of your network will determine what network topologies and cable types can be used on the network. Conversely, when you want to use an already existing cable system, you will want to select data link products that best support it. The data link layer components consist of the network interface cards and card driver programs.

The **network interface card (NIC)** is the component that acts as an interface between the network's data link and physical layers by converting the commands and data frames from the data link layer into the appropriate signals used by the connectors on the physical cable system.

Driver software is needed to control the network card and provide an interface between the data link layer and the network layer software. In order to provide this software interface, Novell has developed a set of driver specifications, called the **Open Data Interface (ODI)**. ODI-compatible drivers allow the network card to be shared by multiple programs running on the workstation or on the file server. For example, ODI drivers allow the NetWare file server to communicate with both Apple Macintosh and IBM PCs attached to the same network.

Microsoft networks, on the other hand, use a driver interface called **Network Device Interface Specifications (NDIS)** to interface network card drivers to Microsoft's network operating system. NDIS-compatible drivers allow software developers to write programs for use on Windows 95 and Windows NT computers without requiring them to write instructions to control the network card—the NDIS drivers perform the hardware functions for them. Microsoft's approach results in fewer programming requirements for applications developers as well as more standardized and reliable networking functionality in those applications.

Because there are two types of driver interfaces, ODI and NDIS, you will need to be sure the network cards you obtain for your network contain the correct driver program for the type of network operating system you will be supporting. Novell provides ODI-compatible driver programs for many popular network cards with NetWare v3.12, but some cards are not supported. The manufacturer of an unsupported card should supply a disk with the ODI-compatible driver program that will interface its NIC to a NetWare file server or workstation. In Chapter 5 you will learn about the standard card drivers that are included with NetWare and how to install them on the server or workstation computers.

 Always try to obtain NICs that work with the standard NetWare ODI drivers whenever possible to make it easier to install and maintain your network system.

So that network cards and drivers from different manufacturers can communicate with each other, certain data link standards need to be followed. These standards are controlled by committees within the Institute of Electronic and Electrical Engineers (IEEE). The two major committees that affect LANs today are the IEEE 802.3 and IEEE 802.5 committees.

In addition to controlling types of signals, data link standards control how each computer accesses the network. Because only one signal can be sent on the network cable at any one time, a **channel access method** is necessary to control when computers transmit in order to reduce collisions that can occur when two or more computers attempt to transmit at the same time. Collisions cause network errors by distorting data signals, making them unreadable. Channel access methods used on today's LANs are either token passing or contention based.

The **token passing method** allows only one computer to transmit a message on the network at any given time. This access to the network is controlled by a **token**, which is a special packet passed from one computer to the next to determine which machine can use the network. When a computer needs to transmit data, it waits until it receives the token packet and then transmits its data frame packet on the network. After the transmission is complete, the transmitting computer releases the token. The next computer on the network can pick it up and then proceed to transmit. In its actual implementation, the token passing system is very complex, involving token priorities, early release of tokens, and network monitoring and error-detection functions. As a result, network cards based on the token passing method are generally more expensive.

 The token passing technology was originally developed by IBM and has now been standardized by the IEEE 802.5 committee.

The **contention access method**, often used on bus networks, allows a node to transmit a message whenever it detects the channel is not in use. Think of the contention access method in terms of CB radio use. When no one is talking on a CB radio channel you are free to transmit your message. When someone else is talking on the radio channel, however, you must wait for his or her transmission to end before you start your own transmission. The main problem with contention-based access arises when two or more computers sense an open channel and start transmitting at the same time. A collision results, and the colliding computers must wait a few microseconds before retransmitting their messages. On a computer network, this contention system is referred to as **carrier sense multiple access with collision detection (CSMA/CD)** and has been standardized by the IEEE 802.3 committee into several different product types, based on speed and cable type. The two most popular IEEE 802.3 committee standards, 10BASET and 10BASE2, will be described presently.

A contention system works very well when network traffic is light, but its performance drops off quickly under heavy network transmission loads. Token-based systems perform better under heavy loads because the performance does not drop off as abruptly. The following sections describe the different types of NICs and data link standards in use today and compare the network topology, performance, and access methods of these products.

Token ring network

IBM originally designed the token ring system for use in industrial environments that require reliable high-speed communications. Today, token ring is widely considered to be the best network system in terms of overall performance and reliability.

 Standard token ring cards originally transmitted at 4 Mbps. Today, however, most token ring cards use 16 Mbps transmission speeds. You cannot mix cards running at 4 Mbps with cards running at 16 Mbps on the same token ring network.

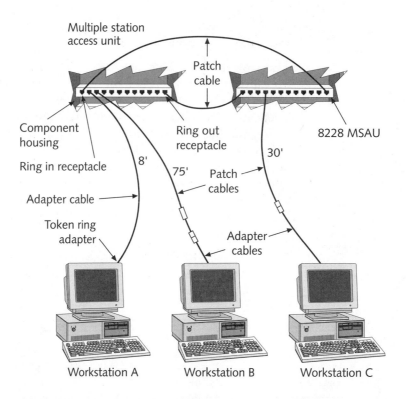

Figure 2-16

Token ring network

The token ring system shown in Figure 2-16 consists of workstations connected by twisted-pair cables to a central hub, called a **multiple station access unit (MSAU)**. Although this appears to be a star arrangement, the network signals actually travel in a ring, which is why it is often referred to as a star ring. A signal originating from workstation A in Figure 2-16, for example, is initially transmitted to the MSAU. The MSAU relays the signal to the cable for workstation B. After receiving the signal, workstation B retransmits the signal and returns it to the MSAU. The MSAU then relays the signal to workstation C, and workstation C transmits the signal back to the MSAU from whence it is relayed back to its source, workstation A. If the wire running from the MSAU to workstation B is broken or if workstation B is shut down, a relay in the MSAU will automatically pass the signal on to workstation C. In this manner, the token ring system is very resistant to breakdowns.

The IBM Token Ring network is often referred to as a Star-Ring because it combines the physical topology of a star with the logical topology of a ring.

The advantages of token ring systems are speed, expandability, and fault tolerance. In addition, token ring systems are usually easy to troubleshoot because bad connections or cable runs can be quickly isolated. The disadvantages include the extra wiring required by the star topology and the higher cost of most token ring cards over other types of network cards. This added to the cost of an MSAU for every eight computers on your network makes token ring networks quite expensive.

10BASET networks

The **10BASET** network system is very popular in business offices today because it combines the flexibility of the star topology with the lower cost of the CSMA/CD channel access method. The IEEE 802.3 designation of 10BASET stands for 10 Mbps baseband network using twisted-pair cable. The term **baseband** describes a computer network that carries **digital signals**; a **broadband** system carries **analog signals**, like the signals used for television and radio transmissions.

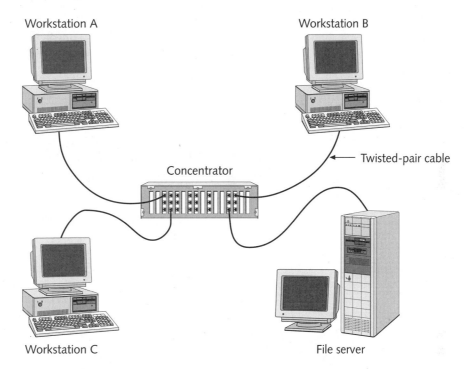

Workstation A   Workstation B

Twisted-pair cable

Concentrator

Workstation C   File server

Figure 2-17

10BASET network

A 10BASET network uses a device called a **concentrator** as a hub to connect all machines in a star topology with twisted-pair cable, as shown in Figure 2-17. Although the 10BASET network uses the same star topology used by a token ring network, the 10BASET signals are not sent from one station to the next as in token ring. They are broadcast to all stations, simultaneously, using the CSMA/CD method standardized by the IEEE 802.3 committee. In many instances a cable system designed for token ring can easily be converted to support 10BASET simply by replacing the MSAUs with concentrators. The concentrator acts as a repeater, receiving signals on one cable port and then retransmitting those signals on all other ports. When two or more network stations attempt to transmit at the same instant, a collision occurs, and the stations must retransmit after waiting a random period of time.

The advantages of 10BASET include high performance under light to medium network loads and low costs for network cards due to the relative simplicity of the CSMA/CD system. Although 10BASET performance can be faster than token ring under light loads, it is more easily slowed due to collisions when many stations are transmitting on the network. Another disadvantage of the 10BASET system is additional cost both for concentrators and for the star topology wiring.

Ethernet

The popular **ethernet** system, shown in Figure 2-18, is based on the linear bus topology and uses the CSMA/CD system standardized by the IEEE 802.3 committee called 10BASE2. The term 10BASE2 comes from the fact that ethernet networks have a transmission speed of 10 Mbps using digital baseband signals over a maximum of two 100-meter cable segments. Thin type RG-58 coaxial cable with T-connectors allows up to 30 machines to be attached to a single cable run or segment. According to the 10BASE2 standards, a segment cannot exceed 607' in length, and no more than five segments can be joined by repeaters to form the entire network. Additionally, a maximum of three of the five segments can have workstations attached. Network professionals often refer to 10BASE2 as **thinnet** because of its thin coaxial cable.

Figure 2-18

Ethernet network

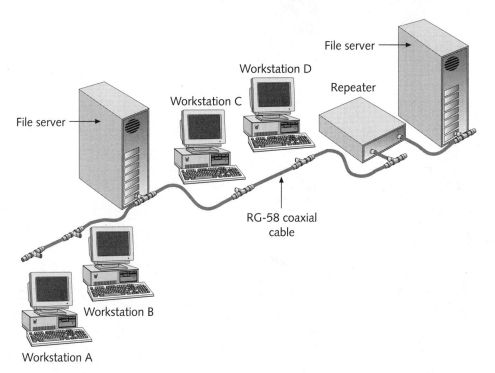

10BASE2 or ethernet cards use the same CSMA/CD system and 10 Mbps speed used by 10BASET cards. Some manufacturers supply cards that can be configured for either the twisted-pair 10BASET system or the RG-58 cable bus. While both ethernet and 10BASET provide excellent throughput under normal network loads, wiring ethernet is simpler and more cost effective than 10BASET in certain environments—those in which groups of computers are located in a small area, such as a computer lab, where one coaxial cable runs machine to machine.

Be sure to obtain cable that meets your local building fire codes if you decide to install new cable above a ceiling or in walls.

ARCnet

Despite its relatively slow speed (2 Mbps), **ARCnet** is popular for small networks because of its low cost and flexible topology. Today, the decreased cost of ethernet and 10BASET systems combined with the lack of IEEE standards for ARCnet and its slower speed make it a poor choice for most networks. Because it has been popular in the past, however, you might encounter networks based on the ARCnet system.

Figure 2-19

ARCnet network

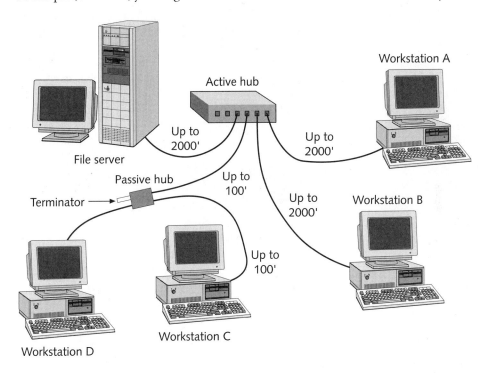

The ARCnet system, shown in Figure 2-19, has a star topology in which an **active hub** acts as a signal repeater, allowing cable runs of up to 2000' from the active hub to the attached workstation computers. **Passive hubs** are simple signal splitters. They can be used at the end of a run to split the cable and allow up to three workstations to be attached to a single cable run. When a passive hub is used, wire length must be limited to 100'. Depending on the ARCnet cards used, either twisted-pair or RG-68 coaxial cable can connect computers. The advantages of ARCnet are low card cost and flexible wiring options. Its disadvantages are slow speed, higher cabling costs based on its star topology, and lack of standardization.

Comparing network systems

Selecting a network system is a complex task that depends on such variables as types and location of computers, existing wiring, and the amount of load expected on the network. In many organizations, multiple network systems are necessary to meet the needs of different departments. Such network systems can be connected with bridges and routers, described in the next section. Figure 2-20 contains a summary of the major network systems.

Figure 2-20

Network comparisons

Network System	Cable Types	Topology	Maximum Number of Nodes	IEEE Standard	Speed	Access Method	Distance
Token ring	UTP, STP fiber	star	96	802.5	4–16 Mbps	token	150' per cable run
10BASET	UTP fiber	star	512	802.3	10 Mbps	CSMA/CD	328' per cable run
Ethernet (10BASE2)	coaxial	linear bus	30 per segment with maximum of 3 populated segments	802.3	10 Mbps	CSMA/CD	607' per segment
ARCnet	RG-62 coaxial UTP	star	255	none	2 Mbps standard	token	2000' from active hub, 100' from passive hub

Bridges and routers

As you have read, each network system presented in this chapter has its own unique limitations. In some cases, you will want to take advantage of certain features found in two different products. For example, in a school environment you might want to implement the ethernet system in computer labs to take advantage of the economical coaxial wiring arrangement. If other computers in the building are located many feet apart in completely separate areas, however, you won't want to connect them this way. You can solve this problem by creating two separate networks—ethernet for the lab and token ring for the office. You then connect the networks together so they share access to the same file server. In other cases, it might be necessary to break a large network into two or more smaller networks to overcome performance problems or cabling distances or to accommodate large numbers of users.

Separate network systems can be connected together with bridges or routers, as shown in Figure 2-21. Whenever two or more networks are attached together, the resultant network is referred to as an **internetwork**. Understanding how bridges and routers can be used to connect networks to form an internetwork will help you meet the needs of your organization.

A **bridge** operates at the data link layer of the OSI model. This means that the bridge sees only the packet's frame information, which consists of the addresses of the sender and receiver along with error-checking information. During network operation, the bridge watches packets on both networks and builds a table of workstation node addresses for each network. When it sees a packet on one network that has a destination address for a machine on the other network, the bridge reads the packet, builds new frame information, and sends the packet out on the other network. Because bridges work at the data link level, they are used to connect networks of the same type. For example, a bridge can connect two different token ring networks and allow more than 100 users to access the same file server. Another use for a bridge might be to break a heavily loaded ethernet or 10BASET network into two separate networks in order to reduce the number of collisions occurring on any one network system. A bridge is often contained in a separate black box but can also consist of specialized software running on a microcomputer that simply contains two network cards.

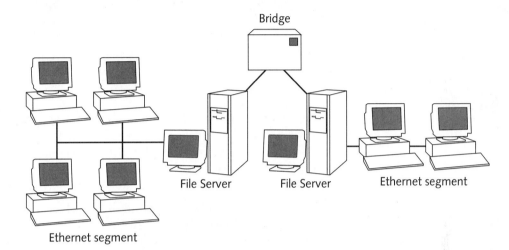

Bridge

File Server   File Server   Ethernet segment

Ethernet segment

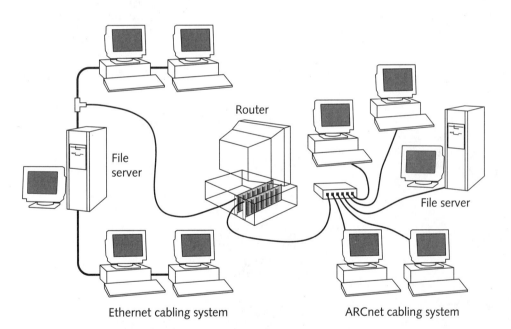

Router

File server

File server

Ethernet cabling system   ARCnet cabling system

Routers are needed to create more complex internetworks. A **router** operates at the network layer of the OSI model and therefore has access to the datagram information containing the logical network address along with control information. When a router is used, each network must be given a separate network address. Remember that a network address is similar in function to a ZIP code. Just as each postal area has a unique ZIP code, each network system must have a unique network address. The router information contained in the datagram packet allows a router to find the correct path and, if necessary, break up a datagram for transmission on a different network system. Two disadvantages of routers are that they require a little more processing time than bridges and that network packets must use a datagram format that the router can interpret.

Generally, networks with different network topologies are connected with routers, whereas networks of the same topology are connected with bridges. Novell uses routers in its NetWare file servers to allow up to eight different network cards to be installed in a single file server computer. This enables you to use the NetWare file server to connect networks of different types and topologies in order to form an internetwork. In Chapter 5 you will learn how to configure a NetWare file server to act as an internal router, connecting two different networks.

PROTOCOL STACKS

The network's **protocol stack** is responsible for formatting requests to access network services and transmit data. While the delivery of the data packets throughout a network system is the responsibility of its data link and physical layer components, the functions of the network, transport, and session layers are built into a network operating system's protocol stack.

Novell's SPX/IPX protocol stack is commonly used to support DOS-based computers on NetWare networks, and a network administrator needs to know how to configure and maintain the IPX protocol. Because today's networks often need to support protocol stacks of computers running other operating systems as well, the CNA should also be familiar with the common protocol stacks used by such operating systems as Macintosh, Unix, and Windows.

In this section you will learn about protocol stacks and some of their advantages and disadvantages, which will enable you to make informed recommendations on what protocol stacks should be supported on a network. You will have an opportunity to use this information later in this book when you learn how to install either the IPX protocol in Chapter 5 or the TCP/IP protocol stack in Chapter 14.

NetWare SPX/IPX

The SPX/IPX protocol is the Novell proprietary system that implements the session, transport, and network OSI layers, as shown in Figure 2-22. Notice that SPX/IPX is not a true implementation of the OSI model, because IPX and SPX functions overlap layers. This is true of many older protocol stacks that were developed before the OSI model was developed and standardized.

Figure 2-22

Novell SPX/IPX protocol

OSI Model Levels

	Physical	Data Link	Network	Transport	Session	Presentation	Application
SPX				X	X		
IPX			X	X			
Ethernet	X	X					
ARCnet	X	X					
Token ring	X	X					
Others	X	X					

IPX (for internetwork packet exchange) is the NetWare protocol that manages packet routing and formatting at the network layer. To function, IPX must be loaded on each network workstation and on the file server. In addition to IPX, each workstation and file server must have loaded a network card driver along with the IPX software in order to transmit the frames containing the packets. IPX software and the network card driver are brought together during the network installation process, as described in Chapter 5. NetWare uses two protocols in addition to IPX to provide network services, SPX and NCP. SPX (for sequential packet exchange) operate at the OSI transport level and provide guaranteed delivery of packets by receiving an acknowledgement for each packet sent.

NCP (NetWare Core Protocol) provides the session and presentation levels at the workstation through the DOS requester program called NETX or the new NetWare 3.12 requester program called VLM. NETX and VLM both establish and maintain network sessions as well as direct information and requests from the workstation and format them for the file server. On the file server, NCP provides network services such as login, file sharing, printing, security, and administrative functions.

TCP/IP

Figure 2-23

TCP/IP protocol

OSI Model Layers

	Physical	Data Link	Network	Transport	Session	Presentation	Application
TCP				X			
IP			X				
Token ring	X	X					
Ethernet	X	X					
Others	X	X					

As shown in Figure 2-23, **TCP/IP (transport control protocol/internet protocol)** covers the same OSI layers as SPX/IPX. Like the IPX protocol, TCP/IP is responsible for formatting packets and then routing them between networks using IP (internet protocol). IP is more sophisticated than IPX in fragmenting packets and transmitting over wide area network links. When IP is used, each workstation is assigned a logical network and node address. IP allows packets to be sent out over different routers and then reassembled in the correct sequence at the receiving station. TCP (transport control protocol) operates at the transport level and provides the guaranteed delivery of packets by receiving acknowledgments. The acknowledgement system allows the sender and receiver to establish a window for the number of packets to be acknowledged. This allows for better performance over WANs, because each packet does not need to be individually acknowledged before another packet is sent. With NetWare 3.12, this method of acknowledging multiple packets can be implemented in what Novell calls **packet burst mode**.

Today TCP/IP is commonly used on Unix operating systems as well as the Internet. Novell file servers can use the TCP/IP protocol to communicate with Unix-based computers and to route TCP/IP packets between network cards.

The need to implement TCP/IP on a NetWare network is growing rapidly because of the exploding popularity of the Internet and the need for CNAs to provide more network support for Unix-based workstations.

NetBEUI

Microsoft's own protocol stack, **NetBEUI**, is integrated into the Windows 95 and Windows NT products. Of the three protocols described in this section, NetBEUI is the smallest, fastest, and easiest to use. It has few features, however, and cannot be used in large internetwork environments because it does not support the network layer needed for routing packets between networks. As a result, the NetBEUI protocol is limited to communicating with other computers attached to the same network cable system. Another disadvantage of the NetBEUI protocol is that it was developed specifically to support peer-to-peer networking on small networks comprising 30 to 50 workstations.

Figure 2-24

NetBEUI protocol

	OSI Model Layers						
	Physical	Data Link	Network	Transport	Session	Presentation	Application
Net BEUI				X	X		
NBF or NBT			X				
Token ring	X	X					
Ethernet	X	X					
Others	X	X					

The NetBEUI protocol stack consists of NetBIOS and service message blocks (SMBs) at the session layer and NetBIOS frames (NBF) at the transport layer, as shown in Figure 2-24. SMBs and NetBIOS provide a well-defined standard method for servers and workstations to communicate with each other. Many peer-to-peer applications have been written to interface with NetBIOS, allowing an application to span multiple computers. Because NetBIOS-based applications are popular, Novell has provided a NetBIOS interface to work with its SPX/IPX protocol. This allows workstations to run peer-to-peer applications while still accessing services from NetWare file servers. The LANtastic peer-to-peer network product also uses NetBIOS to establish communication among DOS-based computers.

Because NetBEUI's NBF does not maintain routing tables, it is extremely small and fast, making it ideal for networks ranging from 2 to 50 devices. Because the NBF does not support packet routing, however, the protocol is limited to communication among computers attached to a single network. The NetBEUI protocol allows for the replacement of NBF with NBT (NetBIOS over TCP/IP), which allows the protocol stack to communicate directly over large TCP/IP-based networks.

AppleTalk

The AppleTalk protocol suite was originally developed to allow Macintosh computers to communicate in peer-to-peer networks. It currently provides connectivity for a variety of computer systems including IBM PCs running MS-DOS, IBM mainframes, and various Unix-based computers. The AppleTalk protocol suite was developed after the OSI model was conceived and therefore can be mapped reasonably well to the OSI layers, as shown in Figure 2-25.

Figure 2-25

AppleTalk protocol

OSI Model Layers

	Physical	Data Link	Network	Transport	Session	Presentation	Application
Apple Filing Protocol(AFP)						X	
Apple Session Protocol (ASP)					X		
Apple Transition Protocol (ATP)				X			
Data Delivery Protocol (DDP)			X				
AARP	X	X					
Local Talk	X	X					
Ethertalk (Ethernet)	X	X					
Token Talk (Token Ring)	X	X					

On the data link level, the Apple Address Resolution Protocol (AARP) connects the AppleTalk protocol stack to the ethernet, 10BASET, or token ring protocol. AppleTalk supports the routing of packets between networks by using the Datagram Delivery Protocol (DDP). In addition, AppleTalk uses zones to organize the names of service providers logically on large internetworks. Zones limit the number of service providers that are presented at one time, which simplifies the user's choices.

Because of the popularity of the Macintosh and of the AppleTalk protocol, Novell has included a five-user version of AppleTalk with NetWare v3.12 file servers. Loading the AppleTalk protocol on a NetWare file server allows Macintosh or other computers using AppleTalk to see the file server as another AppleTalk service provider.

CHAPTER SUMMARY

Network communication depends on packets of information being passed from one computer to another. Understanding how information packets flow through a network system means knowing the functions of the seven layers of the open systems interconnect (OSI) model. The application layer software is responsible for interacting with the user and providing software tools to perform specific tasks. The presentation layer then translates the data from the application layer into the appropriate ASCII and binary codes. The session layer initiates and maintains a communication session with the file server computer providing an interface between the local DOS and the network operating system. The transport layer is responsible for the reliable delivery of data packets, called segments, and often requires the receiving computer to send acknowledgments confirming the receipt of the segment packets. The network layer places the segment packet in a datagram and handles routing of datagram to the correct computer. The data link and physical layers act as the delivery system by placing the datagram packets in frames and sending them on the network cable system. Special committees of the Institute of Electronic and Electrical Engineers (IEEE) control the physical and data link standards for LAN network systems. The IEEE 802.3 committee controls the contention-based carrier sense multiple access with collision detection (CSMA/CD) system, and the IEEE 802.5 committee controls the token passing standard.

Cable types used with today's LANs include shielded and unshielded twisted-pair wire, coaxial cable, and fiber optic cable. Infrared is a special communication medium that uses light beams rather than cable to transmit information from each computer to a central device. The infrared system is a good alternative for a network in a single room where installing cable can be particularly difficult or expensive. The physical geometry of a bounded medium is called its topology. Major physical topologies include ring, linear bus, and star.

Regardless of the type of topology used, only one machine can transmit on a network at any given instant, and with some a method of access control must be used to avoid data collisions. Network access control methods can be either contention based or token based. Ethernet and 10BASET networks use a contention system, in which computers attempt to transmit whenever they sense an open period on the network. On busy networks, however, when two or more machines sense an open period and try to transmit at the same time, a collision occurs and the machines each wait a random time period before retrying their transmissions—this is CSMA/CD.

Token ring and ARCnet both use a deterministic system called token passing. A token is passed around the network when no data packet is being transmitted. A machine needing to transmit must wait for the token. When it receives the token, it can transmit its packet without any collisions. Collisions cause CSMA/CD systems to slow significantly under heavy network transmission loads whereas token passing systems provide more uniform and predictable performance.

An internetwork consists of two or more network topologies connected together by a bridge or router. Working at the data link layer, bridges are very efficient, but they are limited to moving frames between networks of similar design. Routers are more sophisticated because they work at the network layer and have access to the datagram control information. Because of this access, routers can select the most efficient path for a packet and fragment packets into the correct size to send over the selected network.

Protocols are the languages used to implement the OSI layers. Popular protocols you will probably encounter as a CNA include Novell NetWare's SPX/IPX, the TCP/IP protocol used by Unix and the Internet, NetBEUI used in Microsoft Windows-based networks, and the AppleTalk protocol used for Macintosh computers. NetWare servers use Novell's SPX/IPX protocol by default, but can also be configured to handle TCP/IP and AppleTalk. TCP/IP is becoming a very popular protocol for use in Unix environments and international WANs such as the Internet. Both IP and IPX are network layer protocols that control the routing and flow of packets in the network system. TCP and SPX are similar in that they are both transport protocols that provide guaranteed delivery of packets.

KEY TERMS

10BASE2

10BASET

active hub

analog signals

application layer

ARCnet

backbone network

bandwidth

baseband

bounded media

bridge

broadband

carrier sense multiple access with collision detection (CSMA/CD)

channel access method

collision

concentrator

cyclic redundancy check (CRC)

datagram

data link layer

digital signals

electromagnetic interference (EMI)

ethernet

fiber optic cable

frame

infrared

Institute of Electrical and Electronic Engineers (IEEE)

International Standards Organization (ISO)

internetwork

interoperability

media

message packet

multiple station access unit (MSAU)

NetBEUI network address

Network Driver Interface Specifications (NDIS)

network layer

network media

network topology

open data interface (ODI)

open systems interconnect (OSI) model

packet

passive hub

patch cable

patch panel

physical layer

presentation layer

protocol stack

repeater

ring topology

router

segment

session layer

thinnet

token

token passing method

topology

transport layer

unbounded media

REVIEW QUESTIONS

1. The _Institute of Electrical & Electronic Engineers_ (IEEE) standards organization works on physical cable standards.

2. The _Transport_ layer of the OSI model provides guaranteed delivery of segment packets.

3. The data link layer is responsible for _using the destination address to send the packet through the requested network cable system._

4. Sequence the following OSI layers starting from the hardware level and match the packet types with the OSI layers that use them.

    SEQUENCE LAYER   **PACKET TYPE**

    __3__ session   __6__ a. frame

    __1__ application   __2__ b. message

    __2__ presentation   __4__ c. segment

    __6__ data link   __5__ d. datagram

    __7__ physical   __7__ e. bits

    __5__ network

    __4__ transport

5. The _____Infrared_____ unbounded medium would be well suited for use in a classroom.

6. _Twisted-Pair wire_ is the most common form of bounded medium.

7. What can be done to reduce EMI in electrical cables? _Shield the wire_

8. In a(n) ___Star___ topology, a cable is run from each computer to a central device.

9. Coaxial cable is often used with the _Linear Bus_ topology.

10. An MSAU is used on a(n) _Token Ring_ network system.

11. Under the _____ channel access method, only one node is given permission to transmit a message on the network at any given time.

12. The _Token Passing_ access method performs best under heavy loads.

13. Match the IEEE standards to the appropriate products.

    __a__ Ethernet   a. IEEE 802.3

    __b__ Token ring   b. IEEE 802.5

    __a__ 10BASET   c. No IEEE standard

    __c__ ARCnet

14. A concentrator is used on a(n) _10BASET_ network system.

15. Identify which type of medium is commonly used by each of the following network systems.

    ethernet ————————————————————————

    10BASET ————————————————————————

    token ring ———————————————————————

    ARCnet———————————————————————————

16. A(n) _router_ operates at the network layer of the OSI model and can be used to connect networks of different topologies.

17. A(n) _internetwork_ consists of two or more networks attached together by a bridge or router.

18. A(n) _protocol stack_ is a method of implementing the network, transport, and session layers of the OSI model in a network system.

19. The _transport control protocol/internet protocol_ (TCP/IP) protocol is commonly used by the Unix operating system.

20. The _NetBEUI_ protocol is commonly used with Windows NT and Windows 95 workstations.

21. The _sequential packet exchange/internetwork packet exchange (SPX/IPX)_ is a proprietary protocol used in NetWare networks.

22. _SPX & NCP. SPX_ is the protocol that provides NetWare network services.

23. TCP operates at the _Transport_ layer of the OSI model.

24. IPX operates at the _Network & Transport_ layer of the OSI model.

25. List an advantage and a disadvantage of the NetBEUI protocol.
    adv: It's the smallest, fastest, and easiest to use
    dis: It has few features and cannot be used on large networks

EXERCISES

In these exercises you will use the Novell IPX and NETX commands to demonstrate the OSI layers used to attach your workstation to the network and access the file server. You will then use NetWare commands on the server to view information about all file servers on your Internetwork, log in to a selected file server, and view network and node address information for all users attached to your file server.

Exercise 1: Attaching to the Network

Boot your workstation but do not automatically attach to the file server. If necessary, your instructor will provide you with a floppy disk for this exercise. To load the NetWare data link, network, and transport layers, type **IPX** and press **[ENTER]**. Record the message obtained from loading IPX on the line below:

To load the NetWare shell, which handles the session and presentation layers, type **NETX** and press **[ENTER]**. The session layer of NETX will attempt to make a connection with a file server. It does this by sending out a special Get Nearest Server packet. A session is started with the first server to respond to this packet. After establishing a server connection, NETX maps the first network drive letter, usually F: to the LOGIN directory of the attached file server. DOS then has access to load and run programs from the file server by going through the F drive. Once NETX is loaded in memory, it works with the DOS presentation layer to redirect any requests for network file or print services to the file server. In the space below, record the message you receive after loading the NETX program.

To access files and programs in the file server's LOGIN directory, change to drive F and type **DIR**. Record the names of the files found on the server's LOGIN directory in the space below. Try deleting all the files (don't worry, the file server will not let you do this).

Exercise 2-2: Viewing File Server Information

The SLIST.EXE program displays a list of all file server(s) on your internetwork along with the server's network address and the number of routers you must go through to access the server. Type **SLIST** and press **[ENTER]**. Record the information about your file server(s) in the following table. Highlight your default server.

Server Name	Network Address	Number of Routers

Exercise 2-3: Logging in to a specific file server

The LOGIN command is used to log into your assigned file server. If you enter the command LOGIN username, the shell will attempt to log into the default file server. In most cases this will be your assigned file server. If the shell is attached to a different server, however, or if you want to access services on another server, you need to specify the name of the server when you enter the LOGIN command. This is done by specifying the name of the desired file server followed by a slash and then your username. For example LOGIN RLHOST386\TEDSIM could be used to log Ted Simpson into the RLHOST386 file server. On the line below, write the command to log into your file server regardless of the default server.

Test this command and record the results below:

Exercise 2-4: Viewing User Information

The USERLIST command can be used to obtain network information about each user's connection, including the workstation's network card address and the logical address of the network to which the workstation is attached. The network card's address is used on each data frame packet. The network address is included in the datagram packets sent out by the IPX protocol. Use the USERLIST /E or USERLIST /A command to record at least one workstation from each logical network address in the space below. You will probably see only your network address unless your file server is attached to multiple networks and users from other networks are attached to your file server.

Username	Network Address	Node Address

Exercise 2-5: Using the SESSION Menu Utility

In this exercise you will learn how to use the NetWare SESSION utility to look up network information and send a message to another user on the network.

1. Type **SESSION** and press **[ENTER]**.

2. Select User Information and record the names of three other users on your network.

   _____

   _____

   _____

3. Send a message to one of the users recorded above telling him or her your name and workstation address.

4. Use the **Groups** option to record the names of two groups on your file server.

   _____

   _____

Exercise 2-6: Log Out

Use the LOGOUT command to log out of the file server. Record the information provided by the log out process in the space below.

EXERCISES

Case 2-1: PC Solutions Company

The PC Solutions company described in Chapter 1 currently has five computers located in the business office (as shown in Figure 2-26) that they need to connect to the network operating system you defined in Chapter 1. Because the company will probably not be staying in its current building very much longer, the management does not want to spend much money to have someone wire the offices. PC Solutions needs you to recommend a topology and network system that will meet the needs of the company. The company also needs you to draw the necessary cable runs on the floor plan and submit it with your network recommendations.

1.   Select the topology and network system.

Topology selected: _____

Justification:

Network system selected: _____

Justification:

2.   Draw your proposed network cable system on the diagram in Figure 2-26.

Figure 2-26

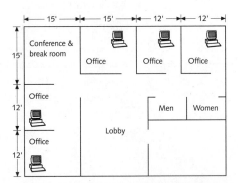

Case 2-2: The ACME Network System

As described in Chapter 1, the ACME Corporation would like to implement a network system to connect its computers together in order to collect quality-control information from the shop floor and save it on the central file server for processing by other computer users. ACME currently has 12 computer workstations all located in the business office with two data collection stations in the shop. One of the problems faced by the computers in the shop is the increased level of electrical interference created by motors and other equipment. Your help is needed to recommend a topology and network system that will meet the needs of the ACME Corporation and then draw the necessary cable runs on the floor plan shown in Figure 2-27.

1. Select a topology and network system.

    Topology selected: _____

    Justification:

    Network system selected: _____

    Justification:

2. Draw your network cable system on the diagram in Figure 2-27.

Figure 2-27

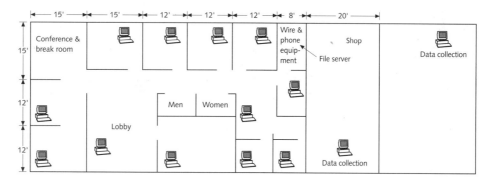

Case 2-3: Court House Network

As described in Chapter 1, the social workers in the county court house are planning to implement a network system to allow 20 users to communicate and share files and printers. In the future additional users in other departments will possibly be added to the network to create a system that will meet the communication needs of the entire court house in the foreseeable future. Using the floor plan shown in Figure 2-28, recommend a topology and network system that will best meet the current needs of the social workers and provide for easy network expansion in the future.

1.   Select topology and network system.

   Topology selected: _____

   Justification:

   Network system selected: _____

   Justification:

2.   Draw your network cable system on the diagram in Figure 2-28.

Figure 2-28

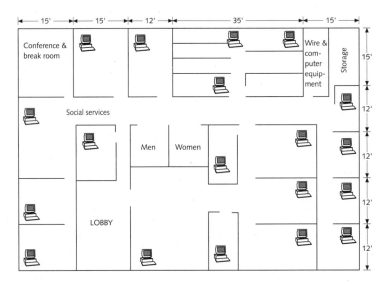

SUPERIOR TECHNICAL COLLEGE PROBLEMS

Project 2-1: Network Design

Based on your recommendation (from Chapter 1), Dave Johnson has decided to proceed with the network project at Superior Technical College. He would like to use either 10BASET or IBM token ring to connect the faculty and staff computers to the file server. To save wiring costs, Dave is exploring the option of using thinnet (10BASE2) in the computer lab. At this time Dave would like you to document a network layout that shows the cabling necessary to implement a UTP star network for the administrative office users and classroom computers along with a linear bus network for the computer in labs A and B. Because token ring and 10BASET both use twisted-pair wire, the same wiring plan should work for either network.

Ethernet Costs:

_____ cards $\times$ \$_____ per card = \$_____

_____ amount of cable $\times$ \$_____ per foot =
\$_____

_____ connectors $\times$ \$_____ each = \$_____

Total \$_____

10BASET Costs:

_____ cards $\times$ \$_____ per card = \$_____

_____ concentrators $\times$ \$_____ each =
\$_____

Total \$_____

Token Ring Costs:

_____ cards $\times$ _____ per card = \$_____

_____ MSAUs $\times$ _____ each = \$_____

Total \$_____

Recommendation:

Figure 2-29

First floor of superior campus

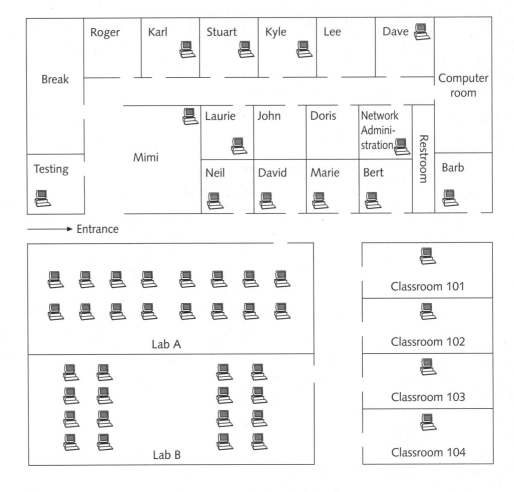

Project 2-2: Estimating 10BASET network costs:

Since the star network you defined in Project 2-1 will support either 10BASET or token ring network systems, Dave would like you to determine the cost differences between 10BASET and token ring and recommend which network system you prefer.

1.　In the table below, use current cost information as identified by your instructor to fill in the projected costs for the Superior Technical College to implement the administration users and the computers in the classrooms on a 10BASET network system.

Estimated 10BASET costs:

Cost per card	Number of cards	Total card cost
Cost per concentrator	**Number of concentrators**	**Total concentrator cost**

Total 10BASET cost: _____

2. In the table below, use current cost information as identified by your instructor to fill in the projected costs for the Superior Technical College to implement the administration users and the computers in the classrooms on a token ring network system.

Estimated token ring costs:

Cost per card	Number of cards	Total card cost
Cost per MSAU	**Number of MSAUs**	**Total MSAU cost**

Total token ring cost: _____

3. **Recommended network system:**

_____

List two reasons for your recommendation in the space below:

Project 2-3: Estimating 10BASE2 network costs:

In addition to the star network, Dave would like you to calculate the costs of implementing the Ethernet 10BASE2 network system in the computer labs. In the table below, use current cost information as identified by your instructor to fill in the projected costs for the Superior Technical College to implement the computer lab workstations on a Ethernet 10BASE2 bus network system.

Estimated Ethernet 10BASE2 costs:

Cost per card	Number of cards	Total card cost
Amount of cable	**Cost per ft.**	**Total cable cost**
Number of T-connectors	**Cost per T-connector**	**Total connector cost**

Total lab network cost: _____

MICROCOMPUTER HARDWARE

In previous chapters you learned about the components of a LAN, focusing on the software and cable systems that support distributed processing. Because LANs support distributed processing on a variety of computer systems, a CNA must also be familiar with how computer hardware components work. This knowledge enables a CNA to manage network processing and file server requirements, make decisions or recommendations involving the upgrade or purchase of new file server computers, and to develop specifications for user workstations.

Microcomputer systems are based on complex and evolving technologies that involve combining components from many manufacturers to meet the growing processing needs of software applications. In order to make sense of many concepts and terms that are used in today's computer environments, a CNA must have a solid background in fundamental microcomputer concepts. This chapter provides a basic background in computer terminology and concepts and describes popular hardware products. This information will both help you meet the computer hard-ware requirements of the Novell CNA test and help you keep abreast of

AFTER READING THIS CHAPTER AND COMPLETING THE EXERCISES YOU WILL BE ABLE TO:

- IDENTIFY THE HARDWARE COMPONENTS THAT MAKE UP A MICROCOMPUTER SYSTEM.

- COMPARE AND CONTRAST MICROPROCESSORS USED ON NETWARE FILE SERVERS AND WORKSTATIONS.

- DESCRIBE THE PURPOSE OF AND USE OF EXPANSION BUSES, I/O PORTS, AND INTERRUPTS IN A MICROCOMPUTER SYSTEM.

- COMPARE AND CONTRAST STORAGE SYSTEMS USED ON NETWARE FILE SERVERS.

- APPLY KNOWLEDGE OF COMPUTER HARDWARE COMPONENTS TO DEVELOPING FILE SERVER SPECIFICATIONS.

developments in microcomputer-based hardware. In addition, the information in this chapter provides a basis for configuring network cards and evaluating file server performance, discussed in future chapters.

COMPUTER BASICS

A microcomputer operates on the same basic internal principles as its larger siblings, mini and mainframe computers. All computers, no matter what their size or capacity, need to perform input, processing, storage, and output operations. The hardware that allows these processes to take place on a microcomputer system is shown in Figure 3-1.

Figure 3-1

The computer model

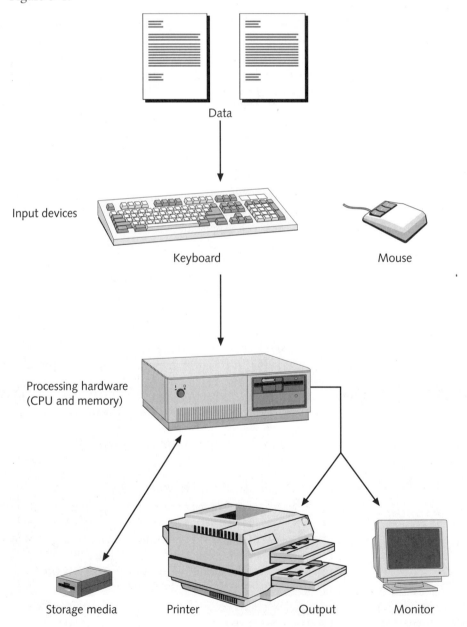

Data

Input devices

Keyboard   Mouse

Processing hardware
(CPU and memory)

Storage media   Printer   Output   Monitor

The input units include such devices as keyboards, scanners, the mouse, and communication ports, which convert data into electronic on/off signals that computer circuits can transmit and store. The processing hardware houses the computer circuits that are responsible for processing the data. As bits of data arrive at the system unit, they are stored in electronic circuits called **memory buffers**. A memory buffer is like a receiving room where the data bits wait until the computer is ready to process them. The central processing unit **(CPU)**, sometimes called a **microprocessor unit** on a microcomputer, contains the electronic circuits that interpret the program instructions stored in memory and then perform the specified operations on the data—including input, arithmetic functions, decision making, and output.

A major component of the processing hardware is the primary memory, also called random access memory or **RAM**. The primary memory stores program instructions and data in a form that is directly accessible to the central processing unit. RAM is temporary, in that its contents are lost when the computer is turned off or rebooted. In order to store software and data for later use, it is necessary to record the information from RAM into a storage system. The storage system of the computer consists of magnetic disks and CD-ROMs that allow the computer system to access software, data files, graphics, and sound directly into its memory for processing.

Output units consist primarily of video monitors and printers. The video monitor of your computer plays a very important role in how fast your computer performs and what software you can run by providing compatibility with several video standards in use today.

The hardware components found in all microcomputers can be divided into six major categories: microprocessors, memory, system boards, storage systems, video monitors, and power systems. This chapter covers the material a CNA is required to know about the basic computer concepts and components that make up each of these major hardware categories and how they can be applied to supporting the distributed processing needs of a network system.

The CNA needs to be familiar with the basics of the binary and hexadecimal systems in order to better understand and configure computer hardware. The binary ones and zeros represent the on/off states of the electronic circuits and are called bits (short for binary digit). The bits are arranged into groups of eight, called **bytes**. A coding system is used to arrange the bits in each byte to represent one character of data. The most common coding system used on microcomputers is the American Standard Code for Information Interchange **(ASCII)** developed by the American National Standards Institute **(ANSI)**. Figure 3-2 contains a partial ASCII chart along with an example: The word NOVELL is translated into binary, decimal, and hexadecimal codes, using the ASCII coding system.

Figure 3-2

ASCII code table

A	01000001	I	01001001	Q	01010001	Y	01011001
B	01000010	J	01001010	R	01010010	Z	01011010
C	01000011	K	01001011	S	01010011		
D	01000100	L	01001100	T	01010100		
E	01000101	M	01001101	U	01010101		
F	01000110	N	01001110	V	01010110		
G	01000111	O	01001111	W	01010111		
H	01001000	P	01010000	X	01011000		

	N	O	V	E	L	L
Binary	01001110	01001111	01010110	01000101	01001100	01001100
Decimal	78	79	86	69	76	76
Hexadecimal	4 E	4 F	5 6	4 5	4 C	4 C

Reading and writing eight bit strings of binary numbers is prone to error due to the chance of transposition of numbers or omission of bits. One solution to this problem is to convert each byte to a decimal number. This is done by starting with the right-most bit position of the byte and then, working from right to left, adding up the value of each bit position that contains one. The possible values of the bit positions in the binary number system are based on powers of 2 with the right-most bit position having the value 1, the next bit position to the left has the value 2, the next 4, then 8, and so on increasing by a power of two giving the left-most bit position in the byte which has the value 128. For example, working from right to left, the ASCII code for the letter "N" (01001110) would have the decimal value of 78 (0 + 64 + 0 + 0 + 8 + 4 + 2 + 0). This makes the maximum value that can be stored in a byte (11111111) equal to 255 (128 + 64 + 32 + 16 + 8+ 4 + 2 +1).

The hexadecimal number system makes binary numbers and ASCII codes more manageable. The hexadecimal system is based on powers of 16, with each position in a number having up to 16 different values. You are already familiar with the symbols for the first 10 of these values (0-9); the other six values are represented by the first six letters of the alphabet (A-F), where the letter A represents ten, B represents eleven, C twelve, D thirteen, E fourteen, and F fifteen. When you divide a byte into two 4-bit sections, called **nybbles**, each nybble has a range from zero (0000) through 15 (1111). This means that each nybble can easily be represented by one hexadecimal digit (0-F). Once you become familiar with the hexadecimal number system you can quickly convert "hex" values to their binary codes.

MICROPROCESSORS

The microprocessor chip is the brain of a microcomputer system. Built into the silicon of modern microprocessors are over one million transistors that make up circuits to interpret and control the execution of program instructions and perform arithmetic and logical operations.

 Experts say that etching all the circuit paths onto a microprocessor chip is comparable to mapping all the highways and streets of Los Angeles onto the head of a pin.

This section describes the different types of microprocessor chips and explains the limitations and capabilities of each. In order to compare microprocessors, you first need to understand the parameters that determine the performance and functionality of microprocessors: clock speed, word size, instruction set, data bus size, and address bus size.

CLOCK SPEED

If the microprocessor is the brain of the computer, then the clock is the heartbeat of the system unit, and its beats are used to synchronize all the operations of the internal components. The microprocessor's **clock** is used to provide precisely timed signal pulses called **cycles**. Each clock cycle consists of an electronic pulse that is transmitted to each component of the system unit to trigger and synchronize processing within the computer system. Each clock pulse received by the microprocessor causes its circuits to perform part or all of an instruction.

Clock speed is measured in millions of cycles per second, called **megahertz (MHz)**. **Wait states** are clock cycles during which the processor does not perform any operations and wait states are necessary to slow down high-speed processor chips and allow them to work with slower devices. In general, higher clock rates mean faster processing speeds. The processing speed, when combined with the speed of a computer's disk storage and monitor, determines its throughput performance.

WORD SIZE

The word size of a microprocessor plays an important part in its performance. A microprocessor chip holds instructions and data temporarily in storage areas called **registers**. Each processor chip has several registers for various purposes. A microprocessor's **word size** is the number of bits each register can hold. A larger word size allows a microprocessor to work on more data per clock cycle. Older processor chips, such as Intel's 8088 and 80286, have 16-bit registers. Newer processors, such as the Pentium, have 32-bit registers.

INSTRUCTION SET

The **instruction set**, also called the **machine language**, is the group of commands that the microprocessor chip has been designed to process. All software must be converted to the microprocessor's machine language before it can be run. This is often accomplished with the aid of a special program called a **compiler**, which converts English-like commands to the binary language of the processor chip. DOS machine language programs use the extension .COM or .EXE. On a NetWare file server, machine language programs have the extension .NLM.

A machine language program can be run only on the processor for which it was designed. Intel and Motorola processors, for example, have very different instruction sets, making it impossible for the Motorola chip to run a machine language program written for an Intel chip. The NetWare v3.12 operating system was written for the instruction set of an Intel 80386 microprocessor, and therefore cannot be run on earlier Intel processors or on Apple computers, which all use Motorola processor chips.

Computers with Intel and most Motorola chips are classified as complex instruction set computers (CISC) because their instructions have a wide range of formats and because one instruction can require many clock cycles. The resultant speed of the microprocessor is often expressed in millions of instructions per second (MIPS).

 Companies such as Cyrix and Advanced Micro Devices produce Intel-compatible processor chips that are used in many IBM compatible systems.

To maximize speed, many engineering workstations running computer aided design (CAD) applications (such as SUN workstations) are based on processors called reduced instruction set computers **(RISC)**. RISC processors are very fast and efficient because their instructions are all the same length and each instruction performs a very specific process. The disadvantage of RISC processors is that the software development is more complex and requires sophisticated compilers to convert programs to the machine language format.

 The biggest advantage of RISC- over CISC-based computers is the increased speed of floating-point math calculations. This speed advantage is the reason RISC-based processors are often used in workstations running engineering, CAD, or scientific applications.

A **math coprocessor** is an extension of a chip's basic instruction set that allows the microprocessor to perform more complex arithmetic operations such as square root and trigonometric functions. Math coprocessors are built into the 80486 and Pentium processors. Math coprocessors can greatly increase the speed of spreadsheet programs and applications used for engineering and CAD, which typically perform many square root and trigonometric calculations.

DATA BUS

As shown in Figure 3-3, the **data bus** is the highway that transfers data bits to and from the microprocessor registers. Just as the number of lanes on a highway determines the amount of traffic that can flow, the size of the data bus determines the number of bits that can be transferred into the microprocessor at one time. Transferring information between the memory unit and the processor is called **fetching**. A 80386SX microprocessor, which has a 32-bit word size and a 16-bit data bus, requires two fetches from memory in order to load one register. A 80386DX microprocessor, which has a 32-bit data bus, can load a register with one fetch.

Figure 3-3

The data bus

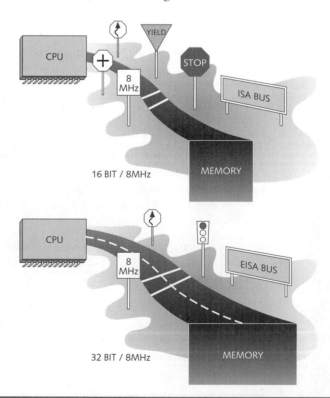

ADDRESS BUS

Just as each box in a post office is given a unique number to identify it, each byte in the computer's memory is identified by a binary number called an **address**. The microprocessor uses an address to identify the memory byte to or from which it is transferring data. The **address bus** consists of wires that carry the address of the memory byte from the microprocessor to the memory unit. When the memory unit receives the address along with a signal to read, it responds by placing the contents of that memory byte on the data bus. The number of bits in the address bus determines the maximum amount of memory the microprocessor can access directly. If an address bus consists of only two wires, for example, its maximum binary number is 11. A computer with this address bus is limited to a maximum of four byte addresses: 00, 01, 10, and 11. In the binary system, each additional bit on the address bus doubles the amount of memory capacity, so a three-bit address bus has a maximum of eight-byte addresses: 000, 001, 010, 011, 100, 101, 110, and 111. The 16-bit address bus commonly found on microprocessors before 1980 could access only 64 Kbytes of RAM; the 20-bit address bus found on the 8088 can access up to 1 Mbyte; the 24-bit address bus on the 80286 and 80386SX can access up to 16 Mbytes; the 32-bit address bus on the 80386DX, 80486, and Pentium can access up to 4 Gbytes.

INTEL MICROPROCESSORS

The Intel family of microprocessor chips are probably the best known because of the wide acceptance of IBM-compatible computers based on this processor design. You need to know the basic features of Intel processor chips and how they relate to the capabilities of the computer systems you are likely to encounter. Knowing the capabilities and limitations of the processors can help you make the best use of existing systems on a network as well as select the correct processor chip when a new system needs to be purchased.

Intel Family History

The Intel's 8088 processor chip, introduced in 1982, started the IBM PC-compatible industry. The 8088 has a 4 MHz clock speed, a 20-bit address bus that can access up to 1 Mbyte of RAM, and a 16-bit register system. It allowed designers to create everything a personal computer user would need in the then-foreseeable future. Running the instruction set that comes with the original Intel 8088 microprocessor is referred to as operating in **real mode**. Real mode instructions use 16-bit data registers and can directly access only 1 million bytes of memory. The DOS operating system—and the thousands of DOS software applications still in use—were specifically designed for the original 8088 microprocessor. This means that even if you have the latest and fastest Intel processor chip, your workstation computer is limited to 640 Kbytes of RAM and 16-bit instructions when it runs DOS-based software in real mode.

The need for more powerful processor chips led to the development of the 80286 processor, which provided up to seven times the performance of the 8088 processor while providing compatibility for real mode programs. Introduced in 1984, the 80286 microprocessor added three new capabilities.

- The address bus was increased to 24 bits to allow for up to 16 Mbytes of system RAM.

- The clock speed was increased to between 8 and 20 MHz.

- It can switch between real mode and protected mode.

Real mode operation allows the micro-processor to act like a very fast 8088; **protected mode** allows it to run multiple programs more reliably by preventing one program from affecting the operation of another. For example, if you are using real mode to run a new program in your computer and the program attempts to write data into memory cells used by DOS, the computer can crash and interrupt all other applications. When the new program is run in protected mode, however, its attempt to write the data will be recognized as invalid and will be terminated while other programs continue to operate normally.

With over 375,000 transistors, the 80386 chip represents a significant advancement over earlier chips while still retaining compatibility with software written for the older processors. Because of its popularity, you will probably encounter a significant number of workstation computers based on the 80386 processor chip. Although the 80386 is capable of 32-bit processing (because of its 32-bit internal registers and data paths), most PC add-on boards and software were designed for older 8- or 16-bit processors and are therefore unable to make optimum use of the 80386's 32-bit capability. Because of this, Intel introduced a less expensive version of the 80386 chip, the 80386SX, and named the original chip the 80386DX. The main difference between the SX and DX versions is that the 80386SX has the same 16-bit external data bus and 24-bit address bus as the 80286 processor. It is therefore limited to a maximum of 16 Mbytes of system RAM and generally runs at a slower speed. In addition to providing 32-bit processing, the 80386DX incorporated the following new features:

- It can directly access up to 4 Gbytes of system RAM.

- It has the ability to switch between real and protected modes without the need to reset the processor.

- The use of **virtual memory** allows the 80386 processor to use hard disk space to simulate a large amount of internal RAM. While the use of virtual memory slows down the computer's throughput, it also allows you to run large programs that would not otherwise fit in the existing RAM.

- The addition of **virtual real mode** allows multiple real-mode programs to run simultaneously.

- It can run at a variety of clock speeds ranging from 16–40 MHz.

 The NetWare v3.1x file server requires an 80386 processor because it was written for the virtual real mode instruction set. This requirement is why you cannot use a computer based on the Intel 80286 or 8088 processor chips as a NetWare file server.

Current Intel Microprocessors

Although you will still encounter workstations and older file servers based on earlier versions of the Intel processors, these early members of the Intel microprocessor family are no longer being produced and all new Intel based workstations and file servers you install will be based on either 80486 or Pentium processors. The 80486 and Pentium processors both provide compatibility with software written for earlier processors and the computing power needed for high-speed graphics-based software. They can also support the powerful file servers that accommodate multiple high-speed workstations.

80486. The 80486 chip is a supercharged version of the 80386 chip that incorporates over one million transistor components. Many workstations you are likely to encounter as a CNA will contain this processor. The 80486 includes the following features:

- Clock speeds are higher, ranging from 33–100 MHz.

- An 8-Kbyte high-speed memory cache allows the processor to access commonly used memory locations without going through the slower external data bus.

- A math coprocessor is built-in.

There are two main versions of the 80486 chip. The 80486DX chip contains all the features just described. The 80486SX is a less expensive version of the 80486DX chip and does not include the math coprocessor. (Interestingly, the 80486SX actually has the math coprocessor, which has been disabled to allow Intel to market the chip at a lower price.) A modified 80486DX chip, called the 80486DX2, uses a clock-doubling technique that doubles the processing throughput of the chip. An 80486DX at 33 MHz becomes an 80486DX2 at 66 MHz. Yet another version of the 80486 chip, called the 80486DX4, can provide clock speeds of up to 100MHz.

Pentium (80586). Intel's Pentium chip represents a major leap ahead of earlier Intel chips by incorporating two 80486-type microprocessors on a single chip which can process two instructions simultaneously. The Pentium chip can operate at over 120 MHz with 64-bit registers and over three million transistors. The Pentium math coprocessor has been redesigned to achieve a 300% improvement in geometric computations over 80486 chips, allowing graphic-intensive applications to operate at much faster speeds.

Initial versions of Pentium processor chips have a known problem with the math coprocessor circuits which produce incorrect results when performing calculations with large floating point numbers. Because a NetWare file server is not required to perform floating point arithmetic, this problem should not affect Pentium-based NetWare file server computers.

The 80586 processor was named Pentium to distinguish Intel's microprocessors from the increasing number of clone microprocessors manufactured to be compatible with Intel chips. Companies such as Cyrix and Advanced Micro Devices specialize in designing and manufacturing Intel-compatible microprocessors that are often priced lower and offer faster performance than equivalent Intel microprocessors.

ADDITIONAL PROCESSORS

Some workstations you will encounter as a CNA are not based on Intel or Intel-compatible microprocessors. Apple Macintosh computers are based on the Motorola 68000 line of microprocessors; Apple PowerMac computers are based on the PowerPC microprocessor.

Motorola Processors

Motorola makes two lines of processors used in the Apple Macintosh line of computers; the MC680x0 line and the PowerPC line. The MC680x0 line includes the following models; the 68000, 68020, 68030, and the 68040. The 68000 chip is the equivalent of the Intel 8088 chip. The 68020 chip is the equivalent of the 80286 chip. While the 68030 and 68040 chips are comparable to the 80386 and the 80486 series of chips respectively. The 68040 chip represented the first Motorola 680x0 chip to offer an internal memory cache, a build-in math co-processor and clock speeds up to 66 MHz.

The 68000 chip was used in the original all-in-one MAC and MAC Plus models (and other low cost models). The 68020 was used in the original Macintosh II model and the original LC model. The 68030 was used in all of the Macintosh II models (except the original) and all the PowerBook 100 series (except the PowerBook 100 and 190). The 68040 was used in the PowerBook 500 series, Centris and Quadra line of MACs. The 68040 is currently available in the LC580, LC630, and PowerBook 190 models (the LC models are now sold as Performa models). The MC680x0 line of processors is about to be phased out of the Apple Macintosh lineup of computers. It is being replaced by the IBM, Apple, Motorola designed PowerPC Risc series of processors.

Power PC

The PowerPC processor, developed cooperatively by Motorola, IBM, and Apple, is a member of the RISC family of microprocessors. Because it is based on the RISC architecture, the PowerPC achieves much higher processing speeds than the existing CISC-type Motorola processors in the 68X family. Both Apple and IBM are using special versions of PowerPC processors to produce high-speed computers that can support both existing software and newer PowerPC-specific software. They do this with special emulator software that resides in ROM and translates 68000-based instructions into PowerPC instructions automatically. Although emulation slows down the effective speed of the systems, it provides functionality in the initial phase of the new product's release when there are few programs written for it.

The Apple Power Macintosh uses the first PowerPC chip, the PowerPC 601, which runs at between 60 and 80 MHz. Microsoft has a PowerPC version of the powerful Windows NT operating system that is intended to make the PowerPC chips more widely used on networked workstations. Newer versions of the PowerPC chip, such as the 603, 604, 615 and 620, will provide lower power usage, higher clock speeds, and a larger word size. The PowerPC 620 has 64-bit registers along with a 64-bit external data bus to provide extremely high-speed processing required by such applications as speech recognition. As a CNA you will need to keep abreast of the developments and products that become available for the PowerPC family of processor chips and how they will affect the processing needs of your network system. Figure 3–4 lists the basic specifications of the Motorola and Intel families of microprocessors for easy comparison.

The PowerPC RISC processor is currently available in several PowerMAC desktop and PowerBook models, as well as several Apple authorized MAC clones (from Power Computing, UMAX and DayStar).

Figure 3-4

Microprocessor specifications

Microprocessor	Word Size	Data Bus	Address Bus	Maximum Clock Speed	Math Coprocessor	Millions of Instructions per Second (MIPS)
8088	16	8	20	10 MHz	no	.33
80286	16	16	24	20 MHz	no	3
80386SX	32	16	24	33 MHz	yes	5
80386DX	32	32	32	33 MHz	no	11
80486SX	32	32	32	33 MHz	no	41
80486DX	32	32	32	66 MHz (DX2)	yes	80
Pentium P5	32	64	128	120 MHz	yes	>100
Motorola 68000	16	16	24	8 – 16 MHz	no	1*
Motorola 68020	32	32	32	12 – 16 MHz	yes	5*
Motorola 68030	32	32	32	>40 MHz	yes	12*
PowerPC 601	64	64	64	150 MHz	yes	>100
Motorola 68040	32	32	32	66 MHz	yes	22*

* Mac User 1500 Special Issue 1993

MEMORY

The purpose of the computer's primary memory unit is to store software and data in a manner that allows the microprocessor unit to access each storage cell directly. Memory is composed of millions of tiny switches built into silicon memory modules that can be turned on or off to represent a binary one or zero. The memory switches are arranged in groups of eight to form memory cells called bytes. Every byte is assigned a unique number or address that identifies it from other memory bytes. Each memory byte can then be used to store one character of data or part of an instruction. The microprocessor can access memory by sending the address number of the desired byte on the address bus and then receiving the contents of the memory cell(s) on the data bus. On a 32-bit data bus, four sequential memory bytes can be sent to or from the microprocessor with one memory access.

MEMORY TYPES

There are four primary types of memory used in microcomputer systems: random access memory (RAM), read only memory (ROM), complementary metal oxide semiconductor (CMOS), and high-speed cache. Each of these memory types has a specific function in the processing of information in a computer system. In this section you will learn about each type of memory and its role in the operation of a computer system.

RAM

RAM is considered a volatile form of memory because it depends on constant power; when power is turned off, the contents of the RAM are erased. A computer's RAM is its primary workspace where programs and data are stored during processing. More

RAM in workstations allows the use of larger and more complex software applications. In a NetWare file server computer additional RAM is used for file and directory caching. (As described in Chapter 1, file caching is the process of storing often-used disk information in memory.) Because memory is more than 100 times faster than disk access time, the amount of memory available for file caching directly affects the performance of a file server computer.

ROM

ROM, or read only memory, as its name suggests, cannot be changed. On most microcomputer systems, **ROM** is used to store boot instructions and control such basic hardware functions as the inputting of data from the keyboard or access to the disk drive. Because they cannot be changed, instructions stored in ROM are referred to as firmware. Because ROM is slower than RAM, most 80386 and later microprocessors allow moving the contents of ROM into RAM during booting—a process known as **RAM shadowing**. RAM shadowing can significantly increase the speed of such hardware-oriented operations as accessing the screen and keyboard.

CMOS

CMOS memory (complementary metal oxide semiconductor) is used to store system configuration information. Because CMOS memory uses very little power, its contents can be maintained when the computer's power is off with a small on-board battery. The CMOS battery is recharged whenever the system is powered. Be aware that the battery can completely discharge when a computer is turned off for an extended period of time, causing loss of configuration information.

Cache

Cache memory is very high speed memory made of chips called **SRAM** (static RAM). Most RAM consists of relatively inexpensive chips called **DRAM (**dynamic RAM**)**. Although inexpensive, DRAM bears a hidden cost; it needs a special clock cycle to maintain its memory contents. Because of this extra refresh cycle, DRAM is slower than SRAM because it requires wait states when used with processors running at speeds above 20 MHz. SRAM's speed advantage over DRAM makes it more suitable for caching the most recently used memory locations. It increases the speed of processing by allowing the processor to access data or instructions without using wait states. High-speed (33 MHz and above) computers typically need 64-128 Kbytes of cache memory to improve their performance. While the Intel 80486 processor typically has 8 Kbytes of cache memory built into the processor chip, additional cache can be installed to increase system performance.

SINGLE IN-LINE MEMORY MODULES

Most RAM is currently provided on small memory cards called **single in-line memory modules** (SIMMs), shown in Figure 3-5. SIMMs are arranged on the system board in banks. A bank can contain from one to four SIMM sockets, and a computer's system board contains several memory banks. Memory is added in banks by filling all SIMM sockets in the bank with the same type of SIMM chip. The number of SIMM banks determines the maximum amount of memory that can be placed on the system board as well as the ease of memory expansion. If a memory board does not contain enough SIMM banks, you can replace existing SIMMs with SIMMs of higher capacity in order to expand the computer's memory.

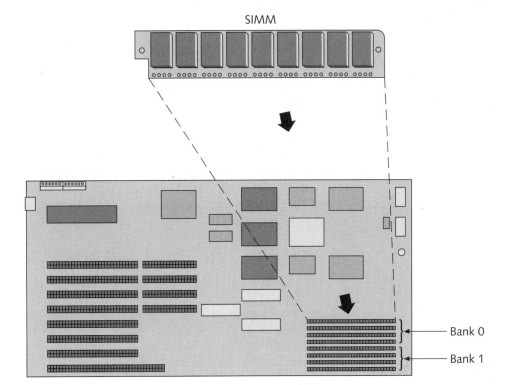

Figure 3-5

Single in-line memory module

Most SIMMs contain 1, 4, 8, or 16 Mbytes of RAM and are supplied in either 30-pin or 72-pin models: 30-pin SIMMs supply 8 bits to the data bus per module; 72-pin SIMMs supply 32 bits per module. When 30-pin SIMMs are used with an 80386SX processor, each bank must contain two SIMMs (8 bits × 2 SIMMs = 16-bit data bus width). If 30-pin SIMMs are used in an 80486 system which has a 32-bit data bus, each bank must contain four SIMMs (8 bits × 4 SIMMs = 32-bit data bus width). Make sure to choose system boards that use 72-pin SIMMs when you purchase computers based on 80486 or Pentium processors.

As mentioned previously, each memory bank must be filled with the same type of SIMM—SIMMs of different capacities cannot be mixed within a bank. Assume, for example, you are using an 80386SX processor that has a 16-bit data bus with two SIMM slots per bank, and that your computer currently has four 1-Mbyte SIMMs in bank one for a total of 4 Mbytes of RAM. You want to add more memory so you will need to install SIMMs in matching pairs. You need to install at least two more 1-Mbyte SIMMs giving you a total of 6 Mbytes. You could not place one 1-Mbyte SIMM in bank two for a total capacity of 5 Mbytes. The next step up would be to add two 4-Mbyte SIMMs in bank two, for a total capacity of 10 Mbytes.

In addition to obtaining the correct capacity for the SIMMs, you need to make sure that the SIMMs are fast enough to keep up with the clock speed used for the memory banks. SIMMs that are too slow will cause the computer to crash. The speed of the memory chips is measured in nanoseconds (billionths of a second). The speed of most SIMMs ranges between 60 and 80 nanoseconds. When adding SIMMs to a computer, you should check the system's manual to verify the appropriate chip speeds.

MEMORY USAGE

The DOS operating system was designed to run on an 8088 processor in real mode, and therefore is limited to managing 1 Mbyte (1,024 Kbytes) of RAM. As shown in Figure 3-6, the first 640 Kbytes of this 1-Mbyte memory area is referred to as **conventional memory** and is used by DOS to run software applications. The memory between 640 Kbytes and 1 Mbyte is called **upper memory** and is reserved for hardware use. For example, part of upper memory is used by your video card to store data displayed on the screen. The CNA might need to use this memory area when configuring certain network cards (as described in Chapter 4). The memory above 1 Mbyte is called **extended memory** and is available to microprocessors running in either protected or virtual mode. Because DOS was not designed to use extended memory, it requires special driver software, called the extended memory system (XMS), to access this memory. An example of an XMS memory manager is the HIMEM.SYS driver that is often included in the CONFIG.SYS file of a DOS workstation and provides access to the extended memory necessary to load the DOS operating system.

 Operating systems that do not rely on DOS—Window 95, Windows NT, Unix, OS/2, and NetWare—can access extended memory directly without the need for special drivers.

Figure 3-6

Memory map

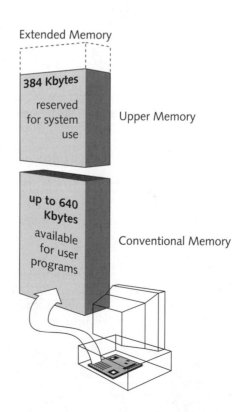

Extended Memory

384 Kbytes
reserved for system use — Upper Memory

up to 640 Kbytes
available for user programs — Conventional Memory

Many memory management programs, such as those found in DOS 5.x and 6.x, use the virtual mode of the 80386 processor to make memory bytes from the extended memory area act as if they were bytes within the upper memory area. This allows the workstation to load memory-resident programs such as Novell's IPX and NETX programs into upper memory blocks, thus saving space in conventional memory for other application software.

You might hear the term expanded memory in connection with IBM compatible computers. **Expanded memory** is an older technology that places RAM chips on a separate expansion card that is then added to the IBM-compatible system. Expanded memory was originally designed as a combined effort by Lotus, Microsoft, and Intel to provide a method for running large programs and worksheets with the DOS operating system on 8088-based computer systems. Because expanded memory is placed on a separate expansion card it requires special software called an expanded memory system **(EMS)** to swap information or program instructions stored on this card into page frames located within the upper memory area. This swapping process causes computers using expanded memory to run more slowly than computers using extended memory. MS-DOS includes a special EMM386.EXE memory driver that can be used to make extended memory act like an expanded memory card in order to support applications written to use expanded memory. Today, application and system software is designed to use extended rather than expanded memory. You might still encounter IBM-compatible computers that are configured to use expanded memory in order to support older applications.

NetWare Memory Requirements

The NetWare file server uses extended memory to run the network operating system, to run the utility modules called NetWare Loadable Modules (NLM), and to keep available in RAM memory information frequently accessed from the hard disk. Adding more memory to a file server generally increases file server performance because it allows more disk information to be kept in RAM, thereby reducing read and transmission time. Adding memory to a file server will not enhance the performance of applications stored and used on the individual workstations, however, because each workstation's memory is managed by its own local operating system—the file server providing only data and communication services.

In order to run efficiently, a NetWare v3.12 file server should contain at least 8 Mbytes of RAM. To calculate the approximate memory requirements for a file server you can use the equation shown in Figure 3-7.

The equation for calculating server memory requirements has four variables: disk space, file cache, operating system requirements, and NLMs. Disk space is calculated by taking the total disk capacity in Mbytes divided by the block size—which, you remember, is set at 4 Kbytes by default. The file cache is calculated by multiplying the number of users by .4 Mbytes, and the operating system size of NetWare v3.12 is fixed at 3 Mbytes. While the amount of memory for NLMs depends upon what extra functions the server will perform, at least 1 Mbyte should be reserved for running the required NLMs.

Figure 3-7

NetWare memory
requirements

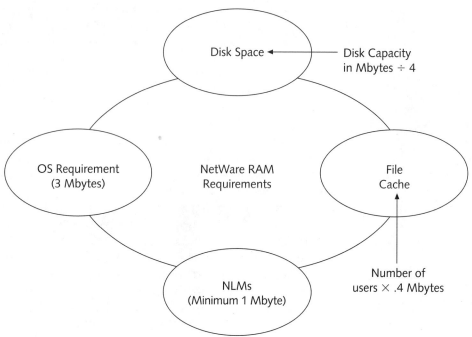

Server RAM in Mbytes = (Disk space × .008) + File Cache + NLMs + OS Requirement

A sample calculation follows. If a file server has a 500-Mbyte disk capacity and supports 10 users, the memory requirement is calculated as: 3 Mbytes for the operating system plus .008 times 125 (1 Mbyte) for disk space, plus 4 Mbytes for file caching, plus 1 Mbyte for NLMs. The memory requirement for this file server is 8 Mbytes of RAM. You will need to add extra memory if you plan to add more disk space, to load additional protocols such as TCP/IP or AppleTalk, or to support more users. Increasing the number of users to 50, for example, would increase the memory requirements to 25 Mbytes (3 + 1 + 20 + 1).

Another kind of memory to consider is **error checking and correcting (ECC) memory**. ECC memory employs algorithms that increase a server's ability to continue operating, despite a single-bit memory error, by actually correcting minor memory errors. If a company's file server controls a mission-critical application, ECC memory can be worth its expense. (A **mission-critical application** is one that an organization depends upon for the day-to-day operation of its business. In a mail order business, for example, the order entry system is considered mission critical because a system failure directly influences the company's profits.)

 A 1991 Gallup poll of Fortune 1000 companies determined that each time a network server goes down it costs a company an average $5, 000 in lost productivity and profits.

THE SYSTEM BOARD

The **system board** (also called the motherboard) is the most important component of a microcomputer because it links all the individual system components. The design of the motherboard directly affects the performance of a computer system. Figure 3-8 illustrates the 4 major components of a motherboard.

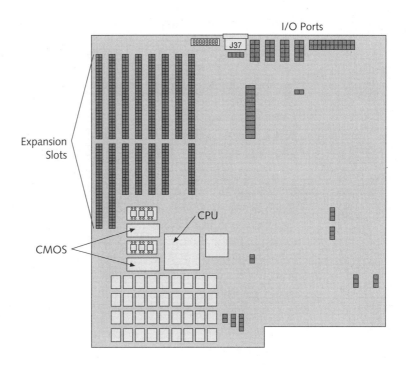

Figure 3-8

Motherboard
components

The circuit that connects the various components of the motherboard is referred to as the **local bus** of the computer. A Direct Memory Access **DMA channel** is the part of the local bus that is used to automate the transfer of data betweeen the computer's memory and external devices such as disk drives and LAN cards. Because DMA channels are assigned to specific devices, when configuring a device such as a network card, you need to be sure to assign a DMA channel number that is not currently in use by another device. Because the local bus is so closely associated with the functions of the processor chip, most motherboard local buses are designed to support the data and address bus of a specific processor. This makes it impossible to upgrade the microprocessor chip on the system board. When you decide to upgrade a system from an Intel 80386SX to an Intel 80486 processor, for example, you need to replace the motherboard.

 Some computers have motherboards that are designed to allow easy upgrading to a newer processor chip. These special motherboards are often initially more expensive, however, and might not be able to take advantage of the new microprocessor chip's capabilities.

INTERRUPTS AND I/O PORTS

In order to provide for input from and output to the computer system you need to be able to attach such devices as keyboards, printers, monitors, network cards, and the mouse. These devices are commonly known as **peripherals** because they are added on to the motherboard. Each peripheral device attached to the motherboard—from the hard disk to the keyboard—must be controlled and monitored by the microprocessor. This monitoring is accomplished by input/output (I/O) ports and interrupts. You need to know how I/O ports and interrupts Work in order to configure adapter cards correctly. (Chapter 5 tells you how to configure network adapter cards and software when you install NetWare on both server and workstation computers.)

Common Interrupts

An **interrupt request** (**IRQ**) is a signal that a device or controller card sends to the processor to inform it that the device or controller needs attention. Your telephone is a good example of how an interrupt request works in a computer. When the phone rings, it means someone is trying to contact you, and you normally try to answer it as soon as possible before you lose the opportunity to speak with the caller. On a network, when a packet arrives at the network card of the file server, it signals the server by "ringing" its interrupt. When the file server detects the interrupt signal of a packet arrival, it temporarily stops its work and spends a few microseconds putting the data packet from the network card into memory before returning to its work.

Each device in a computer system needs to have its own unique interrupt so that the processor will not misinterpret the source of the interrupt signal. If your doorbell is wired so that it also causes your telephone to ring, you cannot be sure which to answer when you hear them. A wrong guess results in the loss of information. In a similar way, two devices using the same interrupt number in a computer system cannot interact correctly with the processor, and your system performance will be sporadic at best.

Because of the limited number of system interrupt numbers, it is impossible to assign unique numbers to every category of computer peripheral. There are some general usage guidelines for system interrupts, however. Figure 3-9 shows interrupt numbers used on several of the most common system devices. Each manufacturer allows you to adjust the interrupt setting of its peripheral device, so you can choose an interrupt setting that does not conflict with other system devices.

Figure 3-9

Common interrupt usage

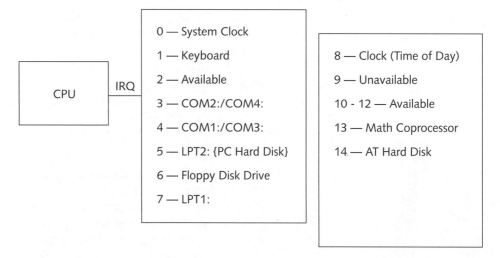

Input/Output ports

An **input/output** or **I/O port** is a memory location that the processor uses to send control commands to a peripheral device and read back status information. To communicate with each device separately, each peripheral attached to the computer system needs a unique I/O port address range. Figure 3-10 lists I/O port addresses for several common peripherals. To avoid conflicts with other devices in a computer, each peripheral controller card manufacturer provides a number of different I/O port address options. The CNA's job includes assigning unique I/O port settings for network cards.

Figure 3-10

Common device configurations

Device	Interrupt	I/O Address
COM1	4	3F8–3FF
COM2	3	2F8–2FF
LPT1	7 (if used)	3BC–3BE
LPT2	5 (if used)	378–37A
LPT3	none	278–27A
IDE disk controller	14	IF0–IF8 170–177
XT disk controller	5	320–32F
IBM token ring (primary)	2	A20–A23
IBM token ring (secondary)	3	A24–A27

Parallel ports. The **parallel port** on a computer is commonly referred to as the printer port because almost all printers use a standard parallel port interface. This makes it easy to plug almost any printer into the parallel port of a computer. The term parallel port relates to the way data is transferred from the computer to the peripheral device 8 bits at a time via parallel wires, as shown in Figure 3-11. The use of the parallel port for printers was standardized by the Centronics printer company. The parallel port consists of a 25-pin female connector on the back of the computer and a larger 36-pin card edge connector on the printer. As a result of the early popularity of the Centronics standard, all IBM-compatible computer and printer manufacturers today include the Centronics parallel port on their systems.

Figure 3-11

Parallel port cable

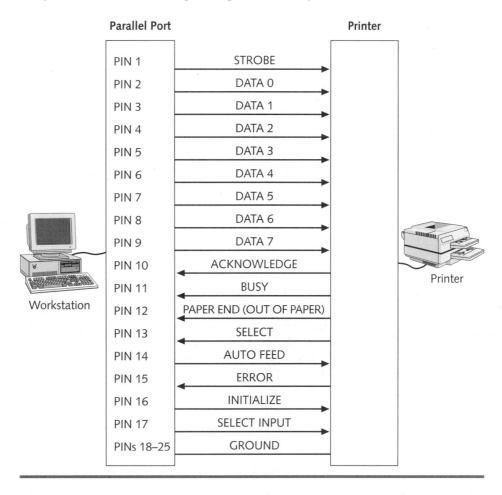

Serial ports. In contrast to parallel ports, which transmit an entire byte at one time, the **serial port** on IBM-compatible computers sends only one bit of data at a time. One advantage of the serial port is its ability to send information between devices over long distances using only a few wires in a twisted-pair cable. In addition, serial ports allow the attachment of devices, such as modems, that can translate bits into an analog signal compatible with telephone systems thereby allowing a worldwide range of computer communications.

Timing is very important in serial communications in order for the receiving device to correctly interpret the signals coming from the transmitter. To understand the principle of serial communication, imagine sending the letter C to a friend using a flashlight. In your code, on represents a one and off represents a zero. First you need to convert the letter C to its ASCII equivalent, 01000011. Next you need to agree on a timing interval—say one second—for each bit, so your friend can determine how many ones or zeros are being sent. You turn the light on or off for each second of the transmission. For the letter C (01000011), the light is off during the first second, on during the second second, off during the next four seconds, and then on again for the final two seconds. The correct timing is critical for your friend to receive the proper signal. If you flash the light on and off in two-second intervals, your friend would get completely different results.

The speed of the serial signal is the **baud rate**. In the example just described, the baud rate is one, indicating one signal change per second. Standard serial port baud rates on a computer range from 300 to 19,200 baud. For digital signals, such as those from the flashlight, the baud rate is equal to the number of bits per second (bps). When a modem sends analog frequencies over the telephone, the bit pattern is represented by a change in frequency, which allows several bits to be transmitted for each baud. In this case, the rate of bits per second is often much faster than the baud rate.

Serial communication can be either synchronous or asynchronous. **Synchronous communication**, commonly used with LAN cards to send packets consisting of 1500 or more bytes between computers, takes place at very high speeds ranging from 4 to over 100 Mbps. Synchronous ports are generally quite expensive because they require special control and timing circuitry. **Asynchronous communication** is much simpler, sending only one character at a time. Asynchronous communication is often used by modems to transmit information between microcomputers, or between a microcomputer and an on-line information service provider such as America Online, Compuserve, or Prodigy.

In asynchronous communication, each character is transmitted separately and is encapsulated with a start and stop bit and an optional parity bit for error checking. See Figure 3-12. The parity bit is set to either odd (off) or even (on). Even parity means that the total number of one bits, including the parity bit transmitted in the data frame, is even. In the case of the letter C, the parity bit is turned on by the transmitter to indicate an even number of one bits. If one of the bits is accidentally changed during transmission, by a bad cable or noise on the line, the receiving computer detects the occurrence of an error because the number of one bits is no longer even. While parity works well for single-bit errors, its reliability falls off when more than one bit is changed.

Figure 3-12

Asynchronous data frame

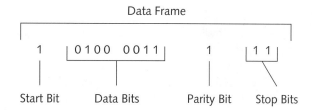

ASCII Character C
Binary Bit Pattern 0100 0011

Data Frame

| 1 | 0 1 0 0   0 0 1 1 | 1 | 1 1 |

Start Bit   Data Bits   Parity Bit   Stop Bits

Most motherboard manufacturers build one or more asynchronous ports into their IBM-compatible systems. These ports are generally referred to as COM1 through COM4, have either 25-pin or 9-pin connectors, and are located on the backs of the computers. Two types of serial port connectors, known as RS232 connectors, were standardized by the Electronic Industry Associate (EIA) in the early days of computing. DTE connectors are used on computers, and DCE connectors are used on modems. This means a simple connector-to-connector cable can connect a computer to a modem, as shown in Figure 3-13. Most of the 25-pin connections on the RS232 cable are not used by standard PC serial communications allowing a 9-pin connector to consist of only the required pin connections. A special type of RS232 cable called a **null modem cable** is used to connect two DTE computers together without the use of a modem. Note that the null modem cable pictured at the bottom of Figure 3-13 has certain wires crossed in order to allow the signals from the sending computer to go to the correct connectors on the receiving computer.

Figure 3-13

RS232 Serial cables

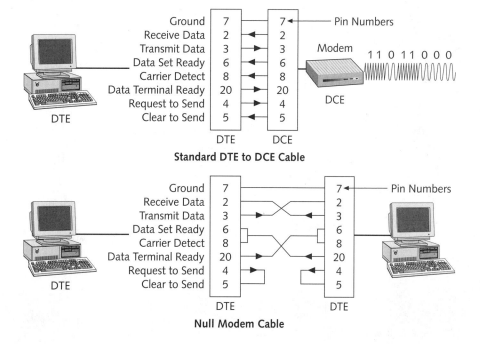

Standard DTE to DCE Cable

Null Modem Cable

CMOS

The original IBM PC bus contained switches that were used to set configuration options such as memory capacity, disk drives, and video. Today's motherboards contain a built-in setup program that is used to store this configuration information in a special memory type called CMOS. If you add a new disk drive or more memory, you will need to run a setup program to update your computer's CMOS configuration. Many CMOS setup programs are built into the ROM of the motherboard and can be executed by pressing a special key sequence (such as the Delete key) while the computer system is initially booted. Some computers need to be booted with a special disk in order to change the CMOS configuration settings.

THE EXPANSION BUS

The **expansion bus** is the part of the motherboard on IBM-compatible systems that allows you to expand the computer system by plugging circuit cards into specially designed expansion slots. Some examples of expansion cards are disk-drive controllers, network cards, internal modems, and sound cards. As the capabilities of microprocessors have improved, the demands placed on the expansion bus have grown. In order to meet the needs of the new hardware, the architecture of the expansion bus has continued to change and improve. To illustrate the differences between various types of card connectors, Figure 3-14 contrasts the popular 16-bit ISA and 16-bit Micro Channel connectors. Notice that an ISA card cannot be used in a Micro Channel expansion slot because of the differences in connector size.

Figure 3-14

ISA vs Microchannel Bus Types

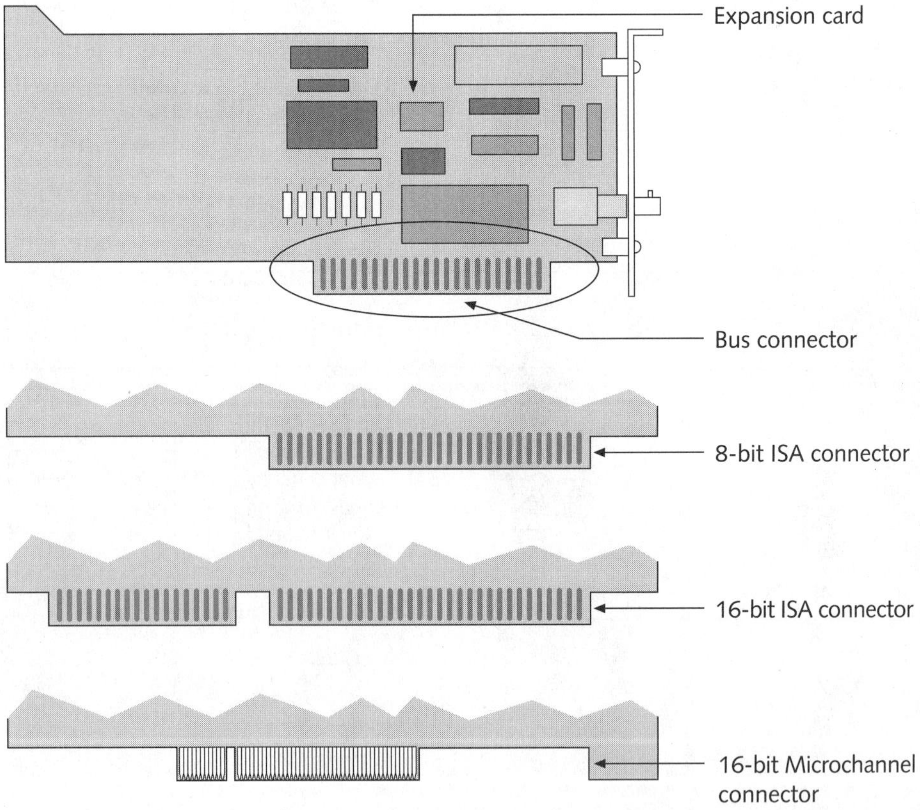

- Expansion card
- Bus connector
- 8-bit ISA connector
- 16-bit ISA connector
- 16-bit Microchannel connector

ISA bus

The industry standard architecture **(ISA) bus** was introduced in 1985 with the IBM-AT computer. It was originally designed for the 80286 microprocessor, and its expansion slots support 16-bit data and 24-bit address buses running at 8 MHz. The motherboard also contains a local bus that can support up to 32-bit data and address paths at high clock speeds (such as 33 MHz) between the microprocessor and memory. Many lower-cost personal computers use the ISA bus because it provides satisfactory performance for many applications and low-end file servers. The main disadvantage of the ISA bus can be seen in graphics applications that require high-speed video processing. Because a video card placed in an ISA expansion slot is limited to a 16-bit data bus and an 8 MHz clock speed, Windows or graphics-based applications run slowly even on a 80486-based computer. To determine if a system has an ISA bus, you can check the system's manual or examine the motherboard. ISA slots on the motherboard will have 16-bit card slots composed of two sockets placed together, one containing 31 pins and the other containing 18 pins.

Micro Channel

The **Micro Channel bus** architecture is owned by IBM and can support 32-bit expansion slots running at high clock speeds (such as 33 MHz). A major advantage of the Micro Channel architecture is that it keeps card configuration information in CMOS memory on the motherboard allowing software setting of card options and configurations. Because CMOS memory is backed up by battery, the settings are preserved when the computer is turned off. IBM owns this architecture, so a royalty must be paid by companies that make products based on it. Because the expansion slots are different, cards designed for the ISA bus cannot be used on a Micro Channel computer.

IBM developed the Micro Channel bus in the late 1980s to provide an expansion path for the 32-bit high-speed 80386DX-based processors. Because manufacturers of IBM compatible computers were outselling IBM with their lower prices, IBM wanted to build the new systems with a proprietary bus and expansion card architecture. This would force clone manufacturers to pay royalties for use of the new bus, and allow IBM to exert control over the market for personal computers. While Micro Channel was used by IBM for its PS/2 line of computers, it never was adopted by the industry in general, and IBM returned to using the ISA bus for many of its less-expensive models.

EISA bus

When IBM introduced its proprietary Micro Channel bus, other PC manufacturers who wanted to sell systems with the increased performance of IBM's 32-bit bus slots were required to pay IBM royalties and redesign their systems. Because the Micro Channel bus does not accept the older ISA cards, users must purchase the more expensive Micro Channel cards even for slower devices such as modems and printers. In reaction to this, a number of IBM-compatible computer manufacturers cooperated on the design of an enhanced version of the ISA bus that would support 32-bit expansion cards and higher clock speeds. The result is the enhanced industry standard architecture **(EISA) bus**, which supports 32-bit data and address expansion slots that can support adapter cards at 8 MHz clock speeds. Because the EISA bus is an extension of the ISA bus, it includes 16-bit expansion slots that accept older ISA cards. Of course, ISA cards placed in these slots still use the limited ISA address and data bus sizes. Because this architecture is not owned by a single company, royalty fees for its use are not required. EISA bus computers became popular for higher speed file server applications. For example, a 32-bit disk interface card placed in an EISA bus slot provides better disk access times than a 16-bit card in an ISA-compatible slot. A typical EISA motherboard includes two 32-bit slots and six 16-bit ISA slots.

Bus mastering, a technique built into EISA and Micro Channel bus systems, allows adapter cards to off-load such tasks as moving information into memory in order to improve overall system performance. Bus mastering is an important option to consider when selecting a file server computer. Much of a file server's processing involves moving information to and from memory. The use of bus mastering can greatly improve the performance of a file server by making the system's CPU available more frequently.

 Systems based on the EISA bus are good choices for medium- to large-capacity file servers that support over 50 users, use more than 500 Mbytes of disk storage, have multiple network cards, and contain additional peripheral devices.

VESA bus

Not long after the 80486 chip was introduced, IBM-compatible motherboard manufacturers struggled to provide systems that would enable the video and hard-drive peripherals to match the increased speed of the latest microprocessors. The Video Electronics Standards Association (VESA) cooperated with Intel to design a new system bus architecture that would allow peripheral cards such as the video adapter to have direct access to the local bus of the motherboard at the same clock speed as the motherboard. The **VESA bus** consists of an extension to the 16-bit ISA slot, enabling the slot to be used either for a VESA-compatible device or 16-bit adapter. This extension allows a card placed in a VESA slot to become part of the local bus of the motherboard and achieve much better data transmission speeds. According to some industry experts, VESA cards can yield performances that are up to 10 times better than the standard ISA bus cards. VESA slots can be included on 80486 and Pentium motherboards that have both ISA or EISA expansion slots. On workstations using graphic-intensive applications, a system's VESA slot is best used for the video card, as this will greatly increase the performance of graphics-based applications, which need to send millions of bits per second to the screen. On file servers, which must be able to move many large blocks of data to and from the disk and the network cards, the VESA slot is often used for high-speed disk controllers and network interface cards.

PCI bus

The latest local bus designed by Intel is called the peripheral component interconnect **(PCI) bus**. The PCI bus improves on the older VESA bus design by avoiding the stand-ard input/output bus and using the system bus to take full advantage of the Pentium chip's 64-bit data path. In addition, the PCI bus runs at the 60 or 66 MHz speed of the processor (compared with the 33 MHz maximum speed of the VESA-standard bus) and, as a result, is being used on many new motherboards designed around the Pentium processors. Another advantage offered by the PCI bus is hard-ware compatibility between Intel-based computers and Apple PowerPC-based machines, due to the use of PCI slots in Apple Macintosh computers. The biggest lim-itation of the PCI bus is that it will support only three to four slots on a motherboard. However, new systems are being designed that will provide multiple PCI buses on the same motherboard in order to provide eight or more PCI slots.

NuBus

The Apple **NuBus** was originally developed by Texas Instruments and was then adopted by Apple for use on its Macintosh line of computers. The NuBus offers a 32-bit address and data bus running at 10 MHz and is similar to Micro Channel in that it supports self-configuring boards. With self-configuring boards, a computer's system will automatically identify and configure each peripheral added to the system, eliminating the need to configure them manually by using DIP switches or jumpers.

STORAGE SYSTEMS

Advances in disk storage systems have been as important to the development of microcomputer systems as the improvements made to processors and memory. Instructions and data need to be retrieved from disks and placed in RAM before the processor chip can act on them. Therefore, the speed and the capacity of disk storage are both critical to the performance of a computer system. Consider a file server's pri-mary purpose for a moment. Its major function involves the shared use of its hard disk drives. The NetWare operating system is specifically designed to maximize the per-formance and reliability of its disk storage system. In this section you will learn about the basic terminology and concepts needed to understand and configure disk systems.

MAGNETIC DISK DRIVES

The magnetic disk drive is the component of the disk storage system in which data is stored by means of magnetic fields representing ones and zeros. The recording sur-face of the disk is coated with a metal oxide that retains magnetic fields. The polarity of each magnetic field is used to represent either a one or a zero. To perform record and playback functions on the disk surfaces, recording heads containing electronic magnets are attached to a device called an **access arm** that allows the recording heads to move back and forth across the disk surface, as shown in Figure 3-15.

Figure 3-15

Disk drive components

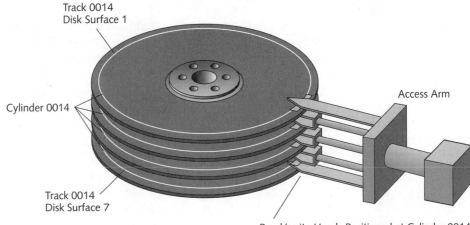

The disk surface is divided into concentric circles called **recording tracks**. The set of recording tracks that can be accessed by the recording heads without the access arm being repositioned is referred to as a **cylinder**. A track, which can contain a large amount of data, is divided into smaller recording areas called **sectors**, as shown in Figure 3-16. Reading or recording information in sectors, which are small, specific areas, allows efficient access to the information.

Figure 3-16

Tracks and sectors

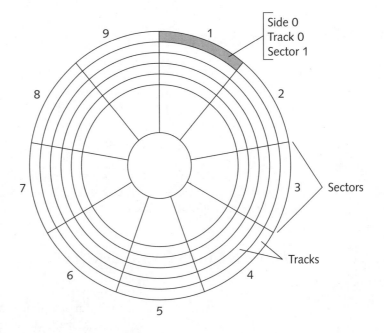

Floppy disk drives

Microcomputer floppy disks are available in two sizes: 5 ¼" or 3 ½". Although the 5 ¼" disks are nearly obsolete, be familiar with their proper use and handling in the event some of your older file server or workstation computers contain 5 ¼" disk drives. The 3 ½" floppy disk provides higher densities, better reliability, and easier storage than the older 5 ¼" disk. Figure 3-17 compares the storage capacities of 5 ¼" and 3 ¼" floppy disks. Although the 3 ½" drives have all but replaced the 5 ¼" floppy disk drives, if at least one computer in your network contains both types of drives, you can always access data on the older disks. Because the primary purpose of the floppy disk drive in a file server computer is software installation and upgrades, a file server computer should always have at least one high-density floppy disk drive for this purpose.

Figure 3-17

Floppy disk capacity chart

Size	Density	Number of Tracks	Number of Sectors	Capacity
5¼"	double	40	9	360 Kbytes
5¼"	high	80	15	1,200 Kbytes or 1.2 Mbytes
3½"	double	80	9	720 Kbytes
3½"	high	80	18	1,400 Kbytes or 1.4 Mbytes

Hard disk drives

A hard drive gets its name because it contains one or more rigid aluminum platters coated with a metal oxide that holds magnetic fields. Each platter has a read/write head positioned above and below each disk surface. Rotating the disk surface at high speeds causes the read/write head to fly just above the disk surface. Because the recording head on hard drives does not touch the disk surface, hard drives do not wear out like floppy disks and can last for several years.

 You cannot assume your data will always be safe even on a hard disk. Component failure, software bugs, and operator errors can and will eventually cause data loss, so it is critical that you establish a regular backup plan for data stored on hard disks.

For information to be recorded or retrieved on the hard disk, the recording head must first be positioned on the proper track. The time it takes to perform this operation is called the **seek time**. Once it is positioned over the correct track, the read head begins looking for the requested sector. The time it takes for the sector to come into position is called the **rotational delay**. When the requested sector comes under the read head, it is read into a computer memory buffer. This is called the **transfer time**. The seek time plus the rotational delay plus the transfer time yields the **access time**. On hard disk drives, the access time is measured in milliseconds (ms). Most current hard disk drive access times range between 15 and 30 ms. The access time for floppy disks is close to 300 ms, making hard disk drives 10 to 20 times faster.

Once installed, a new hard disk needs to be partitioned for use by the operating system. With the exception of Windows, which uses a DOS partition, each operating system requires its own separate hard disk partition. **Partitioning** establishes boundaries within which an operating system formats and stores information on a hard disk. Several different operating system partitions can exist on the same hard disk. When you install NetWare on the file server computer, for example, you need to create one partition for DOS and another for NetWare. Generally the DOS partition is very small—about 5 Mbytes—because it is needed only to boot the computer and then load the NetWare operating system. The NetWare partition contains the storage areas used to store the data and software that will be available to the network. After the partition areas are established, each operating system needs to format its partition for its own use. In DOS this is done by the FORMAT program. The NetWare INSTALL utility allows you to partition and format the disk drive for the file server.

The directory area of the disk partition contains the names and locations of files and other information about each file stored in the partition. Storing an entire file can require many sectors scattered throughout the partition. The **file allocation table (FAT)** links together all the sectors belonging to one file. When you add information to an existing file, the new sectors can be located anywhere in the disk partition. The FAT allows the computer to find all sectors for a file. When you load a file from the disk, the computer first reads the directory to determine the location of the first sector. It then reads each sector of the file as specified by the FAT. In NetWare, the file server keeps the entire FAT and the most frequently accessed directory sectors in memory.

When selecting a hard disk system for your file server, you first need to determine the storage capacity required for your server. Allow at least 80 Mbytes for the NetWare v3.12 operating system files and print queues. Next, determine what software packages you want to store on the file server and record how much storage space is required by each package. To determine how much data storage is required, identify each application and estimate the current storage requirement and future growth over the next three years. Determine how much space each user will be allowed for his or her personal data storage needs along with any shared document storage areas and add these to obtain the estimated total data requirements. After the storage requirements have been estimated, add at least 25% for expansion and overhead to obtain the total hard disk capacity needed.

DISK INTERFACES

Disk interfaces, or **controller cards**, allow a system's microprocessor to control the hard and floppy disk drives in a computer and provide a path for data to be transferred between the disk and memory. The disk controller card plugs into one of the expansion bus slots in a computer's motherboard. There are several types of disk controller cards. This section describes the most common disk controller cards, including the early ST506 controllers used in older computers, the IDE controllers found in most workstations today, and the SCSI controller cards often used in file servers and high-end workstations. A CNA must be able to distinguish among different controller cards in order to configure the NetWare operating system correctly (described in Chapter 5).

ST506 interface

The ST506 controller was developed by the Shugart company in the early 1980s and is normally used with older hard drives that have access times in the 28 to 80 ms range with a data transfer rate of 1 Mbyte/sec (megabyte per second) and are limited to 80 Mbytes of storage capacity. Up to two drives can be attached to an ST506 controller. The second drive on the cable is installed with a terminating resister. ST506 controllers have three cables: one wide cable for control signals, and two narrow data cables, one for each drive. Although the ST506 controllers are no longer installed in new computers, you can encounter this type of controller in older workstations and file servers.

Enhanced small device interface

The enhanced small device interface (ESDI) controller, an updated version of the ST506 controller, was developed by a consortium of disk drive manufacturers. ESDI supports 1.25 Mbytes/sec and is accepted as a reliable technology for midsized drives (up to 400 Mbytes). Because of higher cost and the tendency for ESDI to break down in heavy load environments due to design flaws, most manufacturers have replaced ESDI controllers with the more efficient and reliable IDE controllers.

IDE interface

Today there are two major types of intelligent drive electronics (IDE) hard disk controller cards on the market: IDE and enhanced IDE. **IDE controller cards** are often referred to as paddle cards, are smaller and cost less than the older ST506 disk controllers, which they have replaced because most of the control electronics are built into the disk drive itself. Because few circuits are required for the IDE disk controller, most IDE controller cards come with a floppy disk controller, as well as serial, parallel, and game ports.

Standard IDE controllers can control up to two hard disk drives and support drive capacities between 40 Mbytes and 528 Mbytes along with transfer speeds of 3.3 Mbytes/sec and data access speeds of less than 18 ms. As a result of their low cost and high performance, IDE controllers are very popular and are used on many desktop computers today. While IDE controllers and drives are appropriate for small- to medium-sized file servers having a total disk capacity of less than 528 Mbytes, most file servers use either SCSI or enhanced IDE controller cards.

Enhanced IDE interface

Enhanced IDE controllers and drives offer logical block address (LBA), which allows them to provide up to 8.4 Gbytes (billion bytes), well above the standard IDE limit of 528 Mbytes. In addition, enhanced IDE offers transfer rates of up to 13.3 Mbytes/sec and access times of 8.5 ms. The enhanced IDE speed improvements are achieved by increasing the disk drive rotational speed from 3000 rpm to over 5000 rpm, by employing better read/write heads, and by using an advanced technology that allows the access arm to move from track to track in one-tenth the time required by standard IDE drives. In order to take advantage of the increased transfer speed, the enhanced IDE card must be installed in a PCI or VESA expansion slot. In addition to increased capacity and drive speed, enhanced IDE also provides for up to four devices including nondisk peripherals such as CD-ROM or tape drives. The increased speed and capacity of the enhanced IDE disk system, combined with the ability to connect up to four devices, make it a good choice for many file server environments.

SCSI

The small computer system interface **(SCSI)** is a general-purpose interface card that can control hard disks, tape backup systems, CD ROM drives, and floppy disks. As shown in Figure 3-18, up to seven SCSI devices can be chained together and attached to a single SCSI control card with the last device in each chain having a terminator enabled in order to properly end the cable segment. Multiple SCSI controllers can coexist in the same computer. Each device on the SCSI bus must be given a unique address between zero and six. Because the higher device addresses are given a higher priority, for optimal performance devices such as hard drives should be given the highest numbers and devices such as tape and CD-ROM drives should be given lower numbers.

Figure 3-18

SCSI drive configuration

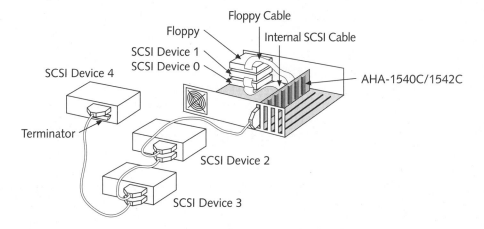

SCSI hard disk capacities normally range from 100 Mbytes to 10 Gbytes or more. Because they are more complex SCSI controller cards and drives are generally more expensive. SCSI controllers use a parallel form of communication sending eight or more bits to a drive at one time. This provides for higher transfer rates to and from the drive. Other controllers use serial communication, transferring only one bit at a time.

SCSI-2

SCSI-2 is an upgrade to the original SCSI specifications that provided a more standard command set along with additional commands to access CD-ROM, tape drives, optical drives, and several other peripherals. A feature of SCSI-2 called **command queuing** allows a device to accept multiple commands and execute them in the order the device deems most efficient. This feature is particularly important for file servers that could have several workstations making requests for information from the disk system at the same time. Another feature of the SCSI-2 controller is a high-speed transfer option called FAST SCSI-2 which, at 40 Mbps, is nearly twice as fast as previous

SCSI transfer speeds. In addition to the FAST SCSI-2 option, the SCSI-2 controller can further increase transfer speeds by using a 16-bit data bus between the SCSI-2 controller card and devices called WIDE SCSI-2. This 16-bit data bus allows for twice as much data to be transferred between the controller and disk drive as could be transferred using the original 8-bit data bus found on standard SCSI controllers.

Because SCSI-2 controller cards accommodate more devices and provide larger storage capacities, they are often the choice for file server computers on medium to large networks requiring over 1 Gbyte of hard disk, along with support for CD-ROM drives and tape drives. SCSI-2 drives have the following advantages over enhanced IDE drives for use in a file server:

- SCSI-2 supports as many as seven devices chained to a single adapter; enhanced IDE supports a maximum of four devices attached to two controller cards.

- SCSI-2 provides multitasking via command queuing, which results in better performance when multiple disk requests are pending.

- The variety of SCSI-2 storage peripherals is far greater than that afforded by enhanced IDE, especially regarding special devices such as magneto-optical drives that are sometimes used for data archiving.

 The forthcoming SCSI-3 interface will provide the ability to transfer data at a rate of 100 Mbps over a six-wire cable as compared to the 40 Mbps maximum of FAST WIDE SCSI-2 over a 128-wire cable.

RAID SYSTEMS

A CNA is concerned with data integrity because network downtime can result in significant losses of revenues for an organization. As a result, the file server computer must be made as reliable as possible. A popular way to increase the reliability of the file server disk system is to use a redundant array of inexpensive disks (RAID). **RAID** provides protection from loss of data due to a bad disk drive. There are three levels of RAID systems: 1, 3, and 5. RAID level 1 is the most common; it uses multiple disk drives and controls along with software to provide basic disk mirroring and duplexing available with NetWare. RAID level 3 is a hardware solution that takes each byte of data off several drives; one drive is used for parity checking and error correcting. If a drive fails in a level-3 RAID system, the parity drive can be used to reconstruct each data byte on the replacement drive.

A level-5 RAID system is more sophisticated. It takes data off the drives by sector. The parity information is embedded in the sectors, eliminating the use of a dedicated parity drive. Many RAID systems also support **hot-swapping**, which allows a drive to be replaced while the computer is running. With hot-swapping, the network administrator can replace a malfunctioning disk drive and have the system resynchronize the drive without interrupting network services. The hot-swapping feature can be well worth its extra cost when your file server needs to support mission-critical applications that cannot be interrupted.

CD-ROM DRIVES

Compact disk - read only memory (CD-ROM) technology is different from that of magnetic disk drives in that it uses light from low-intensity laser beams to read binary ones and zeros from the disk platter rather than sensing magnetic fields contained on hard and floppy disk surfaces. Data is permanently recorded on CD-ROM at the factory and, as the name suggests, the data recorded on the CD-ROM cannot be changed by your computer system. The main benefit of a CD-ROM is its storage capacity. A standard CD-ROM can store over 680 Mbytes of data, the equivalent of over 600 floppy disks' worth of information. This makes CD-ROMs a very good way to distribute and access large software applications, collections of programs, or other data-intensive files such as sound, graphic images, and video.

CD-ROMs store bits of information by using a laser beam to read microscopic "pits" arranged in a single spiral track that winds continually from the outside to the inside of the disk much like the tracks on phonograph records. There are about 2.8 billion pits on a single CD-ROM spiral track. When a CD-ROM is accessed, the drive uses a laser beam to measure the reflections off the pits in the spiral track. These reflections vary in intensity as the light reflects off the pits. The fluctuations in the reflected light are then converted into digital ones and zeros.

The formatting of the data frames or sectors on a CD-ROM is controlled by a standard developed in 1985 by a group of industry leaders that met in the High Sierra Casino and Hotel in Lake Tahoe, California. In this highly motivating setting, the group developed what came to be known as the High Sierra CD-ROM standard. This standard was later adopted by the International Standards Organization as ISO 9660. The ISO 9660 standard ensures that any CD-ROM disk will be accessible in any CD-ROM drive used with IBM PCs, Apple Macintosh, and Unix-based computers.

Because of the large amounts and many types of data available in standard format on CD-ROMs, many users need access to CDs on their workstation computers. This can be provided by installing CD-ROM drives on each workstation, by sharing CD-ROMs from the network file server, or by a combination of both strategies. CD-ROM drives are attached to a computer through either a SCSI or bus interface controller card. Some manufacturers sell their CD-ROM drives with their own proprietary bus-interfaced controllers, designed by the manufacturers to work only with the drives they sell. Although less expensive than SCSI-2 drives, proprietary bus interfaces do not always provide for multiple drive connections and can limit your choice of products to only those of the company that supplied the CD-ROM.

Although it supports floppy and hard disks, the MS-DOS operating system does not have built-in support for devices such as CD-ROMs. Two software items are needed to control a CD-ROM drive on a DOS workstation: the device driver and Microsoft Extensions. A **device driver** is a program that is loaded from the CONFIG.SYS file of a computer when the system is booted. It supplies instructions the computer needs to control a specific device such as the CD-ROM. The CD-ROM controller card typically includes the appropriate device driver (for example, TOSHIBA.SYS or

HITACHI.SYS) and instructions for installing it in your CONFIG.SYS file. The term Microsoft Extensions refers to a program called MSCDEX.EXE that is loaded in an AUTOEXEC.BAT file and allows MS-DOS to access the appropriate CD-ROM ISO 9660 data format. The MSCDEX.EXE program takes the next available drive letter on a system—usually D: or E:—and maps it to the CD-ROM drive so you can access data files and software just as you would from a local hard disk.

 If you accidentally try to store information on the CD-ROM you will receive a Write Protected error message, because the device is read only.

The main advantage of attaching a CD-ROM to a file server rather than attaching separate CD-ROMs to each workstation is that it reduces the cost per workstation, eliminating the cost of multiple CD-ROM device drivers and extension software. When the CD-ROM is attached to the file server, NetWare assigns a drive pointer to the CD-ROM. This allows the information to be accessed and shared across the network, just like any other data on the file server's hard disks. Another reason for installing a CD-ROM drive on your file server is that NetWare v3.12 and NetWare v4.1 are often provided on a CD-ROM. NetWare installation is completed much faster and more reliably with a CD-ROM than with a large number of floppy disks.

When purchasing a CD-ROM for a NetWare file server computer, make sure to obtain SCSI-2 compatible drives that will work with the standard software drives available with NetWare. Before you purchase a CD-ROM drive, it's a good idea to check with the manufacturer to be sure that the drive and the controller card are certified by Novell and that proper NetWare driver software is available.

VIDEO MONITORS

A CNA can be called on to make decisions regarding the types of monitors and adapter cards to be used in workstation computers. This section provides an overview of the video system information that you will need to know in order to meet the requirements of Novell's CNA exam.

The ability of a computer to display graphics depends on the video adapter and type of monitor connected. The **resolution** of a video adapter is measured by the number of pixels on each line and on the number of lines. For example, a resolution of 320 × 200 indicates 320 pixels per line with 200 lines, for a total of 64,000 pixels. A **pixel** (or picture element) is a point on the screen that can be turned on or off. It is composed of three very small dots, one red, one green, and one blue. The dots are adjusted and combined to create the color and intensity of the pixel.

 Dot pitch is a measurement of how close together the dots that make up each pixel are placed. A smaller dot pitch results in a clearer and crisper display screen. A dot pitch of .28 or less is generally desirable for a video monitor.

Non-interlaced monitors are preferable to interlaced monitors. An inter-laced monitor scans every other line on the screen, causing more eye strain. Noninterlaced monitors have a faster scanning system that scans each line from top to bottom to create a smoother screen image.

The video modes available for device drivers also depend on the type of adapter and monitor being used. Video adapters and monitors can be divided into five different classes depending upon their resolution and number of colors: Monochrome, CGA (Color Graphics Adapter), EGA (Enhanced Graphics Adapter), VGA (Video Graphics Array), and Super VGA.

MONOCHROME

Monochrome monitors are the least expensive and are usually satisfactory for use on file server computers. Monochrome monitors fall into three basic categories: TTL, composite, and VGA.

Transistor to Transistor Logic (TTL) monitors were the original green mono-chrome displays offered by IBM on the first IBM PC computers. These monitors pro-vided good text display but were not intended for graphics use. Composite monochrome monitors provide the lowest resolution of all monochrome monitors, providing the same resolution as CGA monitors only without the color. Composite monitors, are the least expensive and can be plugged into any CGA or compatible adapter. The VGA monochrome monitor is perhaps the best choice today for an inex-pensive monitor for use on a file server computer because it can be plugged directly into a standard VGA interface card and provides a good-quality text display.

CGA

The original PC computer with a 8088 microprocessor had a choice of either a TTL monochrome monitor or color monitor. The color monitor used a special color graphics adapter or **CGA** to provide up to 16 colors (four at a time) using the RGB (Red, Green, Blue) digital interface and a resolution of 320 × 200 pixels. In addition, the CGA could support composite monochrome monitors along with text, graphics, and color modes. The main drawback to CGA is the resolution, which is poor in text mode and makes viewing of word processing and spreadsheet applications difficult.

EGA

Along with the 80286 processor and the IBM's AT computer, a new graphics stand-ard, the enhanced graphics adapter **(EGA)** was introduced. Similar to CGA, EGA also used an enhanced version of the RGB digital signal and as a result, the EGA cards work with either CGA or EGA monitors. When working with an EGA monitor, the EGA card provides 640 × 350 resolution with 64 different colors.

VGA

Currently the video graphics array **(VGA)** adapter and monitor have all but replaced the earlier CGA and EGA systems. VGA supports all previous video modes. One big difference between VGA and previous video adapters is its use of analog signals rather than the digital RGB interface. The more expensive analog signal provides many more color variations over the same number of wires. The VGA monitor has the following advantages over EGA and CGA monitors:

- Displays up to 256 colors with 320 × 200 resolution
- Displays 16 colors at 640 × 480 resolution
- Provides emulation for all earlier display modes

SUPER VGA (SVGA)

The super VGA **(SVGA)** adapter is an enhanced version of the VGA adapter which allows better resolution and more color combinations. Additional memory is usually required on VGA adapters in order to provide the enhanced capabilities. Super VGA adapters can display 256 colors with a resolution of 800 × 600, or up to 1024 × 768 when used with 16 colors.

POWER SYSTEM

All system components depend on electricity to operate, so the last but most important part of any computer system is its power system. Power problems can often cause intermittent computer crashes and losses of data that cannot be tolerated on a file server computer. A CNA needs to be familiar with the components that make up a file server's power system. In this section you will learn about the major power components and how you can use them to provide reliable power to a file server.

POWER SUPPLY

A power supply that does not have enough amps or that does not filter out power irregularities can cause system errors or crashes. Because a file server often has multiple high-capacity hard drives along with many other peripherals such as CD-ROMs, tape drives, and network interface cards, the power supply must be able to support the amperage needed by all these devices. A file server should have a switching power supply of at least 300 watts. A **switching power supply** will cease functioning if there is a serious component failure or short in the system. A built-in surge suppressor and a power filter are both good features that will help protect system components from damage resulting from voltage spikes during electrical storms or if your computer is running on the same power line as other high-power electrical equipment such as motors and copy machines.

POWER LINE

The first rule in providing good power to a file server computer is to have an electrician provide a separate power line from the main fuse box to the server room. This power line should have no other equipment or computers attached to it. You should especially avoid attaching laser printers or copy machines to the same power line used by the file server, because these devices can create power fluctuations and electrical noise that adversely affect the system.

POWER FILTERS

The second line of defense in the power system is a good power filter that will remove any noise or power surges from the incoming line. It is a good idea to have your local power company or an electrician use a voltage monitor on your incoming power over a period of several days in order to determine the extent of any electrical noise or power surges experienced in the file server room. You can then use the voltage monitor information to buy the correct power filter to protect your server from unwanted electrical noise and surges.

UNINTERRUPTIBLE POWER SUPPLY

In addition to a high-quality power supply and filter, each file server should be protected from brownouts and blackouts by an uninterruptible power supply or **UPS**. A UPS contains a battery that automatically provides power in the event of a commercial power failure. Depending on the capacity of its battery, a UPS unit can provide power to the server for up to 30 minutes after commercial power has failed. The capacity of most UPS systems is measured in volt-amps (VA). Volt-amps are calculated by multiplying the number of amps needed times the voltage. To determine the correct size of the UPS needed for a server, first make a list of each piece of equipment to be protected (CPU, monitor, external drives, and so on.). Include its nameplate-rated wattage or VA. Then total all wattage and VA to obtain the total wattage and total volt-amps necessary—this total must be less than or equal to the recommended output of the UPS.

Another important feature of a UPS is its ability to send a signal to the computer informing it that the system has switched to battery backup power. NetWare has a UPS monitoring feature that allows the file server to determine how much time the UPS battery will last and shut itself down before all power is drained from the UPS battery. Because a file server keeps much information in RAM cache buffers, if a system's power is turned off prior to the file server being shut down, important information can easily be lost. In many cases the file server will not be able to mount its disk volumes after an unexpected crash, requiring the network administrator to take the extra step of performing a volume fix.

CHAPTER SUMMARY

Microcomputer systems are similar to those of any other computers, in that they perform four basic processes: input, processing, storage, and output. Input devices take information and commands from the outside world and convert them into the binary one and zero system used in digital computers. The system unit of the computer, comprising several components, allows the computer to process the input data and produce information. The brain of the system unit, the microprocessor chip, is known as the central processor unit (CPU). The CPU fetches instructions and data from memory and then performs the requested function. IBM-compatible computers are based on the Intel line of microprocessors, and Apple Macintosh computers use processor chips made by Motorola. Programs written for the Intel chips will not run on Motorola processors.

The power of a microprocessor chip is based on several factors including clock speed, word size, instruction set, and bus size. Most IBM-compatible computers today use either the 80386 or 80486 processor chip. Newer, more powerful computers use the latest Intel Pentium chip. The Pentium microprocessor actually has two 80486 chips working together to provide processing of more than one instruction at a time.

Memory is the primary storage area for the microcomputer system. All instructions and data must be stored in memory before they can be processed by the CPU. RAM is the computer's work area and is used primarily to contain instructions and data that are currently being processed. Workstations using just DOS can get by with only 1 or 2 Mbytes of RAM. If you are also using Windows on a workstation, you should have between 4 and 8 Mbytes of RAM to provide adequate performance. The NetWare file server uses its RAM to run the operating system and cache information from the hard disk for faster access. While a file server with a small disk drive can run with as little as 4 Mbytes of RAM, between 8 and 12 Mbytes is normally necessary for small- to medium-sized servers. A large server using multiple protocols can have up to 2 Gbytes of RAM. Although placing additional RAM in a file server does not directly affect what applications can be run on the workstation, it does provide for network performance. A shortage of memory in a file server computer can cause it to crash or lock up the network.

The motherboard, or system board, of the computer ties all the system unit components together. In addition it provides expansion slots for peripheral controller cards. The capacities of the expansion slots are controlled by the expansion bus. The ISA expansion bus was designed for the 80286 computer with 16-bit data and 24-bit address buses running at 8 MHz. The EISA bus is an enhanced version of the ISA bus that allows 32-bit busses and higher clock speeds. IBM has used a proprietary bus, called the Micro Channel, that also provides 32-bit bus access at high clock speeds and an automatic configuration utility that makes it much easier to install cards. VESA and PCI are called local bus slots because they provide direct access to the CPU and memory at much higher speeds than either EISA or Micro Channel. You should use the VESA or PCI bus slots for devices—such as video and disk controller cards—that require very high access speeds.

The motherboard uses I/O ports and interrupts to communicate with peripheral devices such as keyboards, video monitors, modems, disk drives and network cards. Parallel ports are most frequently used to connect printers, while serial ports provide longer distance communication. When a device is added with an expansion card, it is attached to a controller card that must be assigned a unique interrupt and I/O port address. This is done by changing settings on the cards or using a setup program. Once the cards have been installed, the card driver software must be configured to use the selected interrupt and I/O address settings.

Hard disk storage consists of the controller card and drive. Older computers used the ST506 controller card to operate slower drives of relatively low capacity. Today's high-speed, large-capacity drives require more capability and reliability than was available from the ST506 controller cards. Modern hard drives are based on either IDE or SCSI controller cards. IDE is a very popular controller for DOS and Windows workstations and small- to medium-sized file servers. The new enhanced IDE controllers provide higher speed and increased storage capacity (up to 8.5 Gbytes), and support up to four devices. SCSI-2 controller cards can be used to attach up to seven different types of devices including disk drives, CD-ROMs, and tape drives. They allow for higher capacity and faster drives than IDE and are used for larger file servers requiring multiple devices and over 1 Gbyte of disk space.

CD-ROMs represent an important new development in storage systems, allowing 680 Mbytes to be stored permanently on a removable disk. CD-ROMs are used to store a variety of data including sound, text, fielded data, graphics, and video. Because of the amount of material available on CD-ROMs, sharing them on a network has become an important function controlled by the network administrator. When CD-ROM drives are used on individual workstations with DOS, driver software and Microsoft extensions must be loaded when the workstation is loaded. If the CD-ROM drives are attached to a file server, special NetWare modules are used to make the information on the CD available to all networked workstations.

The power system of the computer is critical to proper operation. Problems with computers locking up or giving parity error messages can be caused by insufficient or faulty power supplies. You need to be sure that the wattage of your computer's power supply provides the necessary amps for all attached devices. A UPS (uninterruptible power supply) uses a battery to provide continuous power to the computer for a short period of time after a commercial power failure. This gives the network administrator or the file server computer time to save the contents of the computer's memory and properly shut itself down prior to loss of power. All file server computers need to be protected by a UPS and proper power filters.

KEY TERMS

access arm

access time

address

address bus

ANSI

ASCII

asynchronous communication

baud rate

bus mastering

byte

cache

CGA

clock

CMOS memory

command queing

compiler

controller cards

conventional memory

CPU

cycle

cylinder

data bus

device driver

DMA channel

dot pitch

DRAM

EGA

EISA bus

EMS

enhanced IDE

error checking and correcting (ECC) memory

expanded memory

expansion bus

extended memory

fetching

file allocation table (FAT)

hot-swapping

IDE controller cards

input/output (I/O) port

instruction set

interrupt request (IRQ)

ISA bus

KB

local bus

machine language

math coprocessor

megahertz (MHz)

memory buffers

Micro Channel bus

microprocessor unit

mission-critical application

motherboard

NuBus

null modem cable

nybble

parallel port

partitioning

PCI bus

peripherals

protected mode

RAID

RAM

RAM shadowing

real mode

register

resolution

RISC

ROM

rotational delay

RS232

SCSI

SCSI-2

sector

seek time

serial port

single in-line memory module (SIMM)

SRAM

SVGA

switching power supply

synchronous communication

system board

tracks

transfer time

TTL

upper memory

UPS

VESA bus

VGA

virtual memory

virtual real mode

wait state

word size

REVIEW QUESTIONS

1.   List three components that make up the motherboard of a computer system:

   _____

   _____

   _____

2.   A(n) _____ is the amount of storage capacity needed to record one character of data in the computer's memory.

3.   The _____ is the brain of a microcomputer system.

4.   The _____ is used to provide precisely timed signals that synchronize the internal working of the system unit.

5.   A microprocessor's word size is a measurement of the number of bits that can be stored in each _____.

6.   The _____ is the part of the CPU that is responsible for performing calculations.

7.   In addition to the real and protected mode, the 80386 microprocessor adds

   _____.

8.   Which processing mode is used by 8088 microprocessor chips?

   _____

9.   Which processing mode allows access to extended memory?

   _____

10.   The _____ is the highway that transfers bits to and from the memory chips.

11.   The size of the _____ limits the amount of memory the microprocessor can directly access.

12.   Briefly explain a difference between the 80386SX and 80386DX microprocessors in the space below:

13.   Briefly explain a difference between the 80486SX and 80486DX microprocessors in the space below:

14.   The Apple Macintosh computers use the _____ family of processor chips.

15. Match Intel to comparable Motorola processor chips.

    _____ 80286   a. MC68020   e. PowerPC 601

    _____ 80486   b. MC68000

    _____ Pentium   c. MC68030

    _____ 80386   d. MC68040

16. When DOS is used, application programs are limited to running in the _____ memory area.

17. _____ is a very high speed form of memory that does not require refresh clock cycles.

18. The _____ memory area is used by NetWare and other workstation operating systems such as Windows and OS/2.

19. The _____ memory area is used by video cards, ROM, and expansion cards.

20. The _____ expansion bus provides 32-bit busses, and is owned by IBM.

21. The _____ is a local bus slot that provides high-speed direct access to the CPU and memory.

22. _____ memory is used to store configuration information on the system board and is backed up by battery power.

23. What is the minimum amount of memory needed by a NetWare file server that has 700 Mbytes of disk space? (Write your calculations in the space provided.)

24. The _____ expansion bus is a direct competitor of the Micro Channel architecture.

25. _____ memory must be paged in and out of upper memory.

26. _____ is used to store startup and hardware control instructions.

27. To increase the performance of 80486 and Pentium processors, from 64 to 256 Kbytes of _____ memory is used, because it does not require wait states and provides very high speed memory access, being composed of expensive SRAM chips.

28. After low-level formatting, a drive needs to be _____ for use by an operating system.

29. The _____ is used to link together all disk sectors belonging to one file.

30. If mirrored 600-Mbyte disks are used on a small- to medium-sized network, what type of disk controller would you recommend for the file server computer?

     _____

31. List three types of data that can be stored on CD-ROMs.

     _____

     _____

     _____

32. _____ is measured by the number of pixels.

33. _____ is the measurement of the distance between pixels.

34. List two things to consider when you are purchasing a UPS for a file server computer:

35. The _____ is used by a device to send a signal to the CPU.

36. Each device must have a unique _____ that is used to receive commands from the CPU.

37. Which provides the highest quality image, a monitor with .28-dot pitch or one with .35-dot pitch?

     _____

38. The _____ bus provides the best high-speed direct access to a Pentium processor.

39. The _____ bus provides compatibility with older expansion cards while providing 32-bit slots running at 8 MHz for use with disk controllers and network cards.

40. The _____ Apple bus most closely resembles EISA.

EXERCISES

Exercise 3-1: Determining Workstation Hardware Configuration

Use either the Microsoft MS-DOS command or another hardware-documenting program supplied by your instructor to fill out the following worksheet showing the hardware environment of the workstation you are using.

Computer Worksheet

Specification developed by: _____

SYSTEM INFORMATION

Computer make/model: _____

CPU: _____   Clock speed: _____   Bus: _____

Memory capacity: _____

DISK INFORMATION

Disk controller

Type: _____

Manufacturer/model :_____

Drive address	Type	Manufacturer	Cyl/Hd/Sec	Speed/Capacity	DOS Partition size
_____	____	_____	__/__/__	_____	_____

DEVICE INFORMATION

Device name	IRQ	I/O port
_____	_____	_____
_____	_____	_____
_____	_____	_____

 EXERCISES

Case 3-1: Calculating File Server Memory Requirements

The ACME company is planning to obtain a dedicated file server computer to support a 25-user network with 800 Mbytes of mirrored disk capacity. Using the memory formula in this chapter, calculate the amount of RAM that you would recommend for this file server. Show your calculations.

Case 3-2: Developing Workstation Specifications

The PC Solutions company wants to purchase two workstation computers to add to its network. As the CNA for this company, you have been asked to develop bid specifications that will meet the needs of the applications to be run on these systems. Fill out a bid specification form for each of the workstations described below.

John's new workstation is to be a DOS-based computer that will be used to run word processing applications and do basic spreadsheet calculations in addition to the company's payroll application, which requires dBASE IV. dBASE IV is a powerful program, requiring at least 2 Mbytes to run, and will run best on a 32-bit processor. The workstation will require about 80 Mbytes of local disk storage for software and work files plus access to the network.

Ann's new workstation is to be a Microsoft Windows environment and is intended to be used for word processing and desktop publishing applications that need high-resolution graphics and a powerful processor. The workstation will require about 300 Mbytes of local disk storage for software and work files. It should have access to the network so it can share data files and access network printers.

Bid Specification Form

Specification developed by: _____

SYSTEM INFORMATION

Computer make/model: _____

CPU: _____   **Clock speed:** _____   **Bus:** _____

Memory capacity: _____

Estimated cost: _____

DISK INFORMATION

Disk controller

Type: _____

Manufacturer\model : _____

Drive address	Type	Manufacturer	Cyl/Hd/Sec	Speed/Capacity	DOS Partition size
_____	____	_____	__/__/__	_____	_____

NETWORK CARD INFORMATION

Network type	Manufacturer ID	I/O port	Interrupt
_____	_____	_____	_____

NON-NETWORK DEVICE INFORMATION

Device name	IRQ	I/O port
_____	_____	_____
_____	_____	_____
_____	_____	_____
_____	_____	_____

Case 3-3A: Determining File Server Disk Requirements

The Ace Auto Supply Company wants to store its supply catalog information on a file server in order to allow all computers to have access to the parts information. Currently the catalog comes on a CD-ROM, and copying it to the server's hard disk will require about 500 Mbytes of disk storage. The company also wants to move its customer database, which currently takes 50 Mbytes of disk space, to the file server, along with a word processing program. In the space below, record the type of controller and disk system you would recommend for this application. Justify your choice.

Disk controller type: _____

Drive capacity information

Justification:

Case 3-3B: Calculating File Server Memory Requirements

Given the file server disk requirements you recorded above, calculate the amount of RAM the Ace Auto Supply Company's file server computer will require. (Show your calculations.)

Minimum memory requirements: _____

Calculation:

Case 3-4: Developing File Server Specifications

The Animal Health Center wants to purchase a new computer to replace its existing file server computer and has budgeted a maximum of $2,500 to be spent. Its current file server is a 80386SX computer with 4 Mbytes of RAM and an 80-Mbyte hard disk drive. The center's system is running out of storage space, and the file server runs slowly when it performs network printing. In addition, the center recently experienced some disk errors on the file server that required an employee to restore data from backups and then re-enter a day's worth of transactions. If possible, the center wants to avoid disk errors causing this type of problem in the future. As the center's CNA, you have been asked to select a computer system that will meet the needs within the requested budget. Record the system and its specifications on the worksheet provided.

File Server Worksheet

Specification developed by: _____

SYSTEM INFORMATION

Computer make/model: _____

CPU: _____ Clock speed: _____ Bus: _____

Memory capacity: _____

Estimated cost: _____

DISK INFORMATION

Disk controller

Type: _____

Manufacturer\model : _____

Drive address	Type	Manufacturer	Cyl/Hd/Sec	Speed/Capacity	DOS Partition Size NetWare	Mirrored with Controller Drive
_____	__	_____	_/_/_	_____	____ ____	_____

NETWORK CARD INFORMATION

Network type	Manufacturer ID	I/O port	Interrupt
_____	_____	_____	_____

NON-NETWORK DEVICE INFORMATION

Device name	IRQ	I/O port
_____	_____	_____
_____	_____	_____
_____	_____	_____

SUPERIOR TECHNICAL COLLEGE PROBLEM

Dave Johnson is ready to purchase a file server computer for use at the Superior Technical College campus. He would like to hear your ideas for the server specifications. The server will need to store the administrative applications and be available for faculty use. It also needs to accommodate the academic computer lab. Dave would like you to fill out a storage requirements worksheet listing requirements for each area along with estimated total disk space needed for the next two years. In addition, you are to complete a requisition worksheet containing the hardware specifications for the file server you feel will best meet the requirements of all three areas. If possible, Dave would like the cost of the file server to be kept under $5,000. The following paragraphs detail the three areas' needs.

Administration. Each of the four departments shown on the Superior Technical College organization chart in Chapter 1 will need approximately 80 Mbytes for storing shared files along with at least 30 Mbytes reserved for each user's personal files and work areas. The major application software packages used by the administrative department include the placement system, which requires about 50 Mbytes and the testing system, which requires approximately 20 Mbytes for data files and software.

Computer lab. The major use of the server for the computer lab is storage of the software used by the students in the lab, along with the menus and a 20-Mbyte area for faculty members to place files that they want their students to have access to. Along with these storage needs, each workstation in the lab will require a 5-Mbyte work area on the server to store temporary files and configuration settings. Approximate software package storage needs are as follows:

Word processing	10 Mbytes
Spreadsheet	5 Mbytes
Windows	12 Mbytes
Menus	3 Mbytes
Database	10 Mbytes

Storage Requirements

Superior Technical College

Prepared by: _____

NetWare operating system requirements: **80 Mbytes**

Administrative:

_____   _____

_____   _____

_____   _____

_____   _____

                                   Subtotal: _____

Faculty:

_____   _____

_____   _____

_____   _____

                                   Subtotal: _____

Computer lab:

_____   _____

_____   _____

_____   _____

_____   _____

                                   Subtotal: _____

                                   Total: _____

File Server Worksheet

Specification developed by: _____

SYSTEM INFORMATION

Computer make/model: _____

CPU: _____ Clock speed: _____

Memory capacity: _____ Bus type: _____

DISK INFORMATION

Disk controller

Type: _____

Manufacturer\model :_____

Drive address	Type	Manufacturer	Cyl/Hd/Sec	Speed/Capacity	DOS Partition Size NetWare	Mirrored with Controller Drive
_____	__	_____	_/_/_	_____	____ ____	_____

DISK CONTROLLER

Type: _____

Manufacturer\model :_____

Drive address	Type	Manufacturer	Cyl/Hd/Sec	Speed/Capacity	Partition Size DOS NetWare	Mirrored with Controller Drive
_____	__	_____	_/_/_	_____	____ ____	_____

NETWORK CARD INFORMATION

Network type	Manufacturer ID	I/O port	Interrupt
_____	_____	_____	_____

NON-NETWORK DEVICE INFORMATION

Device name	IRQ	I/O port
_____	_____	_____

FILE SYSTEM DESIGN

Designing a file system that will meet the special needs of an organization is an important task performed by a CNA prior to installing NetWare and setting up the network system. The structure of the file system must be designed to facilitate a smooth workflow for those who use the network and to prevent disruption of the information flow that existed before the network was implemented. The NetWare file system provides the following advantages.

- Centralized management of data and backups ensures that duplicate copies of data are always automatically available for restoration of lost or damaged files.

- Improved security prevents users from modifying or accessing data they are not responsible for maintaining.

- Improved reliability and fault tolerance allow data to be backed up at regular intervals and provide a recovery process in the event of lost data or a down file server.

- Shared and private storage areas facilitate the creation of workgroups by allowing users to share files or to transfer files from one user to another

---

AFTER READING THIS CHAPTER AND COMPLETING THE EXERCISES YOU WILL BE ABLE TO:

- DESCRIBE THE COMPONENTS OF THE NETWARE FILE SYSTEM.

- EXPLAIN THE PURPOSE OF EACH NETWARE-CREATED DIRECTORY AND NOVELL-SUGGESTED DIRECTORY.

- WRITE VALID PATH STATEMENTS TO IDENTIFY DIRECTORIES AND FILES.

- APPLY DIRECTORY DESIGN CONCEPTS TO DEVELOPING AND DOCUMENTING A DIRECTORY STRUCTURE FOR AN ORGANIZATION.

- USE NETWARE COMMANDS AND UTILITIES TO VIEW VOLUME AND DIRECTORY INFORMATION.

without having to carry disks between machines. Private storage areas allow individuals to save their own work in a secure area of the file server.

- Access to data by many different operating system platforms—NetWare supports Apple, Unix, and OS/2 file structures in addition to the standard DOS—saves money by eliminating the need for separate servers to handle each operating system. The NetWare file system can allow compatible applications running on Windows and Apple Macintosh platforms, for example Microsoft Word, to share data files. As networks grow, a CNA's skill in integrating the file formats of different operating systems in the network file system is becoming increasingly important.

 NetWare is frequently used by network administrators to integrate desktop computers running DOS, Windows, Macintosh, OS/2, and Unix in order to allow people in an organization to communicate and exchange data easily.

FILE SYSTEM COMPONENTS

The NetWare file system is used to organize and secure the information stored on a network, and a good file system design is necessary to facilitate the setup, use, and growth of a network. As shown in Figure 4-1, the four main components of the NetWare file system are the file server, volumes, directories and subdirectories, and files.

Figure 4-1

NetWare file system components

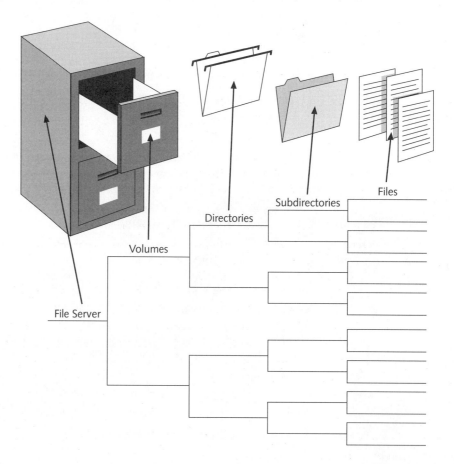

FILE SERVER

The top level in the file system structure is the file server. As defined in Chapter 1, a NetWare file server is a computer system dedicated to running the NetWare operating system. The function of a file server in the network file system is similar to that of a file cabinet in an office because it contains applications and data for access by users on the network. Just as an office needs many file cabinets to organize all its data in an accessible and secure form, an organization's network file system often consists of multiple file servers. In order to provide access to its unique data, each file server is given a name consisting of two to 45 characters. A network user can access files and print services on up to eight NetWare v3.1x servers at one time.

VOLUMES

Just as file cabinets have one or more drawers, the storage space on each file server is divided into one or more **volumes**. Volumes are the major division of NetWare file server storage; all files are accessed through volumes and each volume is associated with a specific file server. A NetWare volume is a physical amount of storage contained on one or more hard disk drives or other storage media, such as a CD-ROM. In DOS terms, a volume is equivalent to a partition of a hard disk drive on a local workstation. However, NetWare v3.1x volumes are more flexible than workstation hard disk drives because each volume can span disk drives and occupy terabytes (Tbytes) of data storage capacity. By allowing a volume to consist of up to 32 disk drives and a maximum capacity of 32 Tbytes, NetWare provides for almost unlimited volume size.

Each NetWare file server is required to have at least one SYS: volume. During installation, NetWare creates and stores its operating system files and utility programs in directories it creates in the SYS: volume. In addition to the required SYS: volume, many network administrators create an additional server volume in which to store the organization's data files separately from the NetWare operating system software. When multiple volumes are used, the SYS: volume is typically reserved for the operating system files, print queues, and general-purpose application software such as spreadsheets and word processors. One or more data volumes are then created to store the organization's files. Placing the organization's data files and special applications in separate volumes provides the following advantages:

- The administrator can ensure that free space is always available in the SYS: volume for NetWare's use.

- Security is enhanced because, by dismounting the volume containing sensitive data, the data can be stored off line when it is not being used.

- Performance is improved when separate volumes hold other operating systems or large graphic and multimedia files. Placing these files in separate volumes allows the network administrator to increase the block size, or add optional filename space support for other operating systems, without decreasing the performance of DOS files stored on other volumes.

- Additional fault tolerance is provided because the server can continue to provide services even when a volume is taken off line for repairs.

Network printing is one reason that additional free space in the SYS: volume is needed. When printed output is sent to a network printer, it is first stored in the SYS: volume in files called print queues until the requested network printer is available. Consider, for example, the following situation. A company has a file server with a SYS: volume that is almost full due to the many large data files stored there. If several users attempt to print rather large desktop publishing jobs on networked printers at the same time, the SYS: volume is inundated with the printed output stored in the print queue. If the SYS: volume runs out of space, the print jobs are canceled and error messages are sent to the users. The print jobs need to be resubmitted, or the network administrator must free up disk space. You will avoid problems like this by keeping data files in separate data volumes and allocating at least 80 Mbytes for the NetWare v3.12 operating system files in the SYS: volume.

If you do run out of space on a volume, you can increase the volume's size by adding another disk drive to the file server and then directing NetWare to use empty space available on the new drive to expand the existing volume. This process is called **spanning** a volume. When a volume spans more than one disk drive, you should mirror the disk drives, because a disk error on either drive makes the entire volume unavailable. Mirroring synchronizes the data on two disk drives so that an error on one drive will not prevent access to the volume's data.

When creating multiple volumes you must use the following naming conventions.

- The volume name must be 2 to 15 characters long.

- Spaces, commas, backslashes, and periods are not valid characters.

- Each physical volume on a file server must have a unique name.

- The physical volume name must be followed by a colon when specified as part of a path.

- A backslash or forward slash must be used to separate the NetWare server name from the physical volume name. Examples of valid volume names include: DATA:, ICS_GRAPHIC16:, CTS-ENGINEERING:, MAC_ATTAC:, and UNIX@WORLD:.

By default, each NetWare volume stores data on the file server drive using a 4-Kbyte block size. A **block** is the amount of data that is read or written to the volume at one time. The block size of a volume is assigned when the volume is created during installation. A larger block size can speed up access time when large files, such as bit-mapped graphic images and CAD applications, are used. However, larger block sizes use up more disk space, which makes them less efficient when a large number of small files need to be stored. Optional block size settings for NetWare v3.1x volumes are 4, 8, 16, 32, and 64 Kbytes.

NetWare 4.1 allows several files to share one block using a technique called **block suballocation**. Block suballocation divides any partially used disk block into 512-byte suballocation blocks allowing the unused space in that disk block to be allocated to another file rather than being left unused.

DIRECTORIES AND SUBDIRECTORIES

The storage space in each NetWare volume can be organized into directories and subdirectories, just as you find in DOS. Creating directories within a NetWare volume is analogous to hanging folders with subfolders in the drawer of a file cabinet. Directories and subdirectories allow you to keep files organized in a volume just as the folders allow you to organize files in a file cabinet's drawer. An important CNA responsibility is to design a directory structure for each volume that will separate software and data according to functionality and use. NetWare's SYS: volume contains several system-created directories that play important roles in the operation of the file server. The following paragraphs describe the names and purposes of the system directories. You will also learn about Novell's recommendations for the directories you will need to create in building a suitable directory structure to store an organization's software and data files.

Required directories

As shown in Figure 4-2, the NetWare operating system stores its required system files and utilities in the SYS: volume by creating four main directories: LOGIN, PUBLIC, MAIL, and SYSTEM. You need to understand how NetWare uses these required directories and where certain types of NetWare system files are stored. This section explains these directories and provides examples of their use by NetWare.

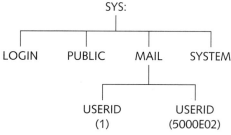

Figure 4-2

NetWare required directories

SYS:LOGIN. The LOGIN directory contains files and programs that can be accessed prior to logging in. You should think of this directory as NetWare's reception area. Just as you enter a reception area when you first go into a business office, a user is placed in the LOGIN directory when he or she first attaches to a file server. As you learned in Chapter 2, attaching to a NetWare file server involves running the IPX and NETX programs. When users complete this step and gain access to the LOGIN directory, they have limited access to any files and programs stored in the directory. Two important programs in the LOGIN directory that you worked with in Chapter 2 are SLIST.EXE and LOGIN.EXE.

When you visit an office building, you need to obtain permission from the receptionist before visiting someone's office. The SLIST.EXE program performs the receptionist's job of checking who is available to see you by listing the names of all file servers on the network. Next the receptionist needs to identify you to the person you want to see. The LOGIN.EXE presents your username and optional password to the file server and then provides you with access to the file server after you are identified as a valid user.

The LOGIN or SLIST programs can be copied from the LOGIN directory and run from a local disk on the workstation. This approach eliminates the need to change to a network drive letter (typically F:) in order to log into the file server. This option can be important when you are creating a DOS batch file and do not know what drive letter a workstation will be using for its network drive.

Many network administrators like to use the SYS:LOGIN directory to store common files and programs used by many workstations during the startup process. This technique allows you to update a new release of these programs simply by copying the new software into the LOGIN directory rather than copying LOGIN and SLIST to each workstation's hard disk drive.

SYS:PUBLIC. The SYS:PUBLIC directory contains utility programs and files that are available to all network users after they have logged in. Many of these programs and files are necessary for users to be able to access and use network services. The USERLIST.EXE, WHOAMI.EXE, SESSION.EXE, and LOGOUT.EXE programs are all examples of NetWare utilities that are run from the PUBLIC directory. For a CNA, the PUBLIC directory is like a toolbox containing many utilities you will need to perform such network tasks as creating new users, managing files, assigning access rights, and working with printers.

SYS:MAIL. As shown in Figure 4-2, the MAIL directory of a server contains a subdirectory for each user which is automatically created whenever a new user is added to the file server. These subdirectories can be used by electronic mail software to pass electronic messages between users, but they are also needed by the NetWare operating system for storing user profile information, such as personal login scripts or special print job configurations. Because the operating system uses these directories, you should not allow users to access the MAIL directories to store their personal files, because this is likely to cause critical NetWare system files to be erased or changed. The CNA needs to keep track of the MAIL directories in order to back up the file server and perform maintenance tasks.

 The name of each user's SYS:MAIL subdirectory is the same as his or her user ID—which is a hexadecimal number of from one to eight digits.

SYS:SYSTEM. The SYSTEM directory contains NetWare operating system files and utilities that are accessible only to the user who is designated the network supervisor. Novell uses the dollar symbol ($) in all filenames that contain system information. The following are examples of SYSTEM files:

- NET$ACCT.DAT contains an audit trail of login and logout information.
- NET$PROP.SYS, NET$VAL.SYS, and NET$OBJ.SYS are the files that contain username and password information.
- NET$ERR.LOG is the supervisor's error log.

Many of the NetWare system files are not accessible from the DOS DIR command; you need to use the NDIR command to display them when you work on the file server. Only the supervisor should be given access rights to the SYSTEM directory to prevent users from erasing or modifying system files and using commands that affect the functioning of the file server. Some network administrators will move certain program files that they do not want the user to run, such as SYSCON, from the PUBLIC directory to the SYSTEM directory. This prevents users from accessing the SYSCON command and using it to change their login process or access restrictions.

Other system directories. In addition to the four major system directories, you can also find ETC, DOC, and DELETED.SAV directories on the SYS: volume of a NetWare server. NetWare v3.12 automatically creates the ETC directory to store the sample files that help configure the server for the TCP/IP network protocol. The DOC directory is optional for NetWare servers and is typically used to contain electronic versions of the NetWare manual.

To help users recover lost files, a CNA should be aware of the purpose and use of the DELETED.SAV directory. The DELETED.SAV directory is automatically created on each NetWare volume and is the part of the NetWare file recovery system that allows the recovery of a file even after the directory that contained the file has been deleted. When files are deleted from a NetWare volume, the blocks on the hard disk that contained the file's information are not immediately reused (as would happen on your local DOS drive). Instead, as NetWare requires more disk space, it reuses disk blocks from the files that have been deleted the longest, allowing you to recover files even after they have been deleted for some time. Normally a file must be recovered in the directory from which it was deleted, but if that directory has been removed the file might still be found in the DELETED.SAV directory. In Chapter 6 you will have an opportunity to practice salvaging deleted files.

Suggested directories

The four required directories just described are automatically created for you during installation and provide the NetWare operating system with the storage areas it needs to perform its functions. In addition, an organization will probably require areas in the file server disk volumes to meet its storage needs. The network administrator is responsible for planning, creating, and maintaining the directory structure necessary to store the organization's data and software on the file server. There are four basic types of directories that Novell suggests should be part of an organization's file system: DOS directories, Application directories, user home directories, and Shared directories. This section describes each of the suggested directories and explains how they can be applied to meet the storage needs of an organization.

DOS directories. Most larger networks have workstations that run different versions of DOS. Because each DOS version will run external commands written for that version only, it is necessary to provide a separate directory for each DOS version. One solution is to have each workstation use its local hard disk drive to contain a directory with the DOS commands used by that workstation. However, this requires each workstation to have a hard drive containing the DOS commands as well as increasing the chance that the DOS commands are accidentally erased or damaged by a computer virus. To deal with this, it is a common practice among network administrators to create subdirectories in PUBLIC for each version of the DOS operating system being used on the network (see Figure 4-3). Each of the subdirectories contains only the DOS external commands, such as DISKCOPY, XCOPY, and FORMAT, that the administrator wants available on the network. This technique saves the administrator from having to keep DOS directories on each workstation's hard disk and updating all workstation hard drives when a newer version of DOS is installed.

The DOS structure shown in Figure 4-3 provides for different machine types and DOS environments by establishing a directory level for each machine type and then dividing the machine types into subdirectories corresponding to DOS versions. This structure is necessary because some PC manufacturers, such as Compaq and IBM, have modified Microsoft DOS to provide special features for their own brands of computers. For example, IBM provides a specialized version of DOS, so the IBM_PC directory is further divided into two subdirectories—one for IBM's DOS version and one for the standard Microsoft DOS versions. Each of the IBM_PC subdirectories can be further subdivided into additional subdirectories for each DOS version. Using the version number for the directory name, as shown in Figure 4-3, allows NetWare to locate the correct DOS directory automatically for the workstation to use when a user logs in.

Figure 4-3

Recommended DOS directory structure

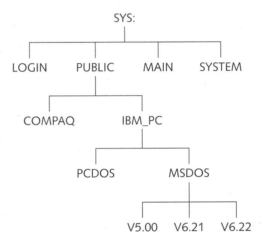

APPLICATION directories.   In addition to creating the required NetWare directories, CNAs will need to create directories and subdirectories for the applications and data needed by network users. The first rule in organizing directories is to keep data and software separate whenever possible. This means you will need to define a directory for each software application that will be stored in the file server. Software applications fall into two basic categories: general-purpose packages, such as WordPerfect and Lotus 1-2-3, and special-purpose applications such as payroll or order-entry software. General-purpose software is often needed by multiple users throughout an organization, so these applications are often stored in directories in the server's SYS: volume. Special-purpose applications are often restricted to small groups of users or departments; they contain their own data directories and files and sometimes have large data storage needs. In order to provide restricted access or prevent the SYS: volume from filling up, some network administrators store special-purpose applications, such as payroll or inventory, in a separate data volume.

HOME directories.   In addition to having access to application directories, each user needs a private **home directory** in which to store files and documents. When planning your disk storage needs, you should anticipate space needed for users to store personal projects and files they use in their work. Generally, only the owner of a home directory has access rights to it; files that are needed by multiple users should be stored in shared directory areas. The location of user home directories depends on the design of the directory structure; they can be placed in a general-purpose USERS directory, as shown in Figure 4-4, or be separated by workgroup as described later in this chapter. User home directories should be named with the user's login name. This allows the CNA to assign a drive letter to the user's home directory when the user logs in. In Chapter 11, you will learn how to use NetWare login scripts to automate the process of mapping drives to user home directories.

Figure 4-4

Novell-suggested directories

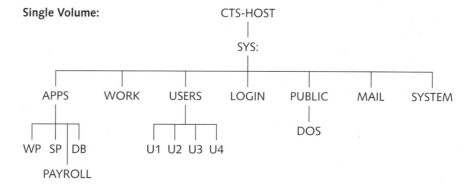

SHARED directories.   One of the benefits of using a network is being able to share files. As a CNA you will need to establish shared work directories that allow multiple users to work with common files and documents. Shared work directories allow one user to save a file and another user working on the same project to access it. Word processing documents and spreadsheet program worksheets stored in a shared directory are available to only one user at a time. Special software is needed to allow a file to be accessed by multiple users at the same time to prevent one user's changes from overwriting the changes made by another. Figure 4-4 shows general-purpose shared directories for use by all users. Later in the chapter you will learn how to create a departmental directory structure that includes shared directories for each workgroup.

FILES

Files contain the actual blocks of data and software that can be loaded from the disk storage system into the computer's RAM. Every NetWare volume contains a **directory entry table (DET)** and a file allocation table (FAT) to keep track of each file's name and location on the disk volume. The DET also stores file attributes and access rights. **Access rights** control what operations a user can perform on a file or directory. **Attributes** are special flags that identify how the file is to be viewed or processed. Examples of common file attributes used in DOS are Read-Only, Hidden, and System. NetWare provides such additional attributes as Sharable and Delete-Inhibit. In Chapter 8 you will learn more about the file access rights and attributes available with NetWare.

NetWare supports DOS file naming conventions with filenames of up to eight characters and an optional three-character extension. The NetWare DET, however, is not limited to DOS filenames because NetWare file servers are often required to store files from workstations running other operating systems such as Windows NT, Apple Macintosh, OS/2, and Unix. As a CNA you will need to know how to set up and manage file storage from workstations running a variety of operating systems. Because non-DOS systems support longer filenames with special attributes, additional logic needs to be added to the NetWare file server, and the DET needs to be expanded for the server volumes that will support files used by the non-DOS systems. Because of the importance of the DET and FAT in accessing files from a NetWare volume, a second copy of both tables is automatically maintained to allow automatic recovery in the event of a disk error that damages the primary tables.

DIRECTORY PATHS

When you log in to a file server, your workstation is assigned to a specific volume and directory known as the **default directory**. To access files located in other directories or to change your default directory, you need to specify the location of the directory or file within the NetWare file system. A **directory path** is a list of file system components that identifies the location of the directory or file you want to access. A **complete directory path** contains the file server's name, volume name, directory, and all subdirectories leading to the target object. For example, the complete path to the U1 home directory, shown in Figure 4-4, is expressed as CTS_HOST\SYS:\USERS\U1. A **partial directory path** lists only the locations leading from the default directory to the target object. Assume, for example, that your default directory is the SYS: volume. In this case, the partial directory path is specified as \USERS\U1. As a CNA, you will often need to use both complete and partial paths when working with the NetWare file system.

COMPLETE PATH

When specifying the complete directory path to an object, you start with the file server's name followed by a slash and then the name of the volume followed by a colon. Directories and subdirectories can then be specified using either a forward slash (/) or backslash (\) to separate the directory and subdirectory names. Although a slash can be added between the volume and directory names, some programs misinterpret the volume name as a directory name. Therefore it is best not to include a slash after the colon in a volume's name. To avoid confusion when you enter DOS paths, you should consistently use backslashes between directory and subdirectory names in NetWare paths because DOS does not accept forward slashes as part of directory paths on local disk drives.

Normally DOS commands do not accept NetWare complete directory paths because they contain unfamiliar objects, such as the file server name and volume name. Figure 4-5 shows an attempt to use the DOS COPY command to copy a file from drive A: to the MARY home directory without having the NetWare shell program loaded. This will result in an error message that says "Too many parameters." DOS cannot correctly interpret SYS: as a valid part of the directory path. Because of the NetWare shell program, however, you can always use the familiar DOS CD command to specify complete paths in the NetWare file system. Figure 4-6 shows an example of a CD command used with a complete path to change to the MARY home directory and then copy the desired file from drive A:.

Figure 4-5

Using a complete path with DOS commands

```
F:\>dir users

 Volume in drive F is SYS
 Directory of F:\USERS

MARY          <DIR>          12-13-94    9:10a
DAVID         <DIR>          12-13-94    9:10a
PETER         <DIR>          12-13-94    9:10a
ROSE          <DIR>          12-13-94    9:10a
JOE           <DIR>          12-13-94    9:10a
        5 file(s)                   0 bytes
                          7,675,904 bytes free

F:\>COPY A:*.* SYS:USERS\MARY
Too many parameters

F:\>_
```

Figure 4-6

Using the CD command

```
F:\>CD SYS:USERS\MARY

F:\USERS\MARY>COPY A:*.* F:
A:89120601.1
A:90990325.1
A:70020501.3
A:70990515.3
A:60900510.2
A:60100610.2
A:54910210.3
          7 file(s) copied

F:\USERS\MARY>_
```

PARTIAL PATH

Entering a partial path is often much quicker than typing a complete path when the directory or file you want to identify is located within the same directory or volume as your default path. In most cases, therefore, you will specify the partial path to a directory or file. DOS commands can often be used with partial paths that do not include a volume name. For example, suppose your default directory path is SYS:USERS and you want to copy all files from the disk in drive A: into the MARY home directory. You could use either of these two partial paths:

F:\USERS>COPY A:*.* \USERS\MARY

F:\USERS>COPY A:*.* MARY

In the first copy command, the backslash at the beginning of the target path specifies that the path to the target directory starts at the beginning of the default volume, which in this case is the SYS: volume. In the second copy command, the backslash has been omitted. This tells DOS that the target path starts with the current directory and proceeds to the subdirectory named MARY. Placing a backslash before MARY would result in an "Invalid path" error message because DOS would look for a directory called MARY on the root of the volume.

DIRECTORY STRUCTURE

Once you understand the components of a file system, you can design a directory structure that will meet the processing needs of an organization. Designing a directory structure can be compared to creating a blueprint for a building. Just as the blueprint allows the builder to determine the construction details and materials needed, the directory structure design allows the network administrator to allocate storage space and implement the file system on a network. Designing the directory structure involves two steps:

1. Defining the directories and subdirectories needed.

2. Placing those directories in the file system structure.

Before you design an organization's directory structure, however, you need to analyze the processing needs of the users in the organization to determine what directories will be needed. When creating the directory structure, you should be aware that there is no single best approach that all network administrators use. Instead, each network administrator develops his or her own unique style for defining and arranging directories. This section explains the concepts and techniques that will help you develop your own style for creating good directory structures.

DEFINE WORKGROUPS

The first step in designing a directory structure is to determine the storage required for the services the file server will provide to the network users. To do this, let's take a look at a sample organization called PC Solutions. PC Solutions is a small but rapidly growing company that markets specialized computer equipment. Its organizational chart is shown in Figure 4-7.

Figure 4-7

PC Solutions organizational chart

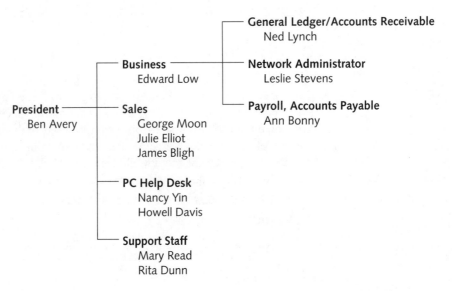

When determining storage needs, you start by examining an organizational chart in order to determine the computer users and any possible workgroups. From the PC Solutions organizational chart you can immediately see that the organization has four possible workgroups: business, sales, help desk, and support staff.

DEFINE DIRECTORIES

After you identify the network users and workgroups, you need to determine—through discussions with the users and department managers—what applications and data storage areas they will need. It is important to get users involved in the design of the network early in the directory design process to ensure that the result will adequately serve and anticipate their needs.

Directories can be divided into four general categories: general-purpose applications, vertical applications, shared data, and home directories. A **general-purpose application** is a software program—such as a word processor, spreadsheet, or CAD product—that is accessed by many different users to create and maintain their own files and documents. A **vertical application** is a software program that performs a specialized process—such as payroll, order entry, or manufacturing requirements planning. Vertical applications are normally restricted to a department or limited number of users and allow for multiple-user access to shared database files within the application's directory structure.

Shared data areas allow users to exchange files by saving the files where multiple users can access them. In designing directory structures, a network administrator can include a **local shared directory** which restricts access to shared files to the users of the workgroup concerned with them. The network administrator can also provide a **global shared directory** so files can be shared among workgroups.

Let's follow this process for PC Solutions. Assume you have discussed network usage with the PC Solutions staff and have learned the following:

- In the business department, a payroll application is used for weekly payroll processing. In addition, the department uses a spreadsheet package to work on budgets, and these budget spreadsheet files are shared only among the business department users.

- Each user in the sales department has his or her own computer and needs to access an order-entry application to record and process orders. Additionally, sales users periodically share word processing document files when working together on a sales presentation.

- The administrative support personnel use word processing and desktop publishing software to work on shared documents such as sales agreements and catalog files. In addition, the administrative support staff work with all other departments to help format and print documents being sent to customers.

- All staff members at PC Solutions need access to a word processing program to write their own correspondence and memos. To make work easier, everyone would like to share common word processing templates, forms, and customer lists.

As shown in Figure 4-8, the general-purpose software directories for PC Solutions include a word processing application needed by all employees, a spreadsheet application for the business department, and a desktop publishing application for use by support staff. Vertical applications at PC Solutions include the payroll system used by the business department and the order-entry system used by the sales department. Shared directories include a FORMS directory to contain common word processing forms for all users, a BUDGETS directory for the business department, and a CATALOG directory for use by the support staff. There will also be four shared work directories: one for business, one for sales, one for support staff, and one for the entire company. While it would be possible to have one shared directory for the entire company, multiple directories will keep the files separate—making it easier for staff to locate and use only the files they need.

Figure 4-8

PC Solutions directory planning form

Directory Planning Form

Created by: _T Simpson_   Date: _____

Organization: _PC Solutions_

Workgroups:

Workgroup Name	Members
Business	four business users
Sales	three sales users
Support	two secretaries
Everyone	all company users

Directories:

Directory Description	Type	Users	Estimated Capacity in Mbytes
Payroll	vertical application	business	20
Budgets	shared data	business	30
Order entry	vertical application	sales	50
General word processing forms and templates	shared data	everyone	25
Shared files and documents	shared data	sales	25
Catalog	shared data	support	100
Shared documents	shared data	everyone	25
Shared documents	shared data	business	25
Shared documents	shared data	support	25
Word processing	general-purpose application	everyone	5
Spreadsheet	general-purpose application	business	5
Desktop publishing	general-purpose application	support	10
Home directories for each user	private data	9 staff members	25 per User

DESIGN THE STRUCTURE

Once you have determined the directories that are needed, you are ready to design the layout and determine the location of the directories within the file server's volumes. To design the directory structure for your file server, you first need to define the data and software directories needed by your users to perform their processing functions. Then, you organize these directories into a logical and easy-to-use structure that will provide a foundation for your network's file system. In this section, you learn how to analyze the directory needs for an organization, as well as two major ways to organize a directory structure: departmental-oriented and application-oriented. In addition, this section provides you with forms and techniques that will help you design and document your directory structures.

The directory design form

When diagramming a directory structure, you will find it is often difficult to draw all directories and subdirectories for a volume on one sheet of paper. As shown in Figure 4-9, the volume design form is used to document each volume and all directories branching from the root of the volume. The volume design form can also be used to show subdirectories that have simple structures. The PC Solutions SALES and SUPPORT directories are treated this way in Figure 4-9. In addition to layout the directory structure, the volume design form contains fields for specifying block size and total volume.

Figure 4-9

Sample volume
design form

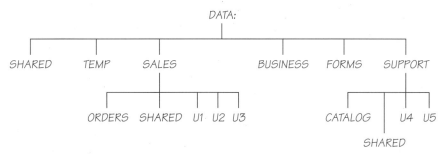

Volume Design Form

Designed by: _Ted Simpson_   Date: _____

Volume name: _DATA:_   Maximum capacity: _600 Mbytes_

Block size: (4Kbytes) 8Kbytes   16Kbytes   32Kbytes

The volume design form does not provide enough space for you to diagram more complex directories. Having separate forms for subdirectories allows you to make alteration to a subdirectory without having to redraw an entire diagram. The directory design form shown in Figure 4-10 illustrates the directory structure for the PC Solutions business workgroup, showing all its subdirectories. You should complete one directory design form for each directory not fully documented on your volume design form.

Figure 4-10

Sample directory
design form

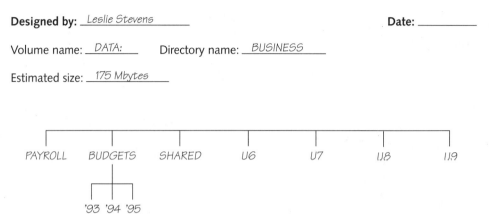

Directory Design Form

Designed by: _Leslie Stevens_   **Date:** _____

Volume name: _DATA:_   Directory name: _BUSINESS_

Estimated size: _175 Mbytes_

Organizing the SYS: volume

The simplest method for organizing the SYS: volume is to branch all directories from
the root of the SYS: volume, as shown in Figure 4-11. The lack of hierarchy in this
directory design, however, makes it inherently difficult to group directories by function or to manage and assign special trustee rights. In addition, storing all files in the
SYS: volume can cause the file server to crash if there is not enough disk space available for the operating system. To avoid these pitfalls, many network administrators separate the SYS: volume from data storage. Not only does this method free up adequate
space in the SYS: volume for system functions, but it also simplifies backup procedures and allows you to perform maintenance activities on the DATA: volume without taking the SYS: volume off line.

Figure 4-11

Simple directory design

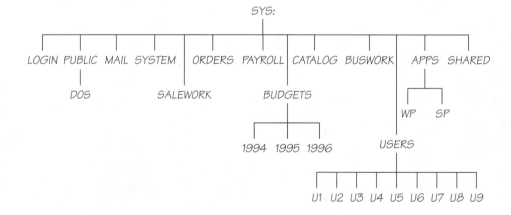

In a multiple volume design, many network administrators place directories for the
DOS operating system and general-purpose applications in the SYS: volume. Figure
4-12 illustrates this multiple-volume approach applied to the PC Solutions SYS: volume structure. Notice that all the general-purpose application packages have been
placed in separate subdirectories under the SOFTWARE directory. This will make it
easy for the network administrator to assign access rights. The remaining directories
for PC Solutions' data and special-purpose applications will be located in a separate

DATA: volume. Because over time these directories will grow in size, placing them in a separate volume will allow the network administrator to monitor and maintain adequate data storage space in the SYS: volume.

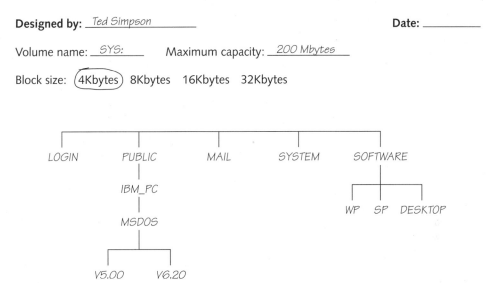

Figure 4-12

PC Solutions SYS: volume

Organizing the DATA: volume

Network administrators generally use two methods to organize directories in a DATA: volume: by application or by department or workgroup. The method you select will depend on your personal preference and on the size and type of processing performed by the organization. Generally, smaller network file systems can be organized by using an **application-oriented structure** that branches all directories from the root of the volume. This keeps the design simple and easy to manage. In larger file systems involving multiple workgroups and many data directories it is often easier to maintain security and locate data when you use a **departmental structure**. This structure places data directories as subdirectories under workgroup directories. In some cases, a combination of both methods will work best for an organization.

 While NetWare will support up to 25 levels of subdirectories, a good rule of thumb is not to exceed six subdirectory layers with no more than 16 subdirectories in any one directory. This way, you can always view all directories on a computer monitor at the same time.

Application-oriented structure. In an application-oriented structure, the directories are grouped by application rather than by department or workgroup. All user home directories, for example, could be placed under a common directory called USERS. The shared directories could then be grouped according to their use, and applications placed in separate directories located on the root of the DATA: volume. Figure 4-13 shows the application-oriented method applied to the PC Solutions structure.

Figure 4-13

PC Solutions application-
oriented structure

Volume Design Form

Designed by: _Ted Simpson_   **Date:** _____

Volume name: _DATA:_   Maximum capacity: _600 Mbytes_

Block size: (4Kbytes) 8Kbytes   16Kbytes   32Kbytes

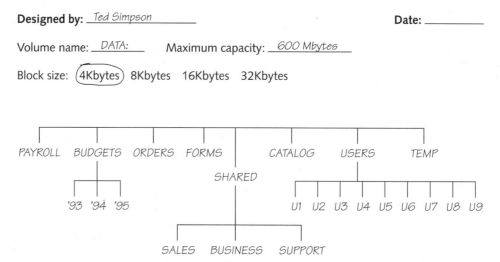

The advantage of an application-oriented structure is that it is fairly shallow, which makes it easier to locate files without going through multiple layers of directories. In large directory structures, however, the shallow nature of the application-oriented structure can actually be a disadvantage—it is difficult to know which directories are used by which departments. In an application-oriented structure, the network administrator will need to make more trustee assignments because rights will not automatically be granted for users to access the directories with the software applications they need.

Departmental structure. In a departmental structure, user home directories, shared work directories, and applications are located within the workgroups and departments that control them. Directories that contain files available to all users are located at the root of the volume. Figure 4-14 organizing the directories for PC Solutions using a departmental structure. The FORMS directory is located at the root of the DATA: volume because it contains files that are used by the entire organization. Notice the shared work directories located in each workgroup's directory structure. These provide separate shared file access for each department. A major difference between the departmental- and application-oriented structures is the location of the user home directories. Notice in Figure 4-14 that the user home directories are located under each department directory rather than all placed together under a general USERS directory.

Figure 4-14

PC Solutions departmental structure

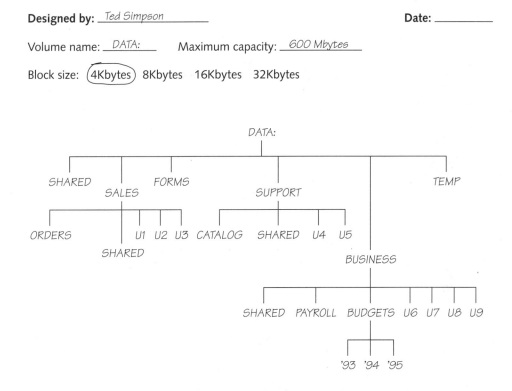

Volume Design Form

Designed by: _Ted Simpson_   Date: _____

Volume name: _DATA:_   Maximum capacity: _600 Mbytes_

Block size: (4Kbytes) 8Kbytes   16Kbytes   32Kbytes

DIRECTORY COMMANDS

NetWare provides several commands and utilities in the SYS:PUBLIC directory. This section describes the NetWare utilities and commands that provide information about the volumes and directory structures on a file server.

VOLINFO UTILITY

The VOLINFO utility, an important CNA tool, quickly displays the directory entries for all volumes on a file server and states the amount of space available. You can use the VOLINFO command to determine where to install new application software based on the space available in all volumes. The VOLINFO command also lets you familiarize yourself with the names and sizes of all volumes on an unfamiliar file server.

The VOLINFO utility, a program that can be run by any user, displays current status information about each volume on the selected file server. VOLINFO is called a **real time program** because the information on its screen changes as new files and directories are added to or deleted from the server. It allows continuous monitoring of changes made to the file server volumes. To run the VOLINFO program, simply enter VOLINFO at the DOS prompt of a workstation that is logged into the network. Each volume's information will be displayed in a separate box, as shown in Figure 4-15. The Kilobytes field shows the total space allocated to a volume and the amount that is still free. The Directories field shows the maximum number of directory entries allowed in the volume followed by the number of directory entries available. Each time a file or directory is created on the volume, the number in the directory total field increases and the number in the free field decreases.

Figure 4-15

Sample VOLINFO
display

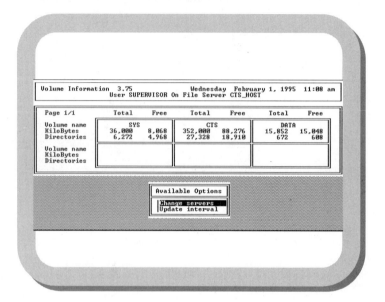

VOLINFO's Available Options menu allows you either to choose to view another file server or to use the Update Intervals option to change how often the KiloBytes Free and Directories fields are updated with new information from the file server. The default update interval is 5 seconds, which is normally satisfactory. As a CNA, you should use the VOLINFO command periodically to keep track of any server volumes that are running low on disk space or directory entries.

CHKVOL COMMAND

The CHKVOL command provides detailed information about a specific volume. Information provided by the CHKVOL command includes the amount of space available to the user and the amount of space used by both current and deleted files. This information can help a CNA determine if more disk space needs to be allocated for a user and if space from deleted files is being properly reused by the operating system.

The CHKVOL command can be run from the DOS prompt by entering CHKVOL followed by the name of the volume, as shown in Figure 4-16. If CHKVOL is entered without any parameters it will display information about the volume that is currently in use.

Notice that the values in the "Total volume space" and "Space remaining on volume" fields match the values displayed on the VOLINFO screen shown in Figure 4-15. The "Space available to SUPERVISOR" field displays how much of the volume space might be used by the workstation's current user. It is important to remember that the space available to a user can be less than the total volume space if special disk space restrictions have been placed on the user by the network administrator.

Figure 4-16

Sample CHKVOL command

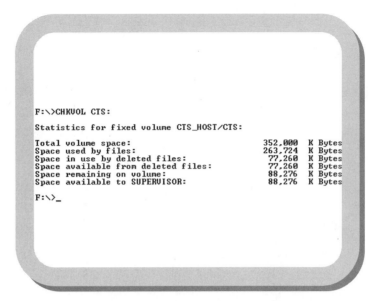

```
F:\>CHKVOL CTS:

Statistics for fixed volume CTS_HOST/CTS:

Total volume space:                     352,000   K Bytes
Space used by files:                    263,724   K Bytes
Space in use by deleted files:           77,260   K Bytes
Space available from deleted files:      77,260   K Bytes
Space remaining on volume:               88,276   K Bytes
Space available to SUPERVISOR:           88,276   K Bytes

F:\>_
```

The CHKVOL command also displays the amount of space used by existing files and by deleted files. By default, when a file is deleted its data blocks are not immediately reused by NetWare, but are held until needed. Blocks from the oldest deleted files are reused first. As long as NetWare has free space on the volume it will not use up the deleted file blocks, so that they can be recovered by the network administrator if it turns out they are needed. You can easily determine how much unused space remains on a volume before NetWare begins to reuse the deleted file blocks. Subtract the space available from deleted files from the space remaining on the volume. In the example shown in Figure 4-16, the result is 11016 Kbytes. This means that there are over 11 MB of new space available in this volume that will need to be used before the system begins to recycle blocks from old deleted files. Use the CHKVOL command periodically to monitor how the disk space in NetWare volumes is being used and how it might affect volume capacity and server performance.

CHKDIR COMMAND

The CHKDIR command reports the amount of disk space occupied by a disk directory and all its subdirectories. You can use this information to determine how much space will be required to back up or move a directory structure to another location. In addition, the CHKDIR command displays how much disk space is available in the volume and how much of that volume disk space is used by the specified directory. NetWare allows a size limit to be placed on a specific directory, and the CHKDIR command can be used to determine if the directory is reaching its limit and whether the directory structure needs to have some of its files deleted or its size expanded (with the DSPACE command described in Chapter 6).

To run the CHKDIR command enter CHKDIR followed by the complete or partial path of the directory you want to check. If no path is specified, the CHKDIR command provides information about the current directory. For example, typing the command CHKDIR SYS:PUBLIC\IBM_PC\MSDOS displays the information shown in Figure 4-17.

Figure 4-17

Sample CHKDIR
command

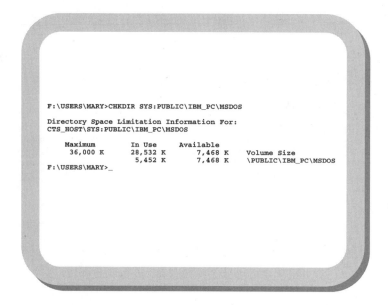

```
F:\USERS\MARY>CHKDIR SYS:PUBLIC\IBM_PC\MSDOS

Directory Space Limitation Information For:
CTS_HOST\SYS:PUBLIC\IBM_PC\MSDOS

     Maximum      In Use     Available
      36,000 K    28,532 K     7,468 K     Volume Size
                   5,452 K     7,468 K     \PUBLIC\IBM_PC\MSDOS
F:\USERS\MARY>_
```

Notice the size of the SYS: volume under the Maximum column. It is the same amount displayed by the CHKVOL and VOLINFO commands. Under the In Use column, the CHKDIR command displays the amount of disk space in use for both the volume and the directory structure. Under the Available column, the CHKDIR command displays the amount of disk space available to both the volume and the MSDOS directory structure. In this example, the amount of space available to the MSDOS directory structure equals the amount of space on the volume. The amount available in the selected directory, however, is sometimes less than the amount available in the volume. This happens when a network administrator, using the DSPACE command, has limited the amount of space used by a directory and its subdirectories. If a user receives a "disk full" error message from the file server, the CNA can determine if there is additional space on the volume by using the CHKDIR command and then, using the DSPACE command, increase the amount of space allocated to the directory structure.

LISTDIR COMMAND

The LISTDIR command displays the names of directories and subdirectories in the specified path. This information is similar to that provided by the DOS TREE command. The NetWare LISTDIR command, in addition, provides options that allow a CNA to view network-specific information about the directories. The LISTDIR command without any options displays the names of the subdirectories in the current directory only. To display a "tree" showing all subdirectories in the directory structure, include the /SUB, or /S parameter. The /SUB will display information about the specified directory along with information on all the subdirectories. Including the /D and /T options displays the creation date and time of each directory and subdirectory. You use the /E option to display the current user's effective rights (Read, File scan, Create, Erase, Write, Modify, or Access control) in each directory. Figure 4-18 shows an example of the LISTDIR command using the /S and /E options to display the effective rights of the user GUEST in all directories of the SYS: volume.

Figure 4-18

Sample LISTDIR
command

```
F:\>LISTDIR SYS: /S /E

The subdirectory structure of CTS_HOST/SYS:
Effective    Directory
-----------------------------------------------------------
[ R    F ] ->LOGIN
[ R    F ] ->  NLS
[ R    F ] ->  OS2
[ R    F ] ->PUBLIC
[ R    F ] ->  NLS
_
```

NDIR COMMAND

NetWare's NDIR command is similar to the DOS DIR command. A CNA can use the NDIR command to display such additional NetWare file information as the last time a file was updated, network attributes on a file, and the user who originally created a file. This information is helpful in locating specific files in a NetWare volume or documenting network file usage. Figure 4-19 shows an example of the NDIR command used to display a list of all files in the FORMS directory of the DATA: volume.

Figure 4-19

Sample NDIR command

```
F:\>NDIR DATA:FORMS
CTS_HOST\DATA:FORMS

Files:              Size       Last Updated        Flags                Owner
------------------  ---------  ---------------  --------------------  ---------
CURRDEV    FRM      1,998   8-30-90   3:12p   [Rw-A--------------]  SUPERVISO
MEMO       FRM        143   8-30-90   3:17p   [Rw-A--------------]  SUPERVISO
ORDER      FRM      1,405   6-21-93   3:02p   [Rw-A--------------]  SUPERVISO
SIRS       FRM      7,146  10-06-90   8:29a   [Rw-A--------------]  SUPERVISO
STAFFDEV   FRM      1,758  10-06-90   8:39a   [Rw-A--------------]  SUPERVISO
TIME       FRM      5,150   6-24-93  12:48p   [Rw-A--------------]  SUPERVISO

        17,600 bytes in    6 files
        32,768 bytes in    8 blocks

F:\>_
```

The NDIR command's /SUB option is useful if you are looking for a specific file in the directory structure and do not know what subdirectory the file is in. For example, the command NDIR DATA:JAN93.WK1 /SUB will scan the entire DATA: volume looking for the file JAN93.WK1. If the file is found, NDIR will display the file's information including its home directory path. The NDIR command has many other options that are useful for obtaining and documenting network file and directory information. Figure 4-20 shows an example of using an NDIR command used to display all files from the DATA:FORMS directory that are larger than 2,000 bytes, in sequence from smallest to largest. Chapter 6 will describe an option that allows you to sort by owner files that have not been accessed since a specified date. This will help you identify files that can be considered for deletion—just one example of how this kind of file information can greatly simplify a CNA's job of managing network file systems.

Figure 4-20

Using NDIR to sort and display selected files

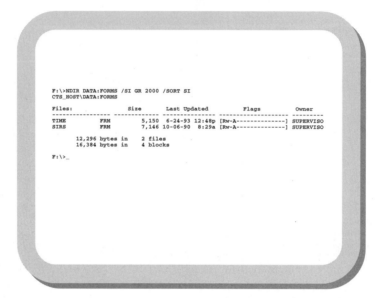

```
F:\>NDIR DATA:FORMS /SI GR 2000 /SORT SI
CTS_HOST\DATA:FORMS

Files:               Size      Last Updated        Flags          Owner
----------------- ---------- --------------- --------------------- ---------
TIME        FRM       5,150  6-24-93 12:48p [Rw-A--------------] SUPERVISO
SIRS        FRM       7,146 10-06-90  8:29a [Rw-A--------------] SUPERVISO

         12,296 bytes in   2 files
         16,384 bytes in   4 blocks

F:\>_
```

TLIST COMMAND

The TLIST command lists all users or groups who have been given a trustee right to the specified directory. One of the major responsibilities of a CNA is to provide the users access to the files they need. At the same time, the CNA needs to prevent unauthorized access to the network file system. The TLIST command is an important tool that allows a CNA to determine what users or groups have been granted a trustee right to the specific directory or file. A trustee right grants a user access rights to the directory or file. The standard eight NetWare access rights are Read, File scan, Write, Create, Erase, Modify, Access control, and Supervisory.

 Each of the access rights flows down the directory structure into the subdirectories unless they are modified by a specific trustee assignment in one of the lower subdirectories or blocked by an inherited rights mask. As mentioned earlier, the LISTDIR /R /S command lists inherited rights mask information for all subdirectories.

The TLIST command with no options displays the trustee rights for the current default directory. Figure 4-21 shows an example of the TLIST command used to check the trustee rights to the SOFTWARE directory of the SYS: volume. Notice that the user (RON) has been granted rights that allow him to maintain the software directory. All other users belong to the group EVERYONE and will be granted Read and File scan rights to the SOFTWARE directory and all its subdirectories. This means all users can run the general-purpose software applications.

Figure 4-21

Sample TLIST command

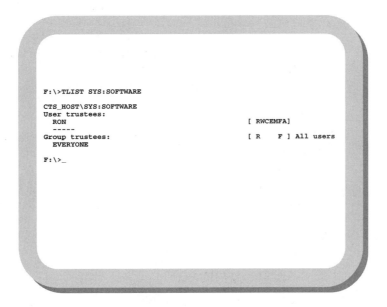

```
F:\>TLIST SYS:SOFTWARE

CTS_HOST\SYS:SOFTWARE
User trustees:
  RON                                     [ RWCEMFA]
  -----
Group trustees:                           [ R    F ] All users
  EVERYONE

F:\>_
```

NCOPY COMMAND

The syntax of the NCOPY command is very similar to that of the DOS XCOPY command. When creating or maintaining the directory structure, a CNA often needs to copy files from a NetWare directory or local disk to another location in the network file system. One advantage of the NCOPY command is that you can specify a complete NetWare path including file server name and volume name. The XCOPY command works only with partial paths containing directory and subdirectory names; it does not accept NetWare complete paths because it does not know about file servers and volumes. Another advantage of the NCOPY command is that it is more efficient than the XCOPY command. When used to copy files between NetWare directories, it does not need to transfer each block of data from the file to the workstation and back. Instead, the file transfers can be completed at the file server—only the status information is sent to the workstation when the transfers are complete. Figure 4-22 demonstrates the use of NetWare's NCOPY command to transfer files from a floppy disk to the FORMS directory of the DATA: volume of the file server named CTS_HOST.

Figure 4-22

Sample NCOPY
command

```
F:\>NCOPY A:*.FRM CTS_HOST\DATA:FORMS
From A:
To    CTS_HOST/DATA:\FORMS
      CURRDEV.FRM    to CURRDEV.FRM
      MEMO.FRM       to MEMO.FRM
      STAFFDEV.FRM   to STAFFDEV.FRM
      SIRS.FRM       to SIRS.FRM
      ORDER.FRM      to ORDER.FRM
      TIME.FRM       to TIME.FRM

      6 files copied.

F:\>_
```

RENDIR COMMAND

In managing directory structures, a CNA sometimes needs to change the name of an existing directory or subdirectory in order to make it more meaningful or to avoid conflicts with other directory or filenames. In these situations, the RENDIR command can be used to change the name of any directory in the file system simply by specifying the current path followed by the new directory name. You do not need to specify the entire path a second time when specifying the new directory's name. Figure 4-23 shows an example of the RENDIR command used to change the name of the BUS directory in the DATA: volume to BUSINESS. Notice that the new directory name does not need to be preceded by the path. The RENDIR command can also be used to rename directories on local DOS disk drives because many versions of DOS do not include a command to rename directories.

Figure 4-23

RENDIR used to rename a directory

```
F:\>RENDIR CTS_HOST\DATA:BUS   BUSINESS
Directory renamed to BUSINESS.

F:\>_
```

CHAPTER SUMMARY

Designing and maintaining a directory structure is one of the most important jobs of a network administrator because it is the foundation of the file system on a server. The NetWare file system consists of four parts: file server, volumes, directories, and files. When NetWare is installed on your file server, the required SYS: volume and system directories are created automatically. The NetWare required directories include LOGIN, PUBLIC, MAIL, and SYSTEM. Each of these directories serves a specific purpose. The LOGIN directory contains files and programs that are available to a workstation before the user logs in. The PUBLIC directory contains NetWare commands and utilities that are available to all users after logging in. The SYSTEM directory is the responsibility of the file server supervisor and contains operating files and supervisor utilities. The MAIL directory contains a subdirectory for each user that is accessed by the system to store user profile information such as personal login script commands and print job configuration files.

In addition to the directories created by NetWare, the network administrator should create additional directories for DOS, application software, shared data, and personal user home directories. There are two major methods of arranging these directories: by application and by department. Application-oriented structures are grouped around applications; departmental structures are grouped around workgroups. Application-oriented structures often work best in small and medium file systems; in large file systems with multiple workgroups and many directories and files, however, the departmental structure usually provides a better structure for directory organization.

A path is used to specify the location of a file or directory in the NetWare file system. A complete path contains all components of the directory structure leading to the specified file or directory. When specifying a complete path, you need to separate the file server's name from the volume name with a slash and separate the volume and directory names with a colon. A partial path consists of the directories and subdirectories leading from your current default directory to the desired file or directory location.

NetWare provides a number of commands that complement standard DOS commands and allow CNAs to view and manipulate the network file system more efficiently. The VOLINFO and CHKVOL commands display volume-specific information. The CHKDIR command displays information about a specific directory structure. The LISTDIR command displays a directory tree showing part or all of the directory structure, including directory creation and access right information. The NDIR command is a network version of the DOS DIR command that allows you to select and sort files to obtain more useful information. The RENDIR command allows you to rename network or local directories. The TLIST command identifies what users or groups have been given specific access rights to a directory. These rights flow down to the subdirectories unless blocked by an inherited rights mask on one of the subdirectories.

COMMAND SUMMARY

Command	Syntax	Definition
CHKDIR	*CHKDIR [path]*	Displays information about the selected directory structure including space used by all files and subdirectories along with space available to the directory.
CHKVOL	*CHKVOL [path]*	Displays volume information including total free space, amount of space used, and amount of space available from deleted files.
LISTDIR	*LISTDIR [path] [/S/D /T /E /R /A]*	Displays all directories in the selected path. The /S option displays all subdirectories in the structure. The /D and /T options display creation date and time. /E displays effective rights in each directory. /R displays the inherited rights mask for each directory and subdirectory. /A includes all information provided by /D, /T, /E, and /R.
NCOPY	*NCOPY [path]filename [path[filename]] [/S /E /V]*	Similar to the DOS XCOPY command except that it is able to use complete NetWare paths.

NDIR	*NDIR [path]* *[/options]*	Displays network directory information including last data updated, file attributes, and owner information. The /SUB option displays files in all subdirectories of the path. The /SORT *order* option allows you to use one of the following orders to control the sequence of the listing by either OWNER, SIZE, or AC (Access Date). The /SIZE *condition number* option lists only the files whose size match the condition specified. The condition can be either GR (greater than), LE (less than), or EQ (equal to) followed by the size you want the files compared to specified in number of bytes. The /OWNER EQ *username* option lists only files owned by the specified username.
RENDIR	*RENDIR oldpath newpath*	Changes the name of a directory by specifying the name of the path and name of the original directory followed by the new directory name. It is not necessary to specify the complete path to the new directory.
TLIST	*TLIST [path]*	Displays each user or group that has been assigned a trustee right, along with the access rights granted.
VOLINFO	*VOLINFO*	Provides real-time volume information showing the amount of free space and directory entries available.

KEY TERMS

access rights

application-oriented structure

attributes

block

block suballocation

complete directory path

default directory

departmental structure

directory entry table (DET)

directory path

general-purpose application

global search directory

global shared directory

home directory

local shared directory

partial directory path

real time program

spanning

vertical application

volume

REVIEW QUESTIONS

1. List three benefits of the NetWare file system:

   or damaged files 1) Centralized management of data & backups ensures duplicates of lost

   2) Others cannot access data they are not responsible for.

   3) Workgroups can share files or transfer file from one user to another

2. List the file system components in sequence from major to minor:

   File Server, Volumes, Directories, Sub-directories, files.

3. A(n) _netware volume_ is a physical amount of storage contained on one or more hard disk drives or other storage media.

4. A volume can span up to _32_ disk drives.

5. What fault tolerance capability should you consider before spanning a volume over multiple disk drives?

   Mirror the disk drives - prevents access to volumes data

6. The maximum length of a volume name is _15_ characters.

7. Identify each of the following as either a valid or invalid character in a volume name:

   $ _valid_

   # _____

   , _invalid_

   (_____

   + _____

   \ _invalid_ - must be used to seperate the NetWare server name from physical volume name

   . _invalid._

8. _storage space_ is the name of the required NetWare volume.

9. _sys: public_ is the directory containing NetWare utilities that can be accessed by all users after they log in.

10. The _SYSTEM_ directory contains files and utilities available only to the supervisor.

11. When you compare a network file system to a file cabinet, which file system component corresponds to each of the following:

    cabinet: _file server_

    drawer: _volume_

    hanging folder: _directory_

    manila envelope: _sub-directories_

12. The _LOGIN.EXE_ directory contains the files that are used to store username and password information.

13. The _DELETED.SAV_ directory is created in each volume to contain deleted files.

14. Briefly explain under what conditions files are placed in the DELETED.SAV directory.

When files are deleted from a NetWare volume

15. List four types of Novell-suggested directories:

DOS directories
APPLICATION directories
HOME directories
SHARED directories

16. Given the following directory structure, write a complete path to the JAN95.WK1 file.

HOST1\DATA:\BUSINESS\BUDGETS\JAN95.WK1

Figure 4-23

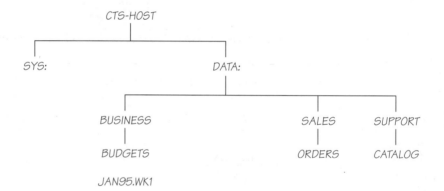

CTS-HOST

SYS: DATA:

BUSINESS   SALES   SUPPORT

BUDGETS   ORDERS   CATALOG

JAN95.WK1

17. Use the directory structure from question 16 to write a CD command that uses a partial path to change your current directory from the FORMS directory of file server HOST2 to the PAYROLL directory on HOST1.

cd HOST1\DATA:\BUSINESS\PAYROLL

18. In a(n) _____ directory structure, the user home directories would be located under a common directory called USERS.

19. What is the first step in designing a directory structure?

You need to define the data and software directories need by your users to perform thier processing functions

20. Briefly describe at least one disadvantage of storing data files in the SYS: volume.

So there is enough space for the print queue

For questions 21 through 30, use the directory structure provided in question 16 and assume that your default directory is in the SYS: volume of a file server named HOST1.

21. Write a command to list all directories on the DATA: volume along with your effective rights.

LISTDIR   DATA: /s /E

22. Write a command to find a file named BUDGET95.WK1 in the BUSINESS directory of the file server HOST1.

NDIR   DATA:BUDGET95.WK1 /sub

23. What command would you use to view the status of all volumes on the HOST1 server?

VOLINFO HOST1

24. What command would you use to determine the amount of space used by deleted files in the DATA: volume?

CHKVOL DATA:

25. Write a command to determine how much space in the DATA: volume is occupied by the BUSINESS directory and all its subdirectories.

CHKDIR   DATA:\BUSINESS /s

26. Write a command to view all trustee assignments for the BUSINESS\BUDGETS directory.

27. Write a command to copy all files with the .DOC extension from the FORMS directory of the HOST2 file server to the FORMS directory on the DATA: volume of server HOST1.

NCOPY HOST2\SYS:\FORMS *.DOC   HOST1\DATA:\FORMS

28. Write the appropriate NetWare command to list all files in the DATA: volume that are larger than 1 Mbyte.

29. Write the appropriate NetWare command to rename the INV subdirectory of SALES to INVENTRY.

RENDIR   HOST\DATA:\SALES\INV   INVENTRY

30. Write a DOS command to change your default directory to the FORMS directory of the HOST2 file server.

EXERCISES

Exercise 4-1: Checking Volume Information

In this exercise you will use the VOLINFO and CHKVOL commands to obtain volume information about your classroom file server. As a CNA, you will need to know how to use the information these two NetWare commands provide to make such decisions as determining a location on the file server in which there is room to install a new application.

1. Use the VOLINFO command to fill in the following table with one line of information for each of the volumes on your file server.

Volume name	Volume size	Free space in Kbytes	Number of directory entries	Number of available directory entries
SYS	600,000	561,100	26,080	22,786
DATA	622,864	620,404	64	61

2. Use the CHKVOL command to determine the following information about the SYS: volume.

    Amount of space in use by deleted files: __8 568__

    Amount of space available from deleted files: __8 568__

    Amount of space available in the volume: __561,100__

3. Calculate the amount of unused disk space that is available without any deleted files being recycled and record your work in the space below.

    591 432

4. Use the above information from step 3 to answer the following question. Will saving a 100-Kbyte file on the SYS: volume require reclaiming space from deleted files? YES or (NO)

    Briefly explain your reasoning.

    There is lots of space above and beyond the 100-Kb required for the file

Exercise 4-2: Using CHKDIR

Use the CHKDIR command to determine the amount of disk space used by each of the four directories on the root of your file server's SYS: volume.

Directory name	Space used	
LOGIN	1,528	Kbytes
PUBLIC	18,396	Kbytes
MAIL	4	Kbytes
EXAMPLE	500	Kbytes

Exercise 4-3: Using LISTDIR

Use NetWare's LISTDIR command to list the directory structure of the SYS:EXAMPLE directory. Use a copy of the volume design form to document all subdirectories in the EXAMPLE directory structure. Next, use the TLIST command to display the trustees along with their access rights for each of the directories and then record the trustee information next to each directory's name.

Exercise 4-4: Using the NDIR Command

Use NetWare's NDIR command to display all files with the filename extension .DOC that are located in the SYS:EXAMPLE directory structure.

Command used: ndir *.doc /sub.

FileName	File size	Complete path
Customer	2,611	\SALES\ORDERS
CISDEV	1,998	\SUPPORT\WORK
FILEFIVE	4,608	\SUPPORT\WORK
FILEFOUR	4,608	\SUPPORT\WORK
FILEONE	4,608	\SUPPORT\WORK

Exercise 4-5: Using the TLIST command

In this exercise you will practice using the TLIST command to determine the users and groups that have been given trustee assignments to specified directories. Use NetWare's TLIST command to determine the trustees of the directories indicated in the following table.

Path	Trustee	Rights
SYS:PUBLIC	Everyone	[R F]
SYS:EXAMPLE	Students	[R F]
SYS:EXAMPLE\SUPPORT\POLICY	No Trustees	
SYS:MAIL	Everyone	[C]

Exercise 4-6: Working with Directories

In this exercise you will practice using the LISTDIR command to find your home directory by checking your effective rights in the directories of each volume. Your home directory should have the same name as your username and provide you with all access rights.

1. Enter the command LISTDIR volumename: /E to list all the directories in the specified volume along with your effective rights. Repeat this command for each volume you identified in Exercise 1 and record each directory in which you have all rights in the space below:

   SYS: 50ADMIN   DATA:
            50 STC

2. Use a CD command along with a complete NetWare path to change your default directory to your ##ADMIN directory, as recorded in step 1.

3. Use the DOS MD command to create a subdirectory called CHAP4 in your ##ADMIN directory and then use the DOS CD command to make CHAP4 your default directory.

4. Within the CHAP4 subdirectory, create subdirectories called LETTERS and BUDGETS.

5. Use the LISTDIR volumename: /S > PRN command to document your directory structure on the printer.

Exercise 4-7: Working with NCOPY and NDIR

In this exercise you will practice using the NCOPY and NDIR commands with full and partial NetWare paths to find files and then copy those files into the directories you have created. You will then use the NDIR command to verify that the files have been copied successfully into the specified directory locations. If you have not already done so, create subdirectories named LETTERS and BUDGET in yor CHAP4 directory.

1. Suppose you need to copy all Microsoft Word document files from the SYS: volume into the LETTERS subdirectory you just created. Because Microsoft Word uses a .DOC extension, you can use the NDIR command to find and display all the Word filenames by entering the following command: NDIR SYS:*.DOC /SUB. Enter this command and record the path to the DOC files on the line below:

   CTS_HOST\SYS:PUBLIC\UNIX

2. Use the NCOPY command to copy the .DOC files you recorded in step 1 into the LETTERS directory. Record the NCOPY command you use on the line below:

   ncopy SYS:Public\unix*.doc   SYS:50Admin\chap4\letters

3. Suppose you want to copy all Lotus 1-2-3 spreadsheet files with the extension .WK1 to your BUDGET directory. First, use the NDIR command to determine the path to the files in the SYS:EXAMPLE subdirectory that contain the filename extension .WK1. Record the files' path on the line below:

   CTS_HOST\SYS:Example\ADMIN\BUDGET

4. Use the NCOPY command to copy the files that start with a month name BUDGET from the directory specified in step 3 to your BUDGETS directory. Record the command you use to complete this step on the line below.

ncopy sys:Example\Admin\Budgets\ *.wk1   SUS: 50Admin\Chap 4\ budgets

5. Use the RENDIR command to rename the directory LETTERS to DOCS. Record the command you use to do this on the line below.

RENDIR letters docs.

Exercise 4-8: Finding Your SYS:MAIL Subdirectory

Your SYS:MAIL subdirectory is used by the NetWare operating system and some electronic mail packages to store system files and messages. As a result, you have been given rights to your mail directory as well as the Create right to other users' mail directories. In this exercise you will follow the steps described below to find your mail directory and view your rights.

1. Use the CD command to change to the MAIL directory of your assigned file server.

2. Use the TLIST command to view trustees of the SYS:MAIL directory. Record up to five trustees and their rights below:

Trustee/Name	Rights
No user trustees	
Everyone	[C]

3. Use the LISTDIR command to display the subdirectories of the SYS:MAIL directory. If you are logged in using your assigned student login name, the only subdirectory you will see is your mail subdirectory. Record the name of your subdirectory on the line below.

→ 35000001

4. Use the TLIST command to view the trustees of your mail directory and record any trustee in the space below.

Trustee/Name	Rights
50ADMIN	[RWCEMF]
No group trustees.	

EXERCISE

Case 4-1: Creating an Application-Oriented Structure

TopTapes is a small business that rents a large inventory of video cassettes and accepts orders for special movies that it does not stock. The current tracking system at TopTapes consists of two computers at a checkout counter. Each computer has a separate copy of the video tape inventory system and catalog lookup system. TopTape's problem is that, whenever changes are made to information in either of these systems, employees must update files on both computers. TopTape's manager, Kim Crowley, has a problem with the amount of time it takes to look up the location of tapes. If there is a third computer in the store, customers can locate their movie selections themselves.

Because she does not want to maintain three separate copies of the store's inventory files, Kim is planning to implement a NetWare file server to share the store's tape catalog and inventory files. In addition, she wants to move the general ledger business system and payroll systems to the file server to provide a centralized backup and allow access to the payroll system only during business hours by the accountant. Finally, Kim wants all staff to have access to a word processing program and be able to store files in either a shared directory or in their own private areas.

Kim has hired you as a consultant to develop a directory structure to meet the processing needs of the TopTapes video store. Kim said she recently had the NetWare file server installed and that she would like to keep the directory structure as simple as possible. After checking the TopTapes file server, you discover that it consists of a SYS: volume of only 500 Mbytes. In order to receive your consulting fee, you will need to document the TopTapes directory structure using a blank volume design form.

SUPERIOR TECHNICAL COLLEGE PROBLEM

In Chapter 3, you identified the storage capacity requirements that were used to help develop the specifications for the file server computer that has recently been ordered by Dave Johnson and is scheduled to arrive next week, before the new NetWare file server computer arrives.

While you wait for the new NetWare file server computer to arrive, Dave Johnson would like you to develop a directory structure to meet Superior Technical College's processing needs that he has documented in a memorandum. Read the memorandum shown in Figure 4-24, and then, using volume and directory design forms, document your directory structure design.

Figure 4-24

MEMORANDUM

DATE:	Yesterday
TO:	Network Administrator
FROM:	Dave Johnson, Data Processing Manager
SUBJECT:	Directory Structure for the Superior Campus

I appreciate your prompt work in developing the specifications for the file server computer and want to inform you that the computer has been ordered and should arrive in about a week. In the meantime, I would like you to develop a directory structure for the file server that will accommodate the processing needs that follow. I would like the directory structure to separate the computer lab environment from administrative and faculty usage.

Computer Lab:

The computer lab should have access to its own copies of the following software packages: word processing, spreadsheet, database, and menu system. This separation is necessary because the configuration of these packages will need to be different from that of the administrative system. The computer lab area should contain a directory called CLASSES and subdirectories for all faculty members. This will allow the faculty to place files in their directories for students to access when they complete assignments. In addition, each workstation should have a subdirectory for temporary file storage and configuration information. This can be done by giving each workstation a login name and home directory. Finally, the computer lab should contain a directory called STUDENTS that can be used to contain home directories for students who are enrolled in advanced computer classes and are required to have individual access to the server in order to perform their work.

Administration:

Each user in the administrative department will need his or her own directory to store personal work and configuration files. Recently the student services department acquired a student recruitment system. You will need to install the recruitment system for them. In the future, the faculty also want access to recruitment system information in order to follow up on potential students. The student services staff also wants to be able to put the aptitude testing software on the server so students can take these tests on any one of the department's computers. The administrative secretaries will need to have a shared directory to allow them to work jointly on projects as well as be able to pass files to and from faculty members. An additional directory should be set up to allow shared access to standardized forms that are used to print letters to students and businesses.

Faculty:

Faculty members are anxious to be able to pass files directly to the secretaries and to the computer lab rather than carrying them around on a floppy disk. Make sure your structure provides shared directories that the faculty can use for these purposes. Also provide a separate shared directory that will allow faculty members to pass files among themselves. We are looking into a software package that handles grade records. If we obtain the software, it will require its own software directory. In your design, you should provide a directory for the future location of the system software.

Please fill out a volume design form showing the directory structure and storage requirements for each volume. If possible place only the DOS directories and software packages for administrative use in the SYS: volume, as this is the practice we have been following in the administrative office. Use directory design forms to define the computer lab and administrative directory structures separately.

Again, thanks for all your hard work. You're doing a great job and I look forward to working with you on the setup of the file server directory structure. If you have any questions, be sure to give me a call.

INSTALLING NETWARE

Now that you have designed your NetWare file system and have a file server computer to work with, you are probably anxious to get down to the business of working with NetWare and setting up your network system. A CNA must know the software components that make the network operate and be able to install and configure the NetWare operating system. In this chapter you will learn the steps for loading and running NetWare on a file server and on the attached workstations. You will also examine alternate NetWare installation options and solutions to some common installation problems.

NetWare installation can be divided into two major parts: file server installation and workstation installation. File server installation includes loading the NetWare operating system on the hard drive of the file server computer, setting up the NetWare partitions on each drive, creating volumes, and loading the necessary drivers to access the network interface cards. Workstation installation involves loading the software and drivers on your workstations that will allow them to access the file server computer and use the network.

AFTER READING THIS CHAPTER AND COMPLETING THE EXERCISES YOU WILL BE ABLE TO:

- DESCRIBE THE STEPS INVOLVED IN INSTALLING NETWARE ON THE FILE SERVER COMPUTER.

- IDENTIFY AND LOAD COMMON DISK AND LAN DRIVERS.

- LOAD AND UNLOAD NETWARE LOADABLE MODULES.

- USE THE NETWARE INSTALL PROGRAM TO CREATE NETWARE DISK PARTITIONS AND VOLUMES.

- USE NETWARE CONSOLE COMMANDS TO CHECK YOUR SERVER INSTALLATION AND CONFIGURATION.

- INSTALL THE SOFTWARE COMPONENTS THAT ALLOW A DOS WORKSTATION TO ACCESS THE FILE SERVER.

FILE SERVER INSTALLATION

There are six main steps to installing NetWare v3.1x on a file server computer:

1. Plan the network layout and complete a file server information worksheet.

2. Create a DOS partition on the bootable hard drive, copy the NetWare files into the DOS directory, and start the server program.

3. Load the correct disk driver, using the INSTALL program to create a NetWare partition on each drive, and then create the volumes defined in the file system design (see Chapter 4).

4. Load the SYSTEM and PUBLIC files from floppy disks, from a CD-ROM, or from another server on the network.

5. Load the LAN driver.

6. Create automatic startup files.

This section illustrates these steps by following the installation of NetWare on a file server for PC Solutions.

DOCUMENTING THE FILE SERVER ENVIRONMENT

Before you start the file server installation, you must document the network system and hardware configuration of your file server computer properly. The initial part of the file server installation plan, preparation of the volume and directory design forms, was covered in Chapter 4. Now you need to complete the plan by documenting the network layout and file server hardware configuration using the file server worksheet. A sample of a completed file server worksheet for PC Solutions is shown in Figure 5-1.

Defining the network layout

Defining the network layout requires understanding and documenting the network system in which the file server computer will be installed. A **network layout** consists of the following components:

- The file server's name and internal network number

- The network topology and network cards used

- The network address of each cable system where the file server is to be connected

- The frame type to be used on each network cable system

To obtain this information, you need to look first at the network system. A good way to do this is to make a simple pencil sketch of the network system which will include the network layout information. Figure 5-2 illustrates a network plan consisting of one file server attached to a single ethernet cable system.

Figure 5-1

File server worksheet

File Server Worksheet

Installed by: _Ted Simpson_

File server name: _CTS_HOST_   Internal network number: _293847_

SYSTEM INFORMATION

Computer make/model: _Kludge 1_
CPU: _80386DX_   Clock speed _33MHz_   Bus _ISA_
Memory capacity: _8Mbytes_

DISK INFORMATION
Disk controller 1
     Type: _IDE_   Manufacturer/model: _____
     Interrupt: _14 (E hex)_   I/O address: _IFO_   DMA channel: _none_
     Memory address: _____ - _____
     Disk driver name: _IDE_

Drive address	Type	Manufacturer	Cyl/Hd/Sec	Speed/capacity	Partition size DOS NetWare	Mirrored with controller drive
Master	IDE	Western Digital	989/15/56	15ms/420Mbytes	1413 Mbytes	None

Disk controller 2
     Type: _SCSI_   Manufacturer /model: _Adaptec_
     Interrupt: _5_   I/O address: _340-343_   DMA channel: _3_
     Memory address: _____
     Disk driver name: _AHA1540_

Drive address	Type	Manufacturer	Cyl/Hd/Sec	Speed/capacity	Partition size DOS NetWare	Mirrored with controller drive
6	SCSI	SeaGate	/ /	12ms/350M	0 350M	None
—	—	—	/ /	—	— —	—

NETWORK CARD INFORMATION

Network type	Manufacturer ID	LAN driver	I/O port	Memory address	IRQ/DMA	Frame type	Network address
ethernet	SMC	SMC8000	300	0D000	10/None	802.3	10BA5E2

NONNETWORK DEVICE INFORMATION

Device name	IRQ	I/O port	DMA	Memory address
COM1	4	3F8-3FF		

Figure 5-2

Network with a
single file server

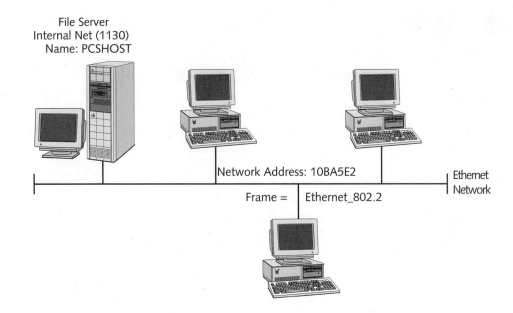

A **file server name** is a unique identification of the server, distinguishing it from other machines on the network. It is important that each file server be given a name that is both meaningful and unique. When assigning a file server name, consider including the location and function of the file server as part of its name, such as PCS_CORP for PC Solutions' primary file server. File server names can be from 2 to 47 characters long and can include any alphanumeric character, hyphens, or underscores; spaces and periods are not allowed.

Additionally, a file server must be assigned a unique **internal network number**. This number is used by the NetWare operating system for communication among its device drivers. Although you can assign your own internal network number, most installations use the random server number suggested by the NetWare installation program. Some network administrators use the server program's serial number as the internal network number. This keeps the serial number handy when you need to contact Novell for NetWare operating system software upgrades.

Chapter 2 defined a network address as a number assigned to each LAN system. The number is used to route packets between networks. With Novell IPX, a network address consisting of between one and eight hexadecimal digits must be assigned to each network interface card.

The network addresses you assign your cable systems should help you identify a network when you see its address on a report or error message. As you read in Chapter 3, hexadecimal digits are limited to the numbers 0-9 and the letters A-F. This might seem to limit your choices for names but, with a little imagination, you can create network addresses that are easy to remember. For example, the network address 10BA5E2 used in Figure 5-2 is the IEEE standard for a thin ethernet system. (Notice the use of the digit 5 in place of the letter S.)

In addition to the network address, a network cable system must have one or more packet frame types assigned to it. As explained in Chapter 2, a frame type defines the formatting of the physical packet that is transmitted over the network. In order to communicate on the network, all machines must use the same frame type. There are several popular packet frame types in use. The two most common ethernet frame types used with NetWare are IEEE802.3 and IEEE802.2. IEEE802.2 is the most up-to-date frame type and is the default for NetWare v3.12. If you are installing a file server on an existing network with machines that use IEEE802.3, you can convert all workstations and servers to IEEE802.2 or you can load both frame types on your new server.

Loading two frame types is a good temporary solution until you can get all machines converted to IEEE802.2. This approach slows down performance, however, because each frame type must be treated as a separate logical network.

Adding a second file server to an existing network creates what is known as a **multiple file server network**, shown in Figure 5-3. Notice that although each file server is given a unique name and internal network number, they both use the same network address and frame type for the LAN cable system on which they communicate.

Figure 5-3

Network with multiple file servers

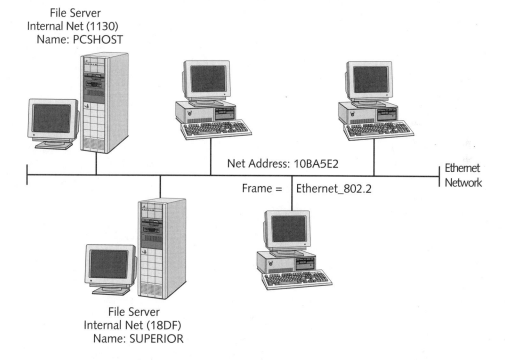

Multiple networks can be connected to form an **internetwork**. As discussed in Chapter 2, an internetwork consists of networks connected together by bridges and routers. Figure 5-4 illustrates an internetwork created by adding a different network topology to the system. Notice that each network cable system in the internetwork is assigned a different network address. The file server SUPERIOR is referred to as an **internal router** because it transfers packets between networks in addition to performing its file server activities.

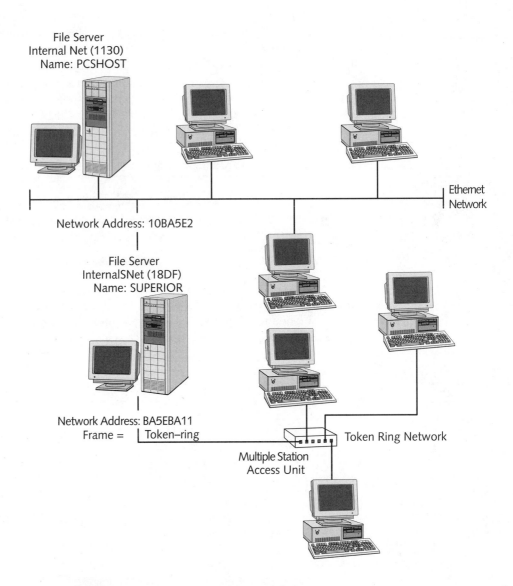

Figure 5-4

Internetwork

File Server
Internal Net (1130)
Name: PCSHOST

Ethernet
Network

Network Address: 10BA5E2

File Server
InternalSNet (18DF)
Name: SUPERIOR

Network Address: BA5EBA11
Frame =   Token–ring

Token Ring Network

Multiple Station
Access Unit

Completing the file server worksheet

Once the network system has been identified, you should record the server's name and internal network number along with the network address and frame type for each network card to be placed in the file server. During the installation process you will also need the file server hardware information listed below:

1. Name of the disk driver program for the controller card

2. Disk controller card settings, including interrupt and I/O port

3. Capacity and configuration of the hard drives attached to the controllers

4. Name of the network card driver program to be used with the network cards

5. Network card settings, including interrupt, I/O port, and memory address range

You can find this information in the documentation supplied with the file server computer and network cards. If you cannot find it there, your hardware vendor can provide the necessary hardware settings. Documenting this information is best accomplished by completing a file server worksheet similar to the sample worksheet shown in Figure 5-1.

The file server worksheet is divided into five main sections: identification, system information, disk information, network card information, and nonnetwork device information. In the identification portion, you record the installer's name, the name of the file server, and the internal network number.

The system information portion contains the make and model of the computer, the microprocessor type, clock speed, memory capacity, and types of expansion slots. Although you won't need this information during NetWare installation, you do need to know that your file server computer meets or exceeds the minimum requirements for the NetWare version you are installing. This information will be useful later if and when you install additional server options or upgrade the file server software. The minimum system requirements for NetWare v3.1x are as follows:

- An IBM PC-compatible computer with an 80386 or later microprocessor

- A minimum of 4 Mbytes of RAM for installation and 6-8 Mbytes to support a small network

- A hard disk with sufficient storage for your network; the minimum is 50 Mbytes: 5 Mbytes for DOS partition plus 45 Mbytes for a NetWare disk partition containing the SYS: volume.

If you plan to install ElectroText, an electronic version of the NetWare v3.12 manuals, you will need an additional 30 Mbytes of disk space.

The disk information portion of the file server worksheet contains documentation for up to two disk controller cards in your file server. You will need this information when you install the file server. In addition, the capacity and partition size information for each disk drive is helpful in planning disk mirroring and duplexing. (Disk mirroring or duplexing requires that each mirrored NetWare partition be the same size.) The settings for the cylinder, head, and sector of IDE disk drives are stored in CMOS. You might need this information to reconfigure the CMOS after a battery or system failure.

The file server described in Figure 5-1 contains both an IDE and a SCSI controller card. The SCSI controller card manages a large capacity drive for the DATA: volume and could be expanded to add a CD-ROM drive and tape backup system that are daisy chained to the SCSI. The SCSI controller card manages a large-capacity drive for the DATA: volume along with a CD-ROM drive and tape backup system that are daisy chained to the SCSI controller card.

You need the controller card information to load the correct disk driver software during installation and to provide NetWare with the necessary configuration parameters. In addition, knowing the hardware configuration information, such as interrupt, I/O port, and DMA channel, will help you avoid hardware conflicts when you install other hardware, such as LAN cards.

One of the first steps in installing NetWare on a file server computer is loading the correct disk driver program to allow the NetWare operating system access to the server's hard drives. Because each type of controller requires a different disk driver, an installer needs to identify the name of the correct drive software before proceeding with the file server installation. Figure 5-5 contains a list of common controllers and the disk driver software that is supplied with NetWare.

Figure 5-5

Common NetWare disk drivers

Bus Architecture	Controller Type	Driver Name
ISA	AT-ST506	ISADISK
	ESDI	ISADISK/B
	IDE	IDE
	SCSI	see vendor
	Novell SCSI	DCB
Micro Channel	ESDI	PS2ESDI
	ST-506	PS2MFM
	IBM SCSI	PS2OPT
EISA	ST-506	ISADISK
	IDE	IDE
	SCSI	see vendor

The IDE.DSK driver shown in Figure 5-5 works with all standard IDE drives. SCSI controller cards, on the other hand, require special disk controllers for each card model or manufacturer. This difference makes installing an IDE drive a little easier than installing a SCSI drive. Notice that there are a number of similar drivers for certain computer models. You should check with your vendor to verify what driver you should use if you have one of these computer models.

It is often the CNA's job to install network cards in the file server and workstation computers. The network card information portion of the file server worksheet contains important information identifying the network cards to be installed in the server along with their configurations. Your first concern is to obtain cards that are appropriate for the network system you are installing and to ensure that the network cards are certified by Novell to work with your version of NetWare. Next you will need to identify the correct network card driver to load during NetWare installation. This will enable NetWare to send and receive packets. To assist you in loading the correct driver, Novell has included network card drivers for many of the common network cards. (See Figure 5-6.) If you have one of the network cards listed or if the documentation that came with your card tells you to use a certain driver, record the name of the LAN driver on the file server worksheet.

Figure 5-6

Common NetWare
card drivers

Cabling System	Network Board	Driver
ARCnet	RX-Net	TRXNET
	RX-Net II	
	RX-Net 2	
Ethernet	NE/2	NE2
	NE/2T	
	NE2-32	NE2-32
	NE1000 (Assy 950-054401)	NE1000
	NE1000 (Assy 810-160-001)	
	NE2000	NE2000
	NE2000T	
	NE2100 (Assy 810-000209)	NE2100
	NE1500T	NE1500T
	NE3200	NE3200
	NE32HUB	NE32HUB
	3COM	3C503
		3C509
		3C523
		3CNLAN
Token ring	NTR2000	NTR200
	IBM token ring	TOKEN

Each network card installed in the file server must be set to use a unique interrupt,
I/O port, and memory address in order to avoid hardware conflicts with other devices
in the computer. Because you might need to enter these hardware settings when first
installing the card driver, it is useful to document the interrupt, I/O port, and memory address of each network card on the file server worksheet.

The last portion of the file server worksheet, nonnetwork device information, allows
you to document other devices and controller cards that are currently in the system.
This information helps you avoid any current or future hardware interrupt conflicts.

LOADING THE SERVER PROGRAM

Once you have identified the network system and hardware specifications and filled
out the file server worksheet, you are ready to roll up your sleeves and start the
NetWare installation process. The time spent planning and documenting the network
and file server environment will pay off by allowing you to avoid problems caused by
loading the wrong drivers or entering incorrect card configurations.

The core of the NetWare operating system is the SERVER.EXE program, which is
located on the System_1 disk along with a few other necessary support files. In addition to supplying network services, the SERVER.EXE program contains the serial
number of your file server and is limited to supporting the number of connections
specified in the license. When installing NetWare, you use DOS to boot the server
computer and then load the NetWare operating system. Once the SERVER.EXE

program has been loaded into memory, it controls the computer and DOS is no longer needed. After starting NetWare, you might actually want to remove DOS from memory to make more space (approximately 64 Kbytes) available for NetWare file caching. (This is discussed further in Chapter 15.)

 Although DOS is initially used to boot server computers, once it is started NetWare functions as a completely separate operating system that directly controls the computer hardware.

While the SERVER.EXE program provides the core NetWare services, such as file and printer sharing, it uses other modules to access hardware devices such as disk drives and network cards or provide additional services such as communications to a mainframe. These modules are shown in Figure 5-7. For this reason, Novell refers to the SERVER.EXE program as a software bus. NetWare 3.1x is a very flexible system that allows the network administrator to add and remove software drivers and services as required without needing to exit the server or reboot.

Figure 5-7

SERVER.EXE software bus

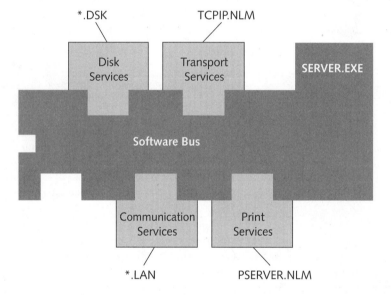

 In earlier versions of NetWare it was necessary to link disk and network card drivers into the operating system prior to starting the server. In order to make changes—such as the configuration or network address of a network card driver—you were required to stop the server, modify or relink the operating system, and then reboot the server computer. In NetWare 3.1x, you can change the configuration of a LAN driver by simply unloading and loading it with the new parameters.

To install the SERVER.EXE program in NetWare v3.11, you manually create a DOS partition, copy the System_1 and System_2 disks into a directory on this partition, and then load the operating system by running the SERVER.EXE program. When the SERVER.EXE program is loaded, it first asks for the file server's name and internal network number. After the server's name and internal network number are entered, the server is up and running, but cannot perform any functions until it can access disk volumes and network interface cards. The installation process from this point on involves loading and configuring the correct drivers and creating the NetWare disk volumes.

NetWare v3.12 can be installed in the manner just described for v3.11. To make installing NetWare v3.12 easier, however, Novell has included an INSTALL batch file that automatically proceeds through the steps of installing SERVER.EXE. There are two ways to use the NetWare v3.12 INSTALL program: either from CD-ROM or from floppy disks. Whether you start the INSTALL program from disk or CD-ROM, it follows the same steps and requires you to have your licensed NetWare System_1 disk and a DOS boot disk containing at least the FDISK and FORMAT programs. The DOS disk is needed for booting the computer and initially creating and formatting a DOS partition, as described in the following steps.

Installing from a CD-ROM

If the server machine has a CD-ROM drive, installing NetWare is much easier and faster—you do not need to insert a floppy disk every few minutes during installation.

 If you are installing NetWare from a CD-ROM onto a server that has a SCSI hard disk controller, the CD-ROM drive should be attached to a controller card that is separate from the one used for the hard disk drives. This is necessary because NetWare uses DOS to access the CD-ROM device containing the SYSTEM and PUBLIC files during installation. After the NetWare SCSI disk driver is loaded, it competes with DOS for control of the CD-ROM and causes errors when the installation program tries to copy files from the CD-ROM to the file server.

When using the INSTALL program to install the SERVER program from a CD-ROM, you follow three steps:

1. Boot the server computer using a DOS boot disk that contains your CD-ROM driver and the Microsoft CD-ROM extension software, as explained in Chapter 3.

2. After the server computer has been booted with DOS, place the NetWare v3.12 CD-ROM in the drive and change to the CD-ROM drive letter.

3. Change the default directory to NETWARE.312\ENGLISH and enter the INSTALL command. See Figure 5-8.

Figure 5-8

Installing NetWare
from a CD-ROM

```
Starting MS-DOS...

CD-ROM device driver Version 02.00.00 09/04/91

# Installed CD-ROM Drive    : 1
# Stock Buffer Memory (Sector) : 10
# Installed IRQ channel : CH2
# Speed : S=1

MSCDEX Version 2.23
Copyright (C) Microsoft Corp. 1986-1993. All rights reserved.
         Drive D: = Driver MSCD001 unit 0
C:\>D:

D:\>CD NETWARE.312\ENGLISH

D:\NETWARE.312\ENGLISH>INSTALL
```

Installing NetWare from floppy disks

Installing NetWare from floppy disks is slow but simple. The biggest disadvantage is the amount of time it takes for NetWare's installation program to copy files from each of the many disks. If you are installing NetWare on a single file server that does not have a CD-ROM drive, however, it might be the only method available to you. The process involves the following steps:

1. Boot the file server computer with a DOS system disk.

2. Place the NetWare System_1 disk in a $3\frac{1}{2}$" high-density floppy drive.

3. Change your default DOS prompt to the floppy drive that contains the NetWare System_1 disk.

4. Enter the INSTALL command and press [Enter]. See Figure 5-9.

Figure 5-9

Installing NetWare
from floppy disk

```
Starting MS-DOS...

Current date is Sun 07-17-1994
Enter new date (mm-dd-yy):
Current time is  9:10:00.93p
Enter new time:

Microsoft(R) MS-DOS(R) Version 6.20
         (C)Copyright Microsoft Corp 1981-1993.

A:\>b:

B:\>INSTALL
```

Running the installation program

Whether you start the server installation process with a CD-ROM or with floppy disks, the INSTALL program performs the same series of installation steps. After a message regarding the use of ethernet frame types, a menu is displayed containing options for a new installation, an upgrade of an existing version, or a display of additional information. See Figure 5-10. Select the appropriate Option and press [Enter].

Figure 5-10

Installation menu

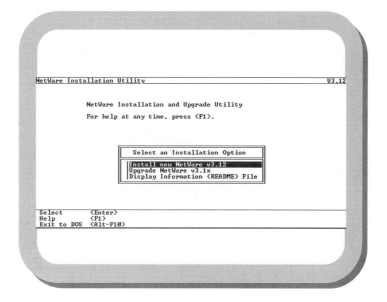

```
NetWare Installation Utility                                      V3.12

                NetWare Installation and Upgrade Utility
                For help at any time, press <F1>.


                    ┌─────────────────────────────────┐
                    │   Select an Installation Option  │
                    ├─────────────────────────────────┤
                    │ Install new NetWare v3.12        │
                    │ Upgrade NetWare v3.1x            │
                    │ Display Information <README> File │
                    └─────────────────────────────────┘


   Select      <Enter>
   Help        <F1>
   Exit to DOS <Alt-F10>
```

NetWare's install program displays any existing hard disk partitions and gives you the option to create a new DOS partition. If there is already a DOS partition on the disk you can retain that partition or delete it and create a new one.

After the DOS partition has been created, the installation process reboots the computer, formats the DOS partition, and then copies the NetWare System_1 disk's contents into a directory called SERVER.312 on drive C:. After starting the SERVER.EXE program, the installation asks for the file server's name. Enter the file server name specified on your file server worksheet. After you enter the file server's name, the install program will suggest a random internal network number for your server. You can overwrite this network number with the network number you recorded on your file server worksheet. If you use the random number supplied by the installation program, be sure to record it on your file server worksheet.

After you select an internal network number, you will be asked to enter the drive letter and path on which you want the SERVER program files installed. You can accept the default installation path, C:\SERVER.312. See Figure 5-11. Once you have selected the path, the installation process copies files to the DOS drive and directory you select. If you are installing from a CD-ROM you still need to place your NetWare System_1 disk into a disk drive in order to copy the SERVER.EXE program and support files.

Figure 5-11

Select source and
destination directories

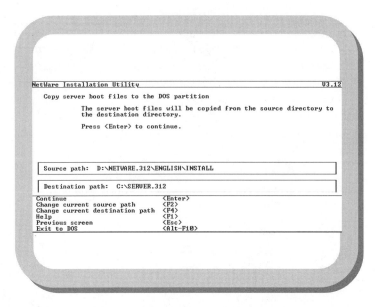

```
NetWare Installation Utility                                          V3.12

    Copy server boot files to the DOS partition

             The server boot files will be copied from the source directory to
             the destination directory.

             Press <Enter> to continue.



     Source path:   D:\NETWARE.312\ENGLISH\INSTALL

     Destination path:   C:\SERVER.312
    Continue                              <Enter>
    Change current source path            <F2>
    Change current destination path       <F4>
    Help                                  <F1>
    Previous screen                       <Esc>
    Exit to DOS                           <Alt-F10>
```

Once NetWare's files have been copied to the DOS partition, the installation program displays a window asking you to select your country code, code page, and keyboard mapping. For standard installations, just press the [F10] key to continue. Next, you need to select either the DOS Filename Format or NetWare Filename Format. In a standard installation, you should select the recommended DOS filename format and press [Enter]. The installation program next asks if you want to enter any startup commands. If your file server has over 16 Mbytes of RAM and you are using a disk controller card in an ISA bus slot that has an address bus limitation of 16 Mbytes, you should select Yes and enter the command SET AUTO REGISTER MEMORY OFF. This prevents NetWare from using memory above 16 Mbytes for the disk driver software. After entering the startup commands, press [F10] to create the startup file and continue.

Finally, the installation process gives you the option of adding the SERVER command to your AUTOEXEC.BAT file to start NetWare whenever you boot your server. Because loading NetWare whenever you boot the machine makes it more difficult to bring the computer up in DOS mode, if it is necessary to perform additional installation processes (such as copying drivers from floppy disk onto drive C:), during your initial installation, select No for this option. When the server is operating correctly you can go back and manually add this command to the AUTOEXEC.BAT file in order to automate the booting process.

The last step performed by the installation program starts the NetWare operating system by running the SERVER.EXE program using the server name and internal network number you supplied earlier. The server program displays the file server computer's speed rating, which is determined by the type of CPU, the clock speed, and memory wait states. A standard 80386DX computer running at 16 MHz, for example, gives a speed rating of 120. You can use this speed rating to compare the performance of different file servers.

After the operating system has been started with a server name and an internal network number, you will see a **console** colon (:) prompt that includes the name of the file server. At this point your computer is no longer a DOS workstation, but has now become a dedicated NetWare file server. Typical DOS commands such as DATE, TIME, and COPY, no longer work on the file server computer because the NetWare console has its own set of commands and utilities. The file server console screen is where the network administrator enters server commands or loads additional modules and drivers programs to perform additional functions, control disk drives, and configure network cards.

Console commands and NetWare Loadable Modules

The SERVER.EXE program requires drivers and other support modules to be loaded to provide access to the disk drives or network cards and to perform specialized functions. This section describes how to use the NetWare console command and utilities to complete the file server installation by loading the correct disk and LAN drivers.

You already know how to issue commands from a DOS prompt. You also know that some commands, such as DATE and COPY, are called internal commands because they are built into the DOS system. Other commands, such as FORMAT and DISKCOPY, are called external commands because they are actually program files (FORMAT.COM and DISKCOPY.COM) that must be loaded and run. NetWare also has its own console commands and external programs that you can load and run from the console prompt. Figure 5-12, for example, shows how you can use the NetWare MEMORY console command to display the amount of RAM in your file server and the SPEED command to display your current file server speed. In order to complete and test the file server installation, you will use several additional console commands to perform the file server operations described in this chapter.

Figure 5-12

The server console commands screen

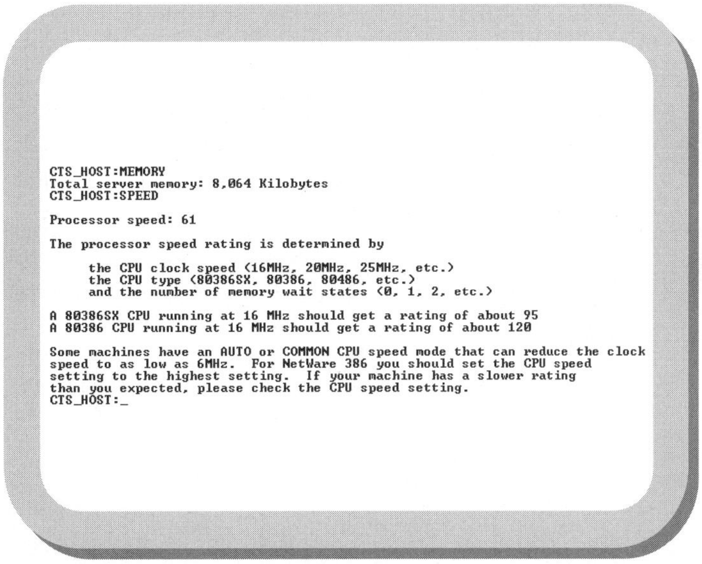

```
CTS_HOST:MEMORY
Total server memory: 8,064 Kilobytes
CTS_HOST:SPEED

Processor speed: 61

The processor speed rating is determined by

        the CPU clock speed (16MHz, 20MHz, 25MHz, etc.)
        the CPU type (80386SX, 80386, 80486, etc.)
        and the number of memory wait states (0, 1, 2, etc.)

A 80386SX CPU running at 16 MHz should get a rating of about 95
A 80386 CPU running at 16 MHz should get a rating of about 120

Some machines have an AUTO or COMMON CPU speed mode that can reduce the clock
speed to as low as 6MHz.  For NetWare 386 you should set the CPU speed
setting to the highest setting.  If your machine has a slower rating
than you expected, please check the CPU speed setting.
CTS_HOST:_
```

In NetWare, external programs are called NetWare Loadable Modules (NLMs). They are invoked with NetWare's LOAD command. Just as DOS uses file extensions to distinguish different types of program files (.COM, .EXE, and .BAT), NetWare distinguishes different types of modules by their file extensions. The extension .NLM identifies general-purpose modules, .DSK identifies disk driver modules, and .LAN identifies network card drivers. Most NetWare Loadable

Modules are stored in the SYS:SYSTEM directory. NLMs can also be stored and loaded from other NetWare directories as well as from floppy drives and from a DOS partition on the server's drive. For example, to load a module from drive A:, you enter the command LOAD A:module-name at the console colon prompt and press [Enter]. For example, to load the VREPAIR.NLM module from the SERVER.312 directory of the DOS C: drive, you enter the command LOAD D:\SERVER.312\VREPAIR at the console colon prompt.

ESTABLISHING A DISK SYSTEM

The computer becomes a NetWare file server when the SERVER.EXE program is loaded, in order to provide shared access to files; the server first needs to be able to manage its own disk system. Before this can happen, you need to install the correct disk driver module for the controller card or cards in your file server computer. These are identified on your file server worksheet. Once the disk driver software has been loaded, you can establish the NetWare disk partitions and then create the required SYS: volume and any additional data volumes defined on the volume design forms you completed in Chapter 4. In this section you will review the process of loading the disk module and then use the INSTALL module to create a NetWare partition and establish volumes.

Loading the disk module

When the SERVER program is first started on your file server, it does not have direct access to the system's disk drives but must make requests for disk drive data through the DOS operating system. Although this is inefficient, it allows access to NetWare Loadable Modules which are stored in the DOS partition. If the disk driver module identified on your file server worksheet is one that is supplied by Novell, you can load the disk driver simply by entering the command LOAD module-name. By default, NetWare uses the DOS partition containing the files copied by the server installation process and loads the requested .DSK module.

 If the controller card in your file server has its own disk driver supplied by the manufacturer and is not included in the standard set provided by Novell, you need to insert the disk containing the required .DSK module and use the LOAD A:module-name command initially to access your drive. You will probably want to copy these modules into the DOS partition of your file server for future use so you can boot your file server without inserting the floppy disk.

Many disk drivers require you to specify configuration information such as a card interrupt and an I/O port when they are first loaded. Figure 5-13 shows the file server console screen after the IDE disk driver for the new file server has been loaded. Notice that the first attempt to load the disk driver failed because an incorrect interrupt number was entered. If you have more than one disk controller card in the file server, a driver program must be loaded for each disk controller. For example, if the file server shown in Figure 5-13 also contained SCSI drives, the correct SCSI disk driver program would also be loaded at this time to provide access to those drives.

Figure 5-13

Loading the IDE
disk driver

```
CTS_HOST:LOAD C:IDE
Loading module IDE.DSK
   NetWare IDE Device Driver
   Version 3.12   April 26, 1993
   Copyright 1993 Novell, Inc.  All rights reserved.
Supported I/O port values are 1F0, 170, 1E8, 168
I/O port: 170
Supported interrupt number values are E, B, F, C
Interrupt number: E
IDE-015: The selected hardware is not available for this IDE driver.
   Module initialization failed.
   Module IDE.DSK NOT loaded
CTS_HOST:LOAD C:IDE
Loading module IDE.DSK
   NetWare IDE Device Driver
   Version 3.12   April 26, 1993
   Copyright 1993 Novell, Inc.  All rights reserved.
Supported I/O port values are 1F0, 170, 1E8, 168
I/O port: 1F0
Supported interrupt number values are E, B, F, C
Interrupt number: E
CTS_HOST:_
```

Loading INSTALL

The INSTALL NetWare Loadable Module is used to perform most of the remaining NetWare installation procedures. As a CNA, you will use the INSTALL module to perform various installation functions, such as creating and mirroring NetWare partitions, creating volumes, and editing the startup files. In the installation process described so far, a DOS program initially copied the files to load and start NetWare's SERVER program. One of the files copied to the DOS partition was the INSTALL.NLM program, which will now be used to perform the remaining NetWare installation steps. After the disk driver has been loaded, you start the INSTALL module by entering the LOAD INSTALL command at the file server's colon prompt. After the INSTALL program is loaded, the opening menu is displayed. See Figure 5-14.

Figure 5-14

INSTALL option menu

```
┌─────────────────────┐
│ Installation Options │
├─────────────────────┤
│ Disk Options        │
│ Volume Options      │
│ System Options      │
│ Product Options     │
│ Exit                │
└─────────────────────┘
```

When installing NetWare v3.11, you should use the command LOAD INSTALL -J. The -J parameter on NetWare 3.11 servers allows you to specify a drive other than A: (such as a CD-ROM drive) when loading the SYSTEM and PUBLIC files to their corresponding directories on the server's SYS: volume.

You can use INSTALL's Disk Options selection to low-level format a drive, to create and delete partitions, to mirror partitions of equal size, or to perform disk tests. Volume Options is used to create new volumes, to add space to an existing volume, or to delete an unwanted volume. System Options allows you to copy SYSTEM and PUBLIC files to the NetWare directories and to work with the startup files. The **startup files** are similar in purpose to the DOS CONFIG.SYS and AUTOEXEC.BAT files in that they provide configuration information, drivers, and commands for NetWare to use when it is first loaded on the server. Product Options is used to install additional services such as Novell's ElectroText electronic documentation. In Chapter 14 you will learn how to use INSTALL's Product Options to install the message handling system (MHS) for electronic mail.

Creating a NetWare partition

A NetWare partition establishes an area of a server hard drive that will be formatted exclusively for NetWare's use. While DOS can access multiple disk partitions on one drive, NetWare can access only one NetWare partition for each disk. If you are planning to mirror two disks, you need to create NetWare partitions of equal size on each hard disk.

Mirroring drives does not require the physical disk drives to have the same capacity as long as the NetWare partitions on each of the mirrored drives are the same size.

In order to create a NetWare partition on a disk drive you first need to select Disk Options from the Installation Options menu and press [Enter]. This displays the Available Disk Options menu, as shown in Figure 5-15.

Figure 5-15

Available Disk
Options menu

Next select the Partition Tables option. If you have more than one disk drive, a window showing details for each drive will be displayed. Select the drive in which you want to create the new partition and press [Enter]. A partition window displaying information for that drive along with the "Partition Options" menu will be displayed. To create a new partition, select the Create NetWare Partition option and press [Enter]. The new Partition Information window containing information similar to that shown in Figure 5-16 will be displayed.

Figure 5-16

Partition Information window

A partition size is specified in cylinders. NetWare's default is all cylinders free on the server's hard drive. If you want to reserve space for another operating system or match the space of another drive for mirroring, you can change the number of cylinders until you obtain the desired NetWare partition capacity.

If you do not want to use the entire disk for NetWare, decrease the partition size by entering a smaller number of cylinders in the Partition Size field. Creating a partition that is smaller than the available disk space is necessary if you need to mirror this NetWare partition with a smaller disk drive. (This is explained in more detail in the following section on disk mirroring.) The Redirection Area is used by Hot Fix to redirect defective blocks from the data area and is normally left at the default of 2% of the partition size.

If you are planning to mirror a partition you should record the number of blocks in its data area on the partition size field of the file server worksheet so you can modify the number of blocks in the redirection size of the new mirrored partition to match this number.

Once you have confirmed that the partition information is correct press [Esc] and select Yes at the prompt to create the new partition. Once the new NetWare partition is created, it will be displayed in the partition information window, as shown in Figure 5-17. If you have additional hard drives to partition, press [Esc] to return to the

Available Disk Options window and select the next drive. After all partitions have been created, press [Esc] until you return to the Available Options menu.

```
        ┌──────────────────────┐
        │   Partition Options  │
        ├──────────────────────┤
        │ Change Hot Fix       │
        │ Create NetWare Partition
        │ Delete Partition     │
        │ Return To Previous Menu
        └──────────────────────┘
```

Mirroring and duplexing

NetWare can keep an exact duplicate of a partition on another disk drive to protect data against the failure of a hard disk or controller. If a second drive containing the duplicate partition is attached to the same drive controller, the process is called mirroring. When the second drive is attached to a different drive controller, the process is called duplexing. Regardless of the drive configuration, the process of using the INSTALL utility to set up either duplexing or mirroring is the same.

To mirror a partition, first select Disk Options from the Installation Options menu. Next, select Mirroring from the Available Disk Options menu. NetWare displays a window detailing the current Partition Mirroring Status, as shown in Figure 5-18. To start the mirroring process you first need to identify the primary NetWare partition that contains the data to be mirrored. To do this, select Logical Partition #1 in the Partition Mirroring Status window and press [Enter]. NetWare displays the Mirrored NetWare Partitions window shown in Figure 5-19. This window shows the mirror status of the selected partition. The message "In Sync" means that the partition is synchronized and ready for use.

After the primary partition has been identified, you identify the secondary partition that will be mirrored, or synchronized, with the primary partition. To do this, press the INS key to display the Available Partitions window, which lists other NetWare partitions available for mirroring. Select a secondary partition and press [Enter]. If the secondary partition is larger than the primary partition, a message warns you that the secondary partition will be reduced to the size of the primary partition. You can then either abort the mirroring process or allow NetWare to match the partition sizes. If NetWare attempts to match the partition sizes and data has already been stored on the larger secondary partition, a message warns you that all data on the larger partition will be lost.

Figure 5-18

Partitions Mirroring Status window

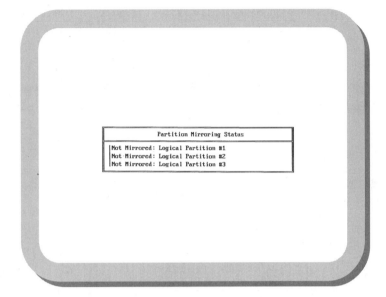

```
              Partition Mirroring Status
|Not Mirrored: Logical Partition #1
|Not Mirrored: Logical Partition #2
|Not Mirrored: Logical Partition #3
```

Figure 5-19

Mirrored NetWare Partitions window

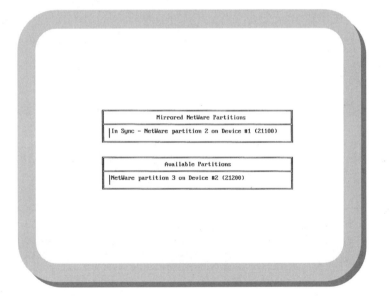

```
            Mirrored NetWare Partitions
|In Sync - NetWare partition 2 on Device #1 (21100)

              Available Partitions
|NetWare partition 3 on Device #2 (21200)
```

If the primary partition is larger than the secondary partition, all data in the primary partition will be destroyed if you continue the mirroring process.

After you select the secondary partition for mirroring, NetWare begins the partition synchronization process by copying data from the primary to the secondary partition. While this process is proceeding, the message on the Mirrored NetWare Partitions screen reads "Out of Sync." The synchronization process can last from several minutes to an hour depending on the size of the partitions. When a primary partition that already contains data is being mirrored, the process can take over an hour.

Once the synchronization process is complete, the Mirrored NetWare Partitions window displays both partitions, as shown in Figure 5-20. When the synchronization process is complete, press the [Esc] key to return to the Installation Options menu.

Figure 5-20

Mirrored NetWare
Partitions window
after mirroring

Creating volumes

Storage space in NetWare partitions must be divided into one or more volumes before it is accessible for use by the operating system. This is where the volume design forms you completed in Chapter 4 are important because they allow you to create a SYS: volume and one or more DATA: volumes of the correct size for your applications. To create the necessary NetWare volumes, start by selecting Volume Options from the Installation Options menu. This displays the Volumes window, which shows any existing volumes. To create a new volume, press the Ins key to display the New Volume Information window shown in Figure 5-21.

Figure 5-21

New Volume
Information window

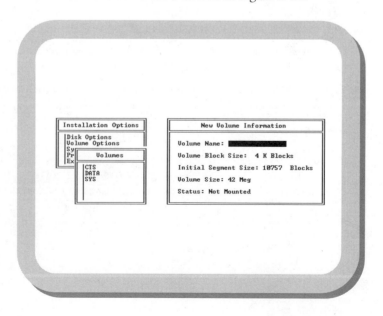

The first NetWare server volume is automatically given the volume name SYS: with a default initial segment that is the size of the entire partition. The Initial Segment Size field is entered in blocks. The default capacity is 4 Kbytes per block. Remember that the volume's block size is set when the volume is created and cannot be changed without recreating the volume and restoring any data.

 The default block size of 4 Kbytes is generally suitable for file storage and should be used for the SYS: volume. As explained in Chapter 4, volumes that are used to store large graphic or multimedia files can benefit from larger block sizes. To create more than one volume you can change the value in the Initial Segment Size field to the number of blocks that will make the volume the size you specified on your volume design planning form.

The size of the new volume is determined in the number of blocks you enter in the Initial Segment Size field. By default this field contains all available disk blocks in the NetWare partitions. If you want to create multiple volumes, you need to reduce the number of disk blocks until the Volume Size field shows the number of megabytes you need for the SYS: volume. After completing all information in the New Volume Information window for the SYS: volume, press [Esc] to create the new volume. If you want to create one or more data volumes, press the Ins key and fill in the New Volume Information window. Include the data volume's name, block size, and correct initial size. After you have created all the volumes you need on the server, press the Esc key until you return to the main Installation Options menu.

INSTALLING SYSTEM and PUBLIC Files

Once the NetWare file server's SYS: volume has been created, the next steps in the server installation process are to create the LOGIN, PUBLIC, MAIL, and SYSTEM directories described in Chapter 4 and then load the NetWare SYSTEM and PUBLIC files from the CD-ROM or floppy disks into these directories. This process involves mounting the volumes and then using the NetWare INSTALL utility to copy SYSTEM and PUBLIC files into their appropriate directories.

Mounting volumes

Before the newly created volumes are available to the system they must be mounted. **Mounting** a volume is the process of loading file allocation table and directory table information into the RAM of the file server. You can use NetWare's INSTALL program to mount a volume by selecting its name from the Volumes window and then changing the Status field from Not mounted to Mounted. To mount all volumes, it is faster to issue the MOUNT ALL command from the server's colon prompt. The MOUNT volume-name command can also be used to mount a specified volume that was dismounted when certain system procedures (such as running the VREPAIR command described in Chapter 15) were performed. **Dismounting** is the process of making a volume unavailable to users on the network and is accomplished by using the DISMOUNT volume-name command.

To return to the console screen, hold down the Alt key while pressing the Esc key (this combination is called the console hot-key sequence) to switch to the next NLM screen. You can return to the INSTALL module by simply repeating the hot-key sequence. Once you have returned to the console colon prompt you can enter the MOUNT ALL command to have NetWare mount all available volumes for you. After completing the installation process, NetWare will automatically mount all volumes for you after it loads the disk drive(s) from the startup files.

You can also use the VOLUMES command to determine what volumes have been mounted. This command lists all mounted volumes along with what operating system names they will support. By default all NetWare volumes support DOS standard filenames. Name space support must be added to the volume to allow the use of special Apple Macintosh and OS/2 filename conventions, as explained in Chapter 15.

Copying SYSTEM and PUBLIC Files

Once the server volumes have been created and mounted, you can use the [Alt][Esc] hot-key sequence to return to the INSTALL module and then use Available System Options to create the required directories and copy the operating system files and utilities into their appropriate directories automatically. Selecting System Options from the Installation Options menu displays the Available System Options menu, which contains the Copy System and Public Files option, as shown in Figure 5-22.

Figure 5-22

Available System Options menu

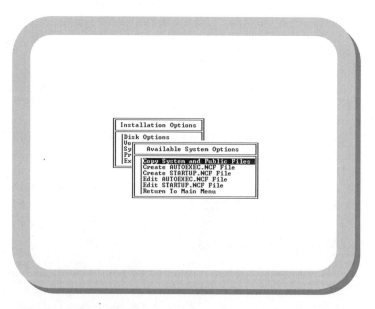

Select Copy System and Public Files and press [Enter] to create the required directories in the SYS: volume. A window asking you to insert the NetWare Install disk in drive A: is displayed. Press [Enter] to copy the NetWare disks from drive A. To copy the files from another drive, such as a CD-ROM, press the F6 key; the install program prompts you to enter the appropriate drive and path.

When installation from CD-ROM is complete, the server will have been booted from the DOS boot disk containing the CD-ROM driver program so the server can access the CD-ROM drive using a DOS drive letter. To install from a CD-ROM located on drive E, for example enter the command E:\NETWARE.312\ENGLISH and press [Enter]. If you need to use drive B to copy floppy disks, you type B: and press

[Enter]. The INSTALL program immediately begins copying the files for the SYSTEM, PUBLIC, and LOGIN directories from the device and path you specify. If you are installing NetWare from floppy disks, you will be asked to insert the necessary disk or disks to complete the process. In either case, it should take at least 15 minutes for the files to be copied to the server.

COMPLETING THE INSTALLATION

Once the SYSTEM and PUBLIC files have been copied into the SYS: volume, completing the installation involves bringing the server on-line by loading the required LAN driver(s) and then testing the installation to see that the server is communicating properly on the network. After you are satisfied that all necessary drivers are loaded and properly configured, the final step in the installation process is creating the startup files that will automate the process of starting the file server by loading the necessary drivers and configuration information. You can then test the startup process by restarting the file server as described at the end of this section.

Loading the LAN driver

After the SYS: volume is mounted and operational, the final step in bringing a new file server on line is loading a LAN driver for each network interface card. You then bind each LAN driver to the correct protocol stack. As mentioned previously, LAN drivers are NetWare Loadable Modules that are normally stored in the SYS:SYSTEM directory having filenames with the .LAN extension.

To load a LAN driver, first use the hot-key sequence to return to the console colon prompt. Next, type the LOAD driver-name command and press [Enter]. If your network card has its own driver program, you need to use the command LOAD A:driver-name (or LOAD B:driver-name) to load the file from its floppy disk. If you are loading a driver with a special frame type, such as an Ethernet 802.3 frame on NetWare v3.12, include the FRAME parameter with the LOAD command. For example, LOAD SMC8000 FRAME ETHERNET_802.3 loads the LAN driver for the SMC ethernet card using the older NetWare 802.3 frame type. Figure 5-23 shows an example of loading a LAN driver for an SMC ethernet card.

Figure 5-23

Loading and binding a LAN driver

```
CTS_HOST:LOAD SMC8000
Loading module SMC8000.LAN
  SMC EtherCard PLUS Server Driver v4.16 (930503)
  Version 4.16   May 3, 1993
  Copyright(c)1993 Standard Microsystems Corporation. All rights reserved.
  Debug symbol information for SMC8000.LAN loaded
Supported I/O port values are 300
I/O port: 300
CTS_HOST:BIND IPX TO SMC8000 NET=10BA5E2
IPX LAN protocol bound to SMC EtherCard PLUS Server Driver v4.16 (930503)
```

Many card drivers require you to enter the I/O port and other hardware settings, such as interrupt or memory address, during loading, so it is important to record these card settings on the file server worksheet. Remember that drivers for Micro Channel and EISA cards can automatically retrieve their settings from the CMOS memory on the motherboard, so configuring these cards and loading their drivers is usually easier.

Binding to the protocol

After the driver software has initialized the network interface card, you might find that you cannot access your new file server. This happens because the LAN driver supplies only the data link layer of the OSI model; the SERVER.EXE program supplies the application and presentation layers. That leaves you with a big gap between the network card and the network operating system. Before the server can communicate with other devices on the network it is necessary to fill this gap by **binding** the network card driver to a protocol stack so that the protocol stack can supply the network, transport, and session layers, which are necessary for communication. The most common protocol stacks were explained in Chapter 2: SPX/IPX, TCP/IP, and AppleTalk. For your convenience, NetWare builds the SPX/IPX stack into the operating system. The TCP/IP and AppleTalk protocol stacks, however, both need to be loaded as NLMs before they can be used.

To bind the SPX/IPX protocol stack to a card driver, use the command BIND IPX TO driver-name. When the SPX/IPX protocol stack is used, the system next asks you to enter the network address to be used for this cable system and frame type. Your completed file server worksheet should show the network address for each frame type according to your network plan. Figure 5-23 provides an example of binding SPX/IPX to the SMC8000 ethernet driver using a network address of 10BA5E2.

Console commands

After binding protocols to the LAN drivers, you can use the CONFIG command to display the network card configuration for the file server, as shown in Figure 5-24. Notice that this command shows such card settings as interrupt and I/O port along with the frame type and network address. The CONFIG command is a good way to verify the information on your file server worksheet or to find out information about an unknown network system.

Figure 5-25 illustrates use of the PROTOCOL command to view what protocols are attached to each of the frame types. Notice that the internal network is displayed as a VIRTUAL LAN with a Protocol ID of zero. In Chapter 15 you will use this command to verify the loading of the TCP/IP protocol. If there are other file servers on your network system, a good way to see if your file server is able to communicate with the other servers is to use the DISPLAY SERVERS command to display all servers on the network followed by the number of routers a packet must pass through to get to the server. Additionally, the DISPLAY NETWORKS command displays the network addresses of all networks accessible to the server including the internal network. Sample DISPLAY commands are included in Figure 5-25.

Figure 5-24

Using the CONFIG command

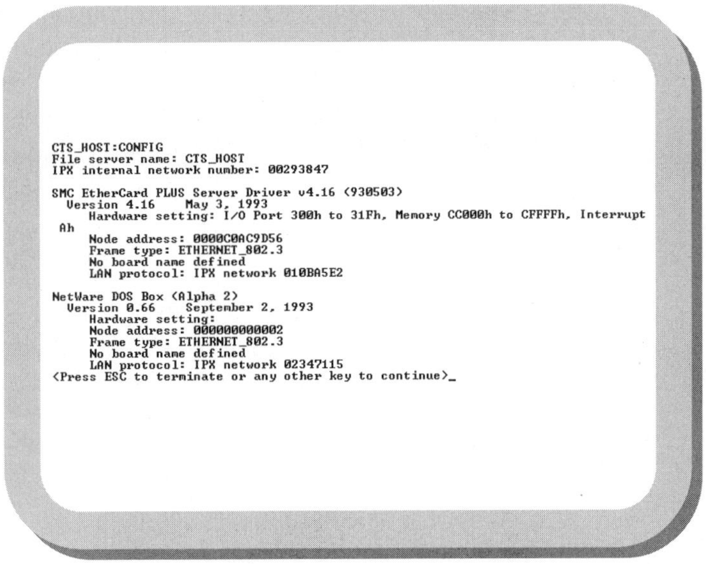

```
CTS_HOST:CONFIG
File server name: CTS_HOST
IPX internal network number: 00293847

SMC EtherCard PLUS Server Driver v4.16 (930503)
    Version 4.16    May 3, 1993
        Hardware setting: I/O Port 300h to 31Fh, Memory CC000h to CFFFFh, Interrupt
Ah
        Node address: 0000C0AC9D56
        Frame type: ETHERNET_802.3
        No board name defined
        LAN protocol: IPX network 010BA5E2

NetWare DOS Box (Alpha 2)
    Version 0.66    September 2, 1993
        Hardware setting:
        Node address: 000000000002
        Frame type: ETHERNET_802.3
        No board name defined
        LAN protocol: IPX network 02347115
<Press ESC to terminate or any other key to continue>_
```

Figure 5-25

Sample console commands

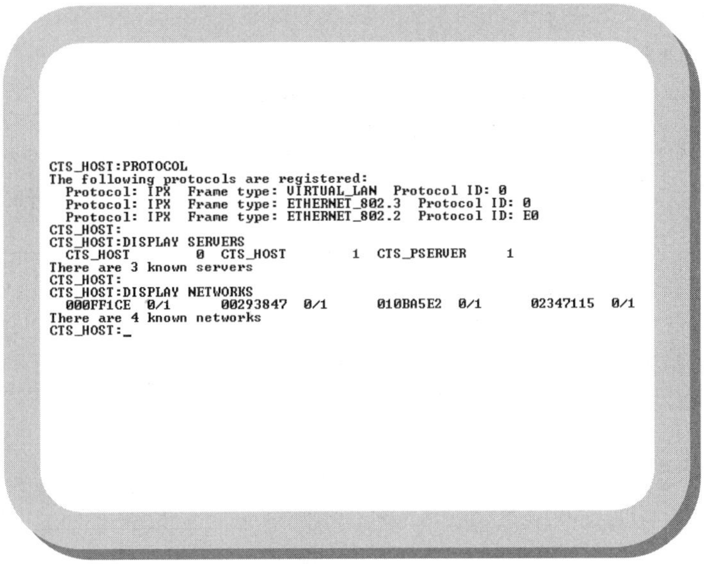

```
CTS_HOST:PROTOCOL
The following protocols are registered:
    Protocol: IPX  Frame type: VIRTUAL_LAN   Protocol ID: 0
    Protocol: IPX  Frame type: ETHERNET_802.3  Protocol ID: 0
    Protocol: IPX  Frame type: ETHERNET_802.2  Protocol ID: E0
CTS_HOST:
CTS_HOST:DISPLAY SERVERS
    CTS_HOST        0  CTS_HOST        1  CTS_PSERVER     1
There are 3 known servers
CTS_HOST:
CTS_HOST:DISPLAY NETWORKS
    000FF1CE  0/1        00293847  0/1        010BA5E2  0/1        02347115  0/1
There are 4 known networks
CTS_HOST:_
```

Now the file server is on line and available for workstations to be connected to it. If the server is not operating correctly, check all cables for bad connections and use the CONFIG command to be sure the IPX protocol is bound to the network cards, that each card is using the correct frame type, and that the network card drivers have the correct interrupt setting. If your file server is not listed by the DISPLAY SERVERS command, use the VOLUMES command to be sure the SYS: volume is mounted.

Creating the startup files

The last step in file server installation is to automate the server's startup process. There are two major startup files used by the NetWare operating system when the server is started: STARTUP.NCF and AUTOEXEC.NCF. **NetWare Control**

Files (NCF) all use the same .NCF file extension and are similar to DOS batch (.BAT) files because they contain a series of commands that the operating system automatically execute.

The STARTUP.NCF file. The STARTUP.NCF file is similar in function to the DOS CONFIG.SYS file and is used to load the disk driver and other basic system configuration parameters. This file must be accessible to NetWare before the disk drivers are loaded and is therefore stored on the DOS partition along with the SERVER.EXE program.

You can create the STARTUP.NCF file by first using [Alt][Esc] to return to the INSTALL program and then selecting System Options from the Installation Options menu. This displays the Available System Options screen; select Create STARTUP.NCF File. The installation program then asks you to enter the path to the STARTUP.NCF file. The default path will be the directory in which the SERVER.EXE program is located. Normally you should press [Enter] to select the default path.

Next, the installation program displays a window showing the command or commands you already used during installation to load the disk driver program along with the I/O port and interrupt. An example of a STARTUP file for a file server using an IDE disk drive is shown in Figure 5-26. Compare the hardware settings on your file server's STARTUP file to the ones on your file server worksheet and make any necessary changes. If you keep your file server worksheet current, it will help you, and others, maintain the server in the future. After verifying the contents of the START-UP file, you can press the [Esc] key to exit the screen and save the file contents.

Figure 5-26

Sample STARTUP.NCF file

```
                   File Server STARTUP.NCF File
load IDE port=1F0 int=E
```

The AUTOEXEC.NCF file. The AUTOEXEC.NCF file contains the file server's name, internal network number, and commands to mount all volumes, load and bind the LAN drivers to the protocol stack, and load other NLMs, such as MONITOR, you want loaded whenever the file server boots.

You can create and edit the AUTOEXEC.NCF file by choosing the Create AUTOEXEC.NCF File from the Available System Options menu. The installation program displays a window showing the initial command to establish the file server's name, the internal network number, and the LOAD and BIND commands you entered previously in order to load the LAN drivers. A sample AUTOEXEC.NCF file for a file server using the SMC8000 LAN drivers is shown in Figure 5-27.

Figure 5-27

Sample AUTOEXEC.NCF file

```
                   File Server AUTOEXEC.NCF File
file server name CTS_HOST
ipx internal net 293847
load SMC8000 port=300 mem=CC000 int=A frame=ETHERNET_802.2
bind IPX to SMC8000 net=10BA5E2
mount all
```

Notice that the LOAD commands for the LAN drivers contain all the hardware settings including I/O port, memory address, and interrupt, along with the frame parameter. In addition to the protocol and card name, the BIND commands also contain the network address for each cable and frame type. For this reason it is best to wait until the server is up and running with its LAN drivers before you create the AUTOEXEC.NCF file.

At this time you can add LOAD commands that automatically load other NLMs, such as MONITOR or a print server. If you load your LAN driver from the floppy disk drive, you might want to modify the LOAD command in the AUTOEXEC.NCF file to remove any reference to the disk drive. You can then copy the LAN driver to the SYS:SYSTEM directory after logging into the file server as Supervisor.

After making any additions, you save the commands shown on the screen in the AUTOEXEC.NCF file by pressing [Esc] and entering **Yes** at the Save AUTOEXEC.NCF File prompt. The AUTOEXEC.NCF file is stored in the SYS:SYSTEM directory and can be accessed by the Supervisor using the NetWare SYSCON utility. The installation process of NetWare is now complete and you can press the Esc key to exit the INSTALL program and return to the console colon prompt.

DOWNING THE FILE SERVER

Once your file server is operational, you should test the startup files to be sure the file server will start correctly the next time you use it. While it is not something a CNA needs to do often, you need to know how to properly stop and restart the file server computer when you maintain hardware or upgrade software.

Downing the file server is the process of stopping the server program by logging off all users, taking the server off line so that it is no·longer available to workstations, and dismounting all volumes to update the disk with any changes currently stored in the memory buffers. All these processes are accomplished using NetWare's DOWN console command.

 Prior to using the DOWN command, you should issue the DISABLE LOGIN command to prevent users from logging into the file server. Next, issue a BROADCAST command to send a short message to any current users. Announce that the file server will be shut down in several minutes and ask users to save their work and log out of the file server.

If there are any users logged into the file server when you issue the DOWN command, the NetWare file server displays a warning on the console, asking if you want to proceed. See Figure 5-28. Continuing with the DOWN command can cause data in files being processed to be lost. To determine if the current users have any files open, you can use the NetWare MONITOR module described in the next section to view existing connections and view any open files. You can then either send a message asking the user to log out or cancel the user's session if no files are open.

Figure 5-28

Downing the file server

```
CTS_HOST:DISABLE LOGIN
Login is now disabled
CTS_HOST:BROADCAST File server going down in 5 minutes - please log out.
CTS_HOST:
CTS_HOST:DOWN
File RCONSOLE.HLP in use by user SUPERVISOR on station 1
File SYS$ERR.DAT in use by user SUPERVISOR on station 1
File SYS$MSG.DAT in use by user SUPERVISOR on station 1
*** WARNING *** There are active files open.
Down server? n
```

After the DOWN command is completed, the console prompt returns. At this time you can continue to use certain console commands and load NetWare modules to perform server maintenance or upgrade functions, or you can use the EXIT command to return to the file server's DOS prompt.

Starting the file server

Starting the NetWare file server involves booting the computer with DOS and then loading the SERVER.EXE program. To start a file server computer you follow three steps:

1. Boot the computer from the DOS partition.

2. Change to the directory containing the SERVER.EXE program. The default directory created by the NetWare installation file is SERVER.312.

3. Enter the command SERVER and press [Enter].

The SERVER program starts by first loading the disk driver specified in the STARTUP.NCF file and then performing the commands in the AUTOEXEC.NCF file. These provide the server name, internal network number, and LAN drivers. You can automate this server startup process by creating an AUTOEXEC.BAT file in the server's DOS partition that contains the following commands:

```
@ECHO OFF
CLS
CD \SERVER.312
PAUSE Use [Ctrl] [Break] keys to abort server startup
SERVER
```

Issuing a PAUSE command in the server's AUTOEXEC.BAT file allows you to stop the computer in the DOS mode before starting the server program. This allows you to perform certain maintenance functions such as copying drivers and software upgrades to the SERVER.312 directory before starting the file server.

Using MONITOR

Once the basic file server installation process is complete, your next task is to get workstations attached to the network and logged into the server correctly. Before leaving the file server console and turning your attention to the workstations, however, it is a good idea to load the MONITOR utility. It provides essential information about the performance of servers and displays workstation connection information.

To start the MONITOR program, enter the command LOAD MONITOR after the console colon prompt and press [Enter]. A MONITOR screen similar to the one shown in Figure 5-29 will be displayed.

Figure 5-29

Sample MONITOR screen

Because many network administrators keep MONITOR loaded for a continuous check on file server status, the MONITOR program also provides a screen saver function. After several minutes of no keyboard activity, the MONITOR program displays a "worm" that moves randomly around the screen. The busier the file server, the longer the worm. This is a quick way for you to see if your file server computer is overloaded with network tasks.

Important MONITOR statistics to be aware of include the Utilization percentage and Total Cache Buffers figure. The Utilization percentage gives you a good idea of how busy the SERVER program is; normal utilization is in the 20%–60% range. Higher utilization numbers might mean that your file server is overloaded and you should consider installing a faster processor, removing additional functions such as print servers, or increasing memory.

The cache buffer information displayed by MONITOR can be used to determine if more memory is needed. The Original Cache Buffers figure represents the amount of memory available for caching files after the SERVER.EXE program was loaded. Mounting volumes and running NLMs reduces the number of buffers originally available and results in the Total Cache Buffers figure, which represents the amount of space available. If the Total Cache Buffers is less than 50% of the Original Cache Buffers, you should consider increasing the amount of memory in the server. If the percentage falls below 20%, you have a critical situation and need to add more memory as soon as possible.

The Connection Information option on the MONITOR Available Options menu can be used to view active connections on the server, the related usernames, and files that are open on those connections. You can use this option before downing the file server to view and clear active connections or send logout messages to individual users. Being able to clear a connection that does not have any files open eliminates the need to go to an active but unattended workstation to shut it down prior to downing the file server.

WORKSTATION INSTALLATION

Once NetWare has been installed on the file server computer, the next task is setting up the workstations that will be attached to the network. Assuming the wiring is already in place and tested, setting up a workstation to use the network involves installing and configuring the network interface card and then installing the client software. As a CNA, you will need to be familiar with these processes in order to upgrade workstation software and install new workstations on the network.

INSTALLING THE NETWORK CARD

To connect a workstation to the network, you must first obtain the network cards appropriate for the topology and system you are using. NetWare is compatible with most network cards on the market, but it is a good idea to obtain cards that have been certified by Novell. They have gone through an extensive testing process in the Novell labs. Before you install the card, you need to determine the correct hardware settings—including interrupt number, I/O port, and memory address—in order to avoid conflicts with other devices in the workstation.

Network cards use either jumpers or software to store configuration settings. The software included on some network cards allows you to store the card's configuration settings in the CMOS memory contained on the network card. Network cards that are designed for the Micro Channel and EISA bus machines have an automatic configuration process that calculates the hardware settings for you and stores them in CMOS memory on the motherboard. The network driver program retrieves up these configuration settings when it runs on the workstation. Using the software setup process allows driver programs to be self-configuring and means you don't need to modify the driver program parameters for different computer configurations.

SOFTWARE COMPONENTS

For a DOS workstation connected to the network to communicate with a file server, it needs three software components: a card driver, a protocol stack, and a shell. The card driver software performs the data link process that controls the network adapter card so it can send and receive packets over the network cable system. Information on the correct driver program for use with NetWare should be included in the manual that comes with your network card. In some cases, the workstation driver software is contained on a disk included with the network card. Sometimes you will be instructed to use one of the many workstation driver programs included with the NetWare installation disks.

The second workstation component is the protocol stack, which includes the network and transport layers responsible for formatting the data within a network packet and routing that packet between networks. NetWare file servers use the default SPX/IPX protocol originally developed by Xerox. Another popular protocol stack often used with workstations running the Unix operating system is TCP/IP. In Chapter 15, you will learn more about the TCP/IP protocol and how NetWare can support workstations using TCP/IP.

 Because of the increased need to support the Unix operating system along with the rapidly growing use of the Internet, both of which use TCP/IP, most CNAs will probably need to support TCP/IP on NetWare networks.

The third workstation component is the shell, or requester, which carries out the session and presentation layer functions by providing access to the network from the local operating system. The DOS shell program, NETX, adapts itself to the version of DOS that is loaded and acts as a front end to DOS by intercepting all requests and routing them to either the file server or local DOS.

Earlier versions of the NETX shell (NET2.COM, NET3.COM, NET4.COM, and NET5.COM) were tailored to work with specific versions of DOS. To make things a little easier, Novell rewrote the shell program to eliminate the need to match the shell program to the DOS version and named it NETX.

In NetWare v3.12, the NETX shell has been replaced by VLMs. While the NETX program works as a front end to DOS, the requester software works with DOS, allowing the requester and DOS to share drive table information, reducing memory requirements and providing better compatibility. Both the shell and requester function by sending a request for the first available file server as soon as they are loaded, then attaching to the first file server that responds and making that server the default file server. After they attach to a file server, the first available drive pointer, normally F, is mapped to the SYS:LOGIN directory of the default file server. The user can then change to drive F and use the LOGIN command to log into the default file server, or the LOGIN servername command to log into another available file server.

INSTALLING NETX SOFTWARE

The NETX shell program works with NetWare versions 2.x through 3.x and, due to some bugs in the early versions of the NetWare VLM software, is still popular on many NetWare v3.12 networks. A CNA should be familiar with installing and using both the VLM and NETX environments. Prior to v3.12, NetWare included a disk labeled WSGEN (workstation generation), which contained an installation program called WSGEN, card drivers, and the NETX programs.

The following sections discuss two different ways to install the workstation software from the WSGEN disk: using WSGEN to create a customized IPX.COM program and using ODI drivers. Most network administrators currently use ODI drivers because they provide multiple protocol capability and are easier to upgrade. Some older network cards, however, do not have ODI-compatible drivers. In those cases you need to use the WSGEN program to create a customized IPX.COM program.

Using WSGEN to create a customized IPX.COM program

This is the original method of installing the workstation software and has the advantage of combining both the card driver and IPX protocol into one program, thereby making the network startup procedure shorter and keeping memory requirements to a minimum. The WSGEN program is used to create an IPX.COM program by linking the network card driver and configuration with the IPX protocol stack.

To use the WSGEN program to create a customized IPX.COM program, first insert the disk labeled WSGEN in any drive, change to the drive containing the WSGEN disk, type WSGEN, and press [Enter]. The WSGEN startup screen containing a welcome message is displayed. Next, press the Enter key to obtain a list of network card drivers included on the WSGEN disk, as shown in Figure 5-30.

Figure 5-30

LAN driver included with WSGEN

If the driver for your network adapter card is not shown, press [Insert]. A screen is displayed that asks you to insert a disk containing your network drivers. Insert the disk that came with your network card and press [Enter]. The NetWare card drivers are loaded from the disk and appear in the driver window.

After the drivers are displayed, highlight the driver program for the network card driver that is correct for the workstation you are installing and press [Enter]. A screen showing possible card configurations for that network card is displayed, as shown in Figure 5-31. Highlight the correct card configuration option and press [Enter]. The WSGEN program then displays the selected card and configuration. Whenever possible you should select Self-Configuring because this option allows the driver to determine the card configuration when it is run. If you use a software program to set the card configuration, select Software Configured to tell the driver to get the card configuration information from the CMOS memory on the card. Using either the Self-Configuring or Software Configured option allows you to change the card configuration without regenerating a new IPX.COM.

Figure 5-31

WSGEN card configuration window

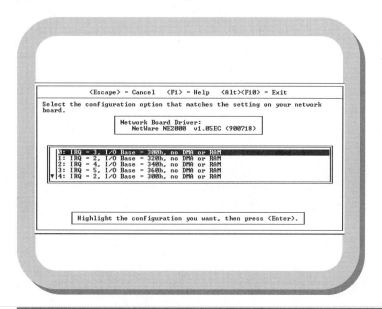

After selecting the card configuration, press [Enter] to create the IPX.COM program. WSGEN now links the driver program with the IPX protocol stack. The installation program might prompt you to insert the card's driver disk during this process. After completion, a message informs you that the new IPX program has been stored on the WSGEN disk. You can press [Enter] to return to the DOS prompt.

After creating the customized IPX.COM program, you next need to copy the IPX.COM and NETX.COM or NETX.EXE programs onto the boot drive of the workstation. (Some versions of the NETX program for NetWare v3.11 use an .EXE filename extension.)

The IPX program should be run first to access the file server from the workstation. This loads the driver and IPX protocol stack. Next the NETX shell program attaches your workstation to the default file server and connects drive letter F to the SYS:LOGIN directory of your file server. The first NetWare drive letter is normally F because by default DOS reserves letters A through E. You can then change to the F drive pointer and use the LOGIN command to log into the file server.

The network drive letter can be affected by the inclusion of the LASTDRIVE= statement in the workstation's CONFIG.SYS file or by loading other network software on your workstation. For example, if your CONFIG.SYS contains the statement LASTDRIVE=K, then the first network drive is L. The shell will allow you to use the left bracket symbol ([ ) as the network drive pointer if the CONFIG.SYS file contains a LASTDRIVE=Z statement.

When the IPX and NETX programs are loaded, they will each need to access a file called SHELL.CFG. If the SHELL.CFG file exists, IPX and NETX will use configuration parameters contained within the file, as shown in Figure 5-32.

Figure 5-32

SHELL.CFG parameters

Parameters Used by NETX	Default Setting
CACHE BUFFERS=n	none
FILE HANDLES=n	40
LOCAL PRINTERS=n	1
LONG MACHINE TYPE=name	IBM_PC
PREFERRED SERVER=name	none
SET STATION TIME=on/off	on

For example, the PREFERRED SERVER= parameter can be used to have the NETX program attach to a specific file server as its default. The LONG MACHINE TYPE= parameter identifies the value for the login script variable %MACHINE, which has a default value of IBM_PC. A more detailed description of the SHELL.CFG parameters will be provided in Chapter 16.

Overview of ODI drivers

One of the main disadvantages of customizing the IPX.COM program for a workstation is the extra work required when Novell updates the IPX software or makes changes to the card driver program—you need to repeat the WSGEN process to relink the card driver to the updated IPX.OBJ file. The process also must be repeated if you change to a newer version of the card driver's software. Another problem with the customized IPX.COM program is that it is only intended to support the IPX protocol on the network card it controls. Increasing numbers of users, however, need to access network services on different types of platforms—word processing documents off a NetWare file server, for example—and run applications on a company's mainframe system. Using IPX.COM, the user would need to reboot his or her workstation in order to load the drivers necessary to access the mainframe system.

To provide support for multiple protocols and to make it easier for network administrators to update card configurations and drivers, Novell developed the open data interface (ODI) software and driver specifications. The ODI driver specifications are standards for network card companies to use in developing drivers that are compatible with Novell's ODI software. In addition, the ODI client software allows the workstation to run multiple protocol stacks on the same network card. The ODI client software, for example, allows a workstation to be configured so it can communicate with a Unix host using TCP/IP while still accessing a NetWare file server attached to the same network cable system and use the IPX protocol. When ODI drivers are used to attach a workstation to the network, they provide another important benefit. The network administrator no longer needs to run the WSGEN program in order to create a customized IPX.COM program. The ODI driver software comprises three components:

1. The link support layer, or LSL.COM.

2. The card driver program.

3. The IPX protocol software called IPXODI.COM.

The LSL program supplied by Novell provides a connection within the data link layer between the protocol stack and the card driver so that more than one protocol stack can share the same network card. For example, the LSL allows you to run both TCP/IP and SPX/IPX simultaneously over the same network card by passing TCP/IP packets to the IP network layer and IPX packets to the IPX network layer.

The ODI driver software's card driver program is supplied either by Novell or by the network card's manufacturer and must be capable of working with the LSL layer according to Novell specifications.

Certain older network cards do not have ODI compatible drivers. You will need to use the WSGEN program to generate a customized IPX program for these cards.

The IPXODI program supplied by Novell provides the SPX/IPX protocol normally used to communicate with the NetWare file server. In terms of the OSI model described in Chapter 2, you can think of the IPXODI program as supplying the functions of the network and transport layers, and the LSL and card driver program as supplying the data link layer.

In NetWare v3.11, the ODI driver software is stored in the DOSODI subdirectory of the WSGEN disk. To use ODI drivers, you need a network card that is compatible with one of the ODI driver files that comes with NetWare, or you need an ODI driver file on a separate disk. In addition to copying NETX.COM or NETX.EXE from the WSGEN disk to the workstation's boot drive, to use ODI you also need to copy LSL.COM, IPXODI.COM, and the correct driver program from the DOSODI subdirectory. If your network card requires a driver program that is not provided in the DOSODI subdirectory, you need to copy that file from the disk provided by the card manufacturer. To use the popular Novell NE2000 driver, for example, you need to copy the files listed to the local boot disk.

FILE	SOURCE
LSL.COM	DOSODI subdirectory of the WSGEN disk
NE2000	DOSODI subdirectory of the WSGEN disk
IPXODI.COM	DOSODI subdirectory of the WSGEN disk
NETX.EXE	The root of the WSGEN disk

Running these four programs in the sequence listed attaches the workstation to the file server if the card configuration for the NE2000 card is set to the factory defaults. If the card is configured to use an interrupt number or network address that is different from the factory default, you need to provide the configuration parameters in a file called NET.CFG. As shown in Figure 5-33, the NET.CFG parameters are divided into two major categories: link support and link driver. The link driver section, containing parameters for configuring the software driver to match the network card interrupt and memory settings, is used most often. The link support section contains the optional BUFFERS parameter that allows the network administrator to configure the number and size of the receiver buffers that will be maintained by the link support layer.

Figure 5-33

NET.CFG file parameters

Parameter Heading	Default Setting
Link support	
BUFFERS number	0
Link Driver drivername	
DMA channel_number	none
INT interrupt_number	none
MEM hex_starting_address hex_length	none
PORT hex_starting_address	none
NODE ADDRESS hex_address	from network card
FRAME frame_type	802.2

 When you use ODI drivers, it is important to place all commands in the NET.CFG file and delete the SHELL.CFG file.

In addition to the parameters shown in Figure 5-33, the NET.CFG file can contain any of the SHELL configuration parameters shown in Figure 5-32. For example, the following statements placed in the NET.CFG file will configure the NE2000 driver to use I/O port 360 and interrupt 5 with a total of three communication buffers.

```
Link Driver NE2000
     PORT=360
     INT=5
Link Support
     BUFFERS 3
```

To have a workstation automatically access the network, you can create a STARTNET.BAT file that contains all the commands to load the ODI drivers, start NETX, and log into the file server. The sample STARTNET.BAT file that follows contains the commands necessary to attach a workstation containing an NE2000-compatible ethernet card to the file server named CTS_HOST.

```
LSL
NE2000
IPXODI
NETX PS=CTS_HOST
F:
LOGIN
```

In this example, the PS parameter following the NETX command causes the shell to attempt to attach to a specific file server. This is a useful option when you want a workstation to log into automatically a specific file server in a multiserver network.

INSTALLING VLM SOFTWARE

The NetWare VLM requester software has several advantages over the older NETX shell program. As previously mentioned, the VLM software provided with NetWare v3.12 shares DOS tables and provides better efficiency and DOS compatibility. The VLM software also provides enhancements such as packet burst mode, better security, and upward compatibility with NetWare v4.x. **Packet burst mode** provides faster communication to the file server by allowing the workstation to receive a number of data packets at once before responding with an acknowledgment. Without packet burst mode, each data packet sent by the server must be acknowledged by the workstation before the next packet can be sent. Packet burst mode is especially effective on lightly used networks. When more workstations are accessing the network, large groups of packets can actually decrease performance for workstations that are waiting to use the network. For this reason, the packet burst mode is automatically adjusted by the VLM shell and file server based on the network load.

The enhanced security of VLMs is provided by unique **packet signatures**, which ensure that packets are sent by authorized workstations. Before the packet signature system, it was possible for another workstation to "forge" a packet and make the file server think it came from a workstation with higher privileges. Packet signatures prevent forged packets by requiring an encrypted code comprising the user's password and workstation connection number to verify that the workstation that originated the packet is authorized to do so.

Like the NETX shell, ODI drivers must be loaded before the VLM requester is initiated. The VLM requester consists of a manager, VLM.EXE, and other virtual loadable modules using the.VLM extension. As illustrated in Figure 5-34, each VLM provides a specific function to the workstation client software. **Multiplexer VLMs** are used to direct requests between other VLMs known as **child VLMs**. The NET.CFG file contains a NetWare DOS requester section that specifies which VLMs will be loaded into the workstation memory. This section is automatically created when you install the VLM software.

Figure 5-34

VLM functions

VLM File Name	Description
CONN.VLM	Connection table manager; tracks network connections and supplies information to other modules.
IPXNCP.VLM	A child of the transport multiplexer; builds the proper IPX packets for use with the NetWare file server.
TRAN.VLM	Transport protocol; a multiplexer VLM that supports other transport protocols.
SECURITY.VLM	Provides packet signature security.
NDS.VLM	Provides support for NetWare v4.1x servers.
BIND.VLM	Provides support for NetWare v3.1x server bindery files.
NWP.VLM	NetWare protocol multiplexer that provides support for its child modules, such as FIO and PRINT.
FIO.VLM	Supports file access on NetWare file servers.
GENERAL.VLM	Provides general functions for other modules.
REDIR.VLM	Works with DOS to handle NetWare redirection tasks.
PRINT.VLM	Works with DOS to handle direction of printer requests to the network.
NETX.VLM	Provides compatibility with applications that use specific NETX functions.
AUTO.VLM	Provides for automatic reconnection of a workstation to the file server.

Instead of the WSGEN program, NetWare v3.12 includes a client installation program called INSTALL. This program can be found on the NetWare's client installation disks or on the CD-ROM in the \CLIENT\DOSWIN directory. To start the workstation installation process, change to the drive and directory containing the client INSTALL program and enter the INSTALL command. The NetWare client installation screen shown in Figure 5-35 is displayed. Notice that the installation process consists of five steps.

Figure 5-35

VLM client installation screen

```
STEP 1. Type client directory name for Client Installation.
        C:\NWCLIENT

STEP 2. Client installation requires "LASTDRIVE=Z" in the
        CONFIG.SYS file and "CALL STARTNET.BAT" added to
        AUTOEXEC.BAT.  Install will make backup copies.
        Allow changes?  <Y/N>:  No

STEP 3. Do you wish to install support for Windows? <Y/N>:  No
        Windows Subdirectory:

STEP 4. Press <Enter> to install the driver for your network
        board.  You may then use arrow keys to find the
        board name.
        Press <Enter> to see list

STEP 5. Press <Enter> to install.

Esc-exit  Enter-select  ↑↓-move  Alt F10-exit
```

Step 1 of the client installation process allows you to specify the location for the client files on the workstation computer—the default is the C:\NWCLIENT directory. Step 2 allows the installation process to modify the CONFIG.SYS and AUTOEXEC.BAT files on the workstation. Step 3 is important if you have Windows installed on the workstation; it automatically includes NetWare drivers and icons to facilitate the use of NetWare while you work in Windows. Step 4 is similar to WSGEN; it allows you to select a network card driver and configuration parameters. Rather than creating an IPX.COM file, however, the INSTALL program copies the correct ODI drivers to your NWCLIENT directory and creates a NET.CFG file with the selected driver configuration. If you are using an ethernet adapter, the default frame type will be 802.2. NetWare 3.12 file servers also default to 802.2 frame types, but if your network contains older file servers that you want to access from this workstation, you might need to use the 802.3 frame type. Finally, step 5 copies the required software from either CD-ROM or floppy disks onto your workstation's hard disk and then creates STARTNET.BAT and NET.CFG files that automatically load the ODI drivers and VLM software. The contents of the NET.CFG file for a sample installation are shown in Figure 5-36.

Figure 5-36

Sample NET.CFG file for VLMs

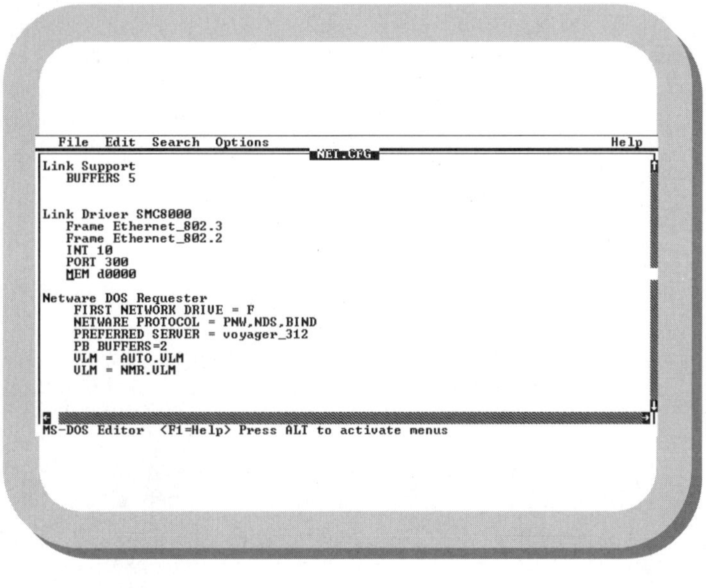

```
   File  Edit  Search  Options                                Help
┌──────────────────────────── NET.CFG ────────────────────────────┐
Link Support
    BUFFERS 5


Link Driver SMC8000
    Frame Ethernet_802.3
    Frame Ethernet_802.2
    INT 10
    PORT 300
    MEM d0000

Netware DOS Requester
    FIRST NETWORK DRIVE = F
    NETWARE PROTOCOL = PNW,NDS,BIND
    PREFERRED SERVER = voyager_312
    PB BUFFERS=2
    VLM = AUTO.VLM
    VLM = NMR.VLM



MS-DOS Editor   <F1=Help> Press ALT to activate menus
```

In the sample, the FIRST NETWORK DRIVE = F parameter specifies the drive letter that will be used when the attached file server is first logged in. If the FIRST NETWORK DRIVE parameter is omitted, the requester uses the drive letter after the last physical drive, which on a workstation with a single hard disk is usually D. Because DOS and the requester share the same drive table, the CONFIG.SYS file should be modified to contain the LASTDRIVE=Z statement. You should check your CONFIG.SYS file to verify that the installation program added this statement.

The STARTNET.BAT file is also created by the installation program and contains the commands needed to attach the workstation to the network and load the DOS requester software. The contents of the STARTNET.BAT file for the sample installation are shown in Figure 5-37.

Figure 5-37

Sample STARTNET.BAT
file

VERIFYING THE INSTALLATION

After completion of the server and workstation installation, you should reboot your workstation to load the new parameters in CONFIG.SYS and run the START-NET program. If you see a "bad command or filename" message when you attempt to log into the file server, it means the requester could not attach to a file server. When using the NETX shell you might see a "file server not found" message. The most common causes of the file server not being found are a defective cable, a faulty ethernet connector, an incorrect frame type, an interrupt being used by both the network card and some other device in either the server or the workstation, or the SPX/IPX protocol not being properly bound to the network card on the file server.

 Sometimes the reason for a problem can be so obvious that it escapes you. Take, for example, the case of a network administrator who spent some time looking for the cause of a "file server not found" message only to discover that someone had broken into the file server room and actually stolen the server. In this case the workstation was correct: the file server could not be found.

Once you verify that the NetWare file server and workstations are communicating correctly you can continue the process of setting up the network by establishing the file server's directory structure along with the user accounts and security as described in the following chapters. Installation is an ongoing process that involves expanding the network to incorporate additional workstations and enhancing the file server. Chapters 15 and 16 provide the concepts and commands that allow a CNA to monitor and improve file server performance.

CHAPTER SUMMARY

The NetWare installation process is divided into two major operations: installing the file server software and installing the workstation software. Installing NetWare on a file server can be divided into five steps. The first step is to complete a file server worksheet to document the network environment and file server hardware configuration. Step 2 involves starting the SERVER.EXE program from the NetWare floppy disk or CD-ROM. This step entails creating a DOS partition, copying necessary NetWare files, starting the SERVER.EXE program, and providing the server name and internal network address. In step 3, you prepare the disk system by loading the correct disk driver and then using the INSTALL program to create NetWare partitions and volumes. Step 4 involves mounting the volumes using either the INSTALL program or the MOUNT ALL console command and then copying the SYSTEM and PUBLIC files from floppy disk or CD-ROM into the NetWare created directories of the SYS: volume. Step 5 is loading the LAN drivers and creating the STARTUP.NCF and AUTOEXEC.NCF startup files.

The workstation computer requires three software components in order to access the NetWare file server. The first component is the network card driver which provides the data link process of transmitting and receiving packets over the network cable system. The second software component is the protocol stack, which is responsible for formatting the packets through the network, transport, and session layers of the OSI model. In NetWare, SPX/IPX is used as the default protocol. The third software component is the requester or shell that provides an interface from DOS to the NetWare file server. NETX is the shell program that acts as a front end for DOS and directs all application and user requests for NetWare services to the network file server. Virtual loadable modules (VLMs) replace NETX. They were first introduced with NetWare v3.12 to work more closely with DOS when it handles network requests. In addition, VLM software provides support that allows it to work with NetWare v4.x and can improve network performance and security through the use of packet burst mode and packet signatures.

When installing NetWare v3.11 systems, you can use either a customized IPX.COM program or Open Data Interface (ODI) drivers. The WSGEN program is used to link a card driver with the SPX/IPX protocol to form a customized IPX.COM program for a certain workstation configuration. The biggest disadvantage of WSGEN in creating a customized IPX.COM program is that it requires you to relink IPX.COM whenever you change a workstation configuration or want to update to a newer version of the IPX or driver software. To access the network from a workstation using a customized IPX program, you enter only two commands: IPX and NETX.

ODI drivers do not require linking, but are copied and loaded separately. ODI drivers include LSL.COM, the card driver, and IPXODI. The configuration information for ODI drivers is in the NET.CFG file; ODI drivers are therefore easier to use when a workstation's configuration is changed. Updating to a newer version of the ODI drivers is simply a matter of copying the new drivers onto the workstation and replacing the older files. ODI drivers also provide the option of using different protocol stacks on a single workstation and being able to switch among them easily. To access an IBM token ring network from a workstation using ODI drivers, for example, you need to load four programs: LSL, TOKEN, IPXODI, and NETX.

NetWare v3.12 and NetWare v41.x both include VLM software and ODI drivers on either floppy disk or CD-ROM. The Novell INSTALL program includes the VLM software and allows you to select the location of the NetWare client files, to modify the AUTOEXEC.BAT and CONFIG.SYS files, to install support for Windows, and to select from a wide range of ODI-compatible network card drivers. After you select the installation options, the INSTALL program copies the necessary files from floppy disks or CD-ROM onto the workstation's hard drive and creates NET.CFG and STARTUP.BAT files. The NET.CFG file contains the configuration statements for the ODI-compatible network card driver in addition to control statements for the VLMs.

After installing the workstation software, you should reboot the computer and attempt to log into the file server. Both NETX and VLM will attempt to attach to a file server when they are first loaded. If NETX does not receive a response from a file server within a few moments, it returns a "file server not found" error message. Although the VLM software does not display an error message if the file server does not respond, an "invalid drive" message from DOS will be displayed when you attempt to switch to the network drive and run the LOGIN program. The most common causes of the "file server not found" error message are a bad cable, incorrect frame type, overlapping interrupt assignments, or the SPX/IPX protocol not being properly bound to the network card on the file server computer.

COMMAND SUMMARY

Command	Syntax	Definition
BIND	*BIND IPX TO driver_name*	Allows NetWare to communicate with a LAN card by attaching a protocol stack to the card driver. When the BIND IPX TO driver-name command is issued, NetWare asks for the network address for that cable system. Each bind command requires a unique hexadecimal network address of one to eight digits.
BROADCAST	*BROADCAST message*	This NetWare console command sends the message specified in the command to all users logged into the file server. You should issue this command to warn users that the file server is going to be shut down.
CONFIG	*CONFIG*	In addition to displaying the file server's name and internal network number, this NetWare console command displays configuration information for each LAN driver—including the interrupt, I/O port, frame type, and network address.
DISABLE LOGIN	*DISABLE LOGIN*	A NetWare console command that prevents users from logging into the file server. Users currently logged in are not affected. Use this command before you shut down the file server to prevent additional users from logging in after you have broadcast the warning message.

DISMOUNT	*DISMOUNT [ALL] [volume name]*	This console command takes the specified volume or all volumes off line, making them inaccessible to the network. It is usually used when you need to perform volume maintenance with the VREPAIR module.
DISPLAY	*DISPLAY NETWORKS*	Displays the network address of each network cable system accessible to your file server.
	DISPLAY SERVERS	Displays the name of each file server accessible to the network along with the number of routers that must be crossed.
DOWN	*DOWN*	A NetWare console command that takes the server off line by stopping all network communication and dismounting all volumes. You receive a warning message if active connections to the server exist, and you can terminate the connections or cancel the command.
EXIT	*EXIT*	A NetWare console command that is issued after the DOWN command, EXIT causes the SERVER.EXE program to end and returns the console to the DOS prompt. If DOS has been removed from memory, this command causes the file server computer to reboot.
INSTALL	*LOAD INSTALL -J*	A NetWare Loadable Module that is used to set up and maintain NetWare disk drives and volumes, as well as perform system operations such as copying SYSTEM and PUBLIC files and creating or modifying the startup files. The "-J" option can be used with NetWare v3.11 to allow the INSTALL module to load files from other devices such as CD-ROM. NetWare v3.12 does not require the use of the "-J" option to load files from other devices.
LOAD	*LOAD module-name [parameters]*	Accesses and runs a NetWare Loadable Module in the file server's RAM. By default, modules are loaded from the SYS:SYSTEM directory. Modules remain in RAM until unloaded. Because NetWare is a multitasking operating system, many modules can be loaded at one time. Examples of module names include the INSTALL and MONITOR modules used in this chapter. Additional loadable modules will be introduced in Chapters 15 and 16.

MEMORY	*MEMORY*	A NetWare console command that displays the amount of RAM in the file server computer.
MODULES	*MODULES*	A console command that displays all NetWare Loadable Modules currently in memory from the last loaded to the first.
MONITOR	*LOAD MONITOR [p]*	A NetWare Loadable Module that displays information regarding the performance of a file server. The optional "?" parameter can be used if you want to include an additional "performance" option in the MONITOR main menu.
MOUNT	*MOUNT volume name [ALL]*	This console command allows you to mount a specific volume or all volumes. Mounting a volume loads the file allocation table and directory entry table into RAM. A volume must be mounted before it can be accessed by the network.
NETX	*NETX [ps=server]*	A workstation command that loads the NetWare DOS shell program; allows you to access a file server and log in. The "ps-" option is often used in multiple file server networks to specify the name of the "preferred server" that you want the NETX program to attach to by replacing the "server" parameter in the "ps=server" option with the name of the desired file server.
PROTOCOL	*PROTOCOL*	Displays all protocol stacks that are attached to each network card driver.
SPEED	*SPEED*	Displays the file server's speed in relation to an 80386 CPU along with an explanation of the method used to calculate this speed.
UNLOAD	*UNLOAD/module name*	Terminates execution of the specified module and removes it from memory.
VOLUMES	*VOLUMES*	Console command that displays all mounted volumes along with the workstation operating system name spaces they will support.

KEY TERMS

binding	downing	internal router
child VLM	file server name	internetwork
dismounting	internal network number	mounting a volume

multiple file server network	NetWare Loadable Modules (NLMs)	packet signature startup file
multiplexer VLM	network layout	
NetWare control files	packet burst mode	

REVIEW QUESTIONS

pg 142 **1.** List the five major steps for installing NetWare on a file server computer.

① Plan the network layout

② Create a bootable DOS partition on h/d. Copy NetWare files. *Start Server Program*

③ Run Install Program.

④ Load SYSTEM & PUBLIC files

⑤ Load LAN Driver.   ⑥ Create Automatic startup files.

pg 174 **2.** A(n) ___Internal Network Number___ is used internally by the NetWare operating system to communicate with its device drivers.

pg 174 **3.** A file server's name can be from ___2___ to ___47___ characters in length.

pg 145 **4.** All devices that communicate with each other over a network cable system must use the same ~~frame type~~.

pg 175 **5.** A network containing two file servers is referred to as a(n) ___multiple file server network___   *pg 175*

pg 175 **6.** Multiple networks connected together by routers are called a(n) ___internetwork___.   *pg 175*

pg 175 **7.** A file server that connects two networks is referred to as a(n) ___internal router___.   *pg*

pg 177 **8.** The minimum amount of RAM necessary to run NetWare v3.12 is ___4MB for installation   6-8 MB to support a small network___

pg 179 **9.** Which of the following is an *invalid* network address?

___valid___ A

___invalid___ 10BA5ET *"T" can't be used*

___invalid___ 1AB216A15 *can only be 1-8 chars.*

___valid___ 1EEE8025

10. ? During what step in the installation process is the file server's internal network number required? _____

pg 185 **11.** List three types of NetWare Loadable Modules and their corresponding extensions.

General Purpose Modules	.NLM
Disk Driver Modules	.DSK
Network Card Drivers	.LAN

12. In the space below, write the NetWare console commands that access the
    IDE disk drives and start the INSTALL module.

    LOAD   C: or A: IDE.DSK

    LOAD   INSTALL INSTALL

13. Briefly describe the purpose of the -J option on the INSTALL command
    during installation of NetWare v3.11.

    To load files from other devices.
        eg. CD-ROM.

pg 187 14. When it creates a partition, NetWare by default reserves ___2___ % for
    hot fix redirection.

15. The _Available Disk_ option of the INSTALL program is
    used to mirror two partitions.

16. Before you can mirror two disk partitions, you must be sure that both parti-
    tions are _the same size._

17. List the steps for creating a new volume.
    ① select Volume Options from Installation Options.
    ② press INS Key.

Default
1 block = 4 Kb.

18. Briefly describe how the INSTALL program is used to duplex two partitions.
    ① select Disk Options from Installation Option Menu.
    ② select Mirroring from Available Disk Options.

pg 145 19. The _Frame_ command is used to specify a frame type for
    a LAN driver. LOAD Driver-Name FRAME Frame-Type

pg 116 20. The _Person Installing._ assigns a network address to a network card.

21.? The _Crtl or Alt._ and _ESC_ keys are used to switch the
    server console from one active module to another.

22. In the space below, write a console command that makes all volumes available
    to the network.

    Mount ALL

23. The _CONFIG_ console command displays the net-
    work address and frame types being used on each network card.

24. List the three workstation software components.

    Card Driver

    Protocol Stack

    Shell

25. The ___*NETX*___ program acts as a front end to DOS and must be matched to the DOS version.

26. ___*Packet Burst Mode.*___ increases speed by acknowledging several packets at one time.

27. List two advantages of VLM client software over NETX.

    ① *Shares DOS tables*

    ② *Better efficiency and DOS compatibility*

    ③ *Enhancements: Packet Burst Mode, better security, and upward compatibility with NetWare V4.x.*

28. List two advantages of ODI drivers over a customized IPX.COM program.

    ① *Provide support for multiple protocols*

    ② *Easier to update card configurations & drivers.*

29. The ___*NET.CFG*___ file contains configuration statements used by the ODI drivers.

30. Given a network card that uses an ODI driver program named SMCPLUS.COM, in the space below, write a STARTNET.BAT file that will load the ODI drivers. Run the NETX shell, and log into a file server named PCSHOST.

 EXERCISES

Exercise 5-1: Performing a Complete NetWare 3.12 Installation

In this exercise you will install NetWare v3.12 from a CD-ROM drive. At the end of this exercise, you will also have configured a file server that you can access from a workstation attached to the network. In order to perform this exercise, you will need the following components, which will be supplied by your instructor:

- Access to an 80386SX or later computer with at least 4 Mbytes of RAM and a 40–Mbyte hard disk

- A network interface card and cable to connect to a network that has at least one other workstation attached to it

- A CD-ROM drive that can be attached to the file server computer (An alternative is a CD-ROM drive that is shared on the network.)
- A copy of a NetWare System_1 disk
- A DOS boot disk containing the FDISK and FORMAT commands

Once you have verified that your work area contains these components, use the following steps to install NetWare and initialize your file server computer.

Step 1: Record file server information

1. Sketch a diagram of the network system you are building, including all student file servers and network topologies. Label the diagram with the following information:

   - Name of each file server
   - Internal network number to be used for each server (Indicate RANDOM if you are going to let the installation process select a number for you.)
   - Network topology
   - Network card model and manufacturer
   - Ethernet frame type

2. Obtain a blank copy of the file server worksheet from your instructor.

3. Fill in the identification section by supplying a valid name for your server.

4. Fill in the system information section by identifying the disk controller card type, drive information, and correct NetWare disk driver to be used. Your instructor will tell you where to obtain this information. You might need the documentation sheet included with the computer and system manuals.

5. Fill in the network card information section by reading the settings off the network card or using the network card handout provided by your instructor.

6. List any other equipment in the file server in the nonnetwork device information section and check that no hardware interrupt conflicts exist.

Step 2: Install the SERVER.EXE program

In this step you will use the CD-ROM drive to run the INSTALL batch file. The following steps assume you have access to a CD-ROM drive as a drive letter on your computer:

1. Boot the computer with the DOS disk. This disk should contain the drivers that allow you to access a CD-ROM drive, either one attached to your computer or one shared on the network. Be sure the NetWare v3.12 CD-ROM is in the CD-ROM drive before you continue.

2. Change to the drive letter containing the NetWare CD-ROM.

3. Change to the NETWARE.312\ENGLISH directory and enter the command INSTALL.

4. Select the New Installation option.

5. If your computer already has a DOS partition with at least 30 Mbytes of free space on the disk drive, select the option to retain the DOS partition. If your system does not have a DOS partition, or if the DOS partition uses all the available disk space, you will need to create a new DOS partition. *Be sure to check with your instructor before removing any existing information on the disk drive.*

6. Enter the name and internal network number to be used on your file server. If you accept a random number, record it on your file server worksheet.

7. Unless instructed otherwise, use the default values for each of the remaining options. Record these values in the space below.

8. After the initial installation is completed, the SERVER program is started. Use the _____ command to record the speed rating of the computer you are using.

   Speed rating: _____

Step 3: Disk System setup

In this step you will load the disk driver module, start the INSTALL program, create a NetWare partition, and create the SYS: volume.

1. Use the LOAD command to load the disk driver module you identified in step 1. In the space below, record the command you use along with the interrupt and I/O port address.

2. After the disk module is running, record the next step and the command you need to use.

   Step: _____

   Command used: _____

3. Create a NetWare partition. In the space below, record each of the steps you use.

4. Create the server volumes. If you have over 40 Mbytes of disk space, make the SYS: volume size 40 Mbytes and create a DATA: volume using all but 5 Mbytes of the remaining disk space. You can use the extra 5 Mbytes to extend the size of a volume when performing a file server maintenance exercise later in Chapter 15.

Step 4: Copy System and Public files

In this step you will copy the NetWare SYSTEM and PUBLIC files from the CD-ROM to the required directories of the SYS: volume.

1. Use the hot-key sequence to return to the console prompt. Record the hot-key sequence on the following line:

2. Use the necessary NetWare console command to bring the volumes you have created on line. Record the command(s) below.

3. In the space below, record the steps you need to perform to copy the SYSTEM and PUBLIC files from the CD-ROM drive to the NetWare directories.

4. On the line below, record approximately how long this installation process took.

_____

Step 5: Completing the installation

In the space below, briefly identify each of the processes you will need to perform to complete the file server installation to the point where the server is available to the network and can be rebooted.

1. Use the hot-key sequence to return to the console prompt.
2. On the line below, record the command you used to load the LAN driver.

_____

3. On the lines below, record the command you used to bind IPX to the LAN driver and supply a network address.

_____

_____

4. Enter the CONFIG command and record the following information about your network card and driver.

Network card hardware configuration including interrupt and I/O address:

_____

_____

Network address: _____

Frame type: _____

5. Return to the INSTALL module.

6. Select the option to create the STARTUP.NCF file. Record the contents of your STARTUP.NCF file below.

7. Where is the STARTUP.NCF file stored? _____

8. Save the STARTUP.NCF file. On the line below, write the name of the menu you return to after saving the file.

   _____

9. Select the options necessary to create the AUTOEXEC.NCF file and record the default contents of the file below.

10. Where is the AUTOEXEC.NCF file stored?

    _____

Exercise 5-2: Testing the Installation

For this exercise you need access to a file server console that you have recently installed or one that has been provided to you by your instructor. For each of the following console commands, briefly describe its purpose and why you might use it after performing an installation. In addition, try the command on the console and record the results in the table below.

Command	Purpose	Results
MEMORY		
MODULES		
PROTOCOLS		
DISPLAY SERVERS		
DISPLAY NETWORKS		

Exercise 5-3: Using WSGEN to Install NetWare on a Workstation

In this exercise you will use the WSGEN program to create a customized IPX.COM program that will allow your workstation to access the network file server. In order to do this exercise, you will need the following components, which will be supplied by your instructor:

- A workstation computer with a LAN card and floppy disk drive compatible with the WSGEN disk

- A copy of the WSGEN disk
- A copy of the documentation that was included with the workstation's network card
- The disk that was supplied with the network card (optional)
- The network card hardware settings (Your instructor might give you a copy of the network card manual with the card settings indicated and ask you to determine the hardware configuration given the jumper settings indicated in the diagram.)

Card Make and Model	Other Novell Cards Emulated	Interrupt	I/O Port	Memory Address

1. Use the documentation supplied by your instructor to fill in the following table with the configuration of your network card.

2. Insert the WSGEN disk in a floppy disk drive and change your default DOS prompt to that drive.

3. Enter the WSGEN command.

4. If your network card is not on the list and does not emulate one of the standard cards shown, press the Ins key and insert the disk that was supplied with your network card. The WSGEN program will attempt to read the driver files from the card's disk and display the driver in the window.

5. Select the correct network card and press **[Enter]**. Record the name of the card driver below.

   _____

6. Select the card configuration and press **[Enter]**. Record the configuration number and settings below.

   Configuration number: _____

   Interrupt: _____

   I/O Port: _____

   Memory address range: _____ to _____

7. WSGEN will now generate an IPX.COM for you. Where is the IPX.COM file stored after it has been created?

   _____

8. To inquire about the settings of a customized IPX program, enter the command IPX I. Use this command to confirm the IPX.COM file you have created. In the space below, record the results of the IPX I command.

9. Test your IPX program by doing the following:

- Create a DOS system disk.

- Copy the IPX and NETX programs onto this disk. Make sure the NETX program is the correct one for your version of DOS.

- Boot your workstation with your newly created DOS system disk.

- Run the IPX program. In the space below, record any messages you see.

- Run the NETX program. In the space below, record any messages you see.

- List two items you should check for if the NETX program cannot find the file server on an ethernet network.

_____

_____

Exercise 5-4: Using ODI Drivers to Install NetWare on a Workstation

In this exercise you will use the WSGEN program to create a customized IPX.COM program that will allow your workstation to access the network file server. In order to complete this exercise, you will need the following components, which will be supplied by your instructor:

- A workstation computer with a LAN card and floppy disk drive compatible with the WSGEN disk

- A copy of the WSGEN disk

- A copy of the documentation that came with the card

- The diskette that was supplied with the network card (optional)

- The network card hardware settings (Your instructor might give you a copy of the network card manual with the card settings indicated and ask you to determine the hardware configuration given the jumper settings indicated in the diagram.)

1. Use the documentation supplied by your instructor to fill in the following table with the configuration of your network card.

Card Make and Model	Other Novell Cards It Emulates	ODI Driver	Interrupt	I/O Port	Memory Address

To use ODI drivers to install NetWare on your workstation, perform the following steps:

2. Create a DOS system disk.

3. Change to the DOSODI subdirectory on the WSGEN disk and copy the necessary files to your system disk. In the table below, record the names of the files you copy along with their functions.

4. Copy the NETX program from the root of the WSGEN disk onto your system disk. Be sure the NETX program is the correct one for your version of DOS.

5. Boot your workstation with your newly created DOS system disk.

6. Run the necessary ODI driver programs. In the spaces below, record each ODI program you run along with any messages.

ODI Program	Messages
_____	_____
_____	_____
_____	_____
_____	_____
_____	_____

7. Run the NETX program. In the space below, record any messages you see.

8. List two items you should check for if the NETX program cannot find the file server on an ethernet network.

_____

_____

EXERCISES

Case 5-1: The Animal Health Center

The Animal Health Center has been using NetWare v2.2 for some time. Recently its file server computer was upgraded with NetWare v3.12. Briefly explain at least one reason why, in this situation, the WSGEN utility might need to be used.

In the space below, list one or more reasons why the Animal Health Center should upgrade to use the VLM modules.

Case 5-2: Installing VLM on a Workstation

After discussing the advantages and disadvantages of using VLMs, the Animal Health Center staff decided to convert their primary workstation to use VLMs. In this exercise, you will install the VLM software on the workstation. In order to do this exercise, you will need the following components, which will be supplied by your instructor.

- A workstation computer with a LAN card and a floppy disk drive compatible with the WSGEN disk
- Copies of the three CLIENT installation disks
- A copy of the documentation that came with the card

1. Use the documentation supplied by your instructor to fill in the following table with the configuration of your network card.

Card Make and Model	Other Novell Cards It Emulates	ODI Driver	Interrupt	I/O Port	Memory Address

2. Insert the DOS/WINDOWS client installation disk in a disk drive and type INSTALL.

3. Use the default values for each option unless your instructor tells you to use other options. In the space below, record the value you select for each option:

4. After the installation process is complete, record the contents of the NET.CFG file in the space below:

5. Test your installation by using the STARTNET command. Record any message below:

6.   Try changing to the F: network drive. In the space below, record the message you receive.

7.   Now reboot your workstation and run the STARTNET command a second time. Why is it necessary to reboot the workstation?

8.   Change to the first network drive and run the SLIST command.

9.   If no network drive exists, the VLM cannot find a file server. What are some items you should check?

SUPERIOR TECHNICAL COLLEGE PROBLEMS

The file server computer that you helped develops specification for in Chapter 3, has just been purchased and was installed by the vendor in the computer room. The vendor also installed network interface cards in all of your computers and provided you with documentation showing the card type and configuration. In addition, the cabling company has completed installing the necessary wire and has tested all connections to ensure they will work. In this project, you will simulate installing the NetWare operating system on the file server computer, as well as installing the client software on a workstation in order to log into the network.

Project 5-1: Simulated Server Installation

In this exercise you will simulate a NetWare file server installation by performing many of the processes on a DOS workstation assigned to you by your instructor. Although you will not actually load the SYSTEM and PUBLIC files or even attach your computer to the network, you will be able to review each of these steps and compare them to the installation screens provided in this chapter. Your instructor has set aside several megabytes of disk space on your workstation that have not been given to DOS. You will use this area to create a NetWare partition along with small SYS: and DATA: volumes.

Yesterday, Jake Pence from the Computer Technology Services company delivered and tested the file server computer for the Superior Technical College campus. Your objective today is to install NetWare v3.12 on the server and start attaching workstations. To complete this exercise you will need access to a workstation with the following specifications:

- An 80386SX or later computer with at least 4 Mbytes of RAM
- At least 8 Mbytes of disk space not assigned to the DOS partition
- A network interface card
- A copy of a NetWare System_1 disk
- A DOS boot disk containing the FDISK and FORMAT commands

Once you have verified that your work area contains these components, use the following steps to install NetWare and start up your file server computer.

Step 1: Fill out a file server worksheet

1. Use the diagram of the Superior Technical College network you created in Chapter 2. Label the diagram with the following information.

   ■ Name of each file server

   ■ Internal network number to be used for each server (Indicate RANDOM if you are going to let the installation process select a number for you.)

   ■ The network topology

   ■ The network card model and manufacturer

   ■ Ethernet frame type to be used

2. Obtain a copy of the file server worksheet from your instructor.

3. Fill in the identification section of the file server worksheet by supplying a valid name for your server.

4. Fill in the system information section of the Worksheet by identifying the type of disk controller card, drive information, and correct NetWare disk drive to be used. Your instructor will tell you where to obtain this information. You might need the documentation sheet included with the computer and system manuals.

5. Fill in the network card information section by reading the settings off the network card or using the network card handout provided by your instructor.

6. List any special file server hardware in the nonnetwork device information section of the worksheet and check that no hardware interrupt conflicts exist.

Step 2: Install the SERVER.EXE program

If you are installing NetWare v3.11, perform the following steps:

1. Create a directory on your DOS partition called SERVER.311.

2. Copy the System_1 disk into your SERVER.311 directory.

3. Change to the SERVER.311 directory, type the command **SERVER**, and press **[Enter]**. The SERVER program displays the message "LOADING...".

4. After the SERVER.EXE program is loaded, you are asked to enter the name of the file server. Enter the file server name and press **[Enter]**.

5. Enter the internal network number you recorded on the file server worksheet. The file server now displays its console prompt.

6. After the initial installation is complete, the SERVER program is started. In the space below, record the speed rating of the computer you are using.

   Speed rating: _____

If you are installing NetWare v3.12, perform the following steps:

1. If you are installing the NetWare v3.12 SERVER program from a CD-ROM, insert the NetWare v3.12 CD-ROM and check to be sure the CD-ROM drivers are loaded and that you can access the CD-ROM drive from the DOS prompt. Next, change your default DOS prompt to the NETWARE.312\ ENGLISH directory on the CD-ROM drive. If you are installing the

NetWare v3.12 SERVER program from floppy disks, insert the NetWare INSTALL disk in a drive and change your default DOS prompt to the drive containing the INSTALL disk.

2. Enter the INSTALL command and fill out the screens as described in this chapter. Record each option you select.

Size of existing DOS partition: _____

File server name: _____

Internal network number: _____

Source directory: _____

Destination directory: _____

Country code options: _____

Default name format: _____

Step 3: Disk system setup

In this step you will load the disk driver module, start the INSTALL program, create a NetWare partition, and then create one or more NetWare volumes.

1. Use the LOAD command to load the disk driver module you identified in step 1. In the space below, record the command you use along with the interrupt and I/O port address.

2. After the disk module is running, record the next step and the command you need to use.

Step: _____

Command used: _____

3. Create a NetWare partition. In the space below, record the steps you use.

4. Create a small SYS: volume leaving at least 2 Mbytes of disk space free for each of the other volumes as defined on the volume design forms in Chapter 4. The minimum volume size is 1 Mbyte. After you have created your volumes, use the Esc key to return to the main menu.

Step 4: Copy SYSTEM and PUBLIC files

In this step you will simulate copying the NetWare SYSTEM and PUBLIC files from CD-ROM to the required directories of the SYS: volume.

1. Use the hot-keys to return to the console prompt. Record the hot-key sequence below.

_____

2. Use the necessary NetWare console command to bring all the volumes you have created on line. Record the command(s) you use on the line below.

_____

3. In the space below, record the steps you need to perform to copy the SYSTEM and PUBLIC files from the CD-ROM or floppy disk drive to the NetWare directories.

4. When NetWare asks you to place the INSTALL disk in drive A: use the Esc key to exit and return to the Available System Options menu. (Performing this part of the installation would be a matter simply of inserting the correct disk at the prompt.)

Step 5: Completing the installation

In the space below, briefly identify each of the processes you will perform to complete the file server installation to the point where the server is available to the network and can be rebooted.

1. Use the hot-key sequence to return to the console prompt.

2. For this step in the installation process, your instructor will supply a disk containing the necessary NetWare LAN driver files. (During a complete installation, you would load the standard drivers directly because you would have copied them into the SYS:SYSTEM directory in step 4. Because you did not actually complete step 4 in this exercise, you will load the LAN drivers from floppy disks. It is the procedure you would follow if you were using a LAN driver that did not come with NetWare.) To load a LAN driver from floppy disk, use the command LOAD D:driver-name, where D: is the letter of the floppy disk drive containing the LAN drivers. On the line below, record the command you use to load the LAN driver.

_____

3. On the lines below, record the command you use to bind IPX to the LAN driver and supply a network address.

_____

_____

4. Enter the CONFIG command and record the following information about your network card and driver.

    Network card hardware configuration including interrupt and I/O address:

    Network address: _____

    Frame type: _____

5. Return to the INSTALL module.

6. Select the option to create the STARTUP.NCF file. Record the contents of your STARTUP.NCF file below.

7. Where is the STARTUP.NCF file stored?

    _____

8. Save the STARTUP.NCF file. What menu do you return to after saving the file?

    _____

9. Select the options necessary to create the AUTOEXEC.NCF file and record the default contents of the file below.

Project 5-2: Using MONITOR

Dave Johnson would like you to record the new file server's performance. Later, when the server starts to become more heavily used, the information can be used as a benchmark. Use the MONITOR utility to record the following statistics.

Percent utilization: _____

Original cache buffers: _____

Total cache buffers: _____

Percent of original cache buffers: _____

Packet receive buffers: _____

Directory cache buffers: _____

Service processes: _____

Project 5-3: Downing the File Server

Now that the server is running, you want to test your startup files to see if they can be restarted automatically. To down the server properly and return to the DOS prompt, you decide to follow the steps described in Novell NetWare 3.11/3.12 : Network Administrator. Record each of the commands you use to down the server in the spaces provided. (Make sure to prevent new users from logging in and send a message to all users informing them that the server will be going down soon.)

_____

_____

_____

_____

At this time you might want to reboot your computer and try restarting it as a file server. In the space below, record the results of restarting the server.

FILE SYSTEM UTILITIES

Once the file server installation is complete, it's time to set up the network file system. To perform this important task, you need to understand the NetWare commands and utilities that are used to create and maintain the NetWare file system. In Chapter 4 you were introduced to several NetWare commands that affect the directory structure: VOLINFO, CHKVOL, CHKDIR, NDIR, LISTDIR, NCOPY, and SESSION. In this chapter you will acquire some additional NetWare commands and utilities and study the NCOPY, NDIR, and SESSION commands in more detail.

There are five basic command groups: command line utilities, menu utilities, supervisor utilities, console commands, and NetWare Loadable Modules (NLMs). **Command line utilities (CLUs),** such as CHKVOL and LISTDIR, are commands that are executed from the DOS prompt; they can include parameters and options. Because CLUs are executed from the DOS prompt, they are readily available. They do not contain helpful menus, however, so you need to know which NetWare command to use and what its proper syntax is.

AFTER READING THIS CHAPTER AND COMPLETING THE EXERCISES YOU WILL BE ABLE TO:

- USE NETWARE COMMAND LINE UTILITIES AND MENU UTILITIES TO WORK WITH FILES AND DIRECTORIES IN THE NETWARE FILE SYSTEM.

- DESCRIBE THE USE OF NETWORK AND SEARCH DRIVE POINTERS.

- USE THE MAP AND SESSION UTILITIES TO CREATE NETWORK AND SEARCH DRIVE POINTERS TO DIRECTORIES WITHIN A FILE SYSTEM.

- ESTABLISH A DRIVE POINTER USAGE PLAN FOR YOUR NETWORK SYSTEM.

Menu utilities like VOLINFO and SESSION are interactive programs that contain menus and help messages that allow you to perform more complex tasks. They can be slower to use because they require you to leave the environment in which you are working in order to run the menu utility. **Supervisor utilities** are command line and menu utilities that are stored in the SYS:SYSTEM directory; they are used in system configuration and maintenance. In future chapters you will learn how to use the supervisor utilities to perform such network management tasks as checking system security and fixing system problems.

Console commands are used to perform functions on the file server console; these functions are built into the NetWare operating system. In Chapter 5 you used such console commands as SPEED, LOAD, MOUNT, BIND, MEMORY, CONFIG, BROADCAST and DOWN to perform activities at the file server console. In addition to the built-in console commands, functions such as network printing can be added to the NetWare file server by running NLMs. Chapter 5 discussed three different kinds of NLMs used during NetWare's installation:

- Disk drivers, such as IDE.DSK and ISADISK.DSK

- LAN drivers, such as TOKEN.LAN and NE2000.LAN

- Other NLMs, such as INSTALL and MONITOR

In Chapter 10 you will learn how to use additional console commands and NLMs to create a network printing environment. In Chapters 15 and 16 you will work with the NetWare file server console commands and NLMs to perform additional tasks such as backing up the file system and configuring the server for improved performance.

The information in this chapter is divided into two major sections: File and Directory Management and Drive Pointers. In the next section you will learn about applying certain DOS commands that you are already familiar with to the NetWare file system, working with NetWare command line utilities and options, and using powerful file system menu utilities: FILER, SALVAGE, and DSPACE. In the Drive Pointer section, you will learn about using the MAP command and SESSION menu utility with network drive pointers in order to facilitate information access in your file system. The Drive Pointers section also contains ideas on how to plan the drive pointer usage in your network system.

FILE AND DIRECTORY MANAGEMENT

In Chapter 4, you learned how to design the server's file system using volumes, directories, and subdirectories. In this section you will learn how to apply DOS and NetWare commands when creating and maintaining directories and files for your server. Because setting up and maintaining the file system is one of the important jobs you need to perform as a CNA, you need to be familiar with the NetWare commands and menu utilities that allow you to perform these functions. This section has three parts: DOS commands, NetWare command line utilities, and menu utilities.

DOS COMMANDS

Because of the NetWare VLM or NETX shell, many DOS commands you already use regularly can also be used to manipulate directories and files in NetWare volumes. In addition, the CD (change directory) command is enhanced by the NetWare shell, giving you more features when you access directories in NetWare volumes. DOS commands work with NetWare volumes through the drive letter that is assigned to that volume. When your workstation first loads the NetWare driver and shell, for example, the shell provides DOS with a drive letter, usually F, that is assigned to the SYS:LOGIN directory. This allows DOS to load and run the LOGIN.EXE program and provides you with access to the file server. Once you have logged into the file server, the network drive letter is reassigned by default to the root of the SYS: volume. After that, most DOS commands treat drive F just like another local hard disk. DOS commands such as FORMAT, CHKDSK, and SCANDISK, however, do not work on a network drive letter because these commands are designed to access and control a local disk drive directly and have no direct control of a NetWare volume.

As mentioned previously, the DOS CD command gains additional functionality when it works on a network drive. With NetWare, for example, you can use the CD command to change to another volume or even switch your default path to another file server by entering the complete NetWare path. An example of creating a new NetWare directory structure is shown in Figure 6-1. From your DOS experience you probably know how to use the CD.. command to move up one directory level on a local drive. When you use the CD command on a network drive letter, however, you can use multiple dots to move up more than one layer, as illustrated in the last CD command shown in Figure 6-1.

Figure 6-1

Using MD and CD commands

```
F:\>CD DATA:
F:\>MD FORMS
F:\>MD BUS
F:\>MD SALES
F:\>MD WORK
F:\>CD BUS
F:\BUS>MD IS
F:\BUS>CD IS
F:\BUS\IS>MD UTILITY
F:\BUS\IS>CD UTILITY
F:\BUS\IS\UTILITY>CD ...
F:\BUS>_
```

Although you can use the COPY, XCOPY, and DIR commands to copy and view file information, these commands do not work with complete NetWare paths because they do not recognize volume and file server names. In addition, these DOS commands yield less information and are less efficient than the corresponding NetWare command line utilities, which are designed to take advantage of enhanced NetWare capabilities. Use the NetWare command line utilities discussed in the next section rather than the standard DOS commands whenever you work with files stored in NetWare volumes.

NetWare Command Line Utilities

NetWare command line utilities are software tools specifically designed for the NetWare file system. This section contains a description and the syntax of each of these utilities and gives examples of applying them in a file system management situation. Utilities, such as LISTDIR, CHKDIR, CHKVOL, and RENDIR, that were already described in Chapter 4, need no additional explanation.

NCOPY command

Although the DOS COPY and XCOPY commands and the Windows File Manager can be used to copy files to and from NetWare drives, the NetWare NCOPY command is more efficient and powerful. This is due to the way the copy process is performed. When a DOS copy command or File Manager is used to transfer files between two locations on the file server, each block of the file is read from the source path and must therefore be transmitted to the workstation. The block is then written to the target directory, causing the data to be transmitted back to the file server. NCOPY improves on COPY or File Manager by working directly with the file server to transfer a file from one directory to another. The blocks do not need to be sent to the workstation and retransmitted back to the server. Instead, the transfer is performed internally at the file server; only the status information is transmitted to the workstation that submitted the copy request. If your network cable system is busy, NCOPY can make a noticeable improvement in performance over the DOS copy commands or File Manager for transferring large files.

Another feature of the NCOPY command that makes it more powerful for copying NetWare files than the DOS commands or Windows File Manager, is the way in which NetWare file attributes are handled. A **file attribute** is a flag, stored in the directory along with the file's name and location, that gives the file certain characteristics such as making it Read Only, Hidden, or Sharable. By default, the NCOPY command copies all the file attributes that are supported by the target server or local hard disk. The DOS copy command, in contrast, does not transfer NetWare file attributes. As shown in Figure 6-2, the syntax of the NCOPY command is similar to that of the DOS XCOPY command with the addition of the /C, and /I, options.

Figure 6-2

NCOPY command
syntax

NCOPY[source-path] filename [to] target-path /[options...]

Option	Description
/S	Copies the subdirectory structure, including all subdirectories and files, to the target path.
/E	Used with the /S option to create copies of any empty subdirectories in the target path.
/V	Verifies that each file created on the target path is identical to the source file.
/A	Copies only files that have the Archive attribute set. The archive attribute is set automatically whenever the data in a file is changed.
/M	Use this option if you want the NCOPY command to turn off the Archive attribute on the source file after successfully copying it to the target path.
/C	Copies files without including the attributes on the copied files. By default, NCOPY copies all attributes and name space information supported by the target server or local hard disk.
/I	Warns when the target device will not support the file attributes or name space information of a source file.

Figure 6-3 illustrates an NCOPY command to copy a file from the SYS: SOFTWARE\SP directory to the BUDGETS directory of the DATA: volume. The results of the NDIR commands shown at the top and bottom of the figure indicate that the file contains Read Only (RO) and Rename inhibit (R) attributes and that the attributes were copied along with the file.

Figure 6-3

Using the NCOPY
command

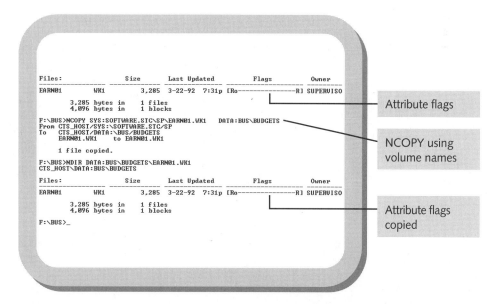

Figure 6-4 illustrates the results of copying the same file with the DOS XCOPY command. Notice that the NDIR command at the bottom of Figure 6-4 shows that the Netware file attributes, Read Only and Rename-Inhibit were not copied with the new file.

Figure 6-4

Using the
XCOPY command

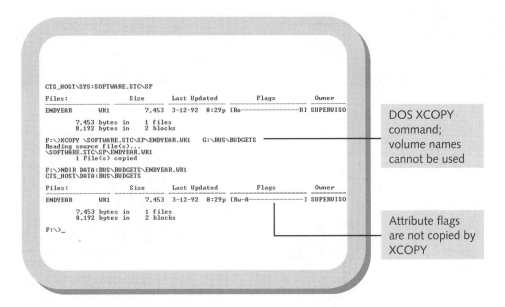

Figure 6-4

Using the
XCOPY command

You can use the /C option to prevent file attributes from being copied. Assume you want to create a new word processing form based on STAFF.DEV in the FORMS directory of the DATA: volume. You want to copy the STAFF.DEV form to your current directory and then alter its design. A file in the FORMS directory presumably has the Read Only file attribute flag set to protect it from inadvertent change or deletion. Because you want to alter STAFF.DEV, you do not want to copy the Read Only attribute when you copy the file. To copy STAFF.DEV from the FORMS directory into your current directory on drive F and give it a new name without any attributes, issue the following command:

F:\WORK>NCOPY DATA:FORMS\STAFF.DEV FACULTY.DEV /C

Like the XCOPY command, the NCOPY command can be used to copy to a new location an entire directory structure and all its files. For example, assume you are going out of town for a business meeting and would like to take a copy of all the files and subdirectories in your home directory structure along with you on your notebook computer. To copy all the directories and files from your home directory onto the notebook computer, use the following NCOPY command:

NCOPY DATA:BUS\USERS\yourname*.* C:\yourname*.* /S /E /I

In this case, the main advantage of the NCOPY command is its ability to copy the attributes along with each file's data. The /S and /E options cause the NCOPY command to create all the necessary subdirectories on the target path even if the source directory does not contain any files. Notice the use of the /I option to inform you of any file attributes that could not be transferred to the notebook computer.

NDIR command

Although the DOS DIR command works fine when used to display filename and size information on network disk drives, it does not recognize NetWare complete paths and displays DOS file information only. It does not display such information as the date the file was last updated or the NetWare file attribute information. The NDIR command displays the basic network information about files and directories and in addition can be used as a management tool that allows the network administrator to list, for example, files that have not been accessed for several months in sequence by file size or all files over 2 Mbytes in sequence by owner. The syntax for the NDIR command is shown in Figure 6-5.

Figure 6-5

NDIR command syntax

NDIR [path] [/option] [/FO] [/DO] [/SUB]

Parameter	Description
/FO	Displays only file information.
/DO	Displays only subdirectory information.
/SUB	Displays directory infomation for entire directory structure.
Sort Options	
/[REV] /SORT OW	Sorts in alphabetic sequence by owner name. Use the /REV parameter to sort from Z to A.
[/REV] /SORT SI	Sorts filenames in sequence from the smallest file to the largest. Use the /REV parameter to sort from largest to smallest.
[/REV] /SORT UP	Sorts filenames in sequence by last date updated starting from oldest to latest unless the /REV parameter is used.
[/REV] /SORT CR	Sorts filenames in sequence by file creation date starting from oldest to latest unless the /REV parameter is used.
[/REV] /SORT AC	Sorts filenames in sequence by last data accessed starting from oldest to latest unless the /REV parameter is used.
[/REV] /SORT AR	Sorts filenames in sequence by last date archived starting from oldest to latest unless the /REV parameter is used.
Format Options	
/DATES	Includes all the date information in the display.
/RIGHTS	Includes inherited and effective rights information in the display.
/HELP	Displays help information.
Attribute Options	**Possible attributes:**
[/NOT] /attribute	RO (Read Only), S (Sharable), A (archive), X (execute), H (hidden), S (system), T (transactional), I (indexed), P (purge), D (delete inhibit), R (rename inhibit)
Restriction Options	
/OW [NOT] EQ name	Displays all files created by the specified username.
/SI [NOT] GR|EQ|LE nnn	Displays all files with byte counts that are either greater than, equal to, or less than the number you specify.
/UP [NOT] BEF|EQ|AFT mm-dd-yy	Displays each file having a last creation update date that is either before, equal to, or after the date specified.
/CR [NOT] BEF|EQ|AFT mm-dd-yy	Displays each file having a creation date that is either before, equal to, or after the date specified.
/AC [NOT] BEF|EQ|AFT mm-dd-yy	Displays each file creation having a last access date that is either before, equal to, or after the date specified.

You can obtain a list of command options by entering a /? following the NetWare command. For example, NDIR/? will display all command options for the NDIR command.

You can optionally replace the NDIR [path] variable with either the full or partial NetWare path leading to the directory or file for which you want to display directory information. The /FO option lists files only; the /DO option lists subdirectories only. The /SUB option displays directory information for the entire directory structure including all subdirectories.

Several possible options are available for the [/option] parameter. The options are divided into four categories: sort options, format options, attribute options, and restriction options. **Sort options** allow you to specify the sequence of the directory listings including filename sequence, file size, and owner. Placing the /REV parameter ahead of the sort option sequences the listing in reverse order. Alphabetical sorts, such as filename or owner, are arranged from Z to A. Numerical sorts, such as file size, are arranged from largest to smallest. **Format options** allow you to specify the file information to be displayed by the NDIR command. To list more information regarding file creation and access dates, for example, you can include the /DATES option. **Attribute options** allow you display files that have one or more of the specified attributes. Use spaces to separate multiple attributes. (Information regarding the meaning of the file attributes will be provided in Chapter 8.) **Restriction options** are search parameters that cause NDIR to display information only for files that match the search criteria you specify. To view only files larger than 2 Mbytes, for example, you could include the /SI GR 2000000 (size greater than 2 million) option.

In addition to the /FO, /DO, and /SUB parameters, an NDIR command can consist of one sort option, one format option, one or more attribute options, and one or more restriction options. The slash (/) is required only before the first option; after that options can be separated by spaces.

One common use of the NDIR command is to locate a file when you do not know the complete filename or the directory in which it is located. Suppose, for example, you need to find a spreadsheet file and are quite sure the file's name starts with JAN, and that it is located in the DATA: volume, but you do not know the exact filename or directory path. To locate the file in the DATA: volume, you could enter the following NDIR command:

```
NDIR DATA:JAN*.WK1 /SUB
```

Another good use of the NDIR command is for listing files based on their size, access date, or owner. Assume, for example, the amount of free disk space on the DATA: volume has been gradually shrinking and you are concerned that users have been leaving large files on the server that are either no longer needed or should be copied to a backup medium. To get a printed list of all files over 90 Kbytes that have not been accessed during the last six months, you could use the following NDIR command:

```
NDIR DATA:*.* /SI GR 90000 /AC BEF 01/01/95 /SUB > PRN
```

The > PRN parameter is a DOS option that redirects the output of the NDIR command to the printer port rather than the display screen.

In addition to displaying only certain files, it is often important to sort the directory information by filename, size, or owner in order to make the directory listing more meaningful. The previous NDIR command, for example, might well yield a list that contains many files over 90 Kbytes that are owned by a number of different users. If you give each user a list of his or her files, you can ask users to back up and remove any files no longer needed. To create such a list, you can use the /SORT

OW option with NDIR. The results of executing the following NDIR command are shown in Figure 6-6.

```
NDIR DATA:*.*  /SI GR 90000 AC BEF 01/01/95 SORT OW SUB
```

Figure 6-6

Sample NDIR command

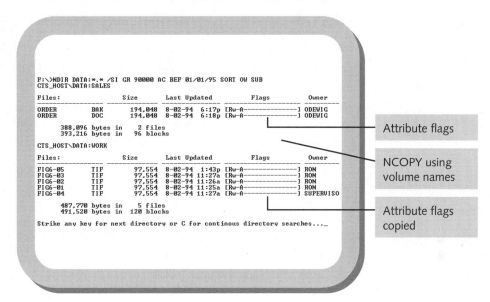

If you want to view information about dates, use the /DATES option with the NDIR command, as shown in Figure 6-7.

Figure 6-7

Using NDIR to display selected file information

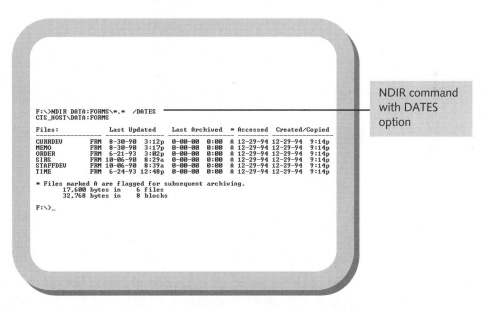

Another use of the NDIR command is to list files by attribute. To obtain a printout of all files in the SYS:SOFTWARE\SP directory that are not protected by the Read Only attribute, for example, use the attribute option along with the /NOT parameter, as shown in the following NDIR command. Then, using the FILER utility or the FLAG command (see Chapter 8), you can alter the file attributes. You can, for example, turn on the Read Only attribute.

```
NDIR SYS:SOFTWARE\*.*  /NOT /RO /SUB
```

The PURGE command

The PURGE command is used to make deleted file space in the specified path immediately available to the NetWare operating system; it permanently deletes the erased files. One reason to use this command is to improve the file server's performance when the disk volume is almost full. It is faster for the operating system to reuse the space from purged files than to search for the oldest deleted file space. Another reason to use the PURGE command is to prevent sensitive information that has been deleted from being salvaged and used.

The syntax of the PURGE command contains the directory path followed by the optional /ALL parameter as follows:

```
PURGE [path] [/ALL]
```

You can replace [path] with either a complete or partial NetWare directory path that contains the deleted files you want purged. If no path is specified, all deleted files in the current directory are purged. The /ALL option purges all files in the subdirectory structure within the path specified. To purge all files in the SYS:SOFTWARE\SP, SYS:SOFTWARE\WP, and SYS:SOFTWARE.DB directories, for example, enter the following command:

```
PURGE SYS:SOFTWARE /ALL
```

The VERSION command

If you have problems with a command or if you want to upgrade your operating system and utilities, you need to know the versions of the commands or utilities you are currently using. The VERSION command provides the date and version number information of the requested programs. To use the VERSION command, simply enter the command VERSION followed by the path and name of the command or utility you want to check. A network administrator often needs to check the version of the RPRINTER.EXE program that enables remote network printing. The following command displays the version of the RPRINTER program:

```
VERSION SYS:PUBLIC\RPRINTER.EXE
```

MENU UTILITIES

The NetWare menu utilities are tools that the system administrator uses to work interactively with the network file system. They allow the network administrator to perform such complex tasks as creating users and groups, salvaging files, restricting disk space, and managing file or directory information. To become a CNA, you need to know how to use these utilities to perform the file system tasks described in this section. All the NetWare menu utilities have a common, straightforward screen interface, including certain keys that perform the same function in all utilities. It is important to learn the key functions in the following list:

Key	Function
[Enter]	Selects an option or item and moves to the next menu level.
[Esc]	Returns back one level in the menu; often used to save the entry you have just completed.
[Ins]	Adds a new entry to a list.
[Del]	Removes an item from a list.
[F1]	Provides additional help information. Pressing the F1 key twice provides a list of keys and their functions.
[F3]	Used by most utilities. Allows you to change the highlighted item. When using the FILER utility, for example, you can use the F3 key to highlight and then change the name of a directory or file.
[F5]	Highlights multiple items in a list. Pressing [F5] a second time removes an item from the highlighted list. In the FILER utility, the F5 key can be used to delete several files from a directory; you mark each file and then press the Del key to delete all files at one time.
[Alt][F10]	This combination directly exits a menu utility without returning to the opening menu.

The NetWare menu utilities often present windows containing information such as a list of objects. If a window has a double-line border, it indicates that you can add, change, or delete objects in the window. If the window has a single-line border, you can view the objects, but you cannot change anything listed in the window. In the following sections you will learn about three menu utilities that play a major role in the NetWare file system: FILER, DSPACE, and SALVAGE.

The FILER utility

The FILER menu utility is the most complex of the file system utilities. It can perform many activities, including manipulating files and directories. It controls NetWare file system security by assigning trustee rights to users and sets attributes on files and directories. This section will give you an overview of the available FILER menu options, and then present examples to show you how to perform the functions. The FILER utility displays a warning if you attempt to perform a function that requires supervisor authority. This section identifies which functions require supervisor authorization.

To use the FILER utility, you first need to log in to the file server, preferably with supervisor rights, and then simply enter the command FILER. The directory path you start FILER from will become the current directory path displayed at the top of the FILER Available Topics window, as shown in Figure 6-8.

Figure 6-8

FILER Available
Topics menu

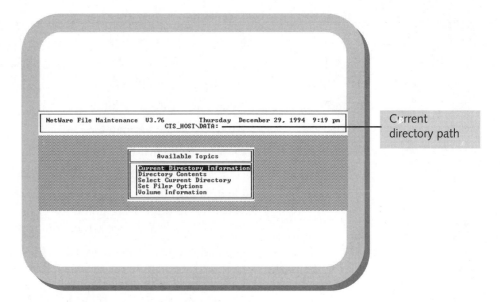

Figure 6-9

Directory Information
window

Current Directory Information. The Current Directory Information option allows you to view and change information in the current directory path displayed at the top center of the FILER window. Selecting this option opens the Directory Information window shown in Figure 6-9. The window has the following options:

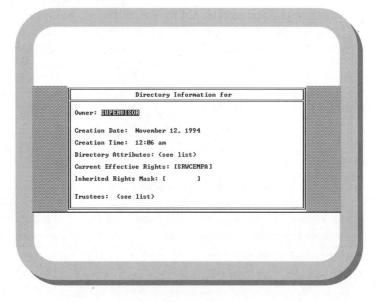

- The Owner field displays the name of the user who created the directory. Supervisor authority is required to change the information in this field.

- The Creation Date and Creation Time fields tell you when the directory was created and can only be changed if you are logged in with supervisor authority.

- The Directory Attributes field contains a pop-up list of all attribute flags assigned to this directory. View the pop-up window by placing the cursor on the field and pressing the Enter key. You can then use the Ins and Del keys to add and remove attributes from the list. You will learn how to use this field to set attributes in Chapter 8.

- The Current Effective Rights field shows your effective access rights in this directory. You cannot directly change the information in this field because it is dependent on the privileges assigned to your username as well as any trustee assignments granted to you or a group you belong to. The information in this field will be described in more detail in Chapter 8.

- The Inherited Rights Mask field contains a list of access rights that the directory will allow to flow into it from its parent directories. The use of this field will be described in Chapter 8.

- The Trustees field contains a pop-up window that lists all users and groups who have been assigned rights to this directory. The Ins and Del keys can be used to add and delete users as trustees of this directory. Assigning trustees to a directory will be explained in more detail in Chapter 8.

Directory Contents.   The Directory Contents option opens a window showing all subdirectories and files that are in the current directory path as displayed at the top of the FILER screen. You can use this option to work with any of the files or subdirectories contained in the current directory. To work with a subdirectory, for example, you first select it by highlighting it using the arrow keys. Then press the Enter key, which displays the Subdirectory Options menu shown in Figure 6-10.

Figure 6-10

Subdirectory Options menu

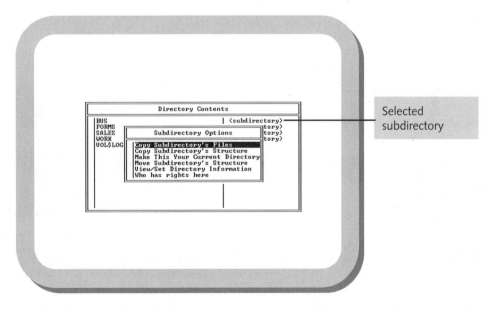

This menu has the following options:

- The Copy Subdirectory's Files option copies all files in the selected directory to the path you specify.

- The Copy Subdirectory's Structure option copies all files and subdirectories to the specified path.

- The Make This Your Current Subdirectory option allows you to change the current directory path displayed at the top of the FILER's screen to the selected subdirectory. The Directory Contents window will then display the subdirectories and files contained in the selected directory.

- The Move Subdirectory's Structure option allows you to relocate a portion of your directory to a different location in the directory structure. This can be very useful if you decide to change the organization of your directory structure.

- The View/Set Subdirectory Information option is an alternate way of displaying the Directory Information screen shown in Figure 6-9 for the selected subdirectory. It is faster to use this option than to change your current directory and then go back to the main menu and use the Current Directory Information option.

- The last option, Who has rights here, is a supervisor-only option that displays a list of all users who have access rights to the selected directory. This option is useful when you want to verify that a directory is secured for use by only the designated users.

The Directory Contents option also allows you to work with files. The File Options menu shown in Figure 6-11 is displayed whenever you select a file from the Directory Contents window and press the Enter key.

Figure 6-11

File Options menu

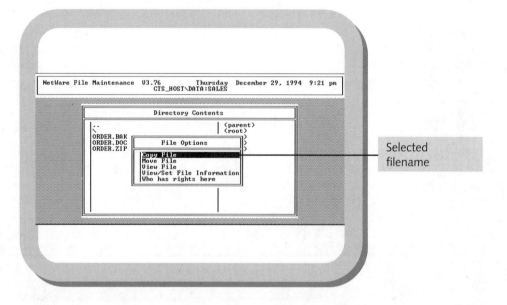

Selected filename

In addition to options for copying or moving files, the File Options Menu provides options for viewing a file's contents or working with a file's directory information. Selecting the Set/View File Information option displays the File Information window shown in Figure 6-12. The File Information window contains the following fields:

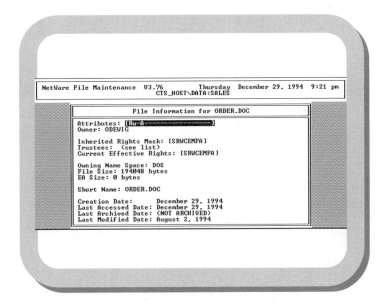

Figure 6-12

File Information
window

- The Attributes field allows you to add or remove attribute flags by displaying a window of existing attributes when you highlight the field and press the F3 (modify) key. You can then use the Ins and Del keys to add or remove file attributes. The use of the NetWare file attributes will be described in Chapter 8.

- The Owner field identifies the user who originally created the file. Only a supervisor can change the contents of the owner field. This is normally done if the name of the user who originally created the file is deleted from the system.

- The Inherited Rights Mask and Trustees fields function the same way they do in the Directory Information window shown in Figure 6-9.

- The Creation Date, Last Accessed Date, Last Modified Date, and Last Archived Date fields are for informational purposes and can be changed only by the supervisor.

- The Short Name and Current Effective Rights fields are for information purposes only and cannot be changed even by the supervisor. The Short Name field is the name of the file used internally by NetWare although the file can have a longer name used by workstations running Macintosh, NFS, and OS/2 operating systems.

If you want to work with several files, use the F5 key to highlight each file's name and then press the Enter key to obtain the Multiple File Operations window shown in Figure 6-13. This menu shows all options available to a supervisor, but if you do not have supervisor authority, your menu will not include the options to change owner or file date information.

Figure 6-13

Multiple File
Operations menu

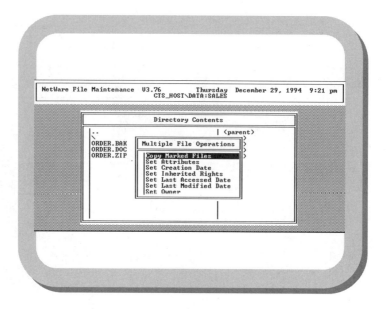

Select Current Directory. You can use the Select Current Directory option to change the current directory path shown at the top of the FILER screen. When FILER asks for the current directory path, you can either enter the complete path to the new location—server_name\volume:directory\subdirectory—or press the Ins key and then select each component of the directory path from a window, as shown in Figure 6-14. After all directories leading to the desired directory path have been selected, use the Esc key to exit the selection window and then press [Enter] to make the selected path your current work directory.

Figure 6-14

Select Current
Directory path

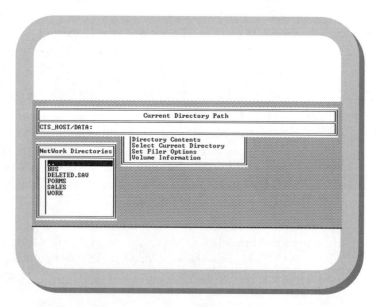

Set Filer Options. You can use the Set Filer Settings window, shown in Figure 6-15, to change FILER settings that control confirmation messages, attributes to be copied, file and directory patterns you want to display, and search attributes. One of the most commonly used fields in the Filer Settings window is the File Search

Attributes field. Normally the Directory Contents window does not show hidden files or system files and directories. To access them, select the File Search Attributes field to display the Search File Attributes window. To see hidden files and system files, add the Hidden and System attributes to the window by pressing the Ins key. This displays the Other Attributes window. Use the F5 key to highlight both the Hidden and System attributes. The selected attributes will be added to the Search File Attributes window after you press the Enter key. You can then use the Esc key to return to the Filer Settings window.

Figure 6-15

Filer Settings window

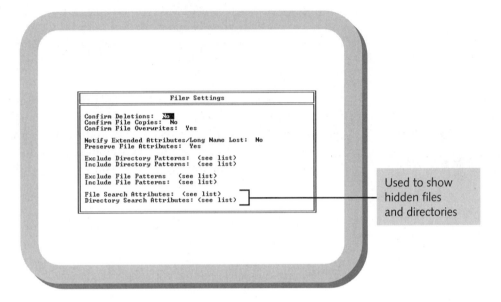

Used to show hidden files and directories

Volume Information.   The Volume Information option allows you to view volume information in the current volume, as shown in Figure 6-16. This window contains the same information displayed by the VOLINFO command and is included in FILER to allow you to view the available volume space without having to exit the FILER utility.

Figure 6-16

Volume Information window

Using FILER to copy or move a directory structure.   One of the powerful file management features of FILER is its ability to copy or move an entire directory structure easily from one location to another. No matter how good a job you do designing a directory structure, it is likely that at some point you will want to make modifications to the structure. This can entail moving a directory and all its files and trustee assignments from one location to another—a process you will need to know how to perform.

To copy or move a subdirectory structure, the Select Current Directory option is first used to select the current directory that contains the subdirectory you want to copy or move. The Directory Contents option from FILER's main menu is then used to display the current directory's files and subdirectories. After you select the subdirectory you want to move, FILER displays the Subdirectory Options menu shown in Figure 6-10.

From this menu you can use the Copy Subdirectory Structure option or the Move Subdirectory option to copy or move the selected directory along with all its file and subdirectories to the location you specify in the target path. After you select the target path, FILER copies all the files and subdirectories from the source subdirectory into the target location you specified. If you select the move option, FILER deletes the source files and subdirectory structure after they are successfully copied to the new location.

Using FILER to copy multiple files.   Although FILER is not the fastest or easiest way to copy files, it is often convenient for the network administrator to use it rather than exit the FILER program, perform the copy process, and then restart FILER to continue working with the file system. To copy files using FILER, the Select Current Directory option is first used to change the current directory to point to the path containing the files you want to copy. Next, select the Directory Contents option to view all subdirectories and files. Use the F5 key to highlight each of the files you want to copy and press [Enter] to display the Multiple File Operations menu, shown in Figure 6-13. Select the Copy Marked Files option and enter the target path to which you want the selected files to be copied. After a valid target path is entered, the selected files are copied into the specified directory.

Using FILER to delete files from a directory.   Deleting files from a directory is similar to copying files. You first change to the current directory containing the files to be deleted, use the Directory Contents option to display all filenames, mark the target files using the F5 key, and press [Del]. You can then select Yes in the Confirm File Deletion window to delete the marked files.

Using FILER to create a directory structure.   FILER allows you to create new subdirectories. The Select Current Directory option is used to select the directory path in which you want to make a new subdirectory. Use the Directory Contents option to display all existing files and subdirectories. To create a new subdirectory, simply press the Ins key and enter the subdirectory name. The new subdirectory appears in the Directory Contents window.

To create subdirectories within the newly created directory, select the newly created directory and press [Enter] to display the Subdirectory Options menu. You can then use the Make This Your Current Directory option to make the newly created directory the current directory. The Ins key can then be used to create subdirectories within the new directory.

Using FILER to rename a directory.   There are times when the name of a directory no longer fits its use or when it conflicts with other directory and filenames. As a CNA you might need to change the name of a user's home directory or the user's login name. You can easily change directory and filenames in FILER by first using the Select Current Directory option to change to the directory containing the target subdirectory. You then use the Directory Contents screen to display the existing files and subdirectories. To change the name of an existing file or subdirectory, simply highlight it and press the F3 key. You can then use the Backspace key to erase the existing name and enter a new name. After you press [Enter], the new subdirectory or filename is displayed in the Directory Contents window.

Using FILER to delete a directory structure.   When revising a directory structure or cleaning up a file server's volume, you sometimes need to delete an entire directory structure, including files and subdirectories. Before you do this, be absolutely certain that any files you or your users need have been backed up or moved to another directory. (Of course, there is a law that says whenever you throw something away you almost immediately find a use for it. If this happens with a file that you delete, you can use the SALVAGE utility described later in this section to recover it from the trash.)

To delete a directory structure, you must first use the Select Current Directory option to change the current directory path to point to the directory or volume that contains the directory structure to be deleted. Next select the Directory Contents option to display all subdirectories and files in the current directory. You can then highlight the target subdirectory and press the Del key or use the F5 key to mark multiple subdirectories to be deleted and then press [Del]. FILER displays the Delete Subdirectory Options menu, giving you the option of deleting the entire subdirectory structure or deleting the subdirectory's files only. The Delete Subdirectory's Files Only option removes all files from the subdirectory but does not delete lower subdirectories or their files. To delete the entire subdirectory structure and all files, highlight the Delete Entire Subdirectory Structure option and press [Enter]. FILER then displays a confirmation box, as shown in Figure 6-17. To delete the entire subdirectory structure and all files, highlight Yes and press [Enter]. The entire subdirectory structure is removed from the volume.

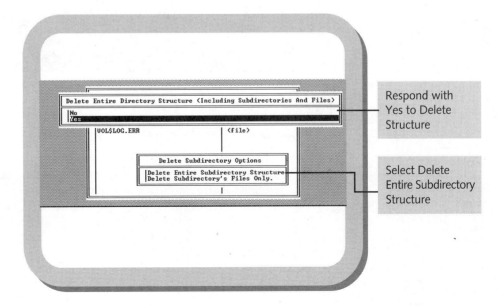

The DSPACE utility

The DSPACE utility allows the network administrator to restrict the amount of disk space available either to a user or to a directory structure. Restricting disk space by user means that in a specific volume the space that can be occupied by files owned by that user is limited. This method of limiting disk space requires supervisor authority.

Restricting disk space by directory structure allows the network administrator to place a limit on how much space a directory, including all its subdirectories and files, can occupy. This option can be used to ensure that disk space allocated during the planning stage is not exceeded by any group or department. The following examples show how a CNA can use the DSPACE utility to restrict disk space both by username and by directory structure.

Using DSPACE to restrict a user's disk usage. Suppose you want to limit to 50 Mbytes per user the amount of disk space used in a volume. You first log into the file server with a username that has supervisor authority and then run the DSPACE utility to display the Available Options menu, shown in Figure 6-18. To restrict the amount of disk space for a user, select the User Restrictions option. This displays a window listing all users on the file server. Highlighting a single username and pressing [Enter] displays a window showing all mounted volumes. Next, select the volume where you want to restrict disk space and press [Enter] to display the User Disk Space Limitation window, shown in Figure 6-19.

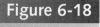

Figure 6-18

DSPACE Available Options menu

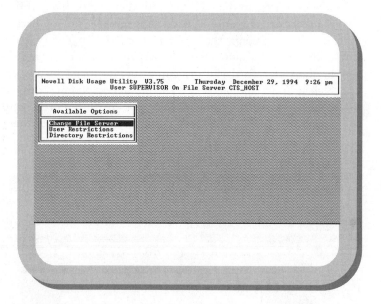

If the User Disk Space Limitation Information window has a single-line border, it means you can only view the information. You do not have the necessary privileges to change user restrictions.

Figure 6-19

User Disk Space
Limitation Information
window

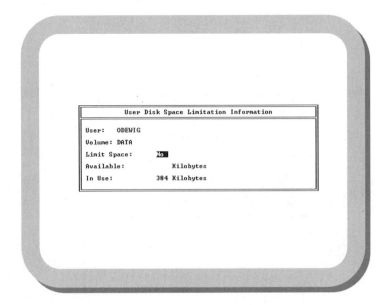

```
      User Disk Space Limitation Information
 User:    ODEWIG
 Volume: DATA
 Limit Space:     No
 Available:          Kilobytes
 In Use:        384 Kilobytes
```

To limit the disk space available to the selected user, press the Enter key and change the No in the Limit Space field to Yes. Press [Enter] a second time to save your entry and move the cursor to the Available field. In the available field, you specify the number of kilobytes (1024 bytes) available to the user. The default entry is 1024 Kbytes, which is equal to 1 Mbyte. To restrict the user to 50 Mbytes, press [Enter], type the number 50000, which is approximately equal to 50 Mbytes, and press [Enter] again to update the field. You can then use the Esc key to save your entry and return to the volumes window. The selected user is now restricted to approximately 50 Mbytes of disk space.

Using DSPACE to limit a directory structure. In many directory structures it is important to restrict a department or an application to the amount of disk space you planned for it. (The planning process is described in Chapter 4.) Restricting the amount of disk space used by a directory structure can prevent a department or application from consuming more than its allocated disk space. To restrict the amount of disk space available to a directory structure, you first need to log in as a supervisor or user who has all rights to the directory you want to restrict. Start the DSPACE utility and select the Directory Restrictions option from the Available Options menu. Next, enter the path to the directory on which you want to place a restriction. As in FILER, a directory path can be entered by either typing the complete path or by using the Ins key to select the path. After you have entered the path to the directory you want to restrict, press the Enter key to display the Directory Disk Space Limitation Information window, shown in Figure 6-20.

To restrict this directory, press [Enter] and change the Limit Space field from Yes to No. Press [Enter] a second time to exit the field and move the cursor to the Directory Space Limit field. In the Directory Space Limit field, you specify the number of kilobytes to which the directory will be limited. To change the Directory Space Limit field, press [Enter] and type the number of kilobytes you want to be used as the space limit for this directory. Remember, approximately 1000 Kbytes equals 1 Mbyte. To limit the space to 100 Mbytes, you would enter the number 100000. To save the restriction and return to the Available Options menu, press the Esc key. The selected directory will now be limited to approximately 100 Mbytes of disk space.

Figure 6-20

Directory Disk Space
Limitation Information
window

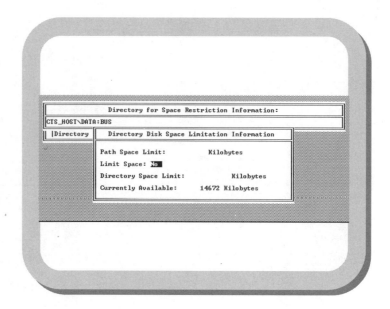

The SALVAGE utility

The purpose of the NetWare SALVAGE utility is to recover files that have been deleted from NetWare directories. The SALVAGE utility will *not*, however, recover files deleted on local DOS drivers. As explained previously, unless a file is purged, the NetWare file server does not immediately use the space from the deleted file. Instead it tracks the deleted file information and only uses a deleted file's space after the space from all files that have been deleted previously has been reused. Knowing how to use the SALVAGE utility is not only a requirement for being certified as a CNA; it can also make you a hero in the eyes of network users by "magically" recovering a valuable file.

In this section you will learn how to use the SALVAGE utility to recover files that have been deleted from an existing directory and even to recover files after their directory is removed. To recover deleted files, you need only the Create and File Scan access rights in the directory in which the deleted file was stored. (This means a CNA can train his or her users to salvage their own files.) To run the SALVAGE utility, simply type SALVAGE from a NetWare drive letter and press [Enter]. The SALVAGE utility uses as the current directory the directory path from which it is started. The current path is displayed at the top of the menu screen, as shown in Figure 6-21.

The Salvage From Deleted Directories option is used to recover a file after the directory it was stored in is deleted. The DELETED.SAV directory is a hidden directory that exists on the root of each volume and is used to contain files that have been deleted from directories that no longer exist. Using this option allows you to search the DELETED.SAV directory for the file you want to recover. Files of the same name can exist in the DELETED.SAV directory. Because each file is stored with its deletion data and time, files with identical names can be identified with this information.

The Select Current Directory option can be used to change the current directory path displayed at the top of the SALVAGE screen. Before recovering a file from an existing directory, you must first make the directory from which the file was deleted the current directory.

Figure 6-21

SALVAGE Utility Main
Menu Options window

Set Salvage Options allows you to specify in what sequence you want SALVAGE to display the deleted files. Possible salvage options include the following:

- By Deletion Date lists first those files deleted most recently. This is handy when you are not sure of the name of the deleted file.

- By Deletor sorts the list by the name of the user who deleted the file.

- By File Size lists first the largest deleted files.

- By File Name, the default sequence, is suitable when you know the name of the file that you want to recover.

The View/Recover Deleted Files option displays information about deleted files in the current directory path and allows you to recover any desired files.

Salvaging a deleted file from an existing directory. To salvage a deleted file from an existing directory, first use the Select Current Directory option of the SALVAGE main menu to change to the directory that contains the deleted file. As with the FILER and DSPACE utilities, you can either enter the complete directory path or use the Ins key to select each directory component starting with the name of the file server and volume. Next select the View/Recover Deleted Files option to display the Erased File Name Pattern to Match window. In this window you can enter a search pattern, such as *.WK1, to view all deleted files with the .WK1 extension, or leave the default global name (the asterisk) to display all deleted files. The SALVAGE utility will next display the Salvageable File window, showing all files that can be recovered from this directory in the sequence specified by the Salvage Options selection in effect. You can either highlight a single file and press [Enter] or use the F5 key to highlight all the files you want to recover and then press the Enter key.

After you select the files to be recovered, the Recover ALL Marked Files window is displayed, as shown in Figure 6-22. Press [Enter] to select Yes. All the files you have marked will be returned to the current directory. If there is a file in the directory using the same name as the deleted file, SALVAGE will ask you to specify a new name for the file that is being recovered.

Figure 6-22

Recovering deleted files

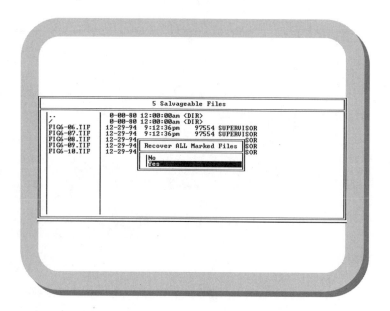

Recovering files from deleted directories.   When a directory is removed, all files in the directory are moved to the DELETED.SAV directory on the root of the volume. Because supervisor privileges are needed in order to access this directory and recover its files, you will need to log in to the file server with a username that has supervisor status prior to recovering files from any deleted directories.

To use the SALVAGE utility to recover a file from a directory that has been deleted, first use Set Salvage Options to select the sort option that will make it easy to spot the target files from the potentially large list of files from other deleted directories. Next select the Salvage From Deleted Directories option. SALVAGE displays a window showing the names of all mounted volumes. Select the name of the volume that contained the files you want to recover and press [Enter] to display the Erased File Name Pattern to Match window. If you know the file's name or extension you can enter it at this time or press the Enter key to accept the global character and display all files from deleted directories. The SALVAGE utility next displays the Salvageable Files window, listing all files in sequence by the salvage option you selected. You can salvage a single file by highlighting the file's name and pressing [Enter] or you can use the F5 key to mark multiple files to be recovered and press [Enter]. After salvaging, the recovered files are placed in the DELETED.SAV directory. You then use the NCOPY command to copy the recovered files from the DELETED.SAV directory to the directory path where they will be used.

DRIVE POINTERS

In both NetWare and DOS environments, drive pointers play an important role in the accessing of files located on different devices and directories. A **drive pointer** is a letter of the alphabet that is used to reference storage areas in the file system. By default, DOS reserves the first five drive pointers (A - E) to reference storage devices on the local workstation. These letters are therefore often referred to as **local drive pointers**. Letters A and B are reserved for floppy disk drives, C and D are normally used for hard disks, and E is often reserved for a CD-ROM or other external storage device. When using a local drive pointer, you can use the DOS CD command to change the pointer to access any directory on that drive.

In a NetWare environment, the network administrator is responsible for establishing the drive pointers to reference software and data locations within the directory structure. These drive pointers must be assigned properly so that DOS and other non-NetWare applications can access network files and directories as if they were on a local hard disk. In this section you will learn about the various types of drive pointers and their use, along with how to assign drive pointers using NetWare's MAP command line utility and SESSION menu utility.

NETWORK DRIVE POINTERS

In the NETX shell, the drive pointer environment is divided into **local drive pointers** that are controlled by DOS and **network drive pointers** controlled by NetWare. The division between the two sets of drive pointers is controlled by the LASTDRIVE= statement in a workstation's CONFIG.SYS file. The default value for the LASTDRIVE= statement is E, giving DOS control of drives A through E. The NETX shell controls the remaining drives, F – Z. The shell program assigns the first network drive letter, by default F, to the SYS:LOGIN directory of the file server to which the workstation is attached.

The VLM requester software works with DOS to share drive pointers, eliminating the need to set aside separate drive pointers for NetWare uses. To allow NetWare and DOS to use all drive pointers (A – Z), you need to place the LASTDRIVE=Z: statement in the CONFIG.SYS file. When the shell first starts, the drive pointer to be assigned to the SYS:LOGIN directory of the attached file server is specified in the FIRST NETWORK DRIVE = statement of the NET.CFG file, as described in Chapter 5.

NetWare drive pointers can be one of three types: regular, root, or search. Regular and root drive pointers are usually assigned to directories containing data files; search drive pointers are assigned to network software directories. A **regular drive pointer** is assigned to a directory path and shows all directories and subdirectories leading to the storage area. A regular drive pointer should be assigned to each volume as well as to commonly used directories. This allows application software packages that cannot use NetWare complete paths to access the data in any volume.

A **root drive pointer** appears to the user or application as if the default path is at the root of the drive or volume. Figure 6-23 shows an example of two drive pointers, G and H, used to access the same directory area. Notice that the G drive pointer is a regular pointer because it shows the entire path leading to the directory, whereas H is a root drive pointer that appears as if it were the first level in the directory structure. Both drive pointers are assigned or mapped to the directory and, as you can see in the figure, have access to the same files. The advantage of the root drive pointer is that it prevents the mapping of the drive pointer from being changed by an application or DOS command to some other location in the directory structure. Root drive pointers are normally used to access user home directories along with shared data directories.

Figure 6-23

Regular and
root drive pointers

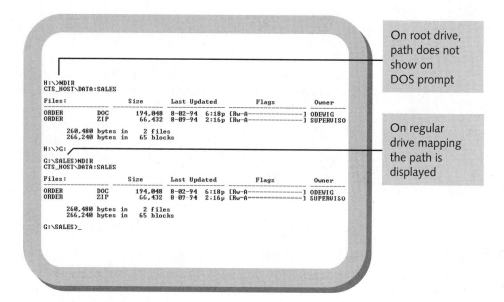

On root drive,
path does not
show on
DOS prompt

On regular
drive mapping
the path is
displayed

A **search drive pointer** is a regular or root drive pointer that has been added to the
DOS path. The DOS path specifies a sequence of locations in which DOS and the
NetWare shell will look for program files that are not in the current directory. Search
drive pointers play a very important role in accessing the file system because they
allow a network administrator to place data files in directories that are separate from
the application software. This enables a user or application located in one directory
path to access software and data located elsewhere in the directory structure. Search
drive pointers should be assigned only to software directories that need to be accessed
from other locations.

Windows applications do not need to use search drives because the
path to the windows application is provided in the application icon
parameters. As a result, the more workstations that become window
environments, the less need there will be for NetWare search drives.

When you enter the command FILER, for example, DOS first determines that the
command is not one of its internal commands. DOS looks in the current directory
for a program or batch file named FILER. If none exists in the current directory, each
search drive specified in the path will be searched, starting with S1 until either the
FILER program is found, or the message "Bad command or filename" is displayed.
You are able to run the FILER menu utility in addition to other NetWare commands
from any directory in the file system because a search drive pointer is automatically
assigned to the SYS:PUBLIC directory during the login process.

Search drives are assigned the letter S followed by a sequential number, from S1 to
S16, and each search drive can point to only one directory location. Subdirectories of
that directory location are not searched unless they are assigned to separate search
drives. In addition to being assigned a sequence number, search drives are given a

drive pointer; Z is assigned to S1, Y to S2, X to S3, and so on. Figure 6-24 illustrates the division of drive pointers between local, regular, and search.

Using search drives is more efficient than using only the DOS path, because search drives allow the requester to work directly with the network, avoiding the need to go through DOS for each search. Search drives also make it easier for the network administrator to add, change, or remove directories from the search sequence using the MAP or SESSION utilities rather than retyping the entire path statement as is necessary in the DOS environment.

Figure 6-24

Drive pointer usage chart

Network and Search Drive Pointers

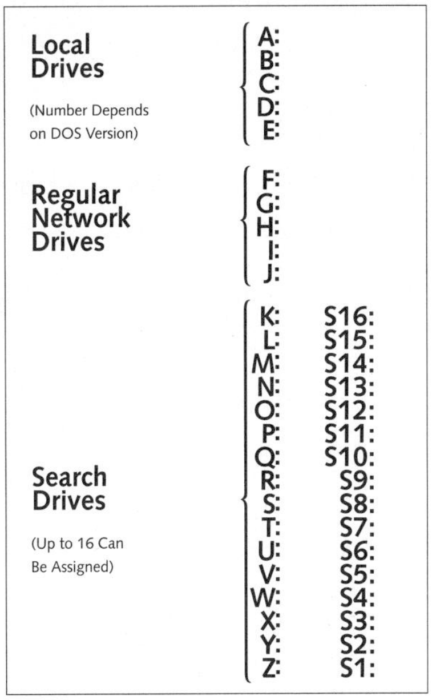

Local Drives (Number Depends on DOS Version)	A: B: C: D: E:	
Regular Network Drives	F: G: H: I: J:	
Search Drives (Up to 16 Can Be Assigned)	K: L: M: N: O: P: Q: R: S: T: U: V: W: X: Y: Z:	S16: S15: S14: S13: S12: S11: S10: S9: S8: S7: S6: S5: S4: S3: S2: S1:

Drive mappings are kept in a table stored in each workstation's RAM. Any changes made using the MAP or SESSION commands are effective only as long as the user is logged into the network. If you want certain drive pointers to be available each time you log in, you can place them in a login script command file. Because each work-station keeps track of its own drive pointers in memory, the same drive pointer can point to different directory locations in different workstations. For example, one workstation can have the F drive pointer mapped to the SYS:PUBLIC directory and its S3 search drive mapped to SYS:SOFTWARE\WP. Another workstation on the network might have the F drive pointer mapped to the DATA: volume and the S3 search drive mapped to the SYS:SOFTWARE\SP directory.

The MAP and SESSION utilities are the major tools used by a network administra-tor to establish and maintain drive pointers. MAP is a command line utility that can be used in login scripts as well as from the DOS prompt. SESSION is a menu utility, which means it can easily manipulate drive pointer assignments. To become a CNA, you need to know how to use the MAP and SESSION utilities to maintain network drive pointers. Additionally, planning and implementing a proper set of network and search drive pointers are important steps in setting up a successful network environment. Later in this section you will read some tips and suggestions for organizing drive pointer usage for your file system.

MAP COMMAND

MAP is a versatile command line utility that is used by network administrators to create, modify, and delete both regular and search drive pointers. This section will help you to learn the required CNA tasks in the following list by describing the purpose of each task, the syntax of the associated MAP command, and an example of its use.

- View current drive mappings
- Create regular drive pointers
- Create root drive pointers
- Change drive pointer mappings
- Create search drive pointers
- Remove a drive pointer
- Change a search drive path

Viewing current drive mappings

Viewing drive mappings allows you to determine the regular and search drive letters that are in use on a network along with the directory paths each drive pointer is assigned to. If a user is unable to access a software application or data file, you should use this command to check that the user's drive pointers are mapped to the correct locations in the directory structure.

Typing the MAP command without any parameters displays all drive pointers and their assigned directory locations, as shown in Figure 6-25. Notice that the drive mappings shown in the figure are divided into regular drive mappings followed by search drive mappings. Root drive pointers are designated by a backslash following the drive pointer's path. From this information you can determine the following:

- Drive pointers A through E are assigned to local disks and controlled by DOS.
- Drive F is a regular drive pointer assigned to the root of the SYS: volume.
- Drive pointer Z is designated as SEARCH1 and is assigned to the SYS:PUBLIC directory.
- Drive Y is designated SEARCH2 and is assigned to the DOS 6.2 subdirectory.

Figure 6-25

Viewing drive mappings

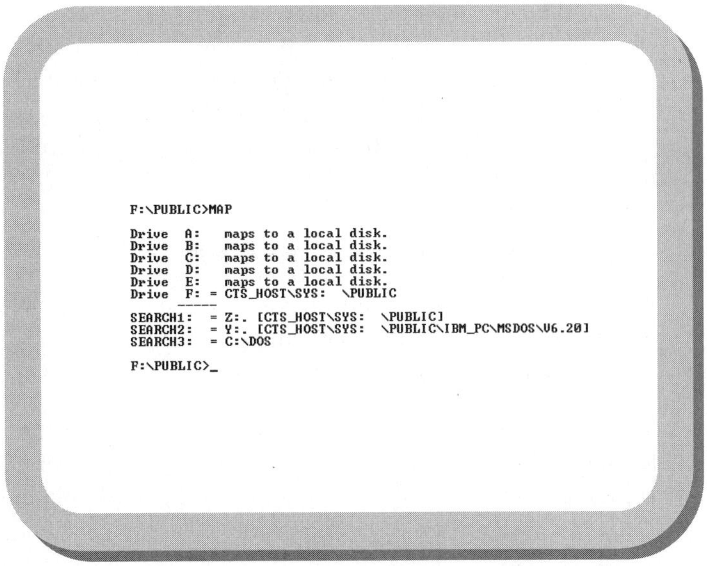

```
F:\PUBLIC>MAP

Drive  A:   maps to a local disk.
Drive  B:   maps to a local disk.
Drive  C:   maps to a local disk.
Drive  D:   maps to a local disk.
Drive  E:   maps to a local disk.
Drive  F: = CTS_HOST\SYS:  \PUBLIC

SEARCH1:  = Z:. [CTS_HOST\SYS:   \PUBLIC]
SEARCH2:  = Y:. [CTS_HOST\SYS:   \PUBLIC\IBM_PC\MSDOS\V6.20]
SEARCH3:  = C:\DOS

F:\PUBLIC>_
```

Drive pointer assignments are initially established for a user when the user logs in. The assignments are made with MAP commands contained in the login script files. A **login script** is a file containing NetWare commands that the LOGIN.EXE program follows when a user successfully logs in to a file server. When a user does not have a personal login script file, the LOGIN program uses default commands to establish the drive mappings shown in Figure 6-25.

Creating regular drive pointers

The MAP command allows you to create regular drive pointers by assigning a NetWare path to a drive letter. Regular drive pointers are important for two reasons:

1. They make it easier to access data files because you do not need to supply a long path.

2. They allow applications and DOS commands that are not designed to work with complete NetWare paths to access files in multiple volumes or multiple file servers.

Suppose your home directory is located in the DATA: volume and your current directory is SYS:SOFTWARE.STC\SP. In order to copy several files from the SYS:SOFTWARE.STC\SP subdirectory into the \BUS\BUDGETS subdirectory using only the F drive pointer, you would need to enter the following NCOPY commands containing the NetWare path:

F:\SOFTWARE.STC\SP>NCOPY JAN95.WK1 DATA:BUS\BUDGETS

As you can see, if you had to copy several files from the directory, this method would entail much typing—and a greater possibility of errors. Using the MAP command to create a separate drive pointer (G) to the BUDGETS directory makes this job a lot easier. The NCOPY command now looks like this:

F:\SOFTWARE\STC\SP>NCOPY JAN95.WK1 G:

To use the MAP command to create a new drive letter, enter the command MAP [drive]:=[path], where [drive] can be any letter of alphabet (A - Z). You can replace the [path] with either a complete or partial NetWare path leading to the target directory. If you omit the path, the MAP command will assign the specified drive pointer to the current path. For example, to assign drive L to the DATA:BUS directory on the CTS_HOST server, use the following MAP command to specify a complete path:

```
F:\>MAP L:=CTS_HOST\DATA:BUS
```

If the current drive (F) is already assigned to the DATA: volume of the CTS_HOST server, you can specify the following partial path:

```
F:\>MAP L:=\BUS
```

You can also use an existing drive mapping as part of the path, as shown in the following command, which assigns the drive letter G to the DATA:BUS\BUDGETS\1995 directory by using the L drive pointer, which is mapped to the DATA:BUS directory as starting point.

```
F:\>MAP G:=L:BUDGETS
```

Notice that there is no slash between the drive letter (G) and the path (BUDGETS). Placing a slash in the command would cause the system to search the root of the DATA: volume for the BUDGETS directory. Because no BUDGETS directory exists in the root of the DATA: volume, an error message indicating an invalid path would be displayed.

You can assign the current path to a different drive pointer by entering the MAP command without specifying a path following the equal sign. The following command makes G and I both point to the same location in the directory structure:

```
G:\BUS\BUDGETS>MAP I:=
```

If you use a local drive pointer (A - E), the MAP command asks if you want to override the local pointer with a network path. If you answer yes, the local drive pointer will access the network path rather than the local drive. This can be useful, for example, when a software package cannot use drive letters after E.

The MAP NEXT [path] command can be used to assign the specified path to the next available drive letter, proceeding from F through Z. This command is useful when you want to map an unused drive letter to a directory path and you do not care what letter is used. Suppose, for example, you have the drive mappings shown in Figure 6-26 and you want to map a drive to the USER subdirectory of the BUS directory. The MAP NEXT command, as shown in the figure, maps the next available drive letter, in this case H, to the USER subdirectory.

Figure 6-26

Mapping regular
drive pointers

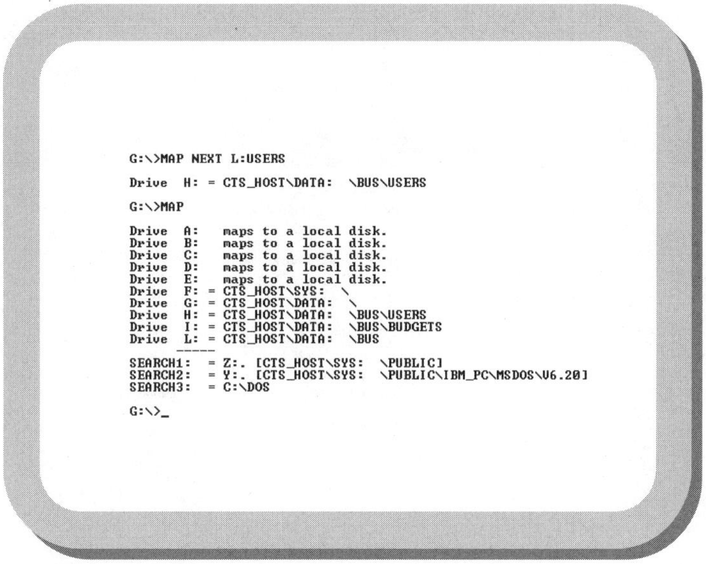

```
G:\>MAP NEXT L:USERS

Drive  H: = CTS_HOST\DATA:  \BUS\USERS

G:\>MAP

Drive  A:    maps to a local disk.
Drive  B:    maps to a local disk.
Drive  C:    maps to a local disk.
Drive  D:    maps to a local disk.
Drive  E:    maps to a local disk.
Drive  F: = CTS_HOST\SYS:   \
Drive  G: = CTS_HOST\DATA:  \
Drive  H: = CTS_HOST\DATA:  \BUS\USERS
Drive  I: = CTS_HOST\DATA:  \BUS\BUDGETS
Drive  L: = CTS_HOST\DATA:  \BUS

SEARCH1:  = Z:. [CTS_HOST\SYS:  \PUBLIC]
SEARCH2:  = Y:. [CTS_HOST\SYS:  \PUBLIC\IBM_PC\MSDOS\V6.20]
SEARCH3:  = C:\DOS

G:\>_
```

Creating root drive pointers

A root drive pointer appears to the user or application program as if the drive pointer is at the beginning of a drive or volume. Root drive pointers are useful for two main reasons.

1. Many applications access files only from the root of a directory path. This can be a problem for a network administrator because users are not usually given rights to the root of a volume and also because you might want to keep the application contained in a certain directory in the structure. NetWare v3.x solves this problem by allowing the network administrator or users to map a drive to a "fake" root containing the application.

2. Root drive pointers make it more difficult for a user or application to change the drive pointer to another location inadvertently. For example, if a user's home directory is mapped to a regular drive pointer and the user issues a CD \ command, the mapping of the drive pointer is changed to the root of the current volume. Root drive mappings on the other hand appear to DOS as the beginning of a drive, causing CD \ to return to the directory to which the root drive is mapped to rather than going to the root of the volume.

The command syntax for mapping a root drive is the same as the syntax for creating a regular drive pointer except that the ROOT option precedes the drive letter.

MAP ROOT drive:=[path]

Figure 6-27 shows an example of mapping H as a root drive to a user's home directory and mapping L as a regular drive pointer to the DATA:BUS directory. When MAP is used to show the drive pointer assignments, the path for the root drive pointer H drive is followed by a backslash while the path for regular drive pointer L does not have a backslash.

Figure 6-27

Mapping regular and
root drives

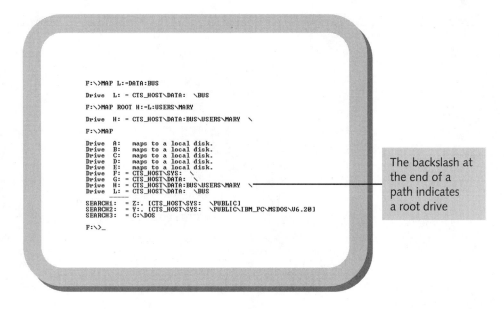

The backslash at
the end of a
path indicates
a root drive

Changing drive pointer mappings

When working with the file system, you will often want to change the path of a drive pointer to access another location. Sometimes you will also want to change a regular drive pointer into a root drive pointer and vice versa. You can change the path of a regular or root drive pointer using either the DOS CD command or the MAP command.

The CD command is perhaps the easiest and most common way to change the path of your current drive pointer. Whenever you use the CD command to change to another directory, you are changing the current drive pointer mapping. Figure 6-28 demonstrates a CD [path] command used to change the F drive mapping from the SYS: PUBLIC directory to the SALES directory of the DATA: volume. The CD command can be used to change to a different volume as well as directory.

Figure 6-28

Changing mappings
using the CD command

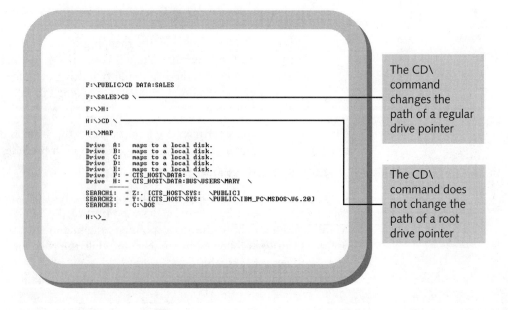

The CD\
command
changes the
path of a regular
drive pointer

The CD\
command does
not change the
path of a root
drive pointer

Although the CD \ command returns a regular drive mapping to the root of the volume, it returns a root drive pointer only to the directory path that was assigned to it. This makes root drive pointers a good choice when you do not want users to change their drive pointers to different locations of the directory structure accidentally.

The MAP [root] drive:=path command can also be used to reassign a specified drive pointer to a new path. To change the mapping of the current drive pointer from the SYS:PUBLIC directory to the SYS:PUBLIC\IBM_PC\MSDOS\V6.2, you could use any of the following MAP commands. Notice that the first command contains a complete path while the second command uses a partial path based on the location of the current drive. The third command is a shortcut that eliminates typing the drive letter if you are changing the path of the current drive.

```
F:\PUBLIC>MAP F:=SYS:PUBLIC\IBM_PC\MSDOS\V6.20

F:\PUBLIC>MAP F:=IBM_PC\MSDOS\V6.20

F:\PUBLIC>MAP IBM_PC\MSDOS\V6.20
```

To change the regular drive pointer L to a root drive, you can use the following command:

```
MAP ROOT L:=L:
```

To change the root drive pointer H to a regular drive pointer you can use the following command:

```
MAP H:=H:
```

Creating search drive pointers

Search drives are drive pointers that are added to a workstation's DOS path in order to allow the workstation to access software that is stored in other directories. A maximum of 16 search drives can be assigned, starting with S1 and ending with S16. New search drives can be added to the list by using the MAP command either to assign the next available search drive number or to insert the search drive between two existing search drives. The syntax of the MAP command that adds new search drives follows:

```
MAP [INS] S#:=[path]
```

When you add a search drive to the end of the list, do not include the INS option and replace # with the next available search drive number from 1 through 16. If you skip search drive numbers, the MAP command will automatically assign the next available number. When you add a new search drive, NetWare automatically assigns the next available drive letter, starting with Z for S1 and ending with K for S16. For example, suppose you have the following search drives mapped:

```
Search1:=Z:. [CTS_HOST\SYS:\PUBLIC]

Search2:=Y:.[CTS_HOST\SYS:\PUBLIC\IBM_PC\MSDOC\V6.20]

Search3:=C:\DOS
```

The next available search drive is Search4 (S4). To map search drive S4: to the SYS:SOFTWARE.STC\SP directory, you can use the following MAP command:

```
MAP S4:=SYS:SOFTWARE.STC\SP
```

When adding new search drives, you cannot skip search drive numbers. For example, if you attempt to map the preceding search drive to S5 before S4 is mapped, NetWare automatically uses the next sequential search drive number, in this case S4, as shown below in Figure 6-29.

Figure 6-29

Adding a new search drive mapping

```
F:\>MAP

Drive  A:    maps to a local disk.
Drive  B:    maps to a local disk.
Drive  C:    maps to a local disk.
Drive  D:    maps to a local disk.
Drive  E:    maps to a local disk.
Drive  F: = CTS_HOST\DATA:        \
Drive  H: = CTS_HOST\DATA:BUS\USERS\MARY   \

SEARCH1: = Z:. [CTS_HOST\SYS:   \PUBLIC]
SEARCH2: = Y:. [CTS_HOST\SYS:   \PUBLIC\IBM_PC\MSDOS\V6.20]
SEARCH3: = C:\DOS

F:\>MAP S5:=SYS:SOFTWARE.STC\SP

SEARCH4: = X:. [CTS_HOST\SYS:   \SOFTWARE.STC\SP]

F:\>_
```

Note Because NetWare will not skip search drive numbers, you can use the command MAP S16:=[path] if you want to add a search drive to the end of the search list and cannot remember the number of the last search drive.

When inserting a search drive between two existing drives, include the INS option and replace # with the number of the search drive before which you want the new drive placed. When you set up search drives, assign the lower search drive numbers to the most commonly used paths. This makes the system more efficient by reducing the number of directories NetWare has to search through when it looks for a program file. For example, assume you have the following search drives mapped.

Search1:=Z:. [CTS_HOST\SYS:PUBLIC]

Search2:=Y: [CTS_HOST\SYS:PUBLIC\IBM_PC\MSDOS\V6.20]

Search3:=X: [CTS_HOST\SYS:SOFTWARE.STC\SP]

Suppose you want to use the word processing program located in the SOFTWARE.STC\WP directory and still maintain the other search drive mappings. In order to make the word processing directory the first in the search order, you could use the MAP INS command shown in Figure 6–30 to create a new SEARCH1 mapping. This will resequence the other search drives, as displayed by the MAP command.

Notice that the drive letter W is assigned to the new search drive and that, while the other search drives are renumbered, they retain their drive letter assignments. The DOS PATH commands shown at the top and bottom of Figure 6–30 illustrate the way the search commands affect the DOS path. NetWare keeps track of search drive numbers by their sequence in the DOS path. Because drive W is now the first drive in the path, it becomes S1.

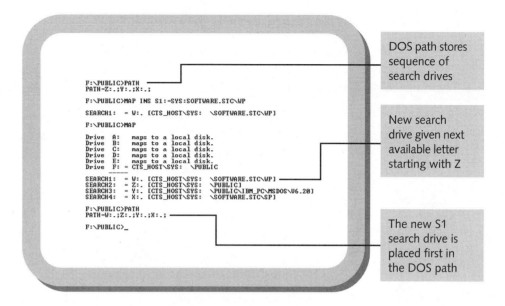

Figure 6-30

Inserting a search
drive mapping

Removing a drive pointer

The advice "everything in moderation" certainly can apply to drive pointers. Too many search drive pointers can slow down the workstation's performance and sometimes overlie existing regular and root drive pointers. Drive pointers also take up some of the file server's memory and can decrease its performance. (This is discussed further in Chapter 15.) In addition, trying to keep track of too many drive pointers can become confusing and counterproductive. A CNA can use the MAP DEL command to remove drive pointers that are no longer being used.

The MAP DEL [drive]: command removes a regular, root, or search drive mapping when [drive] is replaced with the drive letter or search drive to be removed. When you remove a search drive mapping, the remaining search drive numbers are resequenced, as shown in Figure 6-31. The drive letter that was assigned to the deleted search drive is made available for the next search drive that you add. See the next section, "Changing a search drive path."

Figure 6-31

Removing a search
drive mapping

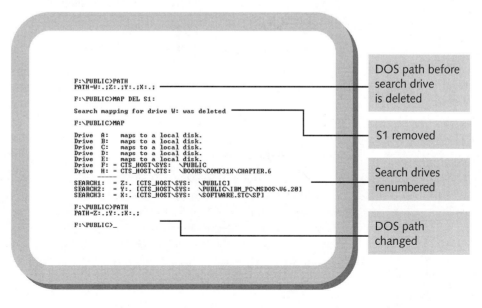

Changing a search drive path

Although most users will not need to change search drive paths once they are established, a network administrator sometimes needs to modify search drives when testing new software packages or reconfiguring a workstation for new applications. At other times, a network administrator might want to modify the search drive paths in a user's menu system rather than adding a new search drive for each software package the user needs to access. This can keep the number of search drives from becoming excessive and slowing down system performance. In this section you will learn the different methods of modifying search drive paths.

There are three methods to change a search drive mapping to point to a different directory:

1. Remapping the existing search drive to the desired path.

2. Deleting the original search drive and inserting a new search drive to the desired path.

3. Using the CD command.

The first method involves overwriting the search drive mapping with a new path. For example, assume you need to use the word processing program and have the following search drives mapped:

```
Search1:=Z:.  [CTS_HOST\SYS:  \PUBLIC]

Search2:=Y:.  [CTS_HOST\SYS:\IBM_PC\MSDOS\V6.02]

Search3:=X:.  [CTS_HOST\SYS:\SOFTWARE.STC\SP]
```

You replace the search drive mapping to the SP directory with the WP path by entering the following command:

```
MAP X:=SYS:SOFTWARE.STC\WP
```

This command causes NetWare to remap the X drive to the WP directory, thereby changing search drive S3 to use the SYS:SOFTWARE.STC\WP path.

The second method deletes the original search drive and then inserts a new search drive using the same search drive number, as follows:

```
MAP DEL S3:

MAP INS S3:=SYS:SOFTWARE.STC\WP
```

The MAP DEL S3: command deletes the S3 drive mapping and resequences the search drive numbers. The second MAP command inserts a new search drive for S3 pointing to the WP directory. This method (described further in Chapter 13) is often used in a batch file or in menus to allow a certain search drive number to be reused for several different applications. It keeps the number of search drives from becoming excessive in situations in which users need to access many different software packages.

Like regular drive pointers, search drive paths can be changed with the DOS CD command as well as with the NetWare MAP command. If a user is unable to run certain network applications, a CNA should investigate for search drive paths that were inadvertently modified by a "power" user using the CD command. Figure 6-32 illustrates using the CD command to change a search drive mapping by first changing the default drive to the search drive to be modified, and then using the CD command to change the path to another directory location. Notice that after the work drive is changed and the MAP command is invoked, the search path for S4 is changed to the path specified in the CD command.

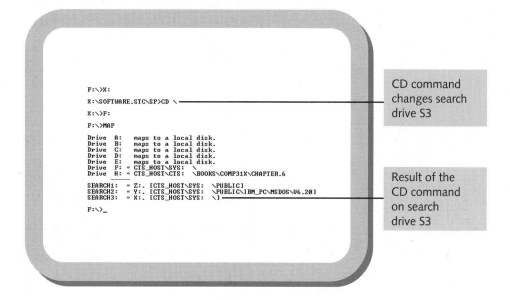

Figure 6-32

Using CD to change search drives

CD command changes search drive S3

Result of the CD command on search drive S3

Changing the drive mapping of SEARCH1 from the SYS:PUBLIC to some other directory will prevent a user from running NetWare utilities; the user will be unable to invoke the LOGOUT and MAP commands from outside the SYS:PUBLIC directory. If this happens, use the CD SYS:PUBLIC command to change to the PUBLIC directory in order to use LOGOUT or other NetWare utilities.

THE SESSION MENU UTILITY

SESSION is an interactive menu utility that allows you to work with both network and search drive pointer mappings to view information about groups and logged in users, and to send messages. Although the SESSION utility is primarily designed for network users, it can also be helpful for the network administrator who needs to set up drive mappings in an unfamiliar directory structure. Remember that any drive mappings you create or change with either MAP or SESSION are only effective as long as you are logged in. When you log out, the drive mappings that were made are no longer available the next time you log in. This means it is necessary to re-establish the drive mappings a user needs each time he or she logs in. In Chapter 12 you will learn how to use NetWare login scripts to automate the process of assigning users the necessary drive mappings each time they log in. Users can then use the MAP command or SESSION utility to establish any temporary drive mappings that will help them in their work.

To use the SESSION utility, simply type SESSION at the DOS prompt. The Available Topics menu shown in Figure 6-33 is displayed. Notice that the top part of the screen identifies the version of the SESSION utility, the current date and time, the user's name, and the name of the current file server. The Available Topics menu in the middle of the screen contains options that allow you to change the current file server, to work with drive mappings, to change the default drive, or to list groups and users. As a CNA you should know why and how to use each of these options. Because SESSION is a menu utility, the same techniques and function keys used for FILER and SALVAGE can be applied to the SESSION utility.

Figure 6-33

SESSION Available
Topics window

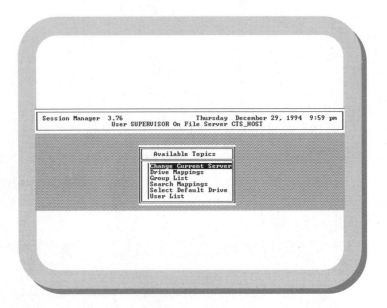

```
Session Manager  3.76                Thursday  December 29, 1994  9:59 pm
                 User SUPERVISOR On File Server CTS_HOST


                              ┌─────────────────────┐
                              │  Available Topics   │
                              ├─────────────────────┤
                              │ Change Current Server│
                              │ Drive Mappings      │
                              │ Group List          │
                              │ Search Mappings     │
                              │ Select Default Drive │
                              │ User List           │
                              └─────────────────────┘
```

Change Current Server

This SESSION option is useful only if you are attached to more than one server and want to view users and group information on a specific server. When you select this option, a window appears listing the servers to which you are currently attached. If the server you want to access is not in this list, press the Ins key to display a list of other available servers. To log in to one of these servers, simply highlight the server's name and press [Enter]. You will then be asked to enter a valid username and password for the selected server. After your login name has been verified, the selected server becomes the current server.

 NetWare v3.x allows you to attach a workstation to a maximum of eight file servers simultaneously.

Drive Mappings

You use this SESSION option to create, change, and delete regular and root drive mappings. For most users it is much easier to use this option to change or add drive mappings than it is to enter a valid MAP command from the DOS prompt. Selecting this option displays the Current Drive Mappings window showing all existing regular and root mappings. See Figure 6-34.

Figure 6-34

Current Drive
Mappings window

```
              Current Drive Mappings
 A   <Local Drive>
 B   <Local Drive>
 C   <Local Drive>
 D   <Local Drive>
 E   <Local Drive>
 F   CTS_HOST\DATA:        \
 H   CTS_HOST\DATA:BUS\USERS\MARY        \
```

To add a new drive mapping to the list, press the Ins key. SESSION displays a window showing the next available drive letter. If you do not want to use the drive letter shown, erase it with the Backspace key, type the drive letter you want, and press [Enter]. Next, SESSION displays the Select Directory window in which you enter the path for this drive pointer. You can enter the path to the desired directory either by typing the complete path or by using the Ins key to select each component of the path starting with the file server. (This process was described in the FILER utility section.) After the path is entered, SESSION displays a window asking "Do you want to map root this drive?" Select Yes to make this a root drive mapping or No to make the new drive a regular drive mapping. When root drive mapping is selected, the new drive pointer and path are displayed in the Current Drive Mappings window.

To change an existing drive mapping to point to a different directory path, simply highlight the drive mapping you want to change and press the F3 key. The Select Directory window showing the current path is displayed. To change the drive mapping, use the Backspace key to erase the existing path. Then either enter the revised path or select it by using the Ins key. After the new path is entered, SESSION again gives you the option of making the drive pointer a root drive mapping. After the root drive mapping question is answered, the revised drive mapping is displayed in the Current Drive Mappings window.

To delete a drive mapping, simply highlight the drive mapping in the Current Drive Mappings window and press the Del key. After you select Yes from the confirmation screen, the highlighted drive mapping is removed from the Current Drive Mappings window.

Group List

SESSION's Group List option displays a window showing all groups on the current file server. The most common reason for using this option is to send a message to all members of a selected group. Avoid sending messages to the group EVERYONE—this can interrupt processing on the network and possibly cause loss of data (and productivity). If you are a member of a group, you can use this option to display such information as the names of other members in the group. A supervisor can view information about all groups.

Search Mappings

The Search Mappings option creates, changes, and deletes search drive mappings. Selecting this option displays the Current Search Mappings window, showing all existing search drive mappings for the user. See Figure 6-35.

Figure 6-35

Current Search Mappings window

To add a new search drive mapping to the list, first press the Ins key to display a window showing the next available search drive number. Because search drives must be assigned sequentially, you cannot enter a number larger than the number shown. If you want to insert a new search drive mapping, you can enter a smaller number corresponding to the search drive number you want assigned to the new search drive. After the search drive number is entered, SESSION displays a Select Directory window in which you enter the path for this drive pointer. You can either enter the path to the software directory by typing the path or use the Ins key to select each component of the path, as described previously. After the Enter key is pressed, the new drive pointer and path are displayed in the Current Search Mappings window.

To change the path of search drive pointer, you simply highlight the search drive pointer you want to change and press the F3 key. The Select Directory window showing the current path will then be displayed. Use the Backspace key to erase the current directory path and then enter the correct path or use the Ins key to select the path, starting with the directory shown in the Select Directory window. After the correct path is displayed in the Select Directory window, press the Enter key to modify the path in the Current Search Mappings window. Pressing the Esc key aborts the change, leaving the existing path unchanged.

To delete a search drive mapping, simply highlight the drive mapping in the Current Search Mappings window and press the Del key. After Yes is selected from the confirmation screen, the highlighted search drive is removed from the Current Search Mappings window, and the other search drives are renumbered.

Select Default Drive

You can use the Select Default Drive option change the default DOS drive pointer to another directory. This can be helpful if you want to work on a specific drive pointer using the DOS prompt. This option displays the Select Default Drive window, which shows all existing drive mappings. From this list, you can select the drive letter you want as your default drive. After you exit the SESSION utility, the drive letter you selected becomes your current DOS drive.

User List

The User List option either displays information about current users of the file server—including login time, station address, and full name—or sends a message to a user. When you select this option, SESSION displays a User window showing all users who are logged in to the current file server. To obtain information or send a message to a specific user, highlight the target username and press [Enter]. The SESSION utility displays a menu containing options for sending a message to the user and displaying user information. To display information about the selected user, highlight the user information option and press [Enter]. A window showing the user's information is displayed. If you have supervisor authority for the selected user, the window displays the user information shown in Figure 6-36.

Figure 6-36

Displaying user
information

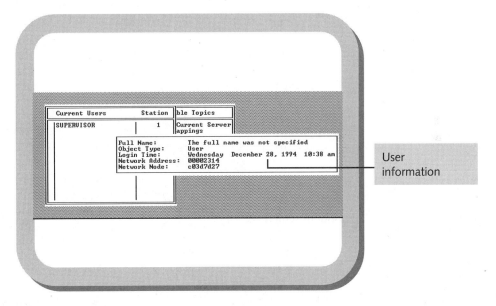

To send a message to a user, highlight the send message option and press [Enter]. A message window appears which allows you to send a one-line message of up to 36 characters to the user. After you type the message and press [Enter], the message is transmitted to the user's workstation. If the receiving user has invoked the CASTOFF command to prevent messages from being received, SESSION displays an error message informing you that the message could not be delivered to the selected user. When a message is successfully sent, the user's workstation displays the message and stops processing until the receiver presses [Ctrl][Enter]. Be aware that if you send a message to a station that is unoccupied, you can interrupt processing that is currently being performed, possibly resulting in loss of data and productivity.

PLANNING YOUR DRIVE MAPPINGS

As a CNA, you will have the important task of assigning the limited number of regular and search drive pointers so that users and applications can access information and software in your file system's directory structure. If each workstation had an unlimited number of drive pointers available to it, you could assign a regular or root drive pointer to each data directory to be accessed along with a search drive to each software package. Even if you had this luxury, however, so many drive pointers would not only be confusing to track, but too many search drives would slow the performance of the workstation because of the number of directories it would need to search through when it loads software. Because of this limitation, you need to plan a minimum set of standard drive pointers that will allow a workstation to run the necessary applications software and provide convenient access to the data with which the user needs to work.

When planning regular drive pointers, you should first determine what regular and root drive pointers are necessary to allow easy access to shared and private files using a drive letter rather than a long NetWare path. It is important to keep these drive pointers to a minimum, because most users cannot keep track of more than five different drive pointers. Typical drive pointers for each user should include:

- a drive pointer to the root of each volume. These drive pointers will allow all users to change to another volume quickly without using the CD volume-name: command. They also provide a standard path for running applications because certain application packages require a drive letter and path to be assigned in order to reference configuration and data file locations. Having the same drive letter mapped to each volume for all users is necessary to run this software. When using a two-volume structure, many network administrators map drive letter F to the SYS: volume and then use another drive letter, such as G to access the DATA: volume.

  Another use for the volume drive pointer is to access shared work directories that are available to all users. For example, if a shared work directory named WORK is created for all users on the root of the DATA: volume, any user can access files in this directory by using the path G:\WORK. Similarly, if a shared word processing forms directory named FORMS is created on the root of the DATA: volume, any user can access a common word processing form by using the path G:\FORMS.

- a root drive pointer mapped to the user's home directory. This drive letter is the starting point for user's personal data storage. It will be a different path for each user. Making this a root drive is important because it prevents the user from accidentally changing the H drive pointer to a different directory location. Users can create subdirectories within their home directories, for example, and then move around within those subdirectories using the CD \ command to bring them back to the beginning of their home directories rather than changing to the root of the volume.

- a root drive pointer mapped to the user's workgroup directory. This drive pointer allows users to access shared files within their workgroups. Users in the business department, for example, can have their L drive mapped to DATA:BUSINESS. The SALES department users can have their L drive mapped to the DATA:SALES directory. If a WORK directory is created for each department, every user in the system can get to his or her work-group's shared work directory using the path L:\WORK.

- application drive pointers. In addition to the standard drive pointers just described and depending on the installation instructions of some application packages, additional drive pointers might be necessary. When these drive pointers are planned, it is important that all users who will run the application can do so with the same drive pointer letter because the software will often be installed using a specific drive letter for accessing its data and work files.

In addition to planning the regular drive pointers, the network administrator needs to plan the use of search drive pointers to allow users access to utilities and software packages that are frequently used. When planning search drive usage, it is important to keep the total number of search drives to less than eight in order to provide better performance and less chance of conflicts with regular drive pointers. Because most users will be running application packages from a menu or Windows environment, application search drive pointers can be temporarily mapped in the menu with the MAP INS command and then removed with the MAP DEL command after the application ends. (See Chapter 13 for more information on setting up NetWare menus.) Users running a Windows environment will not need search drives mapped to the Windows applications because the path to these directories is stored in the properties of the Window icons. As a minimum, most network administrators establish the following search drive mappings:

- Search drive S1 to the SYS:PUBLIC directory

- Search drive S2 to the correct DOS version subdirectory

- Search drive S3 to the network WINDOWS directory if Windows is being run from the network

- Search drive S4-S6 to DOS-based applications such as word processing and spreadsheet software directories

A properly planned set of drive pointers includes the search drives needed to run DOS-based software packages and utilities along with a standard set of regular drive pointers that allow users easy access to data storage directories containing the files with which they need to work. The drive pointer planning form shown in Figure 6-37 shows an example that includes the following drive pointers for each user:

- The H drive pointer to the user's home directory allows each user to access his or her own private data easily.

- The L drive pointer mapped to each user's local department or workgroup allows users to access their department's shared work files by using the path L:\WORK.

- The F drive pointer to the SYS: volume is needed to allow each user access to software or utilities stored in the SYS: volume.

- The G drive pointer mapped to the root of the DATA: volume provides each user with access to the Global data structure for the organization. For example, a user can access the organization's global work directory with the path G:\WORK or access the organization's shared forms directory with the path G:\FORMS. If a department wants its own forms directory, it can be accessed with the path L:\FORMS.

Figure 6-37

Sample drive
planning form

Drive Pointer Planning Form		
Company:		
Planned by:	**Date:**	
GROUP: Everyone		
Letter	**Description of Use**	**Path**
S1:	NetWare utilities	SYS:PUBLIC
S2:	DOS utilities	SYS:PUBLIC\IBM_PC\MSDOS\%OS_VERSION
F:	global SYS: volume	SYS:
G:	global DATA: volume	DATA:
GROUP: Business Department		
Letter	**Description of Use**	**Path**
H:	user home directory	DATA:BUS\USERS\LOGIN_NAME
L:	local workgroup—business department	DATA:BUSINESS
GROUP: Sales Department		
Letter	**Description of Use**	**Path**
H:	user home directory—sales department	DATA:SALES\LOGIN_NAME
L:	local workgroup—sales department	DATA:SALES
GROUP: Support Department		
Letter	**Description of Use**	**Path**
H:	user home directory—support department	DATA:SUPPORT\LOGIN_NAME
L:	local workgroup—support department	DATA:SUPPORT

Planning a good set of drive pointers will make it easier for you to establish login scripts, install software, and work with NetWare menus as well as provide a standard user environment that is convenient for your users to access and you to troubleshoot and maintain.

CHAPTER SUMMARY

NetWare network administrators must master the NetWare commands and utilities in order to set up and manage a network. This chapter described the five different types of NetWare tools available to the network administrator: command line utilities, menu utilities, supervisor utilities, console commands, and NetWare Loadable Modules (NLMs). Console commands and NLMs are used from the file server's console; command line utilities and menu utilities run at the workstations. Command line utilities are similar to DOS commands in that you must know the command and its correct syntax in order to use it. Menu utilities are interactive and more user friendly in that they allow you to select options and provide you with lists and input windows. They use the following set of special function keys:

- The Esc key is used to go back one menu level.
- The F1 key is used to obtain additional help information.
- The F3 key is used to change a highlighted entry in a window.
- The F5 key is used to mark items in a window.
- The Alt and F10 keys are used to exit the menu utility from any level.

Although several DOS commands, such as DIR, COPY, and XCOPY, work with the NetWare file system, you should use the NDIR and NCOPY command line utilities whenever possible because they are specialized for use with the NetWare file system and provide faster performance and better reliability. Some DOS commands, such as MD and CD, are often used on NetWare drives to create directories and change paths, while other DOS commands, such as FORMAT, CHKDSK, DISKCOPY, and SCANDISK, will not work on NetWare drives at all.

In addition to being more efficient than the DOS copy commands, NCOPY has options, such as the ability to copy NetWare file attributes and inform you when the target device will not support the file attributes on the source files. The NDIR command provides additional network information such as owner, network attributes, and last date updated. NDIR can also be used as a management information tool that allows the network administrator to sort and view information for selected files. It can, for example, list in sequence by owner all files that are over 2 Mbytes in size and have not been accessed for the last six months. Other NetWare command line utilities include the PURGE command, which removes deleted files from the system, and the VERSION command, which can be used to determine the version number of another utility.

The primary menu utilities that are used with the file system are FILER, DSPACE, and SALVAGE. A CNA needs to know what functions these utilities perform and how to use them for the tasks described in this chapter. The FILER utility is one of the most sophisticated of the menu utilities and contains the following options: Current Directory Information, Directory Contents, Select Current Directory, Use Filer Options, and Volume Information. These options allow the network administrator to view and maintain current directory information, work with the file and subdirectory contained in the current directory, change the current directory path either by typing the path or by using the Ins key to select each component, select options such as what files to include or exclude, and view information about the current volume. As a CNA, you should know how to use FILER to complete the following:

- Change the current directory using the Ins key or typing the path
- Copy or move a directory structure
- Create directories
- Copy files
- Rename files and subdirectories
- Delete files and directory structures

The DSPACE utility is an important tool that allows network administrators to restrict disk space usage. A CNA needs to know how to use the DSPACE utility to restrict the amount of disk space available to either a username or directory structure. The importance of the SALVAGE utility is its ability to recover files that have been deleted even when the directory structure in which the file was stored no longer exists.

Drive pointers are letters assigned to local drives and network directories for working with the file system and accessing software stored in other directories. The drive pointers A – E are normally reserved for DOS to use with local drives. Drive pointers F – Z are often used by NetWare to point to directory locations. Regular and root drive pointers are assigned to directories that contain data files; search drive pointers are assigned to software directories and work with the DOS path to allow a user to run programs that are not located in the current directory. Up to 16 search drives can be assigned, using letters Z for S1, Y for S2, and so on up to K for S16. Although letters R - K (S9 - S16) are not normally assigned to search drives, using these pointers for regular drives risks conflicting with search paths. This leaves letters F through J always available for regular drive pointer assignments. Root drive pointers appear to DOS and applications as if the directory path were the beginning of a drive or volume. This enables the network administrator to make it more difficult for users or applications to move out of the assigned directory path. All drive pointer assignments are stored in the memory of the workstation until the user logs out. When a user logs in, drive pointers must be reset, either manually using the MAP and SESSION utilities or through the login script.

The MAP command is the utility used most frequently by network administrators to create and maintain drive pointers. As a CNA, you should be able to use the MAP command to perform the following functions:

- View drive pointer assignments
- Create a regular drive pointer
- Create a root drive pointer
- Add a new search drive to the end of the current search drive list
- Insert a search drive within the existing search drives
- Remove a regular drive mapping
- Remove a search drive mapping

The SESSION menu utility is an alternate way to work interactively with regular or search drive pointers. Options of the SESSION utility include the ability to log in to another file server, work with drive mappings, obtain information on groups or send a message to all users in a group, work with search drive mappings, and send a message to or view information about users currently logged in to the file server.

Because drive pointers play a major role in the way the NetWare file system is accessed by users, applications, and menus, it is important for a network administrator to establish standards for drive pointer usage in order to prevent conflicts and software configuration problems. As a general rule you should use a drive pointer planning form similar to one shown in Figure 6-37 to establish for each user a set of drive pointers that includes a regular drive pointer to the root of each volume, a root drive pointer to the user's home directory, and another root drive pointer to the shared work area for the user's workgroup. In addition to the required search drive to the SYS:PUBLIC directory, additional search drives need be allocated for each DOS-based software package and utility that is commonly used. Establishing a standard drive pointer usage plan will make accessing and maintaining the network file system much easier for both the users and network administrator.

COMMAND SUMMARY

Command	Syntax	Definition
DSPACE	*DSPACE*	Menu utility that can be used to restrict disk space used by either a volume or user.
FILER	*FILER*	Menu utility that can be used to work with the file system. Menu options include: Current Directory Information Directory Contents Select Current Directory Set Filer Options Volume Information
MAP	*MAP d:=[path]*	Creates regular drive mappings.
	MAP ROOT d:= [path]	Creates root drive mappings.
	MAP S#:=[path]	Adds a search drive to the end of the search list.
	MAP INS S#:=path	Inserts a search drive before an existing drive number.
	MAP DEL d:	Removes either regular, root, or search drive pointers.
NDIR	*NDIR [path] [/option]*	Displays file information about the specified file and path. Options include: /SORT - Sorts by Owner, Size, Last Accessed. /SI|/OW|/LA GR|LE|EQ value - Selects only files based on the \ value. /DATE/RIGHTS - Displays additional information about a file's creation date, and last accessed or updated dates. /attribute - Displays only the files that have the specified attribute.
SALVAGE	*SALVAGE*	Menu utility that can be used to recover files that have been deleted from an existing directory or from a directory structure that no longer exists. Options allow you to view the deleted files in the sequence you specify. Sequence options are by filename, deletor, deletion date, and file size.
SESSION	*SESSION*	Menu utility that allows you to log into another file server, work with drive mappings, view information on users and groups, send messages, and change the current drive pointer by using the following options:

		Change Current Server
		Drive Mappings
		Group List
		Search Mappings
		Select Default Drive
		User List
VERSION	*VERSION filename*	Displays the version number and date of the file specified by the *filename* parameter.

KEY TERMS

attribute options

command line utility (CLU)

console commands

drive pointer

file attribute

format options

local drive pointers

login script

menu utility

network drive pointer

regular drive pointer

restriction options

root drive pointer

search drive pointer

sort options

supervisor utility

REVIEW QUESTIONS

1. Identify each of the following as being either a command line utility, menu utility, console command, or NetWare Loadable Module (NLM):

    NDIR _____Command line utility_____

    SALVAGE _____menu utility_____

    MONITOR _____NLM_____

    PURGE _____command line utility_____

    CONFIG _____console command_____

    MAP _____command line utility_____

    SESSION _____menu utility_____

2. In the space below, briefly explain an advantage of a command line utility over a menu utility:

    They are slower because you have to leave the evironment that you are working in.

3. Which of the following DOS commands will *not* work on a NetWare drive?

    XCOPY _____

    MD and CD _____

    CHKDSK _____not work_____ } _on a network drive letter_

    FORMAT _____not work_____

    DIR _____

4. In the space below, briefly explain an advantage of NCOPY over the DOS XCOPY command:

   The way the copy process is performed.
   Using NCOPY: blocks don't need to be sent to the workstation and retransmitted back to the server

5. A(n) ___attribute___ is a flag that is set on a file or directory providing certain characteristics such as making a file Read Only.

6. Write an NCOPY command to copy all files with the extension ∗.WK1 from drive A to the BUSINESS\BUDGETS directory of the SYS: volume.

   NCOPY a:∗.WK1   SYS:BUSINESS\BUDGETS

7. Write an NCOPY command to copy the file JAN95.WK1 without its attributes from the USERS\JOHN directory located in the DATA: volume of the CTS_HOST file server to the BUSINESS\BUDGETS directory located in the DATA: volume of the RLHOST file server.

   NCOPY DATA:USERS\JOHN\JAN95.WK1   RLHOST\DATA:\BUSINESS\BUDGETS /C

8. List two advantages of the NetWare NDIR command over the DOS DIR command:

   - Can show more information (ex when file was last updated)
   - can filter files into a list

9. Write an NDIR command to display the contents of the DATA:BUSINESS\BUDGETS directory showing the last accessed and update dates.

   NDIR DATA:BUSINESS\BUDGETS   /DATES

10. Write an NDIR command to display in sequence from the largest file to the smallest the contents of the DATA:BUSINESS\BUDGETS directory.

    NDIR DATA:BUSINESS\BUDGETS   /REV /SORT SI

11. Write an NDIR command to display in sequence by owner all files in the DATA:BUSINESS directory and all its subdirectories that are over 1 Mbyte in size and have not been accessed since January 1995.

    NDIR DATA:BUSINESS /SORT OW /SI GR 1,000,000 /AC BEF 01-01-9

12. Write two commands to delete the file JAN95.WK1 from the DATA:USERS\JOHN directory and then purge the file to immediately reuse its space.

    ① Filer   ② DEL DATA:USERS\JOHN\JAN95.WK1
    PURGE DATA:USERS\JOHN /ALL

13. When the FILER utility is used, the ___F3___ key can be used to change the name of a file or directory.

14. When the FILER utility is used, the ___F5___ key can be used to mark several files for deletion.

15. The ___DSPACE___ utility can be used to restrict the amount of space used by a subdirectory structure.

16. When using FILER to copy JAN95.WK1 from the DATA:BUSINESS\BUDGETS directory to the DATA:BUSINESS\WORK directory, you must first change to the ___TARGET___ directory.

17. ___ROOT & REGULAR___ drive pointers are used to reference data storage locations on the file server.

18. ___SEARCH___ drive pointers are used to reference software storage directories on a file server.

19. When the NETX shell is used, the ___LAST DRIVE =___ statement in the _workstation CONFIG.SYS_ file determines the start of the network drive pointers.

20. Write a NetWare command to view all drive mappings.
    ___MAP___

21. Write a NetWare command to create a new root drive pointer H that will point to the DATA:USERS\JOHN directory.
    ___MAP ROOT H:= DATA:USERS\JOHN___

22. Write a NetWare command to add a search drive pointer to the SYS:SOFTWARE\WP directory after the last search drive number when you don't know the number of the last search drive.
    ___MAP S16:= SYS:SOFTWARE\WP___

23. Write a NetWare command to insert a search drive into the SYS:SOFTWARE\SP directory between the existing S2 and S3 search drives.
    ___MAP INS S3:= SYS:SOFTWARE\SP___

24. The ___SESSION MENU___ NetWare utility can be used to add search drive mappings and send messages to other users or groups.

25. Write commands to change the path of search drive S3 from the SYS:SOFTWARE\WP directory to the SYS:SOFTWARE\UTILITY directory without creating a regular drive pointer from the existing search drive.
    ___MAP X:= SYS:\SOFTWARE\UTILITY___

Given the directory structure shown in Figure 6-38, write MAP commands to map drives to the marked areas.

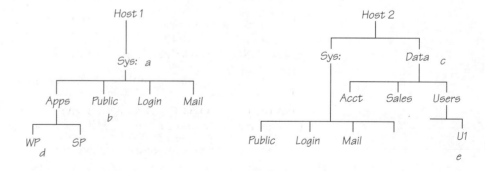

Figure 6-38

Superior Technical College directory structure

26. (a) ___MAP S1:= HOST1\SYS:___
27. (b) ___MAP S2:= HOST1\SYS:\PUBLIC___
28. (c) ___MAP S3:= HOST2\DATA:___

29. (d) _MAP S4:= HOST1\SYS:\APPS\WP_

30. (e) _MAP S5:= HOST2\DATA:\USERS\U1_

EXERCISES

Exercise 6-1: Using NCOPY

In this exercise you will practice using the NCOPY command by copying a sample directory structure from the SYS: volume to a designated location in your home directory. The files and subdirectories in this structure will be used in subsequent hands-on exercises and case studies.

1. Log into your assigned file server using your student username.

2. Before using the NCOPY command to copy all files and subdirectories from the SYS:EXAMPLE directory to your home directory, you need to record the complete NetWare path to your directory. On the line below, record the complete path to your home directory including file server name, volume, and directory names.

    _CTS_HOST\SYS:\50ADMIN_

3. Obtain a printout of the SYS:EXAMPLE directory structure showing all directories and subdirectories.

4. Use the CD command to change the default DOS prompt to point to your home directory. On the line below, record the CD command you use.

    _CD   CTS_HOST\SYS:\50ADMIN_

5. Use the MD command to create a directory for the sample structure at the beginning of your home directory, as shown below.

```
                    VOLUME:
                       |
                    ##ADMIN
                       |
          ┌────────────┘
          |
        Sample
```

6. Use the NCOPY command to copy all files without attributes along with all the subdirectories from the SYS:EXAMPLE directory into the area you created in step 4. On the line below, record the NCOPY command you use.

    _NCOPY   CTS_HOST\SYS:\EXAMPLE   CTS_HOST\SYS:\50ADMIN\SAMPLE   /S /C_

7. Use the LISTDIR command with appropriate options to obtain a printout of your home directory and all subdirectories. Compare this directory listing with the one produced in step 3. Make sure all subdirectories are included. On the line below, record the LISTDIR command you use.

    _LISTDIR   CTS_HOST\SYS:\50ADMIN   /S_

8. Use the NDIR command with the /DATES option to obtain a printout of all files and attributes in the SUPPORT\POLICY\SECTION3 subdirectory of your new sample directory structure. On the line below, record the command you use.

    _NDIR   CTS_HOST\SYS:\50ADMIN\SAMPLE\SUPPORT\POLICY\SECTION3   /DATES   /RIGHTS_

Exercise 6-2: Deleting and Salvaging Files

In this exercise you will practice using FILER to delete files from the
SUPPORT\POLICY\SECTION3 subdirectory of the sample structure and then
practice using the SALVAGE utility to recover the deleted files.

1. Start FILER.

2. Use the Select Current Directory option and then use the Ins key to select
   the path leading to your SUPPORT\POLICY\SECTION3 subdirectory.
   On the line below, record the path you select.

   CTS-HOST\SYS:\50ADMIN\SAMPLE\SUPPORT\POLICY\SECTION

3. Display all files in the SECTION3 directory using the Directory Information
   option.

4. Mark two files to be deleted. On the lines below, record the key you use
   along with the filenames.

   Key used to mark files: ___*F5*___

   Files marked: ___*54910210.3*___
   ___*70020501.3*___

5. Delete the marked files.

6. Use [Alt] [F10] to exit FILER.

7. Obtain a printout showing all files in the SECTION3 subdirectory. Write
   FILES DELETED on this printout.

8. Use the appropriate NetWare command to determine the amount of space
   available from deleted files in this volume. On the line below, record the
   command you use.

   CHKVOL   CTS-HOST\SYS:

9. Start the SALVAGE utility.

10. Change to the directory path you recorded in step 2.

11. Set the Salvage option to sort files by deletion time.

12. Use the appropriate option to display all deleted files.

13. Mark and salvage the files you deleted in step 5.

14. Exit the SALVAGE utility.

15. Use the NDIR command to obtain a printout showing the recovered files in
    the SECTION3 subdirectory. Highlight the names of the salvaged files and
    write FILES SALVAGED on the printout.

Exercise 6-3: Restricting Disk Space

In this exercise you will use the DSPACE utility to restrict the disk space available
to the SALES directory structure of your sample structure to 1 Mbyte.

1. Start DSPACE.

2. Select the appropriate option to restrict the space available to a directory. On
   the line below, record the option you use.

   Directory Restrictions

3. Select the SALES directory from your sample directory structure area and restrict the space available to 1 Mbyte. On the line below, record the path.

CTS-HOST \ SYS : 50ADMIN/SAMPLE /SALES

4. Use the appropriate NetWare command to verify the amount of disk space available in the volume and the SALES directory. On the line below, record the command you use.

CHKDIR   CTS:HOST\SYS:\50ADMIN\SAMPLE\SALES

5. Print the screen showing the output of the command you used in step 5.

Exercise 6-4: Using NDIR commands

In this exercise you will gain practice in using the NDIR command to list selected files from the CHAP4 directory created in Exercises 4-6 and 4-7.

1. Obtain a listing in sequence by owner of all files in your CHAP4 directory structure that have not been accessed since last week and are over 1000 bytes in size. In the space below, record the NDIR command used and the file names listed.

   NDIR COMMAND:

   NDIR   CTS-HOST\SYS:\50ADMIN\ CHAP4 /SI GR1000 /AC BEF 09/22 98 /sub

   Files Listed:

   No Files

2. Start FILER.

3. Use the Select Current Directory option to change to the CHAP4\DOCS directory.

4. Use the Directory Contents option to display all files in the DOCS subdirectory.

5. Select the CISDEV.DOC file and use the appropriate options to view the file contents.   *FILE   DOESN'T   EXIST*

6. Exit FILER.

7. Repeat Step 1. Is the CISDEV.DOC file included in the new listing? Yes or No

8. Explain why the CISDEV.DOC file should NOT be included this listing.

9. Use the NDIR command to obtain a printout showing additional date information on the files in the FORMS directory. On the line below, record the command you use.

    _NDIR   CTS_HOST\SYS:\50ADMIN\SAMPLE\FORMS   /DATES_

Exercise 6-5: Using FILER to Copy Files

In this exercise you will practice using the FILER utility to copy files from one directory on the file server to another directory location.

1. Start FILER and use the "Select Current Directory" option to change to your ##ADMIN directory.

2. Copy all files that end with a number from the SOFTWARE.STC\SP directory into the ADMIN\BUDGETS subdirectory of the sample directory structure. In the space below, record the FILER steps you use to do this.

    1) Select Current Directory of files to be copied
    2) Select Directory Contents and highlight files to be copied
       then Press Enter
    3) Select Copy Marked Files
    4) Enter in the path to be copied to. and hit enter.

Exercise 6-6: Using FILER to Rename Files and Directories

In this exercise you will practice using the FILER utility to change the names of files and directories.

1. If you have not already done so, start FILER and use the "Select Current Directory" option to change to your ##ADMIN directory.

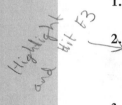

2. Change the name of the worksheet file EARN01.WK1 by replacing the "01" in the filename with the current year (i.e. EARN1995). Change the name of the TAX02.WK1 file by replacing the "02" in the filename with last year (i.e. TAX1994).

3. Change the name of the FORMS directory located in your sample structure to CTIFORMS.

4. Exit FILER.

5. After completing the name changes, use NDIR to obtain a directory listing of the BUDGETS subdirectory. On the line below, record the NDIR command you use.

    NDIR   /sub

6. Use the LISTDIR command to obtain a printout showing the entire structure of your sample directory. On the line below, record the LISTDIR command you use.

    _LISTDIR   CTS_HOST\SYS:\50ADMIN\SAMPLE   /SUB_

Exercise 6-7: Using the MAP Command

In this exercise you will use the MAP command to create both regular and search drive mappings, display your drive mappings on the printer, and then test the search drive. After each of the map descriptions in step 1, record the MAP command you plan to use to create that drive mapping. Do not execute these map commands until step 3.

1. Write MAP commands for the following sample directory areas:

   A regular drive pointer to the sample directory in your student directory.

   MAP S: = CTS-HOST\SYS:\50ADMIN\SAMPLE

   A root drive pointer to Ode Wiggerts's (ODEWIG) home directory located in the SUPPORT department.

   MAP ROOT O: = CTS-HOST\SYS:\EXAMPLE\SUPPORT\ODEWIG

   A search drive pointer after the last existing search drive that points to the UTILITY subdirectory of the DATAPROC directory.

   MAP S16: = CTS-HOST\SYS:\50ADMIN\SAMPLE\DATAPROC\UTILITY

   Insert a search drive before the existing S1 that points to the SYS:SOFTWARE.STC\SP directory.

   MAP INS S1: = CTS-HOST\SYS: SOFTWARE.STC\SP

2. The UTIL program is located in the DATAPROC\UTILITY directory of your sample structure. To illustrate the use of search drives, in this step you will try to run the UTIL program without a search drive and observe the error message. To try running the UTIL program from your current drive, type the command UTIL and press **[Enter]**. In the space below, write the error message you receive and what this message means.

   Bad command or file name.

3. Use MAP commands to create the drive mappings you defined at the start of this exercise.

4. Use the command MAP > PRN to obtain a printout of the drive mapping you have created.

5. What letter is used by the S1 search drive mapping? used the U:

6. Type the command UTIL and press **[Enter]**. If your search drives are mapped correctly, you should receive a message screen. In the space below, record each directory that the computer needed to look in before finding the UTIL program:

   ① CHAP4

   ② SAMPLE

7. Print the screen containing the results of your UTIL command.

8. Enter the command SP to test your S1 search drive mapping.

9. Delete the S1 search drive mapping. On the line below, record the command you use.

   MAP DEL S1

10. Use the MAP command to display the revised search drive list.

Exercise 6-8: Using SESSION

In this exercise you will practice using the SESSION utility instead of the MAP command to create the drive mappings defined in step 1 of Exercise 4.

1. Log out of the file server in order to remove all existing drive pointers.
2. Log into the network again with same username.
3. Display your drive mappings with the MAP command.
4. Use the SESSION utility to establish the drive mappings you identified in Exercise 6-7 and print the screen showing these drive mappings.
5. Exit the SESSION utility and use the MAP command to verify the drive mappings.
6. Enter the command UTIL to test your search drive to the utility directory.
7. Enter the command SP to test your search drive to the spreadsheet software directory.
8. Use SESSION to delete the search drive mapping to the SP directory and print the screen showing the revised search drive mappings.

Exercise 6-9: Moving a Directory Structure

In this exercise you will need to use the FILER menu utility to move the DATAPROC directory structure from the ##ADMIN directory to the ##ADMIN\SAMPLE directory.

1. Start FILER.
2. Change the current directory to point to the ##ADMIN\SAMPLE directory path.
3. Use the Directory Contents option to highlight the DATAPROC directory and press **[Enter]**.
4. Select "Move Subdirectory's Structure."
5. Type the target path, including volume name, to the volume:##ADMIN\SAMPLE\ADMIN, where "##" represents your assigned student number.
6. You are now prompted to enter a new name. Press **[Enter]** to leave the current name unchanged and continue with the moving process.
7. Exit FILER.
8. Use the LISTDIR command to obtain a printout of the new directory structure showing the new location of the DATAPROC directory within the sample directory structure.

EXERCISE

Setting Up a Drive Pointer Environment

ACME Inc. would like you to set up a drive pointer environment for users of its network. Each user needs a drive pointer to be able to access his or her home directory directly without accidentally changing to another location. In addition, all users in each department need to be able to access easily the shared work directory for their department as well as have access to the organization's work directory and word processing forms. The users in the sales department will need a special drive pointer to run the order entry system. All users in the company will need to be able to run either the word processing or spreadsheet application software stored in the SYS:SOFTWARE.STC directory as well as be able to use NetWare and DOS commands.

1. Use the sample directory structure located in the SYS:EXAMPLE directory to complete the drive pointer planning form.

Figure 6-39

Drive Pointer Planning Form

Company: ACME Inc.

Planned by: _____ Date: _____

Group: Everyone

Letter	Description of Use	Path
S1:	NetWare utilities	
S2:	DOS utilities	
	global SYS: volume	SYS:

Group:

Letter	Description of Use	Path

Group:

Letter	Description of Use	Path

Group:

Letter	Description of Use	Path

Group:

Letter	Description of Use	Path

2.   Use MAP commands to implement the drive pointers you recorded in Step 1. Record the MAP commands you use in the space below.

3.   Use the MAP > PRN command to document the drive pointer assignments on the printer.

SUPERIOR TECHNICAL COLLEGE PROBLEMS

Project 6-1: Create the Superior Campus Directory Structure

Now that NetWare has been installed on the campus file server and the user workstations are able to boot up and attach to the network, your next job is to create a directory structure that can support the processing needs of the organization. To perform this task, you recently had a meeting with Dave Johnson and together you have finalized the directory structure you were working on in Chapter 4. Although the final design shown in Figure 6-40 does not exactly match your original design, it has everyone's approval and will meet the processing needs of the campus. The design is departmentalized by computer lab, faculty, and administration. Each department has a work area along with home directories for each user. Now Dave wants you to establish the framework for the directory structure by creating the major directories. The user home directories will not be created at this time, but will be automatically created for you later when you use NetWare utilities to create the user accounts. Dave informed you that the software for administrative use has already been installed in the SOFTWARE.STC directory of the SYS: volume and is ready for use.

Figure 6-40

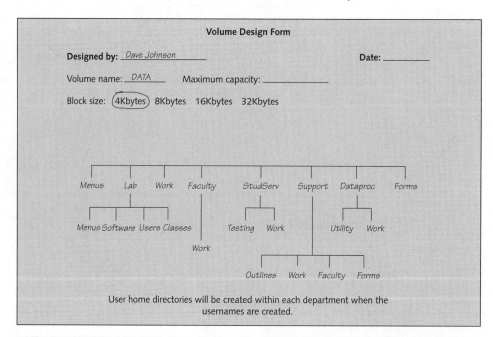

1. Log in to your assigned file server using your student username.
2. Start FILER.
3. Make your home directory your current directory.
4. Use the FILER utility to create the directory structure shown in Figure 6-40.
5. After creating the directory structure, exit FILER.
6. Use the LISTDIR /S > PRN command to print your home directory showing the Superior Technical College directory structure.

Project 6-2: Plan Drive Pointer Usage

Now that the directory structure has been established, Dave would like you to develop a plan for how drive pointers will be defined for users and groups. To help you with this task, Dave has provided you with a copy of the drive pointer assignment form developed for use in the administrative office. Fill out the form showing drive pointers that would be common to all users as well as drive pointer assignments for each department or workgroup. Dave explained, for example, that the computer lab users will need special search drives to the software packages in the lab, while faculty and office staff should have search drives for the software stored in the SYS:SOFTWARE.STC directory. Faculty and office staff users should also have home directories along with drive pointers to their corresponding shared work areas and search drives to the SOFTWARE.STC software directories. The student service staff will also need a way to access the placement and testing applications directories. In this project you should fill out a drive pointer planning form for all users and another form for each workgroup that has separate drive mapping assignments.

Project 6-3: Installing and Testing Utility Programs

Suppose you have some handy utility programs located on your student work disk that you would like to copy onto the file server in the DATAPROC\UTILITY subdirectory of the Superior Technical College structure.

1. Use the NCOPY command to copy all files from the \UTILITY directory of your student work disk into the DATAPROC\UTILITY subdirectory. On the line below, record the command you use.

    _____

2. Set the Sharable and Read-Only attributes on all files in your Superior Technical College UTILITY directory. On the line below, record the command you use.

    _____

3. Next use the NDIR command to obtain a printout of the files contained in the UTILITY directory.
4. Establish a search drive mapping to your UTILITY directory.
5. Use the CD SYS: command to change your default drive to the root of the SYS: volume.

6.   Type the command MENU to run the utility menu from the search drive. Test each of the options and, in the space below, record the results from each option:

Sorted Directory Listing:

Memory Map:

Solitaire:

Document User:

7.   Use the NCOPY command to copy all the files from the FORMS directory of your Student Disk into the FORMS directory you created for the Superior Technical College.

## CHAPTER SEVEN

LOGIN SECURITY

Allowing users convenient access to the file server and at the same time protecting sensitive or private information and services are the primary functions of a network security system. NetWare v3.x provides the capabilities and tools the network administrator needs to establish a sophisticated security system that will meet these needs in a local area network environment. As a CNA you will be expected to know how to use these capabilities and tools to perform the following security system functions:

- Create users and groups
- Determine what administrative functions can be delegated to user accounts and how to assign these privileges
- Protect user accounts from unauthorized use
- Use NetWare accounting to track system usage and charge users for network services
- Assign appropriate access rights and attributes to control access to the file system
- Secure the file server console from unauthorized access

AFTER READING THIS CHAPTER AND COMPLETING THE EXERCISES YOU WILL BE ABLE TO:

- LIST THE THREE TYPES OF NETWARE SECURITY AND DESCRIBE HOW LOGIN SECURITY CAN BE USED TO RESTRICT ACCESS TO THE FILE SERVER.

- DESCRIBE HOW THE NETWARE ACCOUNTING SYSTEM CAN BE USED TO CHARGE FOR NETWORK SERVICES AND FOR KEEPING TRACK OF TOTAL SYSTEM USAGE AND GROWTH.

- CREATE NEW USERS AND GROUPS AND ASSIGN ACCESS RESTRICTIONS USING THE SYSCON, USERDEF, AND MAKEUSER UTILITIES.

- USE THE SECURITY AND BINDFIX COMMAND LINE UTILITIES TO CHECK FOR POSSIBLE SECURITY VIOLATIONS AND FIX PROBLEMS IN NETWARE SECURITY FILES.

To provide these functions, NetWare security has three levels: login security, file system security, and console security. You already worked with login security, which controls initial access to the file server, when you had to enter a valid username to log in to a server. You also used the SETPASS utility to make your account more secure with an optional password. Additionally, you learned that file system security consists of rights and attributes that can be used to control access to the file system.

In this chapter, you will learn about login security and how to use NetWare utilities such as SYSCON, USERDEF, and MAKEUSER to handle NetWare accounting, create users, assign privileges, and establish access restrictions. In Chapter 8 you will learn how file system security can provide users with the necessary access rights to perform their work without affecting other users and limit access to files and directories that contain sensitive or secure information. Chapter 15 contains techniques and commands to make the file server console secure from unauthorized access.

LOGIN SECURITY

Login security is sometimes referred to as initial access security because it controls a user's ability to gain access to a file server. The login security system of NetWare v3.x consists of five components that all work together to provide users with the ability to access the file server and perform their assigned tasks.

1. Usernames

2. Passwords and password restrictions

3. Time restrictions

4. Station restrictions

5. Account restrictions

USERNAMES

When NetWare is first installed and started, two usernames, SUPERVISOR and GUEST, and one group name, EVERYONE, are created automatically for you. The SUPERVISOR username has access to all network services and the entire file system. The GUEST username has no special privileges or access rights and is restricted to performing only those tasks assigned to the group EVERYONE. Initially the network administrator logs in as SUPERVISOR and then creates the directory structure, other users, and access restrictions. When new users are created, they are automatically made members of the group EVERYONE to give them the rights to run programs in the SYS:PUBLIC directory, create files in the SYS:MAIL directory, and send output to standard print queues. In this section you will learn to assign usernames and access privileges and properly construct the user environment.

After creating the file system, the network administrator next needs to create a name on the file server for each user. If a user needs to access information and services on more than one file server, a username must be created on each server the user needs to access. In a multiple server environment, making a user's name the same on all servers avoids confusion.

NetWare v4.x is designed to support multiple file server environments and has a global naming system that makes it possible for a network administrator to create one networkwide login name per user. This login name can access services of any file server on the network. NetWare v4.x also provides many sophisticated management tools that are designed to help the administrator establish and maintain complex multiserver networks.

Although usernames can be up to 47 characters in length, most network administrators try to keep usernames to eight or fewer characters so they can create user's home directories with the same name as the login name. This makes it easier to map drives to user home directories automatically with login script files (explained in Chapter 13).

One of the first considerations in creating usernames is developing a consistent method of constructing a username from each user's actual name. Two common methods are used to construct usernames. One is to use the first letter of the user's first name followed by the first seven letters of his or her last name. For example, the username for Mary Read is MREAD. The advantage of this method is that the username is very similar to the user's actual name. The disadvantages are that most last names need to be truncated and frequent conflicts occur in which two or more users have the same first initial and last name. Such a case would be the username for Michael Read, which is also MREAD.

The second common method for creating usernames is to use the first three letters of the user's first name followed by the first three letters of the user's last name. In this method, for example, Mary Read's username becomes MARREA. The advantages of this method are that the usernames are almost uniformly of a consistent length and there is a smaller chance of duplicates. A disadvantage is that the usernames are less recognizable. Whichever system you choose for creating usernames, you must remember to be as consistent as possible.

NetWare v3.x also allows a network administrator to assign special manager and operator privileges to user accounts so they can perform such basic network administrative functions as creating and maintaining user accounts and working with printers. This delegation of responsibility allows the network administrator to concentrate on more important network functions. Even if you do not want to delegate basic jobs to other users, you can use this capability to create usernames that you use yourself to perform certain functions without having to log in as SUPERVISOR. Logging in as SUPERVISOR every time you need to do a network task that does not require supervisor privileges increases the risk of accidental damage to files or introduction of viruses into the network. (Because the SUPERVISOR username has all access rights to the entire network file system, if your workstation is infected by a computer virus, the virus software can copy itself into other network files and possibly erase network data.)

There is the case of a network administrator who logged in as SUPERVISOR and, while using the FILER utility to clean up the SYS: volume by removing unnecessary directories, accidentally marked and deleted the SYS:SYSTEM directory. This network administrator then had to restore the file server files from the NetWare installation disks.

As supervisor, you can assign one or more of the following six privilege levels to a username:

- Supervisor equivalent
- Workgroup manager
- User account manager
- Print queue operator
- Print server operator
- Console operator

The **supervisor equivalent** privilege level gives a username the same authority as the SUPERVISOR user. Of course, supervisor status should be limited to a small number of users. Most network administrators, however, establish at least one supervisor equivalent username to act as a backup, sometimes called a "back door," in case the SUPERVISOR account is inadvertently disabled or deleted. Later in this chapter, you will learn how the SECURITY command can be used to inform you which users on your file server have been granted supervisor equivalency.

The **workgroup manager** privilege allows a user to create and manage new users and groups without having access to the entire file server. The main purpose of the workgroup manager privilege is to allow the network administrator to delegate control of workgroups or departments to other capable users. In a large network, this privilege level can allow someone with network training in a department to create, delete, and maintain users within his or her domain. This reduces the amount of time the network administrator must spend performing these basic tasks.

The **user account manager** privilege provides the same capabilities as the workgroup manager privilege with the exclusion of creating new users or groups. This means that a user account manager is a user who has been entrusted with the management of one or more other usernames. Managing a username means you can change the user's name, password, and login restrictions, modify the user's personal login script, place or remove the user from groups that you manage, restrict the user's disk space usage, and clear user accounts in the event a user is denied access due to an expired or forgotten password.

The **print queue operator** privilege allows the network administrator to assign the control of a print queue. A **print queue** is a directory on a file server that holds printed output until the designated printer is ready to receive it. The print queue allows multiple users to send output to a printer simultaneously. Print jobs need to be cleared from the print queue periodically due to incorrect printer selection. Print jobs can also be rearranged to allow more important output to be printed first.

The **print server operator** privilege level allows a user to control one or more printers. This privilege is usually assigned to users who have a printer attached to their workstations. Being a print server operator allows the user to perform such printer functions as changing forms, stopping the printer to clear paper jams, restarting the printer at a specific page number, and canceling a print job.

The **console operator** privilege allows a user to use NetWare's FCONSOLE utility to monitor file server status, disable new logins, view server version information, broadcast messages to all users, view detailed user connection information, and send messages to selected users. The one function of FCONSOLE that the console operator is not allowed to perform is downing the file server. To help prevent an accidental downing of the server, only a supervisor or supervisor equivalent user can use FCONSOLE to down the file server. In NetWare v2.x, an important use of the FCONSOLE utility is monitoring file server performance. In NetWare v3.x, this function is performed through the MONITOR NetWare Loadable Module on the file server console.

 Many operators refer to the file server screen that contains the colon prompt as the "server console." You used the file server console screen when installing NetWare on the server computer in Chapter 5.

When a user logs in, the NetWare operating system checks his or her user account to see if it has any of the privileges just described.

PASSWORDS

While usernames and operator privileges provide initial access to the server and delegate network management duties, they do little to prevent unauthorized access to restricted information or server functions. Networks need additional security to restrict who can use the file server in order to protect the information and the integrity of the file server environment. After usernames, the first barrier in a security system is passwords on user accounts, and one of the first tasks of the network administrator after NetWare installation is to log in and establish a password for the SUPERVISOR account. In NetWare v3.x, passwords can be up to 20 characters long, and if you allow users to change their own passwords, you can increase password security by requiring some or all of the password restrictions described in the following paragraphs.

 NetWare provides additional security against guessed usernames and passwords by requiring a password whenever someone attempts to log in using a username that does not exist. This feature makes it more difficult for people to guess usernames because they can never be sure if they have entered a correct username and wrong password or if they have entered an incorrect username.

Setting minimum password length

To prevent the use of passwords that are short and easy to guess, most network administrators use Novell's recommendation of a five-character minimum for password length. In this chapter, you will learn how to change the minimum length of passwords assigned to existing or newly created users.

Forcing periodic password changes

After a while, a user's password can become known to coworkers, and no longer provides protection against unauthorized access to that user's account. Having users run the SETPASS utility to reestablish passwords periodically lessens this problem (as described later in this chapter). NetWare allows you to force selected user accounts to change passwords by establishing a limit on the time period a password remains valid. NetWare's default value of 40 days between password changes might be too frequent for most users. If the time period between password changes is too short, it is not uncommon for users to record their current password near their work areas where it can easily be found and used (under the keyboard and in a desk drawer are common hiding places). As network administrator, you can increase the time between password changes in order to improve file server security. In addition, you should encourage good password and login habits by periodically reminding users not to have their password information recorded near their workstations and to log out whenever they leave their workstations unattended.

Requiring unique passwords

Another way to increase password security is to require users to enter a different password each time they change their password. When you require unique passwords, the file server keeps track of the last 10 passwords that have been used by a user and rejects a new password that repeats one of the previous 10. NetWare's unique passwords option prevents users from alternating among a few favorite passwords, which therefore makes it more difficult for an intruder to log in using a known password. Network administrators often combine this option with forced periodic password changes in order to provide increased safety on security-sensitive user accounts such as the SUPERVISOR account or an account assigned to a payroll clerk.

Limiting login grace periods

When a password has been set to expire, the user is given a default of six logins to use the expired password. This six-login grace period prevents users from accidentally being locked out from the network after their passwords expire, and it also keeps users from using an expired password indefinitely. Each time a user logs in after password expiration, NetWare displays a reminder that the current password has expired and states the remaining number of grace logins. Six grace logins are adequate for most file server installations, but the network administrator or user account manager can change this number on an individual basis or change the default value that is assigned to all new usernames when they are created.

TIME RESTRICTIONS

Time restrictions allow the network administrator or user account manager to increase a user's account security by limiting the times during which the account can be used. This prevents someone who knows a user's password from logging in and accessing the network after business hours. Time restrictions can be set in half-hour increments. For example, a network administrator can establish time restrictions that allow a payroll clerk to use the file server only from 8:00 A.M. until 4:30 P.M. on weekdays. Time restrictions are important on high-security accounts, such as a payroll clerk's, because they prevent an intruder from accessing sensitive payroll information during nonbusiness hours.

STATION RESTRICTIONS

Station restrictions can be used to limit the number of times a user account can be concurrently logged in to the server and to specify from which workstations a user can log in to the network. The NetWare default is that a user can log in from any workstation and be logged in to the network at several workstations simultaneously. A user with SUPERVISOR privileges can change these defaults for newly created user accounts; a user account manager can change the defaults on existing user accounts that are in his or her control.

Setting a username to be valid for logging in from several workstations simultaneously allows a network administrator to create a general-purpose username for multiple users. In most situations, however, limiting user accounts to one workstation at a time is important for the following reasons:

- Logging in from multiple workstations can cause software errors with some programs because certain control files are not sharable and therefore cannot be accessed simultaneously from more than one location by the same user.

- Restricting the username to one workstation at a time helps users who move between multiple workstations remember not to leave a workstation unattended—and thus open to access by unauthorized users.

- Limiting a user account to access from a single workstation prevents an intruder who knows a user's name and password from logging in at an unattended workstation and gaining unauthorized access to the file server.

Restricting a user account to a specific network and workstation node address increases the security of highly sensitive information. A payroll clerk, for example, can be required to log in only on the workstation located in his or her office during normal office hours. In order for an intruder to access the payroll data, he or she would need to know the payroll clerk's username and password, to enter the payroll clerk's office during normal business hours, and to log in to the file server from the clerk's workstation. These limitations prevent all but a very bold intruder and/or a very well-trusted employee from making such an attempt, and his or her actions would likely be noticed by other employees.

Of course, if your SUPERVISOR password is generally known to network users, all security efforts are in vain—anyone with the SUPERVISOR password can log in from any workstation and have access to the entire file server. To thwart this, you might want to enhance SUPERVISOR account security by requiring any supervisor equivalent usernames to access the network from only two workstations that you can constantly monitor. Having your SUPERVISOR account operate from two different workstations, or having a supervisor equivalent username that operates on a separate workstation address, allows you to access the file server with supervisor privileges in the event that one of the workstations is out of order.

ACCOUNT RESTRICTIONS

Account restrictions are conditions defined by the administrator to restrict user accounts. When an account is locked, no one can log in to the file server with that username until the account is reactivated. A CNA needs to know how account restrictions can be used and how to reactivate a user account after it has been locked through any of the following limitations:

- The user account expired.

- The number of grace logins is exceeded.

- The account's balance is depleted.

- The predetermined number of incorrect password attempts that have been made.

Account expiration date

NetWare's account expiration date is used to set a date after which the user account becomes disabled. This is a good way to establish temporary user accounts that you do not want accessed after a certain date. Student user accounts, for example, can be set to expire at the end of a semester or school year. After the expiration date, if a user attempts to log in with an expired username, NetWare requires a password and then displays a message that the account has been disabled. Figure 7-1 illustrates an example of a login attempt with an expired username. Notice that NetWare requires you to enter the password before issuing the error message.

 NetWare's practice of requiring a user to enter a password prior to issuing any error messages makes it harder for an intruder to guess usernames and passwords.

Figure 7-1

Expired username

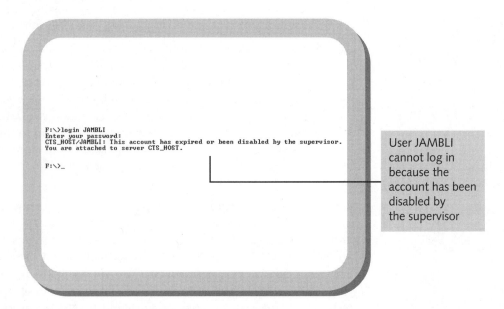

```
F:\>login JAMBLI
Enter your password:
CTS_HOST/JAMBLI: This account has expired or been disabled by the supervisor.
You are attached to server CTS_HOST.

F:\>_
```

User JAMBLI cannot log in because the account has been disabled by the supervisor

Number of grace logins exceeded

Users who are forced to change their password after a specified number of days are granted a fixed number of logins with the old password after it has expired. If a user fails to enter a new password within the granted number of grace logins, the account will be disabled until the SUPERVISOR or user account manager either assigns a new password or extends the number of grace logins. Figure 7-2 shows an example of a login attempt after a user's grace logins are used up.

Figure 7-2

Grace logins expired

```
F:\>LOGIN RON
Enter your password:
Good evening, RON.

Drive  A:   maps to a local disk.
Drive  B:   maps to a local disk.
Drive  C:   maps to a local disk.
Drive  D:   maps to a local disk.
Drive  E:   maps to a local disk.
Drive  F: = CTS_HOST\SYS:  \

SEARCH1:  = Y:. [CTS_HOST\SYS:  \PUBLIC]
SEARCH2:  = X:. [CTS_HOST\SYS:  \PUBLIC\IBM_PC\MSDOS\V6.20]
SEARCH3:  = C:\DOS
SEARCH4:  = C:\WINDOWS
SEARCH5:  = Z:. [CTS_HOST\SYS:  \MHS\EXE]

Password for user RON on server CTS_HOST has expired.
     You have NO grace logins left to change your password.
     This is your LAST CHANCE to change it.
Enter your new password: _
```

Last chance for user to enter a new password

Depleted account balance

If the accounting feature is enabled on a file server, records are kept of usage for such services as disk blocks read or written. Users can be "charged" for these services and the charges are then deducted from the amount in the user's balance field. Supervisors or user account managers can assign the following conditions:

- A balance to an individual user account that determines how much time the user can access the network
- A credit limit that allows the user to draw on an account balance up to the limit
- Unlimited credit to the user
- A default credit limit and account balance that is granted to each new user that is created

When the amount in a user's account balance falls below his or her credit limit, the user's account is disabled until either the SUPERVISOR or user account manager increases the balance or provides more credit. Figure 7-3, on the following page, shows an example of a login attempt after the user balance has been depleted.

Figure 7-3

Depleted account
balance

```
F:\>LOGIN ROB
Enter your password:
CTS_HOST/ROB: You have exceeded your credit limit for this server.
You are attached to server CTS_HOST.

F:\>_
```

Intruder detection

Unlike the other account restrictions that can be set individually for each user, NetWare's intruder detection is a feature that is turned on or off by the SUPERVISOR for all users on a file server. Intruder detection locks an account when a user fails to enter the correct password within the number of attempts specified by the supervisor. The purpose of intruder detection is to prevent someone who knows a user's name from trying to log in to the user's network account by repeatedly entering likely password combinations. The intruder detection feature allows you to place a maximum on the number of times a user can attempt to enter his or her current password within a specified time period, and then set a length of time that the account will be locked when the specified number of attempts has been exceeded. Only the SUPERVISOR or a supervisor equivalent user can release a locked account before the specified time interval. Figure 7-4 shows an example of intruder detection locking up a user account after three login attempts.

Figure 7-4

Intruder detection
lockout

```
F:\>LOGIN SUPERVISOR
Enter your password:
CTS_HOST/SUPERVISOR: Access to server denied.
You are attached to server CTS_HOST.

F:\>LOGIN SUPERVISOR
Enter your password:
CTS_HOST/SUPERVISOR: Access to server denied.
You are attached to server CTS_HOST.

F:\>LOGIN SUPERVISOR
Enter your password:
CTS_HOST/SUPERVISOR: Access to server denied.
You are attached to server CTS_HOST.

F:\>LOGIN SUPERVISOR
Enter your password:
CTS_HOST/SUPERVISOR: Intruder detection lockout has disabled this account.
You are attached to server CTS_HOST.

F:\>_
```

NETWARE ACCOUNTING

NetWare's accounting features allow the network administrator to track resources used on a network. You can monitor user login and logout activity, charge customers for resource usage on the file server, or monitor file server usage in order to allow planning for file server expansion. The SYSCON utility, discussed later in this chapter, is used to install and implement the NetWare accounting functions.

TRACKING USER LOGINS AND LOGOUTS

After accounting is installed on a file server, the server will begin tracking user logins and logouts and storing this information in the NET$ACCT.DAT file in the SYS:SYSTEM directory. This login and logout information is used by NetWare's PAUDIT program to print audit reports showing the time each user logged in, the services used, and when the user logged out. You can use these audit reports to determine activity for specific users. In a school environment, for example, a report can be sent to teachers indicating how often their students are using the network. This can help teachers evaluate whether students are not completing their work because of lack of ability or lack of effort. The PAUDIT program is located in the SYS:SYSTEM directory. Supervisor authority is required to view or print user login and logout information. See the example in Figure 7-5.

Figure 7-5

Using PAUDIT to display login data

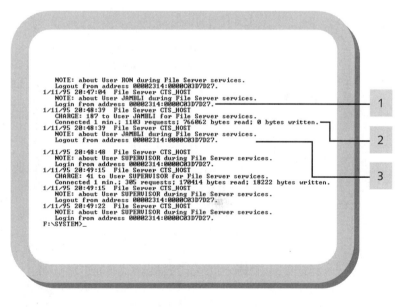

Using the output of the PAUDIT program, you can follow the activity of a user. For example, user JAMBLI first logs into the server from workstation 0000C03D7D27 on 11/27/95 at 20:40 (8:40 P.M.), as shown in Figure 7-5 (1). Notice that the information indicated in (2) shows that the user JAMBLI was logged into the server for one minute, read 766062 bytes, and made 1103 file server requests before logging out from the same workstation as indicated by (3). As you can see, this information can be very useful for auditing purposes.

The contents of the NET$ACCT.DAT file can be summarized and printed with NetWare's ATOTAL program, showing the total usage by service for each week. Because the NET$ACCT.DAT file can become quite large over time, you should establish a schedule for printing reports, backing up the file before erasing it and starting the next reporting period. NetWare automatically recreates the file when the user next logs in.

 The NET$REC.DAT file contains a conversion table used by the PAUDIT and ATOTAL programs to translate the NET$ACCT.DAT information for their reports. Although you erase the NET$ACCT.DAT file to close the accounting period, you must keep the NET$REC.DAT file in the SYS:SYSTEM directory in order for ATOTAL and PAUDIT to work.

CHARGING FOR FILE SERVER USAGE

NetWare's accounting functions can be used to record file server usage by the following categories:

- Disk activity
- Connect time
- Disk storage space consumed
- Service requests

Records of file server usage can be important tools in tracking the growth of a file server, allowing you to budget for future file server needs. Another use of the NetWare accounting feature is to charge users for services. This capability can be useful if your file server is shared by two or more profit centers. Each profit center can then be billed monthly based on its usage of the file server.

 A teacher in a local school system used NetWare accounting to help motivate students to achieve better grades by rewarding good scores with additional credit on the file server. Having credit on the file server allowed students to run games and simulations from the server during their break time.

Types of charges

The **disk activity charge** includes the number of disk blocks read, the number of disk blocks written, or both. The amount to be charged for each block read can be specified in half-hour increments. This allows you to charge one rate during peak business hours—8:00 A.M. to 5:00 P.M.—and another rate for other off-peak periods. The **connect time** figure allows you to charge for the number of minutes a user is logged in to the file server even if no services are accessed. Here, too, you can establish different charge rates for different time periods. The user will be charged the rate you establish for each minute of login time.

The **disk storage** figure allows you to charge for each block of disk space occupied by a file owned by a user. This charge is assigned once per day. The network administrator can select the time of day and charge rate to be used. At the specified time, the file server will scan its directories and compute the charges for each user's disk storage usage. The **service requests** figure allows you to charge for such file server activities as using directory services, accessing bindery files, and sending messages. You can establish different charge rates for different time periods based on half-hour increments. The specified charge rate is applied for each service request.

Charge rate formula

The amount a user is charged for accessing a service is automatically computed by NetWare using a charge rate formula. The charge rate formula is based on a specific amount to be charged for each unit of service and is specified as a ratio consisting of a multiplier and divisor as shown in the following example:

$$\text{Blocks Read Charge Rate} = 1/10$$

Based on this ratio, a user will be charged one unit for each 10 blocks of data read from the disk drive. While the charge amount is arbitrary, Novell suggests that you begin by using one cent for each unit of service and then adjust this ratio as necessary for your network. Suppose, for example, your company maintains a database on a file server for which it needs to collect $150 per month for maintenance. You decide to base your charge for usage of the database on number of blocks read from the disk. Assume that, after using the accounting feature to track network usage, you determine that on an average 10,000 blocks are read from the file server each week. In this case, the charge rate would be 15,000 cents ($150.00 $\times$ 100) divided by 40,000 blocks (10,000 $\times$ 4 weeks). This yields .375, which rounds off to $.38 per block, giving a charge ratio of 38/1. With this charge ratio, users would be charged based on how much information they read from the database in any given month.

Before calculating the charge rate, you need to know how much money you want to obtain per month, what services you want to charge for, and the average usage of that service per month. The amount of money you need to make per month to cover network and administrative expenses is best arrived at by consulting your company accountant. It should be based on operational costs and how much of those costs should be paid by the consumer. Once you calculate the monthly charge figure, you need to determine what services you want to charge for. To keep things simple, you might choose to charge for only one service. If file server storage capacity is a concern for you, you might select the disk storage charge rate. If network utilization is high, you might want to charge for service requests. To prevent users from staying logged in when they are not working, you could charge for connect time.

Finally, to determine the average usage of the selected service, you need to track the total usage for the selected service over a minimum of two weeks. This can be done by performing the following steps:

1. Use SYSCON to assign a 1/1 charge rate for the selected service.

2. Use SYSCON to give all users unlimited credit. This is necessary to prevent user accounts from being disabled during the test period.

3. At the end of the time period, use NetWare's ATOTAL program to obtain the usage results. See the example shown in Figure 7-6. The totals can be used in a spreadsheet to graph server usage.

Figure 7-6

Using ATOTAL to
display usage totals

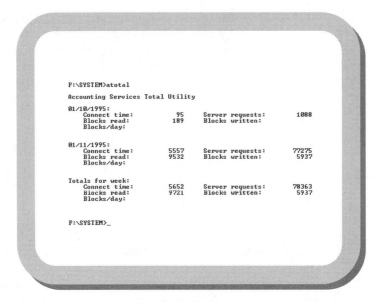

```
F:\SYSTEM>atotal

Accounting Services Total Utility

01/10/1995:
      Connect time:          95      Server requests:        1088
      Blocks read:          189      Blocks written:
      Blocks/day:

01/11/1995:
      Connect time:        5557      Server requests:       77275
      Blocks read:         9532      Blocks written:         5937
      Blocks/day:

Totals for week:
      Connect time:        5652      Server requests:       78363
      Blocks read:         9721      Blocks written:         5937
      Blocks/day:


F:\SYSTEM>_
```

After you have determined the charge rate, you can again use SYSCON to give your customer usernames a balance based on the amount paid for the month, remove the unlimited credit privilege, and optionally assign a credit limit. When a user's credit limit is exceeded, the file server displays a message indicating that the user's account balance has been exceeded and then grants the user several minutes to complete his or her work and log out. At this point, the user's account is disabled and the user cannot log in again until the balance field is updated or additional credit is assigned.

PLANNING FOR EXPANSION

One aspect of NetWare accounting that can be helpful for all network administrators is the ability to monitor file server usage and employ that information in planning for future server expansion. As the usage on your file server grows, you will eventually need to consider adding more disk storage, a faster disk system, more memory, or even a faster file server computer. If these needs are not anticipated and justified, you will probably have a hard time obtaining the budget for network improvements when you need them. With NetWare's accounting functions, the ATOTAL program can gather usage information and then use a spreadsheet program to graph the server usage information to illustrate disk access, storage capacity, and server requests for each week. By extrapolation, the graph you can then draw will project your server expansion needs for budgeting purposes.

NETWARE UTILITIES AND COMMANDS

NetWare provides menu and command line utilities that allow you to create users, implement login security, and work with accounting features. As a CNA, you will be expected to know how to use these utilities to perform the functions described in this chapter. The SYSCON utility is the main tool used by network administrators to create users and manage login security and accounting functions. In this section, you will learn about the various options and menus of the SYSCON utility. Examples of using SYSCON to perform a variety of administrative functions are provided. Although SYSCON is one of NetWare's most powerful utilities, it still requires several steps to create users. The USERDEF and MAKEUSER utilities, also described in this chapter, are designed to streamline the process of creating users by allowing you to create templates or batch files that automate the user creation process. In addition to these menu utilities, the SECURITY and BINDFIX command line utilities play important roles in checking for potential security problems and correcting any problems in the NetWare bindery files, which contain username and password information.

THE SYSCON UTILITY

SYSCON (system configuration) is the main NetWare utility for creating and maintaining users and groups, for working with network accounting, and for managing login security restrictions. Although users can be created with the USERDEF and MAKEUSER utilities, SYSCON is the only utility that can create groups, assign manager privileges to usernames, implement accounting, work with login scripts, and activate intruder detection.

Use of all SYSCON utility functions requires supervisor authority; however, some limited functions are available to other network users. Workgroup managers can access SYSCON, for example, to create users and groups. User account managers can use it to manage their assigned user accounts, and regular users can use SYSCON to view limited information about other users and groups as well as to change some of their own information such as a password or a personal login script.

 Like other menu utilities described in Chapter 6, the SYSCON utility uses the Ins key to add an object to a window, the Del key to remove or delete highlighted object(s), the F1 key for help, the F3 key to change an entry such as the user or group name, the F5 key to mark objects, and the [Alt][F10] key combination to exit.

SYSCON main menu

To use all the options of SYSCON you should be logged in as a supervisor. If you do not have supervisor authority, but are using a workgroup manager username, you will be able to perform all functions except those under the Supervisor Options topic. After logging in to the file server, you can start SYSCON from any directory by typing SYSCON and pressing the Enter key. The SYSCON Available Topics menu shown in Figure 7-7, on the following page, is displayed.

Figure 7-7

SYSCON main menu

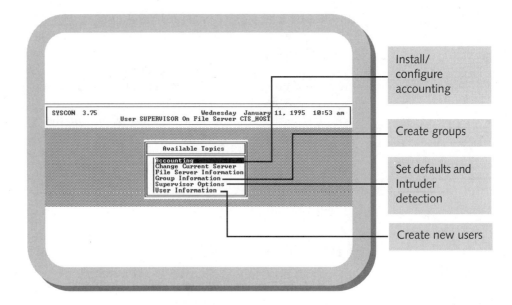

Notice that the top of the SYSCON screen displays the current version number of the SYSCON program along with the current date, username, and file server being accessed. The Accounting option allows you to install and configure NetWare accounting functions and requires supervisor privileges. The Change Current Server option allows you to log in and then change from the server displayed on the top of the screen to another file server. File Server Information can be used to view version and serial number information regarding your current file server. Group Information is used to create and manage groups. As the name implies, the Supervisor Options are available only to the SUPERVISOR or supervisor equivalent users and includes options to set default restrictions, maintain the system login script, create special user types such as workgroup managers and console operators, and turn on or off intruder detection. The last option, User Information, is used to create and manage user accounts.

Accounting.   This SYSCON menu option initiates NetWare's accounting functions on the file server, configures the accounting charge methods, and removes accounting. When you first select the Accounting option, NetWare asks if you want to install accounting on the file server. To install accounting, you select Yes and press Enter. The Accounting menu shown in Figure 7-8 is displayed.

The Accounting Servers option displays a window showing all servers on the network that are currently charging for services. This option can be used to add or remove servers from the accounting system. You can add another server to the list by pressing the Ins key and selecting the print server, as shown in Figure 7-9.

To remove accounting from a file server, you first need to remove the server from the Accounting Servers window by highlighting the server name and pressing the Del key. Next, to remove accounting from the selected file server, press the Esc key to exit the Accounting Servers window and answer Yes to the prompt asking if you want to remove accounting from the selected file server. You can then use the Esc key to return to the SYSCON main menu. The next time you select Accounting, you will again be asked if you want to install accounting on the server.

Figure 7-8

Accounting menu

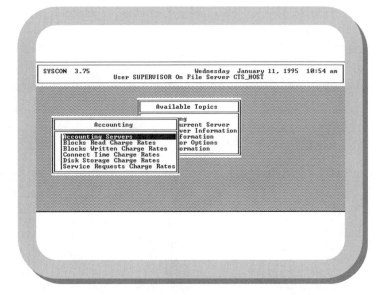

Figure 7-9

Adding an accounting server

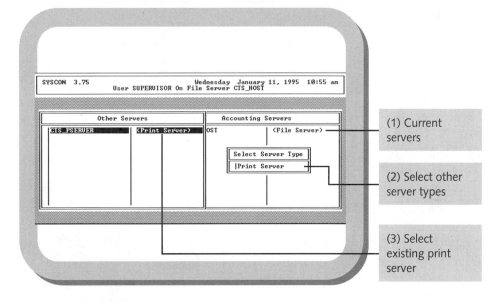

(1) Current servers

(2) Select other server types

(3) Select existing print server

The Blocks Read Charge Rates option allows you to enter the charge ratio you want to use for each block read during the time period specified. Selecting this option displays the Blocks Read Charge Rates screen shown in Figure 7-10.

Notice that times and dates are shown on the right side of the screen, and the existing charge rates are shown at the lower left. The initial screen assigns all time periods a charge rate of 1. Charge rate 1 is always set to no charge. To set a charge ratio of 38 cents for each block read during normal business hours (defined here as Monday – Friday, 8:00 A.M. – 4:00 P.M.), you first highlight the time periods. Use the arrow keys to move the cursor to the 8:00 A.M. row in the Monday column. Next, press the F5 key and use the down arrow and right arrow keys to highlight the times from 8:00 through 4:00 in the columns Monday through Friday. Now press [Enter] to display the Select Charge Rate window. To create a new charge, select the Other Charge Rate option. In the New Charge Rate window, enter the number 38 for the Multiplier and 1 for the Divisor, as shown in Figure 7-11. After entering the new charge, use the Esc key to save the new charge rate and assign it to the selected time range.

Figure 7-10

Blocks Read Charge Rates window

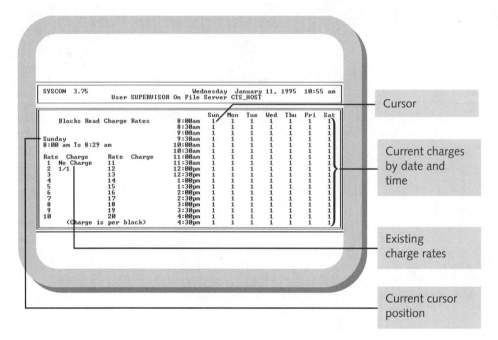

Cursor

Current charges by date and time

Existing charge rates

Current cursor position

Figure 7-11

Entering a charge rate

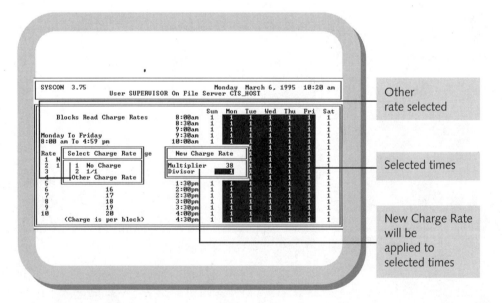

Other rate selected

Selected times

New Charge Rate will be applied to selected times

The charge rate numbers of the selected time periods will change to the newly assigned number. To change time periods and use a different charge rate, use the F5 key to mark the times you want to change and press [Enter]. You can then select a different charge rate or select 1 for no charge.

The Blocks Written Charge Rates option allows you to enter the charge ratio you want to apply to each block written during the time period specified. Selecting this option displays the Blocks Written Charge Rates screen, which has the same format and functions as the Blocks Read Charge Rate screen just described.

The Connect Time Charge Rates option allows you to enter the charge ratio you want to apply to each minute a user is connected to the file server during the time period specified. Selecting this option displays the Connect Time Charge Rates screen, which has the same format and functions as the Blocks Read Charge Rate screen.

The Disk Storage Charge Rates option allows you to enter the charge ratio you want to apply to each block of disk space used per day. Selecting this option displays the Disk Storage Charge Rates screen, which is similar to the Blocks Read Charge Rates screen in Figure 7-10. The method for establishing disk storage charge rates differs slightly from the previous method. To set up the charge ratio for disk storage, first select the time of day you want the system to total the storage used by each user and press the 1 key. The number one stands for the first charge rate. Because no charge ratio has been set for rate 1, SYSCON asks for the multiplier and divisor rates, as it does for the other charge rates. You then enter the desired Multiplier and Divisor and press [Esc] to save the new charge ratio in the charge rates window. Press [Esc] again to return to the Accounting menu.

 Because computing the total storage for users slows down the file server, it is a good idea to have the server do this outside of normal working hours.

The Service Requests Charge Rates option allows you to enter the charge ratio you want to apply to each server request made by a user during the time period specified. Selecting this option displays the Server Requests Charge Rates screen, which has the same format and functions as the Blocks Read Charge Rates screen.

Change Current Server.   This option on SYSCON's main menu displays a window showing all file servers to which you are currently logged in. To change to another file server, simply select that server's name and press [Enter]. The file server name displayed on the top of the SYSCON screen changes to the selected file server. To log in to another file server, press [Ins]. This displays the Other File Server window, which shows all servers on your network. Highlight the name of the server to which you want to log in and press [Enter]. NetWare next asks you to specify a valid username (and password, if required) for the selected file server. After you enter a valid username and password, the new server appears in the Available Servers window. You can then make it your current server by selecting it, as described previously.

File Server Information.   When you select this option, SYSCON displays the Known NetWare Servers window, which lists all file servers to which you are logged in. Select the file server about which you want to view information and press [Enter]. The File Server Information window, as shown in Figure 7-12, will be displayed. Notice that this screen contains information about the version of NetWare running on your server, including the maximum number of connections it will support and its serial number. This information can be important when it is time to upgrade the operating system or when you experience problems that are related to certain NetWare versions. This window also includes the internal network address that was assigned to the file server during installation. Checking this address can ensure that you do not install another file server on the network with the same internal network address.

Figure 7-12

File Server Information window

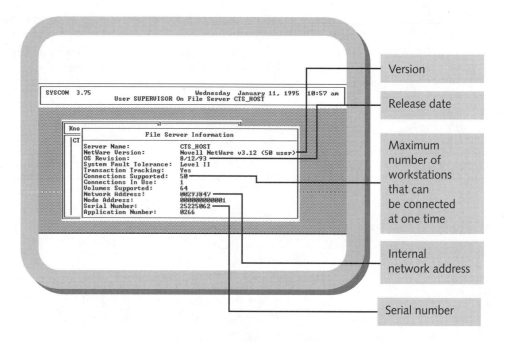

Group Information.   Selecting SYSCON's Group Information option displays the Group Names window, which can be used to create, rename, manage, and delete groups. To create a new group, press the Ins key and enter the name of the group in the New Group Name window, as shown in Figure 7-13. To change the name of a group, highlight the current group in the Group Name window and press the F3 key. SYSCON opens a window showing the existing group name. Use the Backspace key to erase the existing name, type the revised group name, and press [Enter]. The new name for the group will be displayed in the Group Names window.

Figure 7-13

Adding a new group

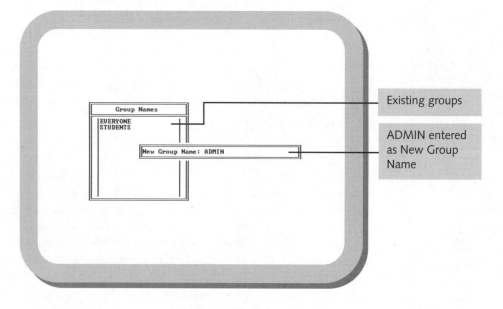

To delete an existing group, use the arrow keys to highlight the name of the group you want to delete and press the Del key. To delete more than one group, use the F5 key to highlight the names of the groups you want to delete and press [Del]. SYSCON displays a confirmation window asking if you want to delete the groups. You can select Yes and press [Enter] to delete the selected groups.

 You can remove unnecessary groups without affecting user accounts. Deleting a group does not delete the user accounts that are members of the deleted group.

If you are logged in as SUPERVISOR, or if you are the manager of a group, you can highlight that group and press [Enter] to display the Group Information window shown in Figure 7-14.

Figure 7-14

Group Information window

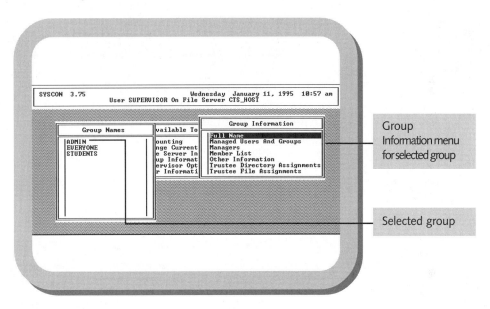

To add members to a group, select the Member List option and use the Ins key to select the usernames you want to include as members of this group. To make another user a manager of the group, select the Managers option and use the Ins key to select the usernames you want to install as managers of this group. The Managed Users And Groups option is used to make all members of this group user account managers of other users and groups included in the Managed Users And Groups windows. The Trustee Directory Assignments and Trustee File Assignments options are used to grant access rights for this group to specific directories or files. The Other Information option can be used to display the hexadecimal group ID assigned to this group for use by the NetWare operating system.

Supervisor Options. To access SYSCON's Supervisor Options menu, shown in Figure 7-15, you must be logged in as either SUPERVISOR or as a supervisor equivalent user. These options allow the supervisor to establish default settings as well as perform such important functions as working with the system login script, viewing operating system information and messages, and providing users with console operator and workgroup manager privileges.

Figure 7-15

Supervisor Options window

The Default Account Balance/Restrictions option is used to set default account balance and credit information along with other account restrictions, as shown in Figure 7-16 for all new users. Any changes that you make in this window do not affect existing user accounts but become the defaults for any new users that are created with the SYSCON utility.

Figure 7-16

Default Account Balance/Restrictions window

The default account balance and restriction information only affects users created with SYSCON; users created with the USERDEF and MAKEUSER utilities are affected by separate default settings.

The "Account has expiration date" field can be used if you want the user accounts that you will create to expire after the date you specify. The expiration date can be entered either by using the mm/dd/yy format or by typing the complete month name followed by the day and year. (For example, 5/5/96 can also be entered as May 5, 1996.) In most cases, you will want to limit the number of workstations from which the new user accounts can log in by changing the "Maximum Connections" field to show a limit of one connection. The "Create Home Directory for User" field is initially set to Yes. This causes SYSCON to create a home directory for each user by asking you to enter the complete path to the directory in which you want the user's directory created. SYSCON then automatically grants the new user all rights to this directory. If you have already created user home directories or if for some other reason you do not want SYSCON to make home directories for the users you will be creating, enter No in this field.

The Require Password option is initially set to No. In most cases you will want to require all users you create to have a password. You should therefore change No to Yes and then specify in the "Minimum Password Length" field a minimum of at least four characters. The "Force Periodic Password Changes" and "Days Between Forced Changes" fields allow a network administrator to require all new users to change passwords within the number of days specified. NetWare will then warn users when their passwords expire. If the user does not enter a new password, his or her account becomes disabled until the supervisor or user account manager changes the password. When you force users to change passwords, it is also important to provide a limited number of grace logins in the "Limit Grace Logins" field. Changing the "Require Unique Passwords" field to Yes prevents users from alternating among a few favorite passwords by requiring them to enter a new password that is different from the previous 10 passwords they have used.

When NetWare accounting is enabled, the "Account Balance" field can be used by a network administrator to assign an initial amount of credit to new users. The "Allow Unlimited Credit" field should be changed to Yes if you do not want user accounts to be disabled when account balances drop below the amount specified in the "Low Balance Limit" field. If you specify unlimited credit, you can keep track of how much file server usage each user has made and won't need to provide the user with an account balance and risk disabling his or her account if the balance drops below the low balance limit.

The Default Time Restrictions screen shown in Figure 7-17 allows the network administrator to prevent users from accessing the file server during specific times or days. The asterisks on the screen indicate the half-hour time intervals that are available to the user.

Suppose you start the file server backup at midnight and you want to be sure no user will access the file server after 11:30 P.M. To restrict all users you create from accessing the server from 11:30 P.M. until 5:00 A.M. on all days, use the arrow keys to move the cursor to 11:30 P.M. in the Sunday column, press the F5 key, and then use the right arrow key to mark the time blocks from 11:30 through 4:30 in all days. Pressing the Del key removes the asterisks from these times and prevents all newly created users from using the file server during this time period.

Figure 7-17

Default Time
Restrictions window

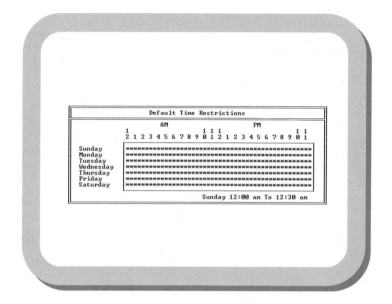

To add access times to the restrictions screen, mark the time periods using the F5 key as described previously and press the Ins key. Asterisks will be inserted in the marked times, indicating that the new users have access during the times indicated with asterisks.

The Edit System AUTOEXEC File option allows the network administrator to view and maintain the AUTOEXEC.NCF file stored in the SYS:SYSTEM directory. Using this option avoids the inconvenience of having to go to the file server console and use the LOAD INSTALL command to access or update the server startup commands.

The File Server Console Operators option allows the supervisor to add or remove users as FCONSOLE console operators. Selecting this option displays a window showing any existing console operators. Pressing the Ins key displays a list of existing users and groups. You can select either a single user or a group or you can use the F5 key to mark multiple users and groups and then press [Enter] to include the selected entities as console operators. If you select a group, then all users who are members of the group will have file server console operator privileges.

Use the Intruder Detection/Lockout option to turn on or off the intruder detection process and set the intruder detection parameters, as shown in Figure 7-18. To enable intruder detection, change the No in the "Detect Intruder" field to Yes. The values that appear in the fields are the default values SYSCON applies when intruder detection is first enabled.

The "Intruder Detection Threshold" contains two fields that allow a network administrator to establish the maximum number of unsuccessful login attempts as well as the amount of time in which the unsuccessful login attempts are accumulated. If a user exceeds the maximum number of login attempts specified in the "Incorrect Login Attempts" field within the amount of time specified in the "Bad Login Count Retention Time" field, NetWare disables the account for the amount of time specified in the "Length of Account Lockout" field.

Figure 7-18

Intruder Detection/
Lockout window

```
SYSCON  3.75                              Monday  March 6, 1995  10:21 am
                     User SUPERVISOR On File Server CTS_HOST


                    ┌────────────────────────────────┐
                    │         Available Topics        │
          ┌─────────┴────────────────────────────────┴─────────┐
          │           Intruder Detection/Lockout               │
          ├────────────────────────────────────────────────────┤tions
          │ Detect Intruders:              Yes                  │
          │                                                     │
          │ Intruder Detection Threshold                        │
          │ Incorrect Login Attempts:      3                    │
          │ Bad Login Count Retention Time: 0  Days  0  Hours  30 Minutes │
          │                                                     │
          │ Lock Account After Detection:  Yes                  │
          │    Length Of Account Lockout:  0  Days  0  Hours  1  Minutes │
          └─────────────────────────────────────────────────────┘
```

The System Login Script option allows you to create, view, or modify the system login script file. The system login script commands are contained in the NET$LOG.DAT file in the SYS:PUBLIC file and are processed by the LOGIN program for all users when they log in. Chapter 12 describes login script files and commands in detail.

The View File Server Error Log option allows the supervisor to view any error messages and warnings that are contained in the SYS:SYSTEM\NET$ERR.DAT file and then clear the file if desired. It is important to use this option periodically to check for any serious warnings or error messages—such as security violations and disk errors. After you view the error log, SYSCON gives you the chance to clear the log file. If you clear the log file periodically, it won't become so long that scanning it becomes too time consuming. The latest messages are added to the end of the error log. Knowing the name of the file is important if you want to archive the file to a local disk before clearing it.

In one reported situation, a NetWare service person found that a file server had been running for over six months with one of its mirrored disk drives down and no one was aware of it. This condition could easily have been detected if the network administrator had viewed the file server error log.

The supervisor can use the Workgroup Managers option to display a window showing a list of all users or groups that have the workgroup manager privilege of creating new users and groups. To add another user or group to the list, simply press the Ins key, highlight the desired user or group name, and press Enter. The F5 key can be used to mark multiple users or groups and add them to the workgroup manager list all at once. If you add a group name to the list of workgroup managers, then all users who are members of the group will have workgroup manager privileges.

The **User Information** option on the SYSCON main menu is one of the most commonly used SYSCON options. It allows you to create, manage, and delete user accounts. Selecting this option displays the User Names window, which lists all existing users on the file server.

To add a new user, simply press the Ins key and enter a valid username in the New User Name window. If the option to create home directories, found in the Supervisor Options menu under Default Account Balance/Restrictions, is turned on, SYSCON asks for the path to the directory that is to contain the user home directories. You can either type the complete NetWare path or use the Ins key to select each component of the path, as described in Chapter 6. If the path to the home directory area does not exist, SYSCON will ask if it is OK to create the directory path. Before answering yes, be sure you have entered the correct path—SYSCON has been known to create paths to nonexistent locations in a directory structure.

To change a username, use the arrow keys to highlight the current user's name and press the F3 key to cause SYSCON to display the current username in a window. You can then use the Backspace key to erase the existing username and then revise it. Pressing [Enter] changes the name in the User Names window. To delete a single user's account, use the arrow keys to highlight the username and press [Del]. You can delete multiple usernames by using the F5 key to mark all usernames you want to delete and then pressing [Del]. To manage an existing user account, highlight the username and press [Enter] to display the User Information window shown in Figure 7-19.

Figure 7-19

User Information window

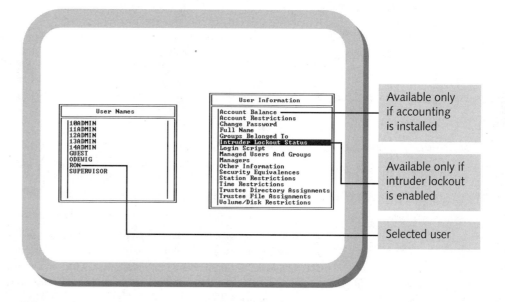

The Account Balance option allows you to enter account balance information—balance amount or credit amount—or provide unlimited credit for the selected user. The Account Balance option only appears when Accounting is installed on the server.

Selecting the Account Restrictions option displays the Account Restrictions window shown in Figure 7-20. Notice that, with the exception of the Create Home Directory for User and Account Balance fields, this window contains the same fields as those contained in the Supervisor Options Default Account Balance/ Restrictions window shown in Figure 7-16. You can use these fields to change the account restrictions for existing users.

The Change Password option allows the supervisor, user account manager, or user to change the account's password. If the Force Periodic Password Changes field is set to Yes for the user's account, the password entered by the supervisor or user account manager will be flagged as expired when the specified period has elapsed. The user is then required to enter his or her own password within the established grace login period. In order to change the password, a user must first enter his or her current password. SYSCON then asks for the new password to be entered twice—for verification purposes.

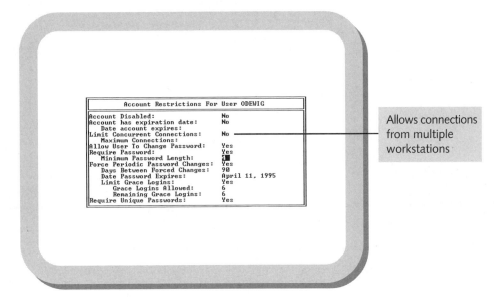

```
         Account Restrictions For User ODEWIG
Account Disabled:                      No
Account has expiration date:           No
   Date account expires:
Limit Concurrent Connections:          No
   Maximum Connections:
Allow User To Change Password:         Yes
Require Password:                       Yes
   Minimum Password Length:            5
Force Periodic Password Changes:        Yes
   Days Between Forced Changes:        90
   Date Password Expires:             April 11, 1995
   Limit Grace Logins:                Yes
       Grace Logins Allowed:          6
       Remaining Grace Logins:        6
Require Unique Passwords:               Yes
```

Allows connections from multiple workstations

The Full Name option allows either the supervisor or user account manager to assign a full name to the user account in addition to the user login name. A user cannot change his or her own Full Name assignment.

Selecting the Groups Belonged To field allows the supervisor or user account manager user to display a window listing all groups to which the user belongs. A user can be deleted from a group by highlighting the group name and pressing the Del key. A user can be made a member of additional groups by pressing the Ins key and then selecting the groups you want to make the user a member of from the Groups window.

A user account manager will be able to add the user only to the groups that he or she manages.

The Intruder Lockout Status option appears only for supervisors and then only when the file server's Intruder Detection function has been activated. The supervisor can use this option to determine the lockout status of an account, as shown in Figure 7-21. As you can see from this screen, the supervisor can view when the account will be available and from what network station address the invalid login attempts were made. Changing the Yes in the Account Locked field to a No unlocks the account and allows the user to log in to the network again.

Figure 7-21

Intruder Lockout Status
window

```
                      Intruder Lockout Status
 Account Locked:          No
 Incorrect Login Count: 0
 Account Reset Time:
 Time Until Reset:
 Last Intruder Address: 00000000:000000000000:0000
```

The Login Script option allows the supervisor, user account manager, or user to create, view, or modify the personal login script command for the account. If a personal login script exists, the commands are executed after the system login script commands. See Chapter 12.

The Managed Users and Groups option allows the supervisor or the user account manager to make the selected user an account manager of other users or groups. To do this, first select this option. This displays the Managed Users And Groups window. Then use the Ins key to add additional users or groups by selecting them from the Other Users and Groups window. If you want to make this user a user account manager of several other users, use the F5 key to mark multiple users and groups and then press [Enter] to add all the selected users or groups to the Managed Users And Groups window. As with the other windows, the Del key can be used to remove the selected users or groups from the Managed Users And Groups window.

Adding a group to a user's Managed Users And Groups window does not allow the user to manage all user accounts in the group. A manager of a group is able to add or remove users from the group and perform other group management tasks, as explained under the Group Information option.

The Managers option displays the Managers window, which lists all users or groups that are user account managers for the selected user account. A supervisor or user account manager can assign a manager to this user by pressing the Ins key and then selecting the new manager from the Other Users and Groups window.

The supervisor, user account manager, or user can use the Other Information option to display information about a user account, as shown in Figure 7-22. The Disk Space In Use field can be used to determine how much disk space is occupied by files owned by this user. This information can be useful in determining if this user account should have a disk space limitation placed on it. The User ID field contains the hexadecimal ID that the NetWare file server uses internally for keeping track of user profile and security information. Knowing the User ID is helpful in determining the user's mail subdirectory because the name of the user's SYS:MAIL subdirectory is the same as the User ID. Being able to locate a user's mail subdirectory is important when system maintenance tasks—such as removing print jobs or working with personal login scripts—are performed.

Figure 7-22

Other Information window

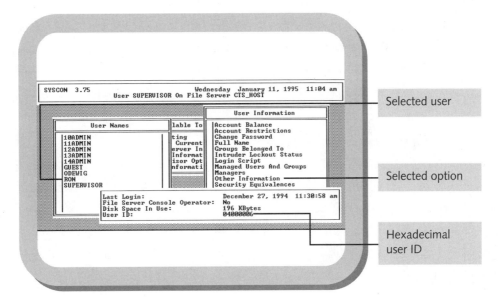

profile and security information. Knowing the User ID is helpful in determining the

Selected user

Selected option

Hexadecimal user ID

Selecting the Security Equivalences option displays the Security Equivalences window, which lists all user accounts to which the selected username is equivalent. Being security equivalent to another account provides the user with all the account privileges and trustee assignments of the users and groups included in this window. The supervisor or user account manager can use the Ins or Del keys to add or remove users and groups from the Security Equivalences window. A user account manager can make the user equivalent only to another user or group he or she manages. A supervisor can use this option to make a user account equivalent to the supervisor by pressing the Ins key and selecting the SUPERVISOR username from the Other Users and Groups window.

The Station Restrictions option can be used by the supervisor or user account manager to limit the user to logging in from only the specified stations. Selecting this option opens the Allowed Login Addresses window, which lists the network and node addresses of all workstations from which the user can log in. A login address consists of two parts: the network address and the node address. The network address is the hexadecimal number assigned to the cable system by the BIND command during server startup. The node address is the hexadecimal number contained in the read only memory of the network interface card and must be unique for each workstation on the cable.

If there are no stations in this list, the user can log in from any workstation on the network. To restrict the user to logging in from a specific station, press the Ins key to display the Network Address window and then enter the address of the network to which the workstation is attached. (If you are not sure of this information, it can be obtained by using USERLIST /E or the SESSION utility.) Next SYSCON asks if you want to allow the user to log in from all nodes on this network. To restrict the user to one or more workstations, select No and then enter the node address of a workstation from which you want the user to be able to log in, as shown in Figure 7-23. The network and node address of the workstation will then appear in the Allowed Login Addresses window.

Figure 7-23

User Station Restrictions screen

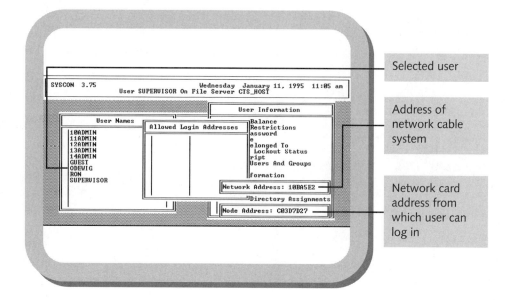

The supervisor, user account manager, or user can choose the Time Restrictions option to view the Allowed Login Times window for the selected user account. The supervisor or user account manager can add or remove asterisks from the window to modify the allowed login time. Each asterisk specifies a half-hour block of time during which the user can access the file server. (For an explanation of how to change the allowed access times, refer to "Time Restrictions" under the "NetWare Security" heading. See also Figure 7-17.

The supervisor, user account manager, or user can access the Trustee Directory Assignments option to display the Trustee Directory Assignments window, which lists all access rights the selected user account has been granted to directories in the file system. In Chapter 8, you will learn how to use this option to add, modify, and delete directory trustee assignments for user accounts.

A supervisor or user account manager can access the Trustee File Assignments option to display the Trustee File Assignments window, which lists all access rights the selected user account has been granted to specific files in the directory structure of the file system. In Chapter 8, you will learn how to use this option to add, modify, and delete file trustee assignments for user accounts.

A supervisor, user account manager, or user can access the Volume/Disk Restrictions option to view any disk space restrictions that have been assigned to volumes of the file server for the selected user account. The supervisor or user account manager who has supervisor rights to a volume, as described in Chapter 8, can use this option to assign a disk space restriction to the user account for the specified volume. Figure 7-24 shows the User Volume/Disk Restrictions window after a restriction of 10 Mbytes has been assigned to a user account for the DATA: volume.

Figure 7-24

Volume/Disk Restrictions
window

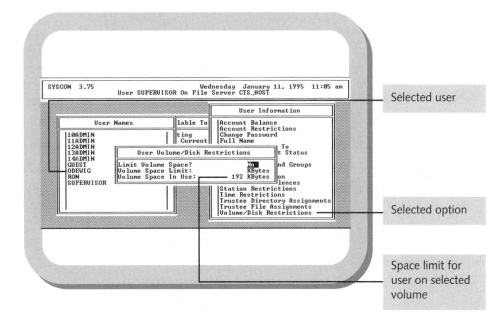

Selected user

Selected option

Space limit for
user on selected
volume

Working with multiple user accounts at one time

It is often desirable for a system administrator to perform an operation on several user
accounts at one time rather than having to repeat the same operation for each user.
SYSCON provides this capability by allowing you to use the F5 key to highlight multiple user accounts from the User window. You then press [Enter] to obtain the Set
User Information menu shown in Figure 7-25.

Figure 7-25

Set User Information
menu

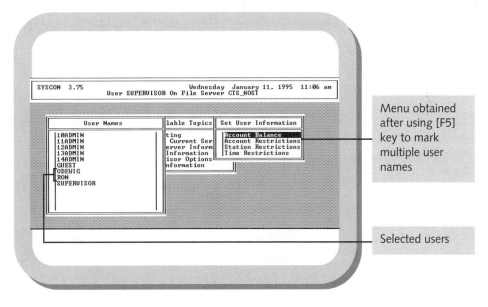

Menu obtained
after using [F5]
key to mark
multiple user
names

Selected users

The Account Balance option appears only if accounting is installed. It allows you to
give all selected users a new account balance or to provide them with unlimited
credit. The Account Restrictions option displays the same user restrictions window
shown in Figure 7-20. It allows the supervisor to set connection restrictions and password requirements for all selected users. The Station Restrictions option allows the
administrator to restrict selected users to one or more workstations. The Time

Restrictions option can be useful if you want to prevent all users from accessing the file server during time periods you schedule for backup or maintenance. Suppose, for example, you want to down the file server after 5:00 P.M. on Wednesday in order to install a new network card. To make sure all users are off the system by this time, you can use the SYSCON Time Restriction option by first marking all your users and then selecting the Time Restrictions option to display the Default Time Restrictions window (Figure 7-17). Using the F5 key, you then mark the period from 5:00 P.M. to 10:00 P.M. in the Wednesday row and press [Del] to remove the asterisks. Press the Esc key to confirm that you want to make the changes to time restrictions for all the marked users. After you have completed the network card installation, you again use the Time Restrictions option from the Set User Information menu to return the time restrictions to their normal settings.

THE USERDEF MENU UTILITY

Although SYSCON is a very versatile and powerful utility, it requires you to perform several steps to create a new user when you want to create a home directory for the user and also assign the user to one or more groups. These multiple steps can involve quite a bit of time and increases the chance of introducing errors if you need to create several new users. The USERDEF menu utility is designed to streamline the process of creating multiple users by allowing the network administrator to create user templates. The templates are then used to create one or more user accounts. **User templates** also allow the network administrator to establish standard user configurations for each department or workgroup. This simplifies the process of creating users in a department, in that the network administrator does not need to look up the location of the home directories for users in that department, the groups to which the users in that department belong, or the print jobs used by the department. All this information is contained in each department's template.

To use the USERDEF utility you need to be logged in to the network with supervisor privileges. After logging in to the file server you can start USERDEF from any directory by typing USERDEF and pressing the Enter key. The USERDEF Available Options screen, shown in Figure 7-26, is displayed.

Figure 7-26

USERDEF Available Options menu

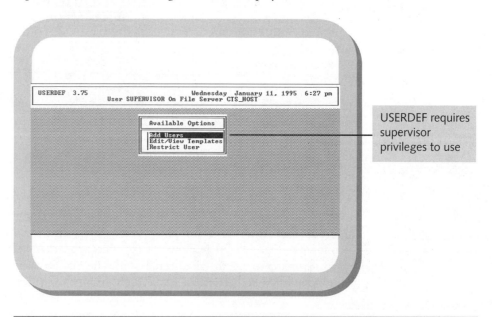

USERDEF requires supervisor privileges to use

Add Users

The Add Users option creates new user accounts. The selected template supplies such information as location of the user's home directory, groups to which the user will belong, print jobs, and account balance and restriction information. To create a new user, first select the Add Users option to display the Templates window and then select either the default template or one of the templates you created previously.

After a template is selected, USERDEF displays the Users window, which lists all existing users on the file server. To add a new user to the list, simply press the Ins key and enter the user's full name. Notice that USERDEF asks for the user's full name first. After the user's full name is entered, USERDEF displays the Login Name window, which shows the full name you entered previously. Because the user's login name is usually different from the full name, you need to use the Backspace key to erase the default login name. Then enter the login name for this user and press [Enter]. The new user's login name is then added to the Users window with the word (New) beside it, as shown in Figure 7-27. You repeat this process to add additional names to the User's window.

Figure 7-27

USERDEF Users window
with new user added

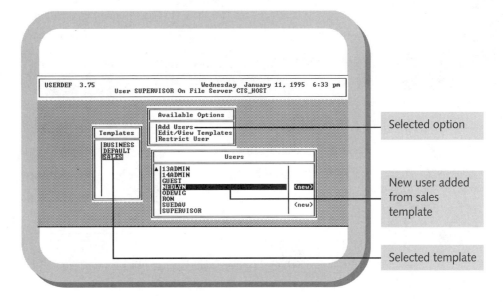

To create the new user accounts on the file server, press the Esc key and then select Yes in the Create New Users Using Template window. USERDEF now attempts to create accounts for the new users using the template selected. If there are errors in the template, such as a group or directory that does not exist, USERDEF displays error messages and the new user accounts will not be created. If you can correct the errors without exiting USERDEF, you can return to the Users window and try to create the new user accounts again. If you exit the USERDEF utility to perform some remedial functions (such as creating groups or directories), however, you need to re-enter the user's names as described previously.

After the new user accounts are created, USERDEF displays the MakeUser Results for Template window, which lists all usernames that have been created. After verifying the results, use the Esc key to return to the Templates window. If you want to repeat the process to create additional users with a different template after you use the Esc key to return to the Templates window, select the desired template. You use the Ins key as described previously to create new usernames with the selected template.

Edit/View Templates

Before creating users, you should employ this option to create or modify templates that will be used for workgroups. Selecting the Edit/View Templates option displays the Templates window, which lists all existing templates. To create a new template, press [Ins] and enter the name of the template you want to create. To change the name of a template, highlight the template name and press the F3 key. USERDEF then displays a window containing the current template's name. Use the Backspace key to erase the existing name and enter a revised name for the template. After you press the Enter key, the revised template name appears in the Templates window. To delete an existing template, highlight the template name and press [Del]. After you confirm the deletion of the template, it is removed from the Templates window. To modify or view information about an existing template, highlight the template name and press [Enter]. After you enter or select a template name, USERDEF displays the Template menu for the selected template, as shown in Figure 7-28.

Figure 7-28

Templates menu

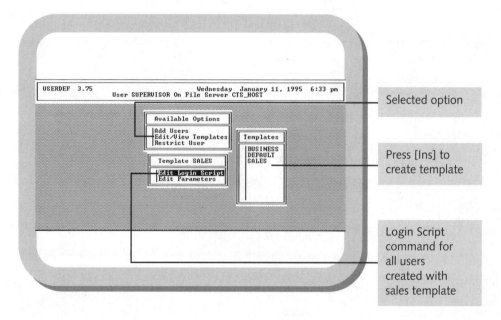

Select the Edit Login Script option to create or modify a personal login script that will be applied to all users created with this template. This option will be described in more detail in Chapter 12. Select the Edit Parameters option to display the Parameters for Template window shown in Figure 7-29. You can then enter or modify any of the fields as described in the following paragraphs.

In the Default Directory field, you enter the complete NetWare path on which the home directories for users created with this template will be created. When USERDEF creates the new users it will attempt to create home directories for the users on the directory path you specify in this field. Because of this, each department's template should contain the path to the directory on which the user home subdirectories exist for that department.

 With USERDEF you cannot use the Ins key to select each component of the directory path as you can with such other menu utilities as FILER, SESSION, and SYSCON.

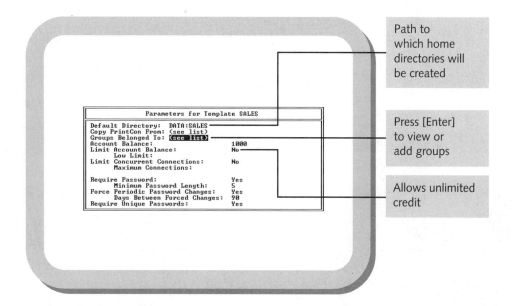

Figure 7-29

Parameters for Template window

In the Copy PrintCon From field, you specify usernames from whom you want to copy print jobs. This allows the new users to have a standard set of print jobs that are the same as those of the selected users. To add or modify entries in the field, highlight the field and press [Enter] to display a window listing any existing usernames. Use the Ins or Del keys to add or remove users from the window.

The Groups Belonged To field displays a window showing the groups to which you want each user created with this template to belong. Use the Ins or Del keys to add or remove groups from the window.

In the Account Balance field, you specify a starting balance to be used for all users created with this template. The Limit Account Balance and Low Limit fields allow you to specify a credit limit. If you leave the No entry, the new users will have unlimited credit.

The Limit Concurrent Connections and Maximum Connections fields are used to limit the number of times a user can be logged into the file server at one time. If you leave the default No, users created with this template will be able to log in to the file server simultaneously from multiple locations.

The Require Password and Minimum Password Length fields allow you to specify that a password of the minimum length specified is required for all users created with this template. By default, USERDEF gives users an initial password that is the same as their username. Because this password is expired, a new user will have a default of six grace login times to enter a new password before his or her account is disabled.

The Force Periodic Password Changes and Days Between Forced Changes fields allow the network administrator to specify that the passwords of all users created with this template will expire in the specified time interval. Because USERDEF automatically invalidates the user's password, they will then need to enter a new password within the number of grace login periods specified on their user accounts, normally left at the default of six.

The Require Unique Passwords field allows the network administrator to specify that all users created with this template must enter a different password each time they renew their password. The server keeps records of the last 10 passwords a user has specified.

Restrict User

The USERDEF Restrict User option is used to restrict the amount of disk space a user can use on the selected volume. You can use this option to select the username and volume as shown in Figure 7–30.

Figure 7-30

Restrict User Option
window

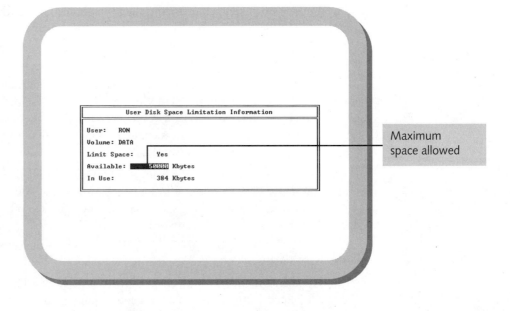

After you select the volume, USERDEF displays the User Disk Space Limitation Information window. To restrict the amount of disk space the selected user can use on the volume indicated, change the Limit Space field to Yes and then enter the amount of disk space in kilobytes (1024 bytes) in the Available field. To restrict a user to 50 Mbytes, for example, you enter 50000 in the Available field, as shown in Figure 7–31. The user disk space restriction function can also be performed with the DSPACE or SYSCON utilities.

Figure 7-31

User Disk Space
Limitation Information
window

THE MAKEUSER UTILITY

MAKEUSER is a batch-oriented utility, which means it uses a command file that contains statements and the statements are used to create the specified user accounts. MAKEUSER command files are ASCII text files that consist of lists of statements containing keywords and parameters that are used by the MAKEUSER program to determine how to create the specified user accounts. MAKEUSER is a good way to create and delete users quickly when you are setting up a group consisting of many user accounts.

Figure 7-32

MAKEUSER keywords

Keyword	Example
#ACCOUNT_EXPIRATION *month day year*	#ACCOUNT EXPIRATION July 20, 1995
#ACCOUNTING *balance, lowlimit*	#ACCOUNTING 10000, –500
#CLEAR or #RESET	#CLEAR
#CONNECTIONS *number*	#CONNECTIONS 1
#CREATE username [;*fullname*] [;*password*] [;*group*] [*directory* [*rights*]]	#CREATE MARREA; PASS;Mary Read; ADMIN, BUSINESS
#DELETE *username* [;*username*]	#DELETE JOHCAR; JAMBLI
#GROUPS *groupname* [;*groupname*]	#GROUPS BUSINESS
#HOME_DIRECTORY *path*	#HOME_DIRECTORY DATA:BUSINESS\USERS
#LOGIN_SCRIPT *path*	#LOGIN_SCRIPT SYS:PUBLIC\SCRIPTS\BUSINESS.LOG
#MAX_DISK_SPACE *vol, number*	#MAX_DISK_SPACE DATA, 500
#NO HOME_DIRECTORY	Use if you do not want MAKEUSER to create user home directories
#PASSWORD_LENGTH *length*	#PASSWORD_LENGTH 5
#PASSWORD_PERIOD *days*	#PASSWORD_PERIOD 90
#PASSWORD_REQUIRED	#PASSWORD_REQUIRED
#PURGE_USER_DIRECTORY	#PURGE_USER_DIRECTORY
#REM *statement*	#REM Create users for business department
#RESTRICTED_TIME *day, start, end* [;*day, start, end*]	#RESTRICTED_TIME everyday, 11:30 A.M., 5:00 P.M.
#STATIONS *network address, node address* [;*node address*]	#STATIONS 0FF1CE, 10FE, 2D40; 11EE
#UNIQUE_PASSWORD	#UNIQUE_PASSWORD

MAKEUSER command keywords

MAKEUSER command files consist of statements constructed from the keywords shown in Figure 7-32. While MAKEUSER can create user home directories, it cannot create the directory path that is specified to contain the user home directories. In addition, MAKEUSER does not create groups. Before you use MAKEUSER, therefore, you need to create any groups and directory paths that will be specified in the command parameters:

- The #ACCOUNT_EXPIRATION keyword is used to specify the date the user accounts created with MAKEUSER will expire.

- Use the #ACCOUNTING keyword if you need to give all new users a starting balance or credit limit.

- The #CLEAR and #RESET keywords are used to reset all parameters and are normally used at the beginning of a MAKEUSER command file or between groups of #CREATE statements when the second group of users will have different specifications.

- The #CONNECTIONS keyword is used to limit the number of workstations to which the new user accounts can be logged in at the same time. Most users should be restricted to logging in to one workstation at a time by including the #CONNECTIONS 1 statement.

- The #CREATE keyword has a complex syntax. It creates user accounts and also assigns the new users to groups or grants them access rights to the file system. The following sample #CREATE command will create a user account for the user Mary Read with the password of PASS and place her in the ADMIN and BUSINESS groups.

  ```
  #CREATE MARREA;PASS;Mary Read;ADMIN,BUSINESS^
  ```

  Notice that a comma separates the two group names and that the caret symbol (^) at the end of the command tells MAKEUSER that there are no more options.

- If the #HOME_DIRECTORY keyword has been specified, a subdirectory named MARREA will be created for this user in the path specified in the #HOME_DIRECTORY statement.

- The #DELETE keyword can be used to delete users along with any information relative to those users. If, for example, the #HOME_DIRECTORY and #PURGE_USER_DIRECTORY options have been specified, the user home directory and all subdirectories and files will also be deleted.

- You can use the #GROUPS keyword to place all new users that are created with this MAKEUSER file in the specified groups. As stated previously, you must use SYSCON to create the specified groups before you will be able to create the users with MAKEUSER.

- If you want MAKEUSER to create home directories for the new users, you include the #HOME_DIRECTORY keyword with the path to the directory in which the user home directories are to be created.

- The #NO_HOME_DIRECTORY keyword is useful if you do not want MAKEUSER to create user home directories.

- The #LOGIN_SCRIPT keyword is useful if you want MAKEUSER to include the statements in the file you specify in the new user's personal login scripts. (You will learn more about the content of personal login script files in Chapter 12.)

- To limit the amount of disk space each of the new users can use, include the #MAX_DISK_SPACE keyword followed by the maximum space utilization specified in blocks (4096) for the specified volume. You will need to place one of these statements for each volume in which you want to limit disk space.

- Use the #PASSWORD_LENGTH keyword to specify the minimum length of passwords for the newly created users.

- The #PASSWORD_PERIOD keyword can be used to specify an expiration period for passwords.

- The #UNIQUE_PASSWORD keyword prevents users from alternating among a few favorite passwords.

- The #REM keyword is short for "REMARK" and can be used to place comment lines in the .USR file that will not be executed. Use it to document the functions being performed by the command file.

- Use the #RESTRICTED_TIME keyword to specify time periods during which new users cannot log in to the file server. Replace "day" with a specific day of the week or with the word "everyday." Replace "start" and "end" with regular time-of-day formats. To prevent users from logging in between 11:30 P.M. and 5:00 A.M., for example, enter the following statement:

  `#RESTRICTED_TIME everyday, 11:30 am, 5:00 pm`

- The #STATIONS keyword restricts newly created users to logging in only from stations that have one of the specified network and node addresses. To allow new users to log in only from stations 10FE, 2D40, and 11EE on network 0FF1CE, for example, use the following statement:

  `#STATIONS 0FF1CE, 10FE, 2D40, 11EE`

MAKEUSER main menu

To use the MAKEUSER utility, you can be logged in as either a supervisor equivalent user or workgroup manager. After logging in to the file server, change to the directory in which you want to store the MAKEUSER text files and start the program by typing MAKEUSER and pressing the Enter key. The MAKEUSER Available Options menu shown in Figure 7-33 is displayed.

Figure 7-33

MAKEUSER Available
Options menu

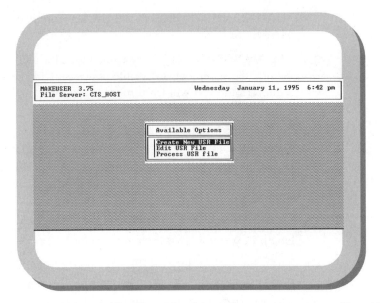

Create New USR File.   Use this option to create a new file with the .USR extension consisting of the keyword statements just described. All keywords that affect the new user accounts should be specified prior to the #CREATE statements. After all statements have been entered, use the Esc key and respond with Yes to save the file. MAKEUSER then asks you to enter the name of the file. Enter a valid DOS filename without the extension. You do not need to specify an extension for the filename because MAKEUSER automatically uses the filename extension .USR for all its filenames. After the file is saved, MAKEUSER returns to the Available Options menu.

Edit USR File.   This option allows you to access an existing USR file for viewing or editing. When you select this option, MAKEUSER displays the Enter the USR filename window. You can either type the name of the file without the extension or press the Ins key to obtain a window showing all USR files in the current directory. You then highlight the desired .USR file and press [Enter]. After the desired filename appears in the Enter the USR filename window, press [Enter] to bring up the edit window containing the contents of the selected USR filename. You can now use standard editing keys such as [Ins] and [Del] to modify the contents of the existing file. To delete a block of text from the file, use the arrow keys to move to the beginning of the block and then press the F5 key to start marking the block. Then use the arrow keys to mark the block and press [Del] to delete the marked text. After all editing changes have been made, use the Esc key to end the editing and respond with Yes to save the changes you made to the original file.

Process USR File.   Use this option to execute the statements in the selected USR file. When you select the option, MAKEUSER asks for the name of the USR file you want to process. You can either type the name of the file without the extension or press the Ins key to obtain a window listing all USR files in the current directory. You highlight the desired USR file and press [Enter]. After the desired filename appears in the "Enter the USR filename" window, press [Enter] to execute the MAKEUSER commands.

If MAKEUSER finds errors in your command file it will not create any users. Instead, it will display an error screen showing each invalid statement along with an error message indicating the problem. You should then use the "Edit USR File" option to correct the indicated errors. Use Process USR File again to re-execute the

USR file statements. Upon successful execution of the USR file, MAKEUSER displays a message telling you that the results are in a file with the same name as the USR file but with the filename extension .RPT. You can then use the Esc key to exit MAKEUSER and return to the DOS prompt where you need to use the DOS TYPE command to display the contents of the specified file having the extension .RPT.

Using MAKEUSER

Suppose you want to create a group of temporary users who will enter data for the SALES department. You want these user accounts to have the following configuration parameters:

- Home directories in the DATA:SALES\TEMPUSER directory
- Limited to 5 Mbytes of personal disk space on the Data: volume
- Members of both the SALES and TEMP groups
- Required to have passwords of at least five characters
- All new temporary user accounts are to expire at the end of the month
- All new temporary user accounts restricted to the login period between 8:00 A.M. and 4:30 P.M.
- The MAKEUSER commands necessary to create the temporary users with the above configuration parameters are shown below:

  #HOME_DIRECTORY DATA:SALES\TEMPUSER

  #MAX_DISK_SPACE DATA 1250

  #GROUPS SALES;TEMP

  #PASSWORD_REQUIRED

  #PASSWORD_LENGTH 5

  #UNIQUE_PASSWORD

  #ACCOUNT_EXPIRATION November 30, 1996

  #RESTRICTED_TIME everyday,8:00 am,4:30 pm

  #CREATE SALTEMP1;TEMPORARY 1; PASS 1^

  #CREATE SALTEMP2;TEMPORARY 2; PASS 2^

  #CREATE SALTEMP3;TEMPORARY 3; PASS 3^

A separate #CREATE command is used to create each temporary user including the user's login name, full name, and initial password separated by semicolons. Notice that each #CREATE statement ends with a carat (^) symbol in order to signal that no additional parameters are being included.

Before creating the new users with MAKEUSER, you first need to be sure the groups specified in the #GROUPS statement and the directory path specified in the #HOME_DIRECTORY statement exist. Next you need to determine where to store the MAKEUSER command file and then change your default path to that directory. One alternative is to create a directory on the root of the SYS: volume with a meaningful name such as USRFILES. After you have changed the default directory path to the MAKEUSER work directory, you can enter the command MAKEUSER to display the Available Options menu. To create the new command file, select the Create New USR File option to display a blank entry screen. Enter the keyword statements shown in Figure 7-34.

Figure 7-34

Sample MAKEUSER file

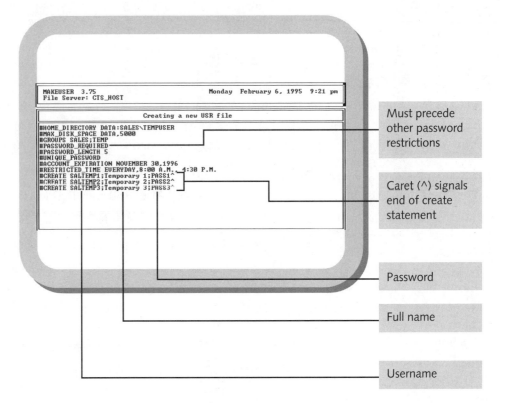

After all statements have been entered, press the Esc key and enter the name (SALTEMP) of the .USR file. Do not include an extension with the filename—the MAKEUSER program automatically adds the .USR extension. After you save the file, MAKEUSER returns you to the Available Topics menu.

To process the MAKEUSER command file and create the new users, select the Process USR File option from the Available Options menu and enter the name of the .USR file in the Enter USR Filename window. If you cannot remember the filename, use the Ins key to display a window showing all .USR files in the current directory. After you enter the .USR filename and pressing [Enter], MAKEUSER begins processing the keyword statements. If there are any syntax errors, or if a group or directory does not exist, MAKEUSER displays an error message and no users are created. You must go back and use the Edit USR File option to correct the problem and run the Process USER File option again. After processing the command file, MAKEUSER displays a completion message, as shown in Figure 7-35. Use the Esc key to exit the MAKEUSER program and check the results.

To display the results in the .RPT file, enter the command TYPE SALTEMP.RPT, as shown in Figure 7-36, to display the MAKEUSER report. You can now log in as each of the new users and test each account to be sure it is working correctly.

Figure 7-35

MAKEUSER completion screen

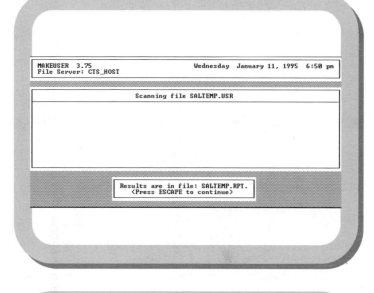

```
MAKEUSER  3.75                    Wednesday  January 11, 1995  6:50 pm
File Server: CTS_HOST

                          Scanning file SALTEMP.USR




                      Results are in file: SALTEMP.RPT.
                         <Press ESCAPE to continue>
```

Figure 7-36

Displaying the MAKEUSER .RPT file

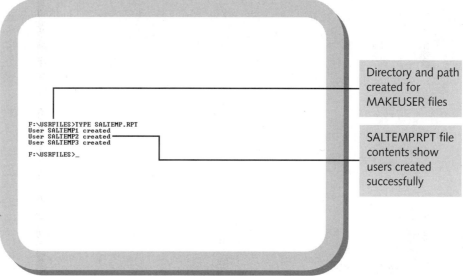

```
F:\USRFILES>TYPE SALTEMP.RPT
User SALTEMP1 created
User SALTEMP2 created
User SALTEMP3 created

F:\USRFILES>_
```

Directory and path created for MAKEUSER files

SALTEMP.RPT file contents show users created successfully

THE SECURITY COMMAND

A supervisor or supervisor equivalent user can use the SECURITY command—which is stored in the SYS:SYSTEM directory—to check for possible security violations. The following are possible security problems identified by the SECURITY command:

- No password assigned. Failing to require a secure password for each user is a major weakness in network security. As a result all usernames that do not have assigned passwords will be reported.

- Insecure passwords. Network security can be compromised by users who have passwords that are easy to guess. The SECURITY command reports all usernames that are not required to have a password of at least five characters, are not required to change their passwords at least every 60 days, have unlimited grace logins, or are not required to use a new and unique password each time they change their password.

- Supervisor equivalence. The SECURITY command reports all users who have supervisor equivalency. As a new administrator of an existing file server, one of the first things you want to know is what user accounts have supervisor equivalency. Unless you feel it is necessary in order to maintain or back up the file server, you should not have more than one "backup" supervisor equivalent user.

- Root directory privileges. Granting a user trustee rights to the root of a volume causes the user to inherit these rights to all directories and subdirectories of that volume unless those rights are specifically revoked or blocked at a lower level. The SECURITY command reports any users that have been granted trustee rights to the root of a volume.

- User login scripts. The SECURITY command reports any users who do not have a personal login script. The user's personal login script is stored in the subdirectory of the SYS:MAIL directory. By default, all users have Create rights to the SYS:MAIL directory in order to allow them to send e-mail messages to other users. If a user does not already have a login script file, another user or an intruder can create a login script file for this user that contains commands to copy or erase files. As a network administrator you need to be sure all users have a personal login script file even if it only contains the EXIT command. Login script files are covered in detail in Chapter 12.

- User account managers. Any user account managers are identified along with the number of users and groups that they manage.

- Groups and users that do not have full names. Although an incomplete name is not a security concern, this information can be used by a network administrator to fill in any missing user or group names.

Figure 7-37 shows an example of the SECURITY command running on a small network. The output of the SECURITY command often fills several screens. Because of this, it is designed to stop automatically after each screen is full unless you use the /C option for continuous output. Normally the /C option is used when the output of the SECURITY command is directed to the printer, written as SECURITY /C > PRN.

Figure 7-37

SECURITY command
sample output

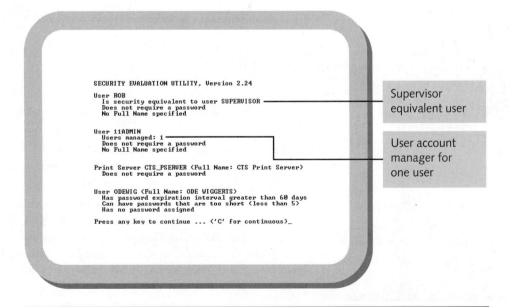

BINDFIX AND BINDREST COMMANDS

NetWare tracks usernames, passwords, and other login security information in files called the **bindery**. In order to back up the system and recover from system problems properly, a CNA needs to know about the function of the bindery files. The bindery consists of three hidden files stored in the SYS:SYSTEM directory: NET$OBJ.SYS, NET$PROP.SYS, and NET$VAL.SYS. The NET$OBJ.SYS file contains the names of the users, groups, print queues, and other objects that exist on the file server. The NET$PROP.SYS file contains the properties or characteristics of each bindery object (for example, password requirement, account restrictions, account balances, and group members). The NET$VAL.SYS file contains the values assigned to an object's properties (for example, the actual password, the number of grace logins, or the time and station restrictions). Because the bindery files are always open and flagged with the hidden and system attributes, some third party backup program will not copy properly when making a backup. You should know how to use the NBACKUP program included with NetWare v3.11 or the SBACKUP software included with NetWare v3.12 to properly backup the binderies as described in Chapter 14.

The NetWare bindery files sometimes become corrupted due to a system error. This can also happen if your workstation crashes while you are adding or modifying user information. The following types of errors can occur as a result of errors in the NetWare bindery files:

- A username cannot be created, deleted or modified.

- A user's password cannot be changed.

- A user's trustee rights cannot be modified.

- The error "unknown server" occurs during printing even though you are printing to the current file server.

- Error messages referring to the bindery are displayed at the server console.

To correct bindery problems, NetWare includes a program called BINDFIX, which can be used to re-synchronize the bindery files. By logging in as the supervisor or as a supervisor equivalent user, a network administrator can use the BINDFIX command to correct problems that occur as a result of errors in the NetWare bindery files.

To use the BINDFIX program, you need to be logged in as a supervisor equivalent user and be certain that no other users are logged into the file server. BINDFIX needs uninterrupted access in order to rebuild the bindery files successfully. While rebuilding the bindery files, BINDFIX displays a list of the tasks it is performing and gives you the option of deleting the mail directories and trustee rights of users who no longer exist. See the example shown in Figure 7-38.

BINDFIX renames the existing bindery files to NET$OBJ.OLD, NET$PROP.OLD, and NET$VAL.OLD before creating new versions. If the reconstructed versions of the files do not solve your problem or if power fails while BINDFIX is running, you can use the BINDREST command to restore the .OLD bindery files, as shown in Figure 7-39.

Figure 7-38

Using the BINDFIX
command

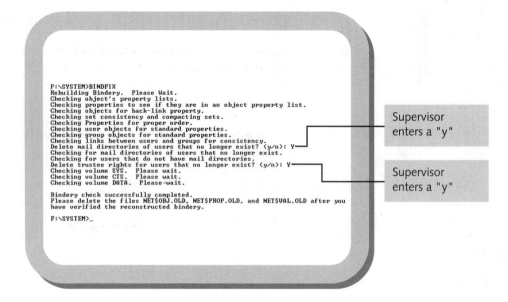

```
F:\SYSTEM>BINDFIX
Rebuilding Bindery.  Please Wait.
Checking object's property lists.
Checking properties to see if they are in an object property list.
Checking objects for back-link property.
Checking set consistency and compacting sets.
Checking Properties for proper order.
Checking user objects for standard properties.
Checking group objects for standard properties.
Checking links between users and groups for consistency.
Delete mail directories of users that no longer exist? (y/n): Y
Checking for mail directories of users that no longer exist.
Checking for users that do not have mail directories.
Delete trustee rights for users that no longer exist? (y/n): Y
Checking volume SYS.  Please wait.
Checking volume CTS.  Please wait.
Checking volume DATA.  Please wait.

Bindery check successfully completed.
Please delete the files NET$OBJ.OLD, NET$PROP.OLD, and NET$VAL.OLD after you
have verified the reconstructed bindery.

F:\SYSTEM>_
```

Supervisor
enters a "y"

Supervisor
enters a "y"

Figure 7-39

Using the BINDREST
command

```
F:\SYSTEM>BINDREST

The BINDERY has been successfully restored.

F:\SYSTEM>_
```

Many network administrators make a backup copy of a file server's bindery
by copying the .OLD files created by the BINDFIX command to a floppy
disk or local hard disk drive. A bindery can then be restored by copying the
.OLD files back to the SYS:SYSTEM directory and running BINDREST.

CHAPTER SUMMARY

The NetWare security system allows a network administrator to limit access to data
and services on the file server in three different ways: login security, file system security, and console security. The login security system described in this chapter consists
of usernames, passwords, time restrictions, station restrictions, and account restrictions.
Usernames can be a maximum of 47 characters and often consist of the user's first

initial followed by the last name, or of the first three letters of the first and last names, combined to make usernames of six letters. Usernames can be given privileges to allow users to perform special administrative functions such as creating users or working with printers. Supervisor equivalent users have the same rights as the SUPERVISOR account: workgroup managers are allowed to create users and groups, and user account managers can maintain user account information such as passwords, login restrictions, login scripts, and group membership. A print queue operator or print server operator privilege provides users control of the printing system. A file server console operator can use the FCONSOLE utility to disable logins and view user connection information.

NetWare provides additional security by allowing the network administrator to establish password requirements and access restrictions. Password requirements that can be placed on each user account include requiring passwords of a specified minimum length, forcing users to change passwords within a specified number of days, and requiring users to select a different or unique password rather than alternating among a few favorite passwords. Time restrictions allow a network administrator to increase the security on an account by specifying what times the user can be logged in to the file server. Station restrictions provide further security by restricting a user account to one or more workstation addresses. Account restrictions along with intruder detection provide additional methods to disable a user's account when certain limits such as account expiration date or a maximum number of login attempts are reached.

NetWare accounting allows the network administrator to establish charge rates for such services as blocks read, blocks written, connection time, disk space used, and file server requests made. Using this feature, NetWare will deduct charges from the user account balances until the user account balance exceeds the credit limit at which time the user account is disabled until the administrator assigns a new balance or increases the credit limit. In addition to charging users for services, the accounting system can be used to keep track of file server usage and print summary reports at the end of each accounting period.

NetWare v3.1x provides three utilities that allow a network administrator to create and secure user and group accounts. The SYSCON utility is the most powerful and can perform a variety of tasks related to login security including creating users and groups as well as establishing accounting and other access restrictions, such as intruder detection. The Supervisor Options of the SYSCON utility allow a network supervisor to establish default account restrictions as well as perform such system functions as viewing the error log, maintaining server startup files, creating workgroup managers, and managing the system login script. The USERDEF utility is a convenient method for the SUPERVISOR or supervisor equivalent user to create user accounts with templates to provide standard settings such as location of home directory, groups to which the users belong, password restrictions, and starting account balances. The MAKEUSER utility allows the network administrator or workgroup manager to create a file containing a number of keyword statements that establish parameters and create user accounts with the specified parameters. MAKEUSER is an efficient way to create groups of users simultaneously that have standard needs.

In addition to the menu utilities described in this chapter, NetWare contains three command line utilities that play an important role in checking system security and fixing problems with the security system. The SECURITY command is an important supervisor command line utility that provides information on possible security violations such as users with no passwords, users who are not required to change passwords at least every 60 days or who have passwords that are less than five characters, supervisor equivalent users, users who have rights in the root of a directory, and user accounts that do not have personal login scripts. The BINDFIX command line utility is another supervisor-only utility that is stored in the SYS:SYSTEM directory along with the SECURITY command. It is used to fix problems with the bindery files (NET$OBJ.SYS, NET$PROP.SYS, and NET$VAL.SYS) that can cause such errors as not being able to change passwords or create or modify usernames. Before constructing new bindery files, the BINDFIX utility makes backups of the current bindery files using the .OLD extension. These .OLD files can be copied to a disk to provide a backup of the bindery. If problems persist or the BINDFIX program crashes, the BINDREST program can be used to restore the original bindery by changing the .OLD bindery files back to the .SYS files.

COMMAND SUMMARY

Command	Syntax	Definition
BINDFIX	*BINDFIX*	BINDFIX is a supervisor command line utility that is stored in the SYS:SYSTEM directory and is used to repair the bindery files (NET$OBJ.SYS, NET$PROP.SYS, and NET$VAL.SYS) in the event of errors occurring when new user accounts are created, passwords are changed, or the current file server is being printed to. The BINDFIX utility creates backup copies of the bindery files with the .OLD extension. The .OLD files can be backed up to disk or restored by the BINDREST program.
BINDREST	*BINDREST*	BINDREST is a supervisor command line utility that is stored in the SYS:SYSTEM directory and can be used to restore the bindery files from the backup .OLD files. It can be used if problems persist after BINDFIX is used or if the BINDFIX program crashes and damages the bindery files being reconstructed. BINDREST can also be used to restore the bindery files from a backup of the .OLD files by copying the .OLD files from the backup disk to the SYS:SYSTEM directory and then running the BINDREST command.
MAKEUSER	*MAKEUSER*	The MAKEUSER utility is used to create, edit, and process ASCII text files that have the .USR extension. It allows the supervisor or workgroup manager to create batches of users. The main advantage of MAKEUSER over SYSCON and USERDEF is its ability to create many users quickly from a standard set of statements containing certain keywords.

SECURITY	*SECURITY [/C]*	SECURITY is a supervisor command line utility that is stored in the SYS:SYSTEM directory and is used to provide a list of possible security violations. The /C parameter causes the listing to be displayed without a pause after each screen.
SYSCON	*SYSCON*	The SYSCON utility contains options to install and configure NetWare accounting, display file server information, create and maintain groups, perform supervisor tasks, and create and maintain user accounts.
USERDEF	*USERDEF*	The USERDEF utility is used by the supervisor to create templates and users. Its main advantage over SYSCON is that it allows use of templates to speed up the creation of multiple-user accounts, in which the users have similar needs.

KEY TERMS

bindery	print queue	user account manager
connect time	print queue operator	user templates
console operator	print server operator	workgroup manager
disk activity charge	service request	
disk storage	supervisor equivalent	

REVIEW QUESTIONS

1. List the three levels of NetWare security.

    login security

    file system security

    console security

2. NetWare keeps track of usernames, passwords, and other access restrictions in the _____ files.

3. The _NET$OBJ.SYS_ file contains the names of the users, groups, and other objects.

4. The _____ file contains the properties of each file server object, such as the fact that a username has a password.

5. The _____ file contains such information as the user's password and the allowed login times.

6. List the five login security components that work together to provide you with the ability to access the file server and perform your assigned tasks.

1) Usernames
2) Passwords & password restrictions
3) Time restrictions
4) Station restrictions
5) Account restrictions.

7. In the space below, list what users and groups exist after NetWare is first installed on a file server.

usernames   *group*

Supervisor   *Everyone*

Guest

8. A username can be up to ___*47*___ characters in length.

9. In the space below, briefly explain why many network administrators try to keep usernames to eight or fewer characters.

So they can create home directories with the login name.

10. The ___*Supervisor equivalent*___ privilege level gives the username the same authority as the SUPERVISOR.

11. The ___*workgroup manager*___ privilege level gives the username the ability to create other users and groups.

12. The ___*user account manager*___ privilege level gives the username the ability to manage the user accounts assigned to it.

13. What privilege does being a console operator give a username?
FCONSOLE utility

14. What privilege level do you need in order to rearrange the sequence of print jobs?
Print queue operator

15. List three restrictions you can assign to password security.
Setting minimum password length
Forcing periodic password changes
Requiring unique passwords
limiting login grace periods

16. In the space below, give an example of how time restrictions can be used to help secure a payroll clerk's workstation.

The file sever can only be accessed between working hours. So people can't login later on.

17. In the space below, briefly describe two ways station restrictions can be used to provide better security.

① number of time a user can be logged in at the same time.

② which workstations a user is allowed to log in from.

18. List the four ways an account can be disabled.

① users account expired

② number of grace logins exceeded

③ account balance is depleted

④ exceed the amount of password attempts allowed

19. List the four types of charges that can be tracked with NetWare's accounting functions.

① Disk activity

② Connect time

③ Disk storage space consumed

④ Service requests.

20. The ___Disk activity charge___ charge rate is most useful if you are charging customers for access to your database file.

21. The ___disk activity___ charge rate is most useful if you are charging customers for the amount of the server's processing time they use.

22. The ___connect time___ charge rate can be used to prevent users from staying logged in to the file server.

23. Which three utilities can be used to create groups?

Syscon

24. Which three utilities can be used to create users?

SYSCON

USERDEF MENU

MAKEUSER

25.   The _Workgroup Managers_ _____ option of the SYSCON utility is used to create workgroup managers.

26.   The _Supervisor Options_ _____ option of the SYSCON utility is used to activate intruder detection.

27.   The _View File Server Error Log_ option of the SYSCON utility is used to view the file server error log.

28.   List four potential security violations that the SECURITY command can detect.

    ① No password assigned   ⑤ User login scripts
    ② Insecure Passwords   ⑥ User account managers
    ③ Supervisor equivalence   ⑦ Groups & users without full names
    ④ Root directory privileges

29.   If you receive an error message when attempting to create a new user or change a user's password, you should run the

    _____ program.

30.   Match the privilege level(s) that can perform each of the following tasks:

    a. SUPERVISOR or equivalent

    b. workgroup manager

    c. user account manager

    d. console operator

Task	Privilege Level
Assigning an account balance to an existing user	
Releasing an account from intruder detection lockout	
Making a user's password expire in 60 days	
Setting a default time restriction for all new users created with SYSCON	
Creating new groups	
Assigning members to a group	
Creating templates with USERDEF	
Using MAKEUSER to create new users	
Using the SECURITY command	
Running BINDFIX	
Running the FCONSOLE program	

EXERCISES

Exercise 7-1: Using SYSCON to Create Users and Groups

In this exercise you will use SYSCON to create three users and two groups and then assign the users to groups. All user and group names you create need to be preceded by your student number in order to separate them from users and groups created by other students.

1. Log in using your assigned student username (it must have workgroup manager privileges).

2. In your ##ADMIN home directory, create a directory named USERS.

3. Start SYSCON and use the appropriate option to create the following three usernames: ##USER1, ##USER2, and ##USER3. Replace the number symbols with your assigned student number. A home directory should be created for each user in the ##ADMIN\USERS directory you created previously. Give each new user an unlimited account balance.

4. Give ##USER1 your full name.

5. If you are logged in as supervisor, use the F5 key to select all user accounts and then use the Account Restrictions option of the Set User Information menu to cause all selected accounts to expire on tomorrow's date. If you are logged in as a workgroup manager, you will need to select each user account separately.

6. Use the appropriate option of SYSCON to create two groups called ##GROUP1 and ##GROUP2. Be sure to replace the number symbols with your assigned student number.

7. From the Group Names window, select ##GROUP1 and use the Member List option to make all three users created in step 3 members of this group.

8. From the Group Names window, select ##GROUP2 and make ##USER2 and ##USER3 members of this group.

9. Exit SYSCON.

10. Change your default directory path to the ##ADMIN\USERS directory.

11. Use the TLIST *.* command to obtain a list of trustee assignments for each of the user home directories.

12. Use the Print Scrn key to print your screen.

13. Log out.

14. Log in as ##USER2.

15. Use the WHOAMI /G command to list all groups of which ##USER2 is a member. Record the result in the space below.

> *You are: 50USER2*
> *Attached to: CTS_HOST, connection 15*
> *Server is Running: NetWare v3.12*
> *Login Time: Tuesday Oct. 13, 1998 8:43am*

groups
EVERYONE
50 GROUP1
50GROUP2

16. Start SYSCON and attempt to change User 2's full name. Record the result in the space below.

> *No Full Name Specified*
> *(Press ESCAPE to continue)*

17. Use SYSCON to give the ##USER2 username a password.

18. Under Account Restrictions, attempt to force your password to be changed every 180 days. Record the results in the space below.

unable to do this

19. Access the User Information menu for ##USER1. In the space below, record the options available in the menu.

Full Name

Groups Belonged To

20. Exit SYSCON.

21. Log out.

22. Log in using your assigned ##ADMIN username.

23. Use SYSCON to delete the users and groups created in this exercise.

24. Exit FILER and log out.

Exercise 7-2: Making a User Account Manager

As described earlier in this chapter, a user account manager is able to manage other user accounts that are assigned to him or her. A user account manager can perform such tasks as assigning the managed users to groups and changing their account restrictions. In this exercise you will create three user accounts and one group, and then make one of the users a user account manager over the other users. You will then log in as the user account manager and change user account restrictions and group membership.

1. Log in using your ##ADMIN assigned username.

2. Start SYSCON.

3. From the User Information option, create three users named ##DAVE, ##MARY, and ##JULIE. Use the Esc key when asked for the path of the user home directory. This skips over creating home directories for these users.

4. Create a group named ##MYGROUP.

5. To make ##MARY a user account manager in charge of ##DAVE and ##MYGROUP, first display the User Information window for user ##MARY and then select the Managed Users and Groups option. Next use the Ins key to display the Other Users and Groups window. Mark ##DAVE and ##MYGROUP using the F5 key and press [Enter] to add the marked user and group to the Managed Users and Groups window for ##MARY.

6. Exit SYSCON.

7. Log out.

8. Log in as ##MARY.

9. Start SYSCON.

10. Use the appropriate SYSCON options to call up the user information for ##JULIE.

11. Can you modify the account restrictions for username ##JULIE to make Julie's account expire in 60 days? Yes or No

12. In the space below, explain the result of step 11.

Don't even have the option to change

13. Use the appropriate SYSCON options to call up the user information for ##DAVE.

Can you modify the account restrictions for username ##DAVE to make Dave's account expire in 60 days? In the space below, explain why.

Yes because ##Dave is under ##MARY.

14. Select the Managers option for the ##DAVE username. In the space below, record the names of the managers.

50ADMIN
50MARY

15. Access the group ##MYGROUP and attempt to make all your users members of this group. Record your results in the space below.

Only Dave can be added.

16. While logged in as ##MARY, attempt to create a new user and group. Record your results in the space below.

won't let me do either

17. What privilege do you need before you are allowed to create new users or groups?

Create.

18. While logged in as ##MARY, try to delete the groups and users created in this exercise. Record your results in the space below.

I can delete 50Dave and 50MPGROUP

19. Log in using your ##ADMIN username and delete any remaining users or groups. In the space below, record the users and groups you delete.

I deleted   50MARY

50JULIE

20. Log out.

Exercise 7-3: Setting Time and Station Restrictions

In this exercise you will determine your current workstation's network and node address and then use SYSCON to create and restrict a user to logging in from only this station during a specified time period.

1. Log in using your ##ADMIN username.

2. Use the SESSION menu utility to call up your ##ADMIN username and determine the network and node address of the workstation on which you are working. Record your workstation address information below.

Network address: _00000041_   Node address: _E02924FDD9_

3. Exit SESSION.

4. Use the USERLIST /E command to verify the information you recorded in step 2.

5. Use SYSCON to create username ##BILL with a home directory in the ##ADMIN\USERS directory.

6. Do not require a password for ##BILL's account.

7. Call up the User Information menu for ##BILL and then use the Station Restrictions option to enter the network and node address recorded in step 2.

8. Use [Print Scrn] to print the SYSCON screen showing ##BILL's station restrictions.

9. Log out.

10. Log in as user ##BILL from your current workstation.

11. Go to another station and attempt to log in as ##BILL. In the space below, record any messages you see.

unapproved workstation

12. Log in using your ##ADMIN username.

13. Call up the User Information menu for ##BILL and then use the Time Restriction option to prevent Bill from logging in during the current hour.

14. Use the Print Scrn key to print the screen showing the time restrictions for ##BILL.

15. Exit SYSCON.

16. Try logging in from your current workstation as ##BILL. In the space below, record the message you receive.

    unauthorized time period.

17. Log in with your ##ADMIN username and delete the ##BILL user account.

18. Use FILER to remove all home subdirectories from your ##ADMIN\USERS directory.

19. Log out.

Exercise 7-4: Supervisor Options

In this exercise you will use Supervisor Options of the SYSCON utility to perform several activities. Because supervisor privileges are necessary to use Supervisor Options, you will need to log in to the file server with a username that has supervisor equivalency to do this exercise. Your instructor will direct you regarding the use of this supervisor equivalent username.

1. Log in using the supervisor equivalent username.

2. Start SYSCON.

3. Create a user named ##JOHN without a home directory.

4. Select Supervisor Options and use the Workgroup Manager option to add ##JOHN as a workgroup manager.

5. View the contents of the AUTOEXEC startup file. *Do not* make any changes. In the space below, record the contents.

6. Call up Intruder Detection/Lockout and record the settings below. *Do not* make any changes to these fields.

   Incorrect Login Attempts: _____

   Bad Login Count Retention Time: _____ Days _____ Hours _____ Minutes

   Length of Account Lockup: _____ Days _____ Hours _____ Minutes

7. Make ##JOHN a user account manager of his own username. In the space below, record the steps you use to do this.

8. Exit SYSCON.

9. Log out.

10. Log in as ##JOHN.

11. Create a new user named ##HELEN without a home directory.

12. Require ##HELEN to change to a different password every 60 days.

13. Delete both ##HELEN and ##JOHN.

14. Were you able to delete the account in which you were logged in? Yes or No

    Can all users delete their own accounts? Yes or No

    In the space below, describe why the user ##JOHN could or could not delete his own account.

15. Log out and then log in as ##ADMIN and delete the user ##JOHN.

Exercise 7-5: Determining Necessary Privilege Levels

In this written exercise you will fill in the following chart showing what privilege levels are required to perform the tasks listed in the left column. Place an X in each privilege column that provides a user with the rights to perform the task. For example, if both a supervisor and workgroup manager can grant supervisor equivalency, you would place an X in both the SUPERVISOR and Workgroup Manager columns.

Task	SUPERVISOR and Equivalent	Workgroup Manager	User Account Manager	Console Operator	Print Queue Operator	Print Server Operator
Grant SUPERVISOR equivalency	X					
Automatically has all rights to the entire file system	X					
Create other users and groups	X	X				
Delete users and groups	X	X	X			
Create a workgroup manager	X	X				
Make a user account manager over other users	X	X				
Run FCONSOLE	X			X		
Manage user accounts	X	X	X			
Use FCONSOLE to down the server	X					
Stop a jammed printer	X				X	X
Rearrange the jobs waiting to be printed	X				X	X

EXERCISES

Case 7-1: Using NetWare Accounting to Track Network Usage

Assume you are working as a lab assistant for your college network administrator and that the administrator would like you to keep track of server usage in order to develop a budget for future file server needs. The previous network administrator had installed accounting and established a charge rate for blocks read. Your network administrator explains that a charge ratio is needed before NetWare will track server usage, but because the previous administrator did not want to have the users charged, he set up a charge at a time when no one should be using the server. Your network administrator wants you to document the charge ratio that was set up by the previous administrator for future reference. The network administrator also wants you to run the ATOTAL program each day and then use this information to create three separate graphs, one for blocks read, one for storage used, and one for the number of file server requests made.

To perform this activity, you first need to use the Accounting option to document the accounting charge rates and record the times there is a charge for the service along with the charge ratio used. Record the information in the following table.

Service charged for: _____

Charge Ratio	Day	Times

To complete the assignment, you will need to run the ATOTAL program each day for the next three days and create graphs similar to the ones shown below showing file server usage.

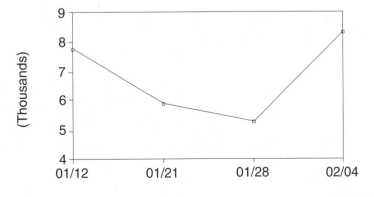

Blocks Read
Storage Space Used

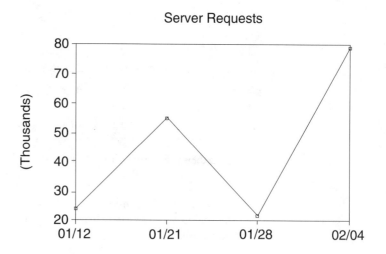

Server Requests

Case 7-2: Creating users with USERDEF

In this case study you will apply USERDEF to create templates and users for the PC Solutions company. Assume you are the network administrator for the PC Solutions company and that you need to create users in both the sales and business departments. As a CNA, you know that the USERDEF utility can simplify the task of creating users by allowing the supervisor to define and use templates that contain account information common to all users in a department. Only the supervisor or a supervisor equivalent user can use the USERDEF utility to create templates and new users; workgroup managers are restricted to creating new users with SYSCON or MAKEUSER. In order to perform this case study, you will need to log in using a supervisor equivalent username. In all cases, substitute your assigned student number for the number symbols (##).

Part 1: Creating the Directory Structure and Groups.

In order to perform this case project, you will need to create a directory structure and workgroups for the PC Solutions Sales and Business departments by following the steps described below:

1. Create a directory structure for the PC Solutions company in your ##ADMIN work area as shown below:

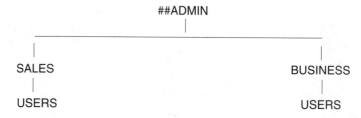

2. Use SYSCON to create ##BUSINESS and ##SALES groups where the "##" represents your assigned student number.

Part 2: Creating templates with USERDEF.

A template contains such information as home directory location, groups the users are to belong to, account balance information, and password requirements. You have decided to use templates to create the users for the business and sales departments. Remember to replace the "##" in object names with your assigned student number.

Follow the next 10 steps to create a template for the business department with USERDEF:

1. Type the command **USERDEF** from the DOS prompt and press **[Enter]**. The USERDEF Available Options menu is then displayed.

2. To create a new template, highlight the Edit/View Templates option and press **[Enter]**. This displays a window showing the existing templates.

3. Press **[Ins]** and type ##**BUS** as the name of the new template.

4. Highlight the Edit Parameters option and fill out the Parameters for Template ##BUS window to place your new users in the ##ADMIN\BUSINESS\USERS directory and make them members of the ##BUSINESS group.

5. In the "Account Balance" field, enter 0. Leave the Limit Credit field set to No to provide unlimited credit.

6. Require all users to have a password of at least five characters and force periodic password changes so that after 120 days the users have to invent a new password that is different from the previous 10 passwords the user has chosen. When a password expires, each user should be given several grace login times before his or her account is disabled. List each user's concurrent connections to 1.

7. After completing the screen, press **[Esc]** to save the entries and return to the Template options screen.

8. Repeat this process, making a template for the Sales department that will create home directories in the ##ADMIN\SALES\USERS directory and make the users members of the ##SALES group.

9. After completing all templates, use **[Esc]** to return to the USERDEF Available Options menu.

Part 3: Creating new users with USERDEF.

Now that the department templates are created, you are ready to create the users for the business and sales departments. Follow the next 19 steps to create the users for the business department with USERDEF:

1. Highlight the **Add Users option** on the USERDEF Available Options menu and press **[Enter]** to display the Templates window showing all templates that have been created.

2. Use the arrow keys to highlight the ##BUS template and press **[Enter]**. A list of current users is displayed.

3. To create a new user, press **[Ins]** and enter the following usernames:

FULL NAME	USERNAME
Ben Avery	##BENAVE
Ned Lynch	##NEDLYN
Ann Bonny	##ANNBON

4. After all usernames have been entered, press **[Esc]**. USERDEF asks if you want to create the new users using the ##BUS template. Respond by pressing **[Enter]**. USERDEF creates the new users and displays the results screen. Because passwords were required in the template, each user is assigned his or her username for a password.

5. Repeat this process to create the following users in the sales department:

FULL NAME	USERNAME
George Moon	##GEOMOO
James Bligh	##JAMBLI
Rita Dunn	##RITDUN

6. After verifying that the user accounts have been created, press **[Esc]** twice to return to the Templates window.

7. Use **[Alt][F10]** to exit USERDEF.

8. Log out.

9. Log in as ##JAMBLI.

10. Enter the command WHOAMI /G.

11. Use the Print Scrn key to obtain a hardcopy of your screen. Keep this printout for instructor verification.

12. Log out.

13. Log in as ##ANNBON.

14. Enter the command WHOAMI /G.

15. Use the Print Scrn key to obtain a hardcopy of your screen. Keep this printout for instructor verification.

16. Test other user accounts by logging in with the user's name, changing to his or her home directory, and using the RIGHTS command to show effective rights.

17. Log in using your supervisor equivalent username.

18. Use SYSCON to remove the users you created in this case study.

SUPERIOR TECHNICAL COLLEGE PROBLEMS

Dave Johnson was pleased with your work installing NetWare and establishing a directory structure for the network file system in such a short time. However, the faculty and staff are anxious to log into the file server and start using the network before school starts. As a result, your next assignment involves establishing user accounts and providing file server security.

Project 7-1: Creating Superior Technical College Campus Users and Groups

Now that the directory structure for the campus has been created, you are ready to undertake the task of creating the users and groups that will be necessary to access the file server. You have discussed the campus needs and the users with Dave Johnson, and he has given you the go-ahead to create the users and workgroups shown in the following table:

GROUP NAME	MEMBERS
##FACULTY	Barbara Rau, Beil Egan, Maria Rodriguez, David Feinstein
##SUPPORT	Lauri Holt, Mimi Ito
##STUDSERV	Karl Dauer, Stuart Chung, Gina Gardini, Kyle Elliott
##ADMIN	Lee Olsen, Dave Johnson, Doris McCabe, John Ross
##LABSTATIONS	##LAB01, ##LAB02 (You will not create these users at this time.)
##EVERYONE	All the users you create including the lab workstations

Dave would like to make Laurie Holt a user account manager of all Support and Student Service department users. Barbara Rau is to be a user account manager of all users in the Faculty department. He has asked you to place reasonable account restrictions on all usernames, including limiting users to logging in from one workstation as well as requiring users to have passwords that expire within 120 days and be at least four characters in length. In addition, Barbara Rau should be limited to logging in only at her assigned workstation during the business hours of 8:00 A.M. through 5:00 P.M. Monday through Friday. Use either SYSCON or USERDEF to create all users along with their home directories located within their associated workgroups. In addition, be sure to make each user a member of his or her appropriate group, including all the users you create as members of the group ##EVERYONE. Making all users members of the group ##EVERYONE is necessary so that you can separate your users from those created by other students. This will be important in future projects in which you assign rights and work with login scripts.

1. Use the SYSCON utility to create these groups. (Make sure to replace the number symbols with your assigned student number.)

You will need to log in as a supervisor equivalent user if you want to create users with the USERDEF utility. In addition, in order for your ##ADMIN username to be able to manage the users you have created with USERDEF, you will need to use SYSCON to select all the users created with USERDEF and insert your ##ADMIN username as manager of these users.

2. Do not create the lab station users at this time. They will be created with MAKEUSER in Project 2.

Project 7-2: Creating Lab Workstation Accounts

Dave Johnson would like you to create a username for each workstation in the computer lab. Most students will use these station names when they log in to the file server to perform their assignments. To make it easier to create a batch of usernames with the same parameters, you will use MAKEUSER to create a .USR file. You can then use the file to create the lab station usernames with the following parameters:

- Home directory path in the ##STJC\LAB\USERS directory
  # HOME-DIRECTORY   SYS:\SOADMIN\
- Log in from only one location at a time

- Login time restricted to 7:00 A.M. through 10:00 P.M.

- No password required

- Disk space on volume restricted to 5 Mbytes

- All workstations belong to groups ##EVERYONE and ##LABSTATIONS.

Before you create all the lab workstation accounts, Dave wants you to develop and test a MAKEUSER command file that creates only the ##LAB01 and ##LAB02 accounts. This file can later be used to create the additional lab accounts simply by adding the necessary #CREATE statements. Follow the steps listed below to create and then test a MAKEUSER file that creates the two lab accounts specified by Dave.

1. Write the keyword statements for the USR file program.

2. Log in to the file server using your ##ADMIN username.

3. Create a subdirectory in the \##STC\LAB directory for your lab users (i.e. ##STC\LAB\USERS).

4. In order to store your MAKEUSER files in the lab users subdirectory, change your default DOS prompt to the directory you created in step 3.

5. Start MAKEUSER.

6. Enter the .USR file.

7. Save the file.

8. Use the "Process USR file" option to create the users. Correct any errors.

9. After users have been created successfully, exit the MAKEUSER program.

10. Print a copy of your .USR and .RPT files and have them checked by your instructor.

11. Start SYSCON.

12. Select all the lab station user accounts and give them all unlimited credit.

13. Restrict all the lab workstation accounts from changing the password. This will prevent one student from placing a password on the account that would then prevent other student's use of the lab station.

14. Exit SYSCON and log out.

FILE SYSTEM SECURITY

After user accounts have been created and secured, the second level of NetWare security involves providing users with access to the NetWare file system. Initially new users have rights only to work in their home directories and run programs from the SYS:PUBLIC directory. An important responsibility of a network administrator is to provide users with the rights to access the network files and directories they need and still protect sensitive network information. NetWare file system security consists of two components: access rights and attributes. Access rights are like a set of keys that are provided to a new employee. Just as keys allow access to rooms, access rights provide the new user with access to the directories that contain files they need to use. Attributes, described in the second half of this chapter, can be attached to files or directories as another means of limiting user access.

AFTER READING THIS CHAPTER AND COMPLETING THE EXERCISES YOU WILL BE ABLE TO:

- IDENTIFY THE COMPONENTS OF NETWARE FILE SYSTEM SECURITY.

- DESCRIBE HOW EFFECTIVE RIGHTS ARE OBTAINED FROM A COMBINATION OF TRUSTEE ASSIGNMENTS, GROUP RIGHTS, AND INHERITED RIGHTS.

- DESCRIBE HOW THE INHERITED RIGHTS MASK MODIFIES EFFECTIVE RIGHTS IN A DIRECTORY OR FILE.

- USE NETWARE UTILITIES TO GRANT TRUSTEE RIGHTS AND DETERMINE USER EFFECTIVE RIGHTS.

- WORK WITH NETWARE FILE AND DIRECTORY ATTRIBUTES.

In previous chapters you were introduced to NetWare access rights and attributes. In this chapter, you will learn how to use access rights along with the Inherited Rights Mask to provide users with the effective rights they need to perform their work. You will also learn how to use attributes and the NetWare utilities to set and maintain them.

 Most software applications are being designed to take advantage of file sharing for workgroup computing. Because of this, the network administrator will need to balance file system security and integrity with providing shared access to directories that contain files used simultaneously by more than one workstation.

ACCESS RIGHTS

The eight access rights, introduced in Chapter 1 are Supervisory, Read, Write, Create, Erase, Modify, File scan, and Access Control. They determine what operations a user can perform in the file system. Figure 8-1 summarizes the access rights functions. Notice that access rights can be assigned to files as well as directories. This important feature of NetWare v3.1x was not available in previous NetWare v2.x operating systems. Being able to assign access rights to a specific file means the network administrator can provide users with the ability to update a certain file or database within the directory while blocking rights to other files that exist in that storage area.

The **Read** and **File scan** rights are often used together to allow users to access files or run programs in a specified directory. All users are given Read and File scan rights to the SYS:PUBLIC directory. Having the **Create** right to a directory allows a user to create subdirectories as well as new files in the specified directory. The Create right allows a user to copy files into the directory as long as there is no other file in the directory with the same name. All users are given the Create right to the SYS:MAIL directory, for example. A user sends a message to another user by copying the message file into the receiving user's directory. Granting the Create right to an existing file might seem meaningless, but it does allow the user to salvage the file if it is deleted.

Be aware that assigning the **Erase** right to a directory allows a user not only to erase files but also to remove the entire directory and its subdirectories. Notice the difference between the **Write** right and the **Modify** right. The Write right allows the user to change or add data to an existing file; the Modify right allows a user to change a file's name or attributes only—it has nothing to do with changing the contents of the file. The **Access control** right allows a user to determine which users can access the directory or file by granting access rights to other users. Because allowing users to grant rights to other users can make it difficult for the network administrator to keep track of file system security, the Access control right should not normally be given to other users. Having the **Supervisory** right is not the same as having all rights because it applies to all subdirectories and cannot be changed at a lower directory. The Supervisory right is also different from the other rights in that it can be assigned only by the SUPERVISOR or another user who has been granted Supervisory rights to the directory. The Supervisory right is often granted to workgroup managers. This allows them to control a specific section of the file system's directory structure. The workgroup manager for the sales department, for example, might be granted the Supervisory right to the DATA:SALES directory structure.

Figure 8-1

NetWare 3.1x
access rights

Access Right	Effect in Directory	Effect in File
Supervisory [S]	Grants all rights to the specified directory and all subdirectories; this right cannot be blocked or reassigned at a lower subdirectory or file level.	Grants all rights to the specified file.
Read [R]	Allows the user to read files or run programs in the directory.	Allows the user to read or run the specified file or program without having Read rights at the directory level.
Write [W]	Allows the user to change or add data to files in the specified directory.	Allows the user to change or add data to the specified file without having Write rights at the directory level.
Create [C]	Allows the user to create files and subdirectories.	Allows the user to salvage the specified file if it is deleted.
Erase [E]	Allows the user to delete files and remove subdirectories.	Allows the user to delete the specified file without having Erase rights at the directory level.
Modify [M]	Allows the user to change file and subdirectory names and use the FLAG and FLAGDIR commands to change the attribute settings on files or subdirectories.	Allows the user to change the name or attribute settings of the specified file without having Modify rights at the directory level.
File scan [F]	Allows the user to obtain a directory of file and subdirectory names.	Allows the user to view the specified file name on a directory listing without having File Scan rights at the directory level.
Access control [A]	Allows the user to grant access rights to other users for this specified directory.	Allows the user to grant access rights to the specified file without having Access Control rights at the directory level.

Users who have the Access control right in a directory, but do not have the Supervisory right, can accidentally restrict themselves from working in the directory by assigning to their usernames fewer rights to the directory or a subdirectory than they need. To avoid this, the Access control right should be granted to a user only when it is absolutely necessary for the user to assign rights to other users.

You will understand better what access rights are necessary to perform functions in the network file system, by looking at specific situations. Figure 8-2 lists typical operations that users need to perform on files and directories and the access rights required to perform the operations.

Figure 8-2

Rights required for common functions

Task	Rights Required
Read a file	Read
Obtain a directory listing	File scan
Change the contents of data in a file	Write
Write to a closed file using a text editor that creates a backup file	Write, Create, Erase, Modify (not always required)
Execute a program file	Read
Create and write to a new file	Create
Copy a file from a directory	Read, File scan
Copy a file into a directory	Create
Copy multiple files to a directory with existing files	Create, File scan
Create a subdirectory	Create
Delete a file	Erase
Salvage deleted files	Read and File scan on the file and create in the directory or on filename
Change attributes	Modify
Rename a file or subdirectory	Rename
Change the Inherited Rights Mask	Access control
Make or change a trustee assignment	Access control

USER TRUSTEE ASSIGNMENTS

A **directory trustee** is a user who has been granted access rights to a directory. The assignment can also be made to a group. Directory trustees are kept track of in the directory entry table of each volume. A directory table entry for a file or directory can hold up to six trustee assignments. If more than six trustees are assigned to a directory, an additional entry in the directory entry table is made for that directory name. It is a good idea, however, to keep trustee assignments to six or less for each directory. You can usually do this by assigning a group as a trustee and then making users who need access to that directory a member of the group.

A **file trustee** is a user (or group) who has been granted access rights to a file. Like directory trustees, file trustees are tracked in the directory entry table. If more than six trustees are assigned to a file, an additional entry in the directory entry table is needed for that filename.

Effective rights consist of a subset of access rights and refer to the functions a user can perform in a specific directory or file. In many cases, a user's effective rights are the same as his or her trustee assignment, however, there are basically four ways a user's effective rights to a directory or file are defined:

1. Direct trustee assignment is made to a username.

2. A user is assigned membership in a group and acquires the trustee rights that have been granted to the group.

3. Group or username rights, or both, are inherited for a file or directory from a directory at a higher level.

4. Rights are blocked by an Inherited Rights Mask.

The simplest and most straightforward way for a user to obtain effective rights in a directory is to be granted a trustee assignment consisting of a specific set of access rights to that directory. This is called a trustee assignment because it makes the user a trustee of the directory. As long as no trustee assignments have been made to any groups to which the user belongs, a user's effective rights will always be equal to his or her trustee assignment. Trustee assignments are usually designated by the first letter of each access right enclosed in brackets. For example, [R F C] specifies that a user has Read, File scan, and Create rights. The word "all" in brackets represents all access rights except Supervisory.

GROUP TRUSTEE ASSIGNMENTS

As described in Chapter 7, groups encompass users who have common network requirements. Grouping users simplifies making trustee assignments. When a group is made a trustee of a directory or file, all members of that group are also considered trustees of the directory or file and have the same rights as the group. A user's effective rights in a directory are then a combination of his or her trustee assignment plus any rights he or she obtains from being a member of a group. Assume, for example, that the marketing group has been granted [R F] rights to the SALES directory, as shown in Figure 8-3. James, George, and Julie are all members of the marketing group. If you want George to be responsible for changing sales data, you can make him a trustee of the SALES directory, with Create, Write, Erase, and Modify rights. George's effective rights are [R F C W E M]: the [R F] rights derived from his membership in the marketing group plus the [C W E M] rights derived from the trustee assignment made to his username.

Figure 8-3

Combining group and user rights

→ indicates assigned rights

INHERITED RIGHTS

By default all files and subdirectories inherit the effective rights a user or group has in the directory. To understand the principle of **inherited rights** better, imagine that in every directory or file each user or group has a container that holds its trustee assignment. If no trustee assignment is made for a user or group in a directory, the user or group's container will inherit the rights from the parent directory. In this way, rights are inherited by each container separately. They flow down from the container in the corresponding higher level. Assume, for example, you want to divide the SALES directory shown in Figure 8-3 into three subdirectories, ORDERS, USERS, and INVENTRY, in order to separate files by application. Because the marketing group has been given Read and File scan rights to the SALES directory, all members of the group have at least Read and File scan rights to the files in the newly created subdirectories. In addition, George inherits Create, Write, Erase, and Modify rights in the new subdirectories. See Figure 8-4.

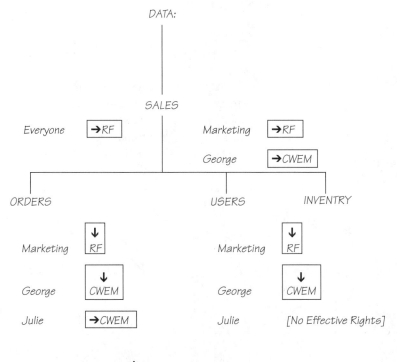

Figure 8-4

Tracking inherited rights

Notice that the effective rights for each user in a directory are a combination of the rights in the user's container and the rights from all group containers of which he or she is a member. In each container, rights can come either from a direct trustee assignment to the user or from a group. If no trustee assignment is made, the user or group inherits any rights it has in the parent directory. Julie, who is a member of the marketing group, has [R F] in the SALES directory because of the trustee assignment of

[R F] made to the marketing group and [R F] in the SALES\USERS directory because of the marketing group's inherited rights. In addition, Julie has the [S R F W C E M] rights in the SALES\ORDERS subdirectory as a result of her personal assignment of [W C E M] combined with the marketing group's inherited [R F] rights. As you can see, using inherited rights can make the job of assigning rights simpler and faster, but the directory structure must be properly organized for it to work.

A user's effective rights in a subdirectory can be modified by making a new trustee assignment to either the username or to a group to which the user belongs. The rights specified in the new trustee assignment will override the inherited rights for that group or username in the specified directory. For example, if the marketing group is given a trustee assignment of [N] for no rights in the USERS subdirectory, this trustee assignment will override the marketing group's inherited rights. The net result is that Julie will have no effective rights in the USERS subdirectory and George will have only [C W E M] rights. See Figure 8-5.

Figure 8-5

Modifying effective rights

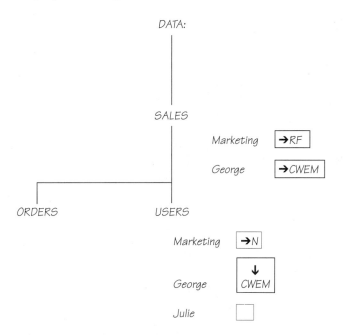

There is one exception to a new trustee assignment overriding inherited rights: when a user or group has been granted the [S]/Supervisory/right to a directory. Assume, for example, that Jim is the manager of the marketing department and you want to grant him all rights to the entire DATA:SALES directory structure. You could do this in one of two ways: either grant him all rights, [S R W C E M F A], to the DATA:SALES directory, or else grant him the Supervisory right [S], to the DATA:SALES directory. If he is granted [S R W C E M F A] rights to DATA:SALES, his rights to the SALES\ORDERS directory could later be changed to [R F] by granting him a trustee assignment of [R F] to ORDERS. If, however, you grant Jim the [S] right to DATA:SALES, the trustee assignment of [R F] to the ORDERS directory would not change his effective rights; he would still have all rights to the ORDERS directory. See Figure 8-6.

Figure 8-6

Assigning the
Supervisory right

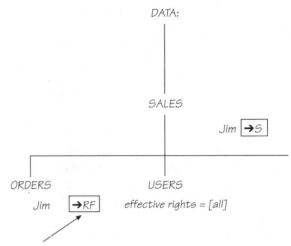

Trustee assignment does not affect Supervisory rights

THE INHERITED RIGHTS MASK

When you do not want user and group rights to be inherited into a lower directory, NetWare allows you to prevent rights from being inherited by providing each directory with what is called an **Inherited Rights Mask (IRM)**. The IRM acts like a filter by blocking selected rights from passing into the lower subdirectory structure. When you first create a directory or subdirectory, the IRM allows all rights to be inherited. Thereafter, removing rights from the IRM prevents the subdirectory from inheriting those rights that are no longer specified in the IRM.

 The IRM filters rights that are inherited from a higher directory, but it does not affect a trustee assignment made to that directory.

In the SALES directory structure shown in Figure 8-7, for example, the IRM—by removing all rights except Supervisory from the IRM of the USERS directory— prevents users and groups from inheriting any rights into the SALES\USERS directory. Notice that while the IRM of the SALES\ORDERS directory has been set to allow only Read and File scan rights to be inherited, it does not change the trustee assignment made to Julie's username. It does prevent George from inheriting his [W C E M] rights.

 The IRM only reduces rights and it never adds to them.

Because the Supervisory right cannot be removed from an IRM, the SUPERVISOR or a user who has been granted the Supervisory rights to a higher directory is not affected by the IRM. Notice that Jim, as the manager of the marketing department, was granted the Supervisory right to the DATA:SALES directory and that he still has all effective rights in each of the subdirectories in the DATA:SALES structure despite the restrictions placed in the IRMs of the subdirectories.

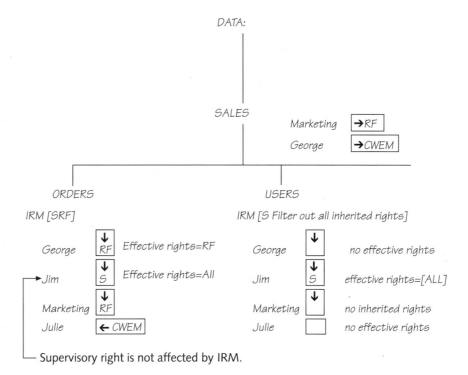

Figure 8-7

Using the Inherited
Rights Mask

PLANNING FILE SYSTEM SECURITY

Computing effective rights can be a complex task when multiple group and user trustee assignments are involved. Good strategies in planning a file system's security include using as few trustee assignments as possible and keeping the use of Inherited Rights Masks to a minimum. If you need to use an Inherited Rights Mask, it might indicate that you should rethink your directory structure or assignment of rights. Imagine, for example, that you are a network administrator for a company and that your predecessor created a directory structure in which word processing document files were stored in subdirectories of the SOFTWARE\WP directory. See Figure 8–8. Because the group EVERYONE is a trustee of SOFTWARE with [R F] rights, all users inherit [R F] rights to the document subdirectories. This creates a security problem because all users have the ability to read any document. To eliminate this problem, you could remove all rights from the IRMs of the document subdirectories to block the inherited rights and then grant appropriate users the necessary trustee assignments to these subdirectories. Although this solution will work, it does not address the real problem: Data directories and software directories should be in separate locations, as described in Chapter 4. The best solution in this example, is to move the document subdirectories to another location in the file system.

Figure 8-8

An example of poor
directory design

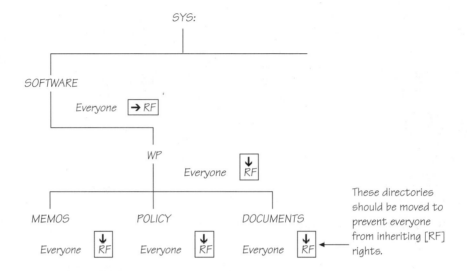

 Word processing programs such as Microsoft Word have enhanced abilities designed to facilitate workgroup computing. Because directories containing shared word processing files should be accessible to all users of the application, placing the shared files in subdirectories of the word processing application directory can provide a good solution to allow workgroups to share files.

To help keep the file system security as simple and effective as possible, Novell suggests that CNAs follow two simple strategies when they plan file system security:

1. Plan rights from the top down.

2. Plan trustee assignments starting with groups.

Remember that rights are inherited from higher directories into lower subdirectories and files. Planning a directory structure from the top down takes advantage of this principle. The following guidelines can help you implement a top-down strategy:

- Place at the top of your directory structure directories that are least frequently accessed. Place the most frequently accessed directories at the bottom.

- Grant only the rights needed based on the needs of the user or group at any given level.

- Use the inheritance principle and use IRMs to protect directories against trustees inheriting unwanted rights.

- Start planning rights at the department or highest level directory and work down to the subdirectories and files within it.

When planning trustee assignments, start by assigning rights to the groups that have the most users and proceed to individual user trustee assignments. This keeps user trustee assignments to a minimum. Some network administrators go to the extreme of never making trustee assignments to users; they make the trustee assignment to a group name instead and then make the user who needs the access rights a member of that group. Although this will increase the number of groups that need to be created and maintained, this approach makes it easier for the network administrator to deal with many users frequently changing job functions—a situation that can arise during company reorganization. This approach is definitely valuable in a company that undergoes frequent reorganization. When assigning trustee rights to groups and users, follow three basic steps:

1. Assign rights to the group EVERYONE.

2. Assign rights to departmental groups.

3. Assign rights to individual users.

COMMAND LINE UTILITIES

NetWare includes command line utilities that enable a CNA to grant trustee rights and to obtain information about a user's effective rights in a directory. The following paragraphs describe these command line utilities, showing the command syntax and illustrating its use in the SALES structure example.

RIGHTS

Use the RIGHTS [*path*] command to determine the effective rights of the currently logged in username in the specified directory path. If no path is specified, the RIGHTS command displays the user's rights in the current directory path. Figure 8–9 shows two examples of the RIGHTS command—one to determine rights in the current directory and one to determine effective rights in the specified directory path.

Figure 8-9

Using the RIGHTS command

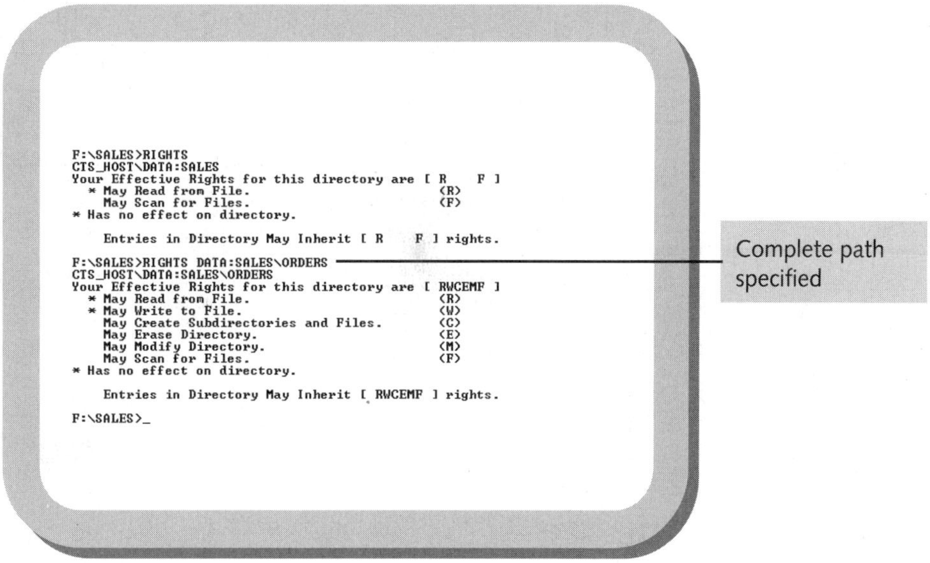

```
F:\SALES>RIGHTS
CTS_HOST\DATA:SALES
Your Effective Rights for this directory are [ R    F ]
    * May Read from File.                      (R)
      May Scan for Files.                      (F)
* Has no effect on directory.

      Entries in Directory May Inherit [ R    F ] rights.

F:\SALES>RIGHTS DATA:SALES\ORDERS ──────────────  Complete path
CTS_HOST\DATA:SALES\ORDERS                        specified
Your Effective Rights for this directory are [ RWCEMF ]
    * May Read from File.                      (R)
    * May Write to File.                       (W)
      May Create Subdirectories and Files.     (C)
      May Erase Directory.                     (E)
      May Modify Directory.                    (M)
      May Scan for Files.                      (F)
* Has no effect on directory.

      Entries in Directory May Inherit [ RWCEMF ] rights.

F:\SALES>_
```

GRANT

If you are logged in as SUPERVISOR or have the Access control right to a directory structure, you can use the GRANT command to make a new trustee assignment to a user or group for the specified directory path. The syntax of the GRANT command is GRANT *rights-list* [FOR *path*] TO *username/group* [/SUB] [/FILES]. Replace *rights-list* with the abbreviations of the rights you want to assign. Separate the abbreviations by spaces; do not place them in brackets. Use the word *all* to specify all rights or the letter N to specify no rights for the user or group in the specified directory. Replace *path* with the complete or partial path leading to the directory in which you want to make the trustee assignment. If you are not a supervisor equivalent user, you will need to have the Supervisory or Access control right to the directory path specified. If no path is specified, the assignment will be made to the current directory. Replace *username/group* with the name of an existing user or group to which you want to make the trustee assignment. The /SUB option, which grants the trustee assignment to all subdirectories within the path, is usually unnecessary because the subdirectories will inherit the rights for that trustee assignment unless you have blocked rights by changing subdirectory IRMs. The /FILES option is similar to the /SUB option except that it makes the trustee assignment to each file in the directory.

To make a trustee assignment of Read and File scan rights to the DATA:SALES directory for all members of the marketing department, use the GRANT command shown in Figure 8-10. The second GRANT command shown in the figure provides Julie with the additional Write, Create, Modify and Erase rights necessary to maintain files in the SALES\ORDERS subdirectory. To prevent the marketing group from inheriting the [R F] rights into the user home directories, use the last GRANT command in Figure 8-10. This eliminates the marketing group rights to the USERS subdirectory by assigning the marketing group no rights.

Figure 8-10

Using the GRANT command

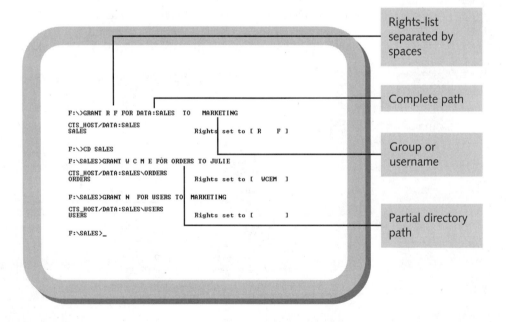

REVOKE

Use the REVOKE command to remove access rights from an existing trustee assignment made to a user or group in the specified directory path. The syntax is REVOKE *rights-list* [FOR *path*] FROM *username/group* [/SUB] [/FILES]. Replace *rights-list* with the abbreviations of the rights you want to remove (separated by spaces). Use the word *all* to specify all rights are to be removed, providing the user or group with no rights to the specified directory. Replace *username/group* with the name of an existing user or group whose trustee assignment you want to revoke. You can specify either a complete or a partial NetWare path. Leaving the *path* parameter off revokes the trustee assignment from the current directory. The /SUB option revokes the rights from all subdirectories within the path if these subdirectories contain a trustee assignment for the specified user. The /FILES option is similar to the /SUB option except that it revokes the rights from each file in the directory that has been granted a trustee assignment for the specified user.

Figure 8-11 shows an example of the REVOKE command. It removes the [M] right from Julie's trustee assignment to the SALES\ORDERS directory. The REVOKE command will not revoke inherited rights from a directory. The second REVOKE command in Figure 8-11 attempts, but fails to revoke the marketing group's rights to the DATA:SALES\USERS directory. The REVOKE command can be issued only at the directory level at which the corresponding trustee assignment was made.

Figure 8-11

Using the REVOKE command

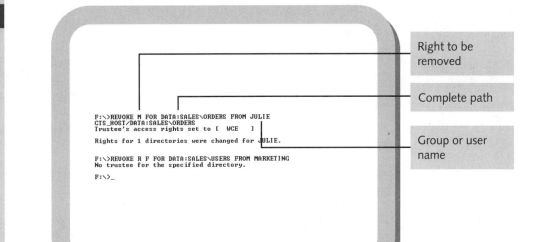

F:\>REVOKE M FOR DATA:SALES\ORDERS FROM JULIE
CTS_HOST/DATA:SALES\ORDERS
Trustee's access rights set to [WCE]

Rights for 1 directories were changed for JULIE.

F:\>REVOKE R F FOR DATA:SALES\USERS FROM MARKETING
No trustee for the specified directory.

F:\>_

Right to be removed

Complete path

Group or user name

TLIST

Use the TLIST [path] command to display a list of all trustee assignments in the specified path. You can replace *path* with either a complete or partial NetWare path. Leaving off the path parameter lists the trustee assignments to the current directory. You can use *.* along with the path to list the trustee assignments made to files and subdirectories within the specified directory path. Unfortunately there is no /SUB option comparable to that available with the LISTDIR and NDIR commands. TLIST lists trustee assignments only for the subdirectories of the specified directory, as shown in Figure 8-12.

Figure 8-12

Using the TLIST
command

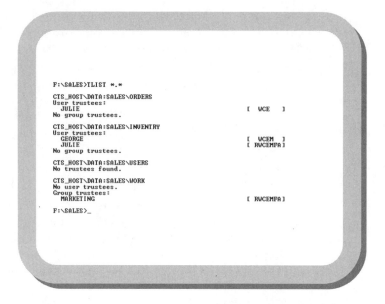

```
F:\SALES>TLIST *.*

CTS_HOST\DATA:SALES\ORDERS
User trustees:
    JULIE                                      [  WCE  ]
No group trustees.

CTS_HOST\DATA:SALES\INVENTRY
User trustees:
    GEORGE                                     [  WCEM ]
    JULIE                                      [ RWCEMFA]
No group trustees.

CTS_HOST\DATA:SALES\USERS
No trustees found.

CTS_HOST\DATA:SALES\WORK
No user trustees.
Group trustees:
    MARKETING                                  [ RWCEMFA]

F:\SALES>_
```

REMOVE

Although the REVOKE command removes specific rights from a trustee assignment, the REMOVE command deletes the entire trustee assignment from the specified path. Its syntax is REMOVE *username/group* [FROM *path*] [/SUB] [/FILES]. Replace *username/group* with the name of the user or group whose trustee assignment you want to delete. Specify either a complete or partial NetWare path. Leaving the path parameter off removes the trustee assignment from the current directory. Use the /SUB or /FILES options to remove the trustee assignment for the specified user from all subdirectories or files. Figure 8-13 shows a REMOVE command to remove Julie's trustee assignment from the SALES\INVENTRY subdirectory.

Figure 8-13

Using the REMOVE
command

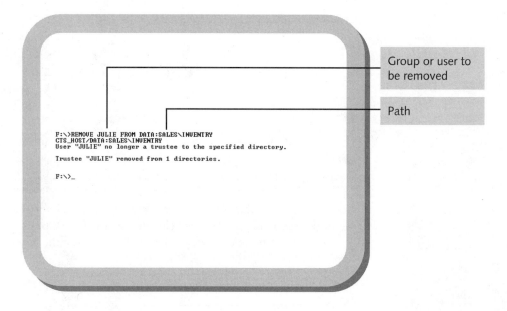

Group or user to
be removed

Path

```
F:\>REMOVE JULIE FROM DATA:SALES\INVENTRY
CTS_HOST/DATA:SALES\INVENTRY
User "JULIE" no longer a trustee to the specified directory.

Trustee "JULIE" removed from 1 directories.

F:\>_
```

In some situations, removing a trustee assignment for a user or group from a subdirectory can actually increase that user or group's effective rights by allowing the subdirectory to inherit rights from the parent directory.

ALLOW

Use the ALLOW command to modify the Inherited Rights Mask of the directory or filename specified in directory path. Its syntax is ALLOW *path* TO INHERIT *rights-list*. Replace *path* with either the complete NetWare path or a partial path leading to the directory or file that contains the IRM you want to modify. If you want to specify the current directory, replace *path* with a period (.) Replace *rights-list* with the rights you want to be contained in the IRM of the specified directory or file. The directory or file will then be allowed to inherit only the rights you specify in the *rights-list* field. The word *all* allows the user or group to inherit all rights; the letter N indicates that no rights are to be passed into this directory or file from higher level directories. Figure 8-14 shows sample ALLOW commands: one that prevents the SALES\USERS subdirectory from inheriting any rights and one that causes the ORDERS directory to inherit only [R F] rights.

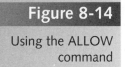

Figure 8-14

Using the ALLOW command

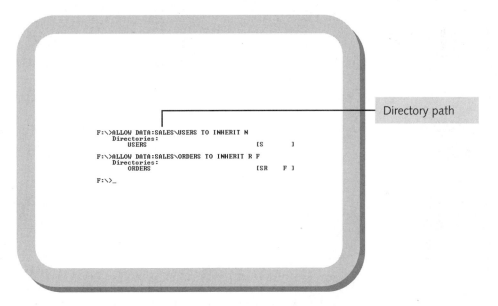

Directory path

```
F:\>ALLOW DATA:SALES\USERS TO INHERIT N
    Directories:
        USERS                          [S      ]
F:\>ALLOW DATA:SALES\ORDERS TO INHERIT R F
    Directories:
        ORDERS                         [SR    F ]

F:\>_
```

WHOAMI

Use the WHOAMI /R command to obtain a list of all the trustee assignments in the entire file system that have been granted to a currently logged in user or to a group of which the user is a member. Figure 8-15 shows an example of the WHOAMI /R command. The logged-in user, Julie, has obtained a listing of all trustee assignments granted to Julie or the marketing group.

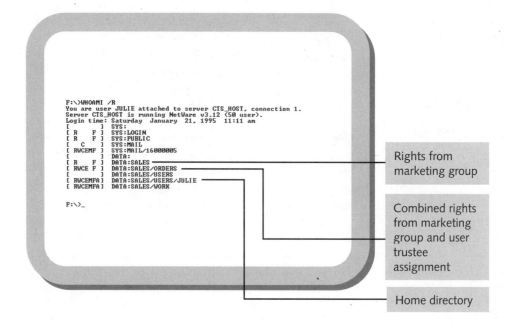

Figure 8-15

Using the WHOAMI
command

Rights from
marketing group

Combined rights
from marketing
group and user
trustee
assignment

Home directory

LISTDIR

Use the LISTDIR command to obtain a list of the current user's effective rights in the specified directory path. Its syntax is LISTDIR [*path*] [/E] [/S]. Adding the /S option displays the effective rights in all subdirectories within the specified path. If no path is specified, the LISTDIR command displays the contents of the current directory. Figure 8-16 shows an example of the LISTDIR command. Julie is still the logged-in user. The command displays all of Julie's effective rights in the DATA: volume. Notice how the IRM in the SALES\USERS directory blocks her effective rights to the USERS directory.

Figure 8-16

Using the LISTDIR
command

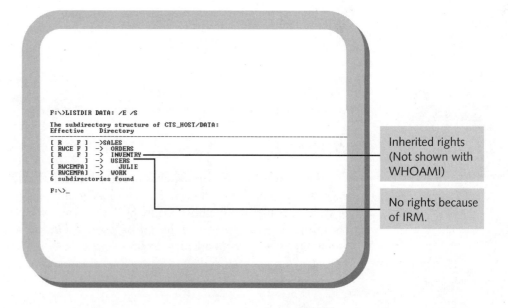

Inherited rights
(Not shown with
WHOAMI)

No rights because
of IRM.

MENU UTILITIES

The NetWare command line utilities can be used efficiently to grant or view trustee assignments from the DOS prompt. They have two drawbacks, however. They entail many keystrokes, especially if you need to make several entries, which of course increases the chance for errors. They also require exact syntax to work correctly. Assigning trustee and effective rights can be simpler and less frustrating with the FILER and SYSCON utilities. Both utilities contain menu options that allow you to assign trustee rights to usernames and groups. In addition, NetWare's FILER utility has a very useful option called Who Has Rights Here. It displays the names of all users and groups along with their effective rights in the selected directory. In this section, you will learn how to use SYSCON and FILER to assign, revoke, remove, and view trustee assignments and effective rights.

Using FILER to manage trustee assignments

Suppose you want to add two users as trustees of the SALES\INVENTRY directory and assign them [R F C E M W] rights. You can perform this task by first starting FILER and then using the Select Current Directory option as described in Chapter 6 to change to the desired SALES\INVENTRY directory. Choose the Current Directory Information option to display directory information for this directory. See Figure 8-17. To work with trustee assignments, simply select the Trustees field. Pressing [Enter] displays a window containing a list of any existing trustees.

Figure 8-17

FILER's Directory Information screen

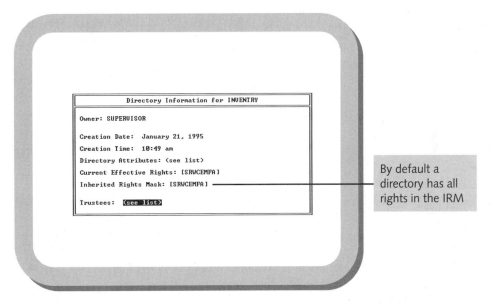

```
          Directory Information for INVENTRY

Owner: SUPERVISOR

Creation Date:   January 21, 1995
Creation Time:   10:49 am
Directory Attributes: (see list)
Current Effective Rights: [SRWCEMFA]
Inherited Rights Mask: [SRWCEMFA]

Trustees:  <see list>
```

By default a directory has all rights in the IRM

To add new trustees to this list, press [Ins] and then use the F5 key to highlight the names of the users you want to add from the Others windows and press [Enter]. The users or groups you have marked will now appear in the trustee window with the default rights of [R F]. To add additional rights to one of the users or groups, use the arrow keys to select the user or group and press [Enter]. The Trustee Rights window, listing the existing rights, will be displayed. To add rights to the Trustee Rights window press [Ins] to display the Other Rights window, as shown in Figure 8-18.

Figure 8-18

Using FILER to add
access rights

Now use the F5 key to mark the rights you want to add to this user or group's trustee assignment and then press [Enter] to have the selected rights added to the Trustee Rights window. To save the updated trustee rights, press [Esc]. The username appears with its assigned rights in the trustee list.

To revoke one or more rights from a trustee assignment, you first select the user or group name from the trustee window and then press [Enter] to display the Trustee Rights window. Use the F5 key to mark the rights you want to remove and press [Del]. FILER will ask you to confirm the deletion. After you confirm the deletion, FILER removes the rights from the Trustee Rights window. Pressing [Esc] returns you to the trustee window, which shows the remaining rights for the selected user or group. This procedure has the same result as using the REVOKE command line utility.

 If necessary, you can remove all rights from a user or group trustee assignment, effectively blocking that user or group's rights to the selected directory.

To remove a trustee of the directory, simply use the arrow keys in the trustee window to select the user or group name and then press the Del key. After you confirm the deletion, the user or group is removed from the trustee window. This is comparable to using the REMOVE command line utility. With FILER, multiple trustees can be removed from the directory. Use the F5 key to mark all the trustees you want to remove and then press the Del key.

Another way to use FILER to assign trustee rights to a subdirectory or file is to select the Directory Contents option from the Available Topics menu. Highlight the name of the directory or file in which you want to make a trustee assignment and press [Enter] to display the subdirectory or file option menu. You can then use the View/Set Information option, as shown in Figure 8-19, to view an information screen similar to the one shown in Figure 8-17. The Trustees field can then be used as described already to add, change, and delete trustee assignments for the selected subdirectory or file.

Figure 8-19

Using Filer's Directory Contents option

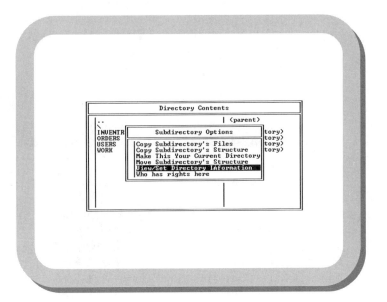

Using FILER to view effective rights

One nice feature that Novell added to FILER in NetWare v3.1x allows a SUPERVISOR or supervisor equivalent user to view the effective rights of all users in a selected directory. This option is available only in the Subdirectory Options menu, so you must first change the current directory to be one level higher than the directory for which you want to view the effective rights. To view who has rights in the DATA:SALES directory, for example, you would need to change your current directory to the root of the DATA: volume. To view users' rights in the SALES\USER subdirectory, you would change the current directory to the DATA:SALES directory. After selecting the directory that contains the subdirectory for which you want to view effective rights, you select the Directory Contents option of FILER's main menu and then highlight the name of the subdirectory you want to examine. Pressing [Enter] displays the Subdirectory Options menu. You can now use the Who Has Rights Here option from the Subdirectory Options menu to display a list of all users and groups who have rights to the subdirectory. See Figure 8-20. The Who Has Rights Here option does not appear on the menu if the logged-in user is not a SUPERVISOR or supervisor equivalent user.

Figure 8-20

Viewing who has rights
in a subdirectory

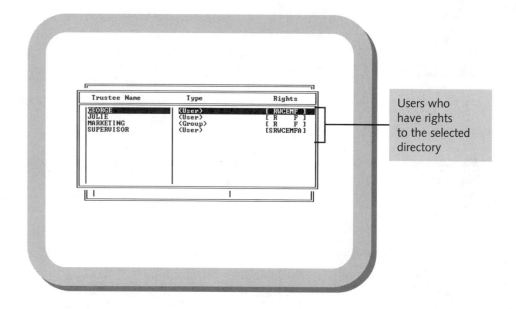

Users who
have rights
to the selected
directory

Using FILER to change the Inherited Rights Mask

The FILER utility makes it easy to view or change the Inherited Rights Mask for a directory. You first select the Select Current Directory option to change to the desired directory and then use the Current Directory Information option to display the Directory Information screen (shown in Figure 8-17). To work with the IRM for this directory, highlight the Inherited Rights Mask field. Pressing [Enter] displays a window containing a list of all rights that this directory can inherit. Use the arrow keys along with the F5 key to highlight any right (except the Supervisory right) you want to remove. Pressing [Del] removes the selected rights. If you need to add rights back to the IRM, press the Ins key and then use the F5 key to mark the desired rights in the "Other Rights" window. Pressing [Enter] includes the selected rights in the IRM. Now press [Esc] to save the new inherited rights and return to the directory information screen.

To use FILER to change the IRM of a subdirectory or file, select the Directory Information option from the Available Topics menu and then highlight the name of the subdirectory or file you want to modify. You can then use the View/Set Directory Information option to view the directory or file information screen and then select the Inherited Rights Mask field to change the IRM of the directory or file, using the steps just described for directories.

Using SYSCON to make a trustee assignment

The SYSCON utility can be used by supervisors and user account managers to make trustee assignments to users and groups they manage. This is convenient—after you create a user you often want to give him or her some special trustee assignments. If you are assigning several trustees to a single directory, it is more convenient to use the FILER utility. When you are assigning a user as a trustee of several different directories, however, it is often quicker to use the SYSCON utility. A CNA should know how to use both methods.

When using SYSCON to make a trustee assignment, start by selecting the User Information option from the Available Topics menu. Then highlight the name of the user to whom you want to grant the trustee assignment and press [Enter]. SYSCON will display the User Information window containing the Trustee Directory Assignments and Trustee File Assignments options. To grant the selected user a trustee assignment to a directory, select the Trustee Directory Assignments option and press [Enter]. SYSCON displays the Trustee Directory Assignments window, showing all the trustee assignments that have been made for the selected user to any directories in the NetWare file system. To add a new trustee assignment for this user, press the Ins key. This displays a window that asks you to enter the directory path. Either type the complete path to the desired directory or press the Ins key and select each component leading to the desired directory. After the path to the directory has been entered, press the Enter key. (If the path you specify does not exist, SYSCON will ask if you want to create the directory. If you get this message because you have entered an incorrect path, select No and re-enter the correct path.) SYSCON adds the new trustee assignment containing the Read and File scan rights for this directory to the user's trustee assignment list, as shown in Figure 8-21.

Notice that the default rights that SYSCON grants for the directory are [R F], the same as FILER. Earlier versions of SYSCON assigned all rights to the directory by default.

Figure 8-21

Using SYSCON to add trustee assignments

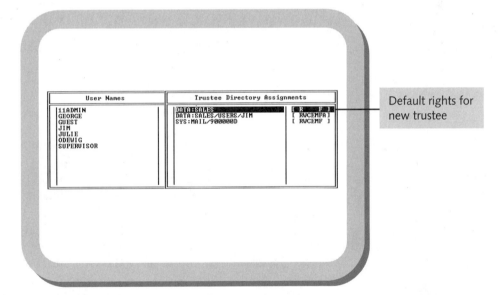

Default rights for new trustee

To modify the rights in one of the user's trustee assignments, highlight the path showing the trustee assignment you want to modify and press [Enter]. SYSCON displays the Trustee Rights Granted window, listing the current access rights. To add rights, press the Ins key to display the Trustee Rights Not Granted window, as shown in Figure 8-22. Use the F5 key to mark the rights you want to add. Pressing [Enter] adds the selected rights to the Trustee Rights Granted window. To delete rights, use the F5 key to mark the rights you want to delete and press the Del key. Pressing [Esc] returns you to the Trustee Directory Assignments window, which shows the updated trustee assignment. To remove a trustee assignment from a user, simply highlight the path showing the trustee assignment you want to remove and press the Del key. After you confirm the deletion, the trustee assignment is removed from the Trustee Directory Assignment window.

Figure 8-22

Using SYSCON
to change
trustee rights

FILE AND DIRECTORY ATTRIBUTES

As introduced in Chapter 6, attributes are flags or codes that can be associated with files and directories. They indicate to the NetWare operating system what type of processing can be performed on the associated file and directory. Attributes are often placed on directories and files by the network administrator in order to provide additional protection against accidental change or deletion. Attributes are also used to specify special processing such as making a file sharable or purging all files that are deleted from a specific directory. Attributes override user effective rights in a directory or file. If a file is flagged with the Read Only attribute, the only operations you can perform on the file—no matter what your effective rights are—are Read and File scan. Assume, for example, a user has the Supervisory trustee right to the SALES directory and therefore would inherit all access rights to the files and subdirectories in the SALES structure. If a file named ZIPCODE.DAT is stored in the SALES directory and is flagged with the Read Only attribute, this user only has Read access to the ZIPCODE.DAT file. Because this user has a Supervisory trustee assignment to the SALES directory, however, he or she can use the Modify right to remove the Read Only attribute and then change or even delete the ZIPCODE.DAT file.

ATTRIBUTES

Figure 8-23 contains a list of all attributes used by NetWare v3.1x along with their corresponding abbreviations. Attributes are used with files; some can be used with directories as well, as indicated in Figure 8-23. The following paragraphs cover the information a CNA needs to know about NetWare attributes.

Figure 8-23

File and directory
attributes

Attribute	Applies To	Abbreviation
Archive Needed	file	A
Copy Inhibit	file	CI
Delete Inhibit	file, directory	DI
Execute Only	file	X
Hidden	file, directory	H
Indexed	file	I
Purge	file, directory	P
Read Only	file	RO
Read Write	file	RW
Rename Inhibit	file, directory	RI
Sharable	file	SH
System	file, directory	SY
Transactional	file	T

Archive Needed

The **Archive Needed** attribute is assigned automatically to files when the contents of a file are modified. Copy or backup utilities can remove this attribute after the file is copied to another storage location. This attribute is important in controlling what files are copied to a backup disk. It is possible to back up only the files that have been changed since the last backup. The use of this attribute along with the backup utilities will be explained in detail in Chapter 15.

Copy Inhibit

The **Copy Inhibit** attribute is used to protect specified files from being copied by Macintosh users. Setting this attribute prevents Macintosh computers running the Apple Filing Protocol v2.0 and above from copying the file. The Copy Inhibit attribute could be used on PC-specific files such as software programs to prevent them from being accidentally copied to a Macintosh computer.

Delete Inhibit

The **Delete Inhibit** attribute prevents a file or directory from being deleted. If assigned to a file, the file's contents can be changed or the file renamed, but the file cannot be deleted unless a user who has been granted the Modify right first removes the Delete Inhibit attribute. The Delete Inhibit attribute is often useful to protect an important data file from accidentally being deleted yet still allows its contents to be changed. You should consider setting the Delete Inhibit attribute on many of your organization's permanent files, such as customer, payroll, inventory, and accounting files.

Setting the Delete Inhibit attribute on a directory prevents the directory's name from being removed, but will not prevent the contents of the directory, its files and subdirectories, from being deleted. You might want to protect the fixed parts of your organization's directory structure from being modified by flagging all main directories with the Delete Inhibit attribute.

Execute Only

The major use of the **Execute Only** attribute is to protect software files from being illegally copied. Execute only can be set only on .EXE and .COM files by a supervisor equivalent user. Once set, Execute Only cannot be removed even by the SUPERVISOR. As a result, do *not* assign Execute Only to files unless backup copies of the files exist. Certain program files will not run when they are flagged Execute Only because these programs need to copy information from their program files into the workstation's memory—the Execute Only attribute prevents this. Because the Execute Only attribute cannot be removed, to get rid of it you need to delete the file and reinstall it from another disk.

Hidden

The **Hidden** attribute is used to hide files and directories from DOS utilities and certain software applications. However, the NDIR, NCOPY, and LISTDIR commands will display hidden files and directories—and show the H attribute, when it is enabled. One simple way to help protect software from illegal copying is to use the Hidden attribute to make the software directories and files hidden from normal DOS utilities. If you move the NCOPY and NDIR commands from the SYS:PUBLIC directory to the SYS:SYSTEM directory or some other location, standard users will not have access to them.

 Another way to protect the NCOPY and NDIR commands from unauthorized use is to place an IRM on the files in question to prevent users from inheriting the [R F] rights to these files and then make a specific trustee assignment to a special group. Only members of the special group can then use the NCOPY and NDIR commands.

The Hidden attribute can be especially useful when you have workstations using the Microsoft Windows environment. With Windows it is very easy for users to explore the directory structure using the File Manager. By hiding directories and files, you can make the file structure much less accessible.

Indexed

The **Indexed** attribute is automatically assigned by the NetWare operating system to files that need over 64 blocks of disk storage. It indicates that the file is indexed for fast access. This attribute will appear when you list attributes for a file. It is for your information only, however. Its setting cannot be changed by the network administrator or user.

Purge

As described in Chapter 6, NetWare allows deleted files to be retrieved with the SALVAGE utility until either the deleted file's space is reused by the file server or the directory is purged using the PURGE command. Space from files that have been purged is no longer available to the operating system, preventing the file from being recovered with the SALVAGE utility. The **Purge** attribute can be assigned to either a file or a directory if you want the NetWare file server immediately to reuse the space from deleted files. When assigned to a file, the Purge attribute causes the file to be purged as soon as it is deleted thereby making its space immediately available to the system for reuse. When Purge is assigned to a directory, any file that is deleted from the directory is automatically purged and its space reused. The Purge attribute is often assigned to directories that contain temporary files in order to reuse the temporary file space as soon as the file is deleted. The Purge attribute can also be assigned, for security reasons, to files that contain sensitive data, thereby preventing an intruder from salvaging and then accessing information from these files after they have been deleted.

Read Audit and Write Audit

The **Read Audit and Write Audit** attributes are not used by NetWare v3.1x through v4.1. Although these attributes can be assigned to files, their use has not yet been defined by Novell. As a result, these attributes are not used by network administrators.

Read Only

The **Read Only** attribute applies only to files. It protects the contents of a file from being modified. The Read Only attribute performs a function similar to opening the write-protect tab on a disk. Files containing data that is not normally changed—such as a ZIP code file or a program file—are usually flagged Read Only. When you first set on the Read Only attribute, the Delete Inhibit and Rename Inhibit attributes are also set by default. If for some reason you want to allow the file to be renamed or deleted but do not want its contents changed, you can remove the Rename Inhibit and Delete Inhibit attributes.

Read Write

The **Read Write** attribute applies only to files. It indicates that the contents of the file can be added to or changed. When files are created, the Read Write attribute is automatically set, allowing the contents of the file to be added to or changed.

Rename Inhibit

The **Rename Inhibit** attribute can be assigned to either files or directories. When assigned to a file, it protects the filename from being changed. During installation, many software packages create data and configuration files that might need to be updated and changed, but those filenames must remain constant in order for the software package to operate properly. After installing a software package that requests certain file or directory names, it is a good idea to use the Rename Inhibit attribute on these file and directories to prevent someone from changing the file or directory name and causing an error or crash in the application. Using the Rename Inhibit attribute on a directory prevents that directory's name from being changed while still allowing files and subdirectories contained within that directory to be renamed.

Sharable

When files are created, they are available to only one user at a time. Suppose, for example, you create a file called BUDGET95.WK1 on the file server and a coworker opens up this file with a spreadsheet program. If you attempt to access the BUDGET95.WK1 file, you will receive an error message that the file is in use or not accessible. With spreadsheet files and word processing documents, if more than one user can access the file at one time, any changes made by one user can be overwritten by another user. Program files and certain database files, however, should be made available to multiple users at the same time. For example, you would want as many users as you have licenses to be able to run the word processing software you just installed or perhaps access a common database of customers. To allow a file to be opened by more than one user at a time, the **Sharable** attribute for that file must be enabled. Normally you need to flag all program files Sharable after performing an installation, as described in Chapter 9.

In addition to sharable, most program files are also flagged as Read-only to prevent users from deleting or making changes to the software. Most document and data files are not flagged as sharable in order to prevent multiple users from making changes to the file at the same time.

System

The **System** attribute is often assigned to files and directories that are part of the NetWare operating system. The bindery files NET$OBJ.SYS, NET$PROP.SYS, and NET$VAL.SYS, for example, are located in the SYS:SYSTEM directory and are flagged with the System attribute. Print queues, described in Chapter 10, are actually subdirectories in the SYS:SYSTEM directory and are also flagged with the System attribute. Like the Hidden attribute, the System attribute hides files from the DOS utilities and application software packages, but also marks the file or directory as being for operating system use only.

Transactional

The **Transactional** attribute can be assigned only to files and is used to indicate that the file will be protected by the **Transaction Tracking System (TTS)**. The TTS ensures that when changes or transactions are applied to a file, either all transactions are completed or the file is left in its original state. The TTS is particularly important for database files—when a workstation is in the process of updating a record and crashes before the update is complete, the integrity of the file is protected. Assume, for example, that a NetWare file server is used to maintain an on-line order-entry system containing customer and inventory files. When an order is entered, at least two transactions are necessary—one to update the customer's account balance and the other to record the inventory item to be shipped. Suppose that while you are entering the order, the workstation you are using crashes after it updates the customer balance and therefore fails to record the item on the shipping list. In this case, TTS cancels the transaction and restores the customer's balance to its original amount, allowing you to re-enter the complete order. Because TTS is a feature used by application software, using the Transactional attribute does not implement TTS protection—you also need to have the proper system design and application software.

COMMAND LINE UTILITIES

The two main command line utilities used in conjunction with attributes are FLAG and FLAGDIR. The FLAG command sets file attributes; the FLAGDIR command sets directory attributes.

FLAG

Use the FLAG command to view or change the attributes of files in the specified directory. Its syntax is FLAG [*path*] *filename* [*flag-list*] [/SUB]. You can replace *path* with either a complete or partial path leading to the desired file or files. If you specify no path, you access files in the current directory.

The *filename* field can be replaced with the name of the file you want to access, or you can use global (*) and wildcard (?) characters to access several files. If no filename is specified, the FLAG command will affect all files in the specified path. To see a list of the attributes on all files in the current directory, simply type FLAG and press [Enter].

Replace the *flag-list* field with the letters, separated by spaces, of the attributes you want to set. Use the letter N to return selected files to the normal attribute settings of Read Write and non–Sharable with no other attributes set. Use the word *all* to flag selected files with all available attributes. Use the */SUB* parameter to view or to change the file attributes in all subdirectories.

Figure 8-24 contains an example of the FLAG command. It sets the Delete Inhibit attribute for all files in the DATA:FORMS directory. The second FLAG command in the figure is used with no options to display the filenames and attribute settings in the directory.

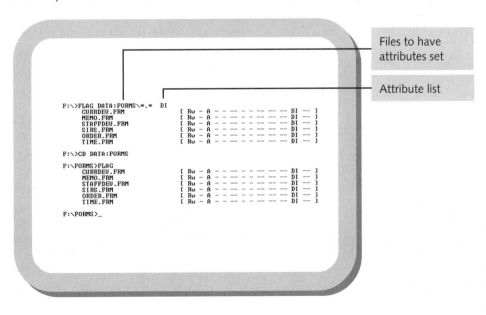

Figure 8-24

Using the FLAG command

FLAGDIR

The FLAGDIR command sets the directory attributes. Only the Hidden, System, Purge, Delete Inhibit, and Rename Inhibit attributes can be applied to directories. The command's syntax is FLAGDIR [*path*] [*flag-list*]. Typing the command FLAGDIR without any options displays the attribute settings of the current directory. You can replace *path* with either the complete or partial NetWare path leading to the target directory. To set attributes for the selected directory, replace *flag-list* with the letters of the attributes you want to set, separated by spaces. Use N to return the selected directory to the normal setting of no attributes set. Figure 8-25 contains an example of FLAGDIR. The command protects the structure of the SALES department directories by setting on the Delete Inhibit attribute. In addition, the Purge attribute is set on the TEMP directory to purge all temporary files as soon as they are deleted. This will provide a slight improvement in file server performance and provide longer times in which other files will be kept for salvaging.

Figure 8-25

Using the FLAGDIR command

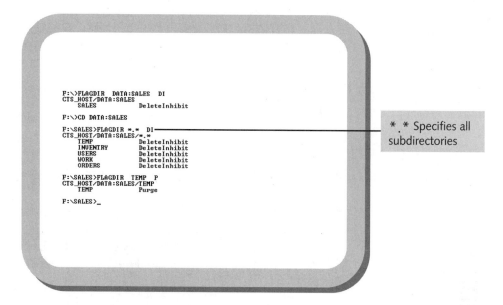

```
F:\>FLAGDIR  DATA:SALES   DI
CTS_HOST/DATA:SALES
     SALES           DeleteInhibit

F:\>CD DATA:SALES

F:\SALES>FLAGDIR *.*  DI
CTS_HOST/DATA:SALES/*.*
     TEMP            DeleteInhibit
     INVENTRY        DeleteInhibit
     USERS           DeleteInhibit
     WORK            DeleteInhibit
     ORDERS          DeleteInhibit

F:\SALES>FLAGDIR  TEMP  P
CTS_HOST/DATA:SALES/TEMP
     TEMP            Purge

F:\SALES>_
```

. Specifies all subdirectories

Neither the LISTDIR nor NDIR command contains options to list all the attribute settings in a directory structure. To see the directory attributes, use the FLAGDIR command, as illustrated in Figure 8-26.

Using FILER to set file attributes

The FILER utility can be used to modify the attribute flags for files and directories. Because FILER is a menu utility, it requires less typing and allows you to select attributes and filenames interactively without having to enter the complete syntax or exact filenames required by FLAG and FLAGDIR. FILER also allows you to set attributes on multiple files. Suppose, for example, you want to set the Read Only attribute on all the previous year's budget files in order to protect them from being changed, deleted, or renamed. You could use the FLAG command to do this, but it would require you to know the name of each of the files and would involve entering the command several times. Instead, you can use the FILER utility to perform this function. You first select the Select Current Directory option to change to the directory containing the budget files. The Directory Contents option displays the names of all files in this directory. Use the F5 key to mark each file on which you want to set attributes and press [Enter]. FILER displays the Multiple File Operations menu shown in Figure 8-27.

Figure 8-26

Viewing directory attributes

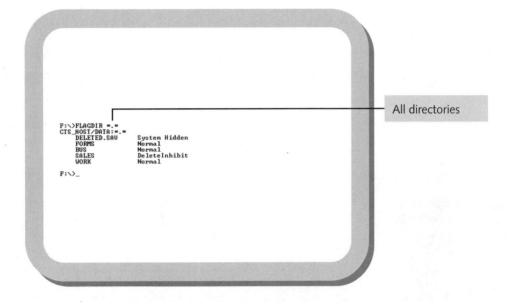

All directories

```
F:\>FLAGDIR *.*
CTS_HOST/DATA:*.*
    DELETED.SAV      System Hidden
    FORMS            Normal
    BUS              Normal
    SALES            DeleteInhibit
    WORK             Normal

F:\>_
```

Figure 8-27

FILER Multiple File Operations menu

```
            Directory Contents
.--                              | (parent)
\                                          >
FIG6-01.TIF  Multiple File Operations      >
FIG6-02.TIF                                >
FIG6-03.TIF  Copy Marked Files             >
FIG6-04.TIF  Set Attributes                >
FIG6-05.TIF  Set Creation Date             >
NET$ACCT.DA  Set Inherited Rights          >
NET$REC.DAT  Set Last Accessed Date        >
PRODUCTS.DA  Set Last Modified Date        >
             Set Owner
```

Use the Set Attributes option to display an empty File Attributes window, in which you set attributes on the selected files. Because multiple files are selected, this window does not show the current file attributes, but does show the new attribute settings you want to make to each of the selected files. The attributes you place in this window replace any attribute settings that currently exist on the selected files. To include the Read Only attribute, you press the Ins key to display the Other File Attributes window. Then use the arrow keys to highlight the Read Only attribute and press [Enter]. See Figure 8-28. If you want to select more than one attribute, use the F5 key to mark them before pressing the Enter key. To set the selected files to the attributes shown in the File Attributes window, press the Esc key and respond with Yes to the Set Marked Files to Specified Attributes window. After setting the attributes, FILER returns to the Multiple File Operations menu. You can then use [Esc] to return to the Directory Contents window.

To view the attribute settings on files, highlight the name of the file you want to view. Pressing [Enter] calls up the File Options menu shown in Figure 8-29. Select the View/Set File Information option to display the File Information window shown in Figure 8-30. Notice that the Read Only (Ro), Delete Inhibit (Di), and Rename Inhibit (Ri) attributes are currently set. To change the file attributes for this file, highlight the Attributes field and press [Enter]. The Current File Attributes window listing the attributes will be displayed, as shown in Figure 8-31. Use the Ins key to select additional attributes from the "Other Attributes" window. Use the Del key to remove the highlighted attribute. To remove multiple attributes, use the F5 key to mark the attributes to be removed and then press Del. After your selections are complete, use the Esc key to return to the FILER Available Topics menu.

Figure 8-28

Using FILER to set file attributes

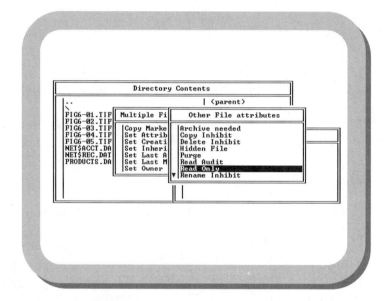

Figure 8-29

FILER's File Options menu

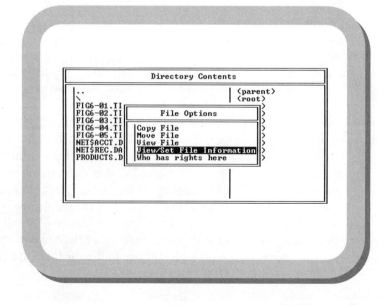

Figure 8-30

Filer's File Information window

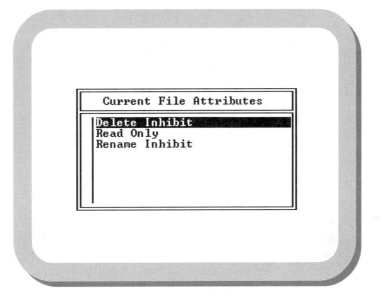

Figure 8-31

Current File Attributes window

Using FILER to set directory attributes

You can use the FILER menu utility to view and set directory attributes. Suppose you want to hide the MENUS directory to prevent curious users browsing the file system from finding the menu files. First use the Select Current Directory option to change to the directory in which you want to set attributes and then select the Current Directory Information option to display the Directory Information window, shown in Figure 8-17. Highlight the Directory Attributes field and press [Enter] to display the Current Attributes window. Using the Ins key displays the Other Attributes window, which lists the available directory attributes, as shown in Figure 8-32. Highlight the attribute you want or use the F5 key to mark multiple attributes and press [Enter]. When you press [Esc], the new attributes are added to the Directory Attributes field shown in the Directory Information window. Press [Esc] again to return to the Available Topics menu.

Figure 8-32

FILER's Directory Attributes window

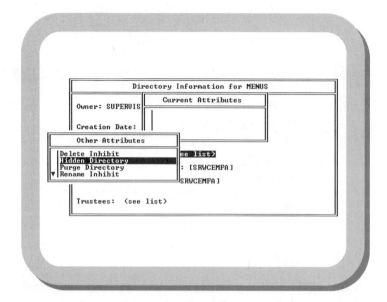

When the Hidden or System attribute has been placed on a directory, that directory will no longer appear in FILER's Directory Contents window unless you use Filer Options, as described in Chapter 6, to include the Hidden or System attributes in the Directory Search Attributes field.

CHAPTER SUMMARY

Just as a physical building, such as a warehouse, needs to be secured with locks and keys, the NetWare file system must also be secured. Trustee assignments provide access rights which, like keys, allow users entry to the file server storage areas they need to access. NetWare v3.1x provides eight access rights: Read, File scan, Write, Create, Erase, Modify, Access control, and Supervisory. The Modify right allows the user to change attributes or rename a file or subdirectory. The Access control right allows a user to assign other rights, except Supervisory, to other users. The Supervisory right can be assigned only by a supervisor equivalent user and provides a user with all rights to the directory and all subdirectories, including the right to assign the Supervisory right to other users. In addition, because the Supervisory right cannot be revoked or blocked at any lower level, assigning the Supervisory right is a good way to make a user act as a supervisor of a portion of the directory structure.

Rights are granted to users or groups for a directory by trustee assignments. Effective rights for a user are a combination of rights given to the user's name combined with the rights given to any groups of which the user is a member. Trustee rights granted to a user or group for a directory are then inherited by all the subdirectories and files within the directory for which the trustee assignment was made. As a result, a user's effective rights often consist of inherited rights that have flowed down to the directory or file from a trustee assignment made to a group or username in a higher level directory.

An Inherited Rights Mask (IRM) exists in each directory and file to control what rights the directory or file inherits from higher level directories. When a file or directory is first created, the IRM allows all rights to flow down into that directory or file. Later you can remove rights from the IRM to block those rights from being inherited into that directory or file.

Several command line utilities are used to set and view trustee assignments and the IRMs. The GRANT command can make a trustee assignment to a user or group for the specified directory or file. The TLIST and WHOAMI /R commands can be used to view the trustee assignments made to directories; the RIGHTS and LISTDIR /E commands can be used to determine your effective rights in the file system. The REVOKE command allows you to remove rights from a trustee assignment, but can only be used in the directory or file where the trustee assignment was made. The REMOVE command allows you to remove a user as a trustee of a directory or file. Sometimes removing a user's trustee assignment can actually increase his or her effective rights, because it allows rights granted to higher level directories to be inherited.

In addition to the command line utilities, the FILER and SYSCON menu utilities both contain options that allow you to make trustee assignments to directories and users. FILER is best used when you want to add several users or groups as trustees to a directory; SYSCON is convenient when you want to add a new user as a trustee to one or more directories.

Attributes play an important role in the file system security because they allow you to protect files and directories from such operations as deletion, renaming, and copying. Attributes can also be used to make files sharable, hidden, or protected by the Transaction Tracking System (TTS). File attributes include: Archive Needed, Copy Inhibit, Delete Inhibit, Execute Only, Hidden, Purge, Read Only, Read Write, Rename Inhibit, Sharable, System, and Transactional. Directory attributes include: Delete Inhibit, Hidden, Purge, Rename Inhibit, and System.

The FLAG command line utility sets attributes on files from the DOS prompt, while the FLAGDIR utility sets directory attributes. Both utilities can be used to view the attributes in either the current directory or in the directory path specified. You can also use the FILER menu utility to view and set both directory and file attributes; FILER options also allow you to view hidden and system directories and files.

COMMAND SUMMARY

Command	Syntax	Definition
ALLOW	*ALLOW [path] TO INHERIT rights-list*	Changes the Inherited Rights Mask of the specified directory or file to include the rights listed. Replace *rights-list* with the rights you want the directory to be able to inherit, separated by spaces. If you do not specify a path, the IRM of the current directory will be changed.

GRANT	*GRANT rights-list[FOR path] TO username/group [/SUB] [FILES]*	Creates a trustee assignment consisting of listed rights to the specified user in the directory path. N indicates no rights, all grants all rights. Use the /SUB option to grant the trustee assignment to each of the directory's subdirectories. Use /FILES to grant the trustee assignment to each of the files in the specified directory path.
LISTDIR	*LISTDIR [path] [/E] [/S]*	Lists the effective rights the current user has in the specified directory path. If no path is specified, the user's effective rights in the current directory will be displayed. The /S option lists effective rights in each subdirectory of the specified path.
REMOVE	*REMOVE username/group [FROM path] [/SUB] [/FILES]*	Deletes the specified user's trustee assignment from the given directory path. The /SUB option removes the user's trustee assignment from all subdirectories. The /FILES option removes the user's trustee assignment from all files contained in the directory path.
REVOKE	*REVOKE rights-list [FOR path] FROM username/group*	Removes the specified rights from the specified user's or group's trustee assignment for the given directory path.
RIGHTS	*RIGHTS [path]*	Lists the current user's effective rights in the specified directory path. If no path is specified, the effective rights in the current directory are displayed.
TLIST	*TLIST [path] [/S/]*	Lists all trustee assignments made to the specified directory. If no path is specified, the trustees of the current directory are displayed. The /S option displays the trustee assignments in each of the subdirectories contained in the specified directory.
WHOAMI	*WHOAMI /R*	Lists all directories in which the user or a group to which the user belongs has been granted a trustee assignment.
FILER	*FILER*	In addition to creating directories and copying files, the FILER utility allows a user to grant trustee assignments, set the Inherited Rights Mask, and view or set file and directory attributes.

NCOPY	*NCOPY [source-path]* *[target-path] [/options]*	Copies specified files and subdirectories from the source path to the target path. Options are the same as those for the DOS XCOPY command with the addition of:

/C – do not copy attributes

/I – Inform if source cannot support attributes

/F – Force copy of spare files |
| **NDIR** | *NDIR [path][/Option]* | Displays file information for the specified file and path. Options include:

/SORT to sort by Size, Owner, Last Accessed

/SI | /OW | /LA GR | LE | EQ value to select only files based on the \value

/DATE/RIGHTS to display additional information about the files creation date, and last accessed or updated dates.

/attribute to display only the files that have the specified attribute. |
| **SYSCON** | *SYSCON* | In addition to creating users and groups, the Group Information and User Information options of the SYSCON utility can be used to grant trustee assignments to directories and files. |
| **FLAG** | *FLAG [[path] filename]* *[flag-list] [/SUB]* | When used without any options, the FLAG command will display the attribute settings of all files in the current directory. To set attributes on one or more files, replace filename with the name of a file or use global file identifiers such as "*", and replace flag list with one or more of the following attributes flags separated by spaces. The/SUB option may be used to assign attributes to files in all subdirectories.

ALL – Set all attributes

A – Archive needed

N – Normal (non-sharable and read and write)

CI –Copy Inhibit |

DI – Delete Inhibit

X – Execute Only

H – Hidden

P – Purge

RW – Read Write

RI – Read Inhibit

S – Sharable

Sy – System

T – Transactional

FLAGDIR   *FLAGDIR [path] [flaglist]*   Used to view or set directory attributes. If no path is specified, the attributes of the current directory will be displayed or changed. Replace *flag-list* with one or more of the following directory attributes separated by spaces.

N – Normal (no attributes set)

DI – Delete Inhibit

H – Hidden

P– Purge

RI – Rename Inhibit

Sy – System

KEY TERMS

Access control	file trustee	Read Write
Archive Needed	Hidden	Rename Inhibit
Copy Inhibit	Indexed	Sharable
Create	inherited rights	Supervisory
Delete Inhibit	Inherited Rights Mask	System
directory trustee		Transaction Tracking System (TTS)
effective rights	Modify	
Erase	Purge	Transactional
Execute Only	Read	Write
file scan	Read Only	

REVIEW QUESTIONS

1. _Access Rights_ define functions that can be performed in the NetWare file system.

2. The _write_ right allows a user to change data within an existing file.

3. The _Access control_ right allows a user to assign rights to other users.

4. The _supervisory_ right cannot be revoked or blocked within the directory structure in which it is defined.

5. _Effective rights_ consists of a subset of the access rights and controls what functions a user can perform in a directory or file.

6. What two components make up a user's effective rights in a directory?

    Trustee rights
    Group or username rights.

7. Given that you are a member of the ADMIN group that has been granted the R F W rights to a directory called BUSINESS, and have a trustee assignment of R F C to the BUSINESS directory, what are your effective rights in the BUSINESS directory?

    Read, File scan, Write, Create.

8. Assume you have been given a trustee assignment of R F C to the BUSINESS directory and a trustee assignment of Erase and Write to the BUSINESS\SPDATA\BUDGETS subdirectory. What are your effective rights in the BUSINESS\SPDATA subdirectory?

    Erase, Write.

    For questions 9-12, use the following rights assignment information:

    You have a trustee assignment of [C W E] to the BUSINESS directory and a trustee assignment of [E W] to the BUSINESS\SPDATA\BUDGETS subdirectory. In addition, you belong to a group that was granted [R F] rights to the BUSINESS directory.

9. What are your effective rights in the BUSINESS\SPDATA\BUDGETS subdirectory?

    Erase, Write.

10. Assume all rights except R and F are removed from the IRM of the BUSINESS\SPDATA subdirectory. What are your rights in the BUSINESS\SPDATA subdirectory?

    Create, write, erase

11. What are your rights in the BUSINESS\SPDATA\BUDGETS subdirectory?

    Create, write, erase, file scan

12. On the two lines below, write the commands to give the user JOEMAN the [C W M E A] rights to the DATA:BUSINESS\BUDGETS directory and the ADMIN group the [R F W] rights to the DATA:BUSINESS directory.

    Grant C W M E A For Data:Business\Budgets to JOEMAN
    Grant R F W For DATA:BUSINESS to Admin.

13. Write a command to remove the Modify and Access control rights from the trustee assignment made for the user JOEMAN in the DATA:BUSINESS\BUDGETS directory.

Revoke M A for Data:Business\Budgets From Joeman

14. Write a command to display all the trustee assignments in the DATA:BUSINESS directory.

TLIST DATA:BUSINESS

15. What command would you use to determine your effective rights in the BUSINESS\SPDATA directory?

Whoami   or   LISTDIR

16. Write a command that would prevent users and groups from inheriting rights in the BUSINESS\USER subdirectory.

Allow

17. Write a command to assign the user MARSIM the Erase and Modify rights in the BUSINESS\SPDATA subdirectory.

Grant EM For Business\SPDATA TO MARSIM

18. Write a command to delete the trustee assignment made to the user JOEMAN in the BUSINESS\SPDATA\BUDGETS subdirectory.

REMOVE JOEMAN FROM BUSINESS\SPDATA\BUDGETS

19. Assume the user JOEMAN was given a trustee assignment of [R F C W E M] to the BUSINESS\SPDATA directory. What are Joe's effective rights in the BUSINESS\SPDATA\BUDGETS subdirectory after his trustee assignment to BUDGETS was deleted in Question 18?

He would have no rights.

20. In the space below, state whether the user JOEMAN gained or lost rights in the BUDGETS directory and explain why.

He lost his rights because none were assigned to him in that directory and any that were in the parent are gone.

21. Write a command that will display all the trustee assignments that have been granted to your username or a group of which you are a member.

WHOAMI /R

22. Write a command that will display your effective rights in each of the subdirectories of the BUSINESS directory structure.

NDIR /RIGHTS /SUB

23. Which menu utility would make it easier for you to make five users trustees of the BUSINESS\SPDATA directory?

Filer

24. Which menu utility would make it easier for you to make the user BILLSIM a trustee of the following three directories: BUSINESS\AR, SALES\INVENTRY, and DATA:PROJECTS?

Syscon

25. Given that your current directory is the BUSINESS directory, which option of FILER would you use to make a trustee assignment to the BUSINESS\PAYROLL subdirectory?

Current Directory Information → Trustees Field.

26. When you set the Read Only attribute, what other attributes are also set by default?

Delete Inhibit & Rename Inhibit.

27. Which of the following attributes are used with directories?

Purge ___*Yes*___

Sharable ___*No*___

Read Only ___*No*___

Delete Inhibit ___*Yes*___

Copy Inhibit ___*No*___

Hidden ___*Yes*___

System ___*Yes*___

28. Write a command setting the attributes to allow software files in a SYS:SOFTWARE\WP directory to be used by more than one user at a time and also prevent the file from being deleted or changed.

FLAG SYS:SOFTWARE\WP*. SH RO*

29. Write a command setting the directory attribute that will prevent deleted files in the SYS:SOFTWARE\TEMP directory from being salvaged.

FLAGDIR SYS:SOFTWARE\TEMP P

30. In the space below, explain the advantages to be gained from setting the Purge attribute on a directory.

The space is immediately available after a file is deleted.

31. What menu utilities can be used to set attributes?

Only Filer

32. What rights do you need in a directory in order to use the TLIST command to view trustee assignments?

Any

33. What rights do you need in a directory to flag all files Delete Inhibit?

Any

34. When a user is first added as a trustee of a directory using the FILER utility, he or she is given the __*[R F]*__ rights by default.

35. What option do you need to set in FILER in order to view Hidden or System directories?

_____

EXERCISES

Exercise 8-1: Working with Access Rights

The objective of this exercise is to provide you with practice assigning access rights to a directory and then attempting to perform several disk operations in that directory to see how the access rights affect using the file system. In the following steps, make sure to substitute your assigned student number for the number symbols (##).

1. Log in using your assigned student username and change to your ##ADMIN directory.

2. Create a directory called CHAP8 within your ##ADMIN directory.

3. Use the NCOPY command to copy all files with the *.WK1 extension from the SYS:SOFTWARE.STC\SP subdirectory into the CHAP8 subdirectory.

4. Use SYSCON to create a username called ##USER with no home directory. Create a group called ##GROUP8 and make ##USER a member of ##GROUP8.

5. Assign ##USER the Access control right to CHAP8 and Read and File scan rights to SYS:SOFTWARE.STC.

6. Log out.

7. Log in as ##USER and change to the ##ADMIN\CHAP8 directory.

8. Use the DIR command to view the files. Record your results below.

   File Not Found.

9. Enter the following GRANT command to grant ##USER File scan rights to CHAP8.

   ```
   GRANT F TO ##USER
   ```

10. Repeat step 8 and record your observations in the space below.

    9 file appear with the wkl extension

11. Try to read the contents of a file by using the TYPE filename command. Record the results in the space below.

    Access denied - JAN00.WKI

12. Use the GRANT command from step 9 to give ##GROUP8 the Read right to the CHAP8 directory.

13. Repeat step 11 and record your observations in the space below.

    Shows a bunch of symbols.

14. Try creating a subdirectory called PRACTICE. Record your observations in the space below.

    Unable to create directory

15. Use the FILER utility to give ##USER only the Create and Access control rights to the CHAP8 directory.

16. Repeat step 14 and record the results below.

    The directory was created.

17. What two ways could you use to make the directories visible?

    Grant F to 5OUSER

    Grant F to 5OGROUP8

18. Map a drive to the SYS volume and then use the COPY command to copy the SP.BAT file from SYS:SOFTWARE.STC\SP to the CHAP8 directory. Record results in the space below.

    Access denied.

    0 file(s) copied.

19. Try using the NCOPY command to copy all files from the SYS:SOFTWARE.STC\DB subdirectory in the CHAP8 directory. Record your results in the space below.

    No files copied

20. Add the File scan right to ##GROUP8 so that you have effective rights of [R F C A] in the CHAP8 directory and then repeat step 19. Record your observations in the space below.

    You cannot copy multiple files to a single file.

21. To add or change data in a file you need the Write right. Use the GRANT command to assign only the Write and Access control rights to ##USER in the CHAP8 directory and use the following commands to add statements to the SP.BAT file.

```
COPY SP.BAT + CON [press Enter]

REM This is the start of my modification.[press
Enter]

PAUSE [press Enter]

REM This is the end of my modification. [press
Enter]

[press F6] [press Enter]

TYPE SP.BAT [press Enter]
```

22. Obtain a hardcopy of the revised SP.BAT file by using the Print Scrn key to print your screen.

23. Log out.

24. Log in using your assigned ##ADMIN username and delete any users and groups you created in this exercise.

Exercise 8-2: Using the Inherited Rights Mask

In this exercise you will create a directory structure and two users and then use NetWare command line utilities to grant trustee assignments and set up an Inherited Rights Mask in order to observe how effective rights are inherited.

Part 1: Create directory structure and users

1. Log in using your assigned student username and change to your ##ADMIN directory.

2. If you have not already done so, create a directory in your ##ADMIN work area named CHAP8.

3. Create two directories in the CHAP8 directory named ORDERS and USERS.

4. Create two users called ##CLERK1 and ##CLERK2. Create home directories for these users in the CHAP8\USERS directory.

5. Create a group named ##CLERKS and make ##CLERK1 and CLERK2 members.

6. Give the group ##CLERKS Read and File scan rights to the CHAP8 directory.

7. Make ##CLERK1 a manager of the CHAP8 directory structure by granting the username the Supervisory right.

8. Make ##CLERK2 a trustee of the CHAP8 directory with [W C E M] rights.

9. Log out.

Part 2: Check effective rights

1. Log in as ##CLERK2.

2. Use the RIGHTS command to record your effective rights in the directories listed in the following table.

Directory Path	Effective Rights
CHAP8	RWCEMF
CHAP8\ORDERS	RWCEMF
CHAP8\USERS	RWCEMF

3. Log out.

Part 3: Modify trustee assignments. In this part of the exercise you will observe how making a new trustee assignment to the group of which a user is a member will change the effective rights inherited by the user to a subdirectory.

1. Log in using your assigned student username and change to your ##ADMIN directory.

2. Use FILER to assign the ##CLERKS group no rights to the CHAP8\ORDERS subdirectory.

3. Log out.

4. Log in as ##CLERK2

5. On the line below, record your effective rights in the CHAP8 directory.

    RWCEMF

6. On the line below, record your effective rights in the CHAP8\ORDERS subdirectory.

    WCEM

7. Why didn't your effective rights in the CHAP8 directory flow down to the CHAP8\ORDERS directory? Explain in the space below.

    Because the group I belong to is
    not granted rights to the directory

8. Log out.

Part 4: Using IRMs to change effective rights

1. Log in using your assigned ##ADMIN username.

2. Use an ALLOW command to remove all rights except File scan and Supervisory from the IRM of the CHAP8\USERS directory. On the line below, record the ALLOW command you use.

    Allow SYS:##ADMIN\CHAP8\USERS F

3. Use FILER to allow the CHAP8\ORDERS directory to inherit only Read and File scan rights. In the space below, record the FILER options you use to do this.

4. Log out.

5. Log in as ##CLERK2.

6. Use the LISTDIR /E command to record your effective rights in the subdirectories shown in the following table.

Directory	Effective Rights
CHAP8	RFWELM
CHAP8\ORDERS	RWCEMF
CHAP8\USERS	F

7. Log out.

8. Log in as ##CLERK1.

9. Use the LISTDIR /E command to record your effective rights in the subdirectories shown in the following table.

Directory	Effective Rights
CHAP8	SRWCEMFA
CHAP8\ORDERS	SRWCEMFA
CHAP8\USERS	SRWCEMFA

Exercise 8-3: Using FILER to Work with Directory Attributes

The objective of this exercise is to provide you with experience using the FILER utility to set directory attributes by creating and then hiding a directory. In order to view the hidden directory, you will then need to use FILER options to activate the correct directory search attributes because, by default, the FILER utility does display hidden or system files and directories.

1. Log in using your assigned ##ADMIN username.

2. Start FILER.

3. Change the directory path to your ##ADMIN directory.

4. Use the Directory Contents option and press [Ins] to create a new directory named MENUS.

5. Select the MENUS directory and use the View/Set Directory Information option of the Subdirectory Options menu to call up the Directory Information screen.

6. Add the Hidden attribute to the MENUS subdirectory and press [Esc] to return to the Directory Contents window. Press the Esc key to return to the Available Topics menu and then re-select the Directory Contents option. If you have successfully hidden the MENUS subdirectory, it should no longer appear in the Directory Contents window.

7. Press [Esc] to return to FILER's Available Topics menu.

8. Select the Set Filer Options from the Available Topics menu to display the Filer Settings window. The File Search Attributes field could be used to set FILER to display Hidden and System files. In this example, however, you will learn to use the Directory Search Attributes field to display hidden and system directories. You can apply the same technique to displaying hidden and system files.

9. Select the Directory Search Attributes field to display the Directory Search Attributes window, which lists any current settings for which FILER will search. You can use the [Ins] and [Del] keys to add or remove attributes from the list.

10. Press [Ins] to display the Other Attributes window.

11. Highlight the Hidden attribute and press [Enter] to add it to the Search Attribute window. (You could also use the [F5] key to mark both attributes and press [Enter], in which case both the System and Hidden attributes would be added to the Search Attributes window.)

12. Press [Esc] to save the attribute settings and return to the Filer Settings window. Press [Esc] a second time to return to the FILER Available Topics menu.

13. Now use the Directory Contents option to view the subdirectories. Record your results below.

7 subdirectories → 1 is Menus
1 file.

14. Use FILER to remove the MENUS directory.

15. Log out.

EXERCISE

Case 8-1: ACME Company Security

Assume that you are the network administrator for ACME, Inc. Lois, John, and Ann are employees of ACME who all work in the business department. The business department's directory structure is shown in Figure 8-33.

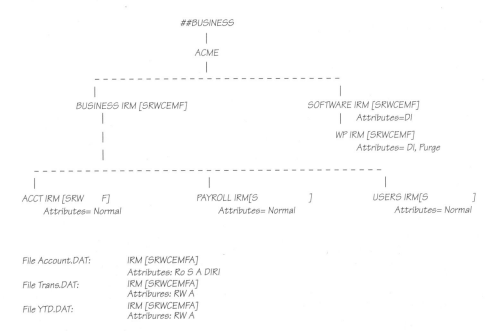

Step 1: Creating a structure.

In order to perform this exercise and answer the questions, you first need to create the directory structure for ACME in your ##ADMIN student work area by performing the following steps:

1. Log in using your assigned student username.

2. Start FILER.

3. Change the current directory to point to your ##ADMIN directory path (see Figure 8-33) and then use FILER to create the directory structure shown in Figure 8-33.

4. Use FILER to set the Inherited Rights Masks for each of the directories as indicated in Figure 8-33.

5. Use FILER to set the Delete Inhibit attribute on each of the directories in the BUSINESS structure.

6. Exit FILER.

7. Use the LISTDIR command to obtain a hardcopy of your BUSINESS directory structure including the IRMs for each directory.

8. Use the FLAGDIR command to display the attributes for each of your BUSINESS directories and subdirectories.

9. Use the Print Scrn key to print the screen showing your directory attributes.

Step 2: Working with files.

In this case study exercise you will need to create the general ledger files for the ACCT directory and use FLAG commands to set attributes necessary to meet the requirements specified in the problem.

1. Use the MAP command to create a root drive mapping (L:) to the ACME directory.

2. Change your default DOS prompt to the L:\BUSINESS\ACCT directory.

3. Use the following COPY command to create the ACCOUNT.DAT file in the ACCT directory.

```
COPY CON ACCOUNT.DAT

    This is the Accounts Database. [press Enter]

    General ledger accounts and their descriptions
are stored here. [press Enter]

    [press F6] [press Enter]
```

4. Use the COPY commands shown below to create the TRANS and YTD files shown in Figure 8-33.

```
COPY CON TRANS.DAT

This is the Accounts Transaction file [press Enter]

Debit and Credit entries are stored here [press Enter]

[press F6] [press Enter]
```

```
COPY CON YTD.DAT

     This is the year to date summary file
[press Enter]

          End of year totals are stored here [press Enter]

     [press F6] [press Enter]
```

File/Directory	Attribute Requirements
ACCOUNT.DAT	Protect the file from being changed and allow shared access.
TRANS.DAT	Protect the file from being erased or renamed, but allow changes to the contents.
YDT.DAT	Protect the file from being erased or renamed, but allow changes to the contents.
SOFTWARE	Hide this directory.
SOFTWARE\WP	Immediately purge any deleted files.

5. Use the appropriate commands to set the file and directory attributes as described in Figure 8-34. On the lines below, record each command you use.

    ACCOUNT.DAT file: _____

    TRANS.DAT file: _____

    YTD.DAT file: _____

    SOFTWARE: _____

    SOFTWARE\WP: _____

6. Use the NDIR command to obtain a hardcopy of all files in the ACCT directory.

7. Use FLAGDIR commands to obtain a hardcopy of all directory attributes. This can be done by adding ">PRN" to the end of the FLAGDIR commands you enter.

Step 3: Creating users and groups.

In this exercise you will create the users and groups needed for the ACME business department. Be sure to replace the number symbols (##) in each username with your assigned student number.

1. Start SYSCON.

2. Create the group ##ADMIN and assign the group [R F] rights to the BUSINESS directory.

3. Create the following user accounts having home directories in the BUSINESS\USERS subdirectory. Make all users members of the ADMIN group.

User	User and Home Directory Name
John Combs	##JOHCOM
Lois Kent	##LOIKEN
Ann Bonny	##ANNBON

4. Exit SYSCON.

Step 4: Assigning trustee rights.

In this case study exercise project you will use the GRANT command to grant trustee assignments for the BUSINESS directory structure to the business department users you created.

1. Because John is the supervisor of the business department, grant him the Supervisory right in the BUSINESS directory structure.

2. Make Ann a trustee of the payroll directory by giving her all rights to the PAYROLL subdirectory.

3. Make Lois a trustee with [R W F C E] rights to the ACCT directory.

4. Grant the ##ADMIN group [R F] rights to the BUSINESS directory.

5. Use the TLIST command to obtain a hardcopy of the trustee assignments for each of the BUSINESS directories.

Step 5: Determining effective rights.

In this case study exercise you will use the appropriate NetWare commands to answer questions regarding the user's effective rights to the directory structure. Following each question are lines for you to record what command you used to determine the rights and who you were logged in as when you used the command. In addition, explain why the user or group has these rights and how the rights were obtained.

1. What are John Combs rights in PAYROLL? _____

   Command used: _____

   Logged in as: _____

   In the space below, explain how John got these rights.

2. In the space below, explain what would you do if you no longer wanted John to have all rights to the PAYROLL subdirectory but still have Supervisory rights in the other subdirectories of the BUSINESS structure?

3. What are Ann's rights in the ACCT directory? _____

   Command used: _____

   Logged in as: _____

   In the space below, explain how Ann got these rights.

4. What are Ann's rights in the PAYROLL directory? _____

    Command used: _____

    Logged in as: _____

    In the space below, explain how Ann got these rights.

5. Enter a command that will prevent Ann from assigning rights to other users.

    Command used: _____

    Logged in as: _____

    In the space below, explain why anyone would want to restrict Ann's ability to assign rights to other users.

6. What are Lois's rights in the ACCT directory? _____

    Command used: _____

    Logged in as: _____

    In the space below, explain how Lois got these rights.

7. Are Lois's rights in the ACCT subdirectory sufficient for her to keep the files updated? _____

    If not, provide her with the necessary rights. On the line below, record the command(s) you use.

    _____

8. Log in as John Combs and determine what John's effective rights in the ACCOUNT.DAT file are. _____

    Command used: _____

    Logged in as: _____

    Try to use the DOS EDIT command to change the contents of the ACCOUNT.DAT file. Record your results in the space below.

9. Explain briefly what John must do if he needs to add information accounts to the ACCOUNTS.DAT file.

10. Use the appropriate command line utility to implement the solution you defined in step 9. On the line below, record the option you use.

_____

11. Ann Bonny needs to be able to post payroll transactions to the TRANS file. Briefly explain what steps you should follow to allow Ann to post to the TRANS file but not allow her access to the other files in the GL directory.

12. Use the FILER utility to implement the process you defined in step 9.

13. Use the TLIST command to obtain a hardcopy of the trustees for the ACCT directory.

    Use the TLIST command to obtain a hardcopy of the trustees for each file in the ACCT directory.

SUPERIOR TECHNICAL COLLEGE PROBLEMS

Dave Johnson is pleased with your progress in setting up the directory structure and creating user accounts for Superior Technical College. He feels the system is starting to come together nicely and is sending you a memo that will help you continue by assigning users the necessary rights to the file system. In the following problems, you will be implementing the trustee assignments defined by Dave along with setting up the necessary file and directory attributes.

For your next task, Dave Johnson would like you to document the trustee assignments for the Superior Technical College campus that are necessary to provide the users with the effective rights they will need in the directories and files while at the same time protecting the file system from accidental erasure as well as preventing unauthorized access by student users who will be sharing the name file server. To do this, Dave has provided you with the following processing requirements for each department:

All users

All campus users will need rights to find and read files in the FORMS directory and have all rights to the campus shared work directory. In addition, they will need the necessary rights to run all software stored in the SYS:SOFTWARE.STC directory.

Student services department

All the users in the student services department need rights in the department's shared work directory to do everything except assign rights to other users.

Support Personnel

Mimi Ito does work for the faculty and will need rights to create, erase, and maintain files in shared faculty directory. Laurie Holt is responsible for working with the outline files and will need all rights to the OUTLINES directory structure. Both Mimi and Laurie need rights to work with files in the shared work directory, but only Mimi should have the ability to clean up the directory by deleting files. Laurie will be given the responsibility of maintaining files in all forms directories.

Faculty

In addition to all rights to their home directories, faculty members need all rights except Access control to the faculty shared work directory, and rights to create, read, and find files in the administrative assistant faculty work area. This will allow the faculty members to place files in the directory for Mimi Ito to work on and then read the file after she has finished. Mimi will be the only user responsible for changing and deleting the files after they have been placed in the directory. In addition, faculty members will need all rights to their class directories in the computer lab directory structure.

Computer lab

Except for all rights to their home directories, the computer workstation users should have only the rights to run programs in the computer lab software directory and read and find files in the CLASSES directory.

Project 8-1: Make trustee assignments

In this Superior Technical College problem you need to make the trustee assignments defined on the directory trustee worksheets. To compare the various utilities, use the GRANT command to assign trustee rights to your ##EVERYONE group; use SYSCON to grant trustee assignments for the student services department and computer lab group. Then use FILER to make the rest of your trustee assignments. In the space below, describe an advantage and disadvantage of using each of the utilities.

     GRANT – Advantage:

            Disadvantage:

     SYSCON – Advantage:

            Disadvantage:

     FILER – Advantage:

            Disadvantage:

Login as the user Laurie Holt and use the NCOPY command to copy the MEMO and STAFFDEV files from your Student Disk's FORMS directory to the FORMS directory for the Superior Technical College. In addition, copy all other files from the FORMS directory of your Student Disk to the SUPPORT/FORMS directory.

Project 8-2: File and Directory Attributes

Dave Johnson would like to see all files in the FORMS directory protected from accidental deletion while still allowing them to be changed. In addition, he would like you to create two TEMP directories: one for the computer lab and one for administration and faculty users. Because the TEMP directories will be used to store work files that are erased after use, both directories should be flagged with the appropriate attribute to prevent these files from being saved for salvaging. Also, the MENUS directory in the computer lab should be hidden to discourage students from browsing through the menus. Finally, you should protect each of the directories in your structure from being accidentally erased.

1. Use the FILER utility to protect all files in the FORMS directory from accidental deletion.

2. Use FILER to set the appropriate attributes on the TEMP and MENU directories along with protecting the directory structure.

3. Use the NDIR command to obtain a hardcopy listing all files in the FORMS directory along with their attributes.

4. Use the FLAGDIR command to print out the attributes on the following directories:

   FORMS

   MENUS

   All subdirectories of the ADMIN directory

   All subdirectories of the LAB directory

5. After your directory structure has been protected, test your system by logging in as one of the users and attempting to access files and delete parts of the directory structure.

6. You are now ready to install the software packages in Chapter 9.

## CHAPTER NINE

INSTALLING APPLICATIONS

Your responsibilities as a network administrator will include the installation, configuration, and testing of application software. Before adding any software on the file server, you need to be sure you do not violate the terms of the software license agreement. Read the software license agreement to determine if it is legal to run the software from a file server and be sure you have the correct number of licenses to cover the number of users who will be accessing the application at one time. As the network administrator, you will be held responsible if the organization you work for is found to be in violation of the software license, so you need to make certain that the software you install on the server does not violate copyrights.

AFTER READING THIS CHAPTER AND COMPLETING THE EXERCISES YOU WILL BE ABLE TO:

- IDENTIFY THREE METHODS OF INSTALLING APPLICATION SOFTWARE.
- FOLLOW STANDARD NOVELL PROCEDURES FOR INSTALLING SOFTWARE.
- USE NETWARE COMMANDS TO MAKE SOFTWARE AVAILABLE TO MULTIPLE USERS AND PROTECT SOFTWARE FROM MODIFICATION OR ILLEGAL COPYING.
- USE NETWARE COMMANDS TO GRANT USERS THE RIGHTS THEY NEED TO RUN SOFTWARE AND ESTABLISH SEARCH DRIVES.
- INSTALL AND TEST SIMULATED APPLICATIONS.

Because software packages have such a wide variety of specialized installation programs and procedures, it is not feasible to provide a detailed set of rules and techniques that will work for installing all applications. Refer to the installation instructions that come with each application to work out the details of installing that product on the file server. There are, however, several general steps that should be followed for most software installations. This chapter describes the following eight steps of software installation:

1. Determine NetWare compatibility

2. Determine single-user or multiuser capability

3. Determine the appropriate directory structure

4. Perform the application installation procedure

5. Set appropriate directory and file attributes

6. Provide user access rights

7. Modify configuration files

8. Test the software

DETERMINING NETWARE COMPATIBILITY

When you install an application on a NetWare server, it is important to first determine the application's level of NetWare compatibility. Most new applications are designed and written for use on networks and can be installed by following the network installation instructions that are included with the software package. Because NetWare is very compatible with DOS, most older applications will also run flawlessly from the server even though they were originally written for a standalone computer. Certain programs, however, cannot be installed on a NetWare drive, and others will not run properly after installation. In this section, you will learn about the three basic levels of NetWare compatibility and how they affect the installation procedure: NetWare incompatible, NetWare compatible, and NetWare aware.

NETWARE INCOMPATIBLE

Certain applications are designed to work only from a local workstation's hard or floppy disks. This is often the case with older applications—especially applications that have copy protection systems built into the software or installation program. Some of these copy protection systems require a special disk containing the software license number to be in the disk drive of the machine running the program. Sometimes these applications will run when installed on a file server; the workstation running the software, however, will need to have the original disk. Other software installation procedures involve writing information, such as the software license, directly to the hard drive of the computer in which the software is installed. Because these installation programs write directly to the DOS partition of the local computer's hard drive, they cannot be used to install the software onto the file server. As a result, these software packages will either fail to be installed into the NetWare file system or not run properly if copied into a NetWare directory.

Today almost all commercially available software packages are designed to run from either a network file server or a workstation's local hard drive. Some software companies, however, have designed their programs to run from a file server only when you purchase the network version of the application. When you attempt to copy the workstation version of one of these programs to the file server and then run the program from an attached workstation, an error message informs you that the application cannot be run from a network drive. This problem is easily solved by purchasing a network upgrade for the software package, which allows the number of workstations specified in your license to access the software from the server at the same time.

NetWare Compatible

There are thousands of software applications that are certified by Novell as being NetWare compatible. **NetWare compatible** means that the software can be installed in the NetWare file system and will then run properly from any workstation just as if it were running from that workstation's local disk drive. Although many programs are not specifically designed for NetWare, the DOS requester (VLM or NETX) makes the NetWare file system appear as a local drive. Most applications, therefore, are not aware of the fact that they are being run from a file server rather than the local hard disk. To deal with these programs, the network administrator usually uses NetWare drive mappings to establish regular or search drives in order to install and run these programs from the file server. To determine if a software package you are considering is NetWare compatible, refer to one of the following sources:

- Novell's NetWire electronic bulletin board
- A regional Novell sales office
- The supplier of the application

NetWare Aware

Many software applications today are designed to take advantage of the features found in local area network operating systems. They therefore often include special NetWare installation options such as setting up network printing or creating separate work and configuration files for each user. These software packages are referred to as being **NetWare aware**.

 Microsoft Windows applications can automatically take advantage of many network functions when Windows is installed on networked workstations. A user running the Microsoft Word application on a networked workstation, for example, can choose to send output directly to a NetWare printer or access a document file using a drive pointer that has been previously mapped to the NetWare file system.

When purchasing an application that is NetWare aware, check with the supplier regarding software license requirements. Some NetWare aware software products have built-in limitations on the number of users that can access the application at one time, based on your license agreement. You need to obtain additional license disks that you then install on the server in order to increase the number of users who can run the software applications with these built-in limitations. For software packages that do not have built-in software license counters, the purchaser is expected to obtain licenses to accommodate the number of users who need to run the software concurrently. It is the network administrator's responsibility to see that this is done.

> Network metering software is available that allows a network adminis-
> trator to place a limit on the number of users who can run a specified
> program at the same time. Installing this type of license-counting soft-
> ware can greatly assist you in enforcing software license agreements on
> your network.

DETERMINING SINGLE-USER OR MULTIUSER CAPABILITY

After you determine that a software package is compatible with your NetWare file server, the next step toward installation is to determine the capability of the application in terms of the number of users it supports. There are three types of network compatible programs: single user, multiple user, and multiuser. This section describes the three capabilities and explains how they relate to installing and using the application on your network.

SINGLE-USER CAPABILITY

Many NetWare compatible software packages are designed to operate from the workstation's local disk drive and are therefore limited to being run by only one user at a time. These are called **single-user applications**. This limitation can be imposed by a software license or by the way the application is designed. Many software programs use temporary files to store the system information the program needs to operate. Because single-user software applications are designed to be used by only one user at a time, when two users attempt to access the application simultaneously, the information written to the temporary file for the second user can overwrite control information needed by the first user. This causes the software application to issue error messages or to crash.

Figure 9-1 illustrates the attempt by two users to run a single-user spreadsheet program. User 1 starts the program first and opens a file named BUDGET.WK1 on a network disk drive. Information about the file, including the file's name, is then written to the temporary file in the spreadsheet software directory. User 2 then starts the spreadsheet program and opens a file called SALES.WK1 on a workstation's local hard drive. The spreadsheet program next writes control information from the SALES files to the same temporary file used to store the control information for the BUDGET file. The result is that the control information for user 1 is erased, causing user 1's spreadsheet program to crash or produce an error message when the file information is needed.

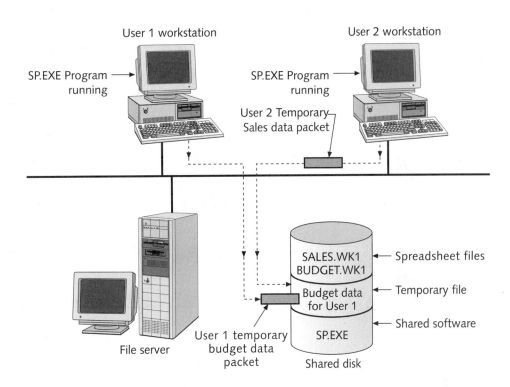

Figure 9-1

Single-user
software application

Even if a software application supports only one user at a time, there are still advantages to placing it on a file server rather than on a local workstation. One advantage is that it can be used by more than one user, as long as it is not done simultaneously. Another advantage is that it prevents users from modifying the configuration files or illegally copying the software to another machine. When a software program is installed on a NetWare file server, you can use access rights and file attributes to prevent files from being changed or copied. A disadvantage of running certain applications from a file server can be the additional load placed on the network cable system, causing the speed of the network to suffer. This is particularly true of software applications that load many overlays in and out of the workstation's memory. Single-user versions of the Aldus PageMaker program, for example, run slower from a network drive than from local hard drives because of the large amount of software and other data loaded during normal program operation. The best way to determine where to place applications to maximize their performance is to load the application on both a server and a work-station and compare its speed during normal operation.

The first step in deciding to place a single-user software package on the server is to consult the license agreement to be sure it is legal for you to run the program from a file server. Even though a single-user application can be run by only one user at a time, some software companies consider placement of their applications on a server a violation of the copyright agreement. Some companies might require you to obtain a network license in order to use the program legally.

MULTIPLE-USER CAPABILITY

A **multiple-user application** is either NetWare aware—and therefore designed to support multiple users—or is designed with enough flexibility so that the applica-tion can be set up to keep each user's work files separated. Figure 9-2 illustrates a multiple-user application. Both user 1 and user 2 are running a multiple-user word processing application and are working with document files on their local hard drives. Because the word processing software is designed for multiple users, user 1's control information for the LETTER1 document file is kept in a temporary file that is separate from the control information for user 2's MEMO2 document file. Keeping each user's temporary and configuration data in separate files is one way multiple-user software applications support simultaneous use of a program.

Figure 9-2

Multiple-user software application

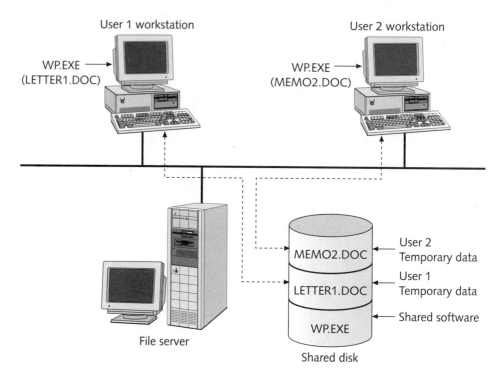

Some applications that are designed for use by a single user on a local workstation can be adapted to support multiple users on a network. This is done by setting up a search drive to the software directory, flagging the program files as sharable, and then providing separate work directories for each user's configuration files. This is a complicated procedure that can be a difficult experience if you are not very familiar with the workings of the program or don't have the advice of someone who has reconfigured an application in this way.

In most network system software, such as Microsoft Windows, and general-purpose software applications, such as word processors, desktop publishing, spreadsheets, and database management software are accessed simultaneously by many users. This means the network administrator needs to maintain only one copy of the applications on the file server rather than keep track of multiple copies installed on separate workstations. NetWare aware programs are designed to support multiple users simultaneously and, provided you obtain the correct number of licenses for the number of users, can be installed by following the instructions for your network system. Multiple-user applications allow users to manage data and document files located anywhere in the network file system. A user in the sales department, for example, can access a spreadsheet program to create a graph showing projected sales for the quarter, while a user in the accounting department runs the same spreadsheet software to do a cash flow analysis report.

While a multiple user application allows more than one user to run the program at the same time to work on separate files, it does not allow two or more users to access the same file simultaneously. Two users can, for example, use the same word processing program, but cannot access the same document file and make changes to it simultaneously. The first user must finish his or her changes and close the file before the next user can access the document to view or change it.

MULTIUSER CAPABILITY

A **multiuser application** is a special type of multiple-user software that allows more than one user to access the same file simultaneously. Multiuser applications are often required in a database system when more than one user needs to access data. This situation occurs, for example, in an order-entry system—like the one shown in Figure 9-3—when two or more records in the customer database files need to be updated by clerks processing orders at the same time. In this illustration, two sales clerks receive calls at the same time from different customers placing orders for widgets. Customer 4 orders 10 widgets; customer 2 orders three widgets. Because the ORDERS.PRG program is designed to allow more than one user to access the customer database, one clerk can be writing customer 4's order to disk at the same time another clerk is updating customer 2's order information, which is stored in a separate database record.

Figure 9-3

Multiuser software application

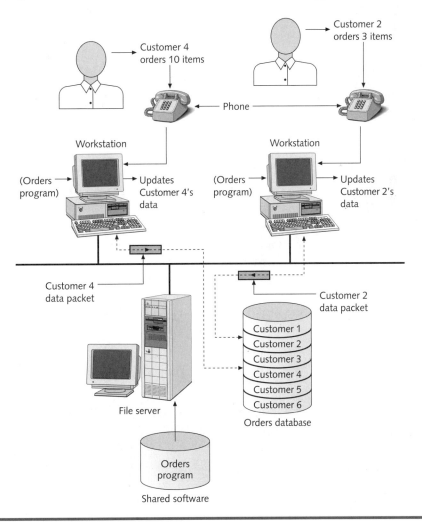

Application systems with multiuser programs—such as order-entry systems or airline reservation systems—often use programs that include special features to prevent one user's changes from overwriting changes made by another user. Record locking is one of the features included with most multiuser applications to protect the database records from corruption in the event two users access the same record simultaneously. **Record locking** allows a multiuser program to prevent users on the network from accessing a specific record in a file while it is being updated. While a sales clerk is working with customer 4, for example, no other user on the network can access customer 4's order information.

In addition to record locking, NetWare includes a feature called the Transaction Tracking System (TTS). The TTS, working with record locking, allows software packages to recover data in the event a workstation crashes in the middle of processing a transaction. Assume, for example, that a clerk's computer crashes after customer 4's order has been written to disk but before the customer's accounts receivable data is updated. Transaction tracking allows the clerk to return the customer order information to its preorder status and then re-enter customer 4's order. Without transaction tracking, customer 4's order could accidentally be placed twice while the account balance is updated only once. Both record locking and transaction tracking require that the application software be written to make use of special multiuser instructions in order to allow the application to implement the record locking and transaction tracking features of Netware.

 In the future, such network applications as word processing will make more use of a process in Microsoft Windows called dynamic linking. This process allows a master document file to consist of multiple object documents. Each object document can then be accessed by a different user, allowing the master document to be updated automatically with any changes that are made to the object documents.

DETERMINING THE APPROPRIATE DIRECTORY STRUCTURE

After you determine the NetWare compatibility level of the application with which you are working, the next step is to decide where the application belongs in the organization's directory structure. Where you place an application's directory in the file system is determined to a large extent by your directory structure design and by what type of application you are installing. This section provides suggestions for placement of an application's directory, based on whether the application is single user, multiple user, or multiuser.

SINGLE-USER APPLICATION

Because single-user applications will be used by only one user at a time, access to them is usually restricted to just a few users in an organization. Because of this, a single-user application is best stored in a location of the directory structure that is closest to the user or users who will be running the application. A single-user payroll application, for example, is normally used by one or two users in an accounting department. The logical location for the directory containing the payroll software and data is therefore within the BUSINESS department's directory structure, as shown in Figure 9-4.

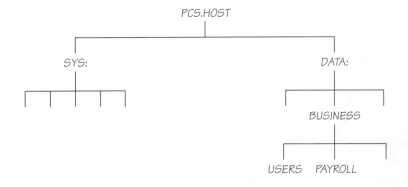

Figure 9-4

Single-user application directory structure

MULTIPLE-USER APPLICATIONS

General-purpose multiple-user applications such as word processors, spreadsheets, graphics or database software applications that are accessed by many users in an organization to maintain their own separate files are often placed in a common directory in the SYS: volume, as shown in Figure 9-5. This directory structure allows the network administrator to use the inherited rights principle (described in Chapter 8) to easily provide Read and File scan rights to the general-purpose applications for all users by assigning the group EVERYONE Read and File scan rights to the SOFTWARE directory.

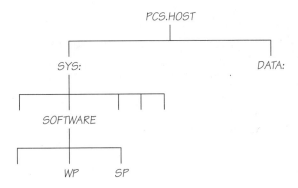

Figure 9-5

Multiple-user application directory structure

When Microsoft Windows is installed on a network, a WINDOWS directory is usually created in the NetWare file system to contain the shared Windows program files. The files in this directory can then be shared by all users after all files are copied into the shared WINDOWS directory with the SETUP-A installation command. This use of shared program files saves much installation time and disk space that would otherwise be required for multiple installations of the same files.

MULTIUSER APPLICATIONS

As described earlier in this chapter, multiuser applications need to be specially written to take advantage of such network features as record locking and transaction tracking. As a result, multiuser applications are usually designed for specific database-oriented applications that handle such tasks as order entry, reservations, or inventory control. Because of the specialized nature of multiuser applications, their location can often be based on the users of each application. An order-entry system that is accessed only by users of the sales department, for example, can be located within the SALES directory structure, as shown in Figure 9-6. An inventory application, on the other hand, might need to be accessed by users in both the sales and accounting departments. It can be located off the root of the DATA: volume, also shown in Figure 9-6.

Figure 9-6

Multiuser application directory structure

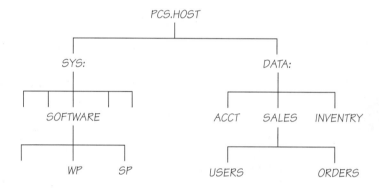

TEMPORARY AND CONFIGURATION FILES

Many NetWare aware software programs need to store configuration information and temporary files for each user. Before you install an application, therefore, it is important to study the installation instructions to determine what options you have for placement of temporary and user configuration files. Temporary files are usually created when a user starts the application and are deleted when the application program is terminated. Configuration files, on the other hand, are permanent files that are normally used to store software settings such as printer type and default data storage path for each user. With separate configuration files, each user can customize the application to accommodate his or her normal usage. Most NetWare aware software installation programs allow the network administrator to specify where the user's temporary and configuration files will be stored. You need to decide where these files will be stored before installing software applications. One option is to store these files on the workstation's local hard disk drive. Using the local hard disk has the advantages of keeping user files separate and reducing demands on the network. A disadvantage, however, is that the user must run the software from his or her assigned workstation to use the customized settings.

A user's Windows environment is created by using the Windows SETUP-N command to copy selected files to the specified directory for that user. This directory can be located on either a local hard disk or within a user home directory on the file server and allows each user to customize his or her Windows environment by storing configuration and temporary files separately for each user.

Because the temporary files involve much more disk activity than configuration files, a good compromise, when possible, is to store configuration files on the network and have the temporary files kept on the local hard disk. When configuration files are stored on the file server, they can be placed in each user's home directory, or all user configuration files for the software package can be placed in a common configuration directory.

The Microsoft Windows application uses temporary files, called swap files, to extend the workstation RAM when multiple applications are run. When you install Microsoft Windows on a network, it is important to place these temporary or permanent swap files on the local hard disk of each workstation rather than on the file server. This prevents serious network performance degradation that results from Windows' need for heavy access to the swap file.

PERFORMING THE APPLICATION INSTALLATION PROCEDURE

The installation procedure for applications generally involves running a batch file or INSTALL program that will ask you for several items of information, including the location of the software disk, the drive or directory path into which you want to install, the location of work and configuration files, printer types, and specialized software configuration parameters. While software configuration parameters depend on the application being installed, the network administrator needs to provide the installation program with a path to the appropriate directory locations and select the proper printers and ports that will work on the network. This section describes some of the installation considerations you need to be aware of when selecting directories and printers.

PLANNING DRIVE POINTER USAGE

Prior to running the installation program for a software product, you need to define any drive pointers that will be needed to install the application. Application installation programs need to know the path to the directory that will contain the application program files as well as the location of the user configuration and temporary files. Because each user who runs this application will need to have access to the application and configuration files, you should plan to use a drive pointer that will be mapped to the same volume for all users. This is important because if the drive letter you select is mapped to a different volume for some users, the directory path will not be found on the specified drive letter when these users attempt to run the application and the application will terminate. Suppose, for example, that you plan to place configuration files in the SYS:SOFTWARE\WP\SETUP directory and during installation you specify the path to the configuration files as F:\SOFTWARE\WP\SETUP, because drive F is currently mapped to the SYS: volume. Assume that after you install the application, a user, who has drive F mapped to the DATA: volume, attempts to run the application. Because the DATA: volume does not contain the \SOFTWARE\WP\SETUP directory, the application program will terminate because it cannot locate the user configuration files. In order for users to be able to run the application package, therefore, it is imperative that the paths specified for software configuration and temporary files use a drive letter that will be mapped to the same path for all users. You can do this by setting up standard drive mappings in the system login script file, as described in Chapter 12.

 When using the SETUP -N command to install Windows on the network for a specific user, make sure that your default drive is the same drive letter that will be mapped to the user's Windows directory when he or she logs in.

When installing software that is not NetWare aware, you might need to use the MAP ROOT command for the drive letter you plan to use to contain the application directory. Mapping a root drive is necessary with installation programs that are not NetWare aware because some installation programs have been known to create their own directory structure at the root of the drive letter you specify. Mapping a root drive will cause these installation programs to create the application directory within the directory structure to which you have mapped the root drive rather than at the root of the NetWare volume. If you wanted, for example, to install a payroll application that is not NetWare aware in the BUSINESS directory shown in Figure 9-4, you would start by first selecting a drive letter, such as P, to be used for the payroll application, and then root mapping the drive P pointer to the BUSINESS directory using the following command:

```
MAP ROOT P:=DATA:BUSINESS
```

Now when the installation program attempts to create a payroll directory in path P:\, it will actually be making the directory in the BUSINESS directory structure.

 When creating a Microsoft Windows program icon for an application, you will need to specify the path to the application, including the drive letter and all directories leading to the executable program file. The drive letter specified in this path must exist and be mapped to the correct volume each time the user logs in and runs the application.

SPECIFYING THE DIRECTORY PATH

Your first step prior to running an installation program is to be sure the drive mappings you plan to use for the application and configuration files have been established. Immediately after starting, most software installation programs will ask you to specify the path to the directory in which the application program files are to be installed. Later during the installation process, you might also have options to enter paths for both temporary and configuration files. When entering the paths, be sure to specify the drive pointers you defined when planning your directory structure.

Figure 9-7 shows a screen that appears during installation of the WordPerfect application, which includes the paths for installing the application on a network drive. Notice that the F network drive letter is being used for installation of the software along with the dictionary and other files used by the WordPerfect program into the SOFTWARE\WP51 directory of the volume, in which the drive F letter is mapped. The default directory for user document files is located on the drive H pointer. This means that, in order to use the application, each user will need to have his or her drive F letter mapped to the volume that contains the WP51 directory along with a drive H pointer mapped to the default document directory, which for most users would be their home directory path.

Figure 9-7

WordPerfect installation screen

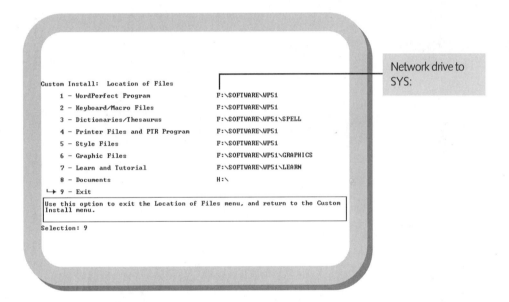

Network drive to SYS:

```
Custom Install:  Location of Files

    1 - WordPerfect Program               F:\SOFTWARE\WP51

    2 - Keyboard/Macro Files              F:\SOFTWARE\WP51

    3 - Dictionaries/Thesaurus            F:\SOFTWARE\WP51\SPELL

    4 - Printer Files and PTR Program     F:\SOFTWARE\WP51

    5 - Style Files                       F:\SOFTWARE\WP51

    6 - Graphic Files                     F:\SOFTWARE\WP51\GRAPHICS

    7 - Learn and Tutorial                F:\SOFTWARE\WP51\LEARN

    8 - Documents                         H:\

↳   9 - Exit
    ┌──────────────────────────────────────────────────────────────────┐
    │Use this option to exit the Location of Files menu, and return to the Custom│
    │Install menu.                                                       │
    └──────────────────────────────────────────────────────────────────┘
Selection: 9
```

The location of the user configuration and temporary files for the WordPerfect program will be the directory from which the WP.EXE program file is started unless a separate path is specified when the WP.EXE program is started. When WordPerfect v5.1 is started, a different location for the temporary files can be specified by including the */D-path* parameter on the command line that starts the WP program. The *D-path* parameter specifies the drive letter and path to the location in which temporary files are to be stored. The command WP /D-F:\SOFTWARE\WP51\TEMP, for example, causes WordPerfect to store all temporary files in a subdirectory of the software directory named TEMP.

SPECIFYING PRINTER TYPES AND PORTS

Most applications allow you to select one or more printer types along with the port used to obtain hardcopy output. Multiple-user applications that include word processors and spreadsheets allow the installer to select many printer types for the user to choose. In these cases, you select the printer types that will be available on the user's workstations or can be shared on the network. If the application is NetWare aware you should be able to select either a printer port, such as LPT1: through LPT3:, or enter the name of a print queue, as described in Chapter 10.

Installation programs for single-user applications might limit you to only one printer type during installation. To allow multiple users to run a software package that is installed for only one type of printer, you might want to place the selected printer on the network as described in Chapter 10. Placing a printer on the network will allow all users to access the same printer type. The best solution is to select the best printer type you can afford for this application and then place that printer on the network, as described in Chapter 10. The printed output from the program can then be redirected to the network printer using the CAPTURE command (also described in Chapter 10) so that the output will be directed to the correct printer type no matter which user is operating the program.

SETTING APPROPRIATE DIRECTORY AND FILE ATTRIBUTES

After you run the software installation program, you need to be sure the application directory and files are secure. If the software is designed for multiple users, you need to provide for its shared use. If the installation program is NetWare aware, it might set the necessary file and directory attributes for you. You might, however, want to add attributes to increase file security or provide extra functions such as transaction tracking. This section discusses what attributes are appropriate for what applications. Figure 9-8 summarizes the attribute settings for each application type.

Figure 9-8

Attribute settings

Application Type	Data Files	Application Program Files
Single-user Example: payroll	Read Write non-Sharable	Read Only non-Sharable (some software programs might allow multiple users to access them even if flagged non-Sharable)
Multiple-user Example: word processor	Read Write non-Sharable	Read Only, Sharable
Multiuser Example: database system	Read Write Transactional Sharable (requires the program to provide record locking and transaction tracking)	Read Only Sharable

The function of the Sharable attribute on a document file is based on the DOS requester and the application program and can be used to allow multiple users to access a specific document file at the same time. While the function of the Sharable attribute on a document file is based on the DOS requester along with the application software, it can sometimes be used if you need to allow multiple users to access a specific document file at the same time.

SINGLE-USER APPLICATIONS

Because a single-user application can be used by only one user at a time, both data files and executable program files require no special attributes—except possibly the Read Only attribute to protect them from accidental erasure or modification either by a user or a software virus. The Read Only attribute is important for applications in which users need to be granted Erase, Modify, or Write access rights in order to work with data or temporary files that are stored in the application's directory. Setting the Read Only attribute, however, can sometimes cause application errors for certain software products that store configuration information in the program files. Make sure to test the application after setting any Read Only attributes to be sure users can perform their necessary functions. An alternative to using the Read Only attribute to protect application files from being renamed or erased and still allow changes to be made, is to use the Delete Inhibit and Rename Inhibit attributes. Setting Delete Inhibit and Rename Inhibit on a file allows the contents of the file to be changed but prevents the file from being renamed or deleted.

Even though program files in a single-user application are not flagged Sharable, in some applications it is possible for two or more users to run the application at the same time, causing program problems or corrupt data files. Test a newly installed application by running it from two different workstations to determine if more than one user can access the programs simultaneously. If more than one user can run the programs at the same time, you need to develop a procedure to prevent multiple access or else install the application in a separate directory for each user. If multiple users need access to the same data files, replace the single-user application with a NetWare aware application that is designed to accommodate multiple users.

MULTIPLE-USER APPLICATIONS

The major difference in attribute settings between a multiple-user application and a single-user application is that the files which run the multiple-user application should be flagged Sharable to allow more than one user to access the software simultaneously. Because most multiple-user applications are NetWare aware, they are designed for shared access, and the installation process might not require you to use the FLAG command to set the Sharable attribute. You should check with the installation instructions, however, to determine if it is necessary to set any additional attributes after installation. Like those for single-user applications, data files for multiple-user applications need to be left non-Sharable and Read Write in order to prevent multiple users from overwriting each other's changes. Leaving the data files non-Sharable will allow only one user at a time to access and modify information in a specific file.

 When WordPerfect is used on a network, a document file can be opened by two users at the same time even when it is not flagged Sharable. However, only the first user to open the document is allowed to save changes to the document under its original name. Changes made by the second user can be saved to a different filename. If the second user attempts to save the file using its original name, an "Access denied" error message is displayed.

MULTIUSER APPLICATIONS

As already stated, a multiuser application is a special form of multiple-user application that allows more than one user to update the same data file simultaneously. The major difference in attribute settings between multiple-user and multiuser applications is that the data files to be shared should have the Sharable attribute set for multiuser applications in order to allow multiple users to access and update the database records simultaneously. In addition, in order that the NetWare Transaction Tracking System is enabled on a shared database system, the database files need to be flagged with the Transactional attribute in addition to being made Sharable. This is illustrated in a sample order entry system, shown in Figure 9-9.

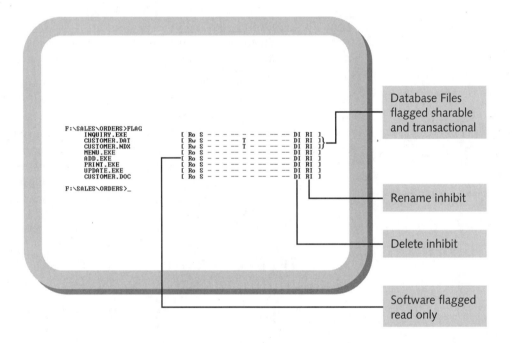

Figure 9-9

Setting multiuser file attributes

Database Files flagged sharable and transactional

Rename inhibit

Delete inhibit

Software flagged read only

Notice that in addition to the Transactional attribute (T), the CUSTOMER database files are also flagged Delete Inhibit (DI) and Rename Inhibit (RI). These additional attributes prevent the files from being accidentally deleted or renamed by users who have been given Erase or Modify access rights. Flagging the *.EXE program files Read Only will prevent them from being changed or deleted by a user or a software virus.

ALL APPLICATIONS

In addition to the attributes already described, you might want to use NetWare's Hidden attribute to make it more difficult for users to copy program files onto a local disk illegally. To prevent an executable file from being copied, you can use the FLAG command to place the Execute Only attribute on the file. This prevents the program file from being copied while still allowing it to be run. The disadvantage of the Execute Only attribute is that once it is set on a file it cannot be removed, even by the SUPERVISOR. Because of this, make sure to have original installation disks or a working backup of the application file before setting the Execute Only attribute. Certain software applications—those that open their executable program files in the read mode in order to access messages and other information—will not run correctly when the Execute Only attribute is set. Because the Execute Only attribute allows the program files to be opened only in run mode, these programs crash when they attempt to read from their program files. Make sure to test the application after you set the Execute Only attribute. Figure 9-10 shows a FLAG command that sets the Execute Only attribute and then an attempt to copy the protected file.

Figure 9-10

Using the Execute Only attribute

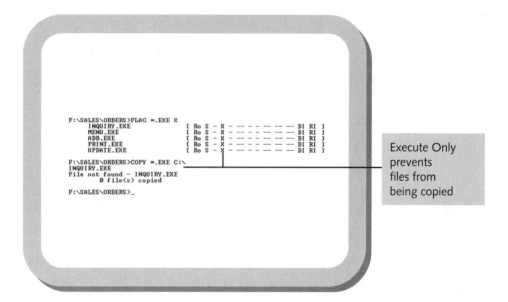

Execute Only prevents files from being copied

Another directory attribute to consider in this context is Purge. Flagging directories that contain temporary files with the Purge attribute will cause the space used by a temporary file to be immediately reclaimed by the NetWare operating system when the temporary file is deleted. Because it is unlikely you would ever want to salvage a temporary file, flagging temporary file directories with the Purge attribute can help improve system performance and provide more time before NetWare will need to reuse space occupied by other deleted data files—ones that might be more in need of salvaging.

PROVIDING USER ACCESS RIGHTS

In order to use a newly installed application, users need access rights to the software directory along with appropriate drive mappings. As a network administrator, you need to determine the minimum set of access rights that will allow users to work with the application software and still prevent them from changing or deleting programs or files that must remain unaltered. In order to separate application software from the data, the network administrator must also define regular and search drives that will allow users to run application software from the directory containing data files. This section discusses several considerations and techniques that will help you plan and provide user access.

ACCESS RIGHTS

At a minimum, all users will need Read and File scan rights to the directory containing an application. Whenever possible, assign trustee rights to groups rather than individual users—this makes it easier to add or change access rights later. In addition to providing these rights, you might need to assign additional rights for either of the following two conditions:

- If you are storing temporary files in the application software directory, you will need to provide users with at least the Create and Erase rights to this directory. In addition, if the software application needs to rename temporary files, you must assign the Modify right. This creates a security problem, however, in that users with the Modify right can change the attributes on program files. You can prevent this either by placing temporary files in a different directory (if possible) or by using the Inherited Rights Mask on each of the program files, allowing them to inherit only Read and File scan rights.

- If the user configuration files are stored in the software directory and you want users to be able to customize their configuration settings, you will need to provide them with at least the Write right. If you place user configuration files in a separate directory, then assign the users Read, File Scan, Write, Create, Erase, and Modify rights to the directory that contains the configuration files.

 To run the WordPerfect application on your network, Novell suggests that you create a group of WordPerfect users and then grant this group the following access rights:

```
F:\SOFTWARE\WP51                    [ R  F]

F:\SOFTWARE\WP51\SETUP              [R W C E M F]

F:\SOFTWARE\WP51\GRAPHICS          [R W C  F]

F:\SOFTWARE\WP51\SPELL             [R W C E M F]
```

DRIVE MAPPINGS

In order for users to run application software and access data files, you need to establish both search and regular drive pointers. (These drive mappings will need to be included in the login script files, as described in Chapter 12.) Regular drive pointers should provide users easy access to the directory location containing their data, with a maximum of three directory layers. The regular drive pointers discussed in Chapter 6 consist of a drive pointer to the root of the volume, a drive pointer to the user's workgroup, and a drive pointer to the user's home directory. These drive pointers should be sufficient to access most application data files. If a data directory is accessed by users in multiple departments, however, a special drive mapping to that directory should be established for all users who need to use the data.

Search drive mappings should be established for all general-purpose software directories. When planning search drive mappings, try to keep the total number of search drives for any user to eight or fewer. This can be done by providing a menu system that will insert a search drive mapping for the application being run and then delete that search drive mapping when the program terminates.

MODIFYING CONFIGURATION FILES

The final step of installing an application involves modifying the CONFIG.SYS files on all workstations that will be running an application. As a network administrator you need to know the statements that might need to be added to the CONFIG.SYS file of each workstation on the network. Installation programs often modify the CONFIG.SYS of the workstation in which you install the software, but the other workstations that will run this application from the network will also need to have their CONFIG.SYS files modified in order to use the application.

Figure 9-11

Common CONFIG.SYS statements

Statement	Example
FILES=n	FILES=25
BUFFERS=n	BUFFERS=15
SHELL=[path]COMMAND.COM/P/E:n	SHELL=COMMAND.COM/P/E:1024 The /E:1024 parameter defines 1024 bytes of environment space.

Figure 9-11 shows three common CONFIG.SYS statements with examples. The FILES statement increases the number of file handles available to DOS. A file handle contains information on each file that is currently open. Most network software will require at least 25 file handles. The BUFFERS statement increases the number of disk blocks that DOS will keep in memory. When NetWare drives are accessed, this number can be kept quite low because most information comes from the network and each block takes up to 532 Kbytes of RAM on the workstation. Between 12 and 15 blocks will be sufficient for most network workstations. The SHELL statement increases the environment space available to hold the DOS paths and search drives. In addition, certain software variables and directory locations are stored here. Because of this, it is often necessary to increase the space to at least 1024 bytes for most network workstations. If you receive the message "Out of Environment Space," you should increase the environment space by an additional 256 bytes.

Certain applications, such as WordPerfect 5.x and Microsoft Windows, require changes to NetWare's NET.CFG file, which is located in the workstation's network startup directory (described in Chapter 5). In Chapter 16, you will learn about additional statements and parameters that can be included in the NET.CFG file in order to enhance a workstation's performance and reliability when it runs network applications.

TESTING THE SOFTWARE

After all steps in the installation process have been completed, the network administrator needs to test the installation by running the application software. First test the application while logged in with Supervisory rights. Use the MAP command to establish the drive mappings you defined for the application software, change to the data directory, and issue the necessary commands to start the application. Test as many functions of the application as possible including data entry, file access, and printing.

When you are confident that the application is installed correctly and the correct drive mappings have been defined, log out and then log back in with a username that will run the application. Repeat the tests you ran as supervisor to make sure users have been granted the rights necessary to work with the application. After you have determined that the software will run from your workstation when you log in as a user, proceed to each user's workstation and test the application to be sure the workstation configurations support the application properly. Finally, check the user's effective rights in each of the directories and program files to make sure the users cannot erase or change critical program files.

CHAPTER SUMMARY

Installing application software can generally be divided into eight steps. The first step is determining the application's level of NetWare compatibility. Some software is not compatible with networks and will run properly only if installed on the local hard drive of a workstation. Because NetWare is designed to work closely with DOS, most applications will run from a NetWare file server without any special features or modifications. Today many software companies design their products to be aware of network features and take advantage of running from a file server.

After you determine that an application will run on a NetWare file server, the second installation step is to determine whether the application has single-user, multiple-user, or multiuser capability. A single-user application allows only one user at a time to operate the software and access the data. A multiple-user application, such as a word processor or spreadsheet program, supports multiple users running the software, but allows only one user to access a specific file at a time. A multiuser application is usually a database system that tracks such information as order entry or inventory—that will support multiple users accessing the same file simultaneously.

The third step in the installation process involves determining the application software directory. Shared multiple-user applications, such as word processors and spreadsheets, are usually stored in a general-purpose software directory located in the SYS: volume. In a departmentalized directory structure, single-user applications and special-purpose multiuser applications are often stored in a subdirectory of a department's workgroup directory structure.

After you decide on the location of the application's directory, the fourth step is to run the installation program and copy the application files into the selected directory path. This process usually involves entering such information as the source and target drives, the path in which to store temporary and configuration files, the type of printer and port, and special settings needed by the particular application.

Once an application's files have been copied, the fifth step is to set file and directory attributes in order to secure the files and allow shared access to multiple-user applications. Files can be protected from illegal copying by flagging them with the Hidden or Execute Only attribute. The directory structure can also be protected by flagging directories Delete Inhibit and Rename Inhibit. To improve performance, you can flag directories that contain temporary files with the Purge attribute. This recovers the file space immediately after file deletion rather than making temporary files available for salvaging.

After the file and directory attributes have been set, the sixth step involves granting trustee assignments to allow users to run the applications. To allow all users to run the general-purpose application software, the group EVERYONE is often assigned the Read and File scan rights to the SYS:SOFTWARE directory. In single-user and special-purpose multiuser application directories, it is sometimes also necessary to provide users with Write, Create, Erase, and Modify rights to enable them to work with configuration and data files that are stored in the same directory in which the application is stored. Whenever possible, configuration and data files should be kept in a separate directory. This avoids the necessity of assigning extra rights to the software directories.

The next step in the installation process is to make any necessary modifications to the DOS CONFIG.SYS file as well as NetWare's NET.CFG file on each workstation that will run the application. Most installations provide information on the necessary settings that need to be included in these files. The instructions will be found either in the software documentation or in README files on the application disks.

After the software installation is complete, you need to test the installation. First run the programs while logged in with Supervisory rights. After you are confident the software has been installed correctly, log in as one of the users of the application and test each of the tasks the users will be expected to perform. The final test of the application is to run the software from each workstation in order to make sure the configuration files are correct. After all testing has been completed, you will be ready to proceed to automating the user environment with login scripts and menus as described in Chapters 12 and 13.

Key Terms

multiple-user application	NetWare aware	record locking
multiuser application	NetWare compatible	single-user application

Review Questions

1. What is the first step a network administrator needs to complete before installing an application?

   The application's level of NetWare compatibility

2. After the application files have been copied into the NetWare directory by the installation program, what is the next step to be performed?

   Setting Appropriate Directory & File Attributes.

3. If you see the message "Out of Environment Space" when running an application, you need to place the _____Shell_____ statement in the _CONFIG.SYS_ file.

4. List the three levels of NetWare compatibility.

NetWare incompatible

NetWare compatible

NetWare aware

5. A(n) _multiple user_ application type allows multiple users to run the software, but only one user at a time can access a specific data file.

6. A(n) _____multiuser_____ application type allows multiple users to access the same file simultaneously.

7. Which of the following would be acceptable locations in which to install a spreadsheet application that will be used by several users in a company? For each unacceptable location, briefly explain why that directory path would not make a good location.
   a. SYS:SYSTEM\SP → want SYSTEM directory to be locked   easier to use indivista rights.
   b. SYS:PUBLIC → yes.
   c. SYS:APPS\WP → not a word processor
   d. DATA:BUSINESS\WP → usually located on SYS: volume.
   e. SYS:WP → Not a word processor.

8. Given the following directory structure, use the line below to write the path to an acceptable location in which to install a multiuser order entry system. The system is to be used only by the sales department to enter customer orders.

   DATA: SALES

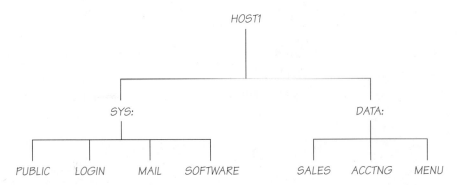

9. What are two important directory locations that the network administrator usually needs to provide during an installation procedure?

   _____

   _____

10. The _Read & File Scan_ attribute should generally be set on all program files.

11. The _____Sharable_____ attribute should also be set on multiple-user program files.

12. The _Execute Only_ attribute can be set on .EXE and .COM files to prevent them from being copied.

13. What directory attribute might you consider setting on the software directories in order to secure them from curious users browsing the network?
Hidden Attribute

14. At a minimum, users will need the _Read & File Scan_ access rights to run the application software.

15. In the space below, briefly explain why it is important that the drive letter you specify in the directory path for the application's work files be one that is mapped to the same location for all users.

16. In the space below, briefly explain why it is important first to test an application logged in with Supervisory rights and then test it again while logged in as a user.
To test the mappings and make sure everything works then fix problems and log on as user to confirm users have appropriate access

17. On the line below, write a NetWare command to make all .PRG files in the DATA:SALES\ORDERS Sharable.
Flag DATA:SALES\ORDERS *.PRG S

18. Assume you install a database application that is designed to be used on a standalone PC on the file server. In the space below, give one reason why you should *not* make the database file sharable.
Because the application is designed to be run on a standalone PC.

19. When would you *not* want to make program files Sharable?
If you are using a multiple user application or a file not to be shared by users.

20. On the lines below, write two NetWare commands that will protect the following SOFTWARE directory structure from being changed and make it more difficult for curious users to find and browse the software structure.
Flag SYS:SOFTWARE DI
Flag SYS:SOFTWARE RI

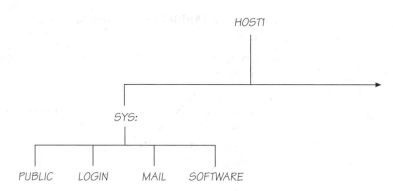

EXERCISES

Exercise 9-1: Sharing a Database

In this exercise you will experiment with using the Sharable attribute to make a database file in a multiuser application accessible to more than one user. To complete this exercise you will need to coordinate your activity with one or more students or have access to two different workstations from which you can log in and test the application. Your instructor will provide you with information about dividing the class into teams.

1. Identify the other student(s) with whom you are to work and exchange usernames.

2. One team member should create DATABASE and CUSTOMER directories in his or her ##ADMIN work area (where ## represents the assigned student user number).

3. Copy the following programs from the SYS:EXAMPLE\SALES\ORDERS directory of the assigned file server to the CUSTOMER directory:

    CUSTOMER.DAT

    CUSTOMER.NDX

    INQUIRY.BAS

    PRINT.BAS

4. Copy the following BASIC language system software from the DOS directory of your local hard drive to the DATABASE directory:

    QBASIC.HLP

    QBASIC.EXE

5. Use SYSCON to create a group named ##SALEGRP that contains the username of each team member.

6. Grant the ##SALEGRP group [R F] rights to the DATABASE directory and [R F W] rights to the CUSTOMER directory.

7. Map a search drive to the DATABASE directory.

8. The team member who owns the ##ADMIN directory should now log in and change to the CUSTOMER directory.

9. Enter the command QBASIC INQUIRY to load the INQUIRY program.

10. Use the [Alt][R] key combination and then select the Start option to run the INQUIRY application program.

11. Another team member should now log in and change to the CUSTOMER directory.

12. To print database records, the other team member(s) will need to map a search drive to the DATABASE directory and then enter QBASIC PRINT to run the PRINT program. In the space below, record the error message you receive when the other team member(s) attempts to run the PRINT program.

permission denied

13. The owner of the directory should now exit the INQUIRY application and use the FLAG command to make the necessary file(s) Sharable.

14. Repeat Steps 9 through 13 to flag all files necessary for both users to run the database program and access the CUSTOMER data. On the lines below, record the name of each file you need to make Sharable in order for multiple users to access the customer database. (You might not need to use all the lines.)

customer.dat needs to be flagged as sharable

15. On the lines below, record the name of each file you need to make Sharable in order for all users to access the customer database. (You might not need to use all the lines provided.)

customer.dat

Exercise 9-2: Testing a Single-User DOS Application

In this exercise you will experiment with creating and sharing a DOS-based application program that is intended for use by a single user. The objective of this exercise is to demonstrate that a single-user application can often be accessed by more than one user at the same time despite the fact that the files are not flagged Sharable. To complete this exercise you will need to coordinate your activity with one or more students or have access to two different workstations from which you can log in and test the application. Your instructor will provide you with information regarding dividing the class into teams.

1. Identify the other student(s) with whom are to work with and exchange usernames.

2. In his or her ##ADMIN work area, one team member should create a SOFTWARE directory that contains subdirectories for word processing and spreadsheet applications.

3. Copy the following programs from the DOS directory of your local computer to the WP directory:

    EDIT.HLP

    EDIT.COM

    QBASIC.HLP

    QBASIC.EXE

4. Grant [R F W C E M] rights for this directory to all team members.

5. Each team member should log in and map a drive to the shared WP software directory.

6. From one team member's workstation, run the EDIT program and create a document file that contains a list of five movies you have seen during the last year.

7. Save the document with the name MOVIES.TXT.

8. Use the FLAG command to record the attributes set on each of the five files in the following list. Record the FLAG command you use on the line below:

File Name	Attribute(s)	
EDIT.HLP	RW	A
EDIT.COM	RW	A
QBASIC.HLP	RW	A
QBASIC.EXE	RW	A
MOVIES.TXT	RW	A

9. Each team member should now change to the WP drive and use the EDIT program to access the MOVIES document. Do you think EDIT will allow multiple users to open the same document without the Sharable attribute? Yes or (No) _____

    Does EDIT allow all team members to access the MOVIES document file? (Yes) or No _____

10. An important reason for making document files non-Sharable is to protect changes made by one user from being overwritten by another user. In this step, each team member should use the EDIT program to call up the MOVIES document and then place his or her name at the top of the document.

11. One user should save his or her document. Then another user should save his or her changes. Does EDIT allow each user to save his or her changes? (Yes) or No _____

    What is the name of the user who saved his or her document first?
    Derek

    What is the name of the user who saved his or her document last?
    Clinton

12. Access the MOVIES document. In the space below, record which users' changes were saved.

    Clinton

13. If both users were able to save their documents, record the name of the user whose changes now appear in the document.

Clinton

14. Based on this test, how should the EDIT program be used on the network? In the space below, record the recommendations you would make.

only by a single user not in shared directories.

Exercise 9-3: Sharing Windows Applications

If you have Windows installed on your networked workstation, you can use this exercise to experiment with the differences between how the Windows Write and Notepad applications share document files on a network. Skip this exercise if you do not have Windows installed on your workstation. One of the objectives of this exercise is to illustrate that setting the Sharable attribute on a document file does not guarantee that more than one user can access the document. This is due to the way the applications access the document files. To complete this exercise you will need to coordinate your activity with one or more students or have access to two different workstations from which you can log in and test the application. Your instructor will provide you with information about dividing the class into teams.

1. Identify the other student(s) with whom you are to work and exchange user-names.

2. To simulate installing a Windows application on a file server, one team member should make a WINAPP directory structure in his or her ##ADMIN work area. The directory structure should share Windows software and data, as shown below:

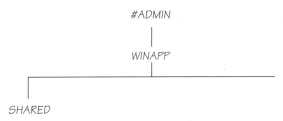

3. To simulate installing the software package, copy the WRITE.EXE program from the WINDOWS directory on the local hard disk to the WINAPP directory.

4. Next, grant each team member [R F] rights to the WINAPP directory and [R F W C E] rights to the SHARED directory.

5. Determine a drive letter to be used to access the WRITE program and shared data. On the lines below, record the drive letters and paths you define.

Application drive letter: _A:_   Path: _SYS: 53ADMIN/WINAPP_

Shared data drive letter: _S:_   Path: _SYS: 53ADMIN/WINAPP/SHARED_

6. Each team member should complete the following:

    a. Map root drive letters to the paths defined in Step 5.

    b. Start Windows.

    c. Create a new program group called NWAPPS (refer to Windows documentation on creating a program group).

    d. Create a program icon for the WRITE application by using the drive pointer defined in Step 5 to access the application. Modify the File Properties setting to make the working directory point to the drive letter containing the shared data files, as defined in Step 5 (refer to your Windows documentation on creating new program icons).

7. Select one team member to use the WRITE program to create a document describing how to create a group icon.

8. In the SHARED subdirectory, save the document file created in Step 7 as ICON.WRI.

9. Each team member should now attempt to use the WRITE application to access the ICON.WRI document. Only the first team member to access the document will be given access.

10. Determine if making the ICON.WRI document Sharable will allow other users to view or change the document. To do this, the owner of the ICON.WRI document should exit Windows and then use the network FLAG command to make the document Sharable. Record the command used on the line below:

    _____

11. Illustrate that flagging a file with the Sharable attribute does not guarantee that the file can be used by more than one user at a time by repeating Step 10. In the space below, record what happens when the team members concurrently attempt to use the Sharable ICON.WRI file from multiple workstations.

Exercise 9-4: Installing a Single-User Application

Certain applications that were originally designed to be installed on a local hard disk can be installed on a file server by tricking the installation program to see the network drive as a local disk. In some cases this can be done by mapping the network drive letter to a local disk drive such as C. In this exercise you will install a copy of the TEST system on the network drive by following the instructions in the README file found in the TESTING directory of your student work disk.

1. Change to the drive containing your student work disk and use the command CD \TESTING to change to the simulated graduate software directory. Use the TYPE README > PRN command to view and then print the installation instructions.

2. On the line below, record the path to the directory in your ##ADMIN work area in which you plan to place the testing application.

_____

3. Perform the installation procedure as described in the README file. In the space below, record any drive mappings you use.

4. Flag the program and data files according to the README instructions.

5. Assign another student user besides yourself access rights to maintain the testing application.

6. Flag all executable files to prevent them from being copied.

7. Provide EVERYONE with rights to run the application.

8. On the lines below, indicate what drive mappings users will need to run this application.

_____

_____

9. Use the NDIR command to obtain a hardcopy listing of all files in the testing directory.

10. Use the TLIST command to list the trustee assignments you made to the TESTING directory and then press the Print Scrn key to obtain a printout of your screen.

11. Test the application while logged in with Supervisory rights.

12. Log in as the user GUEST.

13. Attempt to copy the executable files to your local hard disk.

14. Use the Print Scrn key to record the message you receive.

15. Use the MAP command to create the drive mappings defined in Step 8.

16. Using these drive mappings, attempt to run the testing system. In the space below, record any commands you need to use.

17. Complete a sample test and print your score.

EXERCISE

Case 9-1: OfficePro

The OfficePro company specializes in providing word processing services for other businesses. Currently it employs five word processing staff members, each of whom has his or her own personal computer. Recently OfficePro installed a NetWare network to allow its employees to share laser printers and to have access to common documents. In addition, OfficePro obtained a NetWare aware version of its word processing software, which will allow all users to share the same software package and provide them with special network capabilities. Rita Dunn, manager of OfficePro, has recently asked you to install the new word processing program on OfficePro's file server and has provided you with the installation notes for the software package (shown in Figure 9-12). Rita Dunn also gave you a copy of OfficePro's current file server directory structure (shown in Figure 9-13). Your job is to add the necessary directories to support the word processing application software, install the package, and provide the necessary rights for the users.

Figure 9-12

Word processing installation notes

The LetterPerfect word processing software can either be installed on a local hard disk or a Novell NetWare file server. When using the network installation option, you will need to provide the install program with the type of network to install onto in addition to the location of software, temporary, and configuration files. Follow the instructions below when installing the LetterPerfect software on your network system.

Software Files:

The installation program will ask for the drive and directory to contain the LetterPerfect software package program and work files. Users will need to have a search drive mapped to this directory in order to run the package from any drive or directory in the network file system. All users will need a minimum of Read and File scan rights to this directory unless you plan to keep configuration files in this directory, in which case refer to the following configuration file instructions.

Configuration Files:

Each user must be supplied with a three-letter username that allows the software to separate user configuration files by naming the file LPxxx.CFG where "xxx" is the three -letter username. By default each user configuration file will be stored in the directory from which the LetterPerfect software is started. However, if a user enters a different three-letter username or starts the LetterPerfect software from a different directory, a new LPxxx.CFG file will be created with default configuration information. If you wish to place configuration files in a separate directory, you will need to supply the installation program with the drive and path to the directory that is to contain the user configuration files. In this case, the user LPxxx.CFG configuration files will be stored in that directory rather than the default directory. All users will need to have a minimum of Read, Write, File scan, and Create rights to this directory. Be sure the drive letter you use when entering the location for user configuration files is available when the user runs the LetterPerfect software.

Temporary Files:

Temporary files are used to contain control information such as current filename and location information while the user is running the LetterPerfect software. By default temporary files will be stored in the directory from which the user starts the LetterPerfect software and will be erased when the application is terminated. If you wish you can choose to have temporary files stored in an alternate directory on either the file server or local computer hard disk. Because temporary filenames include the user's three-letter username, multiple user temporary files can be placed in the same directory. Users will need a minimum of Read, File scan, Write, Create, and Erase rights in the directory used to store temporary files. Be sure the drive letter you use when entering the location for user temporary files is available when the user runs the LetterPerfect software.

Figure 9-13

OfficePro directory structure

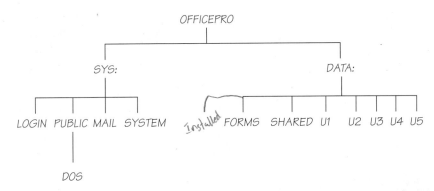

1. Use a copy of the volume design form to design a directory structure that will support the network word processing application.

2. Record any necessary drive mappings below.

   Drive   Path

   _____   _____

   _____   _____

   _____   _____

3. Document the trustee rights for each directory you defined in Step 1.

4. On the lines below, record any FLAG or FLAGDIR commands you need to use to establish special file or directory attribute settings. (You might not need to use all three lines provided.)

   _____

   _____

   _____

SUPERIOR TECHNICAL COLLEGE PROBLEMS

As a result of your work (see Chapter 8), the users at Superior Technical College now have the access rights they need to store and access files in the file system you created. In the following problems, you will apply the concepts and techniques of installing multiple-user and multiuser software packages described in this chapter.

Project 9-1: Install a Multiple-User Application

Superior Technical College recently acquired a network version of the graphics software package that the support staff and faculty will use for campus promotional materials and for classroom training. Dave Johnson has informed you that the application license will support any number of users on one file server. A separate license is required for each server on which the package is to be installed. Your job is to install the package on the file server and make it available both to students in the computer lab and to support staff.

1. Your student work disk contains a copy of the graphics software package to be installed. Place your student work disk in a disk drive and change to that

drive. The \GRAPHICS directory of your student work disk contains the simulated graphics package. Change to the \GRAPHICS directory and use the DOS TYPE > PRN command to print a copy of the README instructions.

2. On the lines below, record the location on the file server in which you plan to place the following files:

   Graphics software package: _____

   Temporary files: _____

   User configuration files: _____

3. Follow the printed instructions to install the application files.

4. Use appropriate NetWare commands to protect the software files and make them available for use by multiple users. On the lines below, record the commands you use.

   _____

   _____

   _____

5. Use appropriate commands to provide users with the access rights they will need to run the software. On the lines below, record the commands you use.

   _____

   _____

   _____

6. Record any necessary drive mappings below.

   Drive   Path

   _____   _____

   _____   _____

   _____   _____

7. Do any statements need to be added to the DOS configuration files? If so, record the statements below.

   _____

   _____

   _____

8. Test the application while logged in with Supervisory rights. On the lines below, write whatever commands are necessary to run the application.

   _____

   _____

   _____

9. Log in as one of the user accounts and test the application by making the necessary drive mappings and entering the necessary startup commands. Record all commands you enter after logging in. These commands will be important to know when you develop your login script and menu in Chapters 12 and 13.

10. Follow the instructions in the README file to check to see if the configuration and temporary files are working correctly.

Project 9-2: Install a Multiuser Database Application

Dave Johnson would like you to install on the file server a copy of the graduate tracking system that Superior Technical College is currently using at the campus. He has obtained a network license and determined that the application is network compatible, but he suggests that you print any documentation or README files from the software disk before you install the software. Your job is to make this application available to all faculty and staff at Superior Technical College. All users in the student services department should be given rights to maintain the graduate system database.

1. Change to the drive containing your student work disk and use the command CD \GRADUATE to change to the simulated graduate tracking software directory. Use the TYPE > PRN README command to view and then print the installation instructions.

2. On the line below, record the path to the directory in which you plan to place the graduate tracking application.

    _____

3. Use the MAP command to create a drive pointer in the acceptable range to the directory you determined in Step 2. On the line below, record the MAP command you use.

    _____

4. Perform the installation procedure as described in the README file. In the space below, record any parameters you select.

5. Use the FLAG command to set the attributes on the program and data files as described in the installation instructions. On the lines below, record the FLAG commands you use.

    _____

    _____

6. Provide the student services users with the necessary access rights.

7. In the space below, write the drive mappings that the student services users will need to run this application.

8. Use the NDIR command to obtain a hardcopy listing of all files in the graduate tracking system.

9. Use the TLIST command to document the trustee assignments you made to the graduate tracking directory.

10. Test the application while logged in with Supervisory rights. In the space below, record the startup commands and any necessary drive mappings you need to use.

11. Log in with the username you created for Karl Dauer.

12. Use the MAP command to create the drive mappings you defined for the student services department (refer to Chapter 6). On the lines below, record the MAP commands you use.

    Drive   Path

    _____   _____

    _____   _____

    _____   _____

13. Using the drive mappings from Step 12, attempt to run the graduate tracking system application. On the lines below, record any commands you need to use.

    These commands will be important in later chapters when you create login scripts and menus.

## CHAPTER TEN

INSTALLING NETWARE PRINTING

Printer sharing is an important benefit of a local area network. Among its advantages are cost savings, increased work space, flexible printer selection, and printer fault tolerance. To become a NetWare CNA, you need to know the NetWare printing system and the NetWare printing utilities that let you set up, customize, and maintain the printing environment on your network. This chapter provides the NetWare printing concepts and skills you will need to understand the NetWare printing components and to implement a sophisticated network printing environment for your organization using NetWare utilities. Chapter 11 provides additional information about managing and customizing network printing to meet special printing needs and properly maintain network printing environments.

AFTER READING THIS CHAPTER AND COMPLETING THE EXERCISES YOU WILL BE ABLE TO:

- IDENTIFY AND DESCRIBE THE NETWARE PRINTING COMPONENTS AND THEIR RELATIONSHIPS TO EACH OTHER.

- USE THE PCONSOLE UTILITY TO CREATE, CONFIGURE, AND WORK WITH PRINT QUEUES AND PRINT SERVERS.

- LOAD A PRINT SERVER ON EITHER A FILE SERVER OR A DEDICATED WORKSTATION AND USE RPRINTER TO MAKE A PRINTER ATTACHED TO A WORKSTATION AVAILABLE TO THE NETWORK.

- USE THE CAPTURE AND NPRINT COMMANDS TO DIRECT OUTPUT FROM A WORKSTATION TO A NETWARE PRINT QUEUE.

NETWARE PRINTING COMPONENTS

Before you can implement a network printing environment, you need to understand the basic network printing components and how they work together. In this section, you will learn about each of the following four network components and how they are implemented in a NetWare printing environment:

- Print queues
- Print server
- Printers
- Workstations

PRINT QUEUES

A **print queue** is a network holding area that stores output from workstations in a form that is ready to be sent directly to a printer. A print queue allows multiple workstations on a network to use the same printer by storing the printer output from each workstation as separate print jobs. In NetWare, print jobs are files that contain output formatted for specific printers. After being stored in the print queue, print jobs are then printed one at a time as the printer becomes available. Figure 10-1 illustrates the principle of print queue use.

Figure 10-1

Print queues

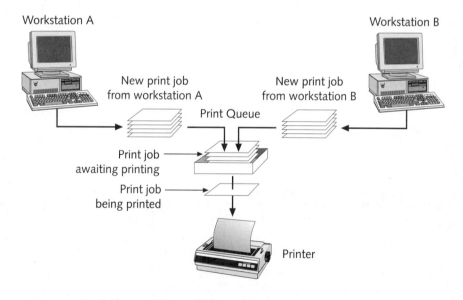

In many ways, having a workstation send output to a print queue is very similar to storing files on a server. When a file is saved on the server, the data is transferred from the workstation to the server and then stored in a file located in the specified directory. An application's printer output is actually data that is transmitted to the printer. Therefore, placing a job in a print queue involves redirecting the printer data from the application to a file, called a print job, that is located in the specified print queue. Print queues are actually directories on the NetWare file server, as illustrated in Figure 10-2.

Figure 10-2

NetWare print queue

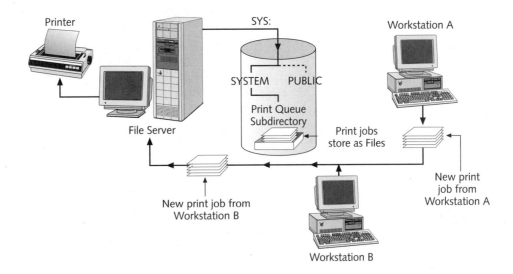

Print queues are created with the PCONSOLE utility, which will be described later in this chapter. When you set up a NetWare printing environment, you create at least one print queue for each networked printer. Output from workstations that needs to be sent to a specific printer can be directed to the print queue associated with that printer by using the NetWare CAPTURE command. Once print jobs have been stored in the print queue, they are processed by the printer assigned to the print queue in the sequence in which they were received. After a job has been printed, it is automatically deleted from the print queue.

A network user who has been designated as a print queue operator is able to rearrange the sequence of print jobs, remove a print job, or place a print job on hold.

If a printer cannot keep up with the number of print jobs that are being generated, you might want to assign two or more printers to that print queue, as illustrated in Figure 10-3. In this example, printer 1 can print output from print job A while printer 2 prints the output from print job B. Whichever printer finishes first will then begin printing job C.

Figure 10-3

Multiple printers per print queue

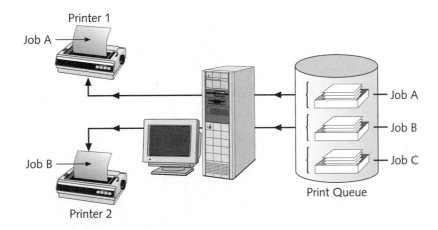

When you want to print high-priority jobs before other jobs that are currently in the print queue, you can either rearrange the jobs in the print queue or you can establish two print queues for the same printer. When two print queues are assigned to the same printer, one print queue can be given a higher priority than the other, as shown in Figure 10-4. When the current job is printed, the next job will be sent to the printer. If there is a print job in the high-priority print queue, it is printed next. If there is no print job in the high-priority print queue, the jobs in the lower priority queues will be printed. Using two print queues for one printer allows you to print high-priority jobs out of sequence by placing them in the high-priority print queue. This can be important if your network uses a printer heavily and you have occasional rush jobs.

Figure 10-4

Multiple print queues per printer

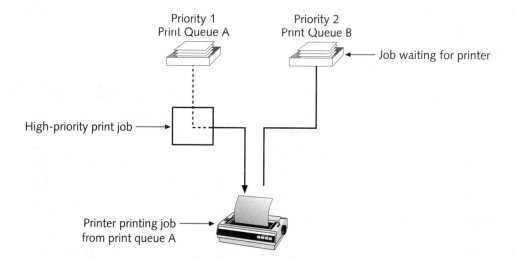

PRINT SERVERS

A **print server** is software that actually controls printing by taking print jobs from a print queue and sending them to the assigned printer, as shown in Figure 10-5. Print servers also are responsible for sending control commands to printers and reporting printer status to the print server operator. In NetWare 3.1x, each print server program can control up to 16 printers. A configuration file determines the name of the print server and the location and hardware settings of each printer. The printer settings include the names and priorities of the print queues assigned to each printer. Up to five of the printers controlled by a print server program can be attached directly to the computer running the program and are called **local printers**. Of the remaining printers, any number can be attached to other networked workstations and are referred to as **remote printers**. A Direct Printer is attached directly to the network cable using its own network interface card and software.

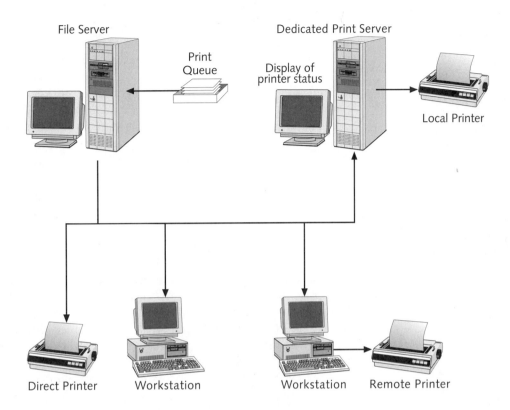

Figure 10-5

NetWare print server

File Server

Print Queue

Dedicated Print Server

Display of printer status

Local Printer

Direct Printer   Workstation   Workstation   Remote Printer

NetWare provides a program, called PCONSOLE, that allows the network administrator to define print queues and the print server. After the print queues and the print server are defined with PCONSOLE, the NetWare print server software can be loaded and run. The PSERVER.NLM program runs as a nondedicated print server from the file server computer. The PSERVER.EXE program allows a workstation to be dedicated to performing print server functions. To reduce the load on your file server—or if you need multiple print servers to support more than 16 network printers—you will want to run a print server from a dedicated workstation. The computer used as a print server must have at least an 80286 processor with a minimum of 640 Kbytes of RAM. It cannot be used for any other application software while the print server is running. A hard disk drive on the dedicated print server computer is not necessary because the print server program does not store any print jobs or work files.

PRINTERS

While there is an almost unlimited number of different printer models and configurations, most printers commonly found on microcomputer systems can be grouped into three general types: dot matrix, laser, and ink jet. Each of these printer types requires different print job formats. As a network administrator, you will need to know the types and models of printers used on your network so that you can correctly configure network printing. This will ensure that the correct output is sent to the appropriate printer. A workstation's word processing program, for example, can support both dot-matrix and laser printers. If a user selects a laser printer and prints a document, the network printing configuration must ensure that the job is sent to the laser printer that the job has been formatted to use.

Printers can be attached to the network in one of three ways: local attachment to the print server, remote attachment through a workstation, or direct attachment to the network cable. You must consider the printer attachment method when you configure the network printing environment. Each attachment method has advantages and will affect the way printers are distributed on the network. Many network administrators use a combination of printer attachments based on the type of printer and its expected usage. In this section, you will learn about each of the printer attachment options and how they affect network printing.

Local attachment

Local printers are attached directly to one of the printer ports of the computer that is running the print server program. Output is sent directly from the print server to the local printers through the local printer ports of the print server computer. Local printers can be attached to the parallel (LPT) or serial (COM) ports of the file server or workstation that is running the print server software. The advantages of a local printer attached directly to the print server include printing performance that is faster than that of remote printers and a reduction in network traffic. The higher printing speed is due to less software overhead. Remote printers that are attached to other networked workstations, in contrast, might be simultaneously running application software for users. In addition, sending print queue jobs from the print server to a printer attached somewhere on the network increases the number of packets on the network and slows the network's response time during busy periods. Figure 10-6 illustrates a local printer attached to the print server.

Figure 10-6

Local printer attachment

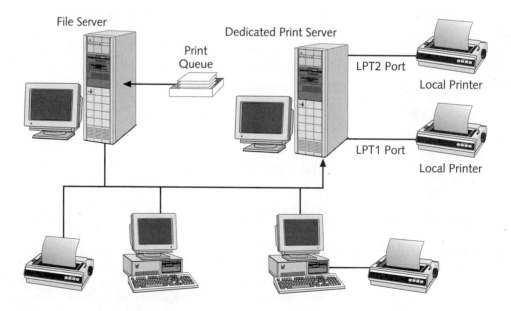

Remote attachment

Remote printers are attached to other workstations on the network, as shown in Figure 10-7. Output is sent from the print server to the workstation that has a remote printer attached via the network cable in packets of printed data. A DOS terminate and stay resident (TSR) program, included with NetWare, can be loaded on a workstation that has attached to it a printer you want to share. The TSR program receives the packets of printer output from the print server and prints them on the attached printer without interrupting any software applications being used on that workstation. An advantage of attaching remote printers to workstations is the convenience of their location. A remote workstation might be more accessible for users retrieving their printed output. Because print servers have a limited number of local printer ports, remote printers can be used to expand the number of network printers supported by a print server.

Figure 10-7

Remote printer attachment

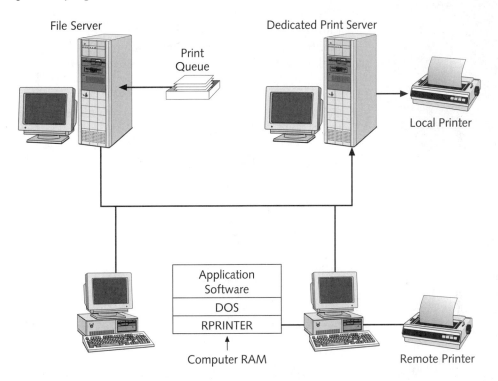

The disadvantages of remote printing include increased network traffic and the need to run the RPRINTER TSR program on each workstation that supports a shared network printer. Running a TSR program to control the remote printer means that both the printer and the workstation must be turned on and attached to the network in order for users to print their output. Another possible problem with running a TSR program on a workstation lies in the compatibility of the TSR program with other application or system software that might be running on the workstation. Finally, in some cases, workstation software conflicts can cause the remote printer to scramble or lose data and, in extreme cases, cause the workstation computer to crash.

> Workstations running Windows 3.1 can experience problems when being used with the NetWare remote printer software (RPRINTER). RPRINTER can affect the operation of the remote printer or cause the workstation to crash. If you experience these problems, be sure to obtain the latest updates for both RPRINTER and Windows.

You can solve the problem of workstation conflict with a remote printer by attaching the printer to another workstation that does not use the conflicting software or by obtaining a printer attachment option for your printer that will allow it to be attached to the network cable and become a remote printer controlled directly by the print server.

Direct attachment

You can attach a printer directly to the network cable by obtaining a special network card option for the printer. Many laser printer manufacturers offer optional network cards that can be installed in their printers to allow the printer to be attached directly to the network cable, as shown in Figure 10-8.

Figure 10-8

Direct printer attachment

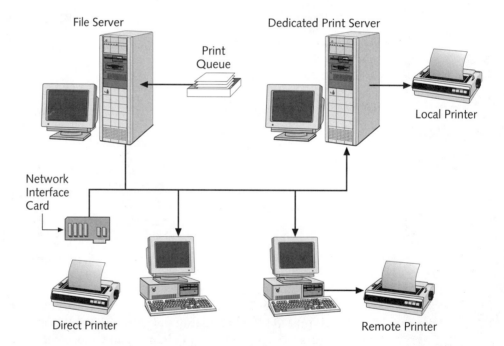

With the direct attachment option, the printer actually becomes its own print server and is able to print jobs directly from a NetWare print queue. The disadvantages of direct printer attachment are the extra cost of the network attachment option needed for each printer and the limited number of printers that have this option available. In addition, making each printer a separate print server can use up network connections to your file server and potentially cause your file server to reach the maximum limit of your NetWare license.

Many network laser printers today are installed with a direct printer attachment option that allows the printer to act as either an independent print server or a remote printer attached to an existing print server.

WORKSTATIONS

The last component of network printing is the user workstation that sends its output to a shared printer. Most existing DOS software applications are designed to send output directly to one of the LPT ports on the local workstation and do not recognize print queues or print servers. Because of this, it is sometimes necessary to redirect the output of these applications to the network card. The output is sent to a print queue and stored as a print job without the application needing to be aware of the network. Both the DOS shell program (NETX) and the VLM requester software are able to capture output being sent from an application to a printer port and transmit it to the selected print queue on a specified file server. The NetWare operating system includes command utilities that allow the output from a workstation to be directed, with a number of customized options, to a specific print queue. As a network administrator you need to know how to use these workstation utilities to establish and maintain a network printing environment that is easy for your users and transparent to your applications.

DEFINING A PRINTING ENVIRONMENT

The first task a network administrator needs to perform when establishing a network printing environment is to define the printing needs supported by the network. Defining the printing environment involves the following steps:

- Define the printing requirements of each user's applications.
- Determine printer locations and types of attachment.
- Define names for all printers and print queues.

In this section, you will learn about each of these steps and how to apply them to defining a network printer environment for your organization by filling out a print server definition form.

DEFINING PRINTER REQUIREMENTS

The first step in defining a printing environment is to identify the number and types of network printers and print servers that will be needed. You start by analyzing the requirements of each user's application software and printing needs. Because a print server can support up to 16 printers, one print server is usually sufficient for most organizations. A sample print server definition form is shown in Figure 10-9. Using the printer definition form will help you define your printer needs by documenting each printer attached to a single print server. A separate print server definition form should be filled out for each print server. In the top part of the form, enter the name of the print server and the file servers that will contain the print queues. Identify the print server as dedicated or nondedicated and enter the name of the file server where a nondedicated print server will be located.

Try to keep the printing system as simple as possible by standardizing the make and model of printer to be used for dot-matrix, laser, and ink-jet printer types. The print server definition form includes columns in which you identify the model and type along with the users and applications for each network printer that will be attached to a print server.

Figure 10-9

Sample print server definition form

Print Server Definition Form

Prepared by: _Ted Simpson_   Date: _____

Organization: _Sample Company_

Print server name: _PCS-PSERVER_   Dedicated: ____ Nondedicated: _X_
                                                     File server: _CTS_HOST_

File servers serviced: _CTS_HOST_

	Printer Name	Printer Type	Make/Model	Attachment Type	Location	Users/Applications	Print Queue Name
0		Laser	HP LaserJet III compatible			business dept. documents	
1		Dot Matrix	Epson LQ1070			business dept. accounting	
2		Color Ink-Jet	Canon BJC-829			everyone/presentations	
3		Laser	HP LaserJet III compatible			sales dept./orders, documents	
4		Dot Matrix	Panasonic KX-P1624			sales dept./invoices	
5		Dot Matrix	Panasonic KX-P1624			sales dept./reports	

Let's look at an example of a print server definition for the business and sales departments of an organization. The business department uses a spreadsheet program to manage budget data along with a payroll and general ledger accounting system. The department needs a dot-matrix printer for local printing of spreadsheet data and a high-speed 24-pin dot-matrix printer that has a wide carriage to print accounting reports and payroll checks. The business department users also need access to a laser printer for output of graphs and word processing documents for presentation purposes. Each member of the sales department uses a personal computer to enter orders and produce price quotations. Price quotations need to be printed on company stationery. What is needed is a laser printer with stationery in tray 1 and standard paper in tray 2. Invoices and packing slips are printed on one dot-matrix printer that has invoice forms always mounted while sales reports are printed on a second dot-matrix printer that has standard tractor-feed paper. The sales department has new presentation software that allows users to produce attractive transparencies for sales presentations. For these they need access to a color printer.

From the preceding information, a print server definition form can be filled in, as shown in Figure 10-9. It defines one print server, named PCS_PSERVER, that controls six printers. As you can see on the form, the business department needs two printers on the network, a dot-matrix printer for accounting and spreadsheet applications and a laser printer for word processing documents and graphs. Three printers have been defined to meet the printing needs of the sales department: a laser printer for printing price quotations and two dot-matrix printers for invoices and sales reports. With two dot-matrix printers, users won't need to change back and forth between invoice forms and standard paper for reports. In addition, users in both the sales and business departments need to send presentation output and graphs to a color ink-jet printer.

PRINTER LOCATION AND ATTACHMENT

Once printer requirements are defined, the next consideration is the location of each printer—including how it will be attached to the network. Use the following guidelines when planning locations and attachment methods for printers:

- Determine if the printer is to be locally attached to the print server, remotely attached to a workstation, or directly attached to the network.

- Place the printer close to the user who is responsible for it.

- Identify the printer port where each printer will be attached.

- Avoid attaching remote printers to workstations running applications that might conflict with the remote printer software. Use a direct attachment option if you are unable to find a workstation that will not conflict with the remote printer software.

Figure 10-10

Sample printer attachments

Printer Server Definition Form

Prepared by: _Ted Simpson_   **Date:** _____

Organization: _Sample Company_

Print server name: _PCS-PSERVER_   **Dedicated:** ___   **Nondedicated:** _X_

File server: _CTS_HOST_

File servers serviced: _CTS_HOST_
_____

	Printer Name	Printer Type	Make/Model	Attachment Type	Location	Users/Applications	Print Queue Name
0		Laser	HP LaserJet III compatible	remote LPT1	business dept. accounting office	bus dept. documents	
1		Dot Matrix	Epson LQ1070	remote LPT1	business dept. payroll office	bus dept. accounting	
2		Color Ink-Jet	Canon BJC-829#	local LPT1	file server, room 100	everyone presentations	
3		Laser	HP LaserJet III compatible	remote LPT1	sales dept. office area	sales dept. orders/document	
4		Dot Matrix	Panasonic KX-P1624	remote COM1	sales dept. office area	sales dept. invoices	
5		Dot Matrix	Panasonic KX-P1624	remote LPT1	sales dept. office area	sales dept. reports	

Refer to Figure 10-10 and notice that in addition to the attachment type, the printer port used to connect the printer is also identified. You will need to know the printer port, the printer number, and attachment information when you use the NetWare PCONSOLE utility to define the printer definitions, described later in this chapter. Notice that the color ink-jet printer (the Canon BJC-829) is locally attached to the LPT1 port of the print server. Depending on the location of the print server computer, this can provide access to the printer to both sales and business department users. A local attachment also reduces network traffic and provides faster and more reliable access for graphics-oriented applications.

NAMING PRINTERS AND PRINT QUEUES

To keep your printing system as simple as possible, select printer and print queue names that allow you to identify the following printer information:

- Location
- Printer model
- Attachment method
- Printer number

One way to create meaningful printer names is to define one- to three-character codes for each of the printer information fields. Each printer name will consist of the codes for the four listed items separated by dashes (-). The printer name BUS-EPS850-R0, for example, identifies the Epson 850 dot-matrix printer that is located in the business department attached as remote printer number 0.

 Printer names can be a maximum of 47 characters and can contain any combination of ASCII characters including spaces and special characters.

Location

The printer location can be a three- to four-character field that identifies the name of the department or place where the printer is located. BUS, for example, can be used to identify a printer located in the business department; a room number, such as 209A, can be used to identify a printer located in a specific room or office. If a printer is moved, its name can be changed to identify its new location. Avoid using a user's name or workstation model to identify a printer. These labels often change and can leave the printer with a name that no longer identifies its location.

Printer model

A three- to five-character code representing the make or use of the printer can be included in its name to help you remember what type of printer output can be sent to this printer. INV, for example, can be used to represent the dot-matrix printer to which invoices are sent; EPS70 can be used to represent an Epson LQ-1070 dot-matrix printer that is available for general use.

Attachment and number

Include an attachment code—L for local, R for remote, or D for direct—along with the port and the number of the printer. The printer number value ranges from 0 to 15 and corresponds to the printer number assigned during configuration of the print server. The code L1, for example, identifies printer 1 as locally attached to the printer server; R2 identifies printer 2 as remotely attached to a port on a networked workstation.

Naming print queues

Print queue names should be the same as the printer name with the addition of the letter Q followed by the priority of the print queue. This allows two or more print queues to be assigned to the same printer. Q1 indicates the highest priority, Q2 the next priority, and so on.

Figure 10-11 shows the sample print server definition form complete with printer names written according to these guidelines. Notice that the color ink-jet printer has been assigned two print queues, which will allow high-priority jobs to be printed while normal jobs wait in the lower priority queue. If two printers use the same print queue, you can omit the printer number from the print queue name. If the business department, for example, has two laser printers, BUS–HP3–R0 and BUS–HP3–R6, assigned to the same print queue, the name of the print queue could be BUS–HP3–Q1.

Figure 10-11

Sample printer and queue names

Printer Server Definition Form

Prepared by: _Ted Simpson_   Date: _____

Organization: _Sample Company_

Print server name: _PCS-PSERVER_   Dedicated: ___   Nondedicated: _X_
File server: _CTS_HOST_

File servers serviced: _CTS_HOST_
_____

	Printer Name	Make/Model	Attachment Type	Location	Users/Applications	Print Queue Name
0	BUS-HP3-R0	HP LaserJet III compatible	Remote LPT1	bus dept.	bus dept. documents	BUS-HP3-R0-Q1
1	BUS-LQ1070-R1	Epson LQ1070	Remote LPT1	bus dept.	bus dept. accounting	BUS-LQ1070-R1-Q1
2	SRV-BJC829-L2	Canon BJC-829	Local LPT1	file server	everyone presentations	SRV-BJC820-R2-Q1 /SRV-BJC820-R2-Q2
3	SAL-HP3-R3	HP LaserJet III compatible	Remote LPT1	sales dept.	sales dept. orders/document	SAL-HP3-R3-Q1
4	SAL-INV-R4	Panasonic KX-P1624	Remote COM1	sales dept.	sales dept. invoices	SAL-INV-R4-Q1
5	SAL-RPT-R5	Panasonic KX-P1624	Remote LPT1	sales dept.	sales dept. reports	SAL-RPT-R5Q1

Print queue names can be a maximum of 47 characters. Unlike printer names, print queue names cannot include spaces, commas, slashes, colons, semicolons, question marks, plus signs, equal signs, greater or less than symbols, or square brackets.

After you define printer names when creating print queues and the print server, it is a good idea to label each physical printer with its assigned name. This will make it easier for both the network administrator and users to identify them.

SETTING UP THE PRINTING ENVIRONMENT

PCONSOLE is the main NetWare menu utility used by network administrators, operators, and users to manage the network printing environment. The network administrator uses PCONSOLE to establish and maintain the network printing environment. Print queue operators and print server operators use it to work with their assigned print queues and servers. Users can also utilize PCONSOLE to view, modify, or remove jobs they have placed in a print queue and determine the length of time before a job will print by viewing its sequence number in the print queue.

In this section, you will learn how to use the PCONSOLE utility to perform the following tasks:

- Create print queues.
- Define print queue users and operators.
- Create the print server.
- Define and configure the printers.
- Assign print queues to each printer.
- Identify print server operators.

CREATING PRINT QUEUES

Only the SUPERVISOR or supervisor equivalent user can access PCONSOLE to create new print queues. To create a print queue, log in with a username that has supervisor equivalency and start the PCONSOLE menu utility. PCONSOLE will display the Available Options menu shown in Figure 10-12. To work with print queues, highlight the Print Queue Information option and press [Enter]. This displays a window showing all existing print queues, as shown in Figure 10-13.

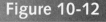

Figure 10-12

PCONSOLE Available Options menu

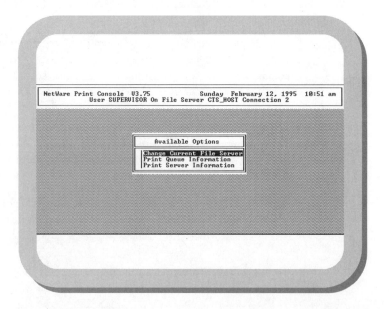

Figure 10-13

PCONSOLE Print
Queue window

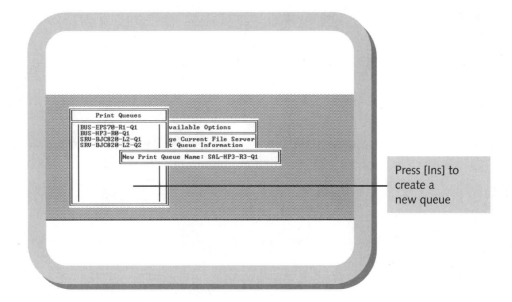

Press [Ins] to
create a
new queue

To create a new print queue, press the Ins key and enter the name of the print
queue. After you press [Enter,] the new print queue name will appear in the Print
Queues window. To change the name of an existing print queue, highlight the
print queue name and press the F3 key. You can then use the Backspace key to
erase the existing name and enter the new name. Finally, to delete an existing print
queue, highlight its name and press the Del key. The print queue will be deleted
after you press [Enter] and respond with a Yes to the delete print queue confirmation window.

DEFINING PRINT QUEUE USERS AND OPERATORS

By default, the group EVERYONE is a user of each print queue and SUPERVISOR
is the print queue operator. To make another user a print queue operator of a print
queue, highlight the name of the print queue and press [Enter] to display the Print
Queue Information menu shown in Figure 10-14. Use the Current Print Job Entries
option to display and manage jobs that are currently in the selected print queue. The
Current Queue Status option allows the print queue operator to take the print queue
off-line, which will prevent users or print servers from accessing it. The Print Queue
ID option can be used to display the name of the SYS:SYSTEM subdirectory that is
used to store print jobs for this print queue.

To make a user an operator of the selected print queue, highlight the Queue
Operators option and press [Enter] to display a window listing existing queue operators. (Initially SUPERVISOR will be the only operator of a new print queue.) To
add a user to the print queue operator window, press [Ins] and highlight the username
from the Queue Operator Candidates window. When you press [Enter], the selected
username will be added to the Queue Operators window. Pressing the Esc key will
then return you to the Print Queue Information menu.

Figure 10-14

Print Queue
Information menu

By default, all users can place jobs in newly created print queues. In certain cases, however, you might want to restrict printer access to a certain user or group of users. The Queue Users option allows the network administrator to limit which users can place jobs in a specified print queue. To restrict the selected print queue, first select the Queue Users option to display a window showing all existing print queue users. Initially this window will show the group EVERYONE as the current user of the print queue. To restrict the selected print queue, you first need to remove the group EVERYONE by highlighting the group's name and pressing the Del key. After you confirm the deletion, the group EVERYONE is removed from the Queue Users window. After the group EVERYONE has been removed as a user of the print queue, not even the SUPERVISOR will be able to send output to the print queue. To allow specified users and groups to place jobs in the print queue, press the Ins key to display the Queue User Candidates window and then use the F5 key to mark the names of the users and groups you want added as users of the selected print queue. When you press [Enter], any selected groups and usernames will be included in the Queue Users window. You can now use the Esc key to return to the Print Queues Information window.

CREATING THE PRINT SERVER DEFINITION

Before you can run the print server software (PSERVER.NLM or PSERVER.EXE), you need to use PCONSOLE to create a configuration file that will define each printer's name, location, port, and associated print queues. To create a print server definition, select the Print Server Information option from the PCONSOLE Available Options menu and press [Enter]. The Print Servers window, showing any existing print servers, will be displayed. To create a new print server definition, simply press the Ins key and enter the name for the new print server definition file.

Print server definition filenames can be a maximum of 47 characters and cannot include spaces, commas, slashes, colons, semicolons, question marks, plus signs, equal signs, greater or less than symbols, or square brackets.

If you want to change the name of an existing print server definition, highlight the current name and press [F3]. You can then use the Backspace key to erase the existing name and then re-enter the new name. To delete a print server definition, highlight the name of the print server to be deleted and press the Del key.

DEFINING AND CONFIGURING THE PRINTERS

After the print server definition has been created, the network administrator configures the printers by providing the name, location, and port for each printer that will be controlled by the print server. To use PCONSOLE to configure the printers, first highlight the print server in the Print Servers window and press [Enter] to display the Print Server Information menu shown in Figure 10-15.

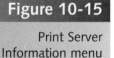

Figure 10-15

Print Server Information menu

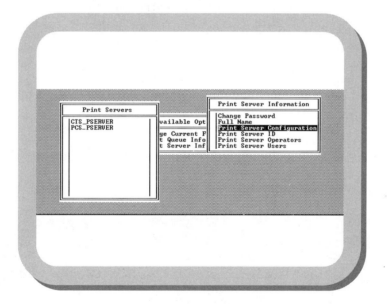

Each print server can be assigned a password and full name. The password prevents an unauthorized operator from loading the print server on a computer. Use the Full Name option to assign a longer name to the print server for documentation purposes. Use the Print Server Operators and Print Server Users options to assign operators and users control of the printer attached to the print server. Users who will need to control printers and respond to problems should be made print server operators.

To configure printers, select the Print Server Configuration option and press [Enter] to display the Print Server Configuration menu shown in Figure 10-16.

Figure 10-16

Print Server
Configuration menu

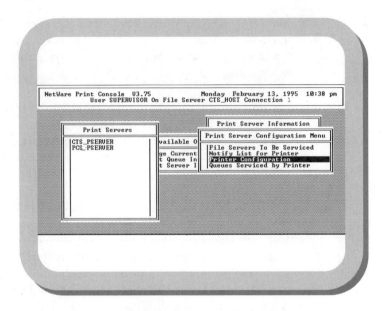

To define the configuration for each network printer, select the Printer Configuration option and press [Enter] to display the Configured Printers window shown in Figure 10-17.

Figure 10-17

Configured Printers
window

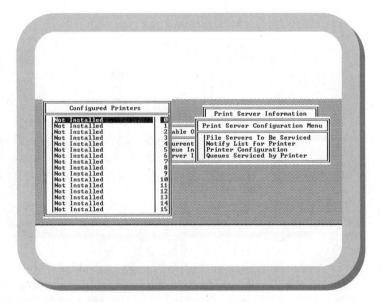

Notice that printers are numbered from 0 to 15 and that initially all printers are marked as Not Installed. To define a printer, highlight the printer number you want to define and press [Enter] to display the printer configuration window shown in Figure 10-18.

Figure 10-18

Printer configuration
window

After entering the name you plan to use for this printer, press [Enter] to advance to the Type field and press [Enter] to display the "Printer types" window shown in Figure 10-19.

Figure 10-19

Printer types
window

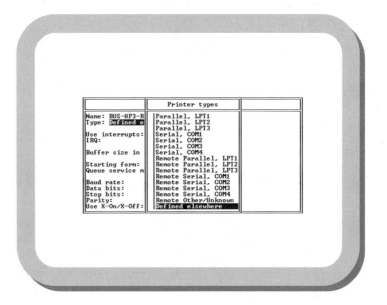

To configure a local printer attached to the LPT port of the print server computer, select the Parallel LPT1 option from the "Printer Types" window and press [Enter]. After selecting the printer type, PCONSOLE will display the printer configuration window shown in Figure 10-20. When all printers have been defined, you can use the Esc key to return to the Print Server Configuration Menu window and continue with the print server configuration.

Figure 10-20

Default remote
printer configuration

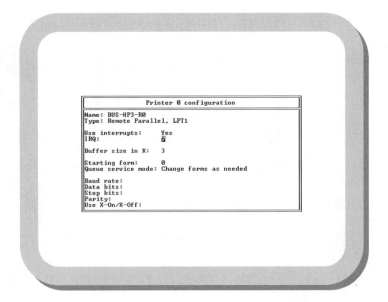

The IRQ field identifies the interrupt that will be used by the remote printer. As described in Chapter 3, interrupts are used to notify the computer's processor that a device or port needs attention. Notice that hardware interrupt 7 is used by default for a remote printer port. Make sure that the printer port of the computer you are using to control the remote printer uses interrupt 7. Because DOS does not require a printer port to use interrupt 7, some lower-cost printer ports do not provide this interrupt and will run very slowly or intermittently in this configuration. A local parallel printer does not require an interrupt, allowing print servers that run on a file server to use the printer interrupt for other devices such as network cards.

Figure 10-21

Local printer
configuration

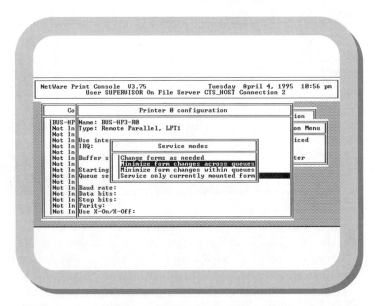

The "Buffer size" field may be used to change the amount of memory used to store output to the selected printer. While the default of 3K is sufficient for most printers, some network administrators increase this value to 5K on printers that will be used to print large print jobs. In addition to the interrupt and buffer settings, the "Queue service mode" field can be used to select the way print jobs with different form types are printed. If you will be using different form types in this printer, highlight this field and press [Enter] to display the possible queue service modes shown in Figure 10-21. The option to "Minimize form changes within queue" will reduce the number of times you will have to change paper in the printer by causing the print server to print all forms of the same type no matter what sequence has been placed in the print queue.

It is important to designate a user as a print server operator. This person will be responsible for receiving messages from printers in his or her work area and can respond to such problems as a printer that is jammed or out of paper. To have a user notified when there is a printer problem, you need to add that user to the notification list for each of the printers in his or her charge.

To add a user to the notification list for a printer, select the Notify List for Printer option from the Print Server Configuration Menu to display a window listing all defined printers. Highlight the target printer and press [Enter]. A window is displayed, which lists the users who will be notified about printer problems. Press the Ins key to display the Notify Candidates window, which lists all available users and groups on the system. You can then use the F5 key to highlight the names of users you want notified and press [Enter] to display the Notify Intervals window shown in Figure 10-22. To accept the default values of 30 seconds until the first message is issued and then 60 seconds between messages, press [Esc] and then press [Enter] to save the changes. The selected usernames will now be added to the notify list for this printer. After updating the notify list for any additional printers, press [Esc] to return to the Print Server Configuration menu.

Figure 10-22

Adding a user to a printer's notification list

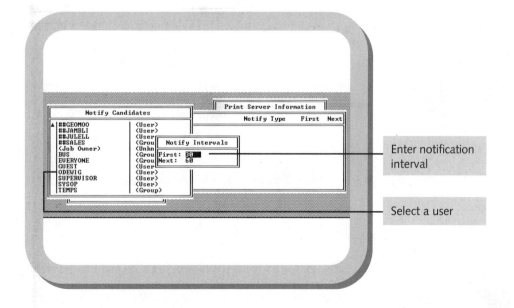

ASSIGNING PRINT QUEUES

Assigning print queues to the printers you have defined is one of the most important steps in configuring your print server because it ties each printer to its corresponding print queue or queues. A common error made by many network administrators hurrying to complete the setup of the printing environment is forgetting to perform this step. To configure a printer to service a print queue, select the Queues Serviced by Printer option from the Print Server Configuration Menu to display a list of all defined printers. Highlight the target printer and press [Enter] to display a window showing any existing print queues that have been assigned to this printer. To add a print queue to be serviced by this printer, press the Ins key to display the Available Queues window, highlight the name of the print queue to be serviced, and press [Enter].

PCONSOLE will then request the print queue priority, as shown in Figure 10-23. Enter priority 1 for your first print queue. This designates the highest level priority. Additional print queues assigned to this printer can be given lower priority settings from 2 on. After you assign a print queue to each printer, your basic print server configuration is complete and you can press [Esc] until you return to the Print Server Information window.

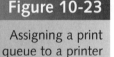

Figure 10-23

Assigning a print
queue to a printer

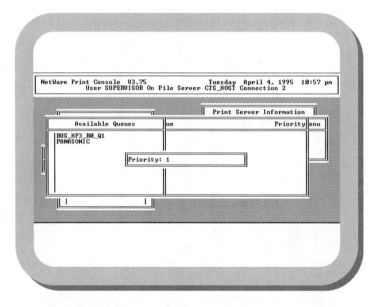

IDENTIFYING PRINT SERVER OPERATORS

The last step in completing a basic print server configuration is assigning print server operators and users. In most cases, the default group EVERYONE will be left to designate print server users. The default print server operator is the SUPERVISOR user. If you add other users to the notification list for printers, however, they should be assigned as print server operators. Print server operators can stop and restart printers in the event of a paper jam or other printing problem. To assign additional print server operators, select the Print Server Operators option from the Print Server Information menu to display a list of the existing print server operators. Initially only the SUPERVISOR user will appear as a print server operator. To add more users, simply press the Ins key to display the Print Server Operator Candidates window. You can then use the F5 key to highlight the names of any users you want to make print server operators and press [Enter] to add the selected users to the Print Server Operators window. After all print server operators are defined, press [Esc] to return to the Print Server Information menu. The printer environment should now be ready for testing. Use the [Alt][F10] key combination to exit the PCONSOLE utility and return to the DOS prompt.

TESTING THE PRINTING ENVIRONMENT

After the printing environment has been established, it is important to test each remote and local printer by placing a job in the appropriate print queue and verifying that it is printed correctly. Testing can be completed by using the following four steps:

- Load the print server.
- Load the remote printing software on each workstation that controls a network printer.
- Place a test job in each print queue.
- Monitor printing results.

LOADING THE PRINT SERVER

The print server software can be run either on a dedicated workstation or from the file server. In most cases, unless the file server is overloaded, the primary print server is run on the file server by loading the PSERVER.NLM NetWare Loadable Module on the file server console. This method is less expensive because it does not tie up another computer system. Because the print queues are on the same machine as the print server, this method also reduces the number of packets that need to be sent over the LAN cable system. Loading the print server on a dedicated computer is necessary if the file server is overloaded or if you need to use more than one print server on the network. In this section, you will learn the techniques necessary to load the print server software on either the file server console or a dedicated computer.

Loading PSERVER on the file server

The SYS:SYSTEM directory contains PSERVER.NLM, a NetWare Loadable Module version of the print server software. To load and run this NLM on your server computer you will need first to have the exact name and password of the print server you want to load. Next, go to the file server console and, if necessary, use the Alt and Esc keys to switch to the console screen. From the colon (:) console prompt enter the command LOAD PSERVER *name*, replacing *name* with the exact name of the print server definition file you created with the PCONSOLE utility. If you cannot remember the exact name of the print server, you can retrieve it by returning to your workstation and using the PCONSOLE utility to view the print server. If you make a typing error or do not enter the exact name, NetWare will ask you to enter a password for the print server. As with usernames, this is intended to make it more difficult to guess a password or print server name.

After loading several support modules, NetWare will start the print server program and display the print server information screen for up to eight printers at a time, as shown in Figure 10-24. You can press the spacebar to view the status of the next eight printers.

Figure 10-24

Print server
information screen

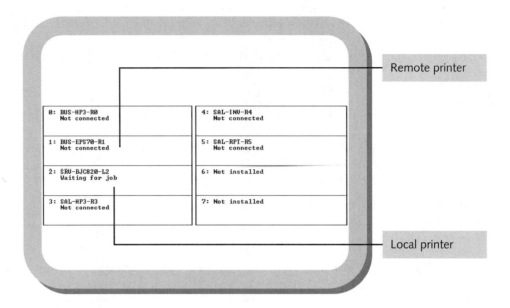

Remote printer

```
0:  BUS-HP3-R0              4:  SAL-INU-R4
    Not connected              Not connected

1:  BUS-EPS70-R1           5:  SAL-RPT-R5
    Not connected              Not connected

2:  SRU-BJC820-L2          6:  Not installed
    Waiting for job

3:  SAL-HP3-R3             7:  Not installed
    Not connected
```

Local printer

Loading PSERVER on a dedicated workstation

To run PSERVER.EXE on a workstation, you need to be certain the workstation computer uses at least an 80286 processor with 640 Kbytes of RAM and has available printer ports and a network interface card. More memory, a color VGA monitor, and a hard disk are all optional features that are not needed by the print server software. The PSERVER.EXE program needs to use the entire computer system—making it completely dedicated to the print server function and unable to run other software while the print server is running. To load and run the PSERVER.EXE software on a dedicated print server, you will first need to modify the NET.CFG file on the computer that is to be the dedicated print server by adding the following statement: SPX Connections = 60. This statement is necessary because the print server must have multiple connections open to each printer and print queue. When this step is completed, reboot the computer to add the extra connection space to the NetWare shell. You can then log in to the network using any username, including GUEST, and enter the command PSERVER *name*, where *name* is the exact name of the print server and press [Enter]. When the print server software is loaded, it will display the printer information screen for up to eight printers at a time. (See Figure 10-24.)

LOADING REMOTE PRINTING SOFTWARE

The second step in implementing network printing is to load the remote printer TSR software on each workstation that will be supporting a remote network printer and supply it with the printer number you defined in the print server configuration. The RPRINTER.EXE program, which is stored in the SYS:PUBLIC directory, is the terminate and stay resident software that, when loaded on the workstation and supplied with the name of the print server and a printer number, will remain in memory and maintain the connection between the workstation's printer and the specified printer definition of the print server. The print server will then be able to take output from the print queue assigned to that printer and send it to the RPRINTER program. The RPRINTER program "listens" for output from the print server and prints the data it receives on the workstation's attached printer. RPRINTER also displays on the print server messages such as "Out of Paper" or "Printer Off-line." Once RPRINTER is loaded on the workstation it will continue to operate whether or not a user is logged in from that workstation. RPRINTER can be started either manually or with a command in a workstation's AUTOEXEC.BAT file.

Notice in Figure 10-24 that the status of all the remote printers is "Not Connected." The status of printer 2, which is a local printer attached to the file server computer, is "Waiting for job." In order to connect the remote printers to the print server it is necessary to load the remote printer software at each workstation that supports a remote printer.

Running RPRINTER interactively

When the RPRINTER program is run without any options, it will prompt the operator to supply the name of the print server and printer to be attached. To start the RPRINTER program and manually attach the current workstation to a remote printer, you first need to log in to the file server from the workstation on which you want to load RPRINTER. You can type any username, including GUEST, that has rights to run programs from the SYS:PUBLIC directory. After logging in, enter the command RPRINTER. Pressing [Enter] displays the Available Print Servers window, which lists all print servers that are currently running on the network. Highlight the target print server. Pressing [Enter] displays the Printer Names and Numbers window, which lists all remote printers that have not yet been assigned to a workstation. (See Figure 10-25.)

Figure 10-25

Attaching a remote printer with RPRINTER

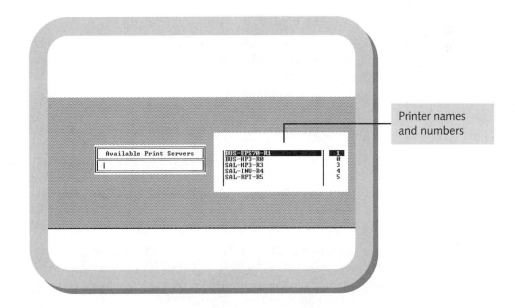

Printer names and numbers

It is very important to select the correct printer number for the type of printer that is attached to the workstation in order for the output from the print queue associated with that printer to be properly printed. If your workstation has a laser printer attached to it, for example, and you select a printer number that is associated with a dot-matrix print queue, dot-matrix print jobs will be sent to the laser printer, causing output to be scrambled.

After you select a remote printer number, RPRINTER displays on the workstation screen a message indicating that the remote printer is installed. Once RPRINTER is loaded into the memory of the workstation, the status of selected printer number on the print server changes to "Waiting for job."

Loading RPRINTER from a batch file

Normally you would not want to rely on your users to load the RPRINTER program correctly each time they boot their workstations. To load RPRINTER automatically you will want to run it from the AUTOEXEC.BAT file on the workstation whenever the workstation is booted. The syntax of the RPRINTER command is:

> **RPRINTER** *printserver* *printernumber* *[/R]*

To use the command in a batch file, replace *printserver* with the name of a currently running print server to which you want to attach. Replace *printernumber* with the number of the remote printer defined in the specified print server's configuration for this network printer. You can include the –R option to remove RPRINTER from the workstation's memory.

To make the system even easier to use, you will want RPRINTER to be loaded without requiring the workstation to be logged in to the file server. To do this you will need to copy the following files from the SYS:PUBLIC directory either to the workstation's local hard drive or to a subdirectory of the SYS:LOGIN directory:

- IBM$RUN.OVL
- RPRINTER.EXE
- RPRINTER.HLP
- RPRINT$$.EXE
- SYS$HELP.DAT
- SYS$MSG.DAT
- SYS$ERR.DAT

A disadvantage of this method is the time required to copy these files to the local hard drive of each workstation running RPRINTER. Another disadvantage of running RPRINTER from the local hard disk is the extra time that is required to update the files on each workstation every time a new version of RPRINTER is released. (If past history is any indicator, this can occur quite often.)

To get around this problem you can create a subdirectory in the SYS:LOGIN directory called RPRINTER and copy the required files into that subdirectory. Because a workstation does not need to be logged in to access the SYS:LOGIN directory, you can simply modify the STARTNET batch file of each workstation so that it changes to the SYS:LOGIN\RPRINTER directory to run the RPRINTER software. To support a remote printer on a NetWare v3.12 client workstation, modify the STARTNET batch file by adding the highlighted statements as shown below:

```
@ECHO OFF
C:
CD \NWCLIENT
SET NWLANGUAGE=ENGLISH
LSL
SMC8000.COM
IPXODI
VLM
F:
CD \RPRINTER
RPRINTER PCS_PSERVER 0
CD \
LOGIN
```

PLACING JOBS IN PRINT QUEUES

Once all the printing components are connected, the next task is to test the printing system by placing jobs in each of the print queues and verifying that they are properly printed. There are four major ways in which jobs can be placed in a print queue for printing:

- Use the PCONSOLE program to insert an ASCII text file into the print queue.

- Use the NPRINT command to transfer an ASCII text file directly to a print queue.

- Use the CAPTURE command to redirect application output to the print queue.

- Use a software application to print directly to the NetWare print queue.

The method of printing directly from an application depends on the software you are using. As a CNA you will only be required to know how to use the first three methods of placing jobs in a print queue. In this section you will learn how to use the PCONSOLE menu utility along with the CAPTURE and PRINT commands to place jobs in print queues.

Using PCONSOLE to insert a job in a print queue

The PCONSOLE utility can be used to place ASCII text files in a print queue. This can be useful if you are working with PCONSOLE and need to print the contents of an ASCII documentation file, such as a README file on a disk, or to print a copy of a DOS batch file. To place a copy of an ASCII text file into a print queue, you need to start PCONSOLE and then select the Print Queue Information option from the Available Options menu. The Print Queue window listing all print queues on the current file server is displayed. Highlight the name of a print queue and press [Enter] to display the Print Queue Information menu. Next select Current Print Job Entries to display a window showing the name and description of any print jobs currently in the print queue. To add a job to the print queue, press the Ins key to display the Select Directory to Print From window.

You can now use either the Ins key to select each component of the path leading to the subdirectory containing the ASCII file, or else type the complete path to the directory and press [Enter]. After you have entered a valid path, PCONSOLE will display the names of all files in the selected directory. You can then highlight the name of the file you want to place in the print queue. Pressing [Enter] displays the Print Job Configuration window, which contains a list of possible print configurations to be used for this file. In Chapter 11, you will learn how to create new print job configurations containing customized parameters. To use the standard parameters for this print job, highlight PCONSOLE Defaults and press [Enter]. PCONSOLE then displays the New Print Job to Be Submitted window containing the default parameters, as shown in Figure 10-26.

Figure 10-26

Print job parameters window

This window allows you to change several parameters, including: the number of copies, how to handle form feeds, the form type, and whether a banner page containing your username is to be printed prior to the job. To suppress printing a banner, change the "Print banner" field from a Yes to a No. You can also use this screen to defer the printing until a specified date and time. This can be handy if you want to print a large job at some later time when the printer isn't being used heavily. The "File contents" field defaults to "Byte stream," telling the print server to send each character as it is to the printer. The other option is Text format, which causes the print server to look for tab codes and convert each tab code it finds to the number of spaces specified. Because most of today's printers convert the codes themselves, the Text option is usually not used.

After making any changes to the defaults, press [Esc] and then choose Yes at the Save Changes prompt to save the job on the print queue using the parameters specified. The new job should now appear in the print job entries window followed by the Ready status. If everything is working correctly, within several seconds the print server will find the job in the print queue and start sending it. When this happens you will see the status change from Ready to Active. In addition, on the print server console the message for the printer in question changes from "Waiting for job" to "Printing Job *filename*." You can use the Esc key to return to a previous menu or else use the Alt and F10 keys to exit the PCONSOLE utility.

Using NPRINT to transfer an ASCII file directly to a print queue

Another method that is often faster than PCONSOLE is to use the NPRINT command to transfer an ASCII text file directly to the specified print queue. The NPRINT command is especially useful for printing copies of README files that are often included on program disks.

 Because NPRINT does not perform any file translation, the file you print must be in ASCII text format so that it can be displayed on the screen using the TYPE *filename* command.

The syntax of the NPRINT command is:

NPRINT *path\filename [options]*

Replace *path\filename* with the directory path leading to the specified filename to be printed. Replace *options* with one or more of the parameters shown in Figure 10-27. If, for example, you want to print the README file from the A: disk drive to the BUS_EPS850_R0 printer with no banner, with a form feed, in byte stream format, and then be notified when the printing is complete, you could enter a command similar to the following:

NPRINT A:README Q=BUS-EPS850-R0-Q1 NB FF NT NOTI

Figure 10-27

NPRINT command options

Parameter	Description
NOTI (notify)	Causes a message to be sent notifying the user who submitted the print job when the job has been printed. By default, the sending user will not be notified.
PS=*printserver*	Normally not needed when the print queue name and file server names are specified.
S=*fileserver*	Names the file server that contains the specified print queue. By default, the current file server's name is used.
Q=*queuename*	The name of the print queue in which you want the output placed.
J=*job configuration*	Specifying a specific PRINTCON job will cause the NPRINT command to get all unspecified parameters from the given print configuration job name.
F=*form* or ##	Specifies the type of form to be used. The default form type is 0. Form types 0–9 may be specified. It is the network administrator's responsibility to identify the type of paper to be used with each form type.
C=*n* (copies)	Specifies the number of copies of the job to be placed in the print queue.
T(tabs)	Specifies the number of spaces to leave for each tab code encountered. The default is eight spaces per tab code.
NT (no tabs)	Specifies that "Byte stream" output format is to be used with no tab codes expanded.
NB (no banner)	Specifies that no banner page is to be printed. By default a banner page will be printed.
NAM=*name*	Specifies the name to appear in the upper part of the banner page. The default is the username.
B=*bannername*	Specifies the name to appear in the bottom part of the banner page. By default the file name is used.
FF (form feed)	By default, this option is enabled. Causes the printer to eject a page after printing the file listing.
NFF (no form feed)	Disables the form feed after the file has printed. Output from the next print job will then start printing on the same page.
D (delete)	Causes the original file to be deleted after it has been printed. By default, the original text file is not deleted after printing.

Use CAPTURE to redirect application output to a print queue

Although the NPRINT command is useful for printing an existing ASCII text file directly to the network printer without viewing it on the screen, it cannot redirect printer output coming from an application package into a print queue. If you are working with an application that does not know about NetWare print queues and you want its output to be printed on a network printer, you need to use the CAPTURE command to redirect the output from the application directly to the print queue.

An important part of using the CAPTURE command is determining when the application has finished its output so the print job can be made available to the print server. There are three ways in which you can have the CAPTURE command determine when a print job is complete and is ready for printing:

- Timeout

- End the application

- End the capture

The timeout method involves establishing a time value that tells the CAPTURE command how many seconds of inactivity to allow before the application is assumed to be finished printing. If you set a timeout value of 7 sec., for example, and then use the spreadsheet program to print a balance sheet, 7 sec. after the spreadsheet program has finished printing the print job will be closed and made available to the print server. The problem with the timeout system is that some applications pause the printing for more than several seconds while they perform calculations or graphics manipulation. When this happens, the output can be separated into two different print jobs, resulting in a broken printout. If you find that your print jobs are broken up on separate pages, increase the number of seconds in the timeout factor.

Another method of ending a print job is to wait for the application to exit before releasing the print job to the print server. In this method, if for example, you use the spreadsheet software to print both a balance sheet and budget reports, you would not receive any printouts until after you exit the spreadsheet program. When the spreadsheet program ends, the print job containing both reports is sent to the print server and printed. This method is referred to as AUTOENDCAP.

The third method of ending a print job is to end the capture function by using the ENDCAP program or logging out of the file server. This method is referred to as NOAUTOENDCAP, and is useful if you want to hold output from all applications until the user issues the ENDCAP command or logs out of the file server. The CAPTURE command syntax is CAPTURE [*options*]. If no options are specified, the CAPTURE command attempts to send output to the default print queue specified in the PRINTCON job or SPOOL command using the default parameters described below. You can replace *options* with one or more of the parameters listed in Figure 10-27 or any of the special CAPTURE parameters described in Figure 10-28. You can, for example, enter the following CAPTURE command to redirect output from the LPT1 port to a laser printer print queue using a timeout of 5 sec., printing a banner page containing the name LESLIE on the top half and BUS_REPORT on the lower half, in byte stream format, with an automatic form feed at the end of the printout, and also notify the user upon completion of the print job:

```
CAPTURE Q=BUS-EPS70-R1-Q1 TI=5 NAM=LESLIE B=REPORT NT FF NOTI
```

Figure 10-28

CAPTURE command
options

Parameter	Description
SH (show)	Displays the current capture status of the printer ports.
TI=*n* (timeout)	Determines when the application is done processing a print job based on no printed output being sent in the specified time period. For example, TI=5 tells the system that the print job is complete if no output is received in a 5-sec. period.
A (autoendcap)	By default, if no timeout is specified, the job will be ready for printing when the application ends. For example, you might print three spreadsheets and not receive any output until you exit the spreadsheet program, at which time all three printouts will be generated.
NA (no autoendcap)	Specifies that no output will be released for printing until the user either logs out or issues the ENDCAP command to end the capture settings.
L=*n* (local)	Specifies the number of the LPT port to be re-routed to the print queue. By default, LPT1 is redirected.
CR=*path* (create)	Creates a file in the specified path that will contain the output in printer format. You can then later use the NPRINT command to print the file, or you might want to include it with a document for documentation or training purposes.
K (keep)	Specifies that the job should be kept on the print queue in the event the workstation crashes before the output is complete. If you do not include the Keep parameter and the workstation "crashes" during the capture process, the file server will discard the data it has received.

To check the capture status of the printer ports, use the CAPTURE SH command, as illustrated in Figure 10-29. Any output sent to the LPT1 port will now be redirected to the BUS-EPS70-R1-Q1 print queue. The screen in Figure 10-29 also shows an example of testing printer redirection by using the DOS TYPE command to send output to the print queue through the LPT1 port.

Figure 10-29

Sample CAPTURE
command

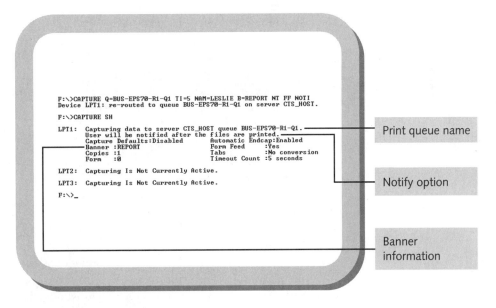

Using ENDCAP

The ENDCAP command is used to return an output port back to the local printer. Its syntax is ENDCAP [L=*n*] [ALL]. Replace *n* with the number of the printer port you want to return to local control. Use the **ALL** option to return all LPT ports to local control. If you issue the ENDCAP command with no parameters, the default is L=1. Suppose, for example, you issue a CAPTURE command to redirect output from your workstation's LPT1 port to a laser printer. After sending the print job, you want to continue working with the dot-matrix printer attached to the LPT1 port of your workstation. To end the capture of the LPT printer output to the laser printer and return to using your local dot-matrix printer, issue the ENDCAP L=1 command. You can also issue ENDCAP with no parameters to get the same result.

Using the SPOOL console command

If the CAPTURE or NPRINT commands are used and no print queue is defined, the output will be sent to the print queue defined in the user's default print job. If no print job file exists for the user, an error message will be displayed and the output will continue to be sent to the local printer. The SPOOL 0 command can be used from the file server console or included in the AUTOEXEC.NCF startup file to establish a default print queue for all users. The syntax of the SPOOL command is SPOOL 0 TO *queuename*. Replace *queuename* with the name of the print queue you want to use for your default network print queue. After the SPOOL command is issued, all users who do not have a default print job and issue a CAPTURE or NPRINT command without a Q=*queuename* parameter will have their output sent to the queuename specified in the SPOOL command.

The origin of the SPOOL command goes back to the earlier days of NetWare. Before print queues were invented, output was "spooled" to a printer number rather than a print queue. Because of this, by default both the CAPTURE and NPRINT commands still send their output to printer 0's spool file. The SPOOL command provides compatibility by allowing you to establish a default print queue for use by both the CAPTURE and NPRINT commands.

The concepts and utilities described in this chapter allow you to define and implement a basic shared printing environment for your network. Once the printing environment is operating correctly, you will want to customize or tune the printing environment to meet the needs of your users and applications. In Chapter 11 you will learn how to customize and control the network printing environment.

CHAPTER SUMMARY

An important task of the network administrator is establishing and maintaining a network printing environment that will provide users with access to a variety of printers. As a CNA, you will be expected to know the printing concepts and utilities described in this chapter and be able to implement and maintain a NetWare printing environment consisting of print queues, a print server, printers, and workstations. A print queue is a subdirectory of the SYS:SYSTEM directory that is used to hold print jobs until the printer is ready to print them. A print server is the software component that controls printing by taking print jobs from the queues and sending them to network printers. The NetWare v3.1x print server consists of a configuration file that defines the print server's printing environment along with two print server programs.

PSERVER.EXE is used when you want a print server to run on a dedicated computer. PSERVER.NLM runs on the file server computer and allows you to use that computer as both a file server and print server. A NetWare v3.1x print server can control up to 16 printers, of which five can be locally attached to the computer running the print server software. The other printers are defined as remote printers and are attached to network workstations running Novell's RPRINTER software.

The first task in establishing the printer environment is defining the printing requirements for each user's applications, determining the types and number of printers necessary to meet these requirements, determining the location of the printers on the network and whether they will be locally attached to the print server or remotely attached to printer ports on the workstations. When printers are attached to the workstations, it is necessary to run a terminate and stay resident program called RPRINTER. Because RPRINTER does not work well with all applications and system software environments, it is sometimes necessary to attach a printer directly to the network by obtaining a special network interface option for the printer. The final step in defining the printer environment is developing a naming system for printer and print queues that will make it easy for you to identify the printer location, type of printer, and method of attachment.

After defining the printing environment, you install the printing system. The PCONSOLE menu utility performs most of the work involved with setting up and maintaining the NetWare printing system. To install the printing system initially, you need to use the PCONSOLE utility to create print queues, assign print queue users and operators, create the print server, define up to a maximum of 16 network printers that will be controlled by the print server, and then assign one or more print queues to each of the printers. Additionally, the printer configuration can include a notification list consisting of usernames to receive printer messages.

The final task in setting up the printing system is loading the PSERVER software either on the file server as a NetWare Loadable Module or on a dedicated workstation. After the print server is up and running, the remote printer software, RPRINTER, needs to be loaded on each workstation that will have a remote printer attached to it. To automate loading RPRINTER on each of the workstations, you need to copy the remote printing software into the SYS:LOGIN directory and modify the network startup batch file for each of the workstations to include the commands necessary to load RPRINTER and attach to the correct printer number.

Once the network printing system is operational, ASCII files that are in a printable format can be placed directly in a print queue using either the PCONSOLE menu utility or the NPRINT command. The CAPTURE command is commonly used to redirect the output of application programs from local LPT printer ports to specified print queues. Parameters added to the CAPTURE and NPRINT commands allow the user to specify such options as name of the print queue, form feeds, an optional banner page, number of copies, and a timeout value for the CAPTURE command to determine when an application has completed printing.

COMMAND SUMMARY

Command	Syntax	Definition
CAPTURE	*CAPTURE [options]*	Redirects output from an LPT printer port to the specified print queue. In addition, the CAPTURE command contains options to determine when printing is complete. Use either the timeout factor or AUTOENDCAP to release the print job when the application program ends. Other options include notification, form feed, banner, and tab codes as shown in Figure 10-28.
NPRINT	*NPRINT path\filename [options]*	Sends an existing ASCII text file directly to the specified print queue. Often used to print documentation and batch files. NPRINT uses many of the same options as used by the CAPTURE command. Figure 10-27 contains a detailed list of NCOPY options.
PCONSOLE	*PCONSOLE*	A menu utility for establishing, maintaining, and controlling the network printing environment. Use PCONSOLE to create print queues and print servers, to configure printers, and to add jobs to an existing print queue.
PSERVER	*PSERVER name*	Takes jobs from print queues and sends them to the network printers. The PSERVER.EXE program can be run on a dedicated workstation attached to the network. The PSERVER.NLM software is designed to run as a NetWare Loadable Module on the file server, eliminating the need to dedicate a computer to the print server function. The PSERVER software can support up to 16 printers, five of which can be locally attached to the computer running the print server software.
RPRINTER	*RPRINTER PS=printservername P= printernumber [-R]*	A TSR program loaded into the memory of a workstation that has a remote network printer attached to it. The RPRINTER program stays in memory and transfers print data from the print server to the attached network printer. In addition, RPRINTER sends printer messages to the print server, informing it of the printer's status.

Replace *printservername* with the name of the print server containing the remote printer definition. Replace *printernumber* with the number of the remote printer to which this workstation is to attach. Include the –R parameter to remove the remote printer software from the workstation memory.

KEY TERMS

local printer

print job

print queue

print server

remote printer

REVIEW QUESTIONS

1. The <u>Print Queue</u> is the network printing component that holds printed output until the printer is ready to print.
2. A(n) <u>Print Server</u> is software that actually makes network printing happen.
3. Up to <u>five</u> local printers can be attached to a print server.
4. On the lines below, list NetWare's two print server programs and their purposes.
   <u>local printers → attached to print server</u>
   <u>remote printers → attached to another networked station.</u>
5. A network printer attached to a workstation is called a(n) <u>remote</u> printer.
6. A print server can control a maximum of <u>16</u> printers.
7. A NetWare v3.1x print queue is actually a subdirectory of the <u>SYS:SYSTEM</u> directory.
8. On the lines below, list three ways of attaching a printer to the network.
   <u>Local attachment → print server</u>
   <u>Remote attachment → network station</u>
   <u>Direct attachment → network cable</u>

9. On the lines below, list the four items of information that should be included in a printer's name.

Location

Printer Model

Attachment Method

Printer Number

10. On the lines below, list in sequence the five steps required to set up a networked printing environment.

① Create Print Queues

② Define print queue users & operators

③ Create the print server

④ Define and configure the printers

⑤ Assign print queues to each printer

11. The ___PCONSOLE___ utility can be used to perform the necessary steps to set up the network printing environment.

12. By default ___all users___ can send jobs to a newly created print queue.

13. What option on the Print Server Information menu defines new printers on the print server?

_____

14. After information in the print server definition is changed, what must be done in order for the changes to be implemented?

15. _____ is a terminate and stay resident program that allows you to run application software, such as a word processing program, on the print server computer.

16. On the lines below, list two ways to run a print server.

Non-dedicated → runs from file server

Dedicated   → runs on standalone

17. What command needs to be placed in the NET.CFG file of a workstation computer when the PSERVER.EXE software is loaded on that computer?

SPX Connections = 60

18. Write an RPRINTER batch command that will attach the current workstation to printer number 1 on the print server named PCS_PSERVER.

RPRINTER PCS_PSERVER 1

19. On the lines below, list three ways jobs can be placed in a print queue.

PCONSOLE

NPRINT

CAPTURE

20. You can use the ___NPRINT___ command line utility to print a file called README from drive A to the BUS-EPS70-R1-Q1 print queue.

21. On the line below, write the command that will print the README file in question 20 with no banner, a form feed, eight spaces per tab code, and notify you when printing is complete.

    NPRINT A:README Q=BUS-EPS70-R1-Q1 NB T NOTI FF

22. On the line below, write a command to direct output from a spreadsheet program to the BUS-EPS70-R1-Q1 print queue with a banner containing your username on the top of the banner page and the message "BUDGET_REPORT" on the bottom. Include a form feed, no tabs, a time-out of 10 sec., and notification when printing is complete.

    CAPTURE Q=BUS-EPS70-R1-Q1 TI=10 NAM=SOADMIN B=BUDGET-REPORT ATFF NOTI

23. In the space below, describe the difference between AUTOENDCAP and timeout on the CAPTURE command.

    AUTOENDCAP → waits until program is exited then sends items to print server.

    Timeout → sends to print queue and waits until its time is up then stops.

24. On the line below, write a command to return all printer ports to the local workstation's printer.

    _____

25. The ___SPOOL___ console command can be used to establish a print queue as the default queue for the NPRINT and CAPTURE commands.

EXERCISES

Exercise 10-1: Creating Print Queues

In this exercise, you will need to log in with a username that has supervisor equivalency in order to establish print queues and print queue operators. If you do not have access to a supervisor equivalent name on your file server, your instructor will need to create the print queues for you.

1. Use PCONSOLE to create the following print queues. (Replace ## with your assigned student number.)

   ##REMOTE

   ##LOCAL

2. Make your student username an operator of each of the print queues.

3. Log out.

4. Log in using your assigned student username.

5. Enter a CAPTURE command to send output from your computer's LPT2 port to the ##REMOTE print queue using a timeout of 5 sec.

6. Enter a CAPTURE command to send output from your computer's LPT3 port to the ##LOCAL print queue using a timeout of 10 sec.

7. Enter the CAPTURE SH command to display the capture status of your computer.

8. Use the Print Scrn key to obtain a hardcopy of the current capture status.

9. Enter the ENDCAP command and then use the CAPTURE SH command to view your results. Record the capture status of each port on the lines below.

    LPT1: _____

    LPT2: _____

    LPT3: _____

10. Enter a command to return all ports to the local workstation. On the line below, record the command you use.

_____

Exercise 10-2: Placing Jobs in Print Queues

In this exercise you will use the NPRINT and PCONSOLE utilities to place jobs in the specified print queues. This exercise assumes that you have two print queues named ##REMOTE and ##LOCAL that either were created by your instructor or by you in exercise 1. These print queues will need to be created before you can complete this exercise.

1. Log in using your assigned student username.

2. Use PCONSOLE to verify the existence of the required print queues. (If the ##REMOTE and ##LOCAL print queues do not exist, complete exercise 1 or contact your instructor.)

3. Use the NPRINT command to print two copies of the CUSTOMER.DOC file located in the SYS:EXAMPLE\SALES\ORDERS software directory. Place the job in your ##REMOTE print queue with a banner page containing your name on the top half and the filename on the lower half. Include a form feed, no tabs, and have the print server notify you when the job is printed. On the line below, record the NPRINT command you use.

_____

4. Use the NPRINT command to place a copy of your workstation's AUTOEXEC.BAT file in your ##LOCAL print queue with no banner, no tabs, no form feed, and forms type 2. On the line below, record the NPRINT command you use.

_____

5. Use the PCONSOLE utility to place a copy of the README.TXT file located in the SYS:EXAMPLE\SALES\ SURVEY directory into your ##LOCAL print queue using the PCONSOLE default settings.

6. Use the Print Scrn key to print the PCONSOLE screen showing all print jobs in the ##LOCAL print queue.

7. Exit PCONSOLE using the [Alt][F10] key combination.

8. Log out.

Exercise 10-3: Redirecting Printer Output

In this exercise you will use the CAPTURE command to redirect printer output from your workstation to a NetWare print queue. This exercise assumes that you or your instructor created two print queues, ##REMOTE and ##LOCAL, for your use. If these print queues do not exist, notify your instructor or complete exercise 1 in order to create the required print queues.

1. Log in using your assigned student username.

2. Use PCONSOLE to verify the existence of the required print queues. (If the ##REMOTE and ##LOCAL print queues do not exist, perform exercise 1 or contact your instructor.)

3. Enter a CAPTURE command to redirect output from LPT1 to print queue ##REMOTE with a timeout of 7 seconds, no tabs, a form feed, and a banner containing your name on the top half and the word REPORT on the lower half. On the line below, record the CAPTURE command you use.

   _____

4. Enter a second CAPTURE to redirect the output sent to the LPT2 port to print queue ##LOCAL using the correct parameter to cause the print job not to be available for printing until after the application program exits. The print job should contain no banner, no tabs, and be kept on the print queue in the event the application program aborts prior to completion. Record the CAPTURE command you use on the line below.

   _____

5. Use the appropriate parameter of the CAPTURE command to display the capture status of all printer ports. On the line below, record the command you use. _____

6. Use the Print Scrn key to print the screen showing the capture status information.

7. Change your default DOS prompt to a drive letter mapped to the SYS: volume. Use the following command to type a copy of each file that ends with the extension .FRM to the LPT2 printer port:

   ```
   TYPE \EXAMPLE\FORMS\filename.FRM > LPT2
   ```

8. Change your default path to the \EXAMPLE\SALES\ORDERS directory.

9. Enter the command QBASIC PRINT and press [Enter] to start the customer print program.

10. Use the [Alt][R] key combination to run the print program and print a copy of the customer report to the print queue assigned to LPT1.

11. Use the [Alt][F][X] key combination to exit the QBASIC software.

12. Use the ENDCAP command to return the LPT2 port back to the local printer.

13. Use the appropriate options of the CAPTURE command to verify the results of the ENDCAP command. On the line below, record the command you use.

   _____

Exercise 10-4: Using a NetWare Print Queue from Windows

If you have access to Microsoft Windows on a networked workstation, you can complete the following exercise to learn how to redirect output from Windows applications to the ##REMOTE and ##LOCAL print queues. This exercise assumes that Windows has been properly installed to work with your network and that the ##REMOTE and ##LOCAL print queues have already been created by either you or your instructor.

1. Log in using your assigned student username.

2. Use the CAPTURE SH command to view the capture status of your workstation. On the lines below, record the capture status.

    LPT1 _____

    _____

    Capture Defaults: _____   Automatic Endcap: _____

    Banner: _____   Form Feed: _____

    Copies: _____   Tabs: _____

    Form: _____   Timeout Count: _____

    LPT2 _____

    _____

    Capture Defaults: _____   Automatic Endcap: _____

    Banner: _____   Form Feed: _____

    Copies: _____   Tabs: _____

    Form: _____   Timeout Count: _____

3. Start Windows.

4. Double-click the Control Panel icon (usually located in the Main program group).

5. Double-click the Printers icon in the Control Panel window.

6. Select a printer type from the Installed Printers window.

7. Click the Connect button.

8. Select the LPT3 port.

9. Click the Network button.

10. Locate your ##REMOTE print queue and connect it to the selected printer port. On the lines below, record the options you use (you might not need all the lines).

    _____

    _____

    _____

    _____

11. Close all Control Panel windows and return to the Main program group.

12. Use the Write application from the Accessories program group to create a short document—maybe describing your plans for this coming weekend.

13. Use the Print option of Write to send output to the network print queue.

14. Use the MSDOS icon to open a DOS window.

15. At the appropriate prompt, enter the CAPTURE SH command and record your capture settings below.

LPT1: _____

LPT2: _____

LPT3: _____

16. In the space below, record your observations about the effect of Windows on the capture status.

17. Exit Windows.

18. Log out.

EXERCISES

In order to perform the case 1 exercise, you will need to log in to the file server with a supervisor equivalent username in order to be able to create and configure print servers and print queues. If you do not have a supervisor equivalent username, follow the steps in case 2.

Case 10-1: Creating a Print Server

The OfficePro company specializes in providing word processing services to a number of different businesses. OfficePro currently has five word processing staff members and two high-quality laser printers that are used to print final output. In addition, each word processor has a dot-matrix printer attached to its workstation that is used to print draft copies of documents for editing. Final output for documents is provided by placing the job in a shared directory. The operator of the computer with an attached laser printer then loads and prints the final documents. This method is becoming inefficient because it interrupts the work of the employee who uses the computer attached to the laser printer. As a result, OfficePro has contacted you to network the two laser printers so that output can be sent directly from each word processing station to one of the laser printers. After evaluating OfficePro's network applications, you decide to connect one laser printer directly to the print server computer and to attach the other laser printer remotely to an existing workstation.

If you are not logged in as a supervisor equivalent user, you will need to log out and then log in using the supervisor equivalent username provided by your instructor. If you do not have supervisor access to your assigned file server, your instructor will provide you with a print server to use.

Part 1: Create and configure the print server

1. Log in using a supervisor equivalent name.

2. If you have not already done so in the exercise, use PCONSOLE to create two print queues named ##LOCAL and ##REMOTE.

3. Use PCONSOLE to create a print server named ##PSERVER.

4. Configure the print server for the following two printers:

   ■ Printer 0 should be locally attached to LPT1 port using hardware interrupt 7 and be assigned to print queue ##LOCAL.

   ■ Printer 1 should be remotely attached to the LPT1 port of a remote workstation using interrupt 7 and be assigned to print queue ##REMOTE.

Part 2: Load the PSERVER program on a dedicated workstation

In this step you will need to cooperate with another student in order to make one of your computers a dedicated print server and the other computer a remote printer.

1. Modify the NET.CFG file on the print server computer to contain the necessary statement. Record the change to the NET.CFG file in the space below.

2. Attach a printer to the print server computer and reboot it in order to load the new settings from the NET.CFG file.

3. Log in to the file server and user the PSERVER command to start the print server. On the line below, record the command you use.

   _____

4. Record the print server status messages for printer 0 and printer 1 on the lines below.

   Printer 0: _____

   Printer 1: _____

Part 3: Test the printing setup

1. Boot the second computer and log in to the file server. Use the RPRINTER command to attach the printer located at this computer to printer number 1 of your print server. On the line below, record the message on the print server status screen for printer number 1.

   _____

2. On the line below, record the number of jobs printed from the ##REMOTE print queue.

3. Map a drive to your ##ADMIN directory.

4. Use the CAPTURE command to redirect LPT1 output to the ##LOCAL printer.

5. Use the DOS EDIT command to create a document file that summarizes the steps involved in using PCONSOLE to create and configure a print server.

6. Use the [Alt][F] key combination to select the file menu.

7. Save your file in the ##ADMIN directory.

8. Use [Alt][F] to select the file menu and use the Print option to print the file to the ##LOCAL printer.

9. Exit the EDIT program.

10. Use the CAPTURE command to redirect LPT1 output to the ##REMOTE printer.

11. Start the EDIT program.

12. Open the document you saved in Step 6.

13. Print the document to the ##REMOTE print queue.

14. Exit the EDIT program.

15. Have your instructor check your printer environment.

16. Log out.

Case 10-2: Troubleshooting an Existing Print Server

This case exercise assumes that a print server and two print queues have already been created for your user account. The print queue names are ##REMOTE and ##LOCAL. Because the print server and print queues already exist, you will not need supervisor equivalency to do this case exercise. You will need to work in a team with another student in order to have at least two workstations to load and test the printer setup. Your instructor will supply you with the name of the print server definition file your team will be using. Because only one team can load a print server at a time, you will need to coordinate your work with other members of your class.

The manager of an animal hospital recently contacted you about a problem the staff is having with the hospital's network printing. After taking a NetWare course, the manager created a print server and two print queues but has been unable to get output sent to the print queues printed on either printer. The manager has asked you to see if you can complete the network printer setup for the hospital.

Part 1: Load the print server

1. Identify the name of the print server your team will be using. On the line below, record the print server name.

   _____

2. Modify the NET.CFG file on the print server computer to contain the necessary statement. Record the change to the NET.CFG file in the space below.

3. Attach a printer to the print server computer and reboot it in order to load the new settings from the NET.CFG file.

4. Log in to the file server and use the PSERVER command to start the print server. On the line below, record the command you use.

   _____

5. Record the print server status messages for printer 0 and printer 1 on the lines below.

   Printer 0: _____

   Printer 1: _____

6. Boot the second computer and log in to the file server. Use the RPRINTER command to attach the printer located at this computer as a remote printer. On the line below, record the message on the print server status screen for printer number 1.

_____

Part 2: Test the print server

1. Use the CAPTURE command to direct output from your LPT1 port to the ##LOCAL print queue.

2. Use the CAPTURE SH command to view the capture status.

3. Press the Print Scrn key twice to place two jobs in the print queue.

4. Does the print server show any printing activity? Yes or No?

5. Start PCONSOLE and record the status and job number of the two jobs you just placed in the print queue.

Job Number   Status

_____   _____

_____   _____

6. What is the most likely reason the jobs are not being printed by the print server?

_____

7. Use PCONSOLE to access the print server file you loaded in part 1.

8. Select the Print Server Status/Control option from the Print Server Information window. This option is available only for print server definitions that are currently running. The option allows a print server operator to control a printer or change its configuration. Note that the changes you make in the Print Server Status/Control option are not saved and therefore will not be effective when the print server is reloaded.

9. Select the Queues Serviced by Printer option. On the lines below, record the print queues that are being serviced by each of the printers.

Printer 0: _____

Printer 1: _____

10. Add your ##LOCAL print queue to the printer that is defined as the local printer.

11. Add your ##REMOTE print queue to the printer that is defined as the remote printer.

12. Use the Esc key to save your changes and return to the Available Topics menu.

13. Select the Print Queue Information option and view the jobs in your ##LOCAL print queue.

14. Record the status of the print jobs you submitted in Step 3.

Job Number   Status

_____   _____

_____   _____

15. On the print server computer, use [Ctrl][Break] to exit the print server program. If [Ctrl][Break] does not work, reboot the print server computer.

16. Start PCONSOLE.

17. Select the Print Server Information option from the Available Topics menu.

18. Does the Print Server Status/Control option appear in the Print Server Information menu? Yes or No?

    If not, in the space below, explain why it no longer appears.

19. Exit PCONSOLE.

20. Log out.

SUPERIOR TECHNICAL COLLEGE PROBLEMS

Project 10-1: Define the Printing Environment

In Superior Technical College's administrative department, both Mimi Ito and Laurie Holt use word processing software to type letters, course outlines, meeting agendas, and final documents for faculty. They currently use a printer switch box to share an HP LaserJet III - compatible printer. This arrangement often slows them down when they both need to print something at the same time. Some faculty members have also expressed interest in having access to a laser printer to print lab assignments, feeling that the output will be more effective than that produced on the dot-matrix printer attached to the faculty computer.

Every two computers in the computer lab share a dot-matrix printer by means of a switch box. Dave Johnson informs you that faculty members want to continue with this system because it is simple and reliable and provides beginning students the experience of working with printers. The college has purchased two laser printers that the faculty want students to use for printing their final output in the desktop publishing class and for resume printing in the written communication class. Both printers will be located in a central area of the lab. If possible, the two laser printers should be installed so that students do not need to specify which printer to send their output to. The system should print laser output on whichever printer is available.

In the student services department, a standard dot-matrix printer is needed to print reports from the graduate and testing systems. Rather than buying two dot-matrix printers for the two systems, however, Karl Dauer has informed you that he would like the department to share one dot-matrix printer for printing application reports and put extra money into buying a laser printer the department can use to print correspondence. Also, the new student recruitment system will eventually need a laser printer to print follow-up letters.

In addition to these stated printing needs, Dave Johnson would like to obtain—using a surplus from last year's budget—a sophisticated high-speed color printer that all staff members can have access to for preparing presentations and special reports using the new graphics software you just installed. Because of the complexity of the graphics data that will be handled by such a computer, Dave is concerned that it might not function satisfactorily as a remote printer. If it is connected locally, however, the department in which it is connected might become possessive of it. He would like to see it located in a central area where it can be better managed.

Complete a print server definition form to define the printer requirements for Superior Technical College.

Project 10-2: Create Print Queues

Use the PCONSOLE utility to create the print queues you defined in project 1. Include your assigned student number at the beginning of each print queue name you create. Make your ##ADMIN username a print queue operator in addition to the user whose workstation has a remote printer attached to it. In order to create the new print queues, you will need to log in using a supervisor equivalent username. If you do not have access to a supervisor equivalent username, your instructor will provide instructions on the use of existing print queues.

Project 10-3: Create a Print Server

Create a print server that will control the printers defined in project 1. Make your ##ADMIN username an operator of the print server and include your username on each of the printer notification lists. If you do not have access to a supervisor equivalent username, your instructor will provide instructions on the use of existing print servers and print queues.

Project 10-4: Test the Printer Environment

To test your printer environment you will need to work with another student in order to have access to a dedicated computer to run your print server.

1. Modify the NET.CFG file on the print server computer.

2. Attach a printer to the print server computer to simulate the local printers and reboot the system.

3. Attach a printer to your workstation to simulate the remote printers.

4. Place a job in each of your print queues. The job placed in the local print queue should be printed on the printer attached to the print server.

5. Load RPRINTER on your workstation using your first remote printer number. The job sent to that print queue should be printed on the printer attached to your workstation.

6. Use the RPRINTER command to remove RPRINTER from memory. On the line below, record the command you use.

    _____

7. Reload RPRINTER on your workstation using the next remote printer number. The job in that print queue should be printed.

8. Repeat Steps 6 and 7 until you have tested all printers.

CUSTOMIZING NETWARE PRINTING

Once the network printing environment has been installed, an ongoing responsibility of the network administrator is managing and customizing the printing environment to meet the ever-changing needs of users and applications. Managing network printing involves such operational tasks as working with print jobs and controlling the print server. In order to reduce the amount of time you spend working with print jobs and controlling printers, you will want to train other users to be print queue and print server operators. In this chapter you will learn how to create commands that can be used in batch files and menus to make managing printers and print queues faster and easier.

Customizing printing to accommodate different types of paper and to provide printer setup features for applications that require special printing is another important part of maintaining a network printing environment. In this chapter you will learn how to use the PRINTDEF utility to help you manage multiple print forms and create printer setup sequences that take advantage of features found in many printers. You will learn how the PRINTCON utility can be used to create and maintain customized print jobs. Users will be able to access many

AFTER READING THIS CHAPTER AND COMPLETING THE EXERCISES YOU WILL BE ABLE TO:

- USE PCONSOLE TO MANAGE JOBS IN A PRINT QUEUE.
- USE PCONSOLE AND PSC TO CONTROL NETWORK PRINTING.
- USE THE PRINTDEF AND PRINTCON UTILITIES TO CUSTOMIZE YOUR PRINTING ENVIRONMENT.
- ACCESS PRINT QUEUES ON OTHER FILE SERVERS.

print system features automatically simply by specifying the name of a print job that contains the parameters they need. You will also learn how to configure your print server to access and print jobs from print queues located on other file servers.

MANAGING THE PRINTING ENVIRONMENT

After you install the network printing system, one of the first tasks you will face is manipulating print jobs and controlling network printers. In this section, you will learn how to use the PCONSOLE utility to manage print queue jobs as well as view and change the status of a print queue in order to make the print queue temporarily inaccessible to users or print servers. Another useful feature of NetWare printing allows you to hold a print job for printing at a later time. This can be helpful if you need to print a job that will take a long time; rather than tie up the printer during the day when it is needed by other users, you can print such a job during off hours.

Another important part of managing the printing environment is being able to control networked printers in order to cancel jobs, change paper, clear paper jams, and properly down the print server. In this section you will learn how you can perform these duties using either the PCONSOLE menu utility or the PSC command from the DOS prompt. The PSC command can be very useful when you want to create automatic commands in menus or batch files. Such files allow a print server operator to issue a control command to a printer without having to complete all the steps associated with PCONSOLE.

MANAGING PRINT JOBS WITH PCONSOLE

Once jobs are placed in a print queue, it is sometimes necessary to rearrange the sequence, to defer printing until a later time, or to change such print job parameters as the banner, the number of copies, or the file contents. These tasks can be performed by either the supervisor or print queue operator using the PCONSOLE utility. As a CNA you will be required to know how to use PCONSOLE to perform the functions described in this section.

Rearranging print jobs

It is sometimes necessary for a print queue operator to rearrange the sequence of jobs in a print queue. This allows a high priority job to be printed ahead of other jobs placed in the print queue before it. For example, suppose the business manager needs a certain print job printed immediately to use as part of a presentation being made to stockholders. If the presentation print job is located after several other large print jobs in the laser print queue, the print queue operator will need to change the sequence number of the presentation print job to cause it to print next. To change the sequence of the jobs in a print queue, start PCONSOLE and select the Print Queue Information option, which displays a list of existing print queues. Next, highlight the name of the print queue containing the jobs to be resequenced and press [Enter] to obtain the Print Queue Information menu. To manage jobs in this print queue, highlight the first option, Current Print Job Entries. Pressing [Enter] displays the current print job entries window, which shows all jobs in the print queue along with their status and job number, as shown in Figure 11-1.

Figure 11-1

Current Print Job
Entries window

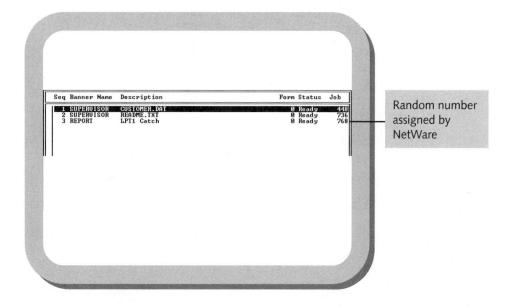

Random number
assigned by
NetWare

The status field indicates the status of the current job entry. A "Ready" status indicates the print job is available for printing by the print server. A status of "Adding..." indicates that a workstation is still placing information in the print job, and the "Active" status indicates the print job is currently being printed. The "Seq" column indicates the order in which the job will be printed. To change the sequence number of a print job, highlight the job you want to change. Pressing [Enter] displays the Print Queue Entry Information window shown in Figure 11-2. Highlight the "Service Sequence" field and change the existing sequence number to reflect the new position of the job in the print queue. In Figure 11-2, for example, changing the sequence number to a 1 would make this job the next one to be printed. Press [Esc] to save the change and return to the window showing the revised sequence numbers of all jobs in the selected print queue.

Figure 11-2

Print Queue
Entry Information
window

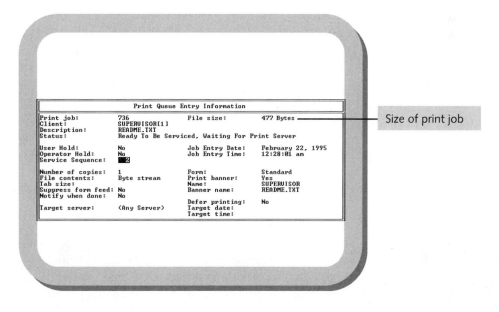

Size of print job

Changing print queue status

To prevent the print jobs from starting to print while you are resequencing a print queue, you need to take the queue offline temporarily. A print queue operator for a print queue can use PCONSOLE to take the print queue offline by selecting it from the Print Queue window and then using the Current Queue Status option to display the Current Queue Status window, as shown in Figure 11-3. To take the print queue off line, highlight the "Servers can service entries in queue" field and change the Yes to a No. The queue will now allow users to place jobs in it, but no jobs will be printed until the status is changed back to Yes. Now press the Esc key to save the status change and return to the Print Queue Information menu.

Figure 11-3

Current Queue Status window

Delaying a print job

You can start printing a long print job late at night and avoid tying up the printer during office hours. This is especially useful with desktop publishing jobs, which typically take a long time to print because of their high-resolution graphics. To delay a print job, first you need to change the status of the print queue to halt printing temporarily. Then place the job in the print queue using the CAPTURE command. Once the job is in the print queue, set the Defer Printing parameter. Use the PCONSOLE utility to select the print queue, and then use the Current Print Jobs option to display the jobs. Highlight the print job you want to schedule and then press [Enter] to display the Print Queue Entry Information window. It will be similar to the one shown in Figure 11-2. To schedule the job to print at a different time, highlight the "Defer printing" option and change No to Yes.

By default, the job will be set to start printing at 2:00 A.M. the following day, as shown in Figure 11-4. You can change this time or press the Esc key to accept the default print date and time and return to the Current Print Jobs window. After you defer the printing of a print job, the status column for that job will change from Ready to Waiting. The Waiting status means the job is set for deferred printing, and, in this example, printing will begin at 2:00 A.M. You can now exit the PCONSOLE utility. The job will be printed at the specified time if the print server computer is running and the printer is ready.

Figure 11-4

Changing the Defer Print Job status

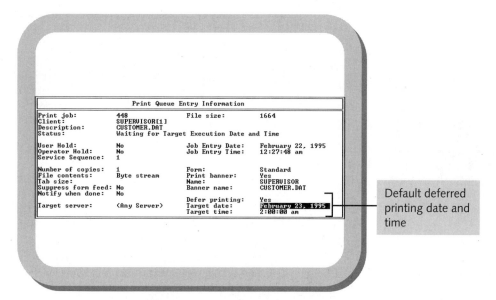

CONTROLLING THE PRINT SERVER

Network printers running on a print server often require the operator to perform certain control functions, such as changing print forms, pausing a printer, canceling a print job, or checking printer status. It is sometimes necessary to attach a print queue temporarily to a different printer or to send printer notification messages to another user if the print server operator is not available. All these functions can be accessed via the Print Server option of the PCONSOLE utility.

In addition to the PCONSOLE menu utility, NetWare also provides a printer control command line utility, called PSC, that can be used to control or view the status of any printers on the network. The advantage of the PSC command is that it can be placed in batch files. In this section you will learn about managing printers using either the PSC command or the PCONSOLE utility.

Using PCONSOLE to control printers

A print server operator might at times, need to change print forms in a printer. There are special paper forms, such as labels or invoices, as well as standard paper for printing reports. The print server operator is notified when a printer requires a print form change. The operator responds by manually changing the paper type in the printer and also by changing the form specification in the Printer Status window. You use the PCONSOLE utility to perform this task by selecting the Print Server Information option and selecting the currently running print server. The Print Server Information menu shown in Figure 11-5 contains the Print Server Status/Control option, which is used to modify or control the currently running print server.

Figure 11-5

Print Server
Information window

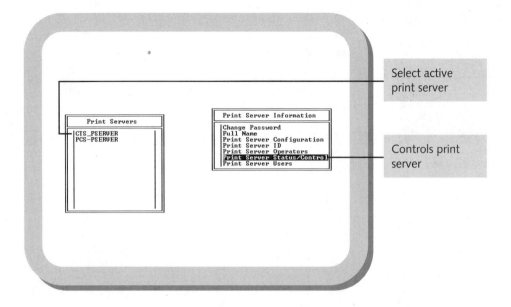

Select active
print server

Controls print
server

The Print Server Status/Control option is only displayed if the print server definition is currently running. As a result, if the Print Server Status/Control option is not displayed, you have either selected the wrong print server, or else will need to start the selected print server before continuing.

After mounting new forms in a printer, select Print Server Status/Control to display the Print Server Status and Control Menu shown in Figure 11-6. To control a specific printer, select the Printer Status option and then select the printer in which the new forms have been mounted from the Active Printers window. PCONSOLE displays the status window for the selected printer, as shown in Figure 11-7. The window in Figure 11-7 shows that the currently mounted form is form 0. Zero is the default form number used by the CAPTURE command. To change to a different form number, highlight the "Mounted form" field and change the form number to the number appropriate for the job you want to print. Later in this chapter you will learn how to use the PRINTDEF utility and the CAPTURE command to assign a form number and name to a print job.

Figure 11-6

Print Server Status
and Control menu

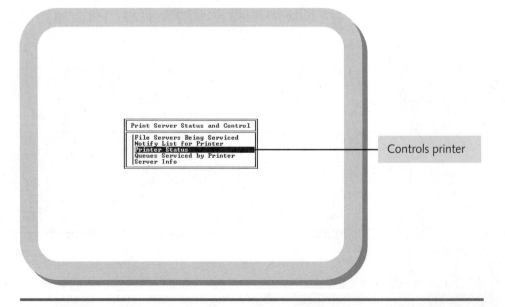

Controls printer

Figure 11-7

Printer status
window

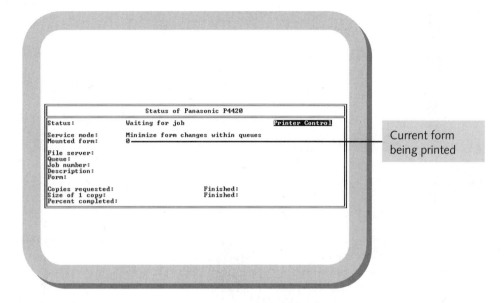

```
                     Status of Panasonic P4420
Status:               Waiting for job                   Printer Control
Service mode:         Minimize form changes within queues
Mounted form:         0
File server:
Queue:
Job number:
Description:
Form:
Copies requested:                          Finished:
Size of 1 copy:                            Finished:
Percent completed:
```

Current form
being printed

Once the form number is changed, the printer will immediately start printing the job. As a result, prior to changing the form number you need to be sure the new forms have been properly mounted. One way to do this is to print a line on the form by highlighting the Printer Control option in the printer status window and pressing [Enter] to display the printer control options shown in Figure 11-8. You can then use the "Mark top of form" option to print a line across the top of the print forms. When you are confident the forms are loaded correctly, you can use the [Esc] key to return to the "Status" window and then change the form number to begin printing on the new forms. After all print jobs requiring the new form have been printed, the print server will display a message. The printer operator can now mount the next form required by the printer and repeat this process to start the printer again.

Figure 11-8

Printer control
options

```
Abort print job
Form Feed
Mark top of form
Pause printer
Rewind printer
Start printer
Stop printer
```

Using PCONSOLE to attach a temporary print queue

If a printer needs to be taken off line for repairs or servicing, you can allow the printing to continue by sending current jobs to a similar printer attached to the network at another location. One way to direct all output in the offline printer's queue automatically to a secondary printer is to attach the queue temporarily to the second printer. Suppose, for example, the business department's laser printer just stopped printing. You have scheduled a service call for tomorrow morning. To allow the department users to continue printing for the remainder of the day, you decide to use the PCONSOLE utility to attach the business laser print queue to the sales department's laser printer temporarily. Because both of these printers use the same printer language, you will be able to send the business department's output to the sales laser printer without modifying the applications or user procedures.

To use PCONSOLE to attach a print queue to a printer without restarting the print server, you select the Print Server Information option and select the currently running print server. Next select the Print Server Status/Control option to display the Print Server Status and Control Menu (shown in Figure 11-6). To add a print queue temporarily to a printer, use the Queues Serviced by Printer option and select the printer to which you want to add the print queue. Next, PCONSOLE displays a window showing all print queues currently attached to the selected printer. To add another print queue to this printer temporarily, press the Ins key and select the print queue you want to attach—in this example it's the business department's print queue. The selected print queue will now be added to the list of queues serviced by the sales laser printer. Using the Esc key saves this change and returns you back to the main PCONSOLE menu. Note that this change is not permanent; the print queue will not be included in this printer's service list when the print server is restarted.

Using PCONSOLE to change a printer's notification list

Suppose that a print server operator will be on vacation for two weeks and you want printer notification messages to be sent to another user during this period. In order to allow another user to receive messages from a printer, you temporarily add the user to the notification list for that printer. Using PCONSOLE, first select the currently running print server and use the Print Server Status/Control option to display the Print Server Status and Control Menu. To add a user temporarily to the notify list for a printer, use the Notify List for Printer option and then select the printer name. This displays a window showing all users who will currently be sent any printer messages affecting this printer. To add another user, simply press the Ins key and then select the user's name from the Notify Candidates window. When you press [Enter], PCONSOLE displays the Notify Intervals window. The default interval is 30, which means the first message is sent 30 sec. after a problem occurs; repeat messages are sent every 60 sec. until the situation is corrected. You can change the default settings or press the Esc key to save the settings. The selected user will now be temporarily added to the notification list for this printer. Use the Esc key to return to the PCONSOLE menu or use [Alt][F10] to exit the PCONSOLE utility. Because this is a temporary change, the user will not be included in the list when the print server is restarted.

Using PCONSOLE to down the print server

Periodically you will need to down the print server, either to reboot the computer or to load a new printer definition file. With the exception of the temporary changes, any changes made to the print server definition file will not be effective until the print server is reloaded. Assume, for example, you want to add a new print queue you just created to an existing printer. To do this, you use the Print Server Configuration option on the Print Server Information menu. Then use the Queues Serviced by Printer option to add the new print queue to the selected printer. Before this change becomes effective, you need to down the print server and then reload it using the updated print server definition file. Although it is possible to down a print server by using the UNLOAD command at the console or by rebooting a dedicated print server computer, these methods can cause print data to be lost if a job is currently being printed somewhere on the network.

To use the PCONSOLE utility properly to down a print server you select the print server to be downed from the Print Server Information window and then use the Print Server Status/Control option to display the Print Server Status and Control Menu. To down the print server, select the Server Info option to display the Print Server Info/Status window. Highlight the "Current server status" field, and press [Enter] to display the Print Server Info/Status window shown in Figure 11-9. To down the print server without losing any print jobs, highlight the "Going down after current jobs" option and press [Enter]. The selected print server will be automatically unloaded after any print jobs currently in progress are completed. Use [Alt][F10] to exit the PCONSOLE utility.

<table>
<tr><td>

Figure 11-9

Print server status
options

</td><td>

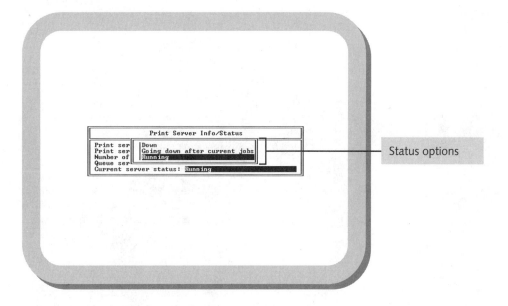

</td></tr>
</table>

 A network administrator, whose name is being withheld to protect the innocent, once made the mistake of entering the command DOWN PSERVER at the console rather than UNLOAD PSERVER. The accident resulted in the downing of the file server rather than the print server as desired.

USING PSC TO MANAGE PRINTERS

As mentioned at the beginning of this section, the PSC command can be used to control the printer directly from the DOS prompt or from a batch file or menu. This enables the network administrator to simplify printer control by setting up the PSC command for each of the print server operators. As a CNA you will be required to know the syntax of the PSC command and how to use it to view printer status, cancel, or stop and restart a network printer. The syntax of the PSC command is **PSC [PS=**_printservername_**] [P=**_printernumber_**] action**. Replace the _printservername_ parameter with the name of the print server that contains the printer to which you want to send the control command. Use the _printernumber_ parameter to identify the number of the printer to which you want to send the control command. Printer numbers ranging from 0–15 are defined in PCONSOLE when you set up the configuration. Replace _action_ with one of the options shown in Figure 11-10.

Figure 11-10

PSC command options

Parameter	Description
STAT (status)	Displays one of the following status messages for the selected printer: Waiting for job, Mount form _n_, Printing job, Paused, Read to go down, Stopped, Not connected, Not installed, In private mode, Off line, Out of paper. _Example: PSC PS=PSC_PSERVER P=1 STAT_
PAU (pause)	Temporarily stops printer output until the start command is received. _Example: PSC PS=PSC_PSERVER P=1 PAU_
AB (abort)	Stops printing the current job. The job is deleted from the queue and the printer continues with the next job in the queue. _Example: PSC PS=PSC_PSERVER P=0 AB_
STO [K] (stop [keep])	Stops the printer and deletes the current print job unless the keep option is specified. _Example: PSC PS=PSC_PSERVER P= 3 STO K_
STAR (start)	Restarts the printer after you have stopped or paused it. _Example: PSC PS=PSC_PSERVER P=1 STAR_
M [_character_] (mark)	Prints a line of whatever character you select. Used for determining where the printer will start printing the page. _Example: PSC PS=PSC_PSERVER P=0 M *_
FF (form feed)	Advances the paper to the top of the next page. _Example: PSC PS=PSC_PSERVER P=1 FF_
MOF=_n_ (mount form)	Informs the print server that you have mounted a new form of the indicated number on the selected printer. _Example: PSC PS=PSC_PSERVER P=0 MOF=2_
PRI (private)	Used from a workstation that is running RPRINTER to reserve the printer for local use only. It should be issued if an application will be printing directly to the local printer in order to prevent output from the local application from being mixed with output from the print server. _Example: PSC PSC= PSC_PSERVER P=1 PRI_
SH (shared)	Changes a workstation that has been placed in private mode back to allowing the print server to send output to the printer attached to its local port. _Example: PSC PS=PSC_PSERVER P=1 SH_
CD (cancel down)	Cancels the PCONSOLE command to down the print server after all jobs have been printed. _Example: PSC PS=PSC_PSERVER CD_

Adding the status option to the PSC command displays one of the messages indicated for the printer you have selected. This is useful if a user needs to check on the status of a printer prior to sending a print job. The pause option temporarily stops the printer. Use it if you want to verify that a job is printing correctly. The start option restarts the printer from the point at which it was stopped when the pause command was issued. The abort option is useful if a job is printing on the wrong printer, on the wrong paper type, or if for some other reason it needs to be stopped and deleted. Note that the abort option deletes the job from the print queue. If you want to stop printing a job but still keep it in the current print queue, use the stop keep option. The form feed option automatically advances the printer to the next page. This is useful for jobs that leave the last page in the printer. Using the form feed option means you don't need to use the buttons on the printer's control panel to advance the paper.

The mount form option specifies printer forms. Assume, for example, a print server operator has been notified that a new form is required in printer number 0 for print server PSC_PSERVER. The operator would first mount the new paper type in the printer. Next he or she would issue the following PSC command from his or her workstation:

```
PSC PS=PSC_PSERVER P=0 MOF=1
```

To make the task automatic, the PSC command could be placed in a DOS batch file or as an option of the print server operator's menu, as described in Chapter 13.

The private option is especially useful for workstations that have remote printers attached to them. The private option takes the remote printer off line and allows the workstation to send a job directly to its locally attached printer rather than routing it through the print queue. If a user sends a job directly to the local printer port without issuing the private option, it is possible the printer will receive lines of output from both the application running on the local workstation and from the RPRINTER program. This causes scrambled results with a loss of data from both applications. To prevent this problem, the user should first issue the private command before printing directly to the local printer port. After the output is complete, the user can issue the shared command to make the printer available for use by the RPRINTER program.

To simplify use of the PSC command, you can use the DOS SET (set environment) command to set a default print server or printer number in the workstation's memory. This allows you to issue commands without typing the print server name or printer number. It can also be useful in developing menus or batch files, because the printer number of the user can be stored in memory. This makes it possible for a common set of PSC commands to be used by all print server operators. The syntax of the DOS SET command that will store the print server and printer information in the environment space of the workstation is **SET PSC=PS**_printserver_ **P**_printernumber_. When you use the SET command to create the PSC variable, replace _printserver_ with the name of the desired default print server and _printernumber_ with the number of the default printer that is to receive the control command. To set default PSC parameters of a workstation to control printer number 0 on the print server named CORP_PSERVER, for example, you could add the following command to the workstation's AUTOEXEC.BAT file:

```
SET PSC=PSCORP_PSERVER P0
```

Now, whenever the workstation is booted, the PSC command to control printer 0 can consist of just the following flaglist options:

PSC STAT   to display the status of printer 0

PSC AB   to abort the current print job

If the operator at this workstation needs to send a command to another printer, the print server name or printer number can be overridden by specifying the printer number or print server in the PSC command. Assuming, for example, that the SET PSC=PSCORP_PSERVER P0 command was issued, the following PSC command can be used to mount form type 2 in printer 1 of the print server named CORP_PSERVER:

PSC P=1 MOF=2

USING PRINT QUEUES ON OTHER FILE SERVERS

Many large local area network systems have more than one file server to provide different services. In a multiple file server network, print queues are often located on each file server in order to allow users to access network printers without having to attach to multiple servers. Rather than creating a separate print server for each file server, however, a single print server can be used to support the print queues on up to eight file servers. To expand an existing print server to support the print queues on multiple file servers, you use PCONSOLE to perform the following three steps:

1. Modify the existing print server to add another file server to the service list.

2. Create a mirrored print server on the additional file server to provide the necessary communication interface between the file server and the print server.

3. Add the print queues in the additional file server for the appropriate printers on the print server.

MODIFYING THE EXISTING PRINT SERVER

To modify an existing print server to service print queues from more than one file server you first need to start PCONSOLE and then use the Print Server Information option to select the print server to be modified. Next select the Print Server Configuration option. Selecting the File Servers to Be Serviced option displays a window showing the currently serviced file servers. To add another file server to the list, press the Ins key to display the Available File Servers window. Highlight the name of the file server you want to add and press [Enter]. The selected file server appears in the File Servers to Be Serviced window. You can then press the Esc key until you return to the PCONSOLE Available Options menu.

CREATING A MIRRORED PRINT SERVER

In order for the print server to work with two or more file servers, each file server that the print server is going to service must have an identical print server definition file with the same name and printer definitions. This allows the PSERVER program to connect with each file server in order to gain access to the jobs stored in its print queues. Assume, for example, the primary print server definition in the main file server is called CORP_PSERVER. Each additional file server to be serviced by this print server will then need to have a print server definition named CORP_PSERVER created on it with the same printer definitions as on the primary print server definition. The only difference between the primary print server definition and a mirrored definition is that the actual printer configuration information exists only on the primary print server, the mirrored print server printer definitions contain "Defined elsewhere" for each of the printer configurations.

To use PCONSOLE to create a mirrored print server definition on another file server, you first need to use the Current File Server option from the Available Options menu. Then select the name of the file server that is to contain the mirrored print server definition. In order to create a print server definition on the newly selected file server, you need to supply the PCONSOLE program with a username and password that has supervisor equivalency on the selected file server. After gaining access to the selected file server, you can create a mirrored print server by first selecting the Print Server Information option from the main PCONSOLE menu and then using the Ins key to enter the exact name of the primary print server that you want to mirror. Next select the new print server and then use the Printer Configuration option from the Print Server Configuration Menu to display the list of configured printers. Select each printer number that exists on the primary print server and use the printer configuration window to give each printer the name used for the corresponding printer number on the primary print server. Leave the Type field at the default "Defined elsewhere" setting for each printer configuration. After all printer numbers on the primary print server have been configured on the mirrored print server, press the Esc key until you return to the Print Server Configuration Menu.

SELECTING PRINT QUEUES TO BE SERVICED

The third and final step in configuring the mirrored print server is to add the print queues to be serviced on this file server to the appropriate printer number. To do this, first select the Queues Serviced by Printer option from the Print Server Configuration Menu to display a list of all configured printers. Next select the printer you want to use for a print queue. Pressing [Enter] displays the print queue. Use the Ins key to display the Available Queues window. You can then highlight the print queue to be used with this printer. Pressing [Enter] assigns the print queue a priority and adds it to the print queue window for the selected printer. Now press the Esc key to save the selected print queue configuration and return to the Defined Printers window. Repeat this process for each print queue that you want assigned to one of the printers. After all printers are attached to the mirrored print servers, press the [Esc] key until you return to the Available Options menu.

To start sending jobs on the newly selected file server to the appropriate printers, you will now need to down the existing print server, if it is currently running, and then restart the print server using the modified print server definition file. Because the primary print server definition file is configured to service other file servers, the PSERVER program will access the other file server and look for the mirrored print server definition file with the same name as the primary print server. It will then take jobs from the print queues specified in the mirrored print server definition and send them to the corresponding printer numbers, as defined in the primary print server configuration.

 One of the advantages of NetWare v4.1 is that print queues do not need to be associated with file servers. They are treated as separate entities that can be serviced from a single print server without the need for creating the mirrored print server required by NetWare v.3.1x.

CUSTOMIZING NETWORK PRINTING

Once the network printing system is operational, the next task is to customize the printing environment. This will make it easier to use, and it will meet any special printing needs of user applications. Factors that make network printing easier to use include defining a form number for each paper type and automating printing configurations for each user. In this section you will learn about form definitions and how to use the PRINTDEF utility to assign names to form numbers. You will also learn about defining printer setup sequences that can be used to change printer modes and functions. These changes are needed by some applications whose output requires the printer to be configured in a special manner. You use the PRINTDEF utility to manage this task as well as for form definitions. With PRINTDEF you can maintain a database of printer modes and functions that can be used to configure a network printer for these print jobs. In this section you will learn how to use the PRINTDEF and PRINTCON utilities to customize printer setup sequences and create print jobs for each user that make accessing special network printing setups easier.

MANAGING FORMS

Unless you have a printer designated for, and preloaded with, each type of paper you use in your organization, it will periodically be necessary to change the paper type in the printers attached to the network. Changing the paper type can cause problems, however, when another user decides to send regular output to the printer containing the special forms. Assume, for example, a payroll clerk has just placed payroll checks in the dot-matrix printer and is getting ready to run a check printing program just as another user sends a report from a workstation to the same dot-matrix printer. Printing the report on the payroll check forms is definitely not what either user wants.

To prevent this kind of mistake, Novell included with NetWare a system for defining and controlling print forms. The default form number, used for standard paper, is predefined as form 0. It is up to the network administrator, however, to establish a set of form numbers that represents the other paper types and printing formats that are going to be used on network printers. Because form number 0 is the default form number used by the CAPTURE and NPRINT commands, the standard paper you use for printing should be defined as form 0. Figure 11-11 contains an example of form numbers defined for some typical paper types.

Figure 11-11

Sample printer forms

Form Number	Description
0	standard $8\frac{1}{2}"$ × 11" paper
1	company letterhead
2	legal $8\frac{1}{2}"$ × 14" paper
3	payroll checks
4	invoice forms
5	labels

To eliminate the problem in the preceding example (a report being printed on payroll check forms), you could place the following CAPTURE command in a batch file that starts the payroll check printing program:

```
CAPTURE Q=BUS_EPS70_R1_Q1 TI=10 NB NT NFF F=3
```

Notice that this CAPTURE command includes the F=3 parameter to indicate that the output requires form type 3 to be mounted in the printer. The print server keeps track of what form number was used on the most recent print job. When it encounters the command containing the form 3 parameter, it will stop and display a message asking for form 3 to be mounted (unless form 3 was the paper type for the previous job as well). Once the form 3 job is completed, the printer will stop again and request the next form needed.

Changing the print queue service mode

The process of starting and stopping the print server can be a problem if users' print jobs often require different forms. Suppose, for example, you have a laser printer that is used for both legal and standard paper. Two users send jobs to this print queue— one user's jobs require legal forms and the other user's jobs require standard forms. The print server operator will spend a lot of time changing paper in the printer. This situation also slows down printer output because of the frequent stops. You can reduce this problem by having the print server print all jobs in the queue that use the same form—regardless of sequence—before asking for the next form to be mounted. This can greatly reduce the number of times the print server operator will need to change paper in a printer.

To change a printer so that it prints all jobs with the same form number before asking for another form to be mounted, you first need to start PCONSOLE and then select the Print Server Information option from the Available Options menu. Next, select the print server definition you want to change and then select Print Server Configuration from the Print Server Information menu. From the Print Server Configuration Menu, select Printer Configuration to display the Configured Printers window, which lists all printers controlled by the print server. Highlight the printer with which you want to work and press [Enter] to display the window which shows that printer's configuration.

To change the way forms are serviced, select the queue service mode field to display queue service mode options, as shown in Figure 11-12. To reduce the number of form changes that need to be made for this printer, select "Minimize form changes within queues" and press [Enter]. When there are multiple jobs in the print queue with different form types, the print server will scan the print queue for all jobs that have the current form type and print them before requesting the next form type. To save your changes and return to the Configured Printers window, press [Esc] and then [Enter]. You can now configure another printer or use the Esc key to return to the Print Server Configuration menu and exit the PCONSOLE utility.

Before the changes you make to the print server configuration become effective, you will need to down the print server and restart it again. The best way to down the print server is to use the PCONSOLE utility as described previously in this chapter. Remember that rebooting a dedicated print server computer or unloading the PSERVER.NLM from the file server can cause print jobs that are in progress to be lost.

CUSTOMIZING PRINTER OUTPUT WITH PRINTDEF

With the PRINTDEF utility, network administrators can customize their printing environments by assigning names to form types and establishing special printer control modes and functions. As a CNA, you will need to know how to use the PRINTDEF utility to assign form names and establish printer control sequences as described in this section.

 NET$PRN.DAT is a database containing standard forms and printer functions. It is maintained by the PRINTDEF program and stored in the SYS:PUBLIC directory.

Assigning names to forms

Assigning names to different form types can make it easier for users and print server operators to work with forms and perform operational tasks such as mounting the correct forms in the printer. For example, if the name PAYCHECK is assigned to form type 3, it will be easier for the print server operator to respond to the message "Mount Forms PAYCHECK" rather than the less transparent "Mount Forms 3." You can use the PRINTDEF utility to assign names to your form types by logging in using a supervisor equivalent username and then starting the PRINTDEF utility from any directory. Starting PRINTDEF displays the PrintDef Options menu shown in Figure 11-13.

Figure 11-13

PrintDef Options menu

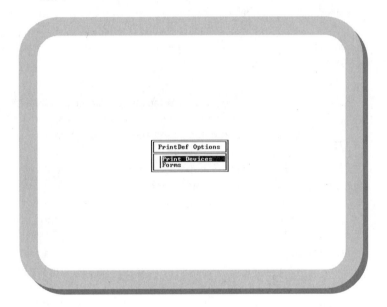

To define form names, select the Forms option. This displays a window showing all existing form definitions in the NET$PRN.DAT database To add a new form type, press the Ins key to display the Form Definition window shown in Figure 11-14.

Figure 11-14

Form Definition window

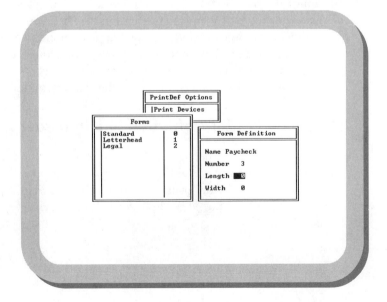

Remember, form 0 is the default form type for the CAPTURE and NPRINT commands. As a result, you should define form type 0 for standard paper before defining additional form types. To define a form type, first enter the name to be used for the form in the "Name" field followed by the form number in the "Number" field. Although values must be placed in the "Length" and the "Width" fields, they are for documentation purposes only and are not used by the print server.

Working with printer functions and modes

There are still many applications in use that are not network aware. Such applications are not able to take advantage of special printer functions such as changing character sizes, paper trays, or paper orientation. Some nonnetwork aware software packages do allow users to select special printing modes, such as condensed print and landscape printing, but they can also leave the printer in that mode and cause the next user's output to be printed incorrectly.

 There are two paper orientations. **Landscape** printing is a function of laser printers in which they print a maximum line width of 11″. **Portrait** printing is more commonly used and has a maximum line width of 8.5″.

PRINTDEF allows the network administrator to manage form types and establish special printer modes and functions by maintaining a printer database called NET$PRN.DAT in the SYS:PUBLIC directory. The NET$PRN.DAT database contains form information along with the printer control commands referred to as modes or functions. A **printer function** is a specific printer escape code sequence that causes the printer to perform one operation, such as changing to landscape mode, selecting a paper tray, changing the character size, or setting page length. A **printer mode** consists of one or more functions that set up the printer for the desired configuration. The legal-landscape mode, for example, might contain functions to change to legal size paper, use landscape format, and then select the lower paper tray in which the legal paper is stored.

Novell has provided printer definition files in the SYS:PUBLIC directory that contain functions and modes for many popular printers. You can use PRINTDEF to merge one or more of the printer definition files into your printer database and then modify them, or you can create new printer definitions by entering your own escape code sequences. Entering your own escape code sequences, however, is slow and prone to error. You will therefore want to use as much as possible the escape code sequences and modes included in the printer definition files.

Merging a Printer Definition File into your printer database

Before you can use the predefined printer functions and modes, you need to merge the printer definition file (PDF) into your printer database. To merge a printer definition file into your network printer database, select the Print Devices option from the PrintDef Options menu. This displays the Print Device Options menu shown in Figure 11-15.

Figure 11-15

Print Device
Options menu

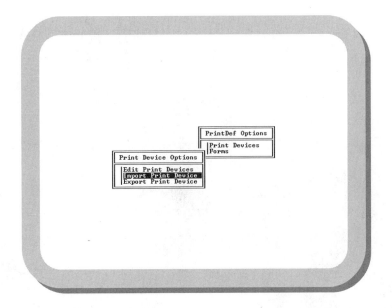

To display a list of all devices currently in your NET$PRN.DAT database, select the Edit Print Devices option. If you have already defined modes and functions for a printer device in your database and want to create a new printer definition file that can be imported to other servers, use the Export Print Device option to select the printer definition and then enter a name for the Printer Definition File (PDF) you want to create. To add another printer definition file to your database, select Import Print Device and press [Enter]. This displays the Source Directory window, which shows your current directory as the default location for the printer definition files. Because the Novell-supplied PDF files are located in the SYS:PUBLIC directory, you will need to enter SYS:PUBLIC to access the standard printer definition files. If you want to load a PDF from another source—a floppy disk drive, for example—you can enter the path to that location.

After you press [Enter] to accept the source directory path, PRINTDEF displays the Available .PDFs window shown in Figure 11-16. This window lists any printer definition files in the specified directory. To work with a laser printer that uses the standard HP LaserJet III language, for example, highlight HP3.PDF and press [Enter]. The print device HP LaserJet III/IIID will then be added to the Defined Print Devices window. You can now press the Esc key until you return to the PrintDef Options menu.

Notice that the printer definition files have abbreviated names to represent the printer make and model. As a result, it is sometimes difficult to determine which printer definition file is the correct one for your printer model. To obtain the correct printer definition file for your printer, select a filename that appears similar to your printer model. After a printer definition file is placed in your printer database, the description of the printer will appear in the "Print Devices" window If you have selected the wrong definition file, you can then use the Del key to remove the printer definition from your database and try selecting another.

Figure 11-16

Available .PDFs
window

 If you try to define a print device that already exists in the database, an
error message informs you that you cannot have two devices with the
same name. After you press [Esc], PRINTDEF allows you to change the
printer name and create a new device in the database. (If you are following along on a computer while reading this chapter, you will need to
add your assigned student number to the beginning of the printer name
in order to create your printer in the database.)

Editing print devices

You can use the PRINTDEF utility to create, modify, or view printer modes and
functions by selecting the Edit Print Devices option on the Print Device Options
menu. To create a new print device, press the Ins key and enter the new device name.
To change the name of an existing print device, highlight the name of the device you
want to change and press the F3 key. You can then use the Backspace key to erase
the existing name and enter the revised name. To delete an existing print device, highlight the name of the device you want to delete, press the Del key, and then press
[Enter] to confirm the deletion of the device.

To view or work with the functions and modes of an existing printer, first select the
Print Devices option from the PrintDef Options menu to display the Print Device
Options menu. Next, select the Edit Print Devices option. This displays the Defined
Print Devices window, which lists all printers that exist in the NET$PRN.DAT
database. To change the modes and functions of an existing printer, highlight the
name of the printer and press [Enter]. This displays the Edit Device Options menu,
which contains options for device modes and device functions. (Remember, modes
consist of one or more functions and are used to establish a printer setup.) To view
or modify the existing modes for the selected printer, highlight Device Modes and
press [Enter]. This displays a list of modes. Figure 11-17 shows the list of modes for
an HP LaserJet printer.

Figure 11-17

HP Laserjet III /IIID
printing modes

Use the up and down arrow keys to view all modes defined for the selected printer.
Notice the last mode is <Re-initialize>. This is a required mode for all print devices
and consists of the functions necessary to reset the printer to the power-on defaults.
The mode is used by the print server at the end of each print job to put the printer
back in standard mode for the next print job. To view the functions that make up
the re-initialize mode of the LaserJet printer, highlight it and press [Enter]. The
<Re-initialize> Functions window, showing the Printer Reset function, is displayed,
as shown in Figure 11-18.

Figure 11-18

HP Laserjet III/IIID
reinitialize functions

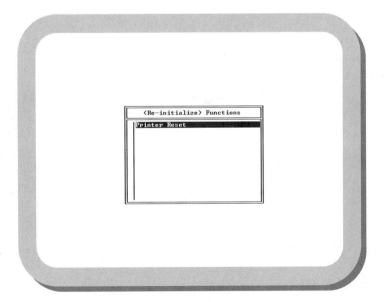

To view the escape code sequence that makes up a reset function, highlight Printer
Reset and press [Enter]. The Printer Reset Escape Sequence or Function window
showing the escape code sequence is displayed, as shown in Figure 11-19.

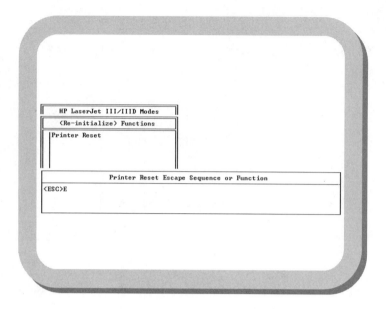

Figure 11-19

Printer reset function for HP LaserJet III/IIID

 You can only view functions when you use the Modes option of the Edit Device Options menu. To add or change printer functions you need to use the Functions option.

Many modes consist of multiple functions. The "Letter landscape, 60 lpp" mode shown in Figure 11-20, for example, consists of five functions. The first function is the printer reset function, which ensures that the printer is returned to its basic settings, even if some other misbehaved application did not reset the printer upon exiting. The other functions include escape sequences to select paper type, paper orientation, and character style and size. You can highlight any function and press [Enter] to view its escape code sequence, as described previously for the Printer Reset function.

Figure 11-20

Viewing a print mode's functions

Adding a new function to a mode

Sometimes you will need to add a function to an existing mode in order to meet your printing needs. Suppose, for example, you plan to use the lower paper tray of an HP LaserJet III laser printer to store standard paper and the top tray to store company letterhead. To be sure that landscape output is printed on standard paper, not on letterhead, you could add the "Paper source – Lower tray" function to the landscape printer mode. This is easily accomplished. First use the Edit Print Devices option to select the laser printer. Then select the Modes option to display all the existing printer setup modes. To add another function to the landscape mode, you need to use the arrow keys to scroll the modes window until you find the desired "Letter landscape" mode and then press [Enter] to display the "Letter landscape" functions window. You can now press the Ins key to display the Additional HP LaserJet III/IIID Functions window and then use the arrow keys to highlight the "Paper Source – Lower Paper Tray" function, as shown in Figure 11-21. Press [Enter]. The Lower Paper Tray function will now be added to the end of the functions list. You can then use the Esc key to return to the HP LaserJet III/IIID Modes window.

Figure 11-21

Adding a new function to a mode

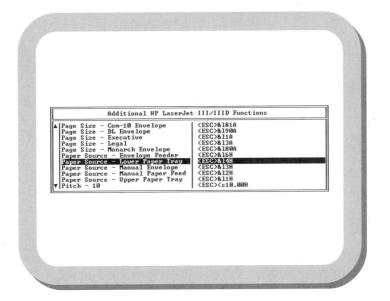

Adding a new mode

If your organization has a special printing need that has not been defined as one of the standard printing modes, you will need to create a new mode to meet that need. Suppose, for example, you need a printer mode that will allow you to print on smaller, executive size paper located in the lower tray of an HP LaserJet III compatible printer. Because this is not one of the standard modes included in the PDF file, you can add your own mode for executive size paper.

First use the Edit Print Device option to select the appropriate printer. Next select the Device Modes option. Pressing the Ins key from the HP LaserJet III/IIID Modes window displays a blank New Mode Name window. Enter a name that describes the new print mode, such as "Executive Paper", and press [Enter]. A blank Executive Paper Functions window is displayed. Press the Ins key and select Printer Reset as the first function. It is important to include Printer Reset as the first function; it ensures that the printer will be set to its power-on defaults before it receives other setup commands. Continue to use the Ins key to select the other functions you want to include in this printer mode. In the Executive Paper mode, for example, you would need to include the Page Size - Executive and Paper Source - Upper Tray functions, as shown in Figure 11-22. After all functions have been selected, press the Esc key to add the new mode to your printer modes window. Use the Esc key to exit the modes window and return to the Edit Device Options menu.

Figure 11-22

Creating a new mode

Adding a new function

One of the more complex tasks that uses the PRINTDEF utility is adding new printer functions. A function consists of an escape code sequence that causes the printer to perform some specific operation, such as setting the character size or paper orientation. You can find the escape code sequence for each function the printer can perform in the printer's operation manual. Assume, for example, you need to set the printer resolution for an HP LaserJet III compatible laser printer when it prints graphic patterns. First, refer to the printer's manual and find the escape code sequence that will set the printer to the desired resolution of 150 dots per inch (dpi). For a LaserJet III compatible printer, the code sequence is [ESC]t150R. [ESC] represents the escape key, which has a decimal value of 27. The code contains the resolution value of 150.

To add this code sequence to your printer database, select the Edit Print Devices option and then select the HP LaserJet III printer. Select the Device Functions option to display the HP LaserJet III/IIID Functions window, which shows all the predefined functions for the HP LaserJet III printer. To add a new function, press the Ins key to display the Function Definition window. Enter a name for the new function, as shown in Figure 11-23. You can enter a descriptive name of up to 32 characters for the new function. The name "Resolution_150dpi" would be appropriate for this example. After entering the function name, press [Enter] to advance the cursor to the Escape Sequence field. Each byte of the Escape Sequence field must be entered using one of the following three formats. NetWare will then automatically convert each byte you enter into its corresponding binary value.

- The exact ASCII character
- The binary value of the byte expressed as a decimal number enclosed in angle brackets (< >)
- The name of an ASCII control character enclosed in angle brackets (< >). A window of ASCII control characters as shown in Figure 11-24 may be displayed by first highlighting a function, pressing the F1 key, and then using the Page Down key.

Figure 11-23

Creating a new function

Figure 11-24

Help screen showing ASCII control characters

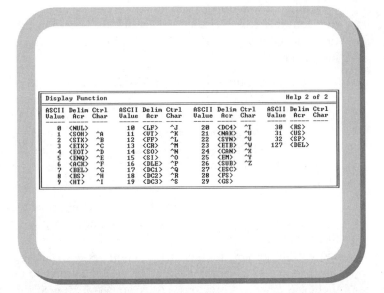

For the example under discussion, the escape sequence can be entered as <ESC>t150R, as shown in Figure 11-25. Once the Function Definition window is completed, use the Esc and Enter keys to save the new function and return to the functions window. When you have no more new functions to add, use the Esc key until you return to the PrintDef Options main menu.

Figure 11-25

Entering an escape
code sequence

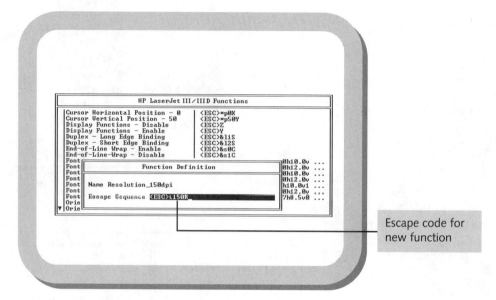

Escape code for
new function

Creating a new print device

If you have a new printer that does not yet have a printer definition file, you might need to create a special printer device in your NET$PRN.DAT database. Suppose, for example, your company has purchased a new color bubble-jet printer and you cannot locate a .PDF file for this printer model. To create this printer definition in the database, you first need to locate the required escape code sequences in the printer documentation and then define what functions and modes your users will need. Regardless of what modes and functions you use, make sure to identify and enter the functions that will reset the printer back to its startup mode. The print server needs these functions when it uses the reinitialize mode to reset the printer upon completing a print job.

After identifying the printer modes you will need and the corresponding functions, use the PRINTDEF utility to create the print device and define the modes and functions. First select Print Devices from the PrintDef Options menu. Use the Edit Print Devices option to display the print devices currently in the NET$PRN.DAT database. To create the new print device, press the Ins key and enter a descriptive name for the new printer. Pressing [Enter] adds the new print device to the Print Devices window.

To add device functions and modes for the new printer, select the new device and press [Enter] to display the Device Edit Options menu. The first step in setting up the new print device is entering the functions. Select the Device Functions option and use the Ins key to enter the functions, as described previously. Next, define the new printer modes. Select the Device Modes option and use the Ins key to enter the modes, as described previously. After you have entered the printer modes, press the Esc key until you return to the PrintDef Options menu. The new printer definition is ready for testing as soon as you exit the PRINTDEF utility and save the changes you have made to your printer database.

Updating the NET$PRN.DAT database

Modifications to the NET$PRN.DAT database are stored in a temporary file. The database itself is not updated until you exit the PRINTDEF utility and select the option to save the database. This allows the network administrator to abort the PRINTDEF process without affecting the current database in case an error is made that damages the current printer configuration files. To exit PRINTDEF and save the changes you have made to the NET$PRN.DAT database, first use the Esc key to return to the PrintDef Options menu. From the PrintDef Options menu, press the Esc key and type Yes to the "Exit PrintDef" query. If you have made changes to the NET$PRN.DAT database, the PRINTDEF utility will display the Exit Options menu shown in Figure 11-26.

Figure 11-26

PRINTDEF's Exit Options menu

Highlight the "Save Data Base, then Exit" option. Pressing [Enter] saves the changes you have made to the current printer database. To exit PRINTDEF and abort any changes, select the "EXIT without saving Data Base" option. To return to the PrintDef Options menu, select the "Do Not EXIT" option. After exiting the PRINTDEF utility and saving the changes to the database, test your printer and forms definitions by using the PRINTCON utility to set up print configuration jobs. This will be described in the next section.

WORKING WITH PRINT JOB CONFIGURATIONS

The network administrator can establish individual printer configurations for each user. The configuration can include special printer modes and functions as well as standard CAPTURE command parameters, such as timeout and banner information. Each set of print job configurations is stored in a file called **PRINTCON.DAT**, located in the user's SYS:MAIL\userid subdirectory. Once print job configurations have been established, a user can issue CAPTURE commands with the J=*jobname* parameter. The output is sent to a print queue with a standard set of parameters automatically; it isn't necessary to include all the parameters with each CAPTURE command.

Any user can access the PRINTCON utility to work with print job configurations in his or her SYS:MAIL subdirectory. Only the network SUPERVISOR or a supervisor equivalent user, however, has the option of copying print jobs. Because PRINTCON affects only print job configurations that are in the current user's SYS:MAIL subdirectory, the network administrator needs to create or modify print job configurations for a user while logged in with that user's name. The network administrator can then log in as SUPERVISOR and use the copy option of PRINTCON to copy print configurations from one user account to other user accounts.

In some organizations, workgroups or departments have unique print job configurations. In these cases, it works well to create a special username for each workgroup. You use that username to maintain the print job configurations for all members of the group. You can log in as SUPERVISOR and copy the print configurations from the special username to all members of that workgroup.

The first print configuration created in a user's PRINTCON database becomes the default print configuration for print jobs created by that user. If a CAPTURE or NPRINT command is issued by that user with no parameters, the print queue, timeout, banner, notify option, and other parameters will be obtained from the default print job configuration. This means that the first configuration you create in a user's PRINTCON database should be the one the user will access most frequently. PRINTCON allows you to change the default print configuration or assign a different print configuration to be the default. While PRINTCON allows you to create, change, and delete print configurations, it does not allow you to delete a user's print configuration database. If you need to remove all print configurations for a user, you have to use the DOS DEL or FILER utility to delete the user's PRINTCON database manually by first changing to the user's SYS:MAIL subdirectory. Then, use the DOS DEL command or FILER utility to remove the PRINTCON.DAT file. To do this, first select the Other Information option of SYSCON's User Information menu to determine the user's eight-digit user ID. Then change to the SYS:MAIL\user ID subdirectory and delete the PRINTCON.DAT file.

A fast way to document the usernames for all mail subdirectories is to enter the command TLIST SYS:MAIL*.* >PRN from any directory.

Using PRINTCON to manage print configurations

To use PRINTCON to work with print configurations, first log in as the user whose print configurations you want to access. Then start the PRINTCON utility from any network directory to display the Available Options menu shown in Figure 11-27. To access the current user's print configurations, select the Edit Print Job Configurations option. This displays the Print Job Configurations window showing any existing print configurations.

To create a new print job configuration, press the Ins key and enter a name for it. The name should identify the print job configuration clearly, but should also be as brief as possible to make it easier to remember when the user issues CAPTURE commands. After the name has been entered for the new print job configuration, PRINTCON displays the Edit Print Job Configuration window, as shown in Figure 11-28. Notice that most of the fields correspond to CAPTURE command parameters. The "File contents" field corresponds to the T (tab) and NT (no tab) options on the CAPTURE or NPRINT command and consists of either **byte stream** or **text** options. (Byte stream corresponds to the no tab (NT) parameter, and text corresponds to the tab parameter.) You should use the byte stream rather than the text option when sending output to sophisticated printers, such as lasers, because the text option will attempt to expand tab codes into several spaces. This can cause incorrect output results on laser printers because the tab codes might actually be part of a special printer setup mode.

Figure 11-27

PRINTCON's Available
Options menu

To send output to a specific printer, select the Print queue field to display a list of print queues on the default file server. You can then highlight the print queue for the desired printer and press [Enter]. To use one of the print modes defined for a printer, highlight the Device field. Pressing [Enter] displays a window showing all print devices in the NET$PRN.DAT database. Highlight the correct printer for the specified print queue and press [Enter] to select that printer.

Figure 11-28

Edit Print Job
Configuration window

After the correct print device has been selected, highlight the Mode field and press [Enter]. This displays a window showing all modes defined for the printer selected in the Device field. You can now select the desired printer setup mode and press [Enter] to attach that mode to this print job. To prevent printing a banner before each print job, select the "Print banner" field and change the Yes to No. To enable a timeout for the CAPTURE command, select the "Enable timeout" field and change the No to Yes. The default timeout, 5 seconds, appears in the "Timeout count" field. You can change the default 5 seconds up to a maximum of 1000 seconds by highlighting the field and pressing [Enter]. Use the Backspace key to erase the existing time and enter a new number of seconds.

 Placing too small a value in the "Timeout count" field can cause printer output to be separated and printed as two different print jobs.

Once the fields on the Edit Print Job Configuration window are changed to your satisfaction, press [Esc] to save the print job in the current user's PRINTCON.DAT database and return to the Print Job Configurations window. Notice that the first print job configuration is automatically defined as the default for this user account.

To change an existing print job configuration, highlight the print job configuration you want to change and press [Enter]. The Edit Print Job Configuration window containing the options shown in Figure 11-28 is displayed. Make any necessary changes and press [Esc] to save the modified print configuration. To delete a print configuration, simply highlight the configuration you want to delete and press the Del key. After the deletion is confirmed, the print configuration is removed from the print configuration database for that user. You cannot delete the default print configuration, however. If you want to remove all print configurations for a user, you need to delete the PRINTCON.DAT file from that user's SYS:MAIL subdirectory.

Using PRINTCON to copy print job configurations

If you are logged in as SUPERVISOR or as a supervisor equivalent user, the Available Options menu will contain an option to copy print job configurations (see Figure 11-27). As a supervisor, you can copy print job configurations from any user's PRINTCON.DAT file, including the supervisor's, to any other user. Before copying the PRINTCON.DAT file from the current user, however, you need to update the database with any changes you have made since you started PRINTCON. Just as with PRINTDEF, changes to the PRINTCON database are stored in a temporary file until you exit the PRINTCON utility and save the changes. After saving the updated PRINTCON database you can then restart PRINTCON and copy the print job configurations to the target users.

To copy new or changed job configurations from one user to another, first save the PRINTCON.DAT database for the current user by pressing the Esc key from the Available Options menu. Select Yes to exit the PRINTCON program. At this point, PRINTCON displays the Save Print Job Configuration window if any changes have been made to the print job configurations. To save the changes you have made, press [Enter] to select Yes. The changes are written to the current user's PRINTCON database. If you don't want to save any changes you have made, highlight No and press

[Enter]. In order to copy the PRINTCON.DAT database from one user's account to another, you must be logged in as a supervisor equivalent user. If you have been working on a user's print configuration logged in as that user and want to copy configurations to other user accounts, you must log out from the current user account and then log back in as SUPERVISOR. (Otherwise, the copy option will not appear on the PRINTCON Available Options menu.)

To copy a user's print configuration database to another user account, start PRINTCON and select the Copy Print Job Configurations option. PRINTCON displays a window asking you to enter the name of the source user—that is, the user from whom you want to copy the print job configurations. Enter the username and press [Enter] to display the Target User window. Now enter the username of the user to whom you want to copy the print job configurations. Pressing [Enter] copies all configurations from the source user to the target user's PRINTCON file. After copying the print job configurations, PRINTCON will return to the Available Options menu. You need to repeat this process to copy the PRINTCON database to each of the other users who need to use these printer configurations.

Accessing print configurations

After print configurations have been established for each user, you can use the CAPTURE and NPRINT commands to access specific configuration parameters by including the name of the print job configuration (J) in the command, as shown in Figure 11-29. If you want to override a configuration parameter, specify the parameter in the CAPTURE command. The second CAPTURE command in Figure 11-29, for example, contains a print queue and timeout factor. The command will send the output to the specified print queue instead of the print queue specified in the landscape print job configuration. The remaining landscape parameters will be effected.

Figure 11-29

A CAPTURE command with a print configuration

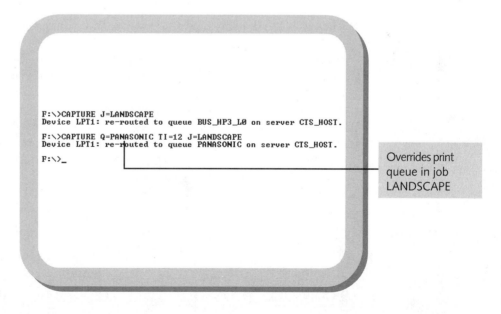

```
F:\>CAPTURE J=LANDSCAPE
Device LPT1: re-routed to queue BUS_HP3_L0 on server CTS_HOST.

F:\>CAPTURE Q=PANASONIC TI=12 J=LANDSCAPE
Device LPT1: re-routed to queue PANASONIC on server CTS_HOST.

F:\>_
```

Overrides print queue in job LANDSCAPE

CHAPTER SUMMARY

After installing the network printing environment, network administrators need to focus attention on the customization and day-to-day management of network printing. Managing network printing involves monitoring network printer status, controlling printers, and working with print queues. The PCONSOLE utility maintains print queues and print server configurations, and can also be used by print server operators to provide such printer controls as mounting new forms, stopping and starting printers, marking the top of the form, and downing the print server. The print server operator can also use PCONSOLE to make temporary changes to a running print server, such as adding a print queue to a printer or including another user in a printer's notification list. The PSC command can be used to issue control commands to network printers directly from the DOS prompt. This makes the PSC command a good choice to use in batch files and menus. It enables users to issue commands to network printers with ease.

NetWare v3.1x printing can be further enhanced by allowing a print server to service print queues on other file servers. This is accomplished in two steps. First, the file server is added to the list of file servers to be serviced by the print server. Then a mirrored print server is created on the other file server. The mirrored print server has the exact names and number of printers as are defined in the primary print server. Because the printer can be defined in only one place, the printer definitions in each of the printer configurations for the mirrored print server are labeled "Defined Elsewhere." The mirrored print server is then used to attach print queues for that file server to the appropriate printer numbers.

Customizing network printing involves establishing form numbers for different sizes of paper and defining special printer setup sequences, called modes. When a paper change is needed, the network printer pauses. A message is issued to the operator asking for the new form. After changing the paper, the printer operator can use the PCONSOLE or PSC command to restart the printer.

The PRINTDEF utility is used to customize the printing environment. It maintains in the SYS:PUBLIC directory a database named NET$PRN.DAT, which consists of special modes and functions for print devices along with print form definitions. You can use the PRINTDEF utility to import printer definition files (PDFs) into the NET$PRN.DAT database. The PDFs contain printer setup modes that consist of one or more printer functions. Each printer function defines a printer escape code sequence that directs the printer to perform a specific function. The PRINTCON utility allows each user to have a customized set of print configurations that simplify access to printers and allow for special printer setup modes using devices defined in the print device database (NET$PRN.DAT). Each user's print configurations are stored in a file called PRINTCON.DAT located in the user's SYS:MAIL\user ID subdirectory.

COMMAND SUMMARY

Command	Syntax	Definition
PCONSOLE	*PCONSOLE*	Creates, deletes, and manages print queues and print servers. Also controls and monitors printers and manages and resequences jobs stored in print queues.

PRINTCON	*PRINTCON*	Creates, maintains, and copies print job configurations. Print job configurations are stored in the PRINTCON.DAT file located in each user's SYS:MAIL\user ID subdirectory and can be used to establish defaults and standard printing configurations used by the CAPTURE, NPRINT, and PCONSOLE commands when jobs are placed in a print queue.
PRINTDEF	*PRINTDEF*	Maintains the NET$PRN.DAT database, located in the SYS:PUBLIC directory. It contains information on print devices and print forms.
PSC	*PSC* *[P=printernumber] Action* *[PS=printservername]*	Sends control commands directly from the DOS prompt or batch file to the specified printer. Replace *printservername* with the name of the print server that controls the printer. Replace *printernumber* with the number of the printer to which you want to send the control command. Command options include mark, status, pause, start, abort, stop, keep, form feed, mount form, private, shared, and cancel down.

KEY TERMS

byte stream option

landscape

NET$PRN.DAT

portrait

PRINTCON.DAT

printer definition file (PDF)

printer function

printer mode

text option

REVIEW QUESTIONS

1. The _____ utility is used to assign names to print forms.

2. Write the path and filename to the database that is used to contain print device and print form information maintained by the PRINTDEF utility.

    _____

3. The _____ utility is used to set up print job configurations for individual users.

4. Assume a user's ID is 12000004. Write the path and filename of the file that is used to contain the user's print job configurations.

    _____

5. What option is not available to users running the PRINTCON utility?

    _____

6. The _____ option of the Print Server Status and Control Menu should be used to down the print server.

7. List five of the seven printer control functions that can be performed from the PCONSOLE utility.

   _____

   _____

   _____

   _____

   _____

8. On the line below, name a print server control function that can be performed from the PCONSOLE utility that cannot be done with the PSC command?

   _____

9. On the line below, name a print server control function that can be performed with the PSC command that cannot be done with PCONSOLE?

   _____

10. On the line below, write a PSC command to view the status of printer number 4 on the PSC_PSERVER print server.

    _____

11. On the line below, write a PSC command to mount form number 3 in printer 1 of the PSC_PSERVER print server.

    _____

12. On the lines below, define two steps in setting up a print server to service print queues on another file server.

    _____

    _____

13. When PRINTDEF is used, a single escape code sequence is referred to as a(n) _____.

14. Write a CAPTURE command to use a print configuration named LTR_LANDSCAPE.

    _____

15. After a printer configuration job is changed for a user, what two steps must be completed before you can copy the revised configuration file to other users' accounts?

    _____

    _____

16. On the line below, write a DOS SET command to allow the PSC command automatically to use printer number 1 on print server PSC_PSERVER.

    _____

17. When a mirrored print server is set up on another file server, the _____ printer type must be selected for each printer defined on the primary print server.

18. On the line below, write a CAPTURE command to use the LABEL print configuration on print queue LASERII with form type 3.

_____

19. Given the following Print Server Information menu options, which option(s) would you use to add a print queue temporarily to printer number 1?

_____ Change Password

_____ Full Name

_____ Print Server Configuration

_____ Print Server ID

_____ Print Server Operators

_____ Print Server Status/Control

_____ Print Server Users

20. Assume you have just made changes to the SUPERVISOR print configurations and then copied them to other users. The users report, however, that their print configurations are not using the new options. In the space below, describe the reason for the problem.

EXERCISES

Exercise 11-1: Managing Print Jobs

In this exercise you will use the PCONSOLE utility to change print job parameters and rearrange the sequence of jobs in print queues. To perform this exercise, you will need to have a print queue, named ##LOCAL, that has your student username defined as a print queue operator. If this print queue does not currently exist, you will need to log in using a supervisor equivalent username, use PCONSOLE to create a print queue named ##LOCAL, and then make your username the print queue operator. If you are not able to access a supervisor equivalent username, your instructor will create this print queue for you.

For the second part of this exercise, your instructor will need to have the classroom print server running, and your username must be an operator of the classroom print server in order to allow you to add your print queue to the classroom printer.

Part 1

1. Log in using your assigned student username.

2. Use PCONSOLE to change the status of the ##LOCAL print queue to prevent print servers from printing jobs.

3. Use PCONSOLE to place the files PRINT.BAS and INQUIRY.BAS from the SYS:EXAMPLE\SALES\ORDERS subdirectory into your ##LOCAL print queue.

4. Issue a CAPTURE command from your workstation to send output to the ##LOCAL print queue with a timeout of 5 sec., no banner, and no form feed. On the line below, record the CAPTURE command.

_____

5. Use the following steps to place three print jobs in your print queue:

   ■ Press the Print Scrn key to print your screen.

   ■ **TYPE C:\AUTOEXEC.BAT > PRN**.

   ■ **TYPE C:\CONFIG.SYS > PRN**.

6. Use the PCONSOLE utility to rearrange the sequence of print jobs in the ##LOCAL print queue so that they appear in the following sequence:

   ■ The CONFIG.SYS file output

   ■ The AUTOEXEC.BAT file output

   ■ INQUIRY.BAS output

   ■ PRINT.BAS output

   ■ The print screen output

7. Use the Print Scrn key to print the screen showing your rearranged output.

8. Change the parameters of the CONFIG.SYS file so that the description reads "Workstation Configuration." Place a banner that includes your name and "CONFIG.SYS" as the banner name.

9. Change the parameters of the AUTOEXEC.BAT file to use form number 2.

10. Change the PRINT.BAS print job to print 20 min. from now.

11. Exit the PCONSOLE utility.

12. Return all printer ports to local mode. On the line below, record the command you use.

_____

13. Use the appropriate option of the CAPTURE command to verify the ENDCAP command.

Part 2

In this part of the exercise you will use the PCONSOLE utility to add your print queue to a printer running on the classroom printer and change the print queue status to allow the classroom print server to get jobs from your print queue.

1. Start PCONSOLE.

2. Use the Print Queue Information option to select your ##LOCAL print queue.

3. Select the option that will make your print jobs available to the print server. On the line below, record the option you use.

_____

4. Use the Esc key to return to the Available Options menu.

5. Use the Print Server option to select the classroom print server.

6. Select the Print Server Status/Control option to display the Print Server Status and Control Menu.

7. Select the option that will allow you to add a print queue to an existing printer. On the line below, record the name of the option.

_____

8. Select printer number 0, which is a local printer attached to the print server. On the line below, record the name of the printer you plan to use.

_____

9. Add your print queue to the printer with a priority of 2.

10. Use the Esc key to return to the Print Server Status and Control Menu.

11. Add your name to the notification list of the printer selected in Step 8.

12. Select the option that will allow you to monitor and control the printer that will be printing your print jobs. On the line below, record the option you select.

_____

13. Wait for the printer to ask for form 2 to be mounted.

14. Change the form number to 2. Record the results below.

_____

15. When the printer asks for form number 0, cancel the print job. On the line below, record the name of the print job that was canceled.

_____

16. Print the remaining jobs using form number 0.

17. Use the Esc key to return to the Available Options menu.

18. Use the Print Queue Information option to view the jobs remaining in your print queue.

19. Wait for your deferred PRINT.BAS job to be printed.

20. Use the Print Server Status/Control option of the Print Server Information menu to remove your print queue from the printer's queue list and your name from the printer notification list.

21. Use [Alt][F10] to exit.

22. Log out.

23. Have your instructor check your printed output.

Exercise 11-2: Managing Print Queues

In this exercise you will locate print queues in the SYS:SYSTEM directory and explore their contents. To perform this exercise, you will need to have two print queues, named ##LOCAL and ##REMOTE, that have your student username defined as a print queue operator. If these print queues do not currently exist, you will need to log in using a supervisor equivalent username and create them with PCONSOLE. Then make your username the print queue operator of each queue. If you are not able to access a supervisor equivalent username, your instructor will create the print queues for you.

1. Use PCONSOLE to find the print queue ID numbers for each of your print queues. Record them below:

    ##LOCAL: _____

    ##REMOTE: _____

2. Use PCONSOLE to place the AUTOEXEC.BAT and CONFIG.SYS print files from your local workstation in the ##LOCAL print queue.

3. Use PCONSOLE to place the file CUSTOMER.DOC from the SYS:EXAMPLE\SALES\ORDERS directory into the ##REMOTE print queue.

4. Exit PCONSOLE and change your default DOS prompt to point to the ##REMOTE print queue.

5. Use the NDIR command to list all files in the print queue directory.

6. Hidden files ending with the extension .SRV contain print server information for the print queue. Hidden files ending with .SYS contain the print queue parameters you see when looking at a job from PCONSOLE. All files with the extension .Q are print jobs. Use the TYPE command to determine which print job is which. In the space below, record their filenames, attributes, and print job descriptions.

7. Although you can delete print job files with the DOS DEL command, the print job parameters that exist in the .SYS file will still be displayed in PCONSOLE. To prove this to yourself, use the DOS delete command to delete the print job containing the AUTOEXEC.BAT printout. On the line below, record the name of the file you delete.

    _____

    Next, start PCONSOLE to display the contents of the ##LOCAL print queue. Because the AUTOEXEC.BAT file is still defined in the .SYS file, the AUTOEXEC.BAT job should appear in the print job window. Does the AUTOEXEC.BAT print job still exist in your print queue?

    Yes or No _____

8. Use PCONSOLE to delete the print jobs from the ##LOCAL print queue.

9. Exit PCONSOLE.

10. Log out.

Exercise 11-3: Controlling the Print Server

In this exercise you will use the PCONSOLE utility and PSC commands to control the printers attached to your print server. You will perform such functions as marking and changing forms, making the remote printer private, and downing the print server. To do this exercise, you will need to have a print queue, named ##LOCAL, that has your student username defined as a print queue operator. If this print queue does not currently exist, you will need to log in using a supervisor equivalent username and use PCONSOLE to create a print queue named ##REMOTE and then make your username the print queue operator. If you are not able to access a supervisor equivalent username, your instructor will create this print queue for you. In addition, your instructor will need to have the classroom print server running, and your username must be an operator of the classroom print server so you can add your print queue to the classroom printer.

1. Log in using your assigned student username.

2. Use a CAPTURE command to direct output from the LPT1 port to the ##REMOTE print queue using a timeout of 10 sec., form type 2, a form feed, no tabs, and a banner containing your name along with the filename REPORT. On the line below, record the CAPTURE command you use.

   _____

3. Change to the SYS:EXAMPLE\SALES\ORDERS directory.

4. Enter the PRINT command to run the report program and print the output to your ##REMOTE print queue.

5. Start PCONSOLE.

6. Use PCONSOLE to place the following jobs in the ##REMOTE print queue:

   ■ The CONFIG.SYS and AUTOEXEC.BAT files from your local workstation

   ■ The README.TXT file located in the SYS:EXAMPLE\SALES\SURVEY directory

7. Change the sequence of the print jobs to make the REPORT job from Step 4 the second job printed.

8. Select the option that will make your print jobs available to the print server. On the line below, record the option you use.

   _____

9. Use the Esc key to return to the Available Options menu.

10. Use the Print Server option to select the classroom print server. On the line below, record the name of the print server selected.

11. Select the Print Server Status/Control option to display the Print Server Status and Control Menu.

12. Select the option that will allow you to add a print queue to an existing printer. On the line below, record the name of the option.

    _____

13. Select a remote printer whose number is your assigned student number minus 10. For example, if your student number is 14, select printer number 4. On the line below, record the name and number of the printer you select.

    Printer number: _____

    Printer name: _____

14. Add your print queue to the printer with a priority of 2.

15. Use the Esc key to return to the Print Server Status and Control Menu.

16. Add your name to the notification list of the printer selected in Step 13.

17. Use the Esc key to return to the Print Server Status and Control Menu.

18. Use the Server Info option to determine the print server status. On the line below, record the status.

   _____

19. Press [Enter] to see the other two status options. On the lines below, record the options.

   _____

   _____

20. Exit PCONSOLE.

21. Run RPRINTER and select the print server identified in Step 10 and printer number defined in Step 13.

22. When the remote printer attached to the print server gets to the REPORT print job, it should stop and send a message to your workstation asking for form 2 to be mounted. Assume you have just changed forms. Now issue the PSC command that will print a test line at the top of the page. On the line below, record the PSC command you use to mark the new form.

   _____

23. To make it easier to issue PSC commands, use the DOS SET command to place in the environment space the name of your print server and the number of the printer you are using. On the line below, record the DOS SET command you use.

   _____

24. To display the contents of the DOS environment space, type **SET** and press **[Enter]**.

25. Issue a PSC command to take the remote printer off line for private use. On the line below, record the command you use.

   _____

26. What is the status message for the Remote Printer after it has been taken offline?

   _____

27. Print your screen. Notice that this output is sent to your local printer.

28. Issue a PSC command to share your remotely attached printer. On the line below, record the command you use.

   _____

29. Issue a PSC command to start the printer with form type 2. On the line below, record the command you use.

   _____

30. After the AUTOEXEC.BAT file has been printed, issue a PSC command to return the printer to form type 0. On the line below, record the command you use.

31. Enter the command RPRINTER /R to remove the remote printer software from your workstation.

32. Use the PCONSOLE utility to remove your ##REMOTE print queue from the printer number recorded in Step 13.

33. Log out.

EXERCISE

Case 11-1: Bayview Window & Door

The Bayview Window & Door company sells and installs customized windows and doors to construction companies in a three-state region. It currently uses a Novell network to support PC applications in its sales department. The sales department uses an HP LaserJet III compatible printer that is used for printing on company letterhead. The letterhead paper is located in the top tray of the printer; standard forms are located in the lower tray. Occasionally the department needs to print on legal forms and has a special legal-size paper tray that can be loaded in the lower paper drawer of the printer. Lately the department has needed to print landscape output on both legal and standard paper, but members have been unable to set the printer up properly for landscape mode with their current application software. They have called on you to help them customize their printing environment so they can print landscape output on both standard and legal paper as well as prevent output that was intended for legal forms from being printed on standard paper. Sales department staff occasionally need to print labels on special label forms. Because the labels are fairly expensive, it's important not to print other jobs on them by mistake.

The work for Bayview Window & Door involves the following tasks:

1. Document the form types and associated form numbers in the table below:

Form Number	Form Name	Description
F##		
F##		
F##		

2. Log in as a supervisor equivalent user.

3. Use PRINTDEF to define the form types you documented in Step 1. Be sure to include "F##" at the beginning of each form number to separate it from forms created by other students.

4. Use PRINTDEF to import the HP LaserJet III printer definition file, and then use the Edit Print Devices option along with the F3 key to change the printer device name to ##HPIII.

5. Use PRINTDEF to remove all printer modes except the following:

Letter Landscape, 45 lpp, 10 cpi

Legal Landscape, 45 lpp, 10 cpi

Letter Portrait, 60 lpp, 10 cpi

Legal Portrait, 78 lpp, 10 cpi

6. Add the lower paper tray function to the printer modes listed in Step 4.

7. Create a new printer mode called Letterhead. Include all the functions from the Letter Portrait mode, replacing the lower paper tray with the upper paper tray.

8. Exit PRINTDEF and save the printer database changes.

9. Start SYSCON and create two sales users named ##SALES1 and ##SALES2. Grant these users Read and File scan rights to the SYS:EXAMPLE directory.

10. Exit SYSCON.

11. Use PCONSOLE to create a ##LOCAL print queue if you do not already have one.

12. Log out.

13. Log in as user ##SALES1.

14. Use PRINTCON to set up the following standard print configurations for the ##SALES1 user.

Print Job Configuration Name	Print Job Description
Standard (default print job) B=Standard	Q=##LOCAL no banner timeout of 10 sec. print mode = Letter Portrait form type = standard paper
Legal B=Legal	Q=##LOCAL no banner timeout of 10 sec. print mode = Legal Portrait form type = legal paper
Standard Landscape B=Standard_Legal	Q=##LOCAL no banner timeout of 10 sec. print mode = Letter Landscape
Legal Landscape B=Legal_Landscape	Q=##LOCAL no banner timeout of 10 sec. print mode = Legal Landscape form type = legal paper
Letterhead B=Letterhead	Q=##LOCAL no banner timeout of 10 sec. print mode = Letterhead form type = standard paper

15. Log in using a supervisor equivalent username. Copy the print configuration from user ##SALES1 to user ##SALES2.

16. Log in as user ##SALES2.

17. Issue a CAPTURE command to use the default print configuration. On the line below, record the command.

18. Use the Print Scrn key to place a job in the ##LOCAL print queue using the default print configuration.

19. Issue a CAPTURE command to use the letterhead print mode. On the line below, record the command.

    _____

20. Change to the SYS:EXAMPLE\SALES\ORDERS directory and use the DOS EDIT command to retrieve the CUSTOMER.DOC file. Use [Alt][F] to print the documentation file using the default print job configuration.

21. Issue a CAPTURE command to use Letter Landscape printer mode. On the line below, record the command.

    _____

22. Change to the SYS:EXAMPLE\SALES\ORDERS directory and enter the PRINT command to print a copy of the customer order report to the ##LOCAL print queue.

23. Remove all print configurations for user ##SALES2. Change to the mail directory for user ##SALES2. On the line below, record the command you use.

    _____

24. Use the NDIR command to list all files. On the line below, record the name of the printer configuration file.

    _____

25. Delete the files listed in Step 23.

26. Use PCONSOLE to view the jobs in your print queue.

27. Have your instructor check your print queue jobs and PRINTCON configuration and sign below when they are satisfactory.

    Instructor signature: _____

28. Log in using a supervisor equivalent username.

29. Use PRINTDEF to remove your form definitions and the ##HPIII print device.

30. Remove the users ##SALE1 and ##SALE2 and log out of the file server.

SUPERIOR TECHNICAL COLLEGE PROBLEMS

Now that the college's network printing environment has been installed and tested, Dave Johnson would like you to customize the printing with form names and special printer modes. Because each department has slightly different printing needs, Dave would also like you to make access to network printer options easier by setting up printer configurations for each department.

Project 11-1: Customizing the Printer Configuration

Laurie Holt, Mimi Ito, and Barbara Rau will be sharing an HP LaserJet III compatible laser printer with letterhead paper in the upper tray and standard forms in the lower tray to perform most of their network printing. Periodically Laurie needs to print labels from the upper paper tray and wants a way to prevent other users from printing from the upper tray when labels are loaded. Mimi occasionally needs to print output from a database file using landscape orientation in order to get all the fields to fit across the page. She would like to have the option of printing in landscape mode on the laser printer.

The student services department has both laser and dot-matrix printers. Staff members would like to have reports generated by both the graduate system and the testing system sent to the dot-matrix printer. Word processing documents should be printed on the laser printer. Letterhead stationery is normally kept in the upper tray of the laser printer and plain paper is kept in the lower tray. Occasionally staff members need to print on legal size forms. They would like to have a way to stop the printer and allow the legal forms tray to be loaded in the lower paper drawer before printing is resumed.

Dave would like you to develop a set of printer configurations for both the support staff and the student services staff and then document these print jobs using the attached print configuration form.

Print Job Configurations

Developed by: _____   Date: _____

File server name: _____

Department: _____

Master username: _____
  (Name of user from whom print configurations are copied)

Form Number	Name	Description

Printer Configuration Jobs

Print Job Configuration Name	Form	Queue	Print Device	Mode	Banner	Timeout	Other
Default							

Project 11-2: Setting Up Forms

After the print configurations and forms are defined to meet the customized print-ing needs of the support and student services departments, your next task is to use the PRINTDEF utility to add the form definitions to the printer device database. If you do not have access to the classroom server as a supervisor equivalent user, your instructor will provide you with a list of forms that have been established for you to use.

Start PRINTDEF and use the Forms option to define the print forms you docu-mented in problem 1. Precede each form name with F##*n*, where ## represents your assigned student number, and *n* represents the form number. Because other students will be setting up forms on the classroom file server, the actual form num-ber you use will be based on the existing form definitions. Record the actual form number and your form name below:

Form Number	Name
_____	_____
_____	_____
_____	_____
_____	_____
_____	_____

Project 11-3: Defining Printer Modes

After all form numbers have been defined, the next task is to import the HP LaserJet III printer definition file and establish the necessary printer modes. If you do not have access to the classroom server as a supervisor equivalent user, your instructor will load the HP LaserJet III printer definition file with the necessary print modes. You can use PRINTDEF to verify and document the printer modes and functions with which you will be working.

1. Use PRINTDEF to import the HP LaserJet III printer definition file and then use the Edit Print Devices option along with the F3 key to change the printer device name to ##HPIII.

2. Modify the letter landscape and letter portrait modes to use the lower paper tray function.

3. Create a new mode, called Letterhead, that contains functions to reset the printer, select portrait orientation, and use the upper paper tray.

Print Mode	Functions

4. Export your modified print device to a printer definition file located on your local disk drive.

5. Document the functions contained in each of the printer modes you documented in problem 1.

Project 11-4: Using PRINTCON to Create Print Jobs

Once the print forms and modes have been defined, the final task in customizing the printer environment is creating the print job configurations you documented in problem 1 for each department. Dave would like you to do this by creating a master PRINTCON user for each department and maintaining the print configurations in that user's PRINTCON database. You can then copy the printer configurations to each of the other users in the department. In this problem you are to create two master PRINTCON users, one for support and one for student services. You can then set up the print job configurations documented in problem 1 for each department's master user and then copy them to all users.

Test your print jobs by using the CAPTURE command to select each print job and then using the Print Scrn key to send output to the print queue. You can then use PCONSOLE to view the print job parameters and compare them to your printer configuration. If you have access to an HP LaserJet compatible printer, attach it to your computer and load your print server. The output should be printed with the appropriate printer configuration.

After you have completed testing the print configurations for each user, have your instructor check your printing environment and sign on the line below.

Instructor signature: _____

## CHAPTER TWELVE

LOGIN SCRIPTS

Once the network directory structure has been established and secured, the user accounts created, the applications installed, and the network printing environment configured, the next challenge for the network administrator is to make this complex system easy to access and use. For most workstations, making the network system easy to use requires creating login scripts and menus. Login scripts make it possible for users to log in to a file server and access network services by establishing drive mappings, providing informational messages, redirecting printer output to default printers, and executing special programs.

AFTER READING THIS CHAPTER AND COMPLETING THE EXERCISES YOU WILL BE ABLE TO:

- IDENTIFY THE THREE CATEGORIES OF LOGIN SCRIPT FILES AND HOW THEY ARE USED.

- IDENTIFY THE PURPOSE AND CORRECT SYNTAX OF LOGIN SCRIPT COMMANDS.

- IDENTIFY THE RECOMMENDED SYSTEM LOGIN SCRIPT COMMANDS.

- WRITE A SYSTEM LOGIN SCRIPT TO MEET THE NEEDS OF A TYPICAL NETWORK SYSTEM.

- WRITE USER LOGIN SCRIPTS TO MEET PERSONAL PROCESSING NEEDS OF USERS.

Workstations logging in with Microsoft Windows or with Apple Macintosh computers do not need a login script to be executed because they can have the workstation drive mappings and printer setup configured in the local workstation's environment.

Because establishing the DOS user environment plays such an important part in the job of a network administrator, Novell requires CNAs to demonstrate their ability to use login scripts and menus. In this chapter, you will learn about login scripts and how to establish the necessary login scripts for your network system. Chapter 13 will cover the NetWare v3.12 menu system and show you how to create menus for the DOS users on your network system.

NETWARE LOGIN SCRIPTS

As you learned in previous chapters, any drive mapping or printer capture commands you establish while you are logged in to a file server are only effective until you log out. The next time you log in, you must again map each drive pointer you want to use and issue CAPTURE commands to redirect printer output to the appropriate print queues. Requiring users to re-establish their drive pointers and print queues not only means they must have much technical knowledge about the system, but also takes time away from productive work. To remedy this problem, NetWare allows you to configure the workstation environment for each user automatically. Each time a user logs in to a file server, NetWare executes a set of commands contained in login script files.

A NetWare **login script** is a file that contains a set of valid NetWare login command statements, as illustrated in Figure 12-1. Each login script command statement must contain a valid login script or NetWare command. The command statements in a login script file form a program that is processed by the LOGIN.EXE program after a user has identified him or herself by providing a valid username and optional password.

Figure 12-1

Login script

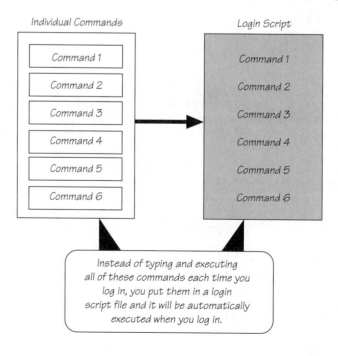

The NetWare login script system consists of three types of login script files: system, user, and default. The three types of login script files enable the network administrator to provide a standard environment for all users and still provide flexibility so the network administrator can meet individual user needs. The **system login script** file allows the network administrator to establish a systemwide standard configuration. The commands it contains are executed for all users when they first log in to the server. Individual user requirements can then be met with **user login script** files. Each user has his or her own personal login script file, which contains additional statements that are executed for that user after the system login script commands are executed. The **default login script** is a set of commands that establishes a default working environment for each user who does not have a defined user login script. After establishing login script files, you will need to disable the default login script, as described later in this chapter. Figure 12-2 contains a simple system login script command file that contains statements to map drive pointers for all users and displays a message that greets users when they log in.

Figure 12-2

Simple system
login script

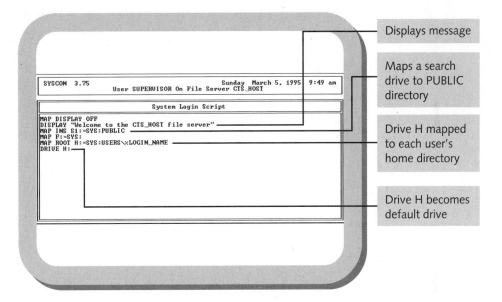

There are a limited number of commands that can be used in login script programs. You need to understand the individual statements before you can design and write login script programs. The following sections present valid login script command statements and how they are used. As a CNA you will need to be aware of the purpose of each login script command and how it can be used to help establish the workstation environment for a user.

Some login script command statements, such as MAP and ATTACH, have corresponding NetWare command line utilities. While the syntax and purpose of these commands are very similar to those of the command line utilities, the login script commands include special options or variables that are not available with the corresponding command line utility.

LOGIN SCRIPT VARIABLES

Many login script commands allow the use of variables as part of the command line. A **login script variable** contains a predefined value that allows login script commands to be used for multiple users. One common use of a login script variable, for example, is to map a drive letter to each user's home directory. If each user's home directory has the same name as his or her username, the following login script command, included in the system login script, will map the drive letter H to the home directory of each user when he or she logs in.

```
MAP ROOT H:=DATA:USERS\%LOGIN_NAME
```

Notice that the variable, LOGIN_NAME, is preceded by a percent sign (%). This identifies LOGIN_NAME as a variable rather than the name of a directory. The LOGIN.EXE program will substitute the name of the user who is currently logging in for the %LOGIN_NAME variable in the MAP command statement. It will then map the H drive letter to the user's specified home directory. Assume, for example, a user logs in with the username MARSIM. The login program will substitute the name MARSIM for the variable %LOGIN_NAME, creating the statement MAP ROOT H:=DATA:USERS\MARSIM.

Login script variables can be divided into several types, based on their usage. The **date variables** contain information about the current month, day, and year in a variety of formats, as shown in Figure 12-3. Date variables are useful for displaying current date information. The login script can also check for a specific day in order to perform special setup instructions. Assume, for example, certain users need to access the DATA:REPORTS directory every Friday. By including a DAY_OF_WEEK variable, you can write a login script command that maps a drive to the REPORTS directory only on Fridays. The value of a date variable is stored as an ASCII string of a fixed length. The DAY variable represents the day number of the current month and might contain only the values 01 to 31. The NDAY_OF_WEEK variable represents the day number of the week with Sunday being day number 1 and Saturday being day number 7.

 When using the DAY variable in an IF statement, it is important to include the leading 0 in front of day numbers 01 through 09 and then enclose the day numbers in quotation marks. (i.e. IF DAY>"09"THEN...)

Figure 12-3

Date variables

Variable	Description
DAY	Day number of the current month. Possible values range from 01 to 31.
DAY_OF_WEEK	Name of the current day of the week. Possible values are Monday, Tuesday, etc.
MONTH	The number of the current month. Possible values range from 01 for January to 12 for December.
MONTH_NAME	The name of the current month. Possible values range from January to December.
NDAY_OF_WEEK	The current weekday number, ranges from 1 for Sunday to 7 for Saturday.
SHORT_YEAR	The last two digits of the current year, for example 95 or 96.
YEAR	The full four-digit year, for example 1995 or 1996.

The **network variables** shown in Figure 12-4 can be used to display or check the network address and name of the default file server of the user who is currently logging in. The **time variables** shown in Figure 12-5 provide a variety of methods to view or check the login time. The GREETING_TIME variable is most often used in WRITE statements to display welcome messages. The difference between the HOUR24 variable and the HOUR variable is that the HOUR variable requires inclusion of the AM_PM variable to specify if the time is before or after noon. The HOUR24 variable is based on a 24-hour system, in which 12 represents noon and 13 represents 1:00 P.M. If you want to specify a time in the login script, the HOUR24 variable is often easier to use. If you want all users who log in before 3:00 P.M. to be notified of a special meeting, for example, you could write login script commands that use the HOUR24 variable to compare the current login hour to 15. If HOUR24 is less than 15, the login script commands could then display a notice of the meeting.

Figure 12-4

Network variables

Variable	Description
NETWORK_ADDRESS	The network address of the cabling system to which the user's workstation is attached. Expressed as an eight-digit hexadecimal number.
FILE_SERVER	The name of the current file server.

Figure 12-5

Time variables

Variable	Description
AM_PM	Day or night (A.M. or P.M.).
GREETING_TIME	Displays welcome messages. Possible values are: Morning, Afternoon, or Evening.
HOUR	The current hour of day or night, ranging from 01 through 12.
HOUR24	The current hour in 24-hour mode, ranging from 01 for 1:00 A.M. through 24 for 12:00 P.M.
MINUTE	The current minute, ranging from 00 through 59.
SECOND	The current second, ranging from 00 through 59.

The **user variables** (see Figure 12-6) allow you to view or check the user's login name, full name, or the hexadecimal ID given to the user in the bindery files. As described previously, the LOGIN_NAME variable is commonly used to map a drive letter to a user's home directory from within the system login script, provided the name of the user's home directory is the same as the user's login name. The FULL_NAME variable can be used to personalize greeting messages by including the user's name as part of the message.

Figure 12-6

User variables

Variable	Description
FULL_NAME	The user's full name, as defined from SYSCON or USERDEF.
LOGIN_NAME	The user's unique login name.
USER_ID	The hexadecimal number assigned by NetWare for the user login name.

The **workstation variables** MACHINE, OS, and OS_VERSION, shown in Figure 12-7, are most commonly used in the system login script when a search drive is mapped to the correct DOS version used on the workstation. The STATION variable contains the connection number assigned to the user's workstation. It can be used by some software packages to separate user temporary files, when the station number is included as part of the temporary filename. You can use the STATION variable to separate temporary files when you create menus (discussed in Chapter 13). The P_STATION variable contains the actual node address of the workstation that is logging in and can be used in login script files to cause certain processing to be performed on specific workstations. Suppose, for example, workstation address DC03D7D27 is used to run CAD software. You could include in the login script commands that use the P_STATION variable to check for station address DC03D7D27, then establish the necessary drive mappings, and start the CAD software.

Figure 12-7

Workstation variables

Variable	Description
OS	The workstation's operating system. Default value is MSDOS.
OS_VERSION	The version of DOS being used on the workstation that is processing the login script. For example, V6.20.
MACHINE	The long machine name that can be assigned in the SHELL.CFG or NET.CFG file. Default value is IBM_PC.
P_STATION	The node address of the network card in the workstation. Expressed as a 12-digit hexadecimal value.
SMACHINE	The short machine name that can be assigned in the SHELL.CFG or NET.CFG file. Default value is IBM.
STATION	The connection number of the current station.
SHELL_TYPE	The workstation's shell version number.

 The node address of any logged in workstation can be determined by the USERLIST /E command.

LOGIN SCRIPT COMMANDS

In many ways, creating login scripts is very similar to writing a computer program. Like any programming language, NetWare login scripts include commands that cause the computer to perform certain processing tasks. Also, like any programming language, login script commands are written according to rules that must be followed in order for the commands to be processed. These rules are commonly referred to as the **syntax** of the programming language. This section will show you the valid syntax of each NetWare login script command and provide examples of how to use it to perform common login functions. Before we turn to the individual login script commands, you should be aware of the following general rules that apply to all login script commands:

- Only valid login script command statements and comments can be placed in a login script file.

- Login script command lines can contain a maximum of 150 characters.

- Long commands can be allowed to "wrap" to the next line if there is not enough room on one line.

- The LOGIN.EXE program reads the login script commands one line at a time, and only one command is allowed on any command line.

- Commands can be entered in either uppercase or lowercase letters. Variables that are enclosed in quotation marks, however, must be preceded by a percent sign (%) and typed in uppercase letters.

- Comments are entered by preceding the text either with the REM command or with one of two symbols, an asterisk (*) or a semicolon (;).

MAP

The MAP command is the most important login script command. It is used to establish automatically the regular and search drive mappings a user needs to work with the NetWare environment from the DOS operating system. The syntax and use of the MAP login script command are very similar to the MAP command line utility described in Chapter 6. In the login script version, however, you can use identifier variables and relative drive letters as part of the MAP command syntax, as follows:

MAP [option] [drive:=path;drive:=path] [variable]

You can replace *option* in the MAP command with one of the following parameters:

Figure 12-8

MAP command parameters

Option Parameter	Description
ROOT	Makes a drive appear as the root of a volume to DOS and application programs
INS	Used with search drives to insert a new search drive at the sequence number you specify and then renumber any existing search drives
DEL	Removes the specified regular or search drive mapping

Replace *drive* with any valid network, local, or search drive. In addition to specifying a drive letter, you can use a relative drive specification, such as *1, to indicate the first network drive, *2 the second network drive, and so on. If the workstation's first network drive letter is F, *1 will be replaced with F, *2 will be replaced with G, and so on. If, on the other hand, a workstation's first network drive is L, *1 will be replaced with L, and *2 will be replaced with M, and so on. Replace *path* with a full directory path beginning with a DOS drive letter or NetWare volume name.

With the login script version of the MAP command, additional drive mappings can be placed on the same line by separating them with semicolons. If you want to map the F drive to the SYS: volume and the G drive to the DATA: volume, for example, you can issue the following MAP command statement:

MAP F:=SYS:; G:=DATA:

As mentioned earlier, login script variables can be included in the MAP statement. Commonly used variables include: %LOGIN_NAME, %OS, %OS_VERSION, and %MACHINE. The %OS, %OS_VERSION, and %MACHINE variables are often used to map a search drive to a specific DOS directory based on the version of DOS being used on the workstation logging in. The values for these variables are determined by the DOS requester or shell program and contain the following default values:

Figure 12-9

Variables for mapping DOS directory

Variable	Default Value
%MACHINE	IBM_PC
%OS	MSDOS
%OS_VERSION	The DOS version running on the workstation, specified as V6.20

If you create the directory structure shown in Figure 12-10 to contain your DOS software versions, you can use the following MAP command statement in a login script file in order to map the second search drive to the appropriate DOS version for the workstation currently logging in:

```
MAP S2:=SYS:PUBLIC\%MACHINE\%OS\%OS_VERSION
```

Figure 12-10

Sample DOS directory structure

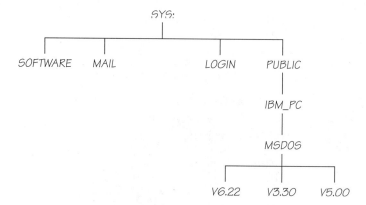

Other special MAP command statements include MAP DISPLAY OFF or MAP DISPLAY and MAP ERRORS OFF or MAP ERRORS ON. By default, MAP DISPLAY is set ON displaying the results of each MAP command in the login script. The MAP DISPLAY OFF command prevents the MAP commands from being displayed on the user workstation while they are executed. This MAP command is often included at the beginning of a login script command to reduce the amount of information that is displayed on the user workstations. The MAP ERRORS OFF command can be used to prevent the display on a user's workstation of error messages generated by MAP commands that specify invalid paths. This command is useful if you include drive mapping commands in a login script that you know will not be valid for all users. Rather than have a user be confused by error messages that do not affect him or her, include the MAP ERRORS OFF command before the MAP commands that contain the invalid drive paths.

COMSPEC

When DOS is booted from a local workstation, it stores the location of the COMMAND.COM file in the DOS environment space. Thereafter, anytime a program exits and COMMAND.COM has to be reloaded, DOS will check the environment space to determine the name and location of the command processor program. If workstations on your network do not have hard disk drives, it is important that you identify a location on the file server from which DOS can reload the COMMAND.COM program. The COMSPEC command allows the network administrator to set a location for loading COMMAND.COM in the DOS environment space. The proper syntax of the COMSPEC command follows:

COMSPEC = [path]COMMAND.COM

You can replace the optional *path* parameter with the location at which DOS can find the proper version of the COMMAND.COM program. Because there can be more than one version of DOS running on the workstations attached to the network, it is necessary to specify a path that will point to the correct COMMAND.COM for the DOS version that the workstation is running. To do this, most network administrators place the COMSPEC command after the MAP command that maps a search drive to the DOS external command directory, as follows:

MAP S2:=SYS:PUBLIC\%MACHINE\%OS\%OS_VERSION

COMSPEC=S2:COMMAND.COM

Notice that there is no forwardslash (/) between S2: and COMMAND.COM. A forwardslash in this position would indicate that the COMMAND.COM file is located on the root of the SYS: volume. When the slash is omitted, NetWare places the proper %OS_VERSION subdirectory name in the DOS environment space. This is illustrated by the DOS SET command shown in Figure 12-11.

Figure 12-11

Result of a
COMSPEC command

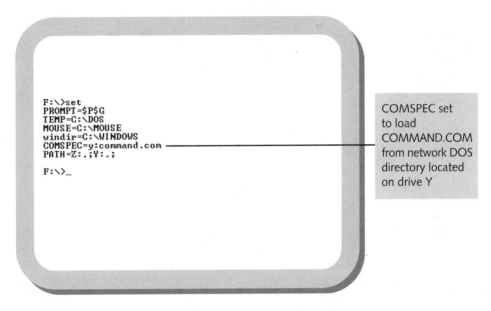

```
F:\>set
PROMPT=$P$G
TEMP=C:\DOS
MOUSE=C:\MOUSE
windir=C:\WINDOWS
COMSPEC=y:command.com
PATH=Z:.;Y:.;

F:\>_
```

COMSPEC set
to load
COMMAND.COM
from network DOS
directory located
on drive Y

WRITE

The WRITE command is used to place simple messages enclosed in quotation marks (" ") on the screen of the workstation. In addition to text, messages can contain identifier variables and special control strings, as shown in the following WRITE command syntax:

WRITE "text [control string] [%variable]"

In addition to replacing the *text* parameter with any message you want displayed when the user logs in, you can add the following control strings anywhere in the text string. Notice that all options must be preceded by a backslash (\). Any options preceded with a forwardslash (/) will be ignored and treated as normal text that appears on the screen.

Figure 12-12

Control characters for the WRITE command

Variable	Default Value
\r	Inserts a return and line feed to display text on the next line
\n	Inserts a blank line
\"	Inserts an embedded quotation mark within the text
\7	Inserts a beep sound on the PC speaker

Login script variables can also be placed into the text by capitalizing all characters of the variable name and preceding it with a percent sign (%). As it does with the MAP command, the login script processor will substitute the value of the variable into the text string before displaying it on the workstation. Login script variables that are often used with the WRITE statement include %GREETING_TIME and %FULL_NAME. The %GREETING_TIME variable contains the current time expressed as either Morning, Afternoon, or Evening. Many network administrators like to include a welcome message at the beginning of their system login scripts similar to the following:

```
WRITE "Good %GREETING_TIME %FULL_NAME \n Welcome to the
       PSC_HOST file server"
```

Figure 12-13 shows an example of the output obtained from the preceding WRITE statement in a login script file.

Figure 12-13

Result of sample WRITE command

```
Good morning, Julie Thiele
 Welcome to the PSC_HOST file server

F:\>
```

You can make sure that all users see and acknowledge important messages by including the following PAUSE statement in your login script:

```
WRITE "File server will be coming down today, March 1, at
       5:00pm for a maintenance call."

PAUSE
```

When the PAUSE command is executed, NetWare stops the login script processing and displays the message "strike any key when ready..." on the screen.

DISPLAY and FDISPLAY

The DISPLAY and FDISPLAY commands show the contents of an ASCII text file on the screen during the execution of the login script. The proper syntax of either command follows:

```
[F]DISPLAY [directory path] filename
```

If the *filename* specified is in the current directory, or if a search drive has been established to the directory containing the *filename*, the directory path is not needed. To show the WELCOME.MSG file stored in the PUBLIC\MESSAGE directory, for example, you can place the following FDISPLAY command in your system login script:

```
MAP INS S1:=SYS:PUBLIC

FDISPLAY S1:\MESSAGE\WELCOME.MSG

PAUSE
```

It is important to follow the DISPLAY command with a PAUSE statement. This gives the user time to read the message file. The difference between DISPLAY and FDISPLAY is that the FDISPLAY command filters and formats the contents of the specified filename so that only the ASCII text itself is displayed. FDISPLAY will not display tabs. The DISPLAY command, on the other hand, displays the exact characters contained in the file, including "garbage" characters such as printer or word processing edit codes. It is usually more appropriate to use FDISPLAY for displaying files that have been created with word processing packages. If you use a word processing package, however, make sure to save the file in ASCII text format or it's possible that, even if FDISPLAY is used, it will not be readable.

Suppose you are a network administrator for a school that wants to display a schedule of events for each day of the week. At the beginning of the week you receive the schedule for the following days. You can use the FDISPLAY command to display the appropriate day's menu by creating files named after weekdays. For example, MONDAY.MSG would contain Monday's schedule, and so on. You can then use the following DAY_OF_WEEK login script variable to display the appropriate day's schedule:

```
FDISPLAY SYS:PUBLIC\MESSAGES\%DAY_OF_WEEK.MSG

PAUSE
```

ATTACH

The ATTACH command can automatically connect the user to additional file servers during the login process. Attaching to another file server requires the user to have a valid username and optional password for the other server, but does not execute any login script commands on that server. The ATTACH command is helpful in multiple server networks in which a user needs access to files or print queues located on a file server other than the one to which he or she is attached. An ATTACH command statement included with MAP statements in the login script can allow users to access data files or software located on other servers without them being aware that another file server is involved. Assume, for example, the following scenario. A business department has its own file server containing accounting and budget data. A sales department has a separate server for its sales data and order system. In order for a user in the business department to access sales data or send output to print queues on the sales file server, he or she needs to attach to that server in addition to the business file server.

The syntax of the ATTACH command is as follows:

ATTACH [*fileserver*[/*username*[;*password*]]]

If the ATTACH command is included in the login script without any parameters, the user will be prompted to enter the server name, followed by username and a password, if required. To prevent the user from having to enter the name of the file server, replace *fileserver* with the name of the server to which the user is to attach. If the user is given an account with the same username and password on this server as on his or her default or primary server, the ATTACH command will automatically connect to the specified server using the current username and password. If the user's name does not exist on the specified file server, NetWare will ask the user to enter a username and password.

> If a user needs to attach to other file servers frequently, you should assign the same username and password for the primary file server and any other file servers. This allows the ATTACH *fileserver* command in the user's login script to connect the user to another server automatically. There will be no need to enter and keep track of another username or password.

So that the user will not need to enter a different username and password to attach to an additional server, you can replace *username* with the correct name needed to access the specified server. In the following example, the user will be asked to enter only his or her password:

ATTACH HOST2/TEDSIM

> Be careful about including passwords for user accounts when you use the ATTACH command in the system login script. All users have access rights to read or print the system login script, which is stored in the NET$LOG.DAT file in the SYS:PUBLIC directory.

The ATTACH command can connect a user to as many as seven file servers in addition to the one to which the user is currently logged in. This means that a user can access information and print queues on up to eight different file servers during one session.

(execute a DOS program)

The external program execution command, #, can load and run an .EXE or .COM program without exiting the LOGIN script processor. When the program is complete, the next login script command line is executed. The syntax of the # command is as follows:

 # [*path*] *filename* [*parameter*]

You can optionally replace the *path* parameter with a full directory path, using either a drive letter or NetWare volume name, that points to the directory containing the program to be run. If no path is specified, the program must exist in either the current directory or be located in one of the paths specified by previous search drive mappings. Replace *filename* with the name of the .COM or .EXE program you want executed. The filename extension is not needed. Depending on the program you are running, you can replace *parameter* with any parameters that are to be passed to the specified program. The format of the entries you place in the parameter string is dependent upon the command being run. To use the # statement to run the CAPTURE command and direct printer output to the BUS_HP3_RO print queue, for example, you could include the following parameters with the #CAPTURE comand:

```
#CAPTURE Q-BUS_HP3_RO TI-5 NB NT
```

The external program execution character, #, is important because it lets you run other command line utilities or DOS commands from inside the login script. Suppose, for example, you want to establish a default network printer for user output. Because CAPTURE is not a login script command, you can use the # command to run the CAPTURE command with the appropriate parameters.

Do not use the # command to load terminate and stay resident programs such as RPRINTER into a workstation. Because the LOGIN program is kept in memory during the execution of the TSR program, the TSR program will be loaded after the LOGIN program, causing the memory from the LOGIN program to be unavailable to the workstation after the LOGIN.EXE program exits.

When application programs are run from a login script, you might encounter an "Out of memory" message indicating that there is not enough room in the DOS 640 Kbyte memory space for the LOGIN.EXE program and the application both to be loaded. When this happens, use the EXIT *filename* command statement to end the login script and then pass control to the application software specified by the *filename* parameter after LOGIN.EXE has exited.

To provide more memory for application software, do not use the # command to run a menu system. The LOGIN.EXE program will take up memory from the menu and any application software that is run from the menu.

IF ... THEN ... ELSE

The IF login statement is used by many network administrators to customize a login script for specific users or groups as well as to perform special processing when a condition—such as a specific day, time, or station—exists. The syntax of a simple IF statement is as follows:

```
IF condition THEN command
```

The *condition* parameter is replaced with a conditional statement that has a value of either true or false. Conditional statements usually consist of an identifier variable and a value enclosed in quotation marks. The following list shows examples of several commonly used conditional statements:

Figure 12-14

Sample conditions for
the IF statement

Condition	Description
MEMBER OF *"group"*	This statement is true if the user is a member of the specified group.
DAY_OF_WEEK="Monday"	This statement is true if the name of the day is Monday. Possible values range from Sunday through Saturday. Uppercase or lowercase letters can be used.
DAY="05"	This statement is true on the fifth day of the month; valid day values range from 01 to 31. It is necessary to include the leading zero for day numbers less than 10.
MONTH="June"	This statement is true for the month of June. You can replace June with any valid month name, from January to December. Either uppercase or lowercase letters can be used.
NDAY_OF_WEEK="1"	This statement is true on Sunday, which is the first day of the week. Valid weekday numbers range from 1 to 7.

The *command* parameter can be replaced with any valid login script command statement. The following is an example of a simple IF statement with a single condition:

```
IF DAY_OF_WEEK = "FRIDAY" THEN WRITE "Hurrah, it's Friday!"
```

More complex IF statements can consist of multiple commands followed by the END statement. The syntax of a multiple statement IF command is as follows:

```
IF condition THEN
    command 1
    command 2
    command n
END
```

In a multiple command IF statement, all commands between the IF statement and the END statement are performed when the condition is true. If you want to map certain drive pointers for the business department users of an organization, for example, you can use an IF command similar to the one shown in Figure 12-15.

Figure 12-15

Multiple statement
IF command

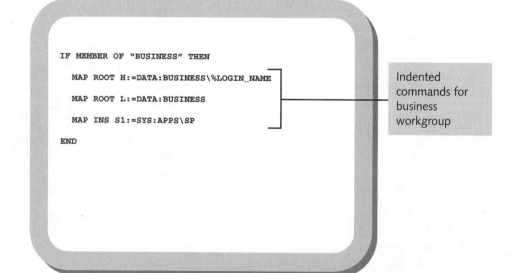

```
IF MEMBER OF "BUSINESS" THEN

    MAP ROOT H:=DATA:BUSINESS\%LOGIN_NAME

    MAP ROOT L:=DATA:BUSINESS

    MAP INS S1:=SYS:APPS\SP

END
```

Indented
commands for
business
workgroup

Sometimes it is desirable to combine multiple conditions using AND or OR. When using OR to connect two conditions, the login command statements will be performed if either condition is true. If you want all members of either the business or sales groups to be informed of a weekly meeting, for example, you can use the following condition:

IF MEMBER OF "SALES" OR MEMBER OF "BUSINESS"

Use the word AND when you want both statements to be true before the commands are processed. Suppose, for example, you want to remind all business users of a meeting on Monday morning. Before displaying the reminder, you want to make sure the user is a member of the business department, the day is Monday, and the login time is before noon. To do this you can use AND to connect these three conditions, as shown in Figure 12-16.

Figure 12-16

Using AND in an IF statement

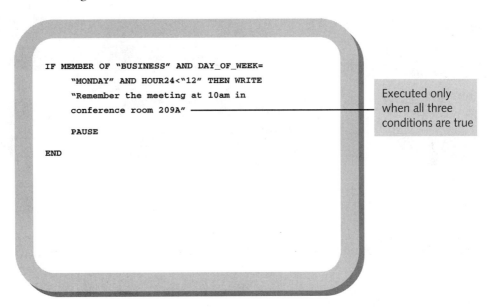

```
IF MEMBER OF "BUSINESS" AND DAY_OF_WEEK=
    "MONDAY" AND HOUR24<"12" THEN WRITE
    "Remember the meeting at 10am in
    conference room 209A" ————————
                                              Executed only
                                              when all three
    PAUSE                                     conditions are true
END
```

The optional word ELSE is an important feature of the IF statement because it allows you to perform either one set of commands or another based on the condition. An example of an IF... ELSE command is shown in Figure 12-17. All members of the business department will have their G drive pointers mapped to the DATA: volume of another file server named BUS_HOST. All other users will have their G drive pointers mapped to the DATA: volume of the primary file server.

Some IF commands can become quite complex, consisting of IF commands within IF commands. The process of placing one IF command within another IF command is called **nesting**. NetWare allows as many as 10 levels of IF statements to be nested. When nesting IF statements, make sure each IF statement has a corresponding END statement, as shown in Figure 12-18. Proper indenting of IF statements as described previously makes this job much easier as well as more accurate.

Figure 12-17

Sample IF...THEN... ELSE statement

```
IF MEMBER OF "BUSINESS" THEN
        ATTACH BUS_HOST
        MAP G:=BUS_HOST\DATA:
ELSE
        MAP G:=DATA:
END
```

Executed when a user does not belong to the business group

Figure 12-18

Nested IF command

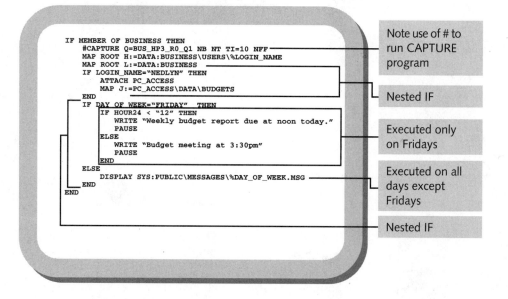

```
IF MEMBER OF BUSINESS THEN
        #CAPTURE Q=BUS_HP3_R0_Q1 NB NT TI=10 NFF
        MAP ROOT H:=DATA:BUSINESS\USERS\%LOGIN_NAME
        MAP ROOT L:=DATA:BUSINESS
        IF LOGIN_NAME="NEDLYN" THEN
                ATTACH PC_ACCESS
                MAP J:=PC_ACCESS\DATA\BUDGETS
        END
        IF DAY OF WEEK="FRIDAY"   THEN
                IF HOUR24 < "12" THEN
                    WRITE "Weekly budget report due at noon today."
                    PAUSE
                ELSE
                    WRITE "Budget meeting at 3:30pm"
                    PAUSE
                END
        ELSE
                DISPLAY SYS:PUBLIC\MESSAGES\%DAY_OF_WEEK.MSG
        END
END
```

Note use of # to run CAPTURE program

Nested IF

Executed only on Fridays

Executed on all days except Fridays

Nested IF

The first nested IF statement shown in Figure 12-18 checks to see if the user is a member of the business department. If the user is a member of the group BUSINESS, the login script does the following:

- Executes the CAPTURE command to establish a default printer

- Maps the user's home drive to the appropriate subdirectory of DATA:BUSINESS\USERS

- Maps a local work drive letter

- Uses a nested IF statement to see if the user is Ned Lynch.

When Ned logs in, the login script will attach him to file server PC_ACCESS and map a drive to the budget directory for Ned to use. Notice that an END statement is associated with each nested IF to mark the end of the commands to be performed for that IF statement.

The second nested IF contains another IF along with the ELSE option in order to display the budget reminder message when a user of the business group logs in before noon on Friday, and a meeting reminder when the user logs in after lunch. The second ELSE statement causes the login script to display the daily message file rather than the budget reminder on all days except Friday. While indenting is not necessary for the IF statement to work, lining up the IF and associated ELSE and END statements and then indenting the commands to be performed is a standard programming practice that makes it much easier to read and maintain complex IF statements.

DRIVE

The DRIVE command is used to set the default drive for DOS to use after the LOGIN.EXE program is executed. The syntax for the DRIVE command is as follows:

> **DRIVE *drive***

Replace the *drive* parameter with either a local or network drive letter. If using a network drive letter, be sure the drive letter has been mapped to a directory path in which the user has the necessary access rights. Most network administrators use the drive near the end of the login script to place the user in either his or her home directory drive or a drive location from which the menu system is run.

EXIT

The EXIT command stops execution of the login script and exits the LOGIN.EXE program. Because the EXIT command ends the LOGIN.EXE program and returns control to DOS, no additional login script commands will be processed after the EXIT command is executed. In addition to ending the login script processing, the EXIT command can also be used to pass a command to DOS by using the following syntax:

> **EXIT "*command-line*"**

Replace the *command-line* parameter with any statement, up to a maximum of 14 characters enclosed in quotation marks, you want passed to the DOS command prompt.

INCLUDE

The INCLUDE command allows you to process login script commands that are stored in another file and then return to the login script statement following the INCLUDE command. The filename specified in the INCLUDE command must contain valid login script commands stored in standard ASCII text format. A standard ASCII text file can be typed from the DOS prompt and edited with a text editor program such as the DOS EDIT command. The proper syntax of the INCLUDE command is as follows:

> **INCLUDE [*path*] *filename***

If the *filename* parameter containing the login script commands is not located in the SYS:LOGIN or SYS:PUBLIC directory, you will need to replace *path* with the complete directory path leading to the specified filename.

The INCLUDE command can be used to make your primary login script file shorter and easier to understand by including other login script files as modules or subroutines that are called from the primary script. Suppose, for example, a school wants to establish a special login script process for all student users. Rather than placing many commands in the system login script or having to maintain a complex login script for each student user, a file named STUDENT.LOG, containing all student login script commands, can be created in the SYS:PUBLIC directory. Because login script files are standard ASCII text files, a text editor program such as the DOS EDIT command can be used to create and edit files containing login script commands. After you create the STUDENT.LOG file, you can use an INCLUDE command in the NetWare system login script, as shown in Figure 12-19, to call the STUDENT.LOG file whenever a student user logs in.

Figure 12-19

Sample INCLUDE command

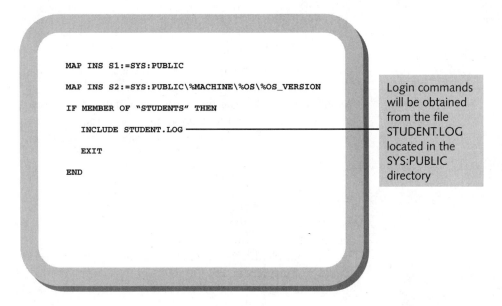

```
MAP INS S1:=SYS:PUBLIC

MAP INS S2:=SYS:PUBLIC\%MACHINE\%OS\%OS_VERSION

IF MEMBER OF "STUDENTS" THEN

   INCLUDE STUDENT.LOG

   EXIT

END
```

Login commands will be obtained from the file STUDENT.LOG located in the SYS:PUBLIC directory

GOTO

The GOTO statement allows you to skip login script statements and continue processing at the specified label. The proper syntax for the GOTO command is as follows:

GOTO *label*

A *label* is a single word that identifies a specific location in the login script. You enter labels into the login script by specifying the label name as a single word ending with a colon (:) and aligned on the left margin. If, for example, you want to continue the system login script at a specific location rather than continuing with the login script after executing a set of commands, you can use commands as shown in Figure 12-20.

Figure 12-20

Sample GOTO command

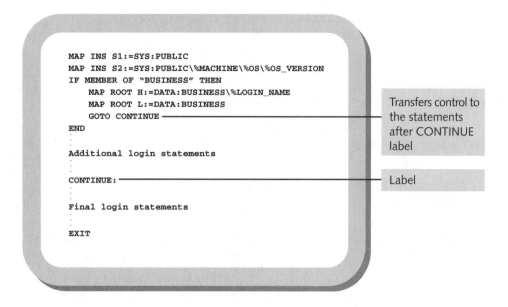

```
MAP INS S1:=SYS:PUBLIC
MAP INS S2:=SYS:PUBLIC\%MACHINE\%OS\%OS_VERSION
IF MEMBER OF "BUSINESS" THEN
    MAP ROOT H:=DATA:BUSINESS\%LOGIN_NAME
    MAP ROOT L:=DATA:BUSINESS
    GOTO CONTINUE
END
.
.
Additional login statements
.
.
CONTINUE:
.
.
Final login statements
.
.
EXIT
```

Transfers control to the statements after CONTINUE label

Label

FIRE PHASERS

The purpose of the FIRE PHASERS command is to make a noise with the PC speaker to alert the operator of a message or condition encountered in the login process.

FIRE [PHASERS] *n* [TIMES]

Replace *n* with a number from 1 to 9 representing how many successive times the phaser sound will be made. The words PHASERS and TIMES are optional and can be omitted from the FIRE login script command. The FIRE PHASERS command is often used in conjunction with the IF statement to notify the user of a certain condition. You can use the FIRE PHASERS statement, for example, to remind the user of a special meeting time, as illustrated in Figure 12-21.

Figure 12-21

Sample FIRE PHASERS command

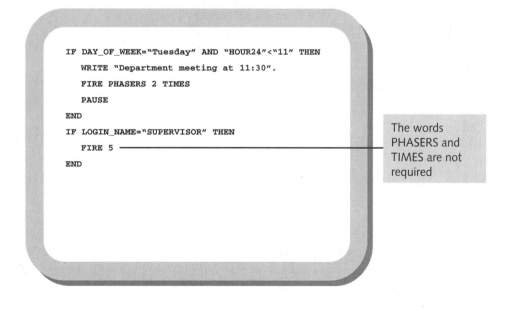

```
IF DAY_OF_WEEK="Tuesday" AND "HOUR24"<"11" THEN
    WRITE "Department meeting at 11:30".
    FIRE PHASERS 2 TIMES
    PAUSE
END
IF LOGIN_NAME="SUPERVISOR" THEN
    FIRE 5
END
```

The words PHASERS and TIMES are not required

Another use of the FIRE PHASERS command is to sound an alarm if someone logs in with the SUPERVISOR username. This can be useful in certain computer lab environments to warn the lab assistant that someone has accessed the SUPERVISOR username. To sound the phaser alarm when anyone logs in as SUPERVISOR, you can place the commands shown at the bottom of Figure 12-17 in your login script.

REM

The REM (for "remark") command can be used with either the asterisk (*) or semicolon (;) to place a comment line in the login script. The LOGIN.EXE program will skip any line that begins with REM, REMARK, *, or ;. Using comments in your login script can make the script much easier for you or another administrator to read and understand. If you place a comment on the same line as other login script commands, however, you will cause errors when the script is interpreted. It is a good idea to precede each section of your login script with a comment identifying the function of that section. Figure 12-22 shows an example.

Figure 12-22

Using REMARK in login scripts

```
REM System Login Script for PCS-HOST file server
REM Written by Ted Simpson 2/95
REM Revision date: 4/18/95
;
* Preliminary Commands
MAP DISPLAY OFF
;
* Required search drive mappings
MAP INS S1:=SYS:PUBLIC
MAP INS S2:=SYS:PUBLIC\%MACHINE\%OS\%OS_VERSION
COMSPEC=S2:COMMAND.COM
```

DOS SET

The DOS SET command can be used to place values in the DOS environment space for later use by menu programs or batch files. Each value placed in the DOS environment space can be assigned to a variable name, as shown in the following syntax:

[DOS] SET *variable*="*value*"

The *variable* parameter must be replaced with a unique and meaningful name that represents the data to be stored. The variable name must consist of a single word with eight or fewer characters. Replace "*value*" with any character string or with a login script variable preceded by a percent sign (%). (Include the quotation marks.) The word DOS is optional and can be omitted from the SET login script command.

The most common use of the DOS SET command is to set the DOS prompt and store certain identifier variables for later use. To set the DOS prompt to display the current directory path and store the user's login name and workstation node address in the DOS environment space, include the following commands in the login script:

```
DOS SET PROMPT="$p$g"
DOS SET USERNAME="%LOGIN_NAME"
DOS SET NODE="%P_STATION"
```

BREAK ON/OFF

The BREAK ON command allows the user to stop execution of the login script by using the [Ctrl] [Break] key combination. BREAK OFF is assumed by default, so if you want to allow users to be able to break out of the system or user login script, you will need to include the BREAK ON command after the necessary login script commands. The BREAK OFF command instructs the login script processor to ignore the use of the [Ctrl] [Break] key combination. Because BREAK OFF is the default condition, the BREAK OFF command is not usually needed unless you have used the BREAK ON command previously. One example of the BREAK OFF command would be providing a "window" in the login script in which a user could press the [Ctrl][Break] key combination to exit the login script, as shown in Figure 12-23.

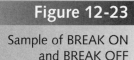

Figure 12-23

Sample of BREAK ON and BREAK OFF

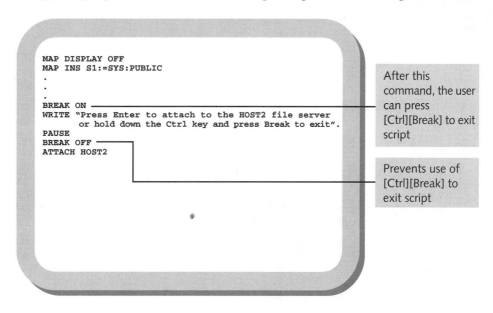

```
MAP DISPLAY OFF
MAP INS S1:=SYS:PUBLIC
   .
   .
   .
BREAK ON
WRITE "Press Enter to attach to the HOST2 file server
      or hold down the Ctrl key and press Break to exit".
PAUSE
BREAK OFF
ATTACH HOST2
```

After this command, the user can press [Ctrl][Break] to exit script

Prevents use of [Ctrl][Break] to exit script

IMPLEMENTING LOGIN SCRIPTS

Once you understand the syntax and function of the login script commands, you can learn how to apply login scripts to establish a network environment for each user's workstation when he or she logs in. Before you implement a login script system, you need to understand how NetWare stores and processes login scripts. This will help you determine the best way to design and implement your login scripts.

TYPES OF LOGIN SCRIPTS

As stated earlier, NetWare offers flexibility by providing three types of login script files: system, user, and default. To become a CNA, you need to know how these login script files work. This will enable you to configure a reliable and efficient login script system for your network. Figure 12-24 contains a flowchart that illustrates the relationships among the login script files.

Figure 12-24

Login script files

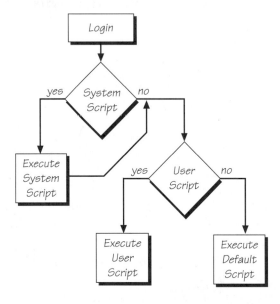

Notice that once the system login script is created, its commands are performed for all users when they log in to the file server. The system login script should therefore contain the commands that establish a standard working environment for your network. Once all commands in the system login script have been executed, NetWare will execute the commands in the user login script, or if there is no personal login script for the user, it will perform the default login script commands. Once you have established a system login script, you do not want the default login script commands to be executed. You will therefore need either to create a personal login script for each user containing at least the EXIT command or to include the EXIT command in the system login script. If you include the EXIT command in the system login script, no user or default login script commands will be executed for any of the users.

The system login script

As stated earlier, the system login script is stored in an ASCII text file named NET$LOG.DAT, which is located in the SYS:PUBLIC directory. When a user logs in, the LOGIN.EXE program checks in the SYS:PUBLIC directory for this file. If the file exists, the LOGIN.EXE program will execute the commands stored in this file. Although the system login script is intended to contain commands that affect all users, most login script commands can be placed in the system login script with IF ... THEN commands separating special commands needed for certain groups or individual users. The system login script should contain at least the following commands:

```
MAP S1:=SYS:PUBLIC
MAP F:=SYS:
```

In addition to these essential commands, many network administrators include the following commands to use DOS directories located in the SYS: volume:

```
MAP S2:=SYS:PUBLIC\%MACHINE\%OS\%OS_VERSION

COMSPEC=S2:COMMAND.COM
```

Because the system login script is an ASCII text file stored in the SYS:PUBLIC directory, any user can access a text editor or the DOS TYPE command to display the contents of the NET$LOG.DAT file, as shown in Figure 12-25. The NET$LOG.DAT file is flagged with the Read Only and Sharable attributes. If you want to use a more sophisticated text editor to maintain the NET$LOG.DAT file, you need to follow these eight steps:

1. Copy the NET$LOG.DAT file to a work file with a different extension (.TXT).

2. Start the text editor program and open the work file.

3. Make the necessary changes and save the file.

4. Use the FLAG NET$LOG.DAT N command to set the file to the normal Read Write, Nonsharable status.

5. Rename the current NET$LOG.DAT file NET$LOG.BAK.

6. Rename the work file NET$LOG.DAT.

7. Use the FLAG NET$LOG.DAT S RO command to flag the file Sharable and Read Only.

8. Test the modified system login script.

Figure 12-25

Displaying the system login script

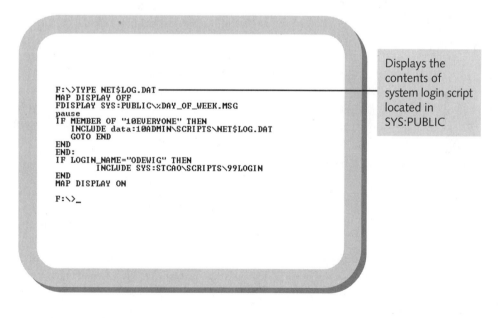

Displays the contents of system login script located in SYS:PUBLIC

```
F:\>TYPE NET$LOG.DAT
MAP DISPLAY OFF
FDISPLAY SYS:PUBLIC\%DAY_OF_WEEK.MSG
pause
IF MEMBER OF "10EVERYONE" THEN
    INCLUDE data:10ADMIN\SCRIPTS\NET$LOG.DAT
    GOTO END
END
END:
IF LOGIN_NAME="ODEWIG" THEN
        INCLUDE SYS:STCAO\SCRIPTS\99LOGIN
END
MAP DISPLAY ON

F:\>_
```

Be very careful when you make changes to the system login script, because errors in the script can prevent users from successfully logging in to the file server. If your system login script file becomes damaged, you will need to fix the problem or restore the backup copy of the NET$LOG file. This can be done by using the ATTACH command, as described in the following five steps, to gain access to the file server as SUPERVISOR. You then use a text editor or SYSCON to make the necessary corrections to the login script or restore the backup copy of the NET$LOG.DAT file.

1. Obtain a copy of the ATTACH command from another file server or from the installation disks.

2. Use the command ATTACH *fileserver*\SUPERVISOR to log in to the problem file server.

3. Change to the first network drive and use the CD SYS:PUBLIC command to change your default path to the PUBLIC directory. (Because you will not have a search drive mapped to the SYS:PUBLIC directory, you will need to use the CD SYS:PUBLIC command before you can run SYSCON.)

4. Use SYSCON to correct any faulty system login script commands.

5. If you have a backup copy of the NET$LOG.DAT file, you might want to flag the current NET$LOG.DAT file to normal settings, rename it as a work file, and then rename the backup file to NET$LOG.DAT and flag it Sharable and Read Only. You can then use a text editor to fix the problems in the work file and later rename it to NET$LOG.DAT as described previously.

The ATTACH command does not execute login script commands and therefore can be used to log in to the file server that has a damaged system login script. Because the ATTACH command is normally stored in the SYS:PUBLIC directory, it is unavailable until after you log in. Although you can obtain a copy from another file server or from the installation disks, this can be an unnecessary frustration. As a safety precaution, therefore you might want to place a copy of the ATTACH command in the SYS:LOGIN directory on your local disk drive so that you have access to it in case you are unable to use the LOGIN command to log in to the file server.

The user login script

The user login script is stored in a file named LOGIN, located in each user's SYS:MAIL*user ID* subdirectory. Unless the EXIT command is executed in the system login script, the LOGIN.EXE program will look in the user's mail subdirectory for this file after completing the commands in the system login script. If the file exists, the LOGIN.EXE program will execute the commands it contains for this user. If a LOGIN file does not exist in the user's mail subdirectory, the LOGIN.EXE program will execute the default login script commands.

The SUPERVISOR, the user account manager, or the user can access the SYSCON program to create or maintain the user login script by selecting the Login Script option from the User Information menu, as shown in Figure 12-26. Most network administrators place as few commands as possible in user login scripts because maintaining many different user login scripts is difficult, and because users can change their own login scripts using the SYSCON utility. A typical user login script will contain special drive mappings and other commands that are unique for that user, along with an EXIT command to link the user to his or her respective menu, as shown in Figure 12-27.

Figure 12-26

Sample of exiting from the system script

```
Rem Mapping for Business workgroup
IF MEMBER OF "BUSINESS" THEN BEGIN
  MAP ROOT H:=DATA:BUSINESS\USERS\%LOGIN_NAME
  MAP ROOT L:=DATA:BUSINESS
  #CAPTURE Q=BUSHP3-R1-Q1 TI=5 NB NT
  IF LOGIN_NAME="EDLOW" THEN BEGIN
    MAP O:=DATA:SALES\ORDERS
  END
  DRIVE M:
  EXIT "NMENU BUSMENU"
END
Rem Mapping for Sales workgroup
IF MEMBER OF "SALES" THEN BEGIN
  MAP ROOT L:=DATA:SALES
  MAP ROOT H:=L:%LOGIN_NAME
  #CAPTURE Q=SAL-HP3-R2-Q1 NT NB TI=10
  MAP ROOT O:=L:\ORDERS
  IF DAY_OF_WEEK = "Wednesday" AND HOUR24 < "09" THEN BEGIN
    WRITE "Remember training at 8:30am"
    PAUSE
  END
  DRIVE M:
  EXIT "SALEMENU"
END
Rem End of Login Script Commands
  MAP DISPLAY ON
EXIT
```

Figure 12-27

Sample user
login script

If you plan to implement user login scripts on your file server, you must include a login script for each user, even if it contains only the EXIT command. This is important for the following reasons:

- If a user does not have a user login script, the LOGIN.EXE program will execute the default login script commands, which can override drive mappings made in the system login script.

- By default, NetWare provides all users with rights to create files in SYS:MAIL and all its subdirectories in order to allow electronic mail packages to send files from user to user. The security problem results because when a user does not have a personal login script, another user can copy a LOGIN file containing login script commands into his or her MAIL subdirectory that will be executed when that user logs in. These login script commands could copy or damage valuable information from the directories to which the user has access.

The default login script

The default login script consists of login script commands that are built into the LOGIN.EXE program. If a user login script file does not exist for the user ID that is currently logging in, the LOGIN.EXE program will execute the default login script commands. The purpose of the default login script is to provide basic drive mappings for users until a system login script has been established. The statements that make up the default login script for NetWare v3.12 are shown in Figure 12-28.

Once the network administrator has established a system login script that contains the basic drive mapping for the network, it is important to prevent the default login script from being executed. Failure to do this will cause drive mappings made in the system login script to either be overwritten or duplicated, as illustrated in Figure 12-29. There are two ways to stop the default login script from being executed. You can provide a user login script for each user on the network, even if the user login script contains only the EXIT command. This method is commonly used; it allows each user to have specialized login script commands. The EXIT NMENU *menuname* statement is often used to link the user to the correct menu.

Figure 12-28

```
WRITE "Good %GREETING_TIME, %LOGIN_NAME."
MAP DISPLAY OFF
MAP ERRORS OFF
MAP *1:=SYS:
MAP INS S1:=SYS:PUBLIC
MAP INS S2:=S1:IBM_PC\MSDOS\%OS_VERSION
MAP DISPLAY ON
MAP
```

The second method is to include an EXIT command in the system login script. The EXIT command ends the LOGIN.EXE program and therefore prevents the execution of either user or default login scripts. Using the EXIT command in the system login script means that it will probably be necessary to maintain a larger system login script, one that contains both systemwide and user-specific commands. Some network administrators actively avoid large or complex system login scripts. Many network administrators, however, actually prefer having one large login script program. In a system with many user login scripts, maintaining those login scripts entails extra work for the network administrator. In this chapter, you will learn how to use both methods. Then you can decide, based on your network environment and personal preference, which method is best for you.

Figure 12-29

Duplicate mappings caused by default login script

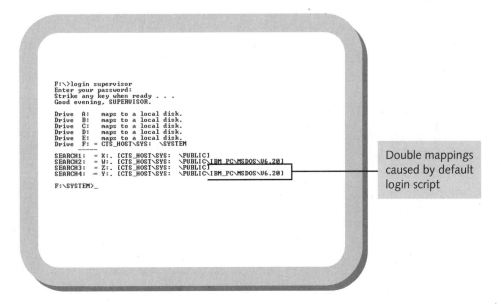

PLANNING LOGIN SCRIPTS

To design a login script system, you start by identifying a standard set of regular and search drive mappings that will be needed by all users to run software and access data in the network file system. Next, identify any special setup needs for each workgroup in the organization. Finally, identify any special setups that are unique for individual users. If most of the user workstation setup needs can be met through the system and workgroup commands, you can choose to place all login script commands in the system login script and use the EXIT command to prevent user or default login script commands from being processed. If your network has many special or individualized setup requirements, you might want to create a simple system login script that contains only the essential commands, such as mapping a search drive to SYS:PUBLIC. You would then implement user login scripts to handle the workstation setup for each individual user. Just as network administrators differ in the ways they design a directory structure, they also implement login script systems differently, depending on their preferences and experience. The important thing is to develop a workable strategy that meets both the needs of your organization and your personal preferences.

WRITING A LOGIN SCRIPT

After you identify your login script needs and strategy, the next step is to write the necessary login script commands. You might find it helpful to use a login script worksheet, such as the one shown in Figure 12-30. A blank copy of this worksheet is included for you to use when you develop login scripts for the exercises and projects at the end of this chapter.

The worksheet is divided into sections by REM statements that define the start of each section. The first part contains sections that are executed by all users. The Preliminary Commands section can contain any initializing commands. The command MAP DISPLAY OFF, for example, will prevent MAP commands from displaying results on the workstation and will clear the screen. The Preliminary Commands section can also be used, as shown in the example in Figure 12-27, to clear the screen and display a message greeting the user. The #C\COMMAND /C CLS command used in the example will clear the screen by running the CLS command from the DOS COMMAND.COM program located in the root of the local workstation's C drive. The #C\ preceding the statement causes the login program to go to the root of the C drive to run the COMMAND.COM program. This means that the #C\COMMAND.COM /C CLS command will not work if the workstation does not boot off its local hard disk. If your network contains workstations that do not have hard drives, you will need to place the #COMMAND /C CLS command in the DOS Setup section of the script after a search drive to the correct DOS directory is mapped, as described below.

The Required Search Drive section should contain any required system search drive mappings that are needed by all users. An example is mapping S1 to the SYS:PUBLIC directory. Other search drive mappings for special products such as the Message Handling System (MHS) described in Chapter 14 can also be placed in this section.

The DOS Setup section is used if you are planning to map a search drive to a network DOS directory and then set the workstation COMSPEC to that DOS directory. Figure 12-28 shows an example of such a mapping. In addition, the DOS Setup section can contain the #COMMAND.COM /C CLS command or a DOS PROMPT statement, as shown, along with any SET commands needed to store information in the workstation DOS environment space. In the example, SET commands are included to store such workstation information as username, connection number, and station address.

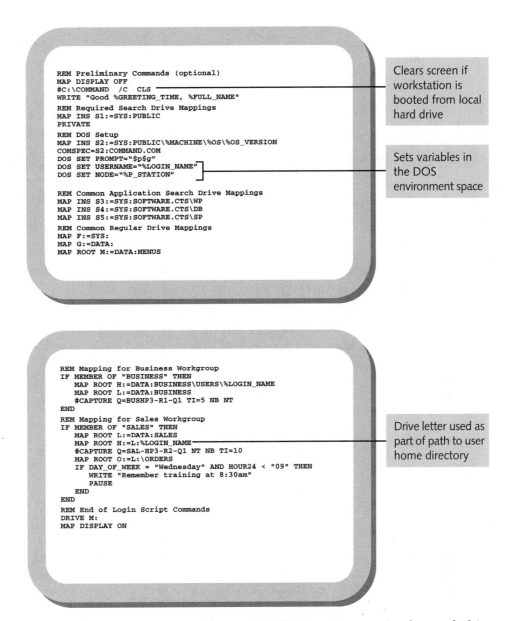

Figure 12-30

Sample system login script worksheet

```
REM Preliminary Commands (optional)
MAP DISPLAY OFF
#C:\COMMAND  /C  CLS
WRITE "Good %GREETING_TIME, %FULL_NAME"
REM Required Search Drive Mappings
MAP INS S1:=SYS:PUBLIC
PRIVATE

REM DOS Setup
MAP INS S2:=SYS:PUBLIC\%MACHINE\%OS\%OS_VERSION
COMSPEC=S2:COMMAND.COM
DOS SET PROMPT="$p$g"
DOS SET USERNAME="%LOGIN_NAME"
DOS SET NODE="%P_STATION"

REM Common Application Search Drive Mappings
MAP INS S3:=SYS:SOFTWARE.CTS\WP
MAP INS S4:=SYS:SOFTWARE.CTS\DB
MAP INS S5:=SYS:SOFTWARE.CTS\SP
REM Common Regular Drive Mappings
MAP F:=SYS:
MAP G:=DATA:
MAP ROOT M:=DATA:MENUS
```

Clears screen if workstation is booted from local hard drive

Sets variables in the DOS environment space

```
REM Mapping for Business Workgroup
IF MEMBER OF "BUSINESS" THEN
    MAP ROOT H:=DATA:BUSINESS\USERS\%LOGIN_NAME
    MAP ROOT L:=DATA:BUSINESS
    #CAPTURE Q=BUSHP3-R1-Q1 TI=5 NB NT
END
REM Mapping for Sales Workgroup
IF MEMBER OF "SALES" THEN
    MAP ROOT L:=DATA:SALES
    MAP ROOT H:=L:%LOGIN_NAME
    #CAPTURE Q=SAL-HP3-R2-Q1 NT NB TI=10
    MAP ROOT O:=L:\ORDERS
    IF DAY_OF_WEEK = "Wednesday" AND HOUR24 < "09" THEN
        WRITE "Remember training at 8:30am"
        PAUSE
    END
END
REM End of Login Script Commands
DRIVE M:
MAP DISPLAY ON
```

Drive letter used as part of path to user home directory

The Common Application Search Drive Mappings section contains the search drive mappings to DOS-based application packages that are to be accessed by all users. In the example login script in Figure 12-28, all users will be able to run the word processing, database, and spreadsheet applications.

The second part of the login script worksheet contains sections for individual workgroups. These contain login script commands that are executed only for users who are members of the specified workgroup. The Common Regular Drive Mappings section contains drive pointers that will be available for all users. On many networks, for example, a drive pointer would be mapped to each NetWare volume as well as a possible drive mapping to the directory containing user menus. In the example, the user who is a member of the business workgroup will have his or her home drive mapped to the BUSINESS\USERS\%LOGIN_NAME directory and an L drive pointer to the BUSINESS directory. In addition, a CAPTURE command has been included to send printer output to the default business laser printer. Notice the # at the beginning of the CAPTURE command; it will cause the CAPTURE.EXE program to be run as an external command. A user who is a member of the sales workgroup will receive an L drive pointer to the SALES directory and a drive to his or her home directory, located in the SALES\USERS directory. Notice the use of the L drive pointer as part of the path specified for the user home directory. In addition to the H and L drive pointers, the sales workgroup users also require a drive pointer to the ORDERS software application. When you specify a drive letter to a software application, it is often necessary to use the same drive letter that was specified during the software installation, as described in Chapter 9.

The End of Login Script Commands section can contain any commands that all users will perform before they exit the login script. In the example, the DRIVE H: command will place all users in their home directory before turning the MAP display on and exiting from the system login script. Because the EXIT command was not included in the sample system login script, NetWare will next execute either the user personal or the default login script commands.

If you do not plan to implement user login scripts, the commands for each workgroup should end with an EXIT statement that links the members of that workgroup to their appropriate menu or application, as shown in Figure 12-31. When user login script commands are not used, it might be necessary to include IF statements in the system login script to provide special setup commands for individual users. Figure 12-31 illustrates an IF statement that is used to map the drive letter O to the SALES\ORDERS directory for a specific user in the business department. This will allow user EDLOW to access the sales order system to obtain accounting information. When user login scripts are not implemented, the EXIT command should be placed in the End of Login Script Commands section. Placing the EXIT command as the last statement in the system login script is important. It ends login script processing for users, such as the SUPERVISOR, who are not members of any specified workgroup.

Figure 12-31

Sample of exiting from the system script

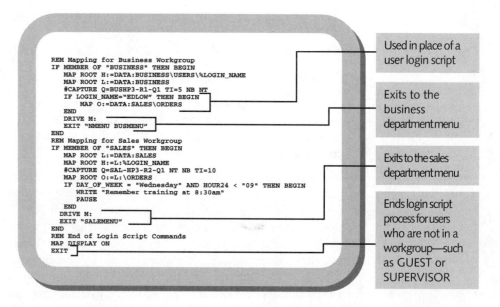

```
REM Mapping for Business Workgroup
IF MEMBER OF "BUSINESS" THEN BEGIN
    MAP ROOT H:=DATA:BUSINESS\USERS\%LOGIN_NAME
    MAP ROOT L:=DATA:BUSINESS
    #CAPTURE Q=BUSHP3-R1-Q1 TI=5 NB NT
    IF LOGIN_NAME="EDLOW" THEN BEGIN
        MAP O:=DATA:SALES\ORDERS
    END
    DRIVE M:
    EXIT "NMENU BUSMENU"
END
REM Mapping for Sales Workgroup
IF MEMBER OF "SALES" THEN BEGIN
    MAP ROOT L:=DATA:SALES
    MAP ROOT H:=L:%LOGIN_NAME
    #CAPTURE Q=SAL-HP3-R2-Q1 NT NB TI=10
    MAP ROOT O:=L:\ORDERS
    IF DAY_OF_WEEK = "Wednesday" AND HOUR24 < "09" THEN BEGIN
        WRITE "Remember training at 8:30am"
        PAUSE
    END
    DRIVE M:
    EXIT "SALEMENU"
END
REM End of Login Script Commands
MAP DISPLAY ON
EXIT
```

Used in place of a user login script

Exits to the business department menu

Exits to the sales department menu

Ends login script process for users who are not in a workgroup—such as GUEST or SUPERVISOR

ENTERING LOGIN SCRIPTS

After you write and check the system login script, the next step is to enter and test it. To enter the system login script, first log in as SUPERVISOR or a supervisor equivalent user and then start the SYSCON program. To create and maintain the system login script, highlight Supervisor Options and press [Enter] to display the Supervisor Options menu. Next, to work with the system login script, highlight the System Login Script option and press [Enter]. A window showing any existing system login script commands is displayed. Enter the system login script commands from your login script worksheet. See the example shown in Figure 12-32.

To erase statements from the login script, place the cursor at the beginning of the text you want to erase and press the F5 key. Use the arrow keys to highlight the text to be erased and press the Del key. To save the system login script, press [Esc] and then respond to the Save Changes message by pressing [Enter]. The System Login Script file will be used whenever a user logs in to the file server.

Figure 12-32

Sample system login script

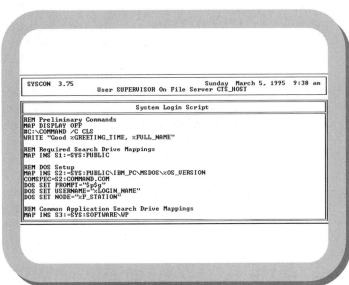

To update user login scripts, first log in as a supervisor equivalent or a user account manager and start SYSCON. Select the User Information option from SYSCON's Available Topics menu, highlight the name of the user whose login script you want to change and press [Enter]. To enter a user login script for the selected user, highlight the Login Script option and press [Enter]. If the user does not currently have a user login script, SYSCON will ask from what username you want to copy a login script. If two or more users have similar login script files, you can simply copy the login script from the first user and then make any necessary changes.

To create a new login script for a user, respond by pressing [Enter] to accept the default of the current username. SYSCON presents you with a blank user login script window. Enter the user login script statements. To delete an incorrect statement, press the F5 key, use the arrow keys to highlight the text to be removed, and then press the Del key to remove the highlighted information. Once the user login script is completed, press [Esc] and then [Enter] to save the user login script in the user's SYS:MAIL\user ID subdirectory. SYSCON will return you to the User Information menu. You can then press [Esc] again and repeat the process to enter a personal login script for another username.

TESTING AND DEBUGGING LOGIN SCRIPTS

After the system and user login scripts have been entered, you should test the login script system for at least one user in each department by logging in with that user's name and checking to be sure all commands are executed properly. If your system login script does not use the EXIT command, it is important to prevent the default login script commands from being executed before you test the login script files. This is done, as described previously, by placing the EXIT statement in each user's personal login script.

To test login scripts, you will need to log in with a username from each workgroup you have defined. After logging in, determine if all commands are being executed properly by first looking for any error messages on the screen. Next, use the MAP command to determine if all drives have been properly mapped for this user. If your login script sets a default print queue, use the CAPTURE SH command to display and check the status of the CAPTURE command to be sure it is directed to the correct print queue.

If you should get a "Bad Command or File Name" message and you cannot execute the MAP or CAPTURE SH commands, then either the user does not have a drive mapping to SYS:PUBLIC or else the user is not a member of the group EVERYONE. To determine which of these problems exists, first try changing to the PUBLIC directory by entering the command CD SYS:PUBLIC. After changing to the PUBLIC directory, you can use the MAP command to determine what drives are currently mapped. You will often be able to determine from the drive mapping information if the user login script or AUTOEXEC.BAT file has overwritten the mapping to the SYS:PUBLIC directory. If the search mapping for the PUBLIC directory has been overwritten, the drive letter, usually Z, will appear with the regular drive mappings, as shown in Figure 12-33. Search drives can be overwritten by the user login script containing MAP S#:=[*path*] commands or by a DOS PATH statement in an AUTOEXEC.BAT file following the LOGIN command.

Figure 12-33

Example of overwritten search drives

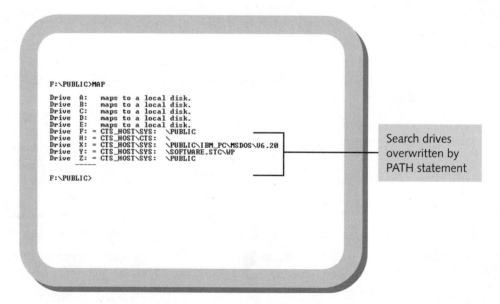

If no drive mapping to the SYS:PUBLIC directory exists, you need to determine if the user has rights to the SYS:PUBLIC directory by using the CD SYS:PUBLIC command to change the default path to the PUBLIC directory. If you cannot change to the PUBLIC directory, then the user must not have Read and File scan rights to

SYS:PUBLIC. The most common reason for a user not having access rights to SYS:PUBLIC is that he or she is not a member of the group EVERYONE, which by default has Read and File scan rights to PUBLIC. In this case, you can use the following commands to change to the SYS:LOGIN directory, log in as a supervisor equivalent user, and then use SYSCON to add the user to the group EVERYONE:

CD SYS:LOGIN

LOGIN SUPERVISOR

 Normally all new users are made members of the group EVERYONE. It is possible, however, for a user to be removed from the group and therefore to have no rights to the SYS:PUBLIC directory.

If the MAP command contains duplicated drive mappings to the SYS:PUBLIC directory, the most likely problem is that the user does not have a personal user login script. When this is the case, NetWare performs the default login scripts, which causes a second drive mapping to be mapped to the PUBLIC and DOS directories. If this happens, you can use the SYSCON program to place the EXIT command in the login script of the currently logged in user in order to prevent the default login script from being executed.

When all login scripts have been debugged, you should document drive mappings and other special setup commands that are performed for each workgroup or user. Because users will need to know certain drive mappings in order to access data and applications through the network file system effectively, it is also important that you provide users with the necessary documentation or training they will need to use the workstation environment provided by the login script. The time spent in documenting and training users in the use of the system will pay off later in fewer problems and support calls.

After you have determined that all users can log in successfully and have their necessary workstation environments established, you are ready to proceed with the final step of automating the user environment—establishing menus, as described in the next chapter.

CHAPTER SUMMARY

Establishing a workstation environment that makes the network easy to use is an important responsibility of the network administrator. NetWare provides a powerful way to automate workstation activities through login scripts. NetWare login script files contain commands that provide drive mappings and other workstation setup functions that are executed during the login process. The login script commands provided by Novell can be used to map drive letters, set the DOS environment of a workstation, display messages and files, execute other programs, and execute certain commands based on whether a given condition is true or false. Using login script variables with commands allows you to create general-purpose login scripts that work for multiple users. Login script variables can be divided into several types, including date variables such as DAY_OF_WEEK, time variables such as HOUR24, user variables such as LOGIN_NAME, and workstation variables such as OS and OS_VERSION. An example of a login script command with a variable mapping a drive pointer to the home directory of each user is MAP ROOT H:=DATA:USERS\%LOGIN_NAME. The percent sign ahead of a variable name tells NetWare to substitute the value of the variable into the login script command when it is executed.

Three types of NetWare login script files can be executed by the LOGIN.EXE program. They are the system login script, the user login script, and the default login script. The system login script is stored in the SYS:PUBLIC directory in a file named NET$LOG.DAT. Its commands are executed for all users when they first log in. After the system login script is executed, the login script processor will look in the user's SYS:MAIL*userid* subdirectory for the existence of a LOGIN file containing the user login script. If no user login script file exists, the login script processor will execute the default login script commands stored in the LOGIN.EXE program. Most login script commands should be stored, whenever possible, in the system login script. By including the EXIT command in the system login script, you can prevent NetWare from executing the user or default login script statements. If you do not place an EXIT command at the end of the system login script, it is very important to create a user login script for each user, even if it contains only an EXIT statement. Creating a login script for each user prevents the default login script from being run and provides additional security. Otherwise it is possible for any user to copy a LOGIN file into another user's SYS:MAIL*userid* directory, causing a security violation.

The SYSCON utility maintains the system and user login scripts. You create and maintain the system login script by selecting Supervisor Options from the SYSCON Available Topics menu. Then, using the System Login Script option, you can edit the login script commands. To maintain the user login script, first select the Users option, which displays a window showing all user accounts. Next, select a username and press [Enter] to display the User Information menu. From the User Information window, select the Login Script option to call up and edit the user's personal login script.

COMMAND SUMMARY

Command	Syntax	Definition
#	*[path] filename[parameter]*	Executes the specified DOS program and returns control back to the login script program. The LOGIN.EXE program remains in memory while the requested program is being run.
ATTACH	*ATTACH [fileserver[/username[;password]]]*	Attaches the user to up to eight file servers to allow him or her to access files and software. If the username and password are not specified, the current user-name and password will be used to attempt to access the specified file server.
BREAK	*BREAK ON/OFF*	The BREAK ON command allows the user to use the [Ctrl][Break] key combination to terminate processing of the login script commands. By default, BREAK OFF prevents the user from halting the login script process.

COMSPEC	*COMSPEC [path] filename*	Specifies the directory path and filename DOS uses to reload the command processor.
DISPLAY	*DISPLAY [directory][path] filename*	Types the contents of the specified file to the screen. If the filename specified is not in the current directory or search drive, include the full NetWare path to the specified filename. The DISPLAY command shows all characters in the file including tabs and other printer control characters. (See FDISPLAY.)
DOS SET	*DOS SET variable="value"*	Allows you to place a value in the DOS environment space using the specified variable name.
DRIVE	*DRIVE [drive:]*	Sets the specified drive letter as the default DOS drive. Unless you specify this command, the default drive will be set to the first network drive letter, usually F.
EXIT	*EXIT "command-line"*	Ends the login script processing and exits LOGIN.EXE. You can replace *command-line* with a command containing up to 14 characters, enclosed in quotation marks, that you want executed after LOGIN.EXE ends.
FDISPLAY	*FDISPLAY [directory path] filename*	Like the DISPLAY command, except that the FDISPLAY command filters out any tab or printer control characters, making files that contain these control characters more readable.
FIRE PHASERS	*FIRE [PHASERS] n [TIMES]*	Produces a phaser sound on the PC speaker the number of times specified, up to nine.
GOTO	*GOTO label*	Transfers control to the specified label. A label is a single left-aligned word ending in a colon.
IF ... THEN ...ELSE	*IF condition(s) THEN command ELSE command END*	The IF statement allows you to specify commands to be executed only when the specified condition is true. Commands following the ELSE statement will be executed if the condition is false. Each IF statement must conclude with an END statement and can contain up to 10 additional nested IF statements.

INCLUDE	*INCLUDE [path] filename*	Causes the login processor to obtain commands from the file specified. If the file is not in the current directory or search drive, you need to specify the complete NetWare *path* leading to the desired file.
MAP	*MAP [option] [drive:=path] [;drive:=path] [variable] d:=path*	Creates both regular and search drive mappings from the login script. The path statement can contain identifier variables preceded by percent signs, e.g., %MACHINE, %OS, %OS_VERSION, %LOGIN_NAME. Special MAP commands include MAP DISPLAY OFF/ON, MAP ERRORS OFF/ON.
PAUSE or **WAIT**	*PAUSE or WAIT*	Suspends login script processing until the user presses any key to continue.
REM	*REM (or REMARK) [text]* ** [text]* *; [text]*	Allows comments to be placed in login script files.
WRITE	*WRITE "text"*	Displays the message string enclosed in quotation marks on the console. Special control codes, such as /r for a new line, along with identifier variables preceded by percent signs can be included within the quotation marks.

KEY TERMS

date variables	**nesting**	**time variables**
default login script	**network variables**	**user login script**
login script	**syntax**	**user variables**
login script variable	**system login script**	**workstation variable**

REVIEW QUESTIONS

1. In the space below, briefly describe the importance of login scripts to a DOS-based workstation.

   To provide a standard environment for all users and still meet individual user needs

2. The COMSPEC command would most likely be found in the _Command.com_ login script file.

3. The _Attach_ command is used to connect the user to another file server on the network.

4. The _Display_ ~~FDISPLAY~~ command is used to write the contents of an ASCII text file to the display screen.

5. The _INCLUDE_ command allows you to execute login script statements contained in a specified ASCII text file.

6. The _WRITE_ command is used to display a brief message on the screen.

7. The system login script commands are stored in the _NET$LOG.DAT_ file located in the _SYS: PUBLIC_ directory.

8. If you are logged in as SUPERVISOR and receive the message "Access denied" when you attempt to change the system login script using a text editor program, what is the problem? Write your answer in the space below.

9. The _USER_ login script is executed before the default login script.

10. The default login script is executed if there is no _USER_ login script file.

11. Suppose you notice that a user has two drive mappings to the SYS:PUBLIC directory. In the space below, explain the most likely reason for this problem. _The Default login script duplicated Mappings from the System Scripts._

12. On the lines below, list two ways you can prevent the default login script commands from being executed.
    ① _A user login script containing only the Exit command_
    ② _End the System login script with the Exit command._

13. The _SYSCON_ utility is used to create and maintain the system login script.

14. The _MAP_ command is most often found in user login scripts because it can be used to link the user to his or her menu.

15. Given that your userid is 14000005, write a NetWare NCOPY command to back up your user login script to drive A of your workstation.
    NCOPY SYS:MAIL\14000005\LOGIN A:

16. Suppose the first network drive on your workstation is L. What drive letter would the login script command MAP *3:=DATA: use to access the DATA: volume?
    _N_

17. On the line below, write a login script command that will display a welcome message containing today's date, including the name of the day, the month, day, and the year.
    Write "Tuesday, November 24, 1998."

18. On the line below, write a condition that can be used to determine if a user is logging in on the third day of the week.

IF DAY_OF_WEEK = "Tuesday" THEN WRITE "Your logged on on the third day"

19. On the line below, write a MAP command that uses identifier variables to map H as a root drive pointer to the user's home directory located in the DATA:USERS directory path.

MAP H:= DATA:USERS\%LOGIN_NAME

20. On the line below, write a search mapping to the SYS:PUBLIC directory and appropriate DOS version assuming the directory structure shown below:

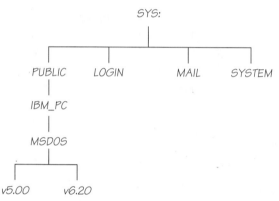

MAP S2:= SYS:PUBLIC\%MACHINE\%OS\%OS_VERSION

21. On the line below, write a login script command to redirect output from the LPT1 printer port to the SAL_HP3_R3_Q1 print queue with a timeout of 5 seconds, no banner, no tabs, and no form feed.

CAPTURE Q=SAL_HP3_R3_Q1 NB TI=5 NT NFF

22. The _____ command can be used to access a file server if the system login script or SUPERVISOR's user login script becomes damaged.

23. The _____ login script command can be used to change to the user's home directory on drive H.

24. Will executing the EXIT command from the system login script prevent the default login script commands from being executed when a user has no user login script file? Yes or No _____*Yes*_____.

25. Assume the home directories for the sales department are stored in the DATA:SALES\USERS directory and the home directories for the accounting department are stored in the DATA:ACCT directory. Write an IF statement for the system login script that will map H as a root drive to the correct home directory path for each sales department user.

IF MEMBER OF "SALES" THEN MAP ROOT H:= DATA:SALES\USERS

Identify and correct any errors in each of the following login script commands:

26. TURN MAP DISPLAY OFF

MAP DISPLAY OFF

27. MAP S2=SYS\PUBLIC\%MACHINE\%OS\%OSVERSION

MAP S2:= SYS:PUBLIC\%MACHINE\%OS\%OS_VERSION

28.   COMSPEC=S2:\COMMAND.COM

COMSPEC = S2: COMMAND.COM

29.   CAPTURE Q=BUS_HP3_R0_Q1 TI=5 NT NB NFF

---

30.   WRITE "Good %Greeting_Time," %Login_name

WRITE " Good %GREETING_TIME %LOGIN-NAME "

EXERCISES

Exercise 12-1: Documenting the System Login Script on Your File Server

In this exercise you will demonstrate your knowledge of login script commands by examining the system login script on your file server and explaining the purpose of each of its commands.

1.   Log in to the file server using your assigned student username.

2.   Change to the SYS:PUBLIC directory and use the FLAG command to identify the attributes set on the system login script file. Record the attributes on the line below.

Ro S A   DI R1

3.   Use the TYPE *filename* > PRN command (where *filename* is the name of the system login script file) to obtain a printout of the commands in your server's system login script file.

4.   Next to each login script command on the printout, briefly describe the command's function in the login script.

Exercise 12-2: Practicing with Login Script Commands

In this exercise you will practice writing and testing several login script commands by creating a practice user and then providing that user with a user login script.

1.   Log in using your assigned student username.

2.   In the space provided, use the LISTDIR /S command to document the DOS directory structure on your assigned file server.

3.   Start SYSCON and create a new user named ##USER, where ## represents your assigned student number.

4.   Change to your ##ADMIN directory and create a subdirectory called WORK. Grant the new user Read, File scan, Write, Create, and Erase rights to your ##ADMIN\WORK directory and Read and File scan rights to the SYS:SOFTWARE.STC directory.

5. Create a user login script for ##USER. The user login script should contain any required comands that are not included in the server's system login script you recorded in Exercise 1.

6. Document the userid for ##USER on the line below.

    C4020003

7. Change to the SYS:MAIL*userid* directory and display the user login script commands.

8. Print the screen.

9. Log out and test the login script you have created by logging in as ##USER. Record any observations in the space below.

10. Log in using your assigned student username and add the following login commands to the user login script for ##USER:

    ■ Write the necessary command to display the daily message file based on the day of the week. For example, on Monday the login script should display a message called MONDAY.MSG, on Tuesday display TUESDAY.MSG, and so on. Record the command on line below.

    IF DAY_OF_WEEK = MONDAY THEN ICLUDE MONDAY.MSG

    ■ If there is another file server on your network, write a command to attach that file server using the username GUEST. Record the command below.

    ATTACH FILESERVER /GUEST

    ■ Write a command to redirect printer output from LPT1 to any print queue on the file server with a timeout of 7 seconds, a banner containing your name, no tabs, and a form feed. Your instructor will provide you with the names of print queues on the file server that you can access. Record the command on the line below.

    CAPTURE Q=? TI=7 NT FF B=%LOGIN_NAME

    ■ Assume the user's birthday is today and include an IF statement that will display a short "Happy Birthday" message along with phaser fire on today's date. Record the IF command on the lines below.

    IF DAY = 24 AND MONTH = 11 THEN

    WRITE "Happy Birthday" FIRE PHASER

    END

    ■ Write a command to map a root drive to your \##ADMIN\WORK directory. Record the command on the line below.

    MAP ROOT G:= SYS:50ADMIN\WORK

■ Write a command to map a search drive to allow the user to run the spreadsheet software located in the SYS:SOFTWARE.STC\SP directory. Record the command on the line below.

MAP S1:==SYS:SOFTWARE.STC\SP

■ Write a command to change the user's default drive to the SYS:SOFTWARE.STC\SP directory. Record this command on the line below.

DRIVE F:\SOFTWARE.STC\SP

■ At the end of the user login script, write an EXIT command to run the SESSION program. Record the EXIT command on the line below.

EXIT "SESSION"

11. Test the login script you have created by logging in as ##USER.

12. Use the Print Scrn key to print the screen after successfully logging in.

13. Enter the MAP command to check the drive mappings.

14. Enter the CAPTURE SH command to check your default capture status.

15. Use the Print Scrn key to print the screen showing drive mappings and capture status.

16. Use the TYPE command to obtain a hard copy of the login script to be checked by your instructor.

EXERCISE

Case 12-1: Designing a System and User Login Script

In this exercise you will use the system login script worksheet included to write a system login script for the Computer Technology Company. The company's directory structure is shown in Figure 12-30. The system login script is to perform the following functions:

■ Include required search drives.

■ Include a drive mapping to each volume of the CTHOST file server.

■ Include a root drive mapping to the MENUS directory.

■ Sales department users should connect to the CTSALES file server with the same usernames they use on CTHOST. Map a drive letter to the SALES\WORK directory.

■ Include search drive mappings to the WP and SP applications for all users.

■ Map a root drive to the home directory for each user, depending on his or her department, as shown in the directory structure (Figure 12-32).

- By default, all users should access the SYS_DOTM_Q1 print queue.

- Save the user's login name in the DOS environment for later use of the menu system.

- All users in the business department except BUDOLS should use the business menu by executing the NMENU BUSINESS command from the SYS:MENUS directory. Bud needs a special menu and will require a drive mapping to the SALES work directory.

- Before noon on Mondays, a message should be displayed for all business department users reminding them of the weekly business meeting in conference room 210A.

- In the sales department, all users except Sally should receive the SALES menus. Sally needs a search drive mapping to the SYS:WINDOWS directory and also needs to load windows by changing the drive to her home directory and executing the command WIN.

Figure 12-34

Computer technology directory

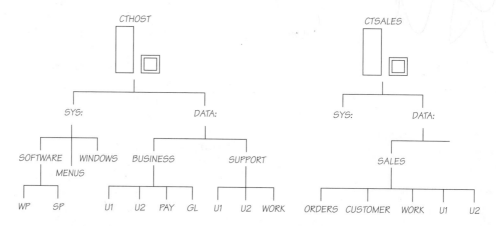

SUPERIOR TECHNICAL COLLEGE PROBLEMS

Now that the network printing environment has been established and the software packages are installed, the Superior Technical College staff is anxious to begin using the network. Before the users can begin to take advantage of the network's capability, however, it is necessary for you to automate the network login process by planning and implementing a login script system that will provide easy and standardized access to network resources.

Project 12-1: Defining the System Login Script

When you analyze the system, you find that users can be divided into three major groups: support services, student services, and faculty. In this problem you will use the system login script worksheet and user login script worksheet included to write the system login script along with any user login script commands. Dave Johnson would like to avoid user login script commands, if possible. He would rather place most or all of the login script processing in the system login script.

Support services

The support staff will both have similar login requirements consisting of the following:

- Search drives to all the SYS:SOFTWARE.STC software subdirectories.

- A root drive pointer to the users' home directories.

- A root drive pointer to the shared work area that allows users to access the outline and faculty directories easily.

- Drive pointers and SET commands to run the graphics software. (The graphics software requires each user to have a separate configuration file stored in the directory path specified during software installation. To create a unique file for each user, Dave Johnson recommends that you use a SET command to store the contents of the LOGIN_NAME variable in the DOS environment space using the variable name specified in the graphics software documentation. Refer to your notes on installing and running the graphics software from Chapter 9.)

- By default, support services' printer output sent to the LPT1 port should be redirected to the laser print queue you identified in Chapter 10.

- A message that is displayed when support services staff log in during the first week of a month. The message is a reminder that there is a meeting agenda due by the end of that week.

Student services

Users in the student services department have the following login script requirements:

- Search drives to all the SYS:SOFTWARE.STC software subdirectories.

- A root drive pointer to users' home directories.

- A root drive pointer to the student services shared work area.

- A root drive pointer to the GRADUATE system directory.

- Default printer redirection to the student services laser printer.

Faculty

In addition to needing search drives to run the application software, faculty users will need the following drive mappings and special commands:

- A root drive mapping to users' home directories.

- A root drive mapping to the shared faculty work area.

- A root drive mapping to the support services faculty work area.

- A drive mapping to the CLASSES directory in the computer lab.

- Default printer redirection to the support services laser printer.

- A reminder message that there is a faculty meeting at 11:30 A.M. on the first Thursday of each month.

Project 12-2: Entering and Testing Login Script Files

Before entering your system login script, you will need to create a directory called SCRIPTS. This is required by the current system login script file in order to include the login script commands you enter into the system login script commands executed by all users in your ##EVERYONE group. The SCRIPTS directory needs to be located in your existing ##STC directory, as follows:

Figure 12-35

The SCRIPTS directory structure

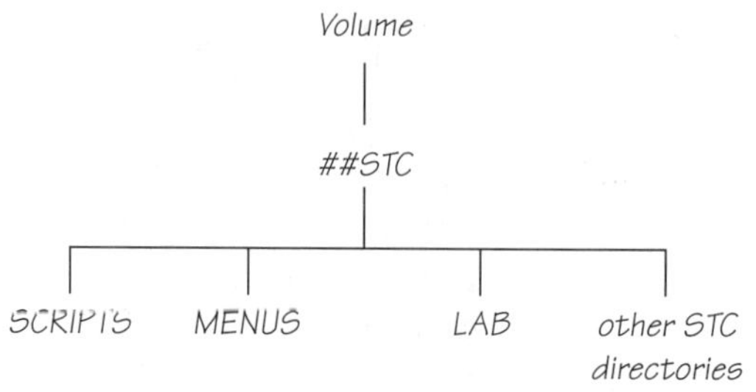

1. Create the SCRIPTS directory as shown.

2. GRANT the ##EVERYONE group Read and File scan rights to this directory.

3. Change to the SCRIPTS directory and use the DOS EDIT command or another text editor of your choice to create a file called NET$LOG.DAT containing your system login script commands.

4. Create another file to contain the login script statements you defined for your student workstation users.

5. Use the SYSCON utility to enter the user login script commands you defined in Project 12-1.

6. Log in as each of the following users and use the MAP command to determine that his or her login script commands are being executed correctly. Use the Print Scrn key to obtain a hardcopy of the results of the MAP command for verification by your instructor.

   Karl Dauer

   Mimi Ito

   David Feinstein

Project 12-3: Testing and Documenting Your System

1. Test the system login script by logging in as one user from each of the groups and use the MAP command to check the users' drive mappings.

2. Print the screen that shows the drive mappings of each of the following groups:

   Student services

   Support services

   Faculty

3. Log in as the user Karl Dauer and change to the drive containing the graduate system. Run the graduate system and create a new user.

4. Print the graduate report and then use PCONSOLE to determine if the report is contained in the student services' laser print queue.

5. Use the TYPE NET$LOG.DAT > PRN command to obtain a hardcopy of both login script files.

Project 12-4: Providing User Documentation

Once the login scripts have been tested, Dave Johnson would like you to prepare instructions for each department informing users of how to use the drive pointers you have established for their departments. These instructions should take the form of a memo written to the head of each department. The memo should inform department heads how to use each drive pointer. The memo should also request the scheduling of a meeting in which you will provide staff training after the menus have been implemented. Use a word processing package to develop and print a memo to each of the following department heads:

Karl Dauer, student services

Lauri Holt, support services

Barbara Rau, faculty

## CHAPTER THIRTEEN

THE MENU SYSTEM

The user interface is the frosting on the cake of the network system. It provides a pleasant environment in which users can easily access their applications. A menu system is one popular kind of user interface that works well with DOS-based applications. It provides users with option lists arranged in main menus and in optional submenus, as shown in Figure 13-1.

AFTER READING THIS CHAPTER AND COMPLETING THE EXERCISES YOU WILL BE ABLE TO:

- IDENTIFY THE COMPONENTS OF THE NETWARE V3.12 MENU SYSTEM.

- DESIGN AND CREATE NETWARE V3.12 MENUS AND SUBMENUS.

- DESCRIBE TWO ALTERNATE METHODS TO RUN THE MENU SYSTEM.

- ASSIGN THE ACCESS RIGHTS NECESSARY FOR MULTIPLE USERS TO RUN NETWARE V3.12 MENUS.

- DESIGN AND IMPLEMENT A NETWARE V3.12 MENU SYSTEM FOR AN ORGANIZATION.

Figure 13-1

Sample menu system

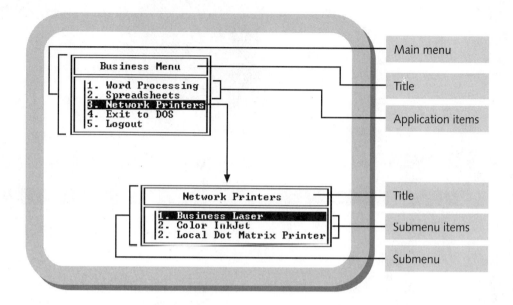

Graphical user interfaces, such as Microsoft Windows or OS/2, are rapidly becoming the standard user environment. However, there are still many DOS-based applications and workstations that run best from a menu system.

The main menu contains the major options to which the user needs quick access. To run the word processing software, for example, the user simply selects option number 1. Options in the main menu can invoke submenus that contain two or more additional options. For example, when the Network Printers option shown in Figure 13-1 is selected from the main menu, it calls up the Network Printers submenu. This submenu offers three choices: sending output to one of two network printers or to a local printer. In this way, menus allow users to perform specific tasks or run applications easily.

Prior to NetWare v3.12, Novell had developed its own menu system. The Novell menu system, while simple to use, lacked some of the features found in other popular DOS-based menu systems. With more recent versions of NetWare, network administrators can design menu systems that allow network users to easily access DOS applications. The new menu system is powerful enough for most applications and still is relatively easy for the network administrator to use.

The NetWare v3.12 menu system is based on the Saber menu system, a popular third-party DOS-based menu system used on many computer systems.

Figure 13-2 shows the menu command statements that produce the menu shown in Figure 13-1. Each menu starts with a MENU statement, indicating the menu's title and the number that is used to access it. The first MENU statement in Figure 13-2 defines menu number 01, naming it Business Menu. Because it is the first menu listed in the source file, it will be the opening or main menu. An ITEM statement defines the text that will be displayed for each menu option and can include an optional parameter. The caret symbol (^) followed by a digit or letter causes the menu system to display that character prior to the menu option. If no digit or letter is defined, a default letter will precede the menu option. The default letters begin with A and proceed through Z. The "^1" preceding the Word Processing option, for example, will cause a 1 to appear before the option name. Otherwise, the letter A would appear. Inclusion of the CHDIR parameter enclosed in braces {} tells the menu system to return to the directory from which it was run after completion of the option. The EXEC statements contain DOS-executable commands that will be processed when a user selects an option. Notice that the word processing option switches to the user's home drive before the WP program is started and the spreadsheet option switches to the BUDGETS directory on drive L before the spreadsheet software is started. When the word processing or spreadsheet program ends, the menu system automatically returns to the default menu directory. Because there are multiple printer selection possibilities, option 3, Network Printers, contains the SHOW command, which links it to menu 02, Network Printers. The Logout option uses the LOGOUT parameter of the EXEC command. This allows the user to log out from the current file server and end the menu program. The Exit to DOS option uses the EXIT parameter of the EXEC command to quit the menu system and return to the DOS prompt. If you want to prevent users from exiting the menu system, you can omit the Exit to DOS option.

Figure 13-2

Sample menu command statements

```
MENU 01,Business Menu
ITEM ^1Word Processing  {CHDIR}
        EXEC H:
        EXEC WP
ITEM ^2Spreadsheet
        EXEC SP
ITEM ^3Network Printers
        SHOW 02
ITEM ^4Exit to DOS
        EXIT DOS
ITEM ^4Logout
        EXEC LOGOUT
MENU 02,Network Printers
TEM ^1Business Laser  {PAUSE}
        EXEC CAPTURE Q=BUS_HP3_R0   TI=5   NB   NT   NFF
ITEM ^2Color Ink-Jet  {PAUSE}
        EXEC CAPTURE Q=SRV_BJC800_L1 TI=10  NB   NT    NFF
ITEM ^3Local Dot Matrix Printer {PAUSE}
        EXEC ENDCAP
```

The second MENU statement in Figure 13-2 defines menu number 02 as the Network Printers menu. Each ITEM statement of menu 02 invokes a CAPTURE command to redirect printer output to the desired print queue. Notice the use of the PAUSE parameter following the ITEM statements. The PAUSE option causes the menu system to pause after it executes the CAPTURE command and ask the user to press any key to continue. This provides the user with an opportunity to view the results of the command and report any problems. Pressing the Esc key will exit the Network Printers menu and return to the Business Menu.

The NetWare menu system's menus have the look and feel of NetWare menu utilities, such as SYSCON and FILER, which link them smoothly to the NetWare menu utilities. As a CNA you will be required to know how to use NetWare's menu system to create, maintain, and debug network menus. In this chapter you will learn about the NetWare menu system and how to create and maintain NetWare menus.

MENU SYSTEM COMPONENTS

In order to develop and implement the NetWare v3.12 menu system on your network, you first need to be familiar with the components of the menu system and how they work together. Figure 13-3 illustrates the NetWare menu system. The source file contains valid menu command statements—such as the MENU, ITEM, and EXEC statements mentioned earlier. Because this file is in ASCII format, a standard text editor program, such as the DOS EDIT command, can be used to create and edit the contents of the source file. The MENUMAKE program translates the source statements into an executable menu file that will display the menu. As it creates the executable file, the MENUMAKE program checks each command for any syntax errors. If errors are discovered, the executable file will not be created and a list of invalid menu command statements will be displayed. When no errors are detected, the MENUMAKE program creates a new executable menu file, with the extension .DAT, that contains the executable menu. Because this file is in a binary format, its contents cannot be viewed or changed with a text editor program. After the executable menu file is created, the NMENU program runs the executable file and displays the menu options on the user's workstation. While the menu is run, certain temporary files are created in the directory from which the NMENU program is run. These temporary files contain statements that link the menu to the application software and then return control to the menu system when the application ends. When the menu system is exited or the user logs out, the NMENU program deletes the temporary files.

Figure 13-3

NetWare menu system components

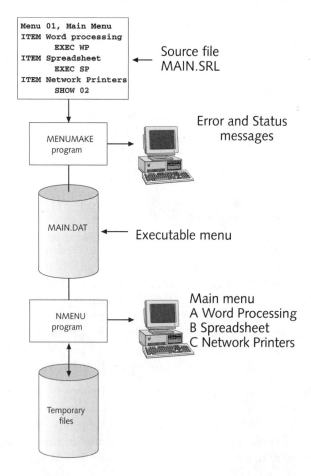

The MENUCNVT program included with NetWare v3.12 can be used to convert a menu file created with the older NetWare menu system to be used with NetWare v3.12. The command is MENUCNVT *oldmenu*.MNU. The MENUCNVT program reads the old menu file, which has the extension .MNU, and creates a file containing the new menu commands. The new file has the filename extension .SRC. The MENUMAKE command then must be used to compile the converted menu to an executable menu file.

CREATING A MENU SYSTEM

A good menu system should be secure and easy to understand and should provide users with the options they need to do their jobs. In order to meet these requirements, a network administrator needs to take care in planning what menus need to be created and how the menu system will be run. Only then can the network administrator proceed to create and test the menu command files. In this section you will learn how to plan a complete menu system. You will follow the creation of a sample menu system for the PC Solutions company. The process entails the following five steps:

1. The menu files are designed.

2. Menus are written, compiled, and tested.

3. Location of the menu files is planned.

4. Access rights are provided to users.

5. Login scripts are modified.

DESIGNING THE MENU FILES

The first step in designing and writing the menu command files is determining what applications and system functions need to be included on each user or workgroup menu and what commands are necessary to start and run each of the menu items. In most cases, a common menu can be designed for all workgroups or departments, even though some items on the menu might not be applicable to all users. Another option is a separate menu for each user. Having a separate menu for each user, of course, makes maintaining the menu system much more difficult because changing an item common to all menus means changing and compiling several menu command files.

A technique that saves time in writing and maintaining the menu system is identifying functions that are common to all menus and placing them in separate submenu files. By placing common commands in separate submenus, you can easily include these commands in each department's main menu simply by including an option that uses the SHOW command to access the desired submenu. For example, assume users in PC Solutions' business department need to run word processing, spreadsheet, payroll, and accounting applications. The users also need to be able to send output to the laser or color ink jet printer as well as to the dot-matrix printer attached to their local workstations. Business department users, like all users in the company, need to be able to perform certain network functions such as changing their passwords, working with drive mappings, and sending messages.

Figure 13-4 illustrates the use of the menu design form to define the menus and submenus that will meet the needs of PC Solutions' business department. The Network Functions submenu contains options, such as changing password and drive mappings, that can be used by all departments. Placing these functions in a menu file and making a separate executable menu allows access to these functions from any department menu, as described later in this section.

Figure 13-4

Sample business department menu design

Menu Design Form

Designed by: _Ted Simpson_   Date:_____

Workgroup name: _Business Department_____

Main Menu

Title: _Business Menu_____
Number: _01_____

Option	Description	Commands/Comments
1	Word Processing	WP
2	Spreadsheet	SP
3	Accounting	L: CD \ACCT GL
4	Payroll	L: CD \PAYROLL PAY
5	Network Printers	Submenu
6	Network Functions	Submenu
X	Exit to DOS	EXIT DOS
L	Logout	LOGOUT

Submenu Name: _Network Printers_
Submenu Number: _02_____

Option	Desc/Commands
1	Business Laser Printer CAPTURE Q=BUS_HP3_R0
2	Color Ink-jet Printer CAPTURE Q=SRV_BJC880_L1
3	Local Printer ENDCAP

Submenu Name: _Network Functions_
Submenu Number: _03_____

Options	Desc/Commands
1	Change Password SETPASS
2	Drive Mappings SESSION
3	Send a Messages SEND
4	Work with Print Jobs PCONSOLE

In the example shown in Figure 13-4, the payroll application option will appear on the menu for all the business department users. Only specified users, however, will be assigned the rights necessary to run the payroll application. If the business user does not have these rights and selects the payroll option, NetWare displays an error message indicating that access is denied.

WRITING MENUS

After you have determined what options you will need for each menu and submenu, the next step is to write the commands necessary to produce each department's menu and then use a text editor, such as the DOS EDIT command, to enter them into the appropriate source files. **Source menu files** consist of a combination of organizational and control commands. **Organizational commands** establish the content and organization of the menus the user sees on the screen; **control commands** tell the NMENU program how to perform an action, such as running a DOS command, starting an application, or linking to a submenu.

Figure 13-5 provides an overview of both organizational and control commands. To become a CNA you need to be familiar with these commands. Keep the following guidelines in mind when you create the source command files:

- The maximum number of menu levels is 11—one main menu followed by 10 submenu levels.

- The maximum number of menu screens is 255.

- The maximum length of a menu name is 40 characters.

- The maximum width of an ITEM line is 40 characters.

- The maximum text file width is 80 characters. If a command wraps to another line, place a plus sign (+) at the end of the line and continue the command on the next line.

- The main menu must be at the beginning of the source file. The main menu then calls up any submenus by menu number.

Figure 13-5

NetWare menu command table

Command	Command Type	Description
MENU	Organizational	Marks the beginning of a new menu or submenu screen
ITEM	Organizational	Identifies a menu option to be included in the menu defined by the preceding MENU statement
EXEC	Control	Instructs DOS to execute the command following the EXEC statement
LOAD	Control	Displays a separate executable menu file as a submenu
SHOW	Control	Displays a submenu included in the current menu file
GETO	Control	Requests optional input from the user prior to executing the next statement in ITEM
GETR	Control	Requests required input from the user prior to executing the next statement in ITEM
GETP	Control	Requests input from the user and then stores the input in parameter variables. The first input is stored in parameter %1, the next in %2, and so on up to %9

The MENU statement

A title and number must be assigned to each menu and submenu that is identified on the menu design form. Use the MENU *number, title* statement to define each menu and submenu. The menu *number* can be any unique number ranging from 1 to 255 that does not exist in this menu file. The number is used with the SHOW command to call up a submenu. Menu numbers do not need to be in sequence. The first menu in the source file becomes the main menu regardless of its menu number. The *title* is the title of the menu that will be displayed above the menu box. The menu title (up to 40 characters) should describe the menu. Figure 13-6 shows the menu statements that correspond to the menu plan shown in Figure 13-4.

Figure 13-6

Sample MENU statements

```
MENU 01,Business Menu

MENU 02,Network Printers

MENU 03,Network Functions
```

The ITEM statement

Each MENU statement must be followed by two or more ITEM statements to define each option that will be displayed in that menu. The ITEM *name [{option}]* statement defines each option that will be a part of the menu defined by the preceding MENU statement. The *name* parameter contains the descriptive name for the menu item that you want displayed in the menu box. A *name* can consist of up to 40 characters and should identify the option's function to the user. Menu items are displayed on the menu in the order in which you enter them in the source file. The NMENU program automatically places a letter, starting with A, before each item name in a menu. If you want to use your own number or character to mark an item, include in the *name* parameter a caret symbol (^) and the number or letter you want to use. If you do assign an item letter or number, you must do so to the rest of the items on the same menu. If you do not, NetWare will assign its default letter sequence, which might duplicate a letter you have chosen. The following ITEM command, for example, marks the menu's exit option with the letter X.

```
ITEM ^XExit the Menu
```

The ITEM command not only identifies a menu option, but can include the options CHDIR, BATCH, PAUSE, or SHOW. These options must be enclosed in braces. The {CHDIR} option, for example, changes the drive and directory back to the path that was in use before the commands contained in the associated ITEM statement were executed. Without this option, the most recent drive and directory used by the application will remain in effect, possibly causing errors in the menu program. It is generally a good practice to include a {CHDIR} option with each menu item that will run an application program. The {CHDIR} option ensures that the menu system will return to the starting directory prior to ending the menu item.

The {BATCH} option removes the menu program from memory before the commands contained in the option are executed. Without this option, a portion of memory is reserved for the menu software (approximately 32 Kbytes), which reduces the amount of memory available to the application software. Because the BATCH option automatically includes the CHDIR option, it is unnecessary to place both BATCH and CHDIR in the same ITEM statement. The {PAUSE} option causes the menu program to stop and display the message "Press any key to continue" after the commands in this item are executed. Use this option to give the user time to view the message or results displayed by the commands in the menu item. The following example shows a {PAUSE} option used after a menu item to display the status of network volumes:

```
ITEM Display SYS Volume Status {PAUSE}

EXEC CHKVOL SYS:
```

The {SHOW} option displays each EXEC command performed in ITEM. The {SHOW} option is useful during testing of the menu. Two or more options can be combined in one ITEM statement by placing both options inside the braces separated by spaces. If you want to include both the SHOW and CHDIR options with the word processing option, you could use the following sample ITEM statement:

```
ITEM Word Processing {CHDIR SHOW}
```

The EXEC statement

EXEC statements must follow each ITEM statement. They start applications or execute DOS NetWare commands and can also perform special menu functions. Figure 13-7 lists the EXEC commands.

Figure 13-7

Special EXEC commands

Command	Description
EXEC EXIT	Exits the menu program and returns to the DOS prompt. Users cannot exit the menu system and return to the DOS prompt unless this command is included in one of the menu items. EXIT must be typed in uppercase letters.
EXEC CALL batch_file	Runs a batch file from the menu program and returns control to the following statement upon completion of the DOS batch file.
EXEC DOS	Runs the DOS command processor (COMMAND.COM) providing the user with a DOS prompt. The menu user can type EXIT at the DOS prompt to return to the menu system. DOS must be in uppercase.
EXEC LOGOUT	Ends a session by logging out of all file servers and exiting the menu system.

The SHOW statement

The SHOW statement is used to access a submenu located in the current menu file using the *number* parameter defined in the MENU command of the desired submenu. Notice that the SHOW command requires the use of the menu's assigned number, not the menu's title.

Figure 13-8 illustrates the ITEM, EXEC, and SHOW commands that will perform the processing required by the options in the PC Solutions' business department main menu. Notice the use of the multiple EXEC statements following the accounting and payroll applications. The first EXEC statement changes the default drive to drive letter L; the second EXEC statement changes to the directory containing the appropriate business application. This requires that the users in the business department will have a drive letter L mapped as a root drive to the business directory structure, which contains the general ledger and payroll software directories. The Exit to DOS option has been included to allow more convenient testing and debugging of the business menu. After the menu is operational, this option will be removed to prevent users from accidentally exiting the menu system.

Figure 13-8

Sample business menu statements

```
MENU  01,Business Menu
ITEM  ^1Word Processing {BATCH}
         EXEC WP
ITEM  ^2Spreadsheets    {CHDIR}
         EXEC SP
ITEM  ^3Accounting      {CHDIR}
         EXEC L:
         EXEC CD \ACCT
         EXEC GL
ITEM  ^4Payroll    {CHDIR}
         EXEC L:
         EXEC CD \PAYROLL
         EXEC PAY
ITEM  ^5Network Printers
         SHOW 02
ITEM  ^6Network Functions
         SHOW 03
ITEM  ^XExit to DOS
         EXEC EXIT
ITEM  ^LLog Out
         EXEC LOGOUT
```

The LOAD statement

The LOAD statement can be used to include other menu files in the main menu. This allows you to keep a complex menu system easier to work with by breaking it into small separate submenu files. The menu files being accessed from a LOAD command must be first translated into executable files by the MENUMAKE program. After the executable submenu files have been created, they can be accessed from the main menu by using the LOAD *filename* statement, where *filename* is replaced with the name of the executable menu file containing the .DAT extension.

Suppose, for example, multiple workgroup menus need to include the network functions found in the Network Functions menu defined previously in the sample menu design form (Figure 13-4). Rather than including the Network Function submenu statements in the source menu file for each workgroup, you can create and compile a separate NETWORK.SRC file containing the network function menu statements. In the main menu for each workgroup you then include the network functions by placing the following menu commands in the main menu:

```
ITEM ^NNetwork Functions
     LOAD NETWORK.DAT
```

Obtaining user input

It is often necessary to obtain information from the user before a command statement can be executed. In order to use the Send Message option under Network Functions, for example, you must obtain the message to be sent and the name of the user to whom the message is to be sent. The Novell menu system handles user input with the following GET statements:

- The GETO command is used when the user's input is optional, such as when asking for optional command parameters. A GETO command might be used, for example, to ask for a volume name to be used with the CHKVOL command. If no volume name is specified, the current volume information will be displayed.

- The GETR command is used when the user's input is required, for example, when user input is needed for the SEND command.

- The GETP command is used when user input needs to be stored. The first input is stored in the variable %1, the second in variable %2, and so on, up to %9.

The syntax of all the GET statements is as follows:

GETx prompt {prepend} length,prefill,[SECURE] {append}

The *prompt* field contains text you want to be displayed when the user is asked to enter a value. It can contain up to 40 characters. The *prepend* field, which must be enclosed in braces, contains characters to be added to the beginning of the user's entry. The *length* field is used to set the characters to be added to the beginning of the user's entry and to set the maximum number of characters for the user input field. The *length* parameter is required, but can be a zero if the user is only required to press the [Enter] key in order to confirm an action. The *prefill* field is used to provide a default response that will be displayed with the prompt. When using the GETO command, the user can accept the default, change the response by typing over the characters, or cancel the selection of the item. The *prefill* field is optional and can be omitted by typing a second comma after the comma that follows the length field. This is shown in the example below. The *append* field must be enclosed in braces {} and is used to contain characters you want added after the user's response. If you want to make sure a colon is placed after the drive letter entered by the user, for example, you could use the append field as shown in the following GETR statement:

```
GETR Enter destination drive { } 1,, {:}
```

This command will force the user to enter a single-character drive letter and then place a colon after the drive letter specified. If you want a default value of drive C to be placed in the destination drive field, place the letter C in the *prefill* field of the GETR command as follows:

GETR Enter destination drive { } 1,C, {:}

The optional SECURE parameter placed before the *{append}* parameter prevents the menu program from displaying the user's input on the screen. This option can be used when the user is asked to enter a password or data that should not be read by others.

When you use the GETO and GETR commands, you must include a space in the *prepend* field in order to separate the user's input from the command line. With the GETO and GETR statements, the user's input is automatically placed after the EXEC statement in the associated ITEM statement. If, for example, you want a menu item that allows a user to view the status of any volume, you can use the GETO statement shown in Figure 13-9. The user input is placed immediately following the EXEC CHKVOL statement. Note the space included in the *prepend* field. If no space is left in the *prepend* field, the volume name the user enters will be placed immediately following the word CHKVOL, causing an error to be displayed. If the user enters the volume name DATA:, for example, the EXEC command becomes EXEC CHKVOLDATA:.

Figure 13-10 illustrates the use of the GETR command to obtain user input for the Send Messages option in the Network Functions menu defined in the sample menu design form (Figure 13-4). Notice that the sequence of the GETR statements must match the syntax of the SEND statements, requiring the user to enter the message followed by the name of the user to whom the message will be sent. In addition, a double quotation mark (") must be included in the *prepend* and *append* fields of the GETR statement. This supplies the quotation marks required by the syntax of the SEND statement. Remember to include a space in the *prepend* field of each GETR statement to separate the message from the username in the final SEND command.

Figure 13-9

Sample GETO statement

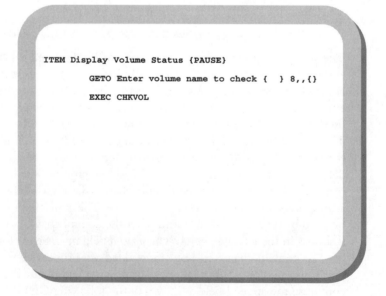

```
ITEM Display Volume Status {PAUSE}
        GETO Enter volume name to check {  } 8,,{}
        EXEC CHKVOL
```

```
MENU  03,Network Functions
ITEM  ^1Change Password
         EXEC SETPASS
ITEM  ^2Drive Mappings
         EXEC SESSION
ITEM  ^3Send a Message {PAUSE}
         GETR Enter message line {   "} 60,,{"}
         GETR Enter username {   } 12,,{}
         EXEC SEND
ITEM  ^4Work with Print Jobs
         EXEC PCONSOLE
```

The GETP statement allows you to control exactly where the user input will be
placed. The variables %1, %2, ... %9 are specified in the GETP statement. Figure 13-11
shows an example of the GETP command with the ITEM for the Send Messages
statement. Notice that with the GETP statement, the sequence of the user input does
not determine the use of the input in the EXEC statement because the %1 and %2
variables can be placed in any sequence. In addition, when the GETP statement is used,
no *prepend* or *append* parameters are necessary; the spaces and quotation marks can be
placed directly in the EXEC command.

```
ITEM  ^3Send a Message {PAUSE}
         GETP Enter username to send message to {} 12,,{}
         GETP Enter message line {} 60,,{}
         EXEC SEND "%2"  %1
```

COMPILING AND TESTING THE MENUS

After you write the menu statements, your next task is to use a text editor, such as the EDIT command, to create and save a menu source file with the filename extension .SRC. At this time, it is wise to place an Exit to DOS option in the main menu to allow you to return to the DOS prompt easily. This will allow you to make any necessary corrections to the menu file or drive mappings when a menu item does not work properly. If the main menu does not contain an Exit to DOS option, you will need to use the logout option to end the menu program and then log in again in order to make corrections to the menu items. After the menu is working properly, you can remove the Exit to DOS option and recompile the menu in order to prevent users from exiting to the DOS prompt.

After the source file has been created, you use the MENUMAKE program to translate, or compile, the source file into an executable menu file with the .DAT extension. Figure 13-12 illustrates the use of the MENUMAKE command to translate the business menu source file, named BUSMENU.SRC, into an executable menu file. Notice the error messages generated as a result of syntax errors in some of the menu command statements. The DOS EDIT program can be used to correct errors in the source file. Then use the MENUMAKE command again to create the executable menu file successfully, as shown at the bottom of Figure 13-12.

Figure 13-12

Using the
MENUMAKE program

To test the menu file, first you need to establish any necessary search and regular drive pointer mappings that are used by the menu items. After all necessary drive mappings have been established, you can run the menu by using the command NMENU BUSMENU. Figure 13-13 shows an example of running the business menu, selecting the Network Functions option and using the Send a Message option. Notice the User Input Requested window generated by the GETR statements (see Figure 13-10). After entering information in each input field, the user must press the F10 key, as shown at the bottom of the input screen, to continue and send the message.

Figure 13-13

Running the sample
business menu

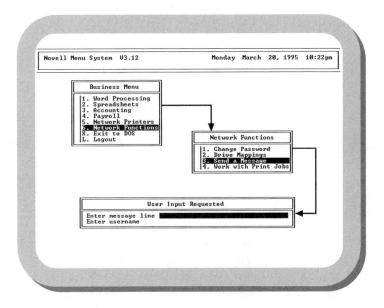

After compiling your menu system, you should test each option. Make notes on any drive mappings or other DOS environment settings you need to run each application. You will use this information to create the environment that users will need to run the menu items.

PLANNING THE MENU DIRECTORY STRUCTURE

Many of the network administrator's activities require decisions and compromises. Planning the menu system directory structure is such a situation. Before setting up the menu system for your users, you first need to determine what menu directories you need and where they should be placed in your file system. In order to make these decisions you need to decide what directory the users will access to run their menus.

The two most popular alternatives used by many network administrators are to have users run the menu system from the menu directory or from their own home directories. The advantages of having users run the menu system from their home directories are that the users have all rights in their home directories for creating and erasing temporary files and that they have access to files and data stored in their home directories without changing to another drive. The major disadvantage of running the menu system from the users' home directories is that you will need to map a search drive to the menu executable directory in order for the users to access the menu command files. Although this is normally not a problem, it does reduce the number of search drives available to your system and can slow down the system somewhat when it searches for programs and files. An alternative to using a search drive is to specify a drive letter ahead of the menu name when the menu is executed. For example, to execute a menu file called BUSMENU located in a directory mapped to the M drive letter, you could use the NMENU M:BUSMENU command from the user's home directory. Although this method does not require a search drive to the MENUS directory, the drive letter must be used each time any reference to a menu file is made.

The second alternative is to run the menus directly from the directory containing the menu executable files. The advantages to this method are that you will not need to use a search drive or include the drive letter to find the menu files and that temporary users, such as GUEST, who might not have a home directory, will be able to run the menu system.

After you decide where users will run their menu files, your next decision is what directory or directories will be used to store the menu source and executable files. One option is to store all the menu files in the SYS:PUBLIC directory rather than creating a separate MENU directory. This not only avoids having to create a separate directory, it also means that all users have a search drive along with Read and File scan rights to the SYS:PUBLIC directory. If you use this method, however, users will need to run menus from their home directories in order to create and delete the temporary files. Another disadvantage to storing menu files in SYS:PUBLIC is that they will be combined with the NetWare utilities and command files, increasing the chances that they will be inadvertently erased or lost when NetWare server upgrades are performed. A disadvantage of storing the source menu files in SYS:PUBLIC is that it allows users to display the contents of the source files and view passwords and other menu options.

Because of the disadvantages associated with storing menus in the SYS:PUBLIC directory, most network administrators create a separate directory for their menu files. Source files can then be separated from the menu executable files by creating a subdirectory called SOURCE, as shown in Figure 13-14. All rights can then be removed from the Inherited Rights Mask on the SOURCE subdirectory to prevent users from inheriting rights into this subdirectory.

Figure 13-14

Suggested menu directory structure

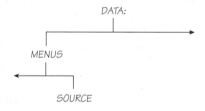

The last decision you need to make is where to store the temporary files. If users are running the menus from their home directories, you can default to having the temporary files stored in the current directory. However, if users will be accessing the menus from the MENU directory where they have only Read and File scan rights, you will need to create a directory for the temporary files, as shown in Figure 13-15, and then give the users Read, File scan, Create, and Erase rights to the temporary file directory. In addition, you can set the Purge attribute on the TEMP directory in order to make the space used by the temporary files immediately available to the system after the files are deleted. This will allow other files to be available for salvaging for a longer time and provide a slight increase in system performance.

Figure 13-15

Menu temporary file structure

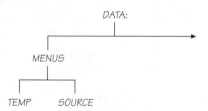

If you plan to use a separate directory to hold temporary files, it is necessary to tell the menu system the name of the path to the temporary directory along with the user's connection number. Because multiple users will be storing their temporary files in the same directory, the user's connection numbers are needed to keep each user's temporary files separate. The connection number is included as part of the temporary filenames.

The DOS SET command can be used to identify the path to the temporary directory as well as the user's connection number. Include the following commands in the system login script after the MAP command to create the M drive printer to the MENU directory:

```
DOS SET S_FILEDIR="M:TEMP\"

DOS SET S_FILE="%STATION"
```

PROVIDING USER ACCESS RIGHTS

To run the menu system, users will need a minimum of Read and File scan rights in the directory containing the menu executable files along with Read, File scan, Create, and Erase rights in the directory containing the temporary files. If users will be running the menus from their home directories, you will need to provide Read and File scan rights to the menu executable directory only, because by default, temporary files will be created and erased from the user's home directory.

When the menus are executed from the directory containing the executable files, you need to either assign Read, File scan, Create, and Erase rights to the executable file directory or separate the temporary files into a different directory. Then assign Read and File scan rights to the executable directory and Read, File scan, Create, and Erase rights to the temporary directory. Figure 13-16 illustrates a grant command used to grant business users the rights to run the menu system.

Figure 13-16

Granting menu access rights

```
F:\>GRANT R F FOR DATA:MENUS TO EVERYONE

CTS_HOST/DATA:MENUS
MENUS                              Rights set to [ R    F ]

F:\>GRANT R F C E FOR DATA:MENUS\TEMP TO EVERYONE

CTS_HOST/DATA:MENUS\TEMP
TEMP                               Rights set to [ R CE F ]

F:\>
```

MODIFYING THE LOGIN SCRIPTS

Once the menus are tested and ready to run, the last step is to automate the menu system by placing the necessary commands in the system and user login scripts. The login script commands to run most menu systems consist of commands to map a drive to the menu directory, optional DOS SET commands, and an EXIT command to link the user to his or her correct menu.

In most cases, you will want to use the system login script to map at least one drive to the directory structure containing the menu system. If users are running the menus from their home directories, you might want to make this a search drive. This will ensure that the menu executable files can be found without inclusion of the drive or path when a menu command file is referenced. If users will be running the menus from the directory containing the executable files, you should map a root drive pointer, such as M, to the menu directory. Using a root drive helps ensure that the path to the drive containing the menu files will not accidentally be changed from an application program or DOS command.

If you plan to store user temporary files in a separate directory, you will need to include DOS SET commands in the system login script. These commands, described in Chapter 12, tell the menu program the path to the temporary directory and the user's connection number. Finally, each user must be linked to his or her appropriate menu. This can be done by including EXIT NMENU menuname as the last or only command in each user's personal login script. If you do not plan to use personal login scripts in your system, you will need to include the EXIT command as the last command executed for each workgroup.

In addition to the EXIT command, you need to be sure the user's default drive points to the directory from which you want the menu system to be run. Use the DRIVE *drive:* login script command in either the system or personal login script. If you want users to run the menu system from their home directories, for example, include the commands shown in Figure 13-17 in the system and personal login scripts. If you want users to run the menu system from the MENUS directory and store temporary files in the MENUS\TEMP directory, include the commands shown in Figure 13-18 in the system and personal login scripts.

Figure 13-17

Login script with Menu run from user home directiory

System Login Script
MAP INS S4:=DATA:MENUS
IF MEMBER OF "BUSINESS"
MAP ROOT H:=DATA:BUSINESS\%LOGIN_NAME
END
Personal Login Script
DRIVE H:
EXIT "NMENU BUSMENU"

Figure 13-18

Login script with Menu run from shared MENU directiory

System Login Script
MAP M:=DATA:MENUS
DOS SET S_FILEDIR="M:\MENUS\TEMP\M"
DOS SET S_FILE="%STATION"
IF MEMBER OF "BUSINESS"
MAP ROOT H:=DATA:BUSINESS\%LOGIN_NAME
END
Personal Login Script
DRIVE M:
EXIT "NMENU BUSMENU"

TRAINING USERS

The final step in implementing a successful menu system is providing training so users understand and can operate the menu system you have designed. This is best done by working with each department separately. First show the users how to move between the menus and submenus with the Esc key. Make sure to stress the importance of logging out prior to leaving the workstation and then show them how they can use the LOGIN command to log back in and redisplay their menu.

Next, explain any special menu options, such as working with drive pointers and selecting network printers. Be sure that each user feels comfortable about using the menu system to access his or her application software and to send output to the correct network printer. Show users how to change their passwords and explain any password restrictions, such as minimum password length and frequency between password changes. Making sure all users know how to use the menu properly to access network resources will increase their efficiency and decrease the problems and frustrations caused by their unfamiliarity with the system.

CHAPTER SUMMARY

A good menu system is necessary for users of DOS-based computers to access the network and perform their jobs easily. The overall impression your users have of the network system is often determined by how well the menu system works. A network administrator needs to be able to establish and maintain a menu system that will meet the needs of users and provide secure access to the network resources.

Although the original NetWare menu system provided a convenient way to create fairly powerful menus, Novell decided with NetWare v3.12 and v4.x, to update its menu system using a specialized version of the Saber menu system. The new menu system uses less memory and includes features found in more powerful menu systems. Among the features are creating executable menu files, linking menus, and preventing users from accidentally exiting the menu system. In addition, the new menu system contains control functions, such as the ability to place temporary files in a separate directory, to return to the original menu directory automatically, and to remove the menu program from memory during the execution of a menu item.

The NMENU system consists of several components.

- The source menu files, having the extension .SRC

- The MENUMAKE program, which compiles source menu statements and creates executable menu files with the extension .DAT

- The NMENU program, which runs the executable menu files

- Temporary files created by the NMENU program to contain the batch commands being executed for a menu item

- The MENUCNVT program, which is used to convert original menu files with the extension .MNU to files containing the new menu commands with the extension .SRC

Creating menus involves planning the contents of each workgroup or user menu and defining common needs and submenus. Commands in the NMENU system can be divided into two classifications. The organizational commands consist of such statements as the MENU statement, which defines a menu's title and number, the ITEM statement, which identifies each item to be displayed in a menu and control options such as BATCH, PAUSE, CHDIR, and SHOW. The control commands consist of such statements as EXEC, LOAD, and SHOW. The EXEC statement causes DOS to execute the specified command or application or perform a special function. Some special function statements are EXEC EXIT to exit the menu system, EXEC CALL to call a DOS batch program, EXEC DOS to display a DOS prompt, and EXEC LOGOUT to end the user's session on the network. The LOAD statement allows you to pass control to another executable menu file; the SHOW statement executes a submenu within the current menu file by using the menu's number.

After writing the menu files, you next need to enter, compile, and test each menu. A standard text editor program, such as the DOS EDIT command, can be used to enter the menu source file and save it with the extension .SRC. Next, you use the MENUMAKE program to translate, or compile, the source menu into an executable menu file. If errors are listed by the MENUMAKE program, you will need to use the text editor to correct the errors and then use the MENUMAKE command again to create an executable menu file. After the executable file has been successfully created, you can proceed to test each menu option. This often involves setting up the necessary drive mappings or copying files to the executable directory and logging in as individual users.

To implement the menu system, first you need to decide on the location from which users will run the menu system, and the location of the menu files. One alternative is to have users run the menus from their home directories. While this allows temporary files to be stored in a user's home directory, it requires a separate search drive to the menu directory as well as requiring all users, including temporary workers, to have a home directory. An alternative is to have users run the menu system directly from the menu executable directory. While this reduces the number of search drives needed and allows any user to run the menu system, it has the disadvantage of requiring the network administrator to establish a location for the temporary files.

Many network administrators create separate directories for the source and executable menu files, allowing users to run menus without being able to display the contents of the source file. In addition, another directory is often created for temporary files which allows users to run the menu system from the menu directory without needing access rights to create and erase files. In this setup, the network administrator needs to assign users Read and File scan rights to the menu directory only. Once the directories are created, you assign users Read and File scan rights in the directory containing the executable files and Create and Erase rights in the directory that will contain the temporary files.

The final step in implementing the menu system is modifying the system and personal user login script files. The system login script needs to contain a drive mapping to the menu directory along with optional DOS SET statements to set the S_FILEDIR and S_FILE environment variables to contain the path to the temporary directory and the user's connection number. If personal login scripts are used, each user's login script needs to be modified to contain the DRIVE *drive:* command in order to place the user in the correct directory to run the menus, and the EXEC "NMENU *menu_name*" command to link the login script automatically to the correct menu file. You then need to log in as each user and verify that the login script and menu system work together to provide the user with an environment that makes the network transparent and easy to use.

COMMAND SUMMARY

Command	Syntax	Definition
EXEC	*EXEC command*	Control command used to start applications or run commands within an ITEM statement. Special commands include EXEC LOGOUT, EXEC DOS, and EXEC EXIT.
GETO	*GETO prompt {prepend} length,prefill, [SECURE] {append}*	Control command used to obtain optional input from the user. The *prompt* parameter contains the message to be displayed. The *prepend* field contains a space followed by any characters you want placed ahead of the user's input. The *prefill* parameter places a default value in the input field. The *append* parameter specifies any characters you want added after the user's input. The optional [SECURE] command suppresses display of user input.
GETP	*GETP prompt {prepend} length,prefill,[SECURE] {append}*	Control command used to store input from the user in labeled variables. The first user input is stored in variable %1, the second in %2, and so on. The *prompt* parameter contains the message to be displayed. The *prepend* field contains a space followed by any characters you

want placed ahead of the user's input. The *prefill* parameter places a default value in the input field. The *append* parameter specifies any characters you want added after the user's input. The optional [SECURE] command suppresses display of user input.

GETR	*GETR prompt {prepend} length,prefill, [SECURE] {append}*	Control command used to obtain required input from users. The *prompt* parameter contains the message to be displayed. The *prepend* field contains a space followed by any characters you want placed ahead of the user's input. The *prefill* parameter places a default value in the input field. The *append* parameter specifies any characters you want added after the user's input. The optional [SECURE] command suppresses display of user input.
ITEM	*ITEM name [{option}]*	Organizational command used to define each option in a menu. Options include CHDIR, PAUSE, BATCH, and SHOW.
LOAD	*LOAD filename*	Control command used to access another menu contained in a separate executable menu file identified by the *filename* parameter.
MENU	*MENU filename.MNU*	Executes NetWare menus before v3.12.
MENU	*MENU number,title*	Organizational command used in a menu source file to define the title and number of a menu or submenu.
MENUCNVT	*MENUCNVT filename.MNU*	Converts early NetWare menu files, creating source files with the extension .SRC, which contain the new menu statements that will implement the original menu in the new menu system.
MENUMAKE	*MENUMAKE filename.SRC*	Compiles a source menu file with the extension .SRC, creating an executable menu file with the extension .DAT, which can be run with the NMENU command.
NMENU	*NMENU filename.DAT*	Executes compiled menu files with the extension .DAT.
SHOW	*SHOW number*	Control command used to display the submenu identified by the menu *number* following the command. The submenu must be contained in the menu file.

KEY TERMS

control commands

organizational commands

source menu files

REVIEW QUESTIONS

1. The _____ NetWare v3.12 menu command is used to access a submenu.

2. List two command categories used in NetWare v3.12 menus.

   _____

   _____

3. List three components of the new NetWare menu system.

   _____

   _____

   _____

4. List the two commands needed to run the MAIN.SRC menu file.

   _____

   _____

5. Menu executable files have the default filename extension. _____

6. Write the two DOS SET login script commands that will store all temporary files in the DATA:MENUS\TEMP directory when drive letter G is mapped to the DATA: volume.

   _____

   _____

7. Write the three commands that will run an original menu file named MYMENU.MNU using the new NetWare menu system.

   _____

   _____

   _____

8. Write a menu command that will cause the menu system to display the option "Database system" and contain options to remove the menu program from memory during the execution of this application and return to the menu default directory.

   _____

9. Write the menu command lines that will provide a menu option to display a directory of the current path, pausing after the last screen is displayed.

   _____

   _____

10. Modify the menu item in question 9 to add a GETx statement that will ask the operator to enter the path for the directory listing. Record all menu statements.

_____

_____

_____

11. Write the menu command to display a DOS prompt and then return to the menu system when the user enters the command EXIT at the DOS prompt.

_____

_____

12. Write a menu item that passes control to another menu file named DOS.DAT.

_____

_____

13. Write a menu item that passes control to a submenu. The submenu is located in a menu control file that starts with the command: MENU 04,Network Control.

_____

_____

14. On the lines below, list the three steps involved in creating the menu system.

_____

_____

_____

15. Indicate the access rights a user needs to the directories that contain the following files:

The directory containing the temporary files: _____

The directory containing the menu executable files: _____

The directory containing the source menu files: _____

16. List below at least one advantage and one disadvantage of running the menu system from a user's home directory.

Advantage:

Disadvantage:

17. The _____ command is used when user input is required.

18. Complete the following statements to create a menu item that uses the GETO statement to ask the user to enter a directory path and then executes the NetWare command necessary to list all filenames in the directory path specified by the user.

    ITEM Directory Listing { _____ **}** _____

    _____ **GETO** _____

    _____ **EXEC** _____

19. Write the GETP and EXEC statements that will obtain input to grant rights to a specified user in the given directory path.

    _____

    _____

    _____

20. List two advantages of using the GETP statement as compared to using GETO.

    _____

    _____

 EXERCISES

Exercise 13-1: Entering and Running a Menu

In this exercise you will need to use the DOS EDIT command or some other text editor to create a simple menu and then use the NetWare menu system to compile and run the menu.

1. Change to your ##ADMIN directory.

2. Create a subdirectory called PRACTICE.

3. Change to the PRACTICE directory.

4. Use the DOS EDIT command or another text editor to enter the sample menu shown in Figure 13-2. Change the title of the menu to contain your name and change the print queue name to one of print queues you created in Chapter 10.

5. Map the necessary search drives to SYS:SOFTWARE.STC, and then use the appropriate menu commands to compile and test the sample menu.

6. Print the screen showing your main menu and attach a printout of your menu source file.

Exercise 13-2: Practicing with Menus

In the following exercise you will learn more about how temporary files are used by developing menu items and viewing the names and contents of the temporary files created by the menu system. In this exercise you will need to create a special menu that can be used to find and view the location of the temporary files.

1. Change to your ##ADMIN directory.

2. Create a subdirectory called MENUS.

3. Make a subdirectory of your ##ADMIN\MENUS directory and name it TEMP.

4. Change to the MENUS directory created in Step 2.

5. Use your text editor program to enter the source file shown in Figure 13-19.

Figure 13-19

Sample menu source file

```
MENU1,TEST MENU
ITEM View temporary filenames (PAUSE)
     EXEC DIR/P
     EXEC DIR\##ADMIN\MENUS\TEMP
     EXCEC DIR\##ADMIN\MENUS
ITEM View temporary file contents (PAUSE)
     GETP Enter tempory filename:()11,,()
     GETP Enter directory path:()20,,()
     EXEC DIR %2
     EXEC TYPE %2\%1
ITEM Display DOS prompt
     EXEC DOS
ITEM Exit to DOS
     EXEC EXIT
```

6. Compile the menu.

7. Run the menu and use the first option to determine the location of the temporary files. Record the location of the temporary files and their filenames in the space below.

8. Exit to the DOS prompt.

Exercise 13-3: Running a Menu from Another Directory

In this exercise you will create a search drive and run a menu from a directory that does not contain the menu executable file.

1. Change to your ##ADMIN directory.

2. Create a subdirectory called PRACTICE.

3. Change to the PRACTICE directory.

4. Use the DOS EDIT command or another text editor to enter the sample menu shown in Figure 13-2. Change the title of the menu to contain your name and add an option to allow you to exit to the DOS prompt.

5. Use the MENUMAKE command to create an executable menu file.

6. Change your default path to the ##ADMIN directory.

7. Use the MAP command to create a search drive mapping to your PRACTICE directory.

8. Execute the menu created in Step 5.

9. Exit to the DOS prompt.

Exercise 13-4: Using NDIR Commands

In this exercise you will use the DOS environmental variable S_FILEDIR to specify a path to your MENUS\TEMP directory for the temporary files.

1. Perform the following steps if you have not done Exercise 13-2.

   a. Create a directory named MENUS within your ##ADMIN directory.

   b. Change to your MENUS directory.

   c. Use the DOS EDIT command to enter the menu shown in Figure 13-19.

   d. Use MENUMAKE to create an executable menu file.

   e. Test the menu options.

2. Change your default path to the ##ADMIN directory.

3. Create a search drive mapping to your ##ADMIN\MENUS directory.

4. Run the menu and use the "View temporary filenames" option to record the location and contents of your temporary files in the space below:

5. Create a subdirectory of MENUS called TEMP.

6. Enter the appropriate command to tell the menu system to store the temporary files in your ##ADMIN\MENUS\TEMP directory.

7. Change your default path to the ##ADMIN directory.

8. Run the menu and use the "View temporary filenames" option to record the location and contents of your temporary files in the space below:

9. Exit to the DOS prompt.

14. Delete the search drive mapping to the menu directory.

15. Run the menu system again.

16. Record the location and names of the temporary files in the space below.

17. Type the contents of the menu temporary file and record the statements in the space below.

18. Exit to the DOS prompt.

19. Did the menu system store the temporary files in the same directory for Steps 5 and 10? Yes or No _____
    If yes, why? Explain briefly in the space below.

Exercise 13-4 Part 2: Multiple Users

One problem associated with a common temporary directory is the possibility of one user's temporary files overwriting another user's temporary files if they both run their menus at the same time. In this exercise you will see how the S_FILE environment variable can be used to separate temporary files by user connection.

1. Determine your connection number by using the USERLIST command.

2. Use the appropriate SET command to set the S_FILE environment variable to your connection number.

3. Run the TEST menu system and determine the name and location of the menu temporary files.

4. Record the temporary filenames in the space below.

5. Display the DOS prompt and see if you can change to the temporary directory and display the contents of the temporary file. Record your observations in the space below.

6. Return to the menu system.

7. Exit to the DOS prompt.

EXERCISE

Case 13-1: The Equity Coop

The Equity Coop is a local cooperative store that uses its network to perform word processing and spreadsheet functions and to maintain an inventory of feeds. The store has a dot-matrix printer for printing output from spreadsheets and inventory reports and a laser printer for word processing and for generating letter-quality documents. Currently the only way staff can use the system and control the printers is from the DOS prompt. They have asked you to set up a NetWare menu system that will contain options to run each of the company's application packages and provide them with an easy way to redirect printer output and perform such printer control functions as stopping and starting the printer and changing forms.

Users first need to change to the SYS:SOFTWARE.STC\WP directory and enter the command WP to run the word processing and spreadsheet software. To run the spreadsheet software, they change to the SYS:SOFTWARE.STC\SP directory and enter the command SP. They run inventory software by first changing to the SYS:SOFTWARE.STC\DB directory and entering the command DB. To send output to the dot-matrix printer, they need to issue the command CAPTURE Q=*queuename* NB NT TI=5 before starting the application software. The command to access the laser print queue is CAPTURE Q=*queuename* NB NT TI=10 NFF. It must be entered before the WP software is started.

Use the menu design form to design a menu system for Equity Coop that will automate the process of running applications and access the network print queues. In addition, create a printer control submenu that uses the PSC commands discussed in Chapter 12 to allow print server operators to start, stop, and change forms in the dot-matrix printer. The form change menu option should ask the user to enter the new form number before the appropriate PSC command is executed. Your instructor will provide you with the following printer information, which you will need to create and test the printer menu items:

Laser print queue name: _____

Dot-matrix print queue name: _____

Print server name: _____

Dot-matrix printer number: _____

1. Change to your ##ADMIN directory and create a subdirectory named COOPMENU.

2. Change to the COOPMENU directory and use the DOS EDIT command to create a source menu file for the Equity Coop store.

3. Compile and test the menu.

4. Obtain a hardcopy listing of your source menu file.

5. Use the NDIR command to obtain a listing of the COOPMENU directory.

6. Use the Print Scrn key to print the screen showing the COOPMENU directory.

7. Have the instructor check your Equity Coop menu and sign on the line below.

   Instructor signature: _____

SUPERIOR TECHNICAL COLLEGE PROBLEMS

Now that you have established system and user login script files for the staff at Superior Technical College, the next step in automating the user environment is creating menus for each workgroup and then combining them with the college login scripts. Because school will be starting soon, Dave Johnson is anxious to have the menu system up and running so you can spend some time training users in the use of the menus and network environment.

Project 13-1: Designing a Menu System

Because Dave has no experience with the new NetWare menu system, he said it is up to you to design and implement the system the best way you see fit. The only thing Dave requires is that the administrative and faculty menu system be separate from the computer lab menu system. To start with, Dave wants you to develop menus for both the support staff and student services. After these users are operational on the network, you will turn to the task of developing menus for both the computer lab and faculty users. Using the menu design form and the following department requirements, design menus for both the support staff and student services personnel:

- Support staff need to be able to run the word processing and graphics software and spreadsheets.

- Student services department users need to access the word processing and spreadsheet software and graduate system applications.

- Users in all departments need to be able to select any printer on the network and send output to it.

- Both the support and the student services staff need a submenu to control their network printers and allow them to stop the printer, start the printer, cancel a print job, view printer status, and mount a new form number in the printer.

- All staff need a submenu containing network options to send messages, change passwords, and run the SESSION FILER, and PCONSOLE utilities.

Project 13-2: Writing and Testing Workgroup Menus

In this project you will write the menu command statements for each of the menus you defined in Project 13-1 and then use a text editor program, such as the DOS EDIT command, to enter and save each of the workgroup menus as separate source files in your ##STC\MENUS directory. Include an option in each menu that will allow you to exit to the DOS prompt while testing the menu options. Be sure to use the extension .SRC for each menu source file. After a menu file has been entered, use the MENUMAKE program to compile the menu file and correct any syntax errors. After one menu file has been successfully entered and compiled, you might want to copy the source file to create another workgroup menu and then use the DOS EDIT command to modify the new source file to meet the needs of the other workgroup. Obtain a final printout of each successfully compiled menu.

After the menus have been compiled, test each menu by making the necessary drive mappings to run the menu applications and then test each menu option to be sure it works correctly. Record the drive mappings you require for each workgroup menu in the following table.

Student Services		Support Staff	
Drive Letter	**Path**	**Drive Letter**	**Path**

Certain application software, as well as the menu system, might require DOS environment variables to be set in the workstation. In the following table, document any DOS environment variables that you need to set:

Environment Variable	Value	Description	Used For

Project 13-3: Providing User Access

After you have tested the menus to be sure all options work with the correct drive mappings and environment setups, you need to implement the menu system in your directory structure by providing for user access.

1. In the spaces provided, document the locations from which you want administrative users to run their menu systems.

Staff Menu System	**Path**	**Access Rights**
Directory to run menu system:	_____	_____
Directory for temporary files:	_____	_____
Location of executable files:	_____	_____
Location of source files:	_____	_____

2. Create the directories listed in Step 1 and provide your users with the access rights you have defined.

3. Use the TLIST command to document the rights you have assigned to each menu directory defined in Step 1.

4. Modify the system login script you created in Chapter 12 so that it provides drive mappings or DOS environment variables necessary to run the menu system and application software.

5. Obtain a printout of your system login script after making any corrections needed to run your menu options. If your system executes everything from the system login script and does not use personal login scripts, modify the system login script to exit to the appropriate workgroup menu. Highlight each statement you added or changed to facilitate the menu system.

6. If your system uses personal login scripts, modify the personal login scripts for all users in the support staff and student services workgroups to run their appropriate network menus.

Project 13-4: Testing the Menu System

Test your menu system by logging in as each of the following users and testing the menu options.

Karl Dauer

Mimi Ito

Gina Gardini

When you believe your menu system is operational, have your instructor check it and sign on the line below.

Instructor signature: _____

Project 13-5: Training Users

Develop and document a training procedure to educate the staff at Superior Technical College in the use of the network menu system. Your plan should include the following:

- Determine the time to spend with each department.

- Develop a brief outline of the information you plan to cover in the training session.

- Write a brief memo to each department head regarding your training plan and the time period in which you want to implement the network for the department. Attach a copy of the training outline to the memo.

- Turn in your outline and memos to your instructor.

MESSAGE HANDLING SYSTEM

The ability to send and receive electronic mail is an essential part of any network system. A CNA needs to understand the concepts and components of e-mail systems and the mechanism by which electronic messages are transmitted in a NetWare environment. An electronic mail system consists of three parts: a user interface for creating, managing, and sending electronic message files, a delivery system, and a notification and retrieval system that allows the recipient to view and extract messages. The **Message Handling Service (MHS)** is the e-mail delivery system standard developed by Novell to move message files. MHS was available for earlier versions of NetWare, but it used to be necessary to purchase it as a separate package. Starting with NetWare v3.12, Novell began including the Basic MHS package with NetWare to provide message delivery for users sharing the same file server. Users on a server running Basic MHS can use any MHS-compatible electronic mail application to send and receive messages or files over the network. Basic MHS includes an electronic mail program called FirstMail, which allows an organization to implement a simplified electronic mail system using MHS.

AFTER READING THIS CHAPTER AND COMPLETING THE EXERCISES YOU WILL BE ABLE TO:

- DESCRIBE THE PURPOSE OF NOVELL'S BASIC MESSAGE HANDLING SERVICE.
- USE THE NETWARE V3.12 FIRSTMAIL SYSTEM TO SEND, READ, AND FILE ELECTRONIC MAIL.
- DESCRIBE THE STEPS REQUIRED TO INSTALL THE BASIC MESSAGE HANDLING SERVICE.
- USE THE ADMINISTRATIVE FUNCTION OF THE BASIC MESSAGE HANDLING SERVICE TO ADD USERS AND CREATE DISTRIBUTION LISTS.

In addition to Basic MHS, the NetWare MHS family consists of Global MHS and Remote MHS. NetWare Global MHS is a scalable full-featured MHS platform that provides message delivery among users on multiple servers scattered throughout an internetwork. The Basic MHS product can be upgraded to Global MHS when message delivery is required between servers connected directly with IPX or over a telephone connection. Global MHS also connects to other electronic mail environments, such as the TCP/IP Simple Mail Transport Program (SMTP) or X.400. This ability is important in large organizations that have multiple systems or when e-mail is sent from one organization to another. Because Basic MHS is 100 percent compatible with Global MHS, you can upgrade to the Global system without having to re-install your e-mail system. Another Novell product, NetWare Remote MHS, allows laptop users to access the MHS network from a dial-up phone line using an asynchronous modem.

The Novell MHS system works by providing a standard interface to application programs. The interface allows an application to call upon MHS to deliver messages and files to other users attached to the network. Each user of MHS must be assigned a unique address consisting of a workgroup name and a username. The **workgroup name** can be the name of the user's primary file server or the name of the organizational or departmental workgroup. In Basic MHS, the workgroup name is optional because all users reside on the same file server. The username can be the same as the user's login name, or it can be the user's full name, which simplifies the addressing of messages.

How Basic MHS Works

To use Basic MHS to transmit a message, a user first needs to create a message file using an MHS-compatible electronic mail application. One such application is Novell's FirstMail program, which is supplied with Basic MHS. The sending user needs to include in the message the e-mail address of the receiving user or the name of a distribution list. In MHS, a user's **e-mail address** consists of the username and workgroup separated by the "@" symbol. A workgroup is defined when you install MHS on a file server. With NetWare's Global MHS, you can organize network users into multiple workgroups by company, division, or department. When you install Basic MHS, however, all users need to belong to the same workgroup. Because of this, with Basic MHS only the username is required for the e-mail address; the workgroup part of the address is optional.

 The format of MHS addresses is similar to the SMTP address system used with the Internet. This provides additional compatibility when messages are transferred between MHS and the Internet system.

A **distribution list** contains the names and e-mail addresses of two or more users who are to receive copies of a message file. Distribution lists are created and maintained in MHS by the network administrator with the ADMIN program, described later in this chapter. When a message is sent to a distribution list, the MHS server checks its database for information on the distribution list. Using this information, the MHS server delivers the message to all the users included in the list. The message can then be read by each user with any MHS-compatible e-mail application.

Figure 14-1 illustrates the use of the MHS system with a compatible e-mail package to send a message from one user to another. In step 1, a user named Mary Read uses an MHS-compatible e-mail application, such as Novell's FirstMail program, to create a message to be sent to Edward Low. After addressing the message with Ed's username, she selects the option to send the message. After a message has been sent from a user's workstation, the MHS server attempts to deliver the message during the next delivery cycle. In step 2, the NetWare MHS server looks up the address EDLOW@PCS, and then uses the information to copy the message to Ed's mailbox. Information about the status of the message will be displayed on the MHS server console. Figure 14-2 shows the MHS server console screen after the mail message is delivered to Ed Low.

Figure 14-1

Sending a message with MHS

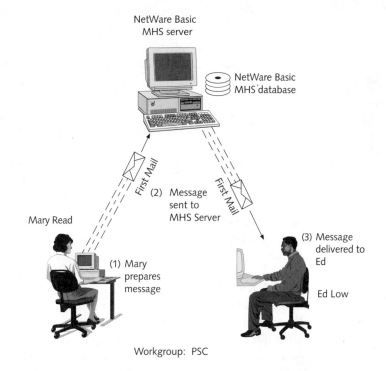

Figure 14-2

MHS server screen

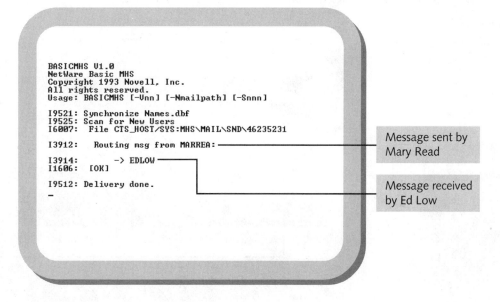

Once the MHS server has delivered the message, the recipient can use any MHS-compatible e-mail application, including FirstMail, to read and process the message. In step 3 of Figure 14-1, Ed receives notification that he has new mail. He then uses the FirstMail program to read the message, extract any files, and return a response to Mary. After he finishes processing the message, Ed can either file it for future reference or delete it.

Common functions included in most e-mail packages are the ability to archive mail after it has been read, reply to mail messages, forward a message to another user, and extract any attached files. The Novell FirstMail system provides all these essential functions, allowing you to implement an e-mail system in your organization quickly. A network administrator needs to know about these e-mail features in order to understand and evaluate mail applications.

USING NOVELL'S FIRSTMAIL

Novell's FirstMail program is a fairly simple electronic mail utility that is available for both DOS and Apple Macintosh computers. It lets users compose and send messages to other users or to distribute lists of users defined in the MHS database of a file server. FirstMail can be used to attach and send documents or data files along with messages. The receiving user can then use the FirstMail extract function to copy the attached file to a directory located on either the network or local hard disk.

Before FirstMail can be used on a network, the network administrator must install MHS (described later in this chapter) and establish a user account for each user who will participate in the messaging system. A user can then log in to the file server and enter the MAIL command from any DOS prompt. Another way to start the FirstMail software is to modify the network menus to include a mail option on each user's menu. A user can then log in and simply select the mail option from the menu to start the FirstMail program. Once the FirstMail software has been loaded, the FirstMail menu shown in Figure 14-3 will be displayed. To select a menu option you can either use the arrow keys to highlight the desired option and press [Enter] or press the letter that precedes the option's description.

Figure 14-3

FirstMail menu

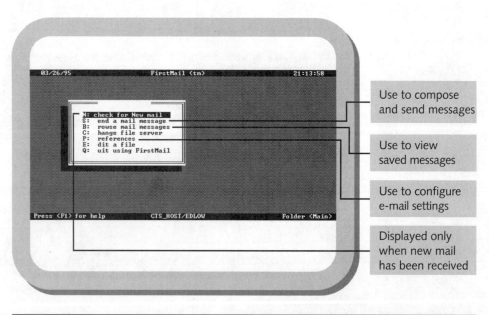

Use to compose and send messages

Use to view saved messages

Use to configure e-mail settings

Displayed only when new mail has been received

The "N: check for New mail" option is displayed only when new mail—mail that has not been read—exists in the user's mailbox. The "S: send a mail message" option is used to compose and send a message to another user or distribution list. The "B: browse mail message" option is used to scan the mail currently in a user's mailbox. The user can read, archive, or delete the existing messages. The "P: preferences" option is used to configure keyboard settings, locate work directories, handle mail, and delete messages. The "E: edit a file" option is used to start a text editor program to create longer, more complex message files.

In addition to the options, there are special function keys that can be used to perform operations. They are shown at the bottom of each screen, enclosed in angle brackets (< >). On all screens, you can use the F1 key to obtain help text relating to the current screen or the F5 key to mark or unmark items from a list. In addition, the [Ctrl][Enter] key combination is used to send a message from the message screen after it has been completed.

E-mail software essentially operates in either sending or receiving modes, as illustrated in Figure 14-4. In sending mode, you compose and send messages to other users or distribution groups. After you send a message, many e-mail packages place you directly in receiving mode. In receiving mode, you read and file messages that have been sent to you. From receiving mode you can enter sending mode by choosing to reply to a message you are currently reading.

Figure 14-4

Basic e-mail modes

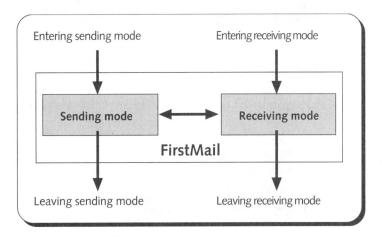

FirstMail stores messages in directories called folders. Initially, FirstMail establishes two folders for each user; a "Main" folder to hold all incoming messages and a "Copies to self" folder to store copies of messages you have sent to other users. FirstMail also allows you to organize your mail. You can create additional folders for specific types of messages and then copy messages from the "Main" or "Copies to self" folders into the folders you have created, as explained later in this section.

COMPOSING AND SENDING MESSAGES

The "S: send a mail message" option activates the sending mode for the FirstMail software. To use the FirstMail application to compose and send an e-mail message to another user, as diagrammed in Figure 14-1, a user first needs to log in to the file server with his or her assigned username. The user then starts the FirstMail software by entering the MAIL command or by using a menu option established by the network administrator. The user then either highlights "S: send a mail message" and presses [Enter] or presses the S key from the mail options menu. The Send Message: Editing Screen shown in Figure 14-5 is displayed.

Figure 14-5

Send Message: Editing Screen

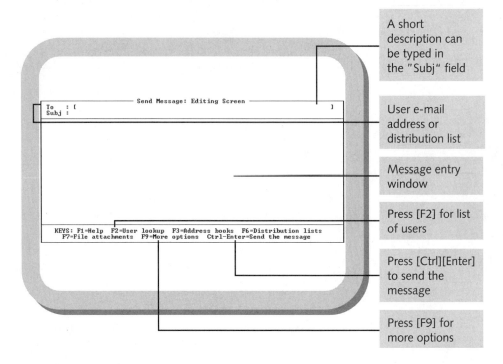

A short description can be typed in the "Subj" field

User e-mail address or distribution list

Message entry window

Press [F2] for list of users

Press [Ctrl][Enter] to send the message

Press [F9] for more options

In the "To" field of the Send Message: Editing Screen, you specify the e-mail address of the user or users to whom you are sending a message. You place e-mail addresses in the "To" field either by typing the recipient's address or by using the F2 key to display a list of all users in the Basic MHS database. If you do not know the e-mail address of the user to whom you want to send a message, for example, you can use the F2 key to display the user directory listing screen shown in Figure 14-6.

Figure 14-6

User e-mail address list

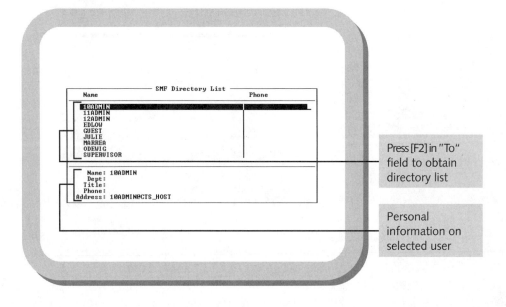

Press [F2] in "To" field to obtain directory list

Personal information on selected user

This screen displays a list of all users and distribution lists that have been created by the network administrator. To select the e-mail address of the user who will receive the message, you can move the arrow keys to highlight the user's name and press the Enter key to insert the user's e-mail address in the "To" field. If you want to send the message to multiple users, you can use the F5 key to mark the target users and then press [Enter] to place all the marked users' e-mail addresses in the "To" field separated by commas. To send the message to all users in a department, you can select the name of a distribution list, such as BUSINESS@PCS. This will send the message to all users in the business department.

 With the [F3] and [F6] keys, a user can maintain his or her own private address and distribution lists to send messages to users on other systems. When Basic MHS is used, however, these function keys are not normally used because mail can be sent only to recipients in the MHS database of the current server.

After selecting the e-mail address of the user or users to whom you want to send the message, press [Enter] to advance to the next field. The optional "subj" field on the Send Message: Editing Screen can be used for a short message description consisting of up to 64 characters. If the message relates to the agenda for the monthly board meeting, for example, the subject description "Monthly Board Meeting" can be typed in the subject field.

You type the body of the message in the message window. The message editor automatically word wraps each line as it is typed and allows you to use the Ins key to insert or type over text. The message window scrolls when a message is longer than the screen. The function keys shown at the bottom of the message window can be used to perform special operations. The [Ctrl][Enter] key combination is used to send the message.

The F7 key allows you to attach one or more files to the message. Use the Ins key to add a filename and path to the Attached to the Message window. Suppose, for example, you want to attach to your message a word processing file containing the minutes from the last board meeting. To do this, press the F7 key to display a list showing any files currently attached to this message. To add a new file to the attachment list, press the Ins key and enter the path to the document file, as shown in Figure 14-7.

Figure 14-7

Attached files window

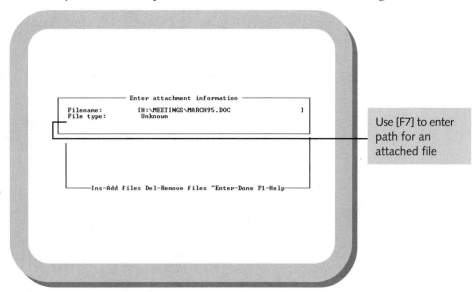

Use [F7] to enter path for an attached file

Just as you can make carbon copies of written memos to be distributed to other people in an organization, FirstMail allows you the option of sending copies, called carbon copies, of an e-mail message to other users on the network. This function is useful when you want other users to be informed of the contents of a message without expecting them to respond. The list of users receiving the carbon copy is included with the message, allowing the receivers to know who else has received the message. To send a carbon copy of the board meeting message to another user, for example, you press the F9 key to display the "Options for your message" window shown in Figure 14-8. To send a carbon copy, move the cursor to the "Cc" field. Then with the F2 key, select the target e-mail address from the directory listing. If you want to send a carbon copy to multiple users, use the F5 key to mark the addresses of all users to whom you want to send the copy and press [Enter]. Another copy option is a Bcc, which stands for blind carbon copy. A **blind carbon copy** is the same as a carbon copy, except that any recipient of the original memo is not notified that a copy has been sent to the recipient of the blind carbon copy.

Before copy machines were common, copies of original memos were often made by carbon paper inserted in the typewriter along with the original. Copies of letters and memos created by other means are still referred to as carbon copies.

Figure 14-8

Additional message options

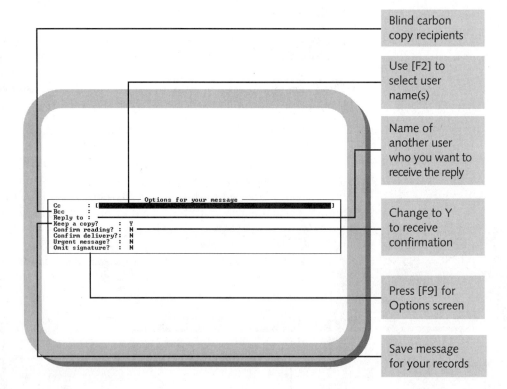

Blind carbon copy recipients

Use [F2] to select user name(s)

Name of another user who you want to receive the reply

Change to Y to receive confirmation

Press [F9] for Options screen

Save message for your records

```
                    ─── Options for your message ───
 Cc        : [████████████████████████████████████████]
 Bcc       :
 Reply to  :
 Keep a copy?      :  Y
 Confirm reading?  :  N
 Confirm delivery? :  N
 Urgent message?   :  N
 Omit signature?   :  N
```

You can store a copy of a message you send. To keep a copy of the board meeting message, for example, you change the "Keep a copy" field to Y. The message will be stored in the "Copies to self" folder. Messages can later be moved from this folder to another folder for organizational purposes, as described in the next section.

Another important e-mail option is to be notified when the receiving user reads your message. It enables you to confirm that the message you sent was received and read by the recipient. It is similar to sending a certified letter through the postal system and receiving a confirmation when the letter is delivered. To be notified when the selected user reads your board meeting message, for example, use the down arrow to move the cursor to the "Confirm reading" field and change the field to Y. You will now receive a confirmation message in your mailbox indicating the date and time the message was read.

To bypass unused fields, simply press the Enter key for each field you do not want to change on the Options screen. After going through all fields, respond with a Y to the "Accept and Continue" prompt and then use the [Ctrl][Enter] key combination to send the message to the selected users.

READING NEW MESSAGES

By default, the MHS server delivers mail every 45 seconds, which is satisfactory for most environments. The default delivery time can be changed, however, by using the Configuration option of the ADMIN program (described later in this chapter).

As mentioned previously, a user needs to be notified somehow that new mail has arrived. With the FirstMail program, the "N: check for New mail" option appears in the main mail menu to indicate that new mail has been received. After a user reads a new message, the mail program will save that message in his or her "Main" folder. With FirstMail, you have the option of creating additional folders. You can then use the Move option to transfer selected messages from the "Main" folder to another folder for filing purposes. When all messages have been read, the "N: check for New mail" option is removed from the mail options menu. Figure 14-9 shows an example of a user named Ed Low viewing his recently received message using the "N: check for New mail" option.

Figure 14-9

New Mail folder

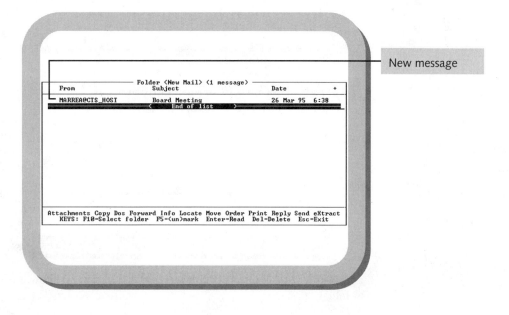

New message

Options listed at the bottom of the Folder <New Mail> screen allow you to perform the functions described in Figure 14-10. To read a new message, highlight the message line for the message you want to read and press [Enter]. The message file is displayed, as shown in Figure 14-11.

Figure 14-10

FirstMail options

Option	Description
Attachment (A)	Allows you to view and extract any files that were attached by the sender.
Copy (C)	Allows you to copy the message to another folder.
DOS (D)	Allows you to shell out to the DOS prompt. The EXIT command can then be used to return to the mail program.
Forward (F)	Sends current message to another user. The message will remain in your new mail folder.
Information (I)	Provides information about the message, such as when it was received, who it is from, its size, if the message was confirmed, and how many attachments it contains.
Locate (L)	Searches for a selected string of characters in the current message or in selected message files.
Move (M)	Moves the selected message to another folder. Normally messages are placed in the "Main" mail folder after they have been read.
Order (O)	Sequences the messages in the current folder by date received, by sender, or by subject.
Print (P)	Prints the contents of the selected message file.
Reply (R)	Allows you to compose a reply message to be sent to the sender of the selected message.
Send (S)	Sends a message directly from the folder to the specified user e-mail address.
Extract (X)	Allows you to move the message to a DOS filename specified in the "Extract message to what file" window.
[F10]	Displays messages in another folder. When you press the F10 key, the Select a Folder window is displayed. This allows you to change your current folder to one of the existing folders or use the Ins key to create a new folder.

Figure 14-11

Reading a
new message

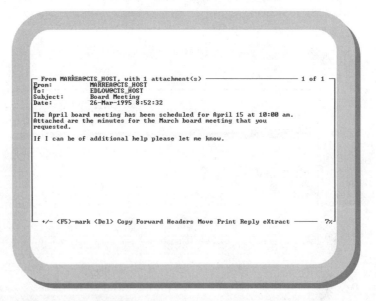

Options at the bottom of the message display screen allow a user to perform the following functions:

- Copy or move the message to another folder.

- Forward the message to another user.

- Display detail header information.

- Print the message.

- Send a reply.

- Extract the message into a separate file. The extracted file contains the contents of the e-mail message, which can then be merged with another document using a word processor or text editor.

Replying to messages

After reading a message, a user has the option of switching to send mode to reply immediately to the current message. To reply to a message you have just read, press the R key to display the "Select reply format" window shown in Figure 14-12. To include the original message as part of the reply, change the general option "Include message" from N to Y. When including the original message as part of the reply, you might want to separate the original message from your reply. To do this you can "comment out" the original message by changing the "Commented" field from N to Y. Each line of the original message will now be preceded with a **comment character**. By default, the comment character is a greater than symbol (>), but a user can change the comment character by using the Editor option of the Preferences menu as described later in this section.

If the original message was sent to multiple users, you can have your reply sent to all users who received the original message by changing the "Reply to all" field to Y. The "Address options" field allows you to extract addresses from the original message to form the "To" field of the reply automatically. To include users who received carbon copies of the original message in the "To" field of the reply, for example, change the "Cc field" from N to Y. A copy of the reply will be sent to all users who received carbon copies in the original message. After it scrolls through all fields on the "Select reply format" window, the FirstMail program will ask you to verify the entries. After your confirmation, FirstMail displays the Send Message: Editing Screen. You can now type the reply and use the [Ctrl][Enter] key combination to send the reply to the users you have selected.

Figure 14-12

Replying to a message

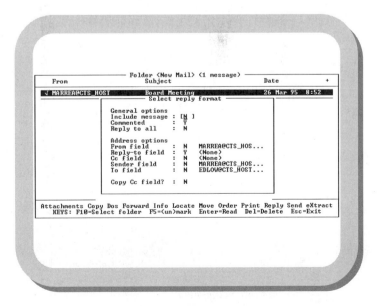

Forwarding messages

Another common e-mail function is forwarding a message to other users if you want them to read it or if you want to solicit their response. To forward a message, you select it from either the "N: new Mail" or "B: browse mail messages" option and press the F key. The "Forward message or file to" window shown in Figure 14-13 is displayed. Complete the options and use the [Ctrl][Enter] key combination to forward the selected message.

Figure 14-13

Forwarding
a message

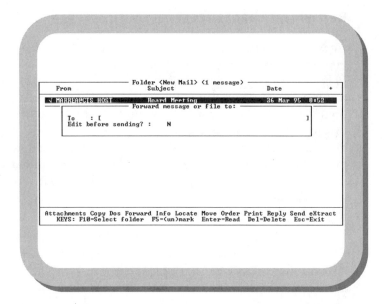

If you change the "Edit before sending?" field to Y, the message is displayed and you can edit it, type additional text, or attach a file before using the [Ctrl][Enter] keys to send the message to the selected address. This option is handy if you want to include comments in a message asking another user to respond to some part of the original message.

BROWSE MAIL MESSAGES

In addition to sending and receiving new messages, an important part of any e-mail system involves organizing and working with messages that have already been sent or received. Saving and organizing messages allows users and managers to track progress on projects. It can provide an audit trail that can be helpful in determining communication problems when activities are not completed as planned. As described previously, FirstMail automatically provides the "Main" and "Copies to self" folders for storing messages after they have been read or sent. The "B: browse mail messages" mail option can be used to view and work with messages stored in the "Main" or "Copies to self" folders, as well as any other folders that you create to organize your messages.

 If you do not want a message you are composing to be saved in the "Copies to self" folder, use the F9 key to change the "Keep a Copy" field from the default of Y to N.

The "B: browse mail messages" option has the same screen format and options found under the "N: check for New mail" option and is used to view, forward, reply, archive, or remove messages after they have been read and stored in a message folder. A **folder** is a directory in a user's mailbox for storing messages that have been read. Initially all users are given a "Main" folder by default, and messages are stored in the "Main" folder after they have been read. When you use the "B: browse mail messages" option, FirstMail always opens the folder with which you were last working, as shown in Figure 14-14.

As on the new mail screen, the options at the bottom of the Folder Main folder window allow you to reply to messages. You can also move or copy messages to another folder and sort, print, delete, or forward them to another user. To change to a different folder, press the F10 key and select the folder name from the existing folders listed in the Select a Folder window. As described in the following section, you can also use the F10 key to create a new folder by pressing the Ins key and entering the new folder name when the Select a Folder window is displayed.

Moving messages

With FirstMail, you can create your own folders and then move messages from the current or "Main" folder to one of the folders you create. Suppose you want to create a separate folder for messages regarding board meetings. To create a new folder called "Board meetings" and move all corresponding messages into this new folder, you switch to receive mode by selecting the "B: browse mail messages" option, which displays all messages in your main folder. Next press the F10 key to display the Select a Folder window shown in Figure 14-15.

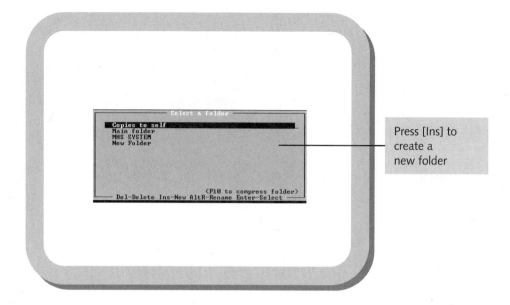

Figure 14-15

Select a Folder
window

Press [Ins] to
create a
new folder

To create a new folder, press the Ins key and enter the full name for the folder (for example, "Board meetings"). The short name field contains the eight-character name of the file that is displayed on the mail options menu. If you do not provide a short name, FirstMail automatically inserts one. In this example, you might choose to enter BOARD in the "short name" field for the "Board meetings" folder. When you press [Enter], the "Board meetings" folder is displayed in the Select a Folder window. To exit the Select a Folder window and return to the currently selected folder window, press the Esc key.

You can now organize your messages by copying messages into the new folder. To copy messages to another folder, use the arrow keys and the F5 key to mark all message files pertaining to board meetings. To move the selected messages to the "Board meetings" folder, select the Move option by pressing the M key. Then select the "Board meetings" folder from the Select a Folder window. The selected messages will then be removed from the "Main" folder and placed in the "Board meetings" folder.

Sorting messages

If a folder contains many messages, you can organize them by ordering them by date, subject, or sender name. To sort messages in the "Board meetings" folder by date, for example, you use the F10 key to make "Board meetings" your current folder and then press the O key to select the Order option. This displays a window in the upper right of the screen showing the possible order sequences—date, name, or subject. See Figure 14-16. Use the down arrow key to select the "sort message by date" option and press [Enter]. The message folder is immediately arranged in date sequence, with the most recent message first.

Figure 14-16

Possible sort
sequences

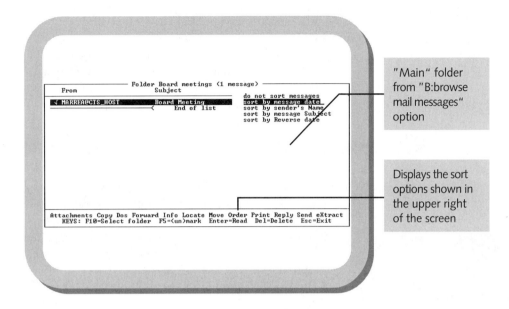

"Main" folder
from "B:browse
mail messages"
option

Displays the sort
options shown in
the upper right
of the screen

Printing a message

In addition to viewing and replying to messages, a user can obtain a hardcopy of any message. To obtain a hardcopy of a message that has already been read, first select the "B: browse mail messages" option. Then use the F10 key to change to the folder that contains the message you want to print. To print the most recent message in the "Board meetings" folder, for example, change to the "Board meetings" folder by pressing the F10 key and selecting the folder name from the Select a Folder window. The "Folder Board meetings" window is then displayed showing all the board meeting messages arranged in sequence by date. To print the latest board meeting message, highlight the first message and press the P key to select the Print option. The "Print settings" window shown in Figure 14-17 is then displayed.

Figure 14-17

Print settings
window

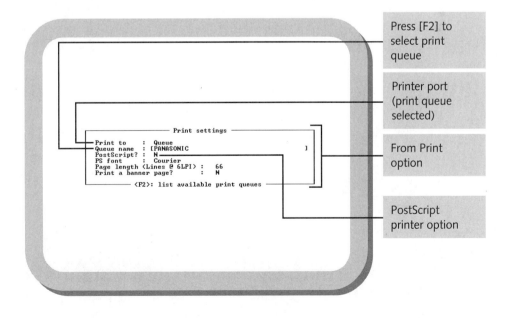

Press [F2] to
select print
queue

Printer port
(print queue
selected)

From Print
option

PostScript
printer option

To send the output to a print queue, change the "Print to" field to "Queue" and then use the F2 key to select the name of the print queue in the print queue field. Unless you are printing on a PostScript printer, leave the other fields unchanged by pressing the Enter key or down arrow for each field. After the last field, press [Enter] to confirm the "Accept and Continue?" prompt. A copy of the selected message will now be sent to the selected print queue.

PERSONALIZING FIRSTMAIL

To meet the personal needs and preferences of individual e-mail users, Novell has included in FirstMail a Preferences option that can be used to customize certain features of FirstMail. The Preferences Menu, shown in Figure 14-18, contains the options for customizing FirstMail. You can use the "Copy-self settings" option to specify a folder in which to store copies of messages you send. The "Editor and keyboard settings" option produces a submenu in which you can change the comment character or specify an editor program to be used when you compose and edit message files.

The "General settings" option produces the submenu shown in Figure 14-19. If you select the "Suppress print dialog?" option, FirstMail will not display the print dialog box each time you print a message. The "Leave read new mail new?" option prevents FirstMail from automatically moving the messages you read to the "Main" folder. This allows you to move the new messages directly to another folder you have created.

The "NetWare MHS/SMF settings" option on the Preferences Menu can be used to specify an MHS username that is different from the user's login name. The "change Home mailbox location" option can be used to specify a directory for storing messages after they have been read or sent. The "Print settings" option is used to specify a printer port or print queue and other default printer setup information such as page length and banner. The "edit or create Signatures" option allows a user to create a small ASCII text file that will automatically be added to the end of each outgoing message.

Figure 14-18

Preferences Menu

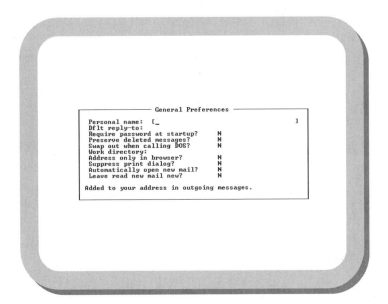

Figure 14-19

General Preferences
window

```
                    ┌──────────── General Preferences ────────────┐
                    │ Personal name:  [_                        ] │
                    │ Dflt reply-to:                              │
                    │ Require password at startup?      N         │
                    │ Preserve deleted messages?        N         │
                    │ Swap out when calling DOS?        N         │
                    │ Work directory:                             │
                    │ Address only in browser?          N         │
                    │ Suppress print dialog?            N         │
                    │ Automatically open new mail?      N         │
                    │ Leave read new mail new?          N         │
                    │                                             │
                    │ Added to your address in outgoing messages. │
                    └─────────────────────────────────────────────┘
```

INSTALLING AND MANAGING MHS

In order to use FirstMail or any MHS–compatible application, you first need to install Novell's Message Handling System on a file server, allowing it to act as the MHS server. MHS can be installed on any NetWare v3.1x or NetWare 4.x file server as long as it has the necessary memory and support software. Before installing the MHS system, check your file server to be sure it has an additional 250 Kbytes of RAM beyond the amount needed to run NetWare and any other options you have installed. To be on the safe side, you might want to have an additional 1 Mbyte beyond the minimum required for your system. For example, because 4 Mbytes are required to run NetWare, you should have at least 5 Mbytes of RAM to install MHS and run the basic server with no other options. Beyond this memory requirement, MHS requires that NetWare BTRIEVE v5.15 or later along with the NetWare CLIB.LLM runtime library v3.11 or later be installed on the server. Finally, if you want the installation program to create MHS users from your existing user's full names, be sure that all users have been assigned full names before you start the installation process.

PREPARE FOR INSTALLATION

Before starting the installation process, you need to determine if your file server has the hardware and software requirements necessary to support Basic MHS operation. Use the MEMORY console command and the VERSION command to determine the total amount of memory your file server computer is using and the current version of NetWare, as shown in Figure 14-20. If your file server has less than 5 Mbytes of RAM, or if you have other products running on your server, such as TCP/IP or NetWare for Macintosh, you will need to add more RAM to the file server computer before attempting to install the MHS software.

Figure 14-20

Determining the
amount of
server memory

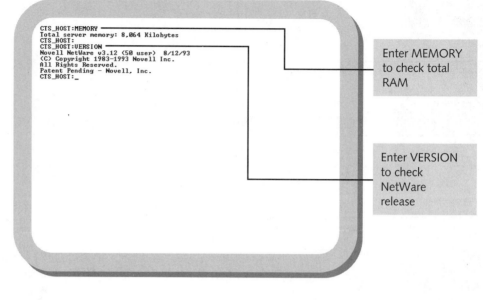

```
CTS_HOST:MEMORY
Total server memory: 8,064 Kilobytes
CTS_HOST:
CTS_HOST:VERSION
Novell NetWare v3.12 (50 user)  8/12/93
(C) Copyright 1983-1993 Novell Inc.
All Rights Reserved.
Patent Pending - Novell, Inc.
CTS_HOST:_
```

Enter MEMORY
to check total
RAM

Enter VERSION
to check
NetWare
release

As shown in Figure 14-21, you can use the MODULES command to determine if the CLIB module currently loaded on your file server is v3.11 or later. If you are using NetWare v3.12, version v3.12 or later of the CLIB module should automatically be loaded and displayed, as shown in Figure 14-21.

Figure 14-21

Determining what
modules are loaded

```
CTS_HOST:MODULES
RSPX.NLM
    NetWare 386 Remote Console SPX Driver
    Version 3.12    March 29, 1993
    Copyright 1993 Novell, Inc.  All rights reserved.
REMOTE.NLM
    NetWare 386 Remote Console
    Version 3.12    May 13, 1993
    Copyright 1993 Novell, Inc.  All rights reserved.
CLIB.NLM
    NetWare C NLM Runtime Library V3.12
    Version 3.12    May 19, 1993
    (C) Copyright 1989-1993, Novell Inc. All rights reserved.
        Patent Pending - Novell Inc.
STREAMS.NLM
    NetWare STREAMS
    Version 3.12    April 19, 1993
    (C) Copyright 1989-1992 Mentat, Inc.
    Portions (C) Copyright 1989-1993 Novell, Inc.
    All Rights Reserved.
NUT.NLM
    NetWare 386 Utility User Interface
    Version 1.13    December 20, 1990
    Copyright 1990 Novell, Inc.  All rights reserved.
<Press ESC to terminate or any other key to continue>
```

Displays
loaded module
information

Version of
module

Modules
displayed in
sequence from
last loaded to
first loaded

Unless you have installed another package that uses BTRIEVE, such as NetWare Connect, the BTRIEVE module will not be automatically loaded and therefore will not show up in the Modules list. If the BTRIEVE module is not currently loaded, use the LOAD BTRIEVE console command, as shown in Figure 14-22, to load the BTRIEVE software. Then verify that the version number is v5.15 or later. If you have an older version, or if BTRIEVE has not been installed on your file server, you will need to install the latest version of BTRIEVE before continuing with the MHS installation process.

Figure 14-22

Loading BTRIEVE

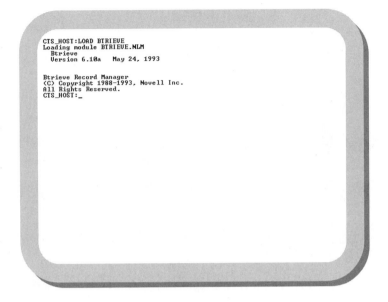

```
CTS_HOST:LOAD BTRIEVE
Loading module BTRIEVE.NLM
   Btrieve
   Version 6.10a   May 24, 1993

Btrieve Record Manager
(C) Copyright 1988-1993, Novell Inc.
All Rights Reserved.
CTS_HOST:_
```

After loading the necessary version of BTRIEVE, you need to verify that BTRIEVE's configuration will support a minimum of two transactions with a page size of at least 4 Kbytes, and that the BTRIEVE startup file contains the necessary commands. To check the number of transactions and the page size, enter the command LOAD BSETUP at the file server console to display the Available Options screen, shown in Figure 14-23. Next, select the Set BTRIEVE Configuration option to view the Current BTRIEVE Configuration window, as shown in Figure 14-24. Now verify that the Number of Transactions field value is larger than 2 and that the Largest Page Size field value is at least 4096 bytes. If necessary, increase the size of the fields to equal or exceed these minimum values. To save the settings, press the Esc key and return to the Available Options menu. Press [Esc] again to exit the BSETUP module.

Figure 14-23

BTRIEVE Available Options menu

```
┌─────────────────────────────┐
│      Available Options       │
├─────────────────────────────┤
│ Set Btrieve Configuration    │
│ Set Rebuild Configuration    │
└─────────────────────────────┘
```

Figure 14-24

BTRIEVE
configuration
settings

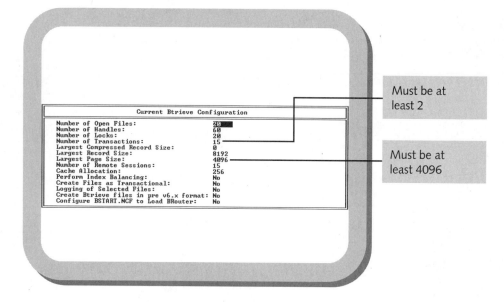

Figure 14-24

BTRIEVE configuration settings

Must be at least 2

Must be at least 4096

The last step in preparing to install the MHS system is to ensure that the BTRIEVE startup file contains commands to load BTRIEVE and BSPXCOM. The BTRIEVE startup file, BSTART.NCF, is stored in the SYS:SYSTEM directory and can be viewed or changed from the file server console by using the EDIT module. To start the EDIT module on the file server console and view the BTRIEVE startup file, enter the command: LOAD EDIT SYS:SYSTEM\BSTART.NCF and press [Enter]. The EDIT program will retrieve and display the startup file, as shown in Figure 14-25. Use the Esc key to exit the EDIT program and save any changes.

Figure 14-25

BSTART.NCF file

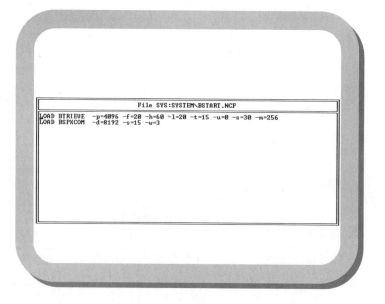

Figure 14-25

BSTART.NCF file

INSTALLING MHS SOFTWARE

The MHS software can be installed from either CD-ROM or floppy disks. You need to specify the path leading to the location of the MHS installation files. If installation is from floppy disks, the path will be either A or B, depending on the location of your

$3\frac{1}{2}$" floppy disk drive. When installing from CD-ROM, you will need to specify the DOS drive letter assigned to your CD-ROM. Make sure that your file server computer loads the necessary CD-ROM drives when it is first booted from DOS. Most CD-ROM drives should appear to DOS as either drive letter D or E, depending on whether you have one or two hard disk partitions. To check your CD-ROM drive, you will first need to down the file server and then use the EXIT command to return to the DOS prompt. You can then place the NetWare CD-ROM in the drive and view the directories of the D and E drives to locate the CD-ROM. After you have determined the CD-ROM drive letter, you can change to your SERVER directory and restart the file server.

After the server is up and running, use the INSTALL module to install the Message Handling System. First enter the LOAD INSTALL command on the file server console. This displays the Installation Options menu. Select Product Options to display the Currently Installed Products window. To install the MHS product, press the Ins key to open a window asking for the path to the new product source medium. If you are installing MHS from floppy disks, insert the MHS-1 disk in the disk drive, enter the drive letter of the disk drive and press [Enter]. Figure 14-26 shows the path to the MHS installation files that was entered for a system with a CD-ROM drive assigned to drive D.

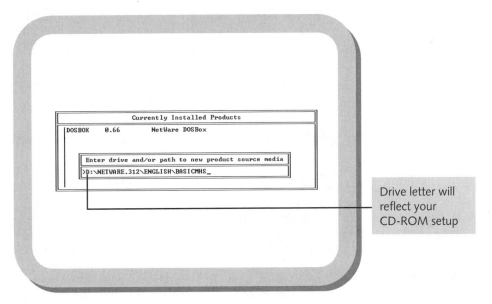

After you enter the path to the MHS product, the installation program will begin the installation process. During installation, you will need to enter the following information.

Workgroup names. The installation program asks for the long name for the workgroup. The default workgroup name is the name of the file server on which you are installing MHS. Novell recommends that you enter N in response to the "Accept Workgroup long name" prompt and enter the name of your organization for the long workgroup name. The short workgroup name is automatically created from the long workgroup name and is used for compatibility with older applications. Enter Y to accept the default short name at the "Accept Workgroup short name" prompt.

A workgroup name can contain any printable characters except: period, at sign (@), double quote ("), semicolon, comma, parentheses, square brackets, and braces. The user address consists of the workgroup name combined with the username. The user address can be up to 253 bytes long.

Mail volume path After you enter the workgroup name, the installation program asks for the path to the MHS MAIL directory. The MHS mail directory contains the users' mailboxes and the Basic MHS database. Normally you should accept the default path to the SYS: volume on the current file server. After the path is selected, the installation program creates the MHS directories, sets directory attributes, and copies files from the floppy disks or CD-ROM into the appropriate directories.

User's mail name—*full name or login name*—After all files have been copied, the installation program asks if you want to enable messaging services for existing users. Enter N if you do not want to add all existing users on your file server to the MHS database. Enter Y to import all users from the group EVERYONE into the mail database. If you choose to import all existing users, the installation software displays the prompt: "Full Name for user's mail name? [Yes|No]:". If you have assigned full names to all your user accounts, you can enter Y to use full names for the mail address. Enter N to use the user login names as the MHS usernames.

"Update System Login?" In response to this prompt, entering Y updates the system login script to include a search drive to the MHS\EXE directory and sets the DOS MV environmental variable to the path to the MHS mail directories (SYS:MHS\MAIL). If you enter N, you will need to add these entries to either the system or user login scripts for all users who are going to access the message system.

"Update AUTOEXEC.NCF File?" In response to this prompt, enter Y to update the AUTOEXEC.NCF startup file for your file server. The startup file will now include the following statements to load the message handling system:

```
SEARCH ADD SYS:MHS\EXE

LOAD BASICMHS
```

The MHS system is now installed and ready to be loaded.

The SEARCH ADD statement in the startup file allows the file server to find the MHS software by adding the SYS:MHS\EXE directory to its search path. Normally the file server checks only in the SYS:SYSTEM directory to find NetWare Loadable Modules. The LOAD BASICMHS command loads the BTRIEVE and MHS modules, which are needed to create a message server.

LOADING BASIC MHS

Once Basic MHS has been installed on your server and the AUTOEXEC.NCF file has been updated, you can start MHS either by downing the server and rebooting or by loading MHS directly from the console. To load MHS from the console, enter the following commands:

```
SEARCH ADD SYS:MHS\EXE

LOAD BASICMHS
```

Whether MHS is installed from the AUTOEXEC.NCF file or directly from the console, the MHS server automatically loads the necessary BTRIEVE modules, synchronizes its database, and begins scanning for new users by displaying the MHS monitor screen shown in Figure 14-27.

Figure 14-27

Basic MHS console
screen

```
BASICMHS V1.0
NetWare Basic MHS
Copyright 1993 Novell, Inc.
All rights reserved.
Usage: BASICMHS [-Vnn] [-Nmailpath] [-Snnn]

I9521: Synchronize Names.dbf
I9525: Scan for New Users
-
```

The MHS monitor screen displays information about each message that is delivered by the MHS system, including the addresses of the sender and receiver as well as the completion status of the delivery. If you experience problems with messages not being properly delivered, this screen can help you determine the source of the problem. When the MHS monitor screen is displayed, your file server console appears to be locked up and won't accept any input. Use the [Alt][Esc] hot key combination to return to the file server's console prompt. You can then use the hot key combination again to return to the MHS monitor screen.

CREATING MHS USERS

Prior to using an MHS-compatible e-mail package such as Novell's FirstMail, you need to establish a user account and e-mail address for each user who will participate in the message system. If you entered Y in response to the "Enable Messaging Services for Existing Users?" prompt during MHS installation, an MHS user account and an e-mail address were created for each user on your file server. In many cases, however, network administrators do not want to set up messaging for all users of the file server. To enable message services for existing users or to add new users to the message service, you use the ADMIN program. The ADMIN program, which performs other MHS configuration functions as well, is located in the MHS\EXE directory and must be run from a workstation by the SUPERVISOR or a supervisor equivalent user.

Prior to running the ADMIN program on your workstation, display the CONFIG.SYS file on the workstation to be sure it is set for a minimum of 30 files and 15 buffers, as shown in the sample CONFIG.SYS file in Figure 14-28. After confirming the number of files and buffers, you need to run the BREQUEST program from the workstation.

The BREQUEST program is needed to communicate with the BTRIEVE software running on the file server. Both BREQUEST and BTRIEVE work together in a client-server relationship to access information from the MHS database, as illustrated in Figure 14-29. BREQUEST takes a request from the ADMIN program and sends it to the BTRIEVE program on the server. The BTRIEVE program then performs the requested database function and returns the results to the BREQUEST program. Running the BTRIEVE software on the file server saves network access time because the BREQUEST program on the workstation does not need to access information in the database; it simply sends a request and waits for the results. BTRIEVE performs the actual work of looking up the requested record directly from the database stored on the file server computer and sends the workstation the results.

Figure 14-28

Sample workstation CONFIG.SYS file

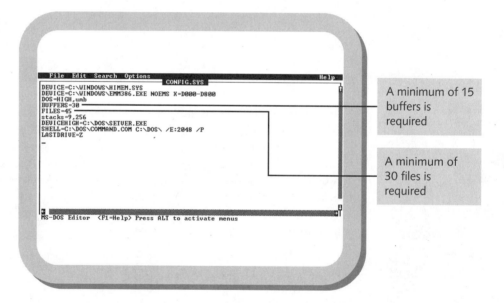

After loading the BREQUEST software, you can use the ADMIN program to add new users to the MHS database by entering the command ADMIN and pressing [Enter].

If you receive the message "Bad Command or Filename," it means that you do not have a search drive mapped to the MHS\EXE directory. When you install MHS you should enter Yes to update the system login script file. This includes the MAP INS S16:=SYS:MHS\EXE command along with DOS SET MV=server\volume:MHS\MAIL. Check the system login script for these commands and then log out and back in again to establish the search drive mapping and environment variable.

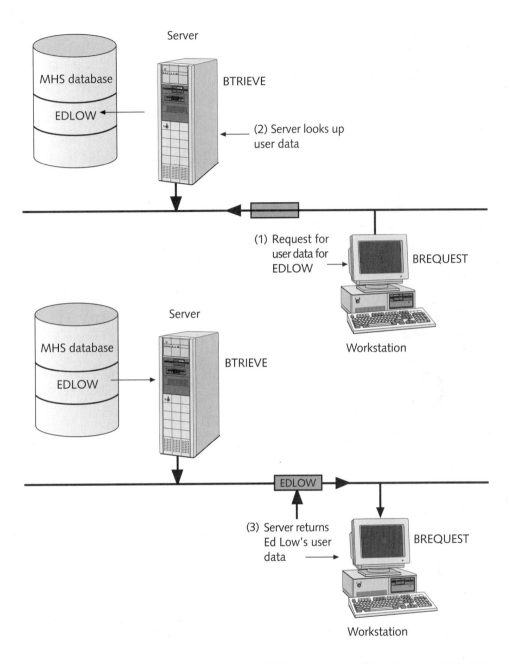

Figure 14-29

The BREQUEST software

After starting the ADMIN program, you will be required to identify your ADMIN user login name and password. Any user of the MHS system can log in to the ADMIN program by supplying his or her user mail name and NetWare password. By default, however, only the SUPERVISOR or supervisor equivalent user is allowed to make changes to the MHS database or configuration. Other users can view existing user-names and distribution lists. After you enter a valid ADMIN username and password, the ADMIN program displays the ADMIN Functions menu, shown in Figure 14-30.

Figure 14-30

ADMIN Admin
Functions menu

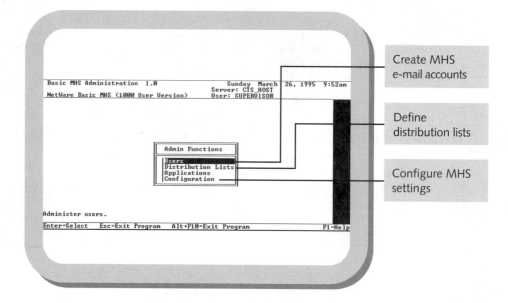

Create MHS
e-mail accounts

Define
distribution lists

Configure MHS
settings

To manage MHS mail users, select the Users option on the ADMIN Functions menu and press [Enter] to display the Users window, which shows all existing MHS users in the database. To add a new user to the MHS database, press [Ins] and enter the user's mail address. If you do not use the user's login name for the mail address, be sure the user's full name is the same as the mail address name. If the mail address does not match either the user's login name or the user's full name, mail cannot be delivered. When you press [Enter], the User Information window shown in Figure 14-31 will be displayed.

Figure 14-31

User Information
window

Notice that the "User's Workgroup" field has been filled with the default workgroup name you supplied during installation; it cannot be changed in the Basic MHS system. The "User's Short Name" field is filled in from the "User's Long Name" field and should be the same as the User's login name. The "Personal Info" field can be used to enter additional user information; the "Applications" field can be used to specify special MHS-compatible applications for this user.

To enter additional information, such as the user's actual name, address, department, and phone number, highlight the "Personal Info" field and press [Enter] to view the Personal Information window shown in Figure 14-32. After all information has been entered for the user, press the Esc key to save it.

 The information contained in the Personal Information window can be displayed at the bottom of the FirstMail screen by pressing [F2].

The ADMIN program will then ask you to enter the login name of the user. Enter the user's login name exactly as it exists in the NetWare bindery files. If the name entered is not a current user, the ADMIN program will automatically create a new user account for the username specified. After the program checks the user's name in the NetWare bindery, it displays the new MHS username in the Users window. Repeat this process for each user you want to include in the MHS e-mail system.

Figure 14-32

Personal Information window

```
                    Personal Information
           Last Name: TEDSIM
First Name and Initial:
 Generation Qualifier:
               Title:
          Department:
        Phone Number:
   Extra Information:
```

CREATING AND MANAGING DISTRIBUTION LISTS

It is often necessary to send a message or memo to multiple users who are members of a department or workgroup. The MHS system allows you to define groups of users and send messages to all members of a group automatically. A distribution list contains the addresses of users who are members of the group to which you want to send a message. You simply address the message to the distribution list. Distribution lists are often arranged by department. You can also create a master distribution list that contains all message users in your organization.

Use the ADMIN program to create or manage distribution lists. First select the Distribution Lists option from the Admin Functions menu. This displays the Distribution Lists window, which shows all existing distribution lists. To create a new distribution list, press the Ins key and enter the information in the Define Distribution List window, as shown in Figure 14-33.

Figure 14-33

Define Distribution
List window

Notice that the "DList Workgroup" field contains the workgroup name you defined during the initial installation of MHS. To define a distribution list, you need to enter both a long and a short distribution list name. These names can be the same, or you can create a more descriptive long name if you like. The "Description" field is optional and can be used to describe the distribution list in more detail. After you have completed the fields in the Define Distribution List window, press the Esc key to save the entry.

The ADMIN program next displays a blank Members window. To add members to the distribution list press the Ins key and use the F5 key to mark the users you want to include. After you have selected all users you want to be members of this distribution list, press [Enter] to add the marked users to the Members window. After all users have been added, press [Esc] to save the new distribution list and return to the Distribution Lists window. The newly created distribution list will appear in the window of distribution lists.

To delete a distribution list, highlight the name of the distribution list and press the Del key. After you confirm the deletion, the ADMIN program removes the distribution list from the MHS database and the Distribution Lists window. To change the name of a distribution list, highlight the distribution list and use the F3 key to call up the Define Distribution List window. You can change any of the information fields described previously. To add or delete members of an existing distribution list, highlight the name of the distribution list and use the Enter key to display the "Members of" window. Now use the Ins or Del keys to add or remove members from the list.

CUSTOMIZING MHS SERVER OPERATIONS

In addition to using the ADMIN program to maintain users and distribution lists, you can also use it to customize the way your MHS server operates and to register new MHS-compatible applications that have been installed on your network. One parameter you can change, for example, is the frequency rate of mail delivery. To modify the MHS server configuration parameters, select the Configuration option on the Admin Functions menu to display the Configuration window shown in Figure 14-34.

Figure 14-34

Configuration
window

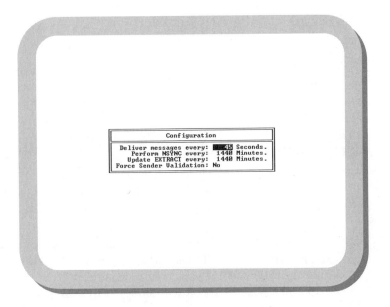

The "Deliver messages every" field is used to control how many seconds MHS will wait before checking for queued messages to be delivered. Decreasing the time will cause mail to be delivered more quickly, but will also decrease the performance of the file server for other tasks. The "Perform NSYNC every" field is used to control how often (in minutes) your server will resynchronize its database files. Unless you are having problems with database synchronization, you should normally leave the default setting of 1440 minutes (24 hours). The "Update EXTRACT every" field determines how often (in minutes) your MHS server will update the extract file. The extract file is an ASCII version of the MHS database that can be used by SMF-compatible applications. Unless you have SMF-compatible applications that need to have the extract file updated more frequently, you should normally leave the default time of 1440 minutes (24 hours).

The "Force sender validation" field allows you to specify whether you want to enable sender validation for applications which support that feature. Sender validation forces the sender of a message to be a registered user in the MHS database. The default setting is No. With the Novell FirstMail program, however, you might want to change the setting to Yes. This will prevent non-MHS users from using the mail application to send messages and files to MHS users. After viewing or changing the configuration settings, use the Esc key to save any changes and return to the Admin Functions menu. To make the changes effective, you will need to unload and reload the MHS server using the following commands on the file server console:

UNLOAD BASICMHS

LOAD BASICMHS

MANAGING THE BASIC MHS SERVER

After your MHS server is installed and operational, you will need to perform such management tasks as backing up the MHS environment and monitoring the log file for error messages. In this section you will learn about each of these MHS management activities and how they relate to your job as a network administrator.

Backing up the MHS server

One of the first management tasks you should perform after installing MHS and setting up your users and distribution lists is backing up the user environment so that you can quickly restore all your users in the event of a major system crash. To back up the MHS system, Novell recommends that you copy the MHS\MAIL\PUBLIC and MHS\MAIL\USERS directories to a backup medium, such as a tape drive or floppy disk. Figure 14-35 shows the files and directories that are included in the MHS\MAIL\PUBLIC directory.

The MHS\MAIL\USERS directory contains a subdirectory for each user's mail. Because these subdirectories initially do not contain any files, you can easily copy the USERS and PUBLIC directories onto one floppy disk, providing a compact backup copy of your initial MHS setup. Once users receive mail and save it in their folders, the user mail subdirectories will take up too much space to make it feasible to back them up on floppy disks. To back up the operational MHS e-mail system, you should include the MHS\MAIL directory in your daily file server backup procedure, as described in Chapter 15. This will allow you to recover your MHS users, distribution lists, and any messages stored in users' mail folders.

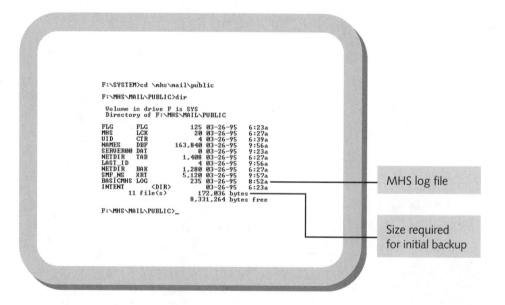

Figure 14-35

MHS directories for backup

Monitoring the log file

Basic MHS maintains a log file in the MHS\MAIL\PUBLIC directory called BASICMHS.LOG. This log contains messages regarding startup, shutdown, and problems in the MHS system. Because the log file is in ASCII text format, you can use a standard text editor, such as the DOS EDIT command, to print or view it. An example of a log file is shown in Figure 14-36. Notice that each log entry consists of the date, time, system message number (preceded by a pound sign (#)), and the system message text. Because some of the error messages are rather cryptic, you might need to refer to the MHS manual for an explanation of a specific error message. The MHS log file is especially useful when you are trying to track a problem, such as a user who is not receiving mail messages. While the MHS log file is normally quite small—less than 10 Kbytes—you should establish a regular monthly schedule of viewing, printing, and archiving the log file, and then deleting it from the MHS\MAIL\PUBLIC directory.

Figure 14-36

Sample MHS
log file

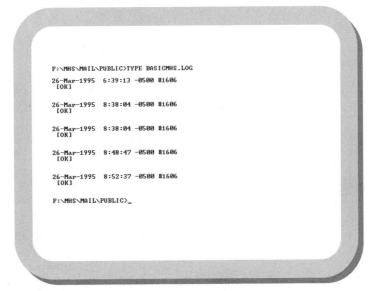

```
F:\MHS\MAIL\PUBLIC>TYPE BASICMHS.LOG
26-Mar-1995  6:39:13 -0500 #1606
   [OK]

26-Mar-1995  8:38:04 -0500 #1606
   [OK]

26-Mar-1995  8:38:04 -0500 #1606
   [OK]

26-Mar-1995  8:48:47 -0500 #1606
   [OK]

26-Mar-1995  8:52:37 -0500 #1606
   [OK]

F:\MHS\MAIL\PUBLIC>_
```

CHAPTER SUMMARY

Electronic messages are rapidly becoming a standard way of communicating within organizations and it is important that the network administrator have an understanding of message handling systems and mail applications. Novell's Message Handling Service (MHS) provides a standard way of delivering messages between MHS-compatible application packages. Standard NetWare v3.12 comes with the Basic MHS system that can support up to 1000 users on a single file server. Basic MHS does not move messages to users on other servers or across routers or wide area networks. To provide message delivery over an internetwork, Novell provides an upgrade from Basic MHS to Global MHS. The Remote MHS system provides users of remote computers and notebooks access to the Global MHS system using their asynchronous modems.

The Novell FirstMail electronic mail application is an MHS-compatible e-mail system that can be used to compose and send messages and attached files between users on the MHS system. Features such as message forwarding, carbon copying, replying to messages, attaching and extracting files, and managing and organizing messages make the FirstMail package a good way to get started in electronic mail. A network administrator needs to understand how to use these features in order to implement an electronic mail system on a network.

Basic MHS is installed on a file server with the Products option of the INSTALL NetWare Loadable Module. Because MHS uses the BTRIEVE client-server database system, it is important to verify that the correct version of BTRIEVE is installed on the server prior to loading the Basic MHS software. Minimum system requirements include a file server with at least 5 Mbytes of RAM to run the MHS system adequately. After MHS is installed, the ADMIN program is used to add MHS users and distribution lists to the MHS database and to check or change any message handling configuration settings.

COMMAND SUMMARY

Command	Syntax	Definition
ADMIN	ADMIN	MHS utility for managing users and distribution lists in the MHS database and modifying MHS configuration parameters, such as the mail delivery frequency rate.
BREQUEST	BREQUEST	Program that sends requests from BTRIEVE-compatible applications running on the workstation to the BTRIEVE database processor running on a file server. It is necessary to load the BREQUEST program prior to running BTRIEVE-compatible software, such as the ADMIN program.
MAIL	MAIL	Starts the Novell FirstMail system and provides a menu containing options to send a message, read new messages, browse existing messages, or personalize e-mail options.
MEMORY	MEMORY	A file server console command that displays the total amount of memory available on the file server computer.
MODULES	MODULES	A file server console command that displays information about each module currently loaded in the file server's memory.
SEARCH ADD	SEARCH ADD	A console command that is used to add a directory to the search path used by the LOAD command on the file server console.

KEY TERMS

blind carbon copy	distribution list	Message handling service (MHS)
carbon copy	e-mail address	
comment character	folder	workgroup name

REVIEW QUESTIONS

1. A(n) _____ can be used to send a message to a group of users.
2. On the lines below, list three options that you can perform with the FirstMail program while reading a message.

    _____

    _____

    _____

3. In the space below, explain what happens to a message after it is read from the "New Mail" folder.

4. In the space below, briefly explain the difference between the "N: check for New mail" and "B: browse mail messages" options.

5. On the lines below, list three options you can select when sending a message.

    _____

    _____

    _____

6. The _____ key is used to create a new folder.

7. On the lines below, list the four steps necessary to move a message from the "Main" folder to another folder called "Meetings."

    _____

    _____

    _____

    _____

    In questions 8–10 identify the FirstMail function key and option that will perform the specified e-mail functions for sending a message.

8. Attach a file.

    Function key: _____

    Option: _____

9. Be notified when the recipient reads the message.

    Function key: _____

    Option: _____

10. Send carbon copies of the message to other users.

    Function key: _____

    Option: _____

    In questions 11–15, identify the FirstMail function key or option that will perform the specified e-mail functions for reading a message.

11. Extract an attachment.

    _____

12. Send the message on to another user.

    _____

13. Search for the word "Skagerrak" in all messages.

     _____

14. Sequence messages by subject.

     _____

15. Move the message to a DOS file located on your local hard disk.

     _____

16. On the lines below, list the three parts of an electronic mail system.

     _____

     _____

     _____

17. _____ is a full-featured platform that will provide message delivery among users on multiple servers scattered throughout the internetwork.

18. Each user of MHS must be assigned a unique address consisting of _____ and _____ .

19. Write the e-mail address for a user who belongs to the PCSALES workgroup and has been assigned the username JSANTEE.

     _____

20. List two e-mail standards to which the Global MHS can be connected.

     _____

     _____

21. True or False? Basic MHS supports multiple workgroups on a single file server.

22. On the lines below, list three steps you should perform in order to prepare for MHS installation.

     _____

     _____

     _____

23. The _____ module is used from the file server console to begin the installation of the MHS software.

24. Which of the following is an invalid workgroup name?

     _____ PC-SOLUTIONS

     _____ PC

     _____ PC SOLUTIONS

     _____ PC.SOLUTIONS

25. If you answer Yes to the "Update System Login?" prompt, what two commands will be added to your system login script by the MHS installation program?

     _____

     _____

26. On the lines below, write the two file server console commands that are needed to load the Basic MHS system.

     _____

     _____

27. The Basic MHS system maintains a log file called BASICMHS.LOG in the _____ directory.

28. True or False? You should never erase the BASICMHS.LOG file.

29. The _____ program is used to create new users in the MHS database.

30. On the lines below, list two of the fields present in the User Personal Information Window when you create a new MHS user.

_____

_____

EXERCISES

Exercise 14-1: Installing MHS

This exercise requires that you have access to an "installation" file server computer and is intended to give you hands-on experience installing the Basic MHS software. Because installing or removing MHS on your classroom server would erase its MHS database containing other students' users, you need to have access to an "installation" file server and take turns with the other students in your class to perform the Basic MHS installation.

1. Follow the preliminary installation steps described in this chapter and record your findings in the space below:

   Amount of memory in the file server computer: _____

   Current version of CLIB: _____

   Current version of BTRIEVE: _____

   Maximum number of BTRIEVE transactions: _____

   Largest BTRIEVE page size: _____

   Contents of BSTART.NCF file:

   _____

   _____

2. Install MHS using your last name as the workgroup name and the default mail volume path. Do not create accounts for existing users. Update both the system login script and AUTOEXEC.NCF files. Record your responses to the installation prompts in the spaces below.

   Workgroup long name: _____

   Workgroup short name: _____

   Mail volume path: _____

   "Enable messaging for existing users?" _____

3. Down the file server.

4. Restart the file server.

5. In the space below, record the contents of the MHS Server screen.

6. Change to the file server console screen and record any messages regarding MHS or BTRIEVE in the space below.

Exercise 14-2: Administering MHS

This exercise requires that you have supervisor equivalent access to the file server to which your workstation is attached. If you are not allowed to login as a supervisor equivalent user on your classroom file server, your instructor can provide you with an installation file server and workstation that you can share with other students to perform this exercise. If you do not have supervisory access to a file server, your instructor might choose to divide the class into groups of three. In the spaces provided in Step 3, record the ##ADMIN names of the students with whom you will be working.

1. Log in as SUPERVISOR or a supervisor equivalent user.

2. Start the MHS administrative program. In the space below, record the commands necessary to run the program.

3. Add three users to the MHS database. If you are sharing the MHS server database with other students, be sure to include your assigned student number prior to entering each username you create. In the spaces below, record the names of the users you create. The MHS program will also create the usernames you specify in the Create NetWare Messaging Users window on the file server. Be sure to use names that do not currently exist on the server.

Mail Username	Short Name	NetWare Username

4. Create a distribution list called ##STAFF and include usernames 2 and 3.

5. Check the MHS configuration settings. In the space below, record the settings.

6. Change the rate of mail delivery to every 20 seconds in order to provide faster delivery times for testing purposes.

7. Use the Print Scrn key to obtain a hardcopy of your MHS configuration settings.

8. Go to the file server computer and change the console so that it displays the MHS server screen.

Exercise 14-3: Sending and Receiving Messages

In this exercise you will practice sending messages to a single user, multiple users, and a distribution list. To enable you to perform this exercise, your instructor will have created two e-mail users named ##USER1 and ##USER2 and a ##GROUP distribution list (where ## represents your assigned student number). The distribution list contains your users along with the instructor's e-mail name. In addition, in this exercise you will learn how to attach a file to a message and receive confirmation when the recipient reads the message.

Part 1: Sending a message and carbon copy to another user

1. Log in using the NetWare username for user 1.

2. Start the FirstMail program and select the option to send a message.

3. Compose a message on the subject of today's weather and send it to user 2 with a carbon copy to user 3. Require a confirmation when the message is read by user 2.

4. Send the message.

5. Monitor the file server's MHS console and record the message indicating your mail was delivered.

Part 2: Sending a message with an attached file

1. Select the option to send a message.

2. Address the message to user 2. Indicate in the "Subj" field that the message relates to the MHS system log.

3. Attach the BASICMHS.LOG file to the message log file.

4. Require confirmation when the message is delivered to user 2.

5. Send the message.

6. Monitor the file server MHS console log for indication that your mail has been delivered.

7. Use the FirstMail program to check for the delivery notification.

Part 3: Reading mail and sending a reply

1. Log in as user 2 and start the FirstMail program.

2. View new mail.

3. Use the Reply option to respond to the weather message with your forecast for tomorrow's weather. Include the original message commented out. Include the carbon copied user as a recipient.

4. Send the reply.

5. Monitor the file server's MHS console for the confirmation of your mail delivery.

6. Log in as user 1 and view new mail.

7. Print the confirmation message showing the time and date that user 2 read the message.

8. Print the reply message from user 2.

Part 4: Extracting an attached file

1. Log in as user 2 and start the FirstMail software.

2. View your new mail.

3. Print the message regarding the MHS message log.

4. Extract the Basic MHS log file and store it on your local hard drive or floppy disk.

5. Send a thank you reply to user 1.

Exercise 14-4: Working with Folders

In this exercise you will use FirstMail to organize messages by creating additional folders and then moving messages fom the "Main" and "Copies to Self" folders into the new folders you have created.

1. Log in as ##USER1.

2. Send four messages to ##USER2. Two of the messages should be on the subject of Weather and two on the subject of using the MHS e-mail system. Save the messages in your "Copies to self" folder.

3. Use the "B: browse mail messages" option to view mail in the "Copies to self" folder.

4. Use the [F10] key to create two folders, one called "Weather" and the other "MHS system."

5. Move all weather-related messages into the "Weather" folder.

6. Move all MHS system messages into the "MHS system" folder.

Exercise 14-5: Removing MHS Users

This exercise, which requires supervisor equivalency, deletes the MHS users and distribution lists you created in Exercise 2. If you did not have the rights to create the users in Exercise 2 and used existing ##ADMIN users to perform Exercises 3 and 4, you should skip this exercise.

1. Start the MHS administration program and log in to MHS as a supervisor equivalent user.

2. With the Users option, delete the three mail users you created in Exercise 2.

3. With the Distribution Lists option, delete the distribution list you created in Exercise 2.

Exercise 14-6: Uninstalling MHS

This exercise requires that you have access to the "installation" file server computer on which you installed MHS. Its purpose is to give you hands-on experience uninstalling the Basic MHS software. Because installing or uninstalling MHS on your classroom server would erase its MHS database containing other students' users, you need to have access to an "installation" file server and work in teams assigned by your instructor in order to uninstall Basic MHS.

1. Before MHS can be uninstalled, you must first unload Basic MHS from the file server computer by using the command UNLOAD BASICMHS.

2. Load the INSTALL module.

3. Select the Products Option option and press **[Enter]**. The Installed Products window will be displayed.

4. Highlight the Basic MHS entry in the Installed Products screen and press **[Del]**.

5. Follow the prompts to remove MHS from the file server.

6. Use the System option of the Install program to view the contents of the AUTOEXEC.NCF file. The MHS command should be removed.

7. Down the server and exit to DOS.

8. Restart the server.

9. Use the MODULES command to verify that MHS has been removed. If you can, log in from a workstation and verify that the MHS directory structure has been removed from the SYS: volume.

 EXERCISE

Case 14-1: Working with e-mail

The Landmark Builder Company specializes in designing and building offices and public buildings using the latest CAD and construction technology. The company has been very successful in this market and has grown rapidly over the last three years. Starting with a single standalone CAD computer, the company now employs several architects each using his or her own workstation. The company also uses computers for office tasks such as desktop publishing and word processing. Recently Landmark decided that an e-mail system would really increase productivity—staff are often out on job sites, making it difficult to talk to them directly. This project simulates setting up and using the FirstMail system to enable Landmark to implement an electronic mail system. To enable you to perform this project, your instructor should have provided you with access to the ADMIN program and a username that will allow you to create MHS users and distribution lists on your classroom file server.

Part 1: Creating users

The following users and departments include the personnel who will be using the Landmark e-mail system:

User	Position	E-mail Address
Bill Tradwell	Owner	_____
Larry Simpson	Manager	_____

Nancy Cann	Designer	_____
Jim Landreth	Designer	_____
Cynthia Olsen	Designer	_____
Dick Herman	Office	_____
Helen Dunn	Office	_____

1. Log in using your assigned student username.

2. Change to your ##ADMIN directory.

3. Create the Landmark directory structure shown in Figure 14–37. In the ACCTNG directory, use the following commands to create a file called PRICES.DAT:

    a. COPY CON PRICES.DAT. Press **[Enter]**.

    b. This is the new price file. Press **[Enter]**.

    c. Cost per square foot is $125.00. Press **[Enter]**.

    d. End of file. Press **[Enter]**.

    e. Press **[F6]**. Press **[Enter]**.

Figure 14-37

Landmark directory structure

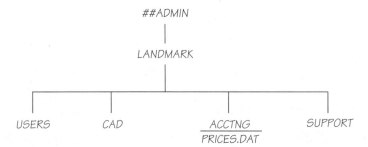

4. Use SYSCON to create usernames and home directories in your USERS directory for each of the users listed above. Give the office users [R F W C E M] rights to the ACCTNG and SUPPORT directories.

5. Use the MHS ADMIN program to create an e-mail address for each of the users. Record the e-mail addresses in the table above. Make sure to precede each user's e-mail name with your assigned student number.

6. Use the MHS ADMIN program to establish a distribution list that includes all Landmark users and separate distribution lists for each department. Make sure to precede each of your distribution lists with your assigned student number. Record the distribution lists and members in the following table:

List Name	Members
##Landmark	

Part 2: Sending a message

Suppose Cynthia Olsen, a designer, is meeting with a client who is planning to build a new office on the outskirts of town. Before she meets with the potential customer she wants to make sure to have copies of the latest building and material prices. To obtain copies of the newest price sheet, she decides to try the new e-mail system. She sends a message to Dick Herman, who is responsible for maintaining the cost files. To be sure Dick reads the message, Cynthia wants a confirmation reply.

1. Log in using Cynthia's username and start the FirstMail application from the menu.

2. Select the "S: send a message" option.

3. Address the message to Dick Herman and include in the "Subj" field the subject Prices.

4. Enter a message requesting a copy of the latest price information.

5. Indicate that the message is urgent and requires a confirmation when the recipient reads the message.

6. Send a carbon copy of the message to Bill Tradwell and Larry Simpson.

7. Keep a copy of the message.

8. Send the message.

9. Log out.

Part 3: Reading and replying to a message

1. Log in using Dick Herman's username and start the FirstMail application from the menu.

2. Read the new mail.

3. Print Cynthia Olsen's message.

4. Create a reply to Cynthia's message. The reply should tell Cynthia that the new price list is just completed and is attached to this message.

5. Use the attachment option to attach the PRICES.DAT file from the accounting outline directory.

6. Keep a copy of the message.

7. Send the message to Cynthia.

8. Log out.

Part 4: Retrieving attached files

1. Log in as Cynthia Olsen and start the FirstMail application.

2. Check for new mail.

3. Read and print the confirmation message.

4. Read and print the message from Dick Herman. Use the Print Settings screen to send the output to the classroom print queue.

5. Extract the attached files and save them in Cynthia's home directory.

6. Return to the FirstMail Mail Options menu.

7. Use the "B: browse message options" option to view messages in the mail folder.

8. Create a folder called "Prices."

9. Move the outline messages from both the "Copies to self" folder and the "Main" folder to the new "Prices" folder.

10. Exit FirstMail.

11. Print a directory listing of Cynthia's home directory showing the extracted files.

12. After checkout, remove the mail users and distribution lists.

 ## SUPERIOR TECHNICAL COLLEGE PROBLEMS

Project 14-1: Defining MHS Users

Dave Johnson is anxious to start implementing e-mail at the campus and was recently involved in helping you install MHS on your file server. To start with, he would like to have you implement e-mail between the student services department and the support staff. Your first job is to define MHS usernames for each of the users of the student services and support departments. Use a table (provided below) to define each user's e-mail and login username. If you do not have SUPERVISOR access to your classroom file server, your instructor will already have installed MHS and included these Superior Technical College users in the mail system using their login names as their e-mail addresses. To determine your users' e-mail addresses, start the FirstMail software and use the [F2] key in the "Send a message" option to record all the usernames in the table.

Username	User Login Name	E-mail Address
Karl Dauer		
Stuart Chung		
Lauri Holt		
Mimi Ito		

Project 14-2: Defining Distribution Lists

After the users have been defined, Dave Johnson would like you to establish distribution lists for all campus staff, for the student services department, and for support staff. Record the distribution lists and users in the following table:

Distribution List Name	Users

Project 14-3: Creating MHS Users

If you have supervisory access to your classroom file server, use the ADMIN program to create the users and distribution lists you defined in Project 14-1.

Project 14-4: Updating Menus

Add a FirstMail option to both the student service and support main menus you defined in Chapter 13. Obtain a printout of each of the main menu source files.

Project 14-5: Testing the System

Test the e-mail system by performing the following activities:

1. Log in as the user Laurie Holt.
2. Copy all the files in the Outline directory on your student work disk to the ##STC\SUPPORT\OUTLINES directory in your Superior Technical College directory structure.
3. Have Laurie Holt send a message to Karl Dauer containing the DOS.CIS outline file that he has requested.
4. Log out.
5. Log in as Karl Dauer and redirect your printer output to the classroom print queue.
6. Read the mail.
7. Extract the DOS.CIS outline file and save it in Karl's home directory.
8. Print the contents of Laurie's message along with the DOS.CIS outline file.
9. Log out.

## CHAPTER FIFTEEN

MANAGING THE FILE SERVER

In the previous chapters of this book you learned how to install and configure a NetWare network. Most of the activities included in establishing the network take place at the workstation. There are, however, times when it is necessary to access the file server console to perform various commands and load modules, such as during installation of NetWare and the Message Handling Services. These activities will have familiarized you with several important console commands and utilities.

Once the network is operational, however, it becomes even more important for the network administrator to know how to use the file server console to monitor network performance, to back up and secure the server, and to expand the network by adding support for other operating systems and network protocols. In this chapter you will learn how the commands you already know fit into the console command system. You will learn additional commands and options that are important for monitoring, backing up, and securing the file server. You will also learn how to access the file server console from another workstation attached either to the local area network or via a modem.

AFTER READING THIS CHAPTER AND COMPLETING THE EXERCISES YOU WILL BE ABLE TO:

- USE NETWARE CONSOLE COMMANDS TO SECURE THE FILE SERVER CONSOLE AND ADD NAME SPACE SUPPORT FOR OTHER WORKSTATION ENVIRONMENTS.

- USE REMOTE CONSOLE MANAGEMENT TO ACCESS THE FILE SERVER CONSOLE FROM A WORKSTATION ATTACHED TO THE NETWORK.

- LOAD SUPPORT FOR TCP/IP PACKETS AND MULTIPLE ETHERNET FRAME TYPES ON A NETWARE FILE SERVER.

- USE THE VREPAIR NETWARE LOADABLE MODULE TO FIX VOLUME PROBLEMS AND REMOVE NAME SPACE SUPPORT.

- USE NETWARE'S STORAGE MANAGEMENT SYSTEM TO BACK UP NETWORK DATA.

CONSOLE OPERATIONS

File server operation entails using commands that can be divided into two major categories: console commands and NetWare Loadable Modules (NLM). Console commands are similar to the DOS internal commands on a workstation in that they are built into the core file server operating system program (SERVER.EXE). NetWare Loadable Modules are external programs that are loaded into the memory of the file server computer and add functionality to the NetWare core operating system. In this section you will learn about the console commands and several of the most common NLMs.

CONSOLE COMMANDS

In order to operate a file server console effectively, you need to know how to use the basic console commands that are built into the NetWare operating system. You should know the purpose and use of each of the console commands described in this section. Because there are many different console commands, the console commands described in this section have been divided into separate functional categories: installation commands, configuration commands, maintenance commands, and security commands. It is not necessary for you to know the command categories. Their sole purpose is to make it easier for you to study and learn the commands by making you focus on a few related commands at one time. The following sections describe the console commands in detail and provide examples.

Installation commands

The commands shown in Figure 15-1 are included in the installation category because they are most frequently used when you first install NetWare on the file server, when you expand the system, or when you install a separate application, such as MHS.

The ADD NAME SPACE command is used to allow non-DOS filenames, such as those used with Macintosh or OS/2, to be used in a NetWare volume. The ADD NAME SPACE command will modify the directory entry table (DET) in the specified volume to allow for the storage of non-DOS filenames. This command needs to be executed only once for each volume in which the non-DOS files are going to be stored. Replace the *name* parameter with the name of the name space module you loaded. Common names are OS/2 and MAC. Replace the *volume_name* parameter with the name of the volume to which you want the specified name space to be added. More information about using the ADD NAME SPACE command for adding name space support is provided later in this chapter.

Figure 15-1

Installation commands

Command Syntax	Description
ADD NAME SPACE *name* [TO VOLUME] *volume_name*	Adds space to a volume's directory entry table in order to support other operating system file naming conventions. Replace *name* with MAC or OS/2. Replace *volume_name* with the volume to which the specified name space is to be added.
BIND *protocol* TO *driver\board_name* [*driver_parameters*]	Attaches a *protocol* to a LAN card. Replace *protocol* with protocol name (e.g., IPX or IP). Replace *driver\board_name* with either the name of the card drive program or an optional name assigned to the network board. You can optionally replace *driver_parameters* with the hardware settings that identify the network interface card (e.g., I/O port and interrupt).
LOAD [*path*]*module_name* [*parameters*]	Loads an NLM in the file server's RAM. Optionally replace *path* with the DOS or NetWare path leading to the directory containing the module to be loaded. Replace *module_name* with the name of the NLM you want to load. Optional *parameters* can be entered, depending on the module being loaded.
REGISTER MEMORY *start length*	Allows servers using a Microchannel or ISA bus to access memory above 16 Mbytes.
SEARCH [ADD *path*] SEARCH [DEL *number*]	Adds or removes a directory path from the search path used by the LOAD command when NLMs are being loaded. When no parameters are specified, the current server search paths are displayed. To add a search path, replace *path* with the DOS or NetWare path leading to the directory from which you want to load NLMs. To delete an existing search path, replace *number* with the number of the search path to be deleted.

The BIND command attaches a protocol stack to a network card and is necessary to allow workstations using that protocol to communicate with the file server. Replace the *protocol* parameter with the name of the protocol stack you want to attach to the network card. The IPX protocol is built into the core operating system and can be bound to a network card simply by using the BIND command. Replace *driver|board_name* either with the name of the card driver loaded previously with the LOAD command or with the name you assigned to the card driver when it was loaded. If you have loaded the driver program more than once on different cards or with different frame types, you can replace *drive_parameters* with a combination of any of the parameters shown in Figure 15-2 that uniquely identify the driver program to which you want to bind the specified protocol.

Figure 15-2

BIND driver
parameters

Parameter Syntax	Description
DMA=*number*	Identifies the DMA channel the LAN driver is using. Use the same DMA channel that you used when you loaded the driver for the board.
FRAME=*name*	Identifies the frame type used when the driver program was loaded.
INT=*number*	Identifies the interrupt the driver is using for the network board. Bind the protocol with the same interrupt that you used when you loaded the LAN driver.
NET=*network_address*	Assigns a network address consisting of one to eight hexidecimal digits to the LAN card.
MEM=*number*	Identifies the memory address used when the driver was loaded.
PORT=*number*	Identifies the I/O port number the driver is using for the network board.
SLOT=*number*	On a micro channel computer, the slot identifies the network board used when the LAN driver was loaded.

Use the *parameters* item to specify options unique to the protocol being loaded. When using the IPX protocol, you are required to specify a network address for use with the cable system to which the card is attached. The following sample BIND command can be used to attach the IPX protocol stack with a network address of 1EEE8023 to an NE2000 driver assigned to an Ethernet card on port 300:

```
BIND IPX TO NE2000 [PORT=300] NET=1EEE8023
```

If the NE2000 network driver assigned to the Ethernet card at port 300 had been assigned a name when it was loaded with the LOAD command, the BIND command could use the name assigned to the driver to specify uniquely the correct card. (See the LOAD command for an example of naming a network card driver.) To bind IPX to a card driver named MEGALAB, you can enter the following command:

```
BIND IPX TO MEGALAB NET=1EEE8023
```

If you want to change the protocol (TCP/IP, for example) on a network card, you first need to use the LOAD command to load the TCP/IP protocol module. After the protocol software has been loaded, you can use the BIND command to attach the protocol to the desired network card. More information on loading and binding the TCP/IP protocol is provided later in this chapter.

The LOAD command reads a NetWare Loadable Module into memory and executes it. By default, the LOAD command searches for the requested module in the SYS:SYSTEM directory unless a different path is specified. Valid paths can include NetWare volume names as well as DOS local drive letters. When a module is loaded into memory it remains there until the console operator ends the program or uses the UNLOAD command to remove the software from memory. Optional parameters can be placed after the LOAD command depending on the needs of the module being loaded.

When a LAN driver is loaded, for example, the I/O port and option name parameters can be included in the LOAD command as follows:

LOAD NE2000 PORT=300 NAME=MEGALAB

This LOAD command will access an Ethernet LAN driver for a card that has an I/O port address of 300 and will assign it the name MEGALAB. The name MEGALAB can later be used to reference this card driver, as described under the BIND command. Several popular NetWare Loadable Modules and their associated parameters are described in more detail in the section on NetWare Loadable Modules.

The REGISTER MEMORY command is used when a NetWare server with either an ISA or MicroChannel bus does not recognize installed memory above 16 Mbytes. To access the memory above 16 Mbytes, replace the start parameter with the starting hexadecimal address at which the memory beyond 16 Mbytes begins. In most cases, the starting address will be 1000000 (which equals 16 Mbytes). Replace length with a hexadecimal number that corresponds to the amount of memory installed above 16 Mbytes. If, for example, a file server computer with an ISA bus has 24M bytes of RAM but reports only 16 Mbytes when you use the MEMORY command, enter the following REGISTER MEMORY command to allow the file server to "see" the additional memory:

REGISTER MEMORY 1000000 800000

Unless a specific path is used, the NetWare server operating system normally checks for modules and files in the SYS:SYSTEM directory. However, just as the MAP INS S1:=path statement allows you to add another directory to the search path of a workstation, the SEARCH ADD statement can be used to specify an additional directory path that contains files or programs to be used by the file server. Using the SEARCH ADD statement to add directory paths for the file server does not affect the search drive mappings of the workstations.

Figure 15-3

Sample SEARCH
commands

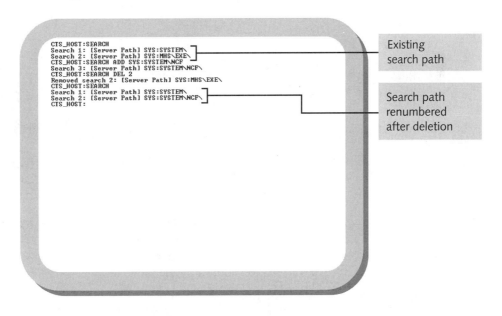

As shown in Figure 15-3, you can enter the SEARCH command by itself to display a list of all active search paths and their corresponding numbers. The SEARCH DEL number command shown in Figure 15-3 deletes an existing search drive by specifying the number of the search drive to be deleted. When a file server is restarted, all current search paths are removed, making it necessary to include SEARCH ADD statements for all necessary directories in the AUTOEXEC.NCF startup file.

Configuration commands

The configuration console commands shown in Figure 15-4 are used to view the configuration of the file server and associated network cards. The information obtained by using these commands helps the network administrator identify the configuration of LAN cards and protocols, view other servers and networks, change the server date and time, and expand the network.

Figure 15-4

Configuration commands

Command Syntax	Description
CONFIG	Displays configuration information about each network card, including hardware settings, network address, protocol, and frame type.
DISPLAY NETWORKS	Shows all networks to which the file server has access, including the number of routers (hops) and the time in ticks ($\frac{1}{18}$ sec.) it takes to reach each network.
DISPLAY SERVERS	Shows all servers in the file server's router table, including the number of routers (hops) to get to each server.
LIST DEVICES	Indicates all devices currently registered with the NetWare operating system.
MEMORY	Displays the total amount of memory available to the file server computer.
NAME	Displays the name of the file server.
PROTOCOL	Displays all protocols that are currently in use.
SET	Allows you to view or change current file server environment settings.
SET TIME [*month/day/year*] [*hour:minute:second*]	Allows you to change the file server's current system date and time.

The CONFIG command displays information about the file server and network card configuration, as shown in Figure 15-5. Notice that, in addition to displaying the file server's name and internal network address, the CONFIG command displays the following information about each network adapter in the file server:

- Name of the LAN driver
- Current hardware settings, including interrupt, I/O port, memory address, and Direct Memory Access (DMA) channel

- Node (station) address assigned to the network adapter

- Frame type assigned to the network adapter

- Board name assigned when the LAN driver was loaded

- Protocol stack that was bound to the network adapter

- Network address of the cabling scheme for the network adapter

Figure 15-5

Sample CONFIG
command

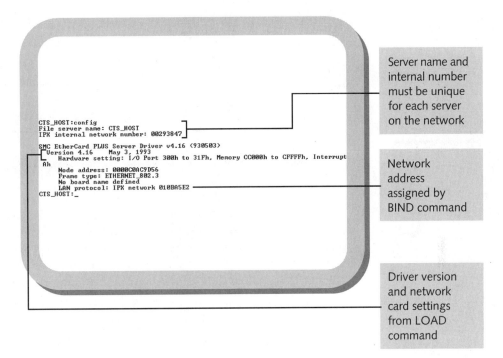

```
CTS_HOST:config
File server name: CTS_HOST
IPX internal network number: 00293847

SMC EtherCard PLUS Server Driver v4.16 (930503)
  Version 4.16   May 3, 1993
    Hardware setting: I/O Port 300h to 31Fh, Memory CC000h to CFFFFh, Interrupt
Ah
    Node address: 0000C0AC9D56
    Frame type: ETHERNET_802.3
    No board name defined
    LAN protocol: IPX network 010BA5E2
CTS_HOST:_
```

Server name and
internal number
must be unique
for each server
on the network

Network
address
assigned by
BIND command

Driver version
and network
card settings
from LOAD
command

Use the CONFIG command before installing memory boards or network adapters in the file server so that you have a current list of all hardware settings on the existing boards. This will help you select unique interrupt and I/O address settings for the new cards. The CONFIG command can also be used to determine the network address of a cable system before you add another file server to the network. If you accidentally bring up another file server using a different network address for the same cable system, router configuration errors between the file servers will interfere with network communications.

The DISPLAY NETWORKS command lists all network addresses and internal network numbers in use on the network system, as shown in Figure 15-6. In addition to showing the address of each network, the DISPLAY NETWORKS command shows the amount of time required to access the network, measured by the number of hops and ticks required to reach each network from the current server. Each *hop* is a router that must be crossed in order to reach the given network. Each *tick* is a time interval of one-eighteenth second. Notice that the DISPLAY NETWORKS command in Figure 15-6 shows that there are three known networks directly accessible to the file server and that only one tick is required to get to each network.

Figure 15-6

Sample DISPLAY
NETWORKS command

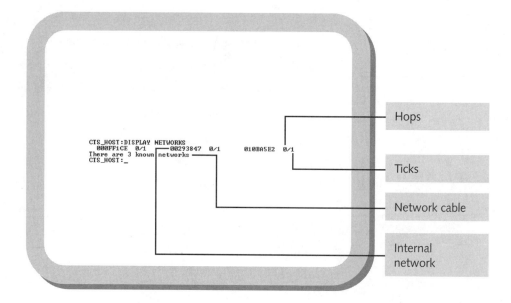

The DISPLAY SERVERS command is useful to determine if the file server is prop-erly attached to a multiserver network. When a file server is first attached to a network, it sends a broadcast to all machines on the network advertising its presence. From these broadcasts, the file servers and workstations on the network build **router tables** that include the names of all servers and routers on the network. The DISPLAY SERVERS command lists all servers that have been inserted into the router table.

If a new server does not appear in other server router tables and if the new server does not "see" the other servers on the network, your file server is not properly commu-nicating with the network. The most common problems causing this are that the IPX protocol has not been bound to the network card or that the network card driver is using a frame type that is different from that of other servers. If the new file server shows up on other file servers, but no file servers appear on the new server, it can mean that the network card in the new server has a conflicting interrupt or memory address and is not able to receive network packets from other servers. In this case, use the CONFIG command to check for an overlapping interrupt or memory address.

The LIST DEVICES command lists information about all storage device drivers attached to the file server, including disk drives, tape drives, and CD-ROMs. Information includes device number, description, and the NetWare assigned device ID, as shown in Figure 15-7, and can be useful when you are checking to see if all devices are loaded.

The MEMORY command allows you to determine the total amount of memory available to the file server. If you have over 16 Mbytes of memory and if the total file server memory displayed is 16 Mbytes or smaller, you might need to use the REGISTER MEMORY command to enable use of the memory above 16 Mbytes. If you have fewer than 16 Mbytes, and the memory displayed is smaller than the total memory in the file server computer, check to be sure that the computer is not load-ing HIMEM.SYS when DOS is booted. Loading HIMEM.SYS can take up part of the extended memory available to the NetWare operating system.

Figure 15-7

Sample LIST DEVICES
command

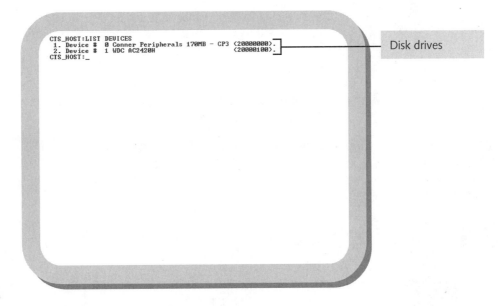

The NAME command simply displays the name of the file server on the console. By default, the NetWare v3.12 and v4.x operating systems display the server name as part of the console prompt, so the NAME command is not needed to identify these file server consoles. With NetWare v3.11 or earlier, however, the file server name does not appear as part of the console prompt. You might find the NAME command useful when you are working in an environment with several older file servers. You can confirm the name of the file server console on which you are working.

As shown in Figure 15-8, the PROTOCOL command displays all protocols that are registered with the file server along with the network frame types associated with the protocol. Initially, only the IPX protocol is registered with the NetWare operating system. Other popular protocols, TCP/IP for example, need to be loaded and registered before they can be used. After being registered, a new protocol can be bound to a LAN driver with the BIND command described earlier. Loading the TCP/IP protocol on a file server is described in more detail later in this chapter.

Figure 15-8

Sample PROTOCOL
command

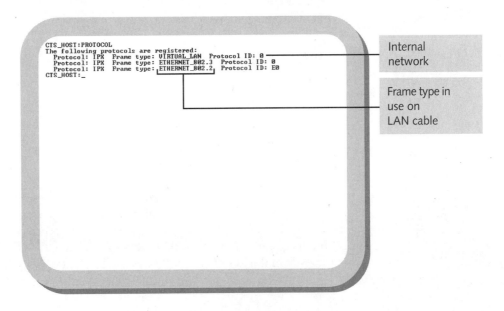

When you load another protocol module, it might be necessary to use the PROTOCOL REGISTER command to assign a frame type and protocol ID number to the new protocol.

Use the SET command to view or change settings for the configuration categories shown in Figure 15-9. The SET parameters in each of these categories will be described in more detail in Chapter 16.

Figure 15-9

SET configuration options

```
CTS_HOST:SET
Settable configuration parameter categories
    1. Communications
    2. Memory
    3. File caching
    4. Directory caching
    5. File system
    6. Locks
    7. Transaction tracking
    8. Disk
    9. Miscellaneous
Which category do you want to view: _
```

Use the SET TIME command to change the current server time or date. The following commands show four variations of using SET TIME to change the file server's current date and time to 3:00 P.M., October 30, 1999:

    SET TIME 10/30/99 3:00p.m.

    SET TIME October 30, 1999 3:00p.m.

    SET TIME October 30, 1999

    SET TIME 3:00p.m.

Maintenance commands

The maintenance commands shown in Figure 15-10 are the console commands commonly used by the network administrator to control access to the file server and volumes, to broadcast messages, to look for network problems, and to shut down the file server for upgrades or maintenance.

Use the BROADCAST command to send a message to all users who are currently logged in to the file server. The message will appear on the user's workstation unless the user has issued the CASTOFF ALL command to prevent all messages from being displayed. The CASTOFF command without the ALL option allows messages from the server to be displayed and ignores messages from other workstations. Users should be discouraged from using the ALL options with the CASTOFF command because it can result in the loss of data if the server is brought down without their knowledge.

Figure 15-10

Maintenance
commands

Command Syntax	Description
BROADCAST *message*	Sends the specified *message* to all currently logged in users.
CLEAR STATION *number*	Terminates the specified workstation connection number in the command.
CLS/OFF	Clears the file server console screen.
DISABLE/ENABLE LOGIN	Prevents or enables new user logins.
DOWN	Closes all files and volumes, disconnects all users, and takes the file server off line.
EXIT	Returns the server to the DOS prompt. If DOS is not loaded, the server computer will reboot.
MODULES	Lists all currently loaded modules starting with the last module loaded.
MOUNT *volume_name* [ALL] DISMOUNT *volume_name* [ALL]	Places a volume on or off line. Replace *volume_name* with the name of the volume you want mounted or use ALL to mount all NetWare volumes.
RESET ROUTER	Rebuilds the file server's router table, including any new servers and removing any servers that do not respond.
SCAN FOR NEW DEVICES	Registers new devices that have been switched on since the server was booted.
SEND *"message"* [TO] *username|connection_number*	Sends a message to a specified user. Replace *message* with a message enclosed in quotes you want sent. Replace *username|connection_number* with either the name of the currently logged in user or the connection number assigned to the user. The *connection_number* can be obtained from the Connection option of the MONITOR NLM.
TRACK ON/TRACK OFF	Displays service advertising packets that are sent or received.
UNBIND *protocol* [FROM] *LAN_driver|board_name*	Removes a protocol from a LAN card. Replace *protocol* with the name of the protocol stack (e.g., IPX) you want to remove from the card. Replace *LAN_driver|board_name* with either the name of the driver program that has been loaded for the network card or the name assigned to the network card by the LOAD command.
UNLOAD *module_name*	Removes a NetWare Loadable Module from memory and returns the memory space to the operating system. Replace *module_name* with the name of the currently loaded module, as stated in the MODULES command.

Use the CLEAR STATION command to terminate a workstation's connection to the file server. A connection to a file server is made when the workstation runs the DOS requester (VLM) or DOS shell (NETX). The connection continues to be active—whether or not a user is logged in to the file server—until the workstation is rebooted or turned off. If a user is logged in when the connection is cleared, data can be lost due to incomplete updating of files that are open at the time the station's connection to the file server is terminated.

Each NetWare operating system is designed to support a maximum number of connections depending on the license purchased. If your maximum number of connections is reached and if you have workstations not currently being used, you can use the CLEAR STATION command to terminate unused connections, making room for other workstations to be attached to the file server. You can use the MONITOR utility, described later in this chapter, to determine which connections are not currently being used.

Another use for the CLEAR STATION command is to force workstations to log off the file server prior to downing the server or performing a backup. Before terminating a connection, however, always use MONITOR to determine if any data files are open and, if possible, use the SEND command to send a message to the user of that station to close the open files and log out.

The CLS and OFF commands can be used to clear the file server console screen, allowing you to see new console messages more easily. A common practice is to use the CLS or OFF command prior to loading new modules or recording error messages.

The DISABLE LOGIN command prevents new users from logging in to the file server. Prior to downing the file server, you should issue the DISABLE LOGIN message to prevent any additional users from logging in. Then use the BROADCAST command to send a message to all connected users telling them that the server will be downed after the specified time period and that they should close all files and log out of the server. If the DISABLE LOGIN command is not issued, new users can log in to the server after the message is broadcast, unaware that the server is about to be downed.

The DOWN command deactivates the NetWare server operating system and removes all workstation connections. Before issuing the DOWN command, you should disable new logins and broadcast a message to all users. You can then use the MONITOR command to be sure all connections are logged out prior to entering the DOWN command. The command sequence is shown in Figure 15-11.

If active sessions exist, the NetWare operating system will issue a warning message asking you if you want to terminate active sessions. If you see this message, you should cancel the DOWN command and use the MONITOR utility to determine which connections have open files. Then send messages to those users to log out. If no one is at the workstation and data files have been left open, you will need to go to the station yourself to close the open files and log out for the user. Remind users that their workstations should not be left unattended while data files are open.

Figure 15-11

Command sequence for
downing a file server

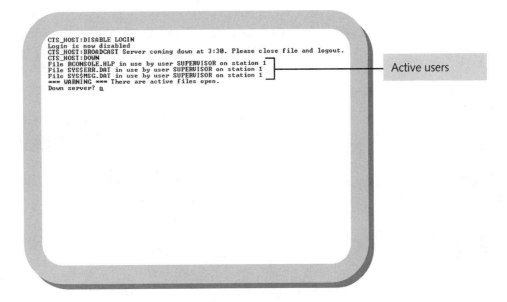

```
CTS_HOST:DISABLE LOGIN
Login is now disabled
CTS_HOST:BROADCAST Server coming down at 3:30. Please close file and logout.
CTS_HOST:DOWN
File RCONSOLE.HLP in use by user SUPERVISOR on station 1
File SYS$ERR.DAT in use by user SUPERVISOR on station 1
File SYS$MSG.DAT in use by user SUPERVISOR on station 1
*** WARNING *** There are active files open.
Down server? n
```

Active users

The EXIT command terminates the NetWare operating system and attempts to return the computer to the DOS prompt. If DOS has been removed from the file server computer with the REMOVE DOS command, NetWare will reboot the file server computer when the EXIT command is executed.

Mounting a volume is the process of loading information from the volume's directory entry table into the file server's RAM. This makes the volume available for access by users and the file server's operating system. The MOUNT command is needed to mount a volume that has been taken off line with the DISMOUNT command or a volume that did not mount correctly when the file server was booted. Normally, the MOUNT ALL command is inserted into the file server's AUTOEXEC.NCF startup file during installation. It attempts to mount all volumes when the file server is brought up. In some cases, however—such as after a file server crash—some volumes might not mount due to errors in their file allocation tables (FATs) or DETs. When this happens, it is necessary to use the VREPAIR module to correct the FAT problem and then use the MOUNT command to bring the repaired volume on line. More information regarding use of the VREPAIR command to fix volume problems is presented later in this chapter.

The MODULES command lists all the currently loaded modules with their names, version numbers, and release dates. The modules are listed in sequence, starting with the last module loaded and ending with the first module loaded. In addition to showing what modules have been loaded, the MODULES command also lets you quickly check the version number and date of a module. You need this information to determine NetWare compatibility or to look for network problems that are known to be caused by defective versions of certain modules.

The Novell NetWire forum, along with the Novell internet home page, are good places to check for information regarding problems with NLMs. They also provide information on obtaining corrected versions of the defective modules.

When a new file server is first brought onto a network, it sends out **service advertising packets (SAPs)** to inform all other machines of its name and network address. Other machines on the network then add the new server to their router tables, allowing them to pass packets to any of the servers. The DISPLAY SERVERS command allows you to view all machines currently in a server's router table. Servers continue to send out SAPs periodically to notify other servers that they are still available as well as to notify new servers of existing server name and address information. When a server is taken off the network, it can take a few minutes for all machines to become aware that the server is no longer sending advertising packets. There is thus a time delay before the inactive server is removed from the router tables. This means that servers can appear in the DISPLAY SERVERS list after they have been taken off the network. The RESET ROUTER command causes a server to rebuild its router table by sending out a broadcast packet asking all servers to identify themselves with their SAPs.

You should normally use the RESET ROUTER and DISPLAY SERVERS commands on a new server to confirm that the new server can communicate with other servers on the network. On a large internetwork it can take several minutes for a downed server to be removed from all server router tables. Because of this, it is a good idea to issue the RESET ROUTER command prior to the DISPLAY SERVERS command, when you want to view the active server list. Then you can be sure all servers listed are currently on the network.

The SCAN FOR NEW DEVICES command causes the NetWare operating system to check for any new devices that have been brought on line since the file server was booted. The most common use for this command is if you have external tape and CD-ROM devices attached to the SCSI interface. If a tape drive or CD-ROM device is not turned on when the file server is booted, it will not be available for use unless you issue the SCAN FOR NEW DEVICES command. On a DOS workstation, you are forced to reboot DOS in order to recognize new devices—such as a mouse or external CD-ROM that has been plugged in to the system after DOS has been loaded. The SCAN FOR NEW DEVICES command allows the NetWare operating system to register new devices without having to be restarted.

The SEND command on the file server console is the same as the SEND command you use from a DOS workstation. The most common use of the SEND command is to request a user to log out prior to downing the file server. Messages can be sent either to a user's login name or to a connection number by enclosing the message in quotation marks and following it with the connection number or username.

The TRACK ON command can be used to view SAPs and router information packets that are either received by or sent from your file server, as shown in Figure 15-12. All servers, including a print server or MHS messaging server, periodically send out SAPs to inform other machines of their presence. In addition to SAPs, file servers periodically (approximately once each minute) send out special packets called **router information packets (RIPs)**. The RIP contains a list of all network addresses and the number of ticks and hops required to reach each network from the sending server.

This router information is used by other servers on the network to maintain their local router tables. The router table on your default server is what allows you to attach or log in to servers located in other areas of the network. Use the TRACK ON command to display any SAPs and RIPs with the name and network address of the sender. This information can help you determine what is happening on the network and whether or not the server in question is functioning properly. If, for example, a server is sending but not receiving any packets, it means the server is using the wrong frame type, other servers on the network are not functioning, or there is a problem with the network cable system.

If a server is on but does not show up in response to the DISPLAY SERVERS command, use the TRACK ON command along with the RESET ROUTER command to determine if the server is sending out SAPs. If the server is sending out SAPs but the SAPs are not being received, it can indicate an error in the network card or cable system. If SAPs are not being sent out from a server, it can mean the server is down or has crashed. You might need to reload the server in order to bring it back on line.

Figure 15-12

Sample TRACK ON command

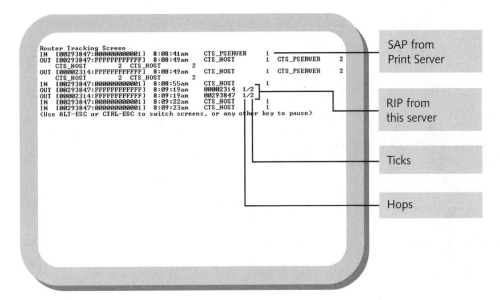

After the TRACK ON command is issued, the console screen displays all SAPs that are being sent or received. You can use the [Alt][Esc] key combination to change back to the console prompt or to any other module. To end the TRACK ON command, use [Alt][Esc] or [Ctrl][Esc] to return to the console prompt. Then enter the TRACK OFF command.

Use the UNBIND command to unload a protocol stack from a LAN driver causing the server to stop communicating with other machines using that protocol. The most common use of the UNBIND command is to take a defective server off the network. Assume, for example, you have bound the IPX protocol to a LAN driver and used the wrong network number for the cable system. Almost immediately, the servers on the network will begin to signal that router is calling the network a different name. To stop this problem, use the UNBIND command to remove the protocol from the network card and then re-issue the BIND command using the correct network address, as shown in Figure 15-13.

Figure 15-13

Sample UNBIND
command

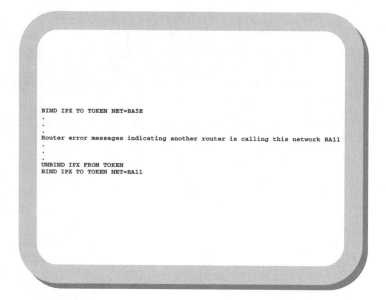

```
BIND IPX TO TOKEN NET=BA5E
.
.
.
Router error messages indicating another router is calling this network BA11
.
.
.
UNBIND IPX FROM TOKEN
BIND IPX TO TOKEN NET=BA11
```

The UNLOAD command terminates a NetWare Loadable Module and removes it from the file server's memory. If your file server has a marginal amount of memory, it might be necessary to remove modules in order to make space for file caching. Chapter 16 describes how to determine how much memory is available for file caching and whether or not it is necessary to unload any modules. Another common use for the UNLOAD command is to disconnect the server from a network card so that you can test or fix a problem without downing the server and affecting users on different networks.

Assume, for example, your server has both token ring and Ethernet cards in it and you need to take the token ring network down to do some maintenance. If you disconnect the server computer from the token ring cable, a string of error messages from the LAN driver indicating the card is not connected will tie up your server console. To prevent this from happening, use the UNLOAD TOKEN command to remove the TOKEN LAN driver prior to disconnecting the cable from the file server. Although the users on the Ethernet network will not be affected, make sure to notify all users on the token ring network that they need to log out before you unload the TOKEN LAN driver and disconnect the server or valuable data might be lost. After performing the necessary work on the token ring network, you re-establish communications with the token ring users by using the LOAD command to load the TOKEN LAN driver module and then using the BIND command to bind IPX to the token driver. The users on the token ring network can then log back in and resume using the server.

Security commands

Securing the file server console is necessary to prevent unauthorized users from entering console commands or loading NLMs. Depending on your organization, the need for file server console security can range from keeping the server in a separate room to providing maximum security from intruders who are attempting to gain access to your network. Locking the server room is one of the first measures of file server security that can be put in place. The security console commands shown in Figure 15-14 allow you to provide extra protection from unauthorized use of console commands.

Command Syntax	Description
REMOVE DOS	Removes DOS from the file server's memory, preventing opera-tors from loading modules from the DOS local drives. Causes the server to reboot when the EXIT command is used.
SECURE CONSOLE	Removes DOS and prevents NLMs from being loaded from any other directory except SYS:SYSTEM.

The REMOVE DOS command can provide some extra security by preventing access to DOS devices. In addition, removing DOS will cause the file server computer to reboot when the operator enters the EXIT command. If you can combine this action with removing the floppy disk drive, using a computer with a power-on password, and creating an AUTOEXEC.BAT file that contains only the commands necessary to start SERVER, you can practically prevent anyone from booting the computer as a DOS machine and running programs that can change information in the NetWare partition.

The SECURE CONSOLE command automatically performs the following security functions intended to prevent several types of breaches in security.

- Removes DOS

- Prevents NLMs from being loaded from any directory other than the SYS:SYSTEM directory

- Prevents keyboard entry into the OS debugger

- Prevents the use of the SET TIME command to change date and time from the console (a console operator or supervisor can still change the date and time by using the FCONSOLE utility from a workstation)

One way an intruder could access or alter information in the file server would be to load a special NLM from the console that directly accesses data files or the NetWare bindery. Because the SECURE CONSOLE command allows NLMs to be loaded only from the SYS:SYSTEM directory, an intruder will not be able to load the offending module from a DOS drive or some other directory on the server in which he or she has rights. For this reason, Novell recommends using the SECURE CONSOLE command. The only way an intruder can load a module after the SECURE CONSOLE command has been issued is to have necessary rights to copy the module into the SYS:SYSTEM directory. Of course, for this part of the SECURE CONSOLE command to be effective in preventing unwanted loading of NLMs, you must be sure that no one has rights to SYS:SYSTEM and that your supervisor accounts are secure.

Some security and accounting features depend on date and time for their enforcement. Suppose, for example, a payroll clerk's username is secured both by a password and by a restriction on when and from what workstation he or she can log in. An intruder learns the payroll clerk's password and gains access to the workstation on a weekend. Because the intruder has the equivalent of a master key, he or she gains access to the file server console and uses the SET TIME command to change the date and time to a normal weekday. The intruder can then access or change the payroll data files. The SECURE CONSOLE command would prevent this by disabling the

SET TIME command. The intruder would then need to log in as SUPERVISOR and use the FCONSOLE utility to change the server's date or time.

Another security measure that is easy to implement is to "lock" the server console and require the operator to enter a password to gain access to it. The MONITOR utility, described later in this chapter, can be used to lock the console and prevent intruders from gaining access to the console prompt.

NETWARE LOADABLE MODULES

One of the major strengths of NetWare v3.1x is its use of NLMs to add functionality to the core operating system. As discussed previously, the SERVER.EXE program provides the core NetWare services and acts like a software bus, allowing NLMs to be added to support hardware devices and software functions such as print servers and electronic messaging. Because NLMs play such an important role in the tailoring of the NetWare network, it is important that a CNA be familiar with the standard NLMs that are included with the NetWare operating system.

As shown in Figure 15-15, NLMs can be classified into four general categories based on their function. Each category has its own extension. In this section you will learn what you need to know about each of these NLMs in order, as a CNA, to manage your file server environments effectively.

Figure 15-15

NLM categories

Category	Extension	Description
Disk drivers	.DSK	Control access to the NetWare disk partitions.
LAN drivers	.LAN	Each network card must be controlled by a compatible LAN driver.
Name space modules	.NAM	Contain logic to support other workstation naming conventions, such as those found on Apple Macintosh computers or OS/2- and Unix-based computers.
General-purpose modules	.NLM	Add additional services and functions to the file server's operating system.

Disk drivers

When you first start the NetWare operating system by running the SERVER.EXE program, it does not have a way of directly controlling the disk drives on the file server computer until a disk driver module is loaded. Accessing the DOS partition of the hard disk and floppy disk drives does not require the disk driver. The DOS partition is available through the local DOS operating system until it is removed from the computer by either the REMOVE DOS or SECURE CONSOLE command. As described in Chapter 5, when NetWare is installed on the file server computer, disk driver modules with the extension .DSK are copied into the DOS partition. The command to load the appropriate disk driver module for your computer is later placed in the STARTUP.NCF file so that, when the SERVER.EXE program starts, it will load the correct disk drive in order to access the NetWare volumes.

LAN drivers

Before a file server can access the network cable, a LAN driver for the network controller card must be loaded and a protocol bound to that LAN driver. Common LAN drivers supplied by Novell with NetWare v3.1x were described in Chapter 5. Standard network drivers all have the extension .LAN and can be found in the SYS:SYSTEM directory after you have installed the NetWare operating system files. If your network card does not use one of the standard drivers, the correct driver software should be included on a disk that comes with the network card. You can initially load the LAN driver off the floppy disk by supplying the drive letter and path to the driver program using the command LOAD A:*path**driver_name*. Once the driver is loaded and you can log in to the network as SUPERVISOR, you will need to copy the driver program from the floppy disk into the SYS:SYSTEM directory so that it will be loaded automatically from the AUTOEXEC.NCF file.

Name space modules

Name space modules add logic to the NetWare operating system that allow it to support non-DOS filenames. By default, NetWare supports standard DOS file specifications consisting of eight-letter filenames and three-letter extensions. To support OS/2, and Macintosh filenames, however, which can contain up to 255 characters including spaces, special symbols, and graphic icon attributes, special NLMs, called name modules that can interpret these filenames must be loaded. Figure 15-16 contains two name modules that are included with NetWare and can be found in the SYS:SYSTEM directory with the .NAM extension. When you use name space support, you need to load the appropriate .NAM modules after the disk driver in the STARTUP.NCF file. Later in this chapter you will learn how to add and remove name space support from a volume.

Figure 15-16

NetWare name
space modules

Name Space Module	Description
MAC.NAM	Supports Apple Macintosh file naming conventions.
OS2.NAM	Supports IBM OS/2 workstation filenames.

General-purpose modules

In addition to special modules for controlling disk and network cards, a number of general-purpose NLMs are included in NetWare's SYS:SYSTEM directory. They have the extension .NLM and provide a wide range of capabilities, as described in Figure 15-17. The rest of this section describes the modules a CNA will use to manage network file servers.

CD-ROM.   The CD-ROM module allows a file server to use a CD-ROM device attached to a device driver as a read-only volume. In order to attach a CD-ROM device to your file server, you first need to obtain a CD-ROM device that has the necessary drivers for use with your NetWare file server, as described in Chapter 3. Most CD-ROM devices attached to NetWare servers today use a SCSI controller card along with associated SCSI disk driver software. You will often need to load additional support modules. If using the Adaptec SCSI controller card with a CD-ROM attached, for example, you would need to load the AHA1540 and CDNASPI modules along with the CD-ROM module in order to access the CD-ROM drive.

Figure 15-17

General-purpose
NetWare Loadable
Modules

Module	Description
CD-ROM.NLM	Provides support for CD-ROM commands.
INSTALL.NLM	Used to work with NetWare partitions, volumes, and system files.
MONITOR.NLM	Used to monitor file server performance, hardware status, and memory usage.
NLICLEAR.NLM	Immediately clears the workstation's connection when the corresponding workstation is shut off or rebooted.
REMOTE.NLM	Provides the ability to view and operate the NetWare server console from a remote workstation. Requires a password.
RSPX.NLM	Allows the REMOTE module to send and receive console screens and commands over the local network cable.
RS232.NLM	Allows the REMOTE module to send and receive console screens and commands over the asynchronous port.
UPS.NLM	Provides the ability to monitor the status of the UPS and down the server prior to depleting the battery.
VREPAIR.NLM	Checks the specified volume for errors and allows the operator to write corrections to the disk.

Sharing CD-ROMs that contain desktop publishing clip art, sound files, and video for multimedia applications is rapidly becoming an important function of the NetWare file server in many organizations.

After loading the CD-ROM module, use the console commands shown in Figure 15-18 to manage the attached CD-ROM devices. Use the CD DEVICE LIST command to obtain a list of volume names and device numbers.

If your CD-ROM is not listed by the CD DEVICE LIST command, check to be sure its power is on and the proper device driver and required support modules for the CD-ROM controller card are loaded.

Use the CD MOUNT command to mount a CD-ROM as a NetWare read-only volume. User workstations can then use a MAP command to assign a drive letter to the CD-ROM volume and access files. Because of the amount of information on CD-ROMs and their relatively slow access times as compared to fixed disk drives, it can often take several minutes to mount a CD-ROM volume.

When working with several CD-ROMs that have large directories, decrease the amount of time required to remount a volume by including the /R option with the CD MOUNT command. The /R option tells NetWare to reuse existing data files instead of rebuilding or recreating them.

Figure 15-18

CD-ROM commands

CD Command	Description
CD HELP	Displays a list of CD-ROM commands and options.
CD DEVICE LIST	Lists all CD-ROM devices that the NetWare operating system can access. Information about the CD-ROM devices includes: device number, name, volume name, and whether or not the CD-ROM volume is mounted.
CD VOLUME LIST	Displays a list of all CD-ROM volumes that are currently mounted.
CD MOUNT [*volume_name*] [*device_number*]	Mounts the volume specified by either the volume name or device number.
CD DISMOUNT [*volume_name*] [*device_number*]	Dismounts the specified volume, freeing up all system resources used by the volume.
CD CHANGE [*volume_name*] [*device_number*]	Allows you to change the CD-ROM mounted in the specified device. The volume specified will be dismounted and you will be prompted for the new volume. The new medium will be automatically mounted as a NetWare volume.
CD DIR [*volume_name*] [*device_number*]	Allows you to view the contents of the root directory of the specified CD-ROM volume. A volume does not need to be mounted for you to use the CD DIR command.

INSTALL.   In Chapter 5 you learned how to use the INSTALL module to perform such installation tasks as creating NetWare partitions and volumes on existing hard drives, copying all system and public files in the SYS: volume, and creating the STARTUP.NCF and AUTOEXEC.NCF files. After NetWare is installed, the CNA needs to know how to use the INSTALL module to add new disk space to an existing volume, maintain the STARTUP and AUTOEXEC files, and install new products such as the Message Handling System.

To add disk space to an existing volume, you need to have additional disk space available in the current NetWare partitions of existing disk drives or you need to add a new disk drive to the file server's computer. Adding disk space from another disk partition to your volume is called *spanning* the volume. One of the biggest problems of spanning a volume across multiple partitions is the increased probability that a failure of any of the drives the volume occupies will bring down the entire volume. Therefore, if you plan to span a volume onto a new drive, you should actually add two drives of the same capacity and then use the mirroring feature (described in Chapter 5) to synchronize the drives. This way, if one of the drives used by your volume fails, the mirrored drive will still allow access to the volume and its data.

A volume can have up to 32 segment assignments, each of which can exist on the same or separate NetWare partitions. Spanning a volume means that two segments of the volume reside on separate partitions.

After adding additional disk space, you can use the INSTALL module to expand a volume's size. First select the Volumes option from the Installation Options menu to list all existing NetWare volumes. Select the name of the volume you want to expand from the Volumes window and press [Enter]. A Volume Information window similar to the one shown in Figure 15-19 will then be displayed.

Figure 15-19

Volume Information
window

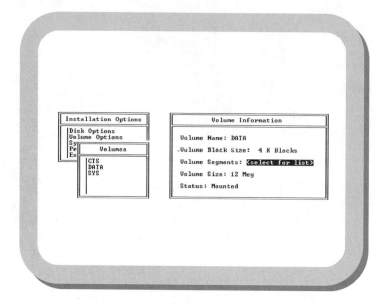

To expand the size of the volume, select the Volume Segments field. Pressing [Enter] displays the Volume Segments window, which shows each segment currently assigned to the selected volume. To add more space to the volume, press the Ins key. If your system contains free space on one or more NetWare partitions, the Free Space Available For Volume Segments window shown in Figure 15-20 will be displayed. The window shows the mirroring status of each partition. You can then select the NetWare partition you want to use in order to expand the volume. If you have free space available on only one partition, the new volume segment size will be displayed immediately after you press the Ins key. This window shows the total space available on the NetWare disk partition you selected, expressed in the number of blocks. To add part of the available partition disk space to this volume, enter the number of blocks you want to add to the volume size and press [Enter]. NetWare then asks you to confirm your entry before it adds the new volume segment to the existing Volume Segments window.

 If you have multiple partitions, select the partition containing the existing segments for the volume, if possible. If you are spanning a volume onto a second NetWare partition, you should mirror that partition to increase reliability and fault tolerance.

MONITOR.   The MONITOR utility module is one of the most powerful NLMs supplied with the NetWare operating system. In this section you will learn how to use the MONITOR utility to lock the file server console, as well as view file server performance, connection information, and disk and network statistics. Use of the MONITOR module to determine memory and resource allocation in the server computer will be described in Chapter 16.

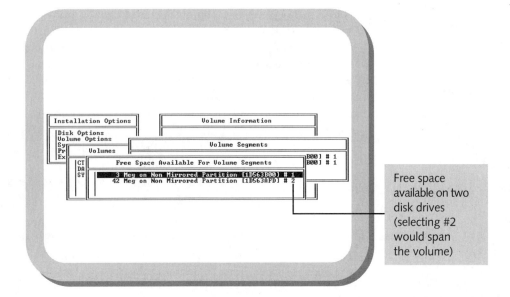

Figure 15-20

Available partitions
window

Free space
available on two
disk drives
(selecting #2
would span
the volume)

After the MONITOR utility is loaded, the main monitor screen shown in Figure 15-21 is displayed. Displayed in the top left of this screen are the version and date of the NetWare operating system. The Information For Server window displays information regarding the file server's available memory and performance.

The Information For Server window will be described in more detail in Chapter 16. For now, you should be aware of the following statistics displayed in the window. File Server Up Time measures the length of time the server has been running since it was last booted. The Utilization field shows the percentage of time the processor is busy. In most cases, utilization should be less than 70%. The Original Cache Buffers field contains the number of buffers (in blocks of 4 Kbytes) that were available when the server was first booted. The Total Cache Buffers field contains the number of buffers currently available for file caching. If the number of total cache buffers is less than one third of the original cache buffers, your server is running low on memory and you should either unload modules or add more RAM as soon as possible.

The Dirty Cache Buffers field contains a count of the number of buffers that have had modifications made but are waiting to be written to disk. A large number of dirty cache buffers indicates the disk system is bogging down and a faster disk or an additional disk controller card might be necessary. The Current Disk Requests field shows how many requests for disk access are currently waiting to be processed. Like the dirty cache buffers, this number can be used to determine if disk performance is slowing down the network.

On the right side of the window, the value in the Packet Receive Buffers field indicates the number of buffers that have been established to process packets that have been received by the server and are waiting to be serviced. In NetWare v3.12, the default value is 100. If the number displayed approaches the default maximum of 400, your file server is falling behind in servicing incoming packets and is therefore slowing down the network. Depending on the other statistics, you might need to add more memory to the file server, install a faster disk drive and controller, obtain a faster file server computer, or reduce the number of users by adding another server to the network.

The Directory Cache Buffers value indicates the number of buffers that have been reserved for disk directory blocks. Increasing the initial number of directory cache buffers available when the server first starts can sometimes improve the performance of the server when it is first booted. This will be described in Chapter 16. The Service Processes value indicates the number of task handlers that have been allocated for station requests. If the number of station requests in the Packet Receive Buffers field exceeds a certain limit, the server will add extra task handlers to execute the requests. Of course, this in turn reduces the amount of memory and processing time for other activities. If the number of Service Processes approaches the default maximum of 20 and you have a high processor utilization percentage, you might need to unload NLMs or add another file server to decrease the load on the current server.

The Connections In Use field can be used to see quickly how many stations are turned on and connected to the server. A station does not need to be logged in to appear in this statistic; any computer running the DOS requester or shell uses up a connection on a file server. You can use the Open Files field to determine if any files are currently open prior to downing the server.

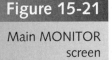

Figure 15-21

Main MONITOR screen

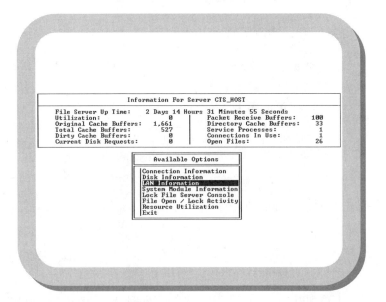

As you can see, the file server Utilization, Total Cache Buffers, and Dirty Cache Buffers statistics together can give you a quick picture of your file server's health. Simply verify that the utilization is under 70%, the total cache buffers figure is at least 50% of the original cache buffers figure, and that the dirty cache buffers figure is less than 30% of the total cache buffers figure.

In addition to the Information For Server window, the MONITOR utility has several options that you can use to view information about the performance and operation of your file server. Selecting the Connection Information option displays a window that shows all active connections and the usernames currently logged in. If no user is logged in to a given connection number, the message "NOTLOGGEDIN" will appear next to the connection number. To view information about any connection, select the connection number and press [Enter]. A window showing connection information for the user logged in to that connection will be displayed.

Also displayed are the names of any currently open files, as shown in Figure 15-22. Notice that the window shows the network address, the number of requests, kilobytes read and written, and currently open files for the selected username.

Figure 15-22

Connection information
window

Use the Disk Information option to check the status of a disk drive. The size of the disk drive, the disk driver, the number of partitions, mirroring, and hot fix status are indicated. A piece of information in the disk information screen that is important to monitor is the number of blocks that appear in the Redirected Blocks field. This number tells you how many times a block of the disk failed to work properly, causing data to be redirected to the redirection area of the disk partition. When the number of redirected blocks starts to grow, it is a sign that the disk drive is wearing out. You will want to make plans to replace it before all the redirection blocks are used up, at which point you will start losing data as a result of disk write errors.

Selecting the LAN Information option displays a window showing all LAN drivers currently loaded on the file server. If you are experiencing sluggish network performance and the file server utilization is low, you should use the LAN Information option to view the error summary for the network card. In addition to recording the total packets sent and received, the LAN Information option keeps track of a number of error statistics. Figure 15-23 lists common LAN error counts and it is important to check these if you experience error problems or slow performance on your network workstations.

The Lock File Server Console option allows you to establish a password lock on the file server. This prevents anyone from entering console commands unless he or she can enter the proper password. To prevent this option from being used to lock out the network administrator, the SUPERVISOR's password can also be used to access the console.

NLICLEAR. The NLICLEAR NLM will automatically clear a user's connection as soon as the user's workstation is rebooted or shut off. Normally a workstation's connection is not cleared until the server has not received any packets for several minutes. Clearing the connection immediately is important on file servers that are nearing the maximum number of connections allowed by their license, because it allows a new workstation to connect as soon as the connected workstation is taken off the network.

Figure 15-23

Common network
error counts

LAN Driver Error Field	Description
No ECB available	This counter increments when a device sends a packet to your file server and a packet receive buffer is not available. When this happens, the server automatically adds more packet receive buffers. If this error continues after the maximum 100 packet receive buffers have been assigned, it indicates the file server cannot keep up with the load. You will need to increase the performance of the server or offload the work by adding another server to the network.
Send packet too big	This counter increments when your server tries to transmit a packet that is too large to be handled by the network card in the server. Increases in this count normally indicate a bad network card or bugs in driver software on one of the workstations.
Receive packet overflow	This counter increments when your server receives a packet that is too big to store in a cache buffer. If this error is registered, you should contact your vendor for an updated version of the LAN software that can properly negotiate packet size.
Send packet retry	This counter increments when your server tries to send a packet until the retry count is reached and is unsuccessful because of a hardware error. If you receive this error frequently, check the network cabling and hardware. The retry count can be increased when a LAN driver is loaded with the LOAD command.
Checksum errors	This counter increments when the checksum byte at the end of a packet does not match the sum of the bytes contained in the packet. These errors are often the result of noise affecting the signal on the cable or bad connectors and cables.
Send abort from excess collisions	This counter is found on Ethernet network cards. It is incremented whenever a packet is not sent due to a large number of collisions on the Ethernet. If this error is registered, you should consider using a bridge to break the Ethernet or 10BA5ET network into two smaller networks. This will reduce the number of collisions.

RS232. The RS232 NLM is part of the remote console management system that allows the file server to be attached to a modem on COM1 or COM2. When used in combination with the REMOTE module, this module allows the network administrator to dial into the server using the ACONSOLE program from a remote computer and gain access to the file server's console screen. More information regarding the use of the RS232 and REMOTE modules is provided in the section Remote Console Management in this chapter.

RSPX. The RSPX NLM allows the remote console management system to communicate with workstations attached to the local area network cable. When used with the REMOTE module, RSPX allows the network administrator to use the RCONSOLE program from any workstation attached to the network and gain access to the file server's console screen.

REMOTE. The REMOTE NLM is the component of the remote console management system that communicates with a workstation running either RCONSOLE or ACONSOLE. It is responsible for sending console screens and receiving input from the remote workstation. REMOTE works with the RS232 module to communicate with remote workstations running ACONSOLE over a dial-up phone line. It also works with the RSPX module to communicate with local workstations running the RCONSOLE program.

When you load the REMOTE module, you will be prompted to enter a password. This helps prevent unauthorized access to the console from a remote workstation. The password can be included when you load the REMOTE module by specifying it after the REMOTE command. This is often done when the REMOTE command is inserted in the AUTOEXEC.NCF file in order to load it when the file server is booted (described in the next section). Whenever a workstation running either RCONSOLE or ACONSOLE attempts to access the server, the user will be prompted to enter this password before being granted access to the console screen. To provide additional security, the date, time, and node address of any workstation that accesses the console through REMOTE is logged to the console screen and file server log file. The file server's error log can be accessed by using the Supervisor Options of the SYSCON utility.

UPS. The UPS module allows your file server to monitor the status of the uninterruptible power system, enabling the file server to down itself in the event of an extended power outage. In order for the UPS module to monitor the status of the UPS, you must obtain a UPS that has a NetWare-compatible interface board. The UPS can be connected to the file server in a number of ways, depending on the type of board. After connecting the UPS, you can then boot the server and load the UPS module using the following syntax:

```
UPS [type port discharge recharge]
```

When you load the UPS module, replace the *type* field with one of the connector types shown in Figure 15-24.

Figure 15-24

UPS connector
types

Connector Type	Description
DCB	The UPS is connected to a Novell Disk Controller Board (DCB). Replace the *port* field with any of the following port addresses: 346, 34E, 326, 32E, 286, or 28E, depending on the card settings.
EDCB	The UPS is connected to a Novell/Enhanced Disk Controller Board. Replace the *port* field with any of the following valid port addresses: 380, 388, 320, or 328, depending on the card settings.
KEYCARD	The UPS is attached to a special Novell key card. Key cards were shipped with earlier versions of NetWare to provide copyright protection by allowing the operating system to check for the correct serial number in the key card. In addition to providing copyright protection, key cards also contain a UPS monitoring port that can be used by NetWare v3.1x. Replace *port* with either 230 or 238, depending on the card settings.
MOUSE	The UPS is attached to the mouse port of the file server computer.

In addition to supplying the *type* and *port* fields, you need to replace the *discharge* field with the number of minutes the network file server can operate on UPS battery power before it depletes the battery. Refer to the UPS battery documentation for these time estimates based on the number of amps required by the equipment attached to the UPS. Next, consult the UPS owner's manual to determine how much time is required for the battery to be recharged after the UPS has been operating on battery power. The *recharge* field can then be used to provide an estimate of the number of minutes the battery will need to recharge after the server has been on battery power. As the battery ages, you should increase the time in the *recharge* field to always allow the battery to recharge fully.

VREPAIR.   The VREPAIR module can often be used to repair the file allocation table of a volume that cannot be mounted. If your file server crashes due to a hardware problem, power failure, or software bug, the file server might not restart because of errors in the FAT of the SYS: volume. In this situation, you can often use the VREPAIR utility to fix the problems in the FAT in order to mount the SYS: volume and get the server up and running again. Because of the importance of VREPAIR for fixing volume errors and in checking for volume problems, a CNA needs to be familiar with the VREPAIR utility. VREPAIR can be used to perform other tasks, such as removing name space support from a volume (described later in this chapter).

The VREPAIR utility is located in both the SYS:SYSTEM directory and the DOS C:\SERVER.31x directory on your file server. The purpose of having a copy in the DOS directory is to allow you to run VREPAIR from the C drive in the event the SYS: volume cannot be mounted due to a FAT or directory error.

VREPAIR can be used only on volumes that are not currently mounted on the server. If you want to use VREPAIR to check an existing volume, you first need to use the DISMOUNT command to close the volume and unload it from the NetWare operating system. When more than one volume is dismounted, VREPAIR displays a window allowing you to select the volume to be serviced. If only one volume is dismounted, VREPAIR assumes that volume is to be repaired and starts checking it immediately after you select the Repair a Volume option from the VREPAIR menu.

After checking a volume, VREPAIR allows you to choose whether or not you want to save the repairs. If you save the repairs to disk, you should then run VREPAIR again to confirm that the volume has been fixed. It sometimes happens that when repairs are written to disk, other volume errors are generated. Running VREPAIR a second time allows you to check and fix any new volume errors that were not detected in the previous run. Once VREPAIR runs with no errors, you can mount the volume.

Another problem that sometimes occurs when VREPAIR runs is that valuable data files are corrupted when VREPAIR writes its fixes to the disk. Any time FAT entries are modified, there is a risk that data in the files being fixed can actually be lost due to incorrect reconnection of FAT chains. In a worst-case scenario, lost or corrupted records in an important database file might not be discovered until several weeks or months have elapsed, causing lost time and money for a company. To help prevent this problem, VREPAIR reports each file in which it finds FAT or directory problems. You can make a note of each file and then thoroughly test or restore the data from any important database or document files.

To use the VREPAIR command to check or fix problems on an existing volume, enter the command LOAD VREPAIR. This displays the Volume Repair Utility menu shown in Figure 15-25. If you are using VREPAIR to fix problems on the SYS: volume that prevent it from being mounted, you will need to load the VREPAIR program from the DOS partition by using the command LOAD C:VREPAIR. Next, select option 2 in order to view and set the VREPAIR options shown in Figure 15-26.

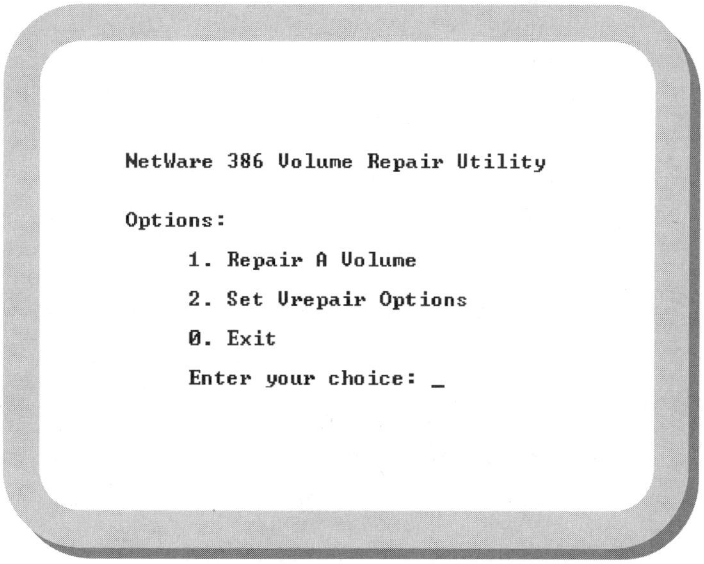

Figure 15-25

VREPAIR main menu

```
NetWare 386 Volume Repair Utility

Options:
        1. Repair A Volume
        2. Set Vrepair Options
        0. Exit
        Enter your choice: _
```

Figure 15-26

VREPAIR options

```
Current Vrepair Configuration:

    Quit If A Required URepair Name Space Support NLM Is Not Loaded
    Write Only Changed Directory And FAT Entries Out To Disk
    Keep Changes In Memory For Later Update
    Retain Deleted Files

Options:

    1. Remove Name Space support from the volume
    2. Write All Directory And FAT Entries Out To Disk
    3. Write Changes Immediately To Disk
    4. Purge All Deleted Files
    0. Return To Main Menu
    Enter your choice: _
```

Notice that the currently active settings are displayed on the top of the screen. Additional options, preceded by numbers, are listed on the lower half of the screen. The default settings are correct for normal needs. If you want to write the entire FAT and directory table to disk, rather than just the repaired entries, you can select option 2. This moves the Write All Directory And FAT Entries Out To Disk item to the top half of the screen. Generally it is best to use the Keep Changes In Memory For Later Update item. This gives you the option of writing the changes to disk after you have noted all files that are being fixed. Use option 0 to return to the VREPAIR main menu after you have finished setting options on the VREPAIR configuration screen.

Select the "1. Repair A Volume" item from the main menu to start the volume repairs. If there is more than one volume currently dismounted, VREPAIR allows you to select the volume to be repaired. If only one volume is currently dismounted, VREPAIR immediately begins scanning that volume. If no volumes have been dismounted, the error message "There are no unmounted volumes" will be displayed. To dismount a volume, use the [Alt][Esc] key combination to access to the console screen. Then use the DISMOUNT command to make the desired volume available to the VREPAIR program.

During the repair process, VREPAIR will stop whenever it encounters a FAT or directory error and report the error message along with the filename. In order to verify that the files are correctly restored by VREPAIR, you should record the error messages and filename. You can then have the appropriate users check the status of the corrected files to determine if they were restored correctly.

Several weeks after using VREPAIR to fix problems on one of the file server's volumes, the network administrator was shocked to learn that a major database file had been damaged by the VREPAIR program and no current backup was available. This problem might have been prevented if the network administrator had noticed that the FAT for the database was corrected by VREPAIR and had then notified users to check the database for any problems.

To record filenames and error messages automatically in a text file for later analysis, press the F1 key to display the additional VREPAIR options as shown in Figure 15-27. Use option 2 to write each message to the text file you specify. Use option 1 to prevent VREPAIR from pausing after each error message. Option 0 allows you to continue with volume repair process.

Figure 15-27

Additional VREPAIR
options

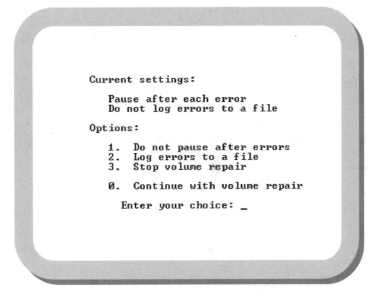

```
Current settings:

    Pause after each error
    Do not log errors to a file

Options:

    1.  Do not pause after errors
    2.  Log errors to a file
    3.  Stop volume repair

    0.  Continue with volume repair

        Enter your choice: _
```

After the volume has been restored, VREPAIR pauses and asks if you want to write the repairs to disk. Normally you should enter Y and press [Enter] to write the new FAT and directory table to the disk. If you have written any changes to disk, you should run the VREPAIR program again to scan the volume and check for any additional volume problems. In some cases, it will take several passes to fix all problems. When you receive a clean report showing that there are no corrections to write to disk, you can exit the VREPAIR program and mount the volume.

REMOTE CONSOLE MANAGEMENT

There are times when it is difficult or time consuming to go to the file server console to check server status, make changes, or fix problems with the NetWare operating system. Sometimes it means spending valuable time driving to the file server's location just to spend a few minutes at the console. To get around this problem, NetWare makes it possible to perform console operations from a workstation computer located on the local network or attached through a wide area network via telephone. Prior to NetWare v3.1, the FCONSOLE utility was the only way to monitor and control a file server from a workstation attached to the network. Although FCONSOLE allows a network administrator to view a NetWare v2.x file server's performance and perform functions such as disabling logins and downing the server, it does not provide remote access to the server's console to enter commands and manage the server's operation.

With NetWare v3.11, Novell developed the **Remote Management Facility (RMF)** to enable a network administrator to manage all file servers, version 3.11 and greater, from one location. RMF actually brings the file server's console screen to the remote workstation, allowing the network administrator to work with the server as if he or she were actually at the file server computer. In addition to providing convenience and time savings of managing all file servers from one location, the RMF can also increase file server security by allowing the network administrator to remove the monitor and keyboard from the file server computer and lock the file server in a restricted area where access can be controlled.

Access to the Remote Management Feature is controlled by assigning a password to each file server console and locating the RCONSOLE and ACONSOLE utilities in the SYS:SYSTEM directory where only the SUPERVISOR has rights to use them. As a result of these measures, only the SUPERVISOR or a remote console operator can use the remote management feature to manage a file server's console. A remote console operator is a user who has been granted the Read and File scan rights to the RCONSOLE program in the SYS:SYSTEM directory and has been given the file server console's password. The SUPERVISOR can also access a file server's console by running the RCONSOLE program from SYS:SYSTEM and supplying the SUPERVISOR's password to gain access to the server console.

 In order for the SUPERVISOR's password to be used to access a file server's console, the file server's SYS: volume must be mounted so that it can read the password from the bindery files.

A CNA needs to be able to perform the following functions to set up and use the Remote Management Feature to manage a remote file server:

- Access a file server and enter console commands from either a remote or locally attached workstation

- Scan directories and edit text files in both DOS and NetWare partitions on a remote file server

- Transfer files to (but not from) a remote file server

- Reboot a file server from the remote console

Understanding remote management

The remote management feature works by using software and hardware to establish with a file server a communication link that enables a workstation to act as the console's keyboard and display screen. Using RMF to control a console over the communication link does not disable actual console operation, but provides for concurrent operation of the file server console from both the file server computer and the remote workstation. This capability means a network administrator can perform certain console operations from a location other than at the file server. Three kinds of RMF communication links can be established: direct link, an asynchronous link, and a redundant link.

In a **direct link**, as illustrated in Figure 15-28, the workstation and file server are attached to the same network system, allowing packets to be sent directly from the workstation's network card to the file server. The advantages of a direct link include high speed, reliability, and the ability to copy files from the workstation directly to the file server.

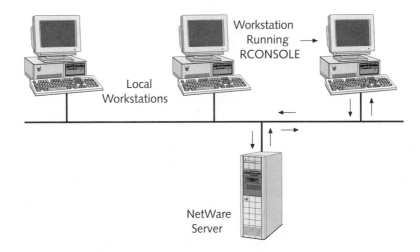

Figure 15-28

RMF direct
communication link

In an **asynchronous link**, as illustrated in Figure 15-29, the workstation and file server are connected by modems using a dial-up telephone line. The asynchronous link provides the ability to support a file server from any PC within reach of a telephone. It also means you can access the server if the network system is down. The major disadvantages of this system are its relatively slow speed and the possibility of communication errors, both of which slow down operations and prevent reliable transfer of large files from the workstation to the file server.

Figure 15-29

RMF asynchronous link

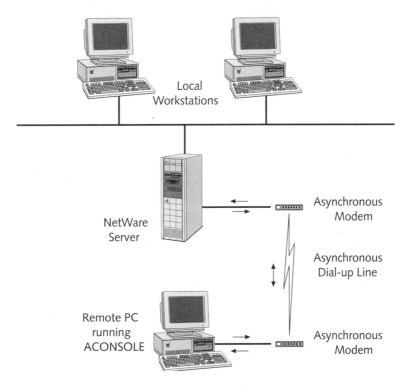

The term *asynchronous link* describes the way data is sent between the file server and the remote workstation. In asynchronous communication, each byte of data is sent separately, encapsulated with a start and stop bit. Asynchronous communication allows the use of lower-cost modems and is very effective for handling keyboard input between a terminal and host computer.

A **redundant link**, as shown in Figure 15-30, allows you to combine the speed advantage of a direct link with the fail-safe ability of an asynchronous link to access the file server console if the network system fails or if the network driver needs to be unloaded so a problem can be fixed or the driver software can be updated.

Figure 15-30

RMF redundant link

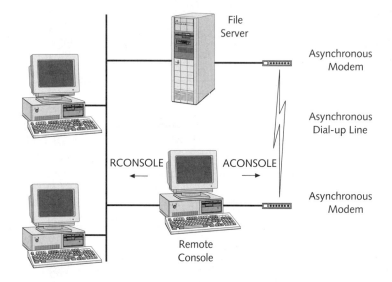

The advantage of a redundant link is the ability to access the server console in more than one way. This allows you to use the faster direct link for normal file server commands and to switch to the asynchronous link if the network fails or you need to unload the LAN driver software.

Before you establish the remote management feature on your network, you need to understand the hardware and software component requirements of both the file server and workstation for supporting communication links. These are illustrated in Figure 15-31.

Figure 15-31

RMF components

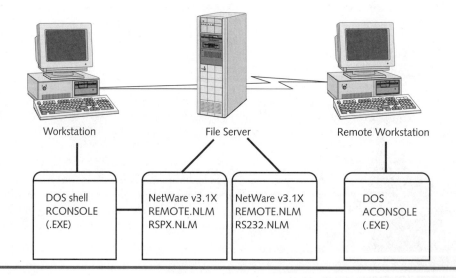

Workstation computer requirements. The workstation computer using a direct connection to the file server requires the following components:

- At least 640 Kbytes of RAM

- A network adapter card

- DOS operating system

- Workstation client software with either the DOS requester VLM or NETX shell

- Access to the RCONSOLE program in the SYS:SYSTEM directory

The workstation computer using an asynchronous connection requires the following hardware and software components:

- At least 200 Kbytes of RAM

- A COM1 or COM2 asynchronous communication port and Hayes-compatible modem capable of communicating at 2400, 4800, or 9600 bps. (currently the ACONSOLE software does not support higher modem speeds, such as 14.4 or 28.8 Kbps)

- A copy of the ACONSOLE program

File server computer requirements. In order to support either direct or asynchronous connections, the file server computer requires the following hardware and NLMs:

- 48 Kbytes of RAM beyond the file server's current minimum requirements

- A Hayes-compatible modem attached to either the COM1 or COM2 port capable of communicating at 2400, 4800, or 9600 bps

- The REMOTE module with a password to provide access to the server console

- The RSPX module to provide access from the REMOTE module to the network system

- The RS232 module to provide access from the REMOTE module to the asynchronous modem

Setting up remote management

Once you have determined that your file server and remote console workstation have the hardware needed to support the connection types you plan to use, the next step is to install RMF on each of the file servers to be managed. Setting up an RMF connection on a file server involves loading the appropriate NLMs for the connection type to be used. Placing commands for the desired connection type in the AUTOEXEC.NCF file will cause the server to load remote console management automatically each time the server is booted.

For a direct link connection, place the LOAD REMOTE and LOAD RSPX commands in the AUTOEXEC.NCF file, as shown in Figure 15-32. It is important to place the LOAD REMOTE command first. RSPX requires the REMOTE module in order to run. Notice the password following the REMOTE command. If no password is specified, the commands following the LOAD REMOTE command will not be executed until the operator enters the password. Placing a password after the LOAD REMOTE command allows the server to load the remote software automatically and continue without waiting for operator input. To support an asynchronous link, replace the LOAD RSPX command with the following command:

LOAD RS232 [*port number*] [*modem speed*]

The port number is either 1 or 2 depending on the communication port to which the modem is attached. *Modem speed* is either 2400, 4800, or 9600 bps, depending on the speed of the modem. If you do not enter a communication port or modem speed, the RS232 module will prompt you to select the communication port number and modem speed. Placing these values after the command allows the file server to start the remote console without operator intervention. For a redundant link, include both the LOAD RSPX and LOAD RS232 statements in the AUTOEXEC.NCF file, as illustrated in Figure 15-33.

Figure 15-32

Sample direct link commands

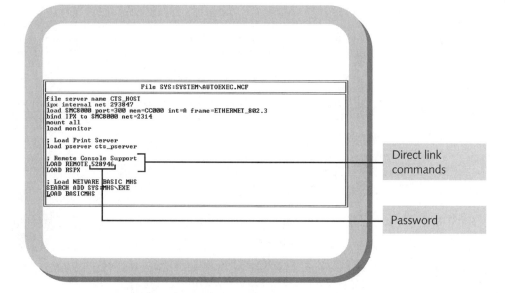

Figure 15-33

Sample redundant link commands

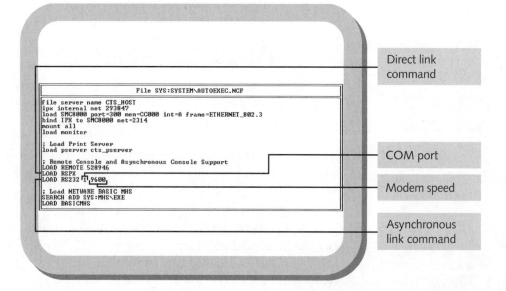

Creating a remote console operator

A remote console operator is a user who has been granted the rights necessary to run the RCONSOLE software and who also knows the password assigned to the REMOTE module. Suppose, for example, a network administrator wants to make a user a remote console operator so that the user can view and respond to any file server error messages when the administrator is unavailable. To create a remote console operator, first log in to the file server as SUPERVISOR and change to the SYS:SYSTEM directory. Use the following command to provide the specified user with the rights to run the RCONSOLE program.

```
GRANT R F FOR RCONSOLE.EXE TO username
```

After the necessary rights are granted, the user needs to be trained to run the RCONSOLE program and given the password needed to access the file server's console.

Starting RCONSOLE

Once the RMF software to support a direct link has been loaded on the file server, you can go to any workstation that meets the necessary hardware requirements and use the RCONSOLE utility to gain access to the console of the file server. First log in as the SUPERVISOR or remote console operator, change to the SYS:SYSTEM directory, and type RCONSOLE to display the Available Servers window. All servers on the network that are running the REMOTE and RSPX modules will appear in this window. Select the file server console you want to access and press [Enter]. The RCONSOLE program prompts you to enter the password for that file server. You can type either the remote operator password supplied when the REMOTE module is loaded or the SUPERVISOR's password and press [Enter]. The console of the selected file server is displayed; it shows whatever screen was last displayed on the server console. (If the MONITOR utility was used to lock the console, you will need to enter the correct password to unlock MONITOR before being granted access to the file server's console.) Now enter any console commands just as if you were operating on the actual file server computer.

One difference between the real console and the remote console is that the [Alt][Esc] key combination (used on the file server computer to switch from one console screen to another) will not work on the remote console. To rotate console screens with the RCONSOLE program you need to use the plus key (+) found on the numeric keyboard. The reason [Alt][Esc] doesn't rotate screens on the remote console is that it might already be programmed to rotate programs running on the local workstation computer, for example, Windows.

The RCONSOLE menu

The RCONSOLE program provides a number of additional functions through the Available Options menu, shown in Figure 15-34. This menu is available by pressing the asterisk key (*) found on the numeric keypad. (The shift-8 asterisk key will not open the menu.)

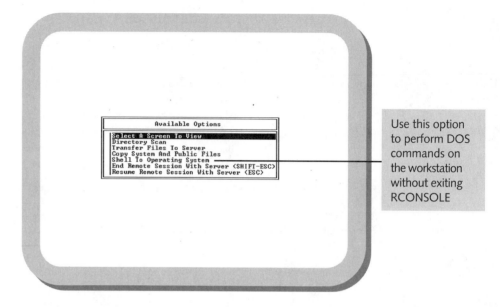

Figure 15-34

RCONSOLE Available Options menu

Use this option to perform DOS commands on the workstation without exiting RCONSOLE

The Select A Screen To View option displays a window containing all tasks currently running on the file server that have a display screen available. You can then change the console to any of the screens simply by entering the number of the screen you want to view and pressing the Enter key. This option is similar to using the [Ctrl][Esc] key combination from the file server computer.

The Directory Scan option allows you to search any DOS or NetWare directory on the file server by specifying the drive letter or volume name, followed by the directory path. You can also include a global file specification to search for specific filenames, as shown in Figure 15-35.

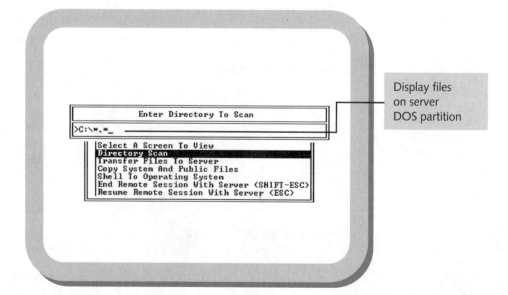

Figure 15-35

Directory Scan option

Display files on server DOS partition

The Transfer Files To Server option can be used to copy files from the local workstation to any DOS or NetWare directory on the file server. To update the DSK driver on the file server, for example, select the Transfer Files To Server option to obtain the Source Path on Workstation window. Then enter the drive letter along with the directory path and filename of the new DSK driver and press [Enter]. The RCONSOLE program displays the Target Path On Server window. To place the new DSK driver in the SERVER.312 directory of the server's DOS partition, type C:\SERVER.312 and press [Enter]. The RCONSOLE program copies the new DSK driver into the SERVER.312 directory of the server's C drive. (This operation will not work if you have issued the REMOVE DOS or SECURE CONSOLE command because the DOS partition will not be accessible to NetWare without the DOS operating system in memory.) To activate the new DSK driver, you need to down the file server and reboot it. This operation can be done from the remote console by following the instructions in the next section.

The Copy System And Public Files option is useful if you need to update the file server to a new release of NetWare while working from the remote console. It can often be more convenient to plug disks into the server from the comfort of your office rather than sitting in a room with the file server inserting disks each time the machine beeps.

The Shell To Operating System option may be used to access the DOS prompt on your workstation. This is handy because it saves you from having to exit the RCONSOLE utility in order to perform a DOS command. After completing the DOS function, you can use the EXIT command to return to the RCONSOLE menu.

Use the End Remote Session With Server option in place of the [Shift][Esc] key combination to exit the current remote console session and return to the Available Servers window. This can come in handy if you forget the [Shift][Esc] key combination.

The Resume Remote Session With Server option simply closes the Available Options menu and returns the remote workstation to the console screen. You can also use the [Esc] key to exit the menu and return to the console screen.

Rebooting the server from RCONSOLE

When disk drivers are updated or when a new version of the SERVER.EXE program is installed, the server computer needs to be downed and rebooted in order to effect the changes. If your file server is located miles away or if you have made the file server inaccessible for security reasons, you might prefer to use the following procedure to reboot the server computer from the remote workstation. To reboot the file server computer from RCONSOLE, you first use the DISABLE LOGIN command to prevent new users from logging in to the server and the BROADCAST command to send a message to all users that the server is going down in a few minutes. Next you need to check the DOS AUTOEXEC.BAT file to be sure it contains the commands necessary to start the file server when the computer reboots. To do this, use the LOAD EDIT C:\AUTOEXEC.BAT command from the remote console to view the current AUTOEXEC.BAT file. Make any necessary modifications to allow the server program to be started when the computer is rebooted. After you have checked the AUTOEXEC.BAT file, press the asterisk key on the numeric keypad to display the RCONSOLE Available Options menu. Then use the Transfer Files To Server option to copy any new files, such as new disk drivers, from your remote workstation to the SERVER.312 directory on the file server computer.

To reboot the file server from the remote console you need to perform the following console commands:

```
REMOVE DOS

DOWN

EXIT
```

The REMOVE DOS command causes the server to reboot automatically when the EXIT command is executed. Normally when the EXIT command is executed, NetWare returns the server computer to the DOS prompt. If DOS has been removed from memory, however, the server computer will reboot rather than return to the DOS prompt. To get around this, you need to remove DOS from memory. The next step is to issue the DOWN command, then the EXIT command—the EXIT command cannot be issued on a file server that is still active. The problem with rebooting the server from the remote console is that, when you issue the DOWN command, your remote workstation loses its connection and you therefore no longer have access to the console in order to type the EXIT command. The solution to this problem is to create a NetWare control file (NCF) that contains the necessary commands to reboot the server. You can then run the NCF from the remote console and the server will automatically go through the process of downing and rebooting itself. An NCF is much like a DOS batch file; it contains console commands that the server will perform when the name of the NCF is entered as a command line on the server console. NetWare control files allow you to create your own console commands that consist of one or more command statements and are stored as files in the SYS:SYSTEM directory with the .NCF extension. To create a NetWare control file called REBOOT.NCF that contains the commands necessary to reboot the file server, issue the following command:

```
LOAD EDIT SYS:SYSTEM\REBOOT.NCF
```

Then enter the statements necessary to reboot the file server. After entering the commands, use the Esc key to exit the EDIT program and save the REBOOT.NCF file in the SYSTEM directory. Now use the plus key (+) to change to the MONITOR screen. Check to make sure all files are closed and all users are disconnected. If necessary, send messages to any remaining users to close their files and log out.

After confirming that all users are logged out (except your current username), you can automatically reboot the file server. Enter the REBOOT command from the remote console. The server goes through the commands in the REBOOT.NCF file, causing DOS to be removed and then downing the server and rebooting through the EXIT command.

Because your workstation is currently logged in, before it goes down, the server displays a message informing you that there are active files open and asking if you want to continue downing the server. Respond with Y to continue downing the file server. The server will now down itself. In a few seconds you will receive a message on your screen indicating that the connection has been lost. Be patient and do not respond to the error message until several minutes have elapsed. Then press [Ctrl][Enter] to regain control of the file server console. If you cannot re-establish contact with the server, you can reboot the workstation, log in as SUPERVISOR, and rerun the RCONSOLE program.

Exiting RCONSOLE

To end the remote console session, first return the console screen to a secure state and then use the [Shift][Esc] key combination to end the remote console function and return to the Available Servers window. If you do not remember the correct key combination, use the asterisk key on the numeric keypad to display the Available Options menu. Then select the End Remote Session With Server option to exit the current file server console session and return to the Available Servers window. Pressing [Esc] from the Available Servers window will exit the RCONSOLE program and return to the DOS prompt.

To exit RCONSOLE without returning to the Available Servers window, use the asterisk key on the numeric keypad to display the Available Options menu. When the Available Options menu is displayed, use the [Alt][F10] key combination to display the Exit Remote Console window. Press [Enter] to exit the RCONSOLE program and return to the DOS prompt.

Using ACONSOLE

The ACONSOLE software is used to access a remote file server's console using an asynchronous communication link with modems over a dial-up telephone line. This capability allows you to access your company's file server console directly from home or even from an island in the South Pacific. ACONSOLE is used by technical support companies to enable CNAs and CNEs to work with customer file servers and assist in installations or upgrades without having to leave their offices.

If you are planning to run the ACONSOLE program from a workstation that is not connected to a NetWare network, you will need to copy the following files from the SYS:PUBLIC directory to the workstation that will be used as a remote console:

```
IBM$RUN.OVL

CMPQ$RUN.OVL

$RUN.OVL

SYS$ERR.DAT

SYS$HELP.DAT

SYS$MSG.DAT
```

In addition to these files, you will need to copy the ACONSOLE.EXE and RCONSOLE.HLP files from the SYS:SYSTEM directory to the remote workstation's disk. The total disk space required for all files is less than 200 Kbytes which can easily fit on one floppy disk.

Once all files have been copied to the remote workstation and the phone line is attached to the modem, you can change to the disk and directory containing the remote files and run the ACONSOLE program to view the menu shown in Figure 15-36. Before using the ACONSOLE program, you need to use the Configure Modem option to configure the modem parameters, as shown in Figure 15-37.

Figure 15-36

ACONSOLE
Main Menu

Figure 15-37

Current Modem
Configuration window

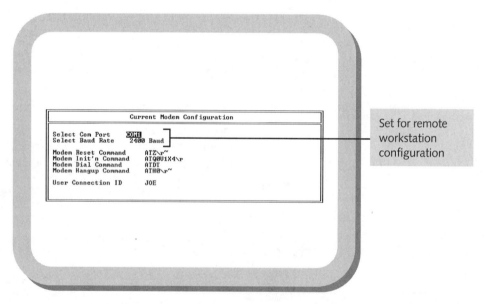

Set for remote
workstation
configuration

The Select Com Port and Select Baud Rate fields should be set to conform to the port and speed of the modem attached to your remote workstation computer. If you are using a Hayes-compatible modem, the default entries in the four modem fields can be left unchanged. The User Connection ID field is used for identification purposes during connection to the file server and must contain an identifying entry. After all fields have been entered, press [Esc] to save the entries and return to the ACONSOLE Main Menu.

After the modem has been correctly configured, select the Connect To Remote Location option to initialize the modem. This displays a window showing the locations and phone numbers of the file servers you can call. Initially this window will be empty. To add a server to the location list, press the [Ins] key and enter the location and phone number of the server to be accessed as shown in Figure 15-38.

Figure 15-38

Adding a new server
location to ACONSOLE

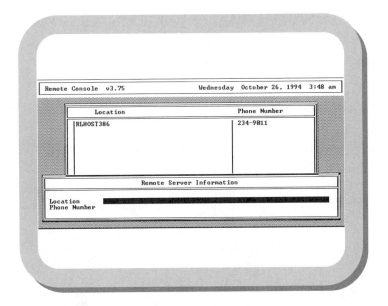

```
Remote Console  v3.75                    Wednesday  October 26, 1994  3:48 am

                Location                        Phone Number
    RLHOST386                            234-9011

                       Remote Server Information
    Location
    Phone Number
```

To call a server, highlight the target server in the location window and press [Enter].
The ACONSOLE program dials the specified number and waits for the remote server
to answer. When the server answers, ACONSOLE establishes an asynchronous communication link and asks you to enter the correct password to gain access to the
remote server's console.

After the correct password has been entered, you will see the current screen on the
server displayed on your remote workstation. At this time you can perform almost all
functions and key combinations that are used with the RCONSOLE program. The
exception is the Copy System And Public Files option. Obviously, copying all system
and public files over a modem, even at 14.4 Kbps, would take hours and probably
result in many corrupt files. An advantage of using ACONSOLE over RCONSOLE
is that you can down the file server or unload the disk driver and LAN driver and still
have control of the console. When you are using RCONSOLE, downing the file
server, dismounting the SYS: volume, or unloading the LAN driver takes the file
server off the network and disables your remote console connection. Because
ACONSOLE communicates through the asynchronous port, however, it does not
require the LAN or disk driver to be loaded in order to operate and can continue the
remote console connection until you issue the EXIT command.

SERVER PROTOCOL SUPPORT

As described in Chapter 2, a protocol defines the rules and formats used for communication between computers attached to a network. In this section, you will learn
what a CNA needs to know about implementing and supporting different types of
protocols on NetWare file servers. Protocols in this section are divided into two types:
lower-level protocols consisting of the OSI data link and physical layers and higher-
level protocols consisting of the OSI network and transport layers.

LOWER-LEVEL PROTOCOLS

Lower-level protocols control the formatting of packets, called frames, that are sent over a specific type of network system, such as Token Ring or Ethernet. As described in Chapter 2, the formatting of data frames is controlled by the data link layer of the OSI protocol stack. The data link layer uses IEEE 802.2 standards to provide control fields that are used to process the packet and extract the data segment information, which is then passed to the higher network layers. Data frames that are formatted with the IEEE802.2 Logical Link Control layer are referred to as 802.2 frame types. While the IEEE802.2 frame type can be used on different topologies, including Ethernet and token ring, some operating systems and protocol stacks might use other frame formats. On Ethernet networks, for example, there are several common frame types, as shown in Figure 15-39.

While different frame types can be used on the same Ethernet network at the same time, only computers using the same frame type can intercommunicate. This means that each frame type forms a different logical network over the same cable system.

Figure 15-39

Ethernet frame types

Frame Type	Usage
ETHERNET_802.2	Standard frame type used with NetWare v3.12. Conforms to IEEE 802.2 Logical Link Control layer specifications.
ETHERNET_802.3	Standard frame type used with versions of NetWare before v3.12.
ETHERNET_II	Frame type commonly used with TCP/IP Unix hosts and AppleTalk Phase I.
ETHERNET_SNAP	This frame type can be used by TCP/IP and AppleTalk Phase II.

Using multiple frame types

A task CNAs commonly encounter is adding a NetWare v3.12 file server to an existing Ethernet network that contains workstations or servers that use an earlier version of NetWare. Before NetWare v3.12, NetWare did not default to the IEEE802.2 Logical Link Control layer to process Ethernet frames. Instead it used a frame format referred to as 802.3. As a result, when a NetWare v3.12 server is installed with the default 802.2 frame type on an existing network that uses 802.3 frame types, the new server will not communicate with v3.11 or older file servers and workstations.

The best way to solve this problem is to convert all existing workstations and file servers to the new 802.2 frame type. On small networks, this can be done quite quickly by using the conversion techniques described in this section. It is often not feasible, however, to convert a large network consisting of hundreds of workstations and several file servers all at once. In these situations, it is often desirable to add support for IEEE 802.3 frame types to the v3.12 server until all the existing servers and workstations can be converted.

Adding two or more frame types to a single network card causes the file server to treat the network card as two separate logical networks, each one having a unique network address. Because this increases both the processing overhead on the file server and network traffic, you should plan to convert computers using the IEEE 802.3 frame type to 802.2 as soon as possible. To add IEEE 802.3 frame type support to a NetWare v3.12 file server, use the following LOAD command to load the Ethernet driver a second time. The command includes FRAME= parameter to specify the 802.3 frame type.

LOAD *driver_namev* FRAME=ETHERNET_802.3 NAME=*board_name*

Replace *driver_name* with the name of the currently loaded LAN driver for the Ethernet card to which you are adding the 802.3 frame type. Replace *board_name* with a name consisting of up to 17 characters that can be used to identify uniquely the 802.3 frame type. (If you do not specify a frame type, NetWare will ask if you want to add another frame type to the previously loaded adapter, as described presently). The message "Previously loaded module was used re-entrantly" will then appear, indicating that the new frame type is attached to the existing LAN driver.

 If you load a driver a second time with a different frame type, NetWare might query if you want to add a second frame type to the previously loaded adapter. Enter Y to add another frame type and then select the desired frame type from the possible selections given.

Because the new frame type is treated as another logical network, before NetWare can use the new frame type to communicate with other servers and workstations you need to bind the IPX protocol to the frame type and assign a network address using the following BIND command:

BIND IPX TO *board_name* NET=*net_address*

Replace *board_name* with the board name you assigned when you loaded the 802.3 frame type. Replace *net_address* with a unique network address consisting of up to eight hexadecimal digits, as described in Chapter 5 under file server installation.

After the IPX protocol has been bound to the 802.3 frame type, use the CONFIG command to view the frame types and network addresses associated with the adapter. An example of an Ethernet adapter is shown in Figure 15-40. Using the DISPLAY SERVERS command on the file server console or the SLIST command on a workstation should now display all file servers on the network.

Figure 15-40

Verifying frame types

```
CTS_HOST:CONFIG
File server name: CTS_HOST
IPX internal network number: 00293847

SMC EtherCard PLUS Server Driver v4.16 (930503)
     Version 4.16    May 3, 1993
          Hardware setting: I/O Port 300h to 31Fh, Memory CC000h to CFFFFh, Interrupt
   Ah
          Node address: 0000C0AC9D56
          Frame type: ETHERNET_802.3
          No board name defined
          LAN protocol: IPX network 010BA5E2
SMC EtherCard PLUS Server Driver v4.16 (930503)
     Version 4.16    May 3, 1993
          Hardware setting: I/O Port 300h to 31Fh, Memory CC000h to CFFFFh, Interrupt
   Ah
          Node address: 0000C0AC9D56
          Frame type: ETHERNET_802.2
          No board name defined
          LAN protocol: IPX network 000FF1CE
CTS_HOST:_
```

HIGHER-LEVEL PROTOCOLS

By default, NetWare uses the internetwork packet exchange, or IPX, as its higher-level protocol, which controls the formatting and routing of packets between networked computers and the file server. IPX is very efficient and reliable for delivering packets throughout a local area network. Its drawbacks, however, are that it is a proprietary system not available on several popular operating systems (Unix and Macintosh, for example) and that it does not support all the features found in certain wide area network protocols, such as TCP/IP. In order for Unix and Macintosh computers to communicate with the file server, it is necessary to add support for the TCP/IP and AppleTalk higher-level protocols and for other operating systems' directory information. In this section, you will learn how to load support for the TCP/IP protocol and add name space support for Macintosh and other operating systems.

Supporting TCP/IP

TCP/IP is the standard protocol used to connect Unix-based computers and to communicate over the Internet. As a result, the use of TCP/IP has grown rapidly, and many network administrators are finding it important to support TCP/IP on their NetWare servers.

In future releases of NetWare, Novell plans to include TCP/IP and IPX as a built-in protocol for communicating between the server and NetWare clients. This will allow organizations to support only TCP/IP on their networks rather than both TCP/IP and IPX, as is required now.

The **TCP/IP** protocol consists of two components, TCP and IP, that make up two layers of the OSI model, as described in Chapter 2. The IP, or internet protocol, layer is responsible for routing packets between different networks. The TCP, or transport control protocol, layer handles such functions as acknowledging the successful delivery of packets and controlling the flow of packets between computers. Higher-level programs, such as Simple Network Management Protocol and Network File System, provide support for managing the network and sharing files and printers. The TCP/IP protocol suite supports standard drivers such as Ethernet and token ring.

There are three major ways in which TCP/IP can be supported on your file server. First is for your file server to be able to act as a TCP/IP router, forwarding TCP/IP packets from one network card to another, as shown in Figure 15-41. In this example, a Unix host computer is located on the same Ethernet network to which your file server is attached. Workstations on the token ring network also need to gain access to the Unix host in order to run programs and access data. With TCP/IP support loaded on the NetWare file server, the file server can act as an IP router, enabling packets from the workstations located on the token ring network to pass across to the Ethernet and be picked up by the Unix host.

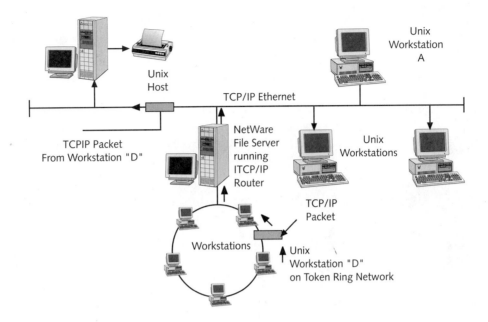

Figure 15-41

Using NetWare as a TCP/IP router

The second type of TCP/IP support is to provide a way for workstations using Novell's IPX protocol to communicate with a file server across a TCP/IP network, as shown in Figure 15-42. In this case, the file server can be located in a remote location. The TCP/IP host is used as a router, sending IPX packets across the wide area network in order to reach the file server. This technique is referred to as **tunneling** because the IPX packets are encapsulated, or "tunneled," inside TCP/IP packets, which allows them to pass through the IP routers.

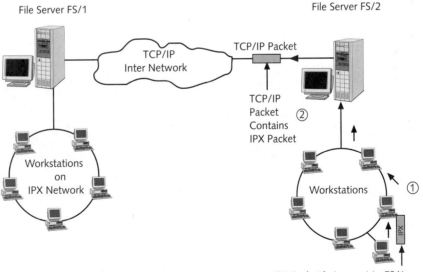

Figure 15-42

Tunneling IPX Packets through TCP/IP

The third type of TCP/IP support is to allow Unix hosts to store and access files in NetWare volumes. This requires that you load the Unix Network File System (NFS) for NetWare on your file server in addition to the TCP/IP protocol. When

NFS is used, both Unix and DOS workstations will have access to common files and printer resources, making NetWare a true integrator of different operating system environments.

Adding TCP/IP support to your file server involves loading several NLMs on the server. Which NLMS you need is determined by the level of support you want to obtain. NetWare v3.1x includes support for routing TCP/IP packets and tunneling IPX packets. If you need to allow Unix hosts to save files or use NetWare printers, you will need to purchase Novell's NFS package, which contains the necessary NLMs to support the Unix Network File System.

Another consideration in implementing the TCP/IP is the correct frame types. One of the first things you need to do in order to support TCP/IP on a token ring or Ethernet network is to add support for the correct frame types to your server's network card driver, as described in the previous section.

TCP/IP addressing

The TCP/IP protocol uses a 32-bit logical address consisting of network and node numbers assigned to each device attached to the network. The 32-bit address is expressed by four decimal numbers separated by periods. One to three of the numbers express the address of the network; the remaining number or numbers identify the station's address. Class A addresses use the leftmost number to represent the network address and the remaining three numbers to represent the node or station address. Class B addresses use the leftmost two numbers to represent the network address and the remaining two numbers to represent the node or station address. Class C addresses use the three leftmost numbers for the network address and the remaining number represents the node or station address. You can determine the class of a TCP/IP address by the value in the leftmost number of the address, as shown in Figure 15-43. All TCP/IP addresses that have a value between 0 and 127 in the first number belong to class A; values between 128 and 191 belong to class B, and values between 192 and 255 belong to class C.

Figure 15-43

TCP/IP address classes

TCP/IP Address Class	Address Range		
Class A	0.0.0.0	through	127.0.0.0
Class B	128.0.0.0	through	191.0.0.0
Class C	192.0.0.0	through	255.0.0.0

When supporting TCP/IP on your file server, you need to understand the different address classes in order to assign a valid address to your file server computer when binding IP to the network card, as described in the following section.

Using a server as a TCP/IP router

In this section you will learn how to load the necessary TCP/IP support on your NetWare file server so that it can act as a TCP/IP router to connect workstations on a token ring network to Unix hosts attached to an Ethernet network system. Before loading TCP/IP support, make sure your file server meets the following hardware requirements:

- An additional 4 Mbytes of RAM.

- An additional 1 Mbyte of disk space on the SYS: volume for TCP/IP files.

- A network adapter that will support TCP/IP frame types. On Ethernet this means supporting Ethernet_II or Ethernet_SNAP frame types. On token ring networks, the driver must support the Token_SNAP frame type.

After you have verified that your computer meets the hardware requirements of TCP/IP, you support the routing of TCP/IP packets through your file server between Ethernet and token ring networks by first issuing the following LOAD commands to add the SNAP frame type support to both your existing Ethernet and token ring LAN drivers.

```
LOAD driver_name FRAME=ETHERNET_SNAP NAME=ETHERNET_TCP
```

```
LOAD TOKEN FRAME=TOKEN_SNAP NAME=TOKEN_TCP
```

Next, issue the following LOAD command to load the TCP/IP support modules into the file server's memory and provide support for routing IP packets.

```
LOAD TCPIP Forward=yes
```

After the TCP/IP support has been loaded, you can use the BIND command to attach the IP protocol stack to the LAN drivers and assign an IP address to each network. The IP address you specify for each network must consist of both network and host components, as defined by the TCP/IP address class you are using. In addition, the network portion of the address must be the same as that used by other hosts that share the cable system. In this example, assume you are using class B addresses that consist of 2-byte network and 2-byte host addresses and that the Unix host on the Ethernet uses an IP address of 1.1.0.1. Based on this, you assign the NetWare server an IP address on the Ethernet of 1.1.0.2 and an IP address on the token ring of 1.2.1.0. The following BIND commands will bring the system onto both the Ethernet and token ring networks:

```
BIND IP TO ETHERNET_TCP NET=1.1.0.1
```

```
BIND IP TO TOKEN_TCP Net=IP=1.2.1.0
```

After binding IP to the network cards, you can use the PROTOCOLS command to verify that the IP protocol has been registered in the server. Use the CONFIG command to verify network card configurations. You can also use the PING *IP_address* command on TCP/IP workstations to determine if the file server and Unix host computers can receive packets. The PING command sends an IP packet to the host identified by the *IP_address* parameter and waits for a reply. When the Unix host or router receives the packet, it returns an acknowledgment, which verifies that the router and host computers can communicate with the workstation. If no response packet is received by the workstation computer, an error message will be displayed, indicating that the specified host does not exist. If this happens, you need to check all your connections, frame types, and the IP address to be sure everything is properly configured. If you are still unable to communicate through the router, you might require the services of a TCP/IP or Unix expert to identify and resolve the problem.

SUPPORTING MULTIPLE NAME TYPES

If your file server is able to support different operating systems—such as Unix, Macintosh, OS/2 or Windows 95—on its workstations, you will want to be able to support the file naming conventions of these operating systems. Because NetWare is separate from DOS or any other local workstation operating system, it is capable of supporting any operating system's file naming conventions. It converts them internally to NetWare core protocol requests, allowing users to see the files and objects in a familiar way. If Macintosh users are connected to the NetWare file server, for example, they can see their files and printer objects on the network represented by the icons and long filenames with which they are familiar. DOS and Windows users can see these same files and printers using filenames and object types that are compatible with their workstation environments. By default, NetWare supports standard eight-character DOS filenames and extensions.

To support other operating system file naming environments, it is first necessary to add logic to the server that enables it to support each workstation's operating system's file naming conventions. Second, it is also necessary to add space in the directory entry tables for each volume that will be using additional file naming systems. The additional name space is needed for the longer names and additional attributes to be stored on that volume.

Before adding name space support to a volume, you need to load the appropriate .NAM name space module for that operating system. This was described in the NetWare Loadable Modules section of this chapter. Once you establish name space support, whenever the file server is booted, the name space module must be loaded. This allows the server to mount the volume that contains the other operating system naming conventions. To ensure that the name space module is loaded before you attempt to mount any volumes, place the load command for the appropriate name space module in the STARTUP.NCF file.

Once the necessary name space support module has been loaded, the next step is to add space for the new file naming conventions to each volume that will be used to store files from that operating system. Before adding name space support to your volumes, you need to determine what volumes are going to be used to support the additional operating system naming conventions. Novell recommends that support should be included for no more than one additional name space on any existing volume and that the SYS: volume should not contain any other operating system naming conventions.

The reason for limiting name space support to only one additional type per volume is that it requires more system overhead in terms of processing time and memory. It becomes more difficult to back up and restore information on the volumes that contain multiple naming conventions. For example, if you want Macintosh users to use the NetWare file server to share files, if possible, you should create a separate MAC: volume and then add name space support only for Macintosh to the MAC: volume. If you do not have the disk space to create a separate MAC: volume, the next best choice is to add Macintosh name space support to the existing DATA: volume, leaving the SYS: volume to support standard DOS filenames only.

To add Macintosh name space support to an existing DATA: volume, first use the LOAD MAC command to add name space support logic for Macintosh filenames to your file server's operating system. Next you need to add space in the directory entry table of the DATA: volume to support longer Macintosh filenames and graphic attributes. This can be done by entering the following ADD NAME SPACE command at the server console:

ADD NAME SPACE MAC TO DATA:

 The ADD NAME SPACE command needs to be entered only once to add space in the DET for Macintosh filenames. Subsequently, use Macintosh filenames on this volume, you need to load the MAC name space module in the STARTUP.NCF file only.

After name space has been added to the volume(s), you next need to modify the STARTUP.NCF file to load the name space support module whenever the file server is booted. To add the LOAD MAC command to the STARTUP.NCF file, you can use either the EDIT C:\SERVERv.31x\STARTUP.NCF command or the INSTALL module to modify the contents of the STARTUP.NCF file.

 If you know you will be adding name space support to a volume, it is more efficient to add name space support when the volume is first created. This will allow NetWare to place the name space extensions closer to the volume's directory entry table and make access to the name space more efficient.

Removing name space support

As your network grows, it might become desirable to move files that require name space support to a separate volume. Assume, for example, your DATA: volume is currently used to store both Macintosh and DOS files and that the DATA: volume is filling up due to the large number of Macintosh files that are stored there. To correct this problem, you have obtained permission to expand the disk system by adding a separate volume for Macintosh files. After the new disk drive and volume have been installed, all existing Macintosh files will be moved to the new volume and name space support for Macintosh filenames can be removed from the DATA: volume.

To remove name space support from a volume, you need to dismount the volume and then use the VREPAIR utility to remove the name space support. First use the LOAD VREPAIR command to display the VREPAIR menu, shown in Figure 15-25 in the NetWare Loadable Modules section of this chapter. In order for VREPAIR to access the extra name space support, it needs additional program logic. You provide this by loading the corresponding VREPAIR name space support module. By default, NetWare includes the V_MAC.NLM and V_OS2.NLM modules to support Macintosh and OS/2 name support.

To load Macintosh name space support for the VREPAIR volume, use the [Alt][Esc] key combination, or the plus key (+) if you are working from the RCONSOLE program, to change from the VREPAIR menu to the file server's console prompt. Next, use the LOAD V_MAC command to load Macintosh name space support into the VREPAIR module. This provides it with the logic necessary to work with the Macintosh name space. Now use the [Alt][Esc] key combination, or the plus key if you are working from the RCONSOLE program, to change back to the VREPAIR menu.

After loading the VREPAIR name space support module, you need to select the option to remove name space support. Select "2. Set Vrepair Options" from the main volume repair menu to display the VREPAIR options screen shown in Figure 15-26. To remove Macintosh name space support from the dismounted volume, identify the name space support to be removed by selecting "1. Remove Name Space support from the volume." Press [Enter] to display a window showing all NetWare-defined name space options. Next select "1. MACINTOSH" and press [Enter] to add the option of removing Macintosh name space to the top of the VREPAIR option screen. Now use option 0 to return to the main VREPAIR menu.

To start the process of removing the selected name space, select "1. Repair A Volume." If you have more than one volume dismounted, the VREPAIR utility will display a window of volume names. Select the appropriate volume name. To remove Macintosh support from the DATA: volume, type the corresponding number and press [Enter]. VREPAIR removes the Macintosh name space support from the DET of the DATA: volume. During the name space removal process, VREPAIR pauses for each filename that needs to be corrected and waits for you to press any key to continue. To continue having to respond to each message, you can use the F1 key to assign a filename to contain the messages, as described earlier in this chapter. This prevents VREPAIR from pausing after each message.

As it does with other volume repairs, after the name space is removed, VREPAIR stops and, if it has found any problems with the volume, asks if you want to write the corrections to the disk. Enter Y to correct any invalid entries and update the volume. Macintosh name space support has now been removed from the DATA: volume. Use the "0. Exit" option to end the VREPAIR module. You can now use the MOUNT command to remount the volume and make it available to users on the network.

PROTECTING NETWORK DATA

An organization's data plays a critical role in today's highly competitive and rapidly changing world of business and industry. A company robbed of its information would certainly suffer major losses and could even be forced out of business. As a network administrator in an organization that relies on the network for data storage and retrieval, therefore, you become the "keeper of the flame." You are responsible for many, if not all, of your organization's critical data files. Management counts on your knowledge to provide a reliable storage system that is secure from unauthorized access and protected from accidental loss due to equipment failure, operator error, or natural disaster.

In previous chapters you learned how the NetWare network can be used to establish a secure directory structure that protects the organization's data from unauthorized access. Another advantage of the NetWare network operating system is its ability to provide a centralized backup-and-restore procedure that can protect valuable data from being lost due to equipment or operator error. With NetWare, you can also implement a disaster recovery procedure that can enable your organization to continue to operate despite the loss of the file server or even an entire building.

THE STORAGE MANAGEMENT SYSTEM

NetWare v3.12 includes a **Storage Management System (SMS)** that allows you to back up even complex networks consisting of data that resides on multiple file servers as well as data on DOS and OS/2 workstations. The file server that runs the backup program and has the tape or other backup medium attached to it is referred to as the **host server**. The file servers and client workstations that are being backed up are referred to as **target machines**. In SMS, the term **parent** refers to a data set, such as a directory or subdirectory. The term **child** refers to a specific subordinate of a data set, such as a file or program. SMS uses NLMs on the host server to communicate with modules on target devices, reading the information from the target devices and sending it to the backup medium as illustrated in Figure 15-44.

Figure 15-44

SMS Backup Process

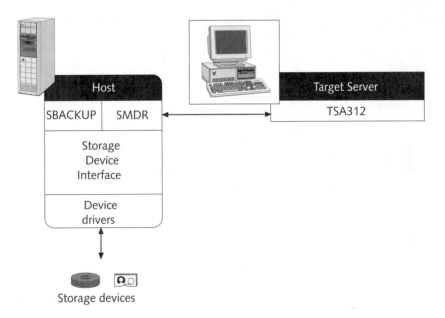

The NetWare SMS consists of the following software components. They can be run on NetWare file servers as well as on DOS or OS/2 workstations.

- Storage device drivers that are loaded on the host server. They control the mechanical operation of various storage devices and media, such as tape drives.

- Target server agents (TSAs) that are loaded on the target servers. They communicate with the SBACKUP program through the store management data requester (SMDR). The purpose of TSAs is to get information from the target server's volumes and send it to the SBACKUP program running on the host server. A server can act as both host and target by running both the SBACKUP and TSA software.

- Workstation TSAs that are run at the DOS or OS/2 workstations. They back up data located on the local drives across the network through the SMDR.

- The SBACKUP utility. This NLM provided with NetWare v3.1x is the principal module that works with the SMS architecture to control the backup process on the host server. It makes requests for data to the SMDR device and then routes the returned data to the storage device interface

(SDI). SDI software is part of the SBACKUP software and uses device drivers to pass commands and data between SBACKUP and the storage device driver. The SMDR software is also loaded on the host server and passes commands and information between the SBACKUP program and the TSAs.

ESTABLISHING A BACKUP SYSTEM

The first step in establishing a backup system for your network is calculating how much data needs to be copied to the backup tape on a daily basis. First, determine what volumes and directories you plan to back up. If possible, you should then try to obtain an SMS-compatible tape backup system that has capacity sufficient to store one day's records on one tape cartridge. In a single-file-server environment, the file server acts as both the host and target devices requiring you to load both the SBACKUP and TSA modules on the same server. An advantage of one file server functioning as both host and target device is that a file server backing up its own data runs almost four times faster than a host file server backing up data across the network from a target file server. When you implement SMS in a multiple-file-server environment, you should plan on making the file server that has the largest amount of data be the host system.

Installing SMS on the file server

In order to use the SMS software to back up data, you need to install a backup tape device along with its software drivers on the host file server. The host file server will need to have 3 Mbytes of RAM above the minimum required to run NetWare and at least 2 Mbytes of free disk space on the SYS: volume for temporary file storage. In addition to storing temporary files on the host server, the SMS also stores temporary files on the target servers. It is important to monitor the size of these files regularly (using the command SYS:SYSTEM\TSA$TMP.*) because they can become quite large. Erase them as necessary.

After the tape backup system has been installed on the file server computer, the next step is to configure the SMS software to use the correct driver software. When the SBACKUP program is loaded on the host file server, it scans in the SYS:SYSTEM\DIBI directory for a file called DIBI2$DV.DAT. It uses this file to load the device driver software that controls the tape drive. To prepare for this, prior to using the SBACKUP software you need to define the backup device driver that is going to be used to control your tape drive. Enter the name of the device driver along with any necessary parameters into the SYS:SYSTEM\DIBI\DIBI2$DV.DAT file by using a text editor program from a workstation or using the EDIT module on the file server console. To modify this file, you first need to log in from a workstation computer, change to the SYS:SYSTEM\DIBI directory, and then use the FLAG command to change the file attributes to normal (Read Write and non-Sharable) as follows:

```
CD SYS:SYSTEM\DIBI

FLAG DIBI2$DV.DAT N
```

Next, use the DOS EDIT command to call up the DIBI2$DV.DAT file. Then modify it to include the device driver you will be using. A sample DIBI2$DV.DAT file is shown in Figure 15-45. When you add a new device driver, it is important to include the exact driver name and any necessary startup parameters for the tape driver software. Then save the file before exiting the EDIT program.

Figure 15-45

Sample
DIBI2$DV.DAT
file

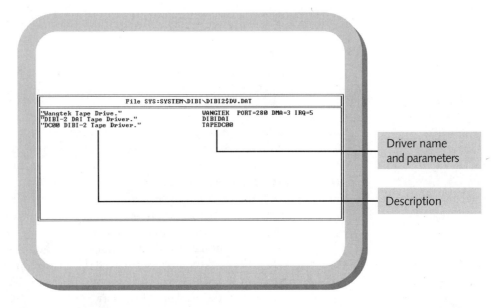

Running SBACKUP

After you modify the DIBI2$DV.DAT file, the next step is to test the SMS installation by backing up your file server data and then testing the backup by restoring selected files from the backup tape. To test the SMS backup, you first need to return to the file server console screen in order to load the TSA software on the host file server. To load the target server software on a NetWare v3.12 file server, enter the command LOAD TSA312 on the console screen. To back up the file server data, enter the LOAD SBACKUP command. This loads the SMC backup software and the necessary driver and support modules specified in the DIBI2$DV.DAT file. If you have more than one device driver in the DIBI2$DV.DAT file, SBACKUP will ask you to select the device driver to be used. After the device driver is initialized, the backup main menu shown in Figure 15-46 will be displayed.

Figure 15-46

SBACKUP main menu

Highlight the Select Target To Backup/Restore option and press [Enter]. This displays a window showing all available target devices currently running the TSA software. Select the target server to be backed up and press [Enter]. You are returned to the main backup menu options screen. To back up data from the selected server, use the Backup Menu option to display the backup menu. Select the Select Working Directory option and enter the path to a working directory in which session log and error files are to be stored. Often this directory is named BACKUPS and is stored off the root of the SYS: volume on the host file server. If the directory specified does not exist, the SBACKUP program can create it for you.

After the working directory has been specified, use the Backup Selected Target option to select the directories and files to be backed up. Once the directories to be included on the backup are selected, complete the backup screen by entering a title for the backup session and pressing the Esc key to start the backup process. When starting the backup process, you will be given options to start the backup either now or later. Starting the backup later, for example, can cause the process to begin sometime during the night when users are not logged in to the file server. If you decide to start the backup now, you should first disable logins and require all users to log out of the file server before the backup process is started. This is necessary to ensure that all files will be copied to the backup tape because files that are currently open and in use will not be copied to the backup. Then start the backup session and insert the tape cartridges as requested.

After a backup has been completed successfully, try testing your backup system by restoring selected files from the backup medium. Doing a complete restore is often not feasible due to time constraints as well as to the possible loss of data should the restore process fail. To restore selected files, select the Restore option from the main SBACKUP menu. Enter the path to the working directory you used when the backup tape was created. Next, select the option to "Restore session" files and select the session you named previously when the backup was created.

 Because of the potential for data loss, before you perform a major restoration, you should start by restoring test files that are not needed or files that have been copied to another disk storage device.

Now fill in the restore screen shown in Figure 15-47 by entering the names of the files or directories you want to be copied from the backup tape to the server.

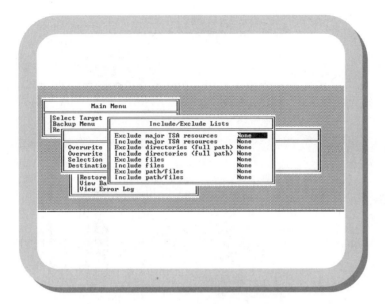

Figure 15-47

Restore screen

After the restore screen is filled in, press [Esc] and select the option to start the restore process. The selected files should be copied back to their appropriate directories. When the restore process is complete, log in from a user workstation and verify that the files have been correctly restored.

Developing a backup procedure

Once the backup system has been tested, you need to implement a reliable disaster recovery plan. This means developing a tape rotation procedure and backup schedule. A procedure that rotates multiple tapes means backups can be saved for long time periods. This is an important part of a disaster recovery plan because it provides a way to restore an earlier backup. It also provides a means of storing backup tapes in a separate building in order to protect them in case of catastrophic damage at your location. It is sometimes important to be able to recover a file from an earlier backup if that file should become corrupted by a software virus, operator error, or software bug and the damage to the file is not discovered for several days or weeks. If you were rotating your backups on a limited number of tapes, by the time such an error is discovered, the original backup containing the valid file might have been overwritten by a backup copy of the corrupted file. To help prevent this scenario, a good tape rotation system should consist of 19 tapes, as illustrated in Figure 15-48.

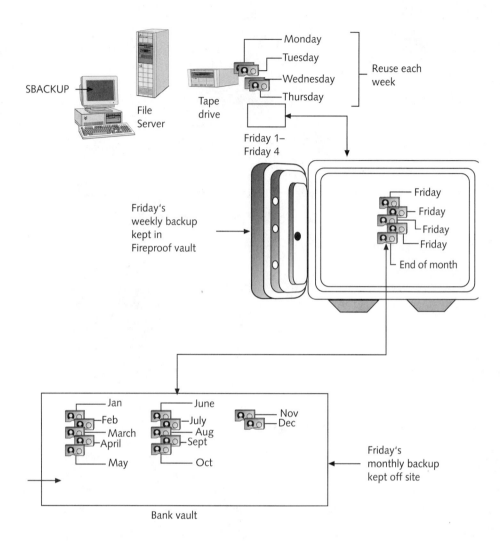

Figure 15-48

Tape rotation procedure

Four tapes are labeled Monday through Thursday and are rotated each week. Four tapes are labeled Friday 1 through Friday 4. Friday 1 is used on the first Friday of the month, Friday 2 on the second, Friday 3 on the third, and Friday 4 on the fourth. In addition, 12 tapes are labeled January through December. These tapes are rotated each year and can be used on the last Friday of each month by replacing the Friday # tape with the appropriate monthly backup. Another alternative, if someone is available to change the tape, is to make the monthly backup on the last Saturday of each month. The storage of the backup tapes is also important in the event of a fire or damage to the building. As a result, many administrators store weekly backups in an onsite fireproof vault and keep monthly backup tapes offsite in a secure location, such as a bank safety deposit vault.

The final step in implementing the backup system is to establish a time for the backup to be performed and to ensure that no users are logged in during the backup process. To prevent interference with user work schedules, many network administrators start the backup each night at about 12:00 midnight. To restrict night owls from working late, and to prevent users from leaving their workstations logged in during the backup, all user accounts, except the username used to backup the system, should have a time restriction to prevent users from accessing the network between 12:00 midnight and 5:00 A.M. This provides a 5-hour time interval that should be sufficient to create the backup. If extra time is needed, the backup can be set to begin at 11:00 P.M. and/or extend to 6:00 A.M., provided user time restrictions are also set for the longer backup period.

You need to develop a procedure to deal with the files in the working directory because the size of these files continues to grow with each backup that is made. The session files in the working directory play an important role in the restore process by allowing you to select quickly the files and directories you want to restore. One way to deal with the restore files is to copy them to a floppy disk each day and store the floppy disk with the corresponding backup tape. If you need to restore a backup tape, you can then copy the corresponding floppy disk into the working directory prior to restoring the files with the SBACKUP program. Using this procedure, each morning you can first check the status of the backup to be sure all files were successfully copied. Next, copy the files from the working directory specified in the SBACKUP program to a floppy disk and delete the session files in the working directory. Finally, store the backup tape and corresponding disk in a secure location. Once the disaster recovery procedure is in place and operating, you can rest easier knowing that you have done all you can to provide a secure environment for your organization's precious data and software.

CHAPTER SUMMARY

Managing the file server computer involves mastering the NetWare console commands and using several NetWare Loadable Modules to perform various tasks on the server computer. Console commands are built into the NetWare operating system and can be divided into four categories based on their use: installation commands, configuration commands, maintenance commands, and security commands. NetWare Loadable Modules are external programs that are loaded into the file server to control devices and add more functionality to the server. NetWare Loadable Modules can also be divided into four categories based on their three-letter filename extensions. Disk drivers have the filename extension .DSK and allow NetWare to control the attached hard disk drives. LAN drivers have the extension .LAN and are used to attach the file server to a network topology. Name space modules have the extension .NAM and provide NetWare with the additional logic needed to translate file naming conventions from other workstation operating systems to NetWare's directory system. General-purpose modules have the extension .NLM and provide services to the network such as the MONITOR utility, which allows you to view file server performance and status; the INSTALL module, which is used for installation; and the PSERVER module, which allows a file server to function as a print server.

For reasons of security, the file server computer is often placed in a location that is not easily accessible. In addition, a network administrator often needs to manage several file servers in different locations. Because of these two factors, it is often more convenient for a CNA to operate the file server console from a workstation in his or her office than it is to go to the file server computer. The Remote Management System allows the file server's console to be accessed from other locations on the network. This is done by loading the REMOTE and RSPX NetWare Loadable Modules on the servers to be managed and then running the RCONSOLE program from the remote workstation. This is referred to as a direct link: the network cards in the file server and workstation provide direct, high-speed communication to the file server console. Security for the console is provided by setting a password on the REMOTE module and by placing the RCONSOLE software in the SYS:SYSTEM directory in which only the SUPERVISOR has access. Users can be made console operators by granting them rights to run the RCONSOLE software and providing them with the necessary REMOTE password. By attaching a modem to a file server and loading the RS232 NLM you can access the server's console over a dial-up telephone line by using the ACONSOLE software on the remote computer. This connection is referred to as an asynchronous link and provides a method of accessing the server from a distant site in addition to providing access to the console in the event of a network failure.

With the growing need to interconnect heterogeneous systems and communicate over the internet, a network administrator often is required to provide support for different protocols and operating system environments. Lower-level protocol supporting often involves supporting multiple frame types on the same network cable system in order to provide an upgrade path for the existing system. Because NetWare v3.12 uses the 802.2 Ethernet frame type by default, the most common lower-layer support problem a network administrator encounters today is the conversion of Ethernet drivers from the 802.3 frame type used with previous versions of NetWare to the 802.2 frame type used with NetWare v3.12. This chapter explained how multiple frame types can be supported in the file server on the same network card.

Unix-based computers use TCP/IP as their standard higher-level protocol, and Apple Macintosh computers use the AppleTalk protocol. In order to allow Unix and Macintosh computers to have access to the file server, you need to add protocol support for these operating systems to the NetWare file server, which by default uses the IPX protocol. With NetWare v3.12, Novell provides support for both TCP/IP and AppleTalk protocols. This is done by loading and configuring additional NLMs. This chapter explained how to load the TCP/IP protocol and provide the NetWare file server with support for routing TCP/IP packets between network cards. It also covered using the file server to tunnel IPX packets through TCP/IP networks in order to allow workstations located on remote TCP/IP-based networks to log in to the NetWare file server. In order to allow a Unix host computer to store and retrieve files on a NetWare server, it is necessary to obtain and load the Novell Network File System (NFS) on your server. NFS allows your server to appear as another Unix host, which can be used to share files and printers.

Protecting critical network data is one of the most important functions of a network administrator. With NetWare v3.12, Novell provides the Storage Management System (SMS). It enables the network administrator to establish a backup-and-restore system that is capable of backing up all file servers as well as data contained on local drives of the DOS and OS/2 workstations. A host server is the file server that contains the backup storage device and is responsible for running the SBACKUP program. Target devices consist of file servers and workstations running the target service agent (TSA) software that can be backed up by the host server. A single file server can be both a host and target device, enabling the server to back up its own data in addition to data contained on other servers or workstations. A network administrator needs to know how to design and implement a backup-and-restore system for a network.

COMMAND SUMMARY

Command	Syntax	Definition
ADD NAME SPACE	*ADD NAME SPACE name volume_name [TO]*	Makes space on the directory table of the given volume to support the specified name space. Possible name space options that come with NetWare v3.12 are MAC and OS/2.
BIND	*BIND protocol TO driver | board_name [driver_parameter]*	Attaches a protocol to the specified LAN driver. Before a file server can communicate with a LAN driver, a protocol must be identified. IPX is the standard protocol built into NetWare. Other protocols, such as TCP/IP and AppleTalk must first be loaded as NetWare Loadable Modules before they can be bound to the network card.
BROADCAST	*BROADCAST message*	Sends the message to all users currently logged in to the file server.
CLEAR STATION	*CLEAR STATION number*	Terminates the specified connection number and makes the connection number available to other workstations.
CLS/OFF	*CLS/OFF*	Clears the file server console screen.
CONFIG	*CONFIG*	Displays the current file server's internal network number and information about each network card, including the card's hardware settings, the frame type and protocol in use, and the network address assigned to that card.
DISABLE LOGIN	*DISABLE LOGIN*	Prevents additional users from logging in to the file server.
DISMOUNT	*DISMOUNT volume_name [ALL]*	Closes a volume and removes it from the network. It is necessary to dismount a volume before you use the VREPAIR utility to check the volume and correct any volume problems.
DISPLAY NETWORKS	*DISPLAY NETWORKS*	Displays all network addresses and internal network numbers currently in the server's router table.
DISPLAY SERVERS	*DISPLAY SERVERS*	Displays the name of each network server currently in the file server's router table, the number of routers that must be crossed to reach the server, and the average number of ticks ($\frac{1}{18}$ second) required to send a packet to this server.

DOWN	*DOWN*	Removes all attachments to the file server, writes all cache blocks to disk, dismounts the volumes, and takes the file server off line. Always use the DOWN command before shutting off the file server computer.
ENABLE LOGIN	*ENABLE LOGIN*	Re-enables user login to the file server.
EXIT	*EXIT*	After the DOWN command has been used to take the file server off line, EXIT is used to end the SERVER.EXE program and return the computer to the DOS prompt. If DOS has been removed, the EXIT command will cause the file server computer to reboot.
LIST DEVICES	*LIST DEVICES*	Displays a list containing information about all device drivers attached to the network file server.
LOAD	*LOAD [path]module_name [parameter]*	Loads the specified module into the file server's memory and executes it. An optional path can be supplied if the specified module is not in the SYS:SYSTEM directory.
MEMORY	*MEMORY*	Displays the total amount of memory in the file server computer.
MODULES	*MODULES*	Lists all currently loaded modules.
MOUNT	*MOUNT volume_name [ALL]*	Opens a volume for use on the network by loading directory table entries into memory. A volume must be mounted before it can be accessed on the network. If the SYS: volume is not mounted, the file server will not show up on the network when the SLIST and DISPLAY SERVER commands are used.
NAME	*NAME*	Displays on the console the name of the file server computer.
PROTOCOL		Displays all protocols currently in use.
PROTOCOL REGISTER	*PROTOCOL REGISTER*	Registers a new protocol for use on the server or obtains a list of all previously registered protocols.
REGISTER MEMORY	*REGISTER MEMORY*	Allows certain file servers to recognize memory above 16 Mbytes.

REMOVE DOS	*REMOVE DOS*	Removes the DOS operating system from memory, providing more memory for file caching and preventing the LOAD command from accessing DOS drives.
RESET ROUTER	*RESET ROUTER*	Causes the file server to send out a packet on the network asking all servers to identify their addresses and names. From this information, the file server rebuilds its router table to show all existing servers and their network addresses.
SCAN FOR NEW DEVICES	*SCAN FOR NEW DEVICES*	Causes the NetWare server to search for any additional devices that have been activated since the server was booted.
SEARCH ADD/ DELETE	*SEARCH [ADD path] {DEL number]*	Specifies another path in which the NetWare operating system will look for modules when you use the LOAD command.
SECURE CONSOLE	*SECURE CONSOLE*	Increases the file server's console security by removing DOS from memory, forcing NLMs to be loaded only from SYS:SYSTEM, preventing the use of the OS debugger program, and not allowing the system time to be changed from the server console.
SEND	*SEND "message" TO] username\connection_ number*	Use the SEND command from the console to send a message (in quotation marks) to a specific user or connection number.
SET	*SET*	Displays a menu of options that allow you to view or change network configuration parameters in the file server.
SET TIME	*SET TIME [month/day/year] [hour:minute:second]*	Used by itself, displays the current server time. Used with date and time settings, changes the time in the server to the specified time and date.
TRACK	*TRACK ON/OFF*	Allows you to view all service advertising packets that are sent or received by the file server. The TRACK OFF command cancels the tracking display.

UNBIND	*UNBIND protocol FROM LAN_driver|board_name*	Removes a protocol stack from a network card, effectively removing the server from that network. The UNBIND command is often used to change the network address of a server because other servers on that network are using a different address.
UNLOAD	*UNLOAD module_name*	Removes a NetWare Loadable Module from memory and returns its memory to the file cache.

KEY TERMS

asynchronous link

child

direct link

host server

parent

redundant link

remote management facility (RMF)

router information packet (RIP)

router tables

service advertising packets (SAPs)

spanning

storage management system (SMS)

target machine

TCP/IP

tick

tunneling

REVIEW QUESTIONS

1. The _____ command is used to provide space on a volume for non-DOS filenames such as Macintosh or OS/2.

2. The _____ command assigns a network address to a LAN driver.

3. The _____ command is used to assign a frame type and I/O port to a LAN driver.

4. The _____ command shows total file memory available on the file server computer.

5. Assume the command in question 4 shows that your file server has 16 Mbytes of RAM rather than the 20 Mbytes of RAM you have installed. The _____ command can be used to cause the server to recognize the additional 4 Mbytes of RAM.

6. The _____ command will cause the file server to load NLMs from the SYS:SYSTEM\NLM directory when it does not find the requested module in the SYS:SYSTEM directory.

7. The _____ console command displays the network addresses assigned to each LAN in the file server.

8. The _____ console command lets you know if your newly installed file server can "see" other file servers on the network.

9. Suppose your file server is up and running and you have just switched on an external CD-ROM drive but it does not show up in the CD-ROM device list. What would you do next?

_____

10. On the line below, write a console command that changes the file server's clock to 11:59 P.M. on December 31, 1999.

_____

11. In the space below, write the sequence of commands a network administrator should enter before turning off the file server computer in the middle of the day.

12. After booting the file server, you notice that the TEXT: volume did not mount because of errors in the file allocation table. In the space below, identify what NetWare Loadable Module can be used to fix the volume and then the command necessary to bring the TEXT: volume back online.

13. Suppose that, after you load the NE2000 Ethernet card driver and bind the IPX protocol with the network address 1EEE8023, your file server begins reporting router configuration errors that indicate other servers on the network are using the network address 10BA5E2 for the Ethernet LAN. In the space below, write the commands you can use to correct the problem.

14. The _____ console command prevents NetWare from loading NLMs from the SYS:PUBLIC\NLM directory.

15. The _____ console command causes the file server to reboot when you enter the EXIT command.

16. NetWare disk drivers all have _____ for a file extension.

17. In the space below, list three commonly used LAN drivers that are included with NetWare v3.12.

18. If the number in the Total Cache Buffers field on the MONITOR screen is less than _____ of the amount in the Original Cache Buffers field, you need to add more memory to your file server.

19. In the space below, enter in the correct sequence the commands that provide a redundant remote console link on your file server.

20. In the space below, list the software modules that must be installed on the host file server so that the SMS backup facility can be used.

21. Suppose you have just installed a new NetWare v3.12 file server. You added it to the existing Ethernet network, which currently has two NetWare v3.11 servers. While the newly installed workstations can see the server, none of the existing servers or workstations will communicate with it. On the line below, identify the most likely problem.

    _____

22. Assume an existing file server is using an Ethernet card with an 802.3 frame type and network address of 10BA5E2. You have just installed a new Netware v3.12 file server using a NE2000 Ethernet card with the 802.2 frame type and a network address of FADE. Write two commands that you could enter at the new file server to allow the existing file server and workstation to access it.

    _____

    _____

23. List two ways TCP/IP can be supported on a NetWare v3.12 server without the need for additional software to be purchased.

    _____

    _____

24. In order for you to use Macintosh name space on a volume, the _____ _____ command needs to be added to the _____ file.

25. Before you run the SBACKUP software on the host file server, the device driver information must be added to the _____ _____ file located in the _____ _____ directory.

EXERCISES

Exercise 15-1: Working with Console Commands

In this exercise, you will use NetWare console commands to perform the specified console operations and obtain requested information. So that you can perform this exercise, your instructor will provide you with access to your classroom's "installation" file server console.

1. Use the CONFIG command to obtain the following information about a network board.

    Driver: _____

    I/O port: _____

    Network address: _____

    Frame type: _____

    Protocol: _____

2. Use the DISPLAY NETWORKS command to document two different networks currently in use in your classroom. On the lines below, identify each network address along with the number of hops and ticks required to reach that network.

Network Address	Number of Hops	Number of Ticks
_____	_____	_____
_____	_____	_____

3. Use the DISPLAY SERVERS command to identify up to three servers available from the classroom network. On the lines below, identify each server's name along with the number of hops to reach that server.

Server Name	Number of Hops
_____	_____
_____	_____
_____	_____

4. Set the date and time on the file server to 8:30 A.M. on December 28, 1999. On the line below, record the command you use.

    _____

5. Down the server by performing the following procedures. In the spaces provided, record each command you use.

    Load MONITOR to determine the number of connections.

    _____

    Prevent any new logins.

    _____

    Send a message to all users that the server is going down.

    _____

    Take the SYS: volume offline.

    _____

    Use the VREPAIR utility from the DOS partition of your file server (drive C) and check the volume for any errors.

    _____

    Bring the volume back online.

    _____

    Remove DOS.

    _____

Try to load the VREPAIR utility from the C disk drive and record the message below.

_____

Clear any existing connections.

_____

Down the server.

_____

Exit to DOS.

_____

Because DOS has been removed from the server, exiting the server should cause the file server computer to reboot. In the space below, record what happened on your file server computer when you exited to the DOS prompt.

Bring the server back online.

_____

6. Use the TRACK ON command to view the router tracking screen. Record an OUT packet message on the line below and identify it as either a SAP or RIP packet:

_____

Type of packet (SAP or RIP): _____

7. Change from the TRACK screen to the console prompt using the Control and Esc keys.

8. Enter the RESET ROUTER command to rebuild the router table. Then use the Alt and Esc keys to rotate to the TRACK screen. In the space below, record any observations regarding the effect of the RESET ROUTER command on the TRACK screen.

9. Use the TRACK OFF command to exit the tracking function.

10. Use the UNBIND and BIND commands to change the network address assigned to the network card from its current address to BEEBEE. In the space below, record the command you use.

11. Change the address back to its original number. In the space below, record the command you use.

12. Use the SEARCH ADD statement to load NLMs from the SYS:MHS\EXE directory.

   Enter the SECURE CONSOLE command. Attempt to load the BASICMHS utility. Record the results below.

   Attempt to change the date back one year. Record the results below.

13. In the space below, record the modules that are currently loaded in the server.

Exercise 15-2: Working with NLMs

In this exercise, you will use NLMs to obtain information but you will not modify the existing file server environment. It can therefore be done on any file server to which the instructor has provided you access.

1. Use the MONITOR NLM to obtain the following information about your file server:

   Version and release date of server: _____

   Original Cache Buffers: _____

   Total Cache Buffers: _____

   Packet Receive Buffers: _____

   Number of connections: _____

   Number of redirection blocks: _____

   Number of redirected blocks: _____

   Total packets received: _____

   Number of packets received that were too large: _____

2. Use MONITOR to lock the console with a password.

3. Load the CD-ROM module.

4. Use the CD HELP command to obtain information on CD-ROM commands.

5. Use the appropriate command to list any existing devices. In the space below, record the fields of information available in the CD DEVICE LIST window.

6. Use the INSTALL module to determine the following:

The size of the SYS: volume in blocks: _____

Whether any free blocks are available to be assigned to an existing volume:

Record the number of free blocks: _____

The size of the DOS and NetWare partitions:

DOS: _____

NetWare: _____

Exercise 15-3: Managing a Remote Console

In this exercise you will load RMF on the file server designated by your instructor and perform the following procedure from the server:

1. Load support for remote console management on the designated server. Modify the startup files to load this support automatically each time the server is booted. In the space below, record the commands you place in the startup file.

Name of startup file containing remote console commands:

_____

Commands included:

2. Create a remote console operator. If you do not have supervisory rights on the server, your instructor will provide you with rights to the RCONSOLE and ACONSOLE programs.

3. Log in as a remote console operator from a workstation.

4. Access the file server console. In the space below, record the console message received as a result of your accessing the remote console.

5. Scan the files in the server's DOS drive.

6. Copy a file from the workstation to the C drive of the server.

7. Print the screen and highlight the new file.

Exercise 15-4: Rebooting a Remote Server

To perform this exercise you will need to have access to a file server that is not currently being used by other students. Your instructor will provide you with a time when—or a file server machine on which—this exercise can be performed.

1. Disable new logins.

2. Broadcast a message.

3. Use the LOAD EDIT C:\AUTOEXEC.BAT command to be sure the server will automatically load when the computer is rebooted.

4. Use the EDIT command to create an NCF file using your name and the extension .NCF. In the NCF file, include the commands necessary to reboot the file server. Record the commands in the space below.

5. Execute the NCF file to reboot the server.

6. Copy the file you created in Step 1 to the C drive of the file server.

Exercise 15-5: Backing Up the Server

In this exercise you will use the SBACKUP program along with the device driver provided by your instructor to back up the SYS:PUBLIC directory on the "installation" file server. In the space below, record each of the steps you perform along with any observations.

 **EXERCISES**

Case 15-1: Multiple Frame Types

The Loch Lomond Beach Club recently expanded its NetWare network to include an additional file server to be used for desktop publishing, e-mail, and some new educational multimedia applications. Assume you have just installed the new NetWare v3.12 file server for the Loch Lomond Beach Club. Currently the club has workstations and file servers attached to an Ethernet network running an earlier version of NetWare. The current network address used by the existing file servers for the Ethernet is 10BA5E2. In the near future the club wants to upgrade all servers to v3.12. In the meantime, it wants to use the standard features of the v3.12 server on newly installed workstations while continuing to support the v2.2 servers.

To simulate this scenario, you will need access to a file server and two workstation computers attached to an existing network. You can perform this exercise by working in teams of two, with one student operating each workstation.

1. Bring up the file server using the default frame type which on an Ethernet network should be 802.2. Assign the network address currently in use by the existing network. Record the network address and frame type on the lines below.

    Frame Type: _____

    Network Address: _____

2. Change the NET.CFG file of one of the workstations to use a different frame type, such as 802.3. This simulates the older v2.2 machines currently used at the beach club.

3. Boot the 802.3 frame type computer and attempt to attach to the v3.12 server. If there are other servers on the network, the SLIST command should not be able to see the v3.12 server. If there are no other computers on your network using the frame type you entered, you will not have a network drive letter available to the workstation. Record your observations below.

4. Boot the standard workstation and attach to the v3.12 server. Record any observations below.

5. Use the LOAD command on the file server console to add the frame type specified in Step 2 to the file server's LAN card. Use the NAME parameter to assign a name to this frame type. This simulates the procedure used at the Loch Lomond Beach Club to allow existing servers and workstations to communicate with the new server.

6. Reboot the workstation with the modified NET.CFG frame type. Why can't the workstation attach to the new file server?

7. Use the BIND command to bind the IPX protocol to the new frame type using the board name assigned in Step 5. This simulates the need to establish a logical network with the existing file servers used at the Loch Lomond Beach Club. When using the BIND command, specify the 10BA5E2 network address used by the v2.2 file servers.

8. Reboot the workstation with the modified NET.CFG frame type and record the results below. If your v3.12 server supports the new frame type, both the workstations should now be able to "see" the file server.

Case 15-2: Supporting TCP/IP

Scampi Manufacturing is a large sailboat manufacturing company with plants on both the East and West coasts. Currently its business office is located on the West Coast. It has a Unix-based mainframe computer located in the West Coast office and another Unix-based minicomputer located in the East Coast facility. The Unix minicomputer is used for inventory and manufacturing control and is online through a wide area network system to the west coast computer for providing summarized inventory and manufacturing data to the mainframe system. In addition to the Unix host, a NetWare LAN is in place at each facility to handle PC-based office needs, such as word processing, scheduling, and shared use of files and printers.

Recently the need to connect the two NetWare LANs has become an important priority. This will allow the two facilities to share PC files and centralize administrative functions. The management at Scampi would like you to find a way for the NetWare file servers to use the TCP/IP WAN in order to send and receive IPX packets so that users in the West Coast office can have access to certain files on the file server located at the east coast facility.

In this assignment you will simulate setting up TCP/IP tunneling in order to allow IPX packets to pass through the TCP/IP wide area network. This assignment requires that you have access to two file servers in order to simulate using the IP tunnel software. Label one server "East Coast" and the other server "West Coast." Assign each server a class B IP address on the same network and record the addresses on the lines below.

Network address: _____._____

East Coast server IP address: _____._____._____._____

West Coast server IP address: _____._____._____._____

1. The East Coast server and at least one workstation should use the frame type and network address assigned to the classroom network. Record the frame type and network address of the East Coast server below:

    East Coast server name: _____

    East Coast server frame type: _____

    East Coast server IPX network address: _____

2. To simulate a different network, the server you designated as the West Coast server should use a different frame type and network address. On an Ethernet network use a frame type of ETHERNET_SNAP. On a token ring network use the frame type TOKEN-RING_SNAP. Using a SNAP frame type will make it easier to use TCP/IP on this server. Record the frame type and network address for the West Coast server below:

    West Coast server name: _____

    West Coast server frame type: _____

    West Coast server IPX network address: _____

3. Using a workstation attached to the classroom network, login to the East Coast file server. Use the SLIST command to verify that the West Coast server is not listed. Why is the West Coast server not listed?

    _____

4. To use TCP/IP to connect the two servers, you will next need to load the SNAP frame type on the East Coast file server. To do this, on the East Coast file server load the LAN driver a second time using the same SNAP frame type you recorded in step 2. Record the load command you use on the line below:

    _____

5. Load TCP/IP on both servers.

6. Bind IP on each server to the SNAP driver using the IP address you recorded earlier. Record each BIND command you use below:

    East Coast Server: _____

    West Coast Server: _____

7. Use the following command to enable IP tunneling on the East Coast file server:

    LOAD IPTUNNEL PEER=(IP address of West Coast server)

8. Use the following command to enable IP tunneling on the West Coast file server:

    LOAD IPTUNNEL PEER=(IP address of East Coast server)

9. To cause IPX packets to pass through the tunnel you have created, you next need to establish an IPX network address for the IP Tunnel. To do this you first need to define a unique IPX network address for use over the IP tunnel. Record the IPX network address you plan to use on the line below:

    IPX Tunnel Address: _____

10. Use the following commands to bind IPX to the IP tunnel on both East and West Coast file servers:

    BIND IPX TO IPTUNNEL NET=(address you defined in 3step 9)

11. To test the IP tunnel, use the SLIST command from the workstation used in step 3. The West Coast file server should now appear. Use the Print Screen key to print the screen.

12. Have your instructor check out your IP Tunnel and initial below when complete.

SUPERIOR TECHNICAL COLLEGE PROBLEMS

Project 15-1: Implementing Name Space Support

Dave Johnson has lost his mind! He actually went out and purchased two Macintosh computers to be attached to the campus network for the purpose of creating and maintaining an in–house system of program flyers. In the past, the campus has always gone to an outside printing company to design and print the program flyers. Dave claims that the number of changes to the existing programs on an annual basis will justify the purchase of the Macintosh computers for use in creating the flyers in-house.

Dave has contracted with a local Apple vendor to install the Macintosh computers and train the users, but now he wants you to add name space support for the Macs to the DATA: volume. This will allow the new Macs to store and share files with each other and with other Windows-type applications currently in use. Dave asks you to document this procedure for future reference.

In this project you will need to use the "installation" computer to add name space support to the DATA: volume by following the process defined in this chapter. Document each step of the procedure you perform.

Project 15-2: Removing Name Space Support

Despite your concerns, the Macintosh computers work out well and save money. However, the Macintosh computers have used up most of the space on your DATA: volume, requiring you to obtain and install an additional disk drive just for the Mac flyer files. Now that the MAC: volume is online, you want to remove the Macintosh name space support from the DATA: volume, returning it to a DOS-only environment.

To do this exercise, you will need to have access to the "installation" computer used in Project 15-1. Go through the steps described in this chapter to remove name space support from a volume. Document each step of the procedure.

## CHAPTER SIXTEEN

MAINTAINING THE NETWORK

You could say that this chapter is about job security. Although installing a network requires skill and knowledge, maintaining and upgrading an existing net–work by installing new software, adding workstations, upgrading existing software, monitoring network performance, and correcting problems is an ongoing task that continues to tap the network administrator's training. In this chapter you will learn how to use NetWare tools such as the WSUPDATE program to assist you in keep-ing the software drives on your workstations current. You will also learn how to use some additional options of the NET.CFG file that will allow you to config-ure your workstations to provide better performance and support for network applications. Packet burst mode, packet signatures, and large internet packets are new features that are included in NetWare v3.12. In this chapter you will learn how these new features affect the performance and security of workstations and how you can configure them to best meet your network needs.

AFTER READING THIS CHAPTER AND COMPLETING THE EXERCISES YOU WILL BE ABLE TO:

- USE THE WSUPDATE PROGRAM TO UPGRADE WORKSTATION SOFTWARE.

- LIST THE PARAMETERS OF THE NET.CFG FILE THAT CAN BE USED TO IMPROVE THE PERFORMANCE OF THE WORKSTATION.

- DESCRIBE NETWARE V3.12 MEMORY POOLS AND HOW THEY ARE USED TO MANAGE FILE SERVER MEMORY USAGE.

- USE THE MONITOR UTILITY AND SET COMMANDS TO VIEW AND CONFIGURE THE FILE SERVER.

- DESCRIBE HOW PACKET BURST AND PACKET SIGNATURE ARE IMPLEMENTED AT THE WORKSTATION.

The file server's performance is going to be one of your ongoing concerns as a CNA. You will need to know how to monitor the file server and identify possible problems before they affect your users. In this chapter, you will learn how NetWare v3.12 manages its memory and how to use the MONITOR utility to obtain memory usage and performance information. This information, in conjunction with the SET command, can be used to modify the server's configuration for improved performance and additional support to user workstations.

MAINTAINING WORKSTATIONS

With the rapid changes that characterize the computer industry, the work of the CNA is never done. Once the network is operational, you might, in fact, have more to do than you did during the initial installation of the server and client software. New versions of application software, upgrades to the network system software, and new workstations and operating systems, such as Windows 95, all require the network administrator to continually change and modify the network environment. In this chapter you will learn how new network software can be efficiently distributed to all the workstations on the network. In the first section of the chapter, you will learn how to use statements in the NET.CFG file to make modifications to the workstation's configuration that will support network applications more efficiently.

With the increased number of changes to computer hardware and software, the number of revised software drivers and utilities is rapidly increasing. As a result, network administrators need to have an efficient method to handle software updates.

UPDATING WORKSTATION SOFTWARE

Keeping the latest version of the NetWare driver and requester software on each of the networked workstations is an ongoing task for all network administrators. Updated versions of software components are usually downloaded from Novell's NetWire bulletin board service, available through the Compuserve information utility, and then copied onto each workstation. In large networks consisting of 100 or more workstations, carrying a floppy disk to each workstation in order to update the software drivers would be a waste of a network administrator's time. To help automate this job and save time for the administrator, Novell supplies a program with NetWare v3.12 called WSUPDATE. This program checks the date of the current programs on each workstation and then automatically updates a program having a date prior to the version stored on the server.

As a CNA, you will periodically need to obtain releases of new NetWare software drivers and then be able to copy these new updates to each of the workstations that use the software. See your instructor for a description of how to access NetWire through Compuserve and then download an updated driver file. In this section you will learn how to use the WSUPDATE software to copy updated software to workstations.

Updating workstation files

After you have downloaded and extracted the files you need, the next task is to update all the workstations that are using the older versions of these files. If you have only a few workstations, this can be done simply by taking a disk containing the new files to each workstation and then copying the files onto those workstations. If you have 50 or more workstations or if your workstations are distributed over a wide area, however, you will want to use the WSUPDATE program provided by Novell to copy the updated files automatically to each workstation that uses them.

The WSUPDATE command can be used from either the DOS prompt or the system login script. It updates files on the client workstation by checking the dates of the specified files and then copying files with more recent dates from the server to a directory on the client workstation. The syntax for the WSUPDATE command is as follows:

> **WSUPDATE [*source_path\filename*] [*target_drive:filename*]**
> **[*/options*]**

Replace *source_path\filename* with the full NetWare directory path, including filename. Replace *target_drive:filename* with the local drive letter and filename you want to be updated. The keyword ALL_LOCAL: or ALL: can be used in place of a drive letter if you want WSUPDATE to search all local drives for the specified file. If the *filename* parameter is not included in the *target_drive:filename* field, WSUPDATE will use the filename specified by the *source_path* as the destination file's name.

One limitation of the WSUPDATE program is that the *target_drive:filename* parameter can contain only a drive letter followed by a colon (:) and the file's name. It does not allow path or global file characters, which make it difficult to update software that is stored in a directory or subdirectory. To get around this limitation, you need to use either the DOS SUBST *drive_letter: path* command to define a drive letter pointing to the directory path that contains the software to be updated or the /S parameter of the WSUPDATE command to cause the WSUPDATE program to search all directories on the specified target drive.

Because the DOS SUBST command is an external DOS program, using the SUBST command will require that the workstation have a path mapped to a DOS directory that contains the SUBST.EXE program.

Searching all directories on a local workstation's hard disk can be very time consuming, so most network administrators prefer to use the SUBST command to define a drive pointer to the path containing the files to be updated.

The WSUPDATE command includes a number of additional parameters that can be used to accomplish the tasks described in Figure 16-1. When WSUPDATE finds an older version of the specified file, by default it prompts the user to replace the old file, rename the old file, or ignore the update and leave the file unchanged. Of course, as a network administrator you do not want to leave this decision to the user. Using the /C parameter will automatically replace the old file with the newer one. When a workstation's system files are flagged Read Only (to prevent accidental erasure), you can include the /O option to overwrite them.

Another important parameter is /F=*filename*. When you have several new files to update, the /F option allows you to specify the name of a file that contains a list of new files to be updated. When you have several files that you want to update, using the /F=*filename* parameter is more efficient than placing several WSUPDATE commands in the system login script. This is because each WSUPDATE command placed in the system login script requires the workstation to load and run the WSUPDATE.EXE program. Running the program once and then using the /F=*filename* option to update several files at one time is much more efficient than running the WSUPDATE program for each new file. When using the /F=*filename* parameter, you need to create the file specified by the *filename* parameter. Then, using a text editor program such as the DOS EDIT command, enter separate command lines for each new file you want to update on the workstations running the WSUPDATE program for each new file:

Figure 16-1

WSUPDATE optional parameters

Option	Description
/F=[path]filename	Add this option if the commands are contained in a separate file specified by the given path and filename.
/C	Include this option to overwrite the old version of the file automatically without pausing.
/R	Include this option to rename the old version of the file automatically with the .OLD extension prior to copying the new version to the workstation.
/O	Include this option to overwrite read only files automatically.
/S	Include this option to search for older versions of the specified file in all subdirectories of the target drive.
/L=[path]filename	Include this option, with the path and filename, when you want a log of all workstations that have been updated. The log file includes the username, date, and network address of each workstation that has been updated.
/N	Add this option when you want to create the file and path on the target drive if they do not already exist. Do not use this option with /S or ALL:.

A common use of the WSUPDATE program is to replace old versions of Novell driver files with new versions that you have recently obtained from NetWire or some other source. Suppose, for example, you have recently downloaded new versions of the workstation driver files LSL.COM and IPXODI.COM and you now want to update all workstations that have older versions with the new files. The best way to perform this task is to include the #SUBST and #WSUPDATE commands in the system login script as illustrated in Figure 16-3.

To use the WSUPDATE program in the system login script, you first need to copy the WSUPDATE.EXE program from the SYS:SYSTEM directory to the SYS:PUBLIC directory. Next you need to create a directory in which to place the new files that you want copied to the workstations. One way to do this is to create a subdirectory in SYS:PUBLIC named NEWVER to store the new software. When the subdirectory NEWVER is created within the SYS:PUBLIC directory, all users inherit Read and File Scan rights to it that allow them to access the new version of the software. After creating the NEWVER subdirectory, you can then copy the new versions of the LSL.COM and IPXODI.COM programs into the SYS:PUBLIC\NEWVER directory. In order to make the update process more efficient, use the /F=*filename* parameter on the WSUPDATE command to cause the WSUPDATE program to read commands from the filename specified.

Before you can run the WSUPDATE command, you need to create—using the DOS EDIT command—an ASCII text file containing WSUPDATE command lines, as shown in Figure 16-2. Notice that drive letter E is used as the target drive in the command lines. It allows you to update files located in a subdirectory of the workstation's local hard disk. You do this by using the SUBST command to assign drive pointer E to the path containing the software to be checked. In order to cause each workstation to run the WSUPDATE software and update its drivers, you next use the SYSCON program to modify the system login script to include the WSUPDATE command, as shown in Figure 16-3. Notice that the SUBST and WSUPDATE commands are preceded by the # login script command. This is because they are external programs. The #SUBST E C:\NWCLIENT command prior to #WSUPDATE runs the DOS SUBST program and assigns drive letter E to the path containing the workstation driver software. As described earlier, the SUBST command is necessary whenever the software to be updated is stored in a subdirectory and you do not want to have the WSUPDATE program search all directories of the hard disk. In addition to assigning drive letter E to the correct directory path of the C drive, it is important to place the #WSUPDATE command after the search drive mapping to the SYS:PUBLIC directory. This allows the workstation to find the WSUPDATE.EXE program.

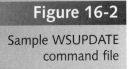

Figure 16-2

Sample WSUPDATE command file

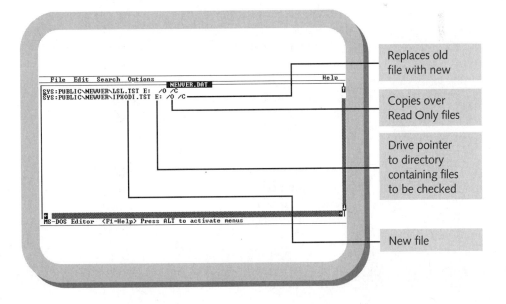

Figure 16-3

WSUPDATE included
in the system
login script

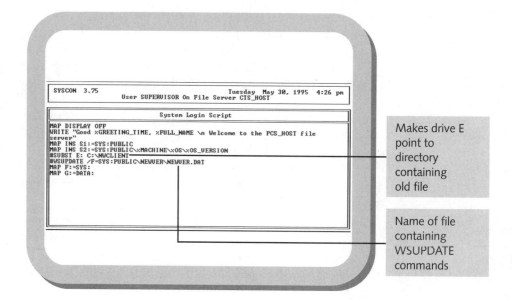

```
SYSCON  3.75                           Tuesday  May 30, 1995  4:26 pm
                    User SUPERVISOR On File Server CIS_HOST

                              System Login Script
MAP DISPLAY OFF
WRITE "Good %GREETING_TIME, %FULL_NAME \n Welcome to the PCS_HOST file
server"
MAP INS S1:=SYS:PUBLIC
MAP INS S2:=SYS:PUBLIC\%MACHINE\%OS\%OS_VERSION
#SUBST E: C:\NWCLIENT
#WSUPDATE /F=SYS:PUBLIC\NEWVER\NEWVER.DAT
MAP F:=SYS:
MAP G:=DATA:
```

Makes drive E
point to
directory
containing
old file

Name of file
containing
WSUPDATE
commands

Once the changes to the system login script are saved, whenever a user logs in the WSUPDATE program checks the C:\NWCLIENT directory and copies the new LSL.COM and IPXODI.COM files into the directory if the dates on the existing files precede the new file dates. After you are sure all workstations have had their driver files updated, you can use SYSCON to modify the system login script. Place a remark command (REM * ;) ahead of the SUBST and #WSUPDATE statements to prevent them from being run each time a user logs in. Later, when you again have new drivers, you can remove the remark prefix and modify the NEWVER.DAT file to update any new software.

USING NET.CFG

As described in Chapter 5, the NET.CFG file contains configuration information for the workstation's network card driver as well as IPX and the DOS VLM requester. This file is initially created for you when you go through the NetWare v3.12 client installation. If a workstation is running Microsoft Windows, is acting as a remote printer or print server, or has other special needs, however, you might need to change the configuration parameters for proper operation. The additional NET.CFG configuration parameters described in this section will help the CNA properly maintain workstation performance.

The network card driver, link support program (LSL), and DOS requester (VLM) each have a section header in the NET.CFG file. This makes it possible for you to find their appropriate parameters, as shown in Figure 16-4. In this section, you will learn how several of these parameters can be used to help configure the workstation environment in order to provide better performance and network functionality.

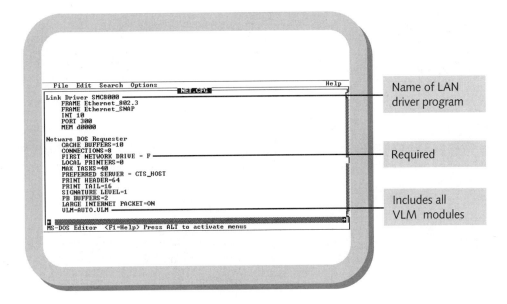

Figure 16-4

Sample NET.CFG
file

Name of LAN
driver program

Required

Includes all
VLM modules

Link Driver Statements

When multiple frame types are included in the Link Driver section of the NET.CFG file, NetWare IPX will communicate using the first frame type specified.

Because servers and clients must use the same frame type in order to communicate, the FRAME *frame_type* statement is sometimes necessary in the Link Driver section of the NET.CFG file to tell the network card driver software what type(s) of frame(s) to process. If necessary, multiple FRAME statements can be placed in the NET.CFG file, as shown in Figure 16-4, in order to allow a workstation to communicate with file servers that are using different frame types. The FRAME statement is most frequently used in Ethernet environments to specify either Ethernet_802.3 or Ethernet_802.2 frame types. Figure 16-5 contains a list of common frame types for both token ring and Ethernet cards, along with their use. In addition to frame type, the Link Driver section also contains the hardware settings for the network card including: interrupt, I/O port address, and memory address. If you change the network card hardware configuration, you will also need to modify these statements in the NET. CFG file to correspond to the card's hardware settings.

Netware DOS Requester.   As introduced in Chapter 5, the NetWare DOS Requester section allows the network administrator to configure the VLM modules. While the default parameters provided by the client installation program are adequate for most workstations, as a CNA, you should also be aware of the effect of the following parameters on a workstation's performance:

Figure 16-5

Popular Ethernet and token ring frame types

Frame Type	Use
ETHERNET_802.2	NetWare IPX v3.12 and above
ETHERNET_802.3	NetWare IPX v3.11 and before
ETHERNET_SNAP	TCP/IP, Apple Ethertalk Phase II
ETHERNET_II	TCP/IP
TOKEN_RING	NetWare IPX
TOKEN_SNAP	TCP/IP, Apple TokenTalk

Cache Buffers.   The CACHE BUFFERS *n* statement is used by the DOS requester FIO.VLM module to provide storage areas for caching of nonshared, nontransaction-tracked files that are open on the file server. While the default value of five cache buffers works adequately for most applications, the efficiency of applications, such as word processors, that read large sequential files can be enhanced by increasing the number of cache buffers to 10 or 15 (see Figure 16-4). Increasing the number of cache buffers reduces the number of read requests that need to be made to the server when sequential files are processed. When database files are shared, the cache buffers will not have any effect on performance because each record must be read from the server to allow for modifications by other users.

Connections.   By default, the DOS requester program can be attached to a maximum of eight file servers during one session. This is the maximum for a NetWare v3.1x environment, but in a NetWare 4.x environment, a workstation can access additional servers. If a workstation needs to access information on as many as 16 file servers, for example, you need to place the CONNECTIONS=16 statement in the NET.CFG file to allow for more connections.

First Network Drive.   In order to log in to a file server initially, the DOS workstation needs to access the SYS:LOGIN directory, which contains the SLIST and LOGIN programs. After connecting to a file server, the DOS requester uses the letter specified by the FIRST NETWORK DRIVE statement to provide access to the SYS:LOGIN directory of the default file server. By default, the client installation software places FIRST NETWORK DRIVE=F in the NET.CFG file when you install NetWare on a workstation.

Local Printers.   The number specified in the LOCAL PRINTERS statement indicates what printer ports on the local workstation can be used for local printing. If a workstation does not have a local printer but is required to send output to a network print queue, you might want to use the LOCAL PRINTERS=0 statement to prevent the workstation from crashing if the operator attempts to send output to the local printer port without using a CAPTURE or an NPRINT command.

On workstations that are running the RPRINTER program, using the LOCAL PRINTERS = 0 statement may be used in order to prevent the user from directly printing to the LPT port that is controlled by the PRINTER software.

Max Tasks.   The MAX TASKS parameter controls the maximum number of tasks that can be active at the same time. Multitasking applications such as Microsoft Windows allow several programs to run at one time. If a workstation is unable to start a new program, you might need to use the MAX TASKS=40 statement to increase the number of tasks available to the CONN.VLM to around 40.

Preferred Server.   By default, when the DOS requester first loads, it attempts to attach to a file server on the network by sending out a "request for server" packet. The requester then connects to the first file server that responds to the "request for server" message. If a workstation is attached to a multiserver network, the fastest or least-busy file server will normally be the one attached to. Because on a NetWare v3.1x network users normally must log in to a specific server, the PREFERRED SERVER statement can be used to force the requester to look for that server and, if possible, attach the workstation to it. If the requested file server does not respond, an error message is displayed and the requester reverts to attaching to the file server that first responds to its "request for server" message.

Print Header.   When PRINTCON is used to specify a particular print device mode, the necessary printer setup escape code sequence is placed in the print header field. By default, the PRINT.VLM module reserves 64 bytes for this print header information. If a printer setup sequence requires more than 64 bytes, the remaining bytes will be truncated. This results in problems when the file is printed. If any of the print modes in the NET$PRN.DAT printer database contain more than 64 bytes of escape code characters, you will need to increase the size of the print header with a PRINT HEADER= n statement, in which n represents the number of bytes required by your print header. Placing the statement in the workstation's NET.CFG file will accommodate the additional size of the setup strings.

Print Tail.   In addition to having a header, each print job has a "tail," which contains the escape codes for resetting the printer to its startup configuration. The reset escape code functions are specified in the reset print mode, which is maintained in the NET$PRN.DAT file by the PRINTDEF utility. If the number of bytes necessary to perform the printer reset mode exceeds 16, remaining escape code bytes will be truncated. This results in the printer not being returned to the correct startup mode, which can, in turn, cause subsequent print jobs to be printed incorrectly (for example, they might contain "garbage" characters). To correct this problem, you can use the PRINT TAIL= n statement, in which n represents the number of bytes required by the print tail. Specify the size of the print tail field to meet the requirements of your network printers.

Signature Level.   To provide additional security after login, in NetWare v3.12 and later, each NetWare IPX packet contains a signature field that can contain a unique "signature" from the workstation. This signature enables the file server to be sure the packet originated from the workstation and is not a forged packet from an intruder workstation. Signatures prevent an intruder from creating packets using the connection number of another user's workstation and thereby fooling the file server into providing the intruder with the same rights as the legitimate user. In high-security environments, you might be required to implement packet signatures on some or all workstations.

Figure 16-6

Possible packet signature levels

Signature Level	Description
0	Workstation does not sign packets. (same as v3.11 server)
1	Workstation signs only if server requests signature
2	Workstation signs if server is capable of signing.
3	Workstation always signs and requires all servers to sign.

Figure 16-6 shows different possible signature levels that can be used with the DOS requester. Signature level 1 causes the DOS requester to sign packets when it communicates with servers that are capable of working with packet signatures, such as v3.12 or v4.x. When it communicates with older NetWare versions, the DOS requester omits signature fields from the packets. If you want to force a workstation always to use packet signatures, you can place the statement SIGNATURE LEVEL=3 in the DOS requester section of the NET.CFG file. The workstation is thereby prevented from communicating with servers that do not support packet signatures.

Because a packet signature takes additional processing time and network overhead, if you are working in an environment that has many workstations that are not concerned with packet signatures, you might want to use the SIGNATURE LEVEL=0 statement in the NET.CFG files of the workstations that do not require this security feature.

PB Buffers.   The PB BUFFERS parameter allows you to configure the number of buffers used to support packet burst protocol on the workstation. **Packet burst protocol** increases network performance by speeding up the transfer of multiple packet requests. Before Novell implemented packet burst protocol in v3.12, each packet that was sent to the workstation from the file server required an acknowledgment before the next packet could be sent. This extra overhead increases traffic on the network and takes extra resources from the file server. When NetWare v3.12 servers with VLMs are used, the file server and workstations "negotiate" the number of packets that will be sent from the server to the workstation before an acknowledgment is required. This technique is referred to as a **sliding window** because the number of packets sent in each burst can be changed to meet the load that exists on the network and file server.

The packet burst protocol is not implemented when workstations communicate with the server using the NETX shell. It is thus necessary to convert workstations to the VLM requester software in order to take advantage of this performance feature. By default, three buffers are reserved to support packet burst protocol. Although packet burst protocol automatically negotiates the number of packets sent in each burst, based on network load, on busy networks (over 75 workstations) it is possible that packet burst actually slows down network performance by preventing workstations from accessing the file server. To avoid this reduced performance, you can disable the use of packet burst on a workstation by placing the command PB BUFFERS=0 in the DOS requester section of the NET.CFG file. Increasing the number of packet burst buffers allows for larger packet bursts and can increase performance over WANs or on lightly used LANs. Increasing the number of packet burst buffers on workstations in a large network may have the disadvantage of causing workstations to wait a longer time to get a network request processed due to each workstation taking a larger block of network bandwidth. As a result, you should usually not increase the number of packet burst buffers unless you have a very small network consisting of only a few workstations.

Large internet packet size

Prior to NetWare v3.12, whenever a workstation communicated with a file server across a router, the default packet size was reduced to 576 bytes (data portion of 512 bytes with 64 bytes of heading information), even if both networks could handle larger packet sizes. By default, a NetWare v3.12 file server will use the large internet packet (LIP) system to allow workstations running the VLM requester to negotiate the packet size with the server. This allows the packet being passed between the file server and workstation to be of maximum size.

Consider the following example. A file server is attached to a token ring network supporting 4202-byte packets, and a workstation is attached to an Ethernet network supporting 1500-byte packets. The LIP system will negotiate a packet size of 1500 bytes, which is equal to the smaller, Ethernet packets, to be used between the file server and workstation. The use of LIP greatly reduces the number of packets that need to be sent between computers. This means a smaller load on the file server and less traffic on the network cables. When implementing LIP, a potential problem occurs when a network that uses small packet sizes connects two networks that use a larger packet size. This situation is illustrated in Figure 16-7. Because workstation "N1" and file server "C" are both on token ring networks, they could negotiate a packet size of 4202 bytes. The Ethernet network that is being used as a backbone supports only 1500-byte packets, however, which results in network errors. In this scenario, workstations that need to communicate with the token ring file server need to include the LARGE INTERNET PACKETS=OFF statement in the DOS requester section of their NET.CFG files. This causes the workstation to default to the standard 576-byte packets when communicating with file servers that are not attached to same local network cable. Another solution to this problem could be to move the file server "A" to the Ethernet backbone network, thereby allowing a packet size of 1500 bytes to be negotiated.

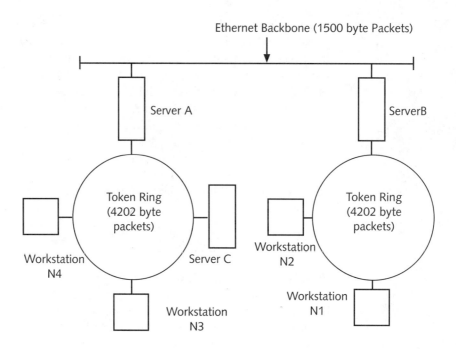

Figure 16-7

Large Internet packets

MAINTAINING FILE SERVER PERFORMANCE

When you assess file server performance, it is important to keep in mind that the main function of a file server is to act as a shared storage device. Getting information to and from the server's disk and the workstation as fast as possible is therefore an important goal of the network administrator managing a local area network. The three main factors in this task are the workstation's configuration, the network cable system, and the performance of the file server. In the previous section, you learned how the NET.CFG file can be used to change workstation configuration settings to enhance processing. This section explains how to monitor the file server environment for possible performance problems and provides solutions to them.

Prior to NetWare v3.1x, a problem faced by many network administrators was properly configuring the file server to make the best use of the server's resources. When Novell developed NetWare v3.x, it provided a solution to this problem and called it dynamic resource allocation. **Dynamic resource allocation** uses artificial intelligence (AI) programming techniques to allow a v3.1x file server to tune and configure itself automatically to best meet the ever-changing processing demands it encounters. Because NLMs also allocate resources on the server, a combination of multiple levels of resource allocation between the NLMs and the operating system can result in degraded performance of the file server. For this reason, an essential element of dynamic resource allocation is the ability to load and unload NLMs. As a CNA, you should be familiar with how to use the MONITOR utility to view your file server's memory usage and be able to use this information to help determine the effects of NLMs on your file server's performance.

In this section you will learn how NetWare v3.1x uses dynamic resource allocation to manage the server's memory. You will learn how to use the MONITOR utility to develop baseline statistics for your file server. You will also see how the MONITOR utility can be used to observe the effects of loading and unloading NLMs. In addition, you will learn how to use several common SET commands to configure your server to meet special network requirements or improve performance by changing certain configuration parameters to more closely match your network baseline information.

MEMORY MANAGEMENT

Over 50% of a file server's memory should be dedicated to the job of moving data from the volumes to the workstations. One of your goals as a network administrator is to optimize the amount of memory available for file caching and to decrease the number of disk read and write requests that the file server must make to provide information to the workstations. Data is stored in the NetWare disk volumes in storage locations called **blocks**. A **buffer**, in contrast, is a location in RAM used to store information read from disk blocks.

A volume's block size is determined when the volume is created and can vary from the default 4 Kbytes to up to 64 Kbytes. Larger block sizes are generally more efficient for processing large graphics-oriented files, one of which can require several Mbytes. Having a larger block size decreases the number of disk read requests necessary to send a large file to a workstation. The disadvantages of large block sizes are the need for file cache buffers for each block and wasted disk space when smaller files are stored.

By default, NetWare buffers are 4 Kbytes, and multiple buffers are assigned to hold larger block sizes. Although the buffer size can be changed by including a SET BUFFER SIZE statement in the STARTUP.NCF file, the buffer size can never be larger than the block size of a volume to be mounted. Allocating a larger buffer size would have very little benefit from a performance standpoint and would have the potential disadvantage of preventing you from mounting volumes having the standard 4-Kbyte block size (possibly the SYS: volume, for example). To improve performance when large files are processed, therefore, leave buffer size at 4 Kbytes even if some of your volumes have larger block sizes.

In order to make the most memory available for file caching and in order to identify performance problems, you need to understand the way the NetWare operating system allocates its memory usage by splitting the server's memory into memory pools and subpools, as shown in Figure 16-8. Because these memory pools are important to understanding how to monitor the server's performance, it is important for a CNA to understand the purpose of each pool and how it can affect memory and performance in the file server computer.

Figure 16-8

NetWare v3.1x
memory pools

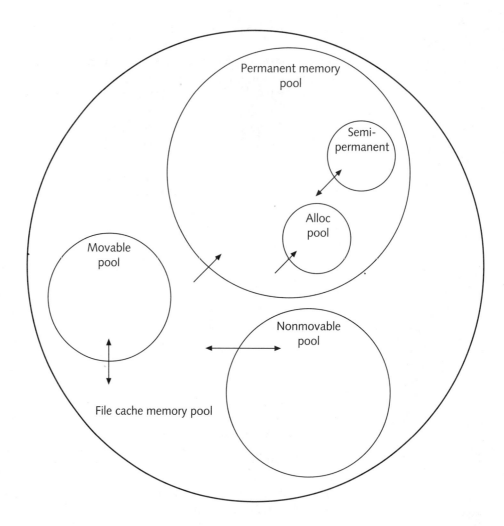

File cache

The **file cache** pool stores the most recently read disk blocks in RAM buffers. This makes access time nearly 100 times faster than rereading the blocks from disk. When the SERVER.EXE program is first loaded, all available memory is placed in the file cache pool. As the server needs memory for other purposes, such as loading NLMs and volume directory tables, memory is taken from this pool and allocated for these needs. To maintain proper performance, Novell recommends that the size of the file cache pool should be at least 50% of the total configured RAM on the file server computer. The file cache pool contains three subpools: permanent, cache movable and cache nonmovable.

Cache movable

The **cache movable** pool is controlled by the NetWare operating system. The size of the tables it contains changes dynamically. It is referred to as the movable pool because the tables can be relocated in memory as necessary to meet the changing size requirements. Memory needed for the tables in the cache movable pool is taken from the main file cache pool and then returned when no longer needed. Tables contained in this pool include directory entry tables, file allocation tables, directory hash tables, transaction tracking system tables, and volume tables. Being able to move these tables in memory allows NetWare to be more efficient by minimizing fragmentation of the file cache buffer allocation.

 A directory hash table acts as an index to speed up—by as much as 30 percent—the process of finding a filename.

Cache nonmovable

The **cache nonmovable** pool stores the program code and fixed data requirements of NetWare Loadable Modules that are currently running in the file server. Memory needed for loading an NLM is initially taken directly from the main file cache pool in a contiguous block of the size required by the NLM software. The block is then returned to the file cache pool when the NLM is unloaded. The cache nonmovable pool is referred to as nonmovable because NLMs cannot be relocated in memory after they have been loaded. The reason for this is that an NLM program initializes specific memory addresses for storage when it is loaded. Moving an NLM to another location after it is running would require re-initialization of these memory addresses.

Because loading an NLM requires a rather large contiguous block of memory to store the NLM code and the fixed data it needs to run, loading and unloading NLMs can cause the memory of the file cache pool to become fragmented. As a result, on a server where NLMs are frequently loaded and unloaded you will sometimes receive an error message indicating that there is not enough memory to run an NLM even though ample memory exists in the file cache pool. The actual problem is one of insufficient contiguous memory availability, and the solution might require downing the file server or possibly unloading other, smaller NLMs and then reloading them after the larger NLM is running.

Permanent memory pool

The **permanent memory pool** is used for long-term memory requests such as the file allocation table and buffers needed for the directory caching and the packet receive buffers used by the data communication subsystem. Memory allocated from file cache for the permanent pool remains in the permanent pool and becomes a source of memory for the semipermanent and alloc short-term subpools. This technique helps to keep the memory in the file cache memory pools from becoming fragmented and therefore harder to allocate in the large contiguous segments needed for NLMs. A possible result of not returning memory to the file cache, however, is that the size of the permanent memory pool can grow beyond its actual needs, making less memory available for file caching and NLM loading. As a CNA, you will need to be able to monitor the size of the permanent memory pool in relation to the actual memory in use. This information is available through the MONITOR utility, described later in this chapter.

Semipermanent subpool

The **semipermanent subpool** is a subdivision of the permanent pool used by NetWare Loadable Modules such as disk and LAN drivers to allocate small memory tables that will be in use for long periods of time. The semipermanent subpool allows the NetWare operating system to reduce memory fragmentation by separating these types of memory needs from the larger tables and buffers found in the permanent pool. When an NLM is unloaded or no longer needs memory allocated to the semipermanent subpool, the available memory is returned to the permanent pool.

Alloc short-term subpool

The **alloc short-term memory subpool** gets its allocated memory from the permanent pool and is used for smaller short-term memory requests that are in a constant state of change. Memory allocated from the permanent pool remains in the alloc pool and is not returned after it is freed up. This allows for alloc memory to be reassigned for other short-term needs without further fragmenting the memory in the permanent pool. The disadvantage of not returning memory to the permanent pool is that the alloc memory pool can become larger than is required, thereby using up memory that would otherwise be available for the permanent or file cache pools. The following are examples of information stored in the alloc memory pool:

- Drive mappings
- Service requests
- Open and locked files
- Router tables
- User connection information
- Messages to be broadcast from the console
- Pop-up menu screens from NLMs
- Print queue management tables

For each drive mapping kept by a workstation, a corresponding entry is kept in the alloc short-term memory, allowing the DOS requester to send a request for data from the mapped directory without including the complete path. Having unnecessary drive mappings in the login scripts can take up valuable file server memory, causing decreased network performance. The CNA should check the size of the alloc pool and, if the server is using too much alloc memory for drive mappings, should attempt to reduce workstation drive mappings to a minimum. In addition, when an NLM that uses pop-up screens to communicate with the console is loaded, it allocates memory in the alloc pool for its screen formats. A possible result of this is alloc memory that is unused after the NLM is unloaded. Because of this, you should avoid unnecessary loading and unloading of NLMs that use many pop-up screens, such as the INSTALL module. If you need to edit the AUTOEXEC.NCF or STARTUP.NCF files, consider using the Supervisor's option of the SYSCON utility or the EDIT NLM rather than loading and unloading the INSTALL module.

NLM management

One of the primary goals of NetWare's memory allocation system is to reduce memory fragmentation while providing the memory resources needed to operate the file server and NetWare Loadable Modules. Reducing memory fragmentation allows the file server to operate more efficiently and provides maximum memory for loading NLMs. Improper loading and unloading of NLMs and the allocation and releasing of temporary memory resources, however, can result in significant memory fragmentation, with the associated reduction in file server performance. One way to improve the performance of a file server that experiences a large amount of dynamic NLM activity is to down the file server periodically in order to release the fragmented memory resources. A preferable solution for most network administrators, however, is to reduce the need to free up fragmented memory resources by proper management of NLM loading.

One rule of loading NLMs is to load permanent NLMs that will stay in memory before loading NLMs that can be unloaded. Examples of permanent NLMs are support programs, such as STREAMS and CLIB, that are needed by other modules and disk drivers and name space NLMs, which are normally loaded from the STARTUP.NCF file when the file server is booted. Examples of NLMs that are often unloaded after use are MONITOR and INSTALL.

Another factor to consider in loading NLMs that are similar in duration of use is the amount of memory the NLM will need to allocate after it is loaded. NLMs that dynamically allocate large resource blocks should be loaded after NLMs requiring smaller memory allocations. Otherwise, NLMs that require large memory allocations will be allocating memory while other NLMs are still being loaded, increasing memory fragmentation.

USING MONITOR

In Chapter 15 you learned how the MONITOR utility can be used to view file server performance and disk and LAN statistics. In addition, MONITOR is an important tool for checking the size of a file server's memory pools and determining resource allocation. In this chapter you will learn how to use the Resource Utilization option of MONITOR to view memory pool usage and determine a file server's baseline performance. The baseline information you develop can help in identifying file server performance problems and in improving the file server's performance by optimizing configuration settings.

Monitoring resource allocation

It is important for a network administrator to periodically check the status of the memory allocation of a file server in order to monitor the server's memory usage and determine if excessive memory has been allocated to any of the memory pools or modules. The ability to track resource allocation and memory usage is provided by the Resource Utilization and System Module Information options on the MONITOR utility's Available Options menu, as shown in Figure 16-9.

Figure 16-9

MONITOR Available Options screen

Resource Utilization. The Resource Utilization option can be used to display the Server Memory Statistics window, shown in Figure 16-10. The first item to observe is the percent of memory available in the cache memory pool (cache buffers). If this percentage is less than 40, your file server's disk performance will be impaired due to the increased need to read information directly from the disk. One of the fastest ways to increase the amount of memory in the cache memory pool is to release memory by unloading unnecessary NLMs. The cache nonmovable memory statistic can help you quickly determine if the server has an excessive number of NLMs loaded by showing you the percent of the server's memory currently in use by NLMs. A percentage over 30 indicates that your server possibly has an excessive amount of its memory locked up by other programs and that you should unload NLMs that are not in use, add memory to the file server computer, or move some of the NLMs, such as the PSERVER.NLM or message handling system, to another file server.

Figure 16-10

MONITOR Resource Utilization screen

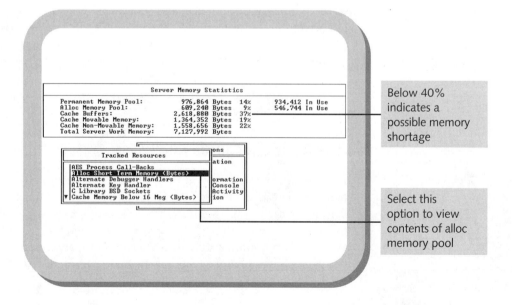

Below 40% indicates a possible memory shortage

Select this option to view contents of alloc memory pool

The statistics in the Permanent Memory Pool and Alloc Memory Pool fields allow you to determine what percent of memory these pools occupy as well as the amount of that memory which is actually used. The number on the far right of the screen indicates the amount of permanent or alloc memory currently in use. If the size of your cache memory pool is less than 40% and the amount of memory allocated to, but not used by, the permanent and alloc memory pools exceeds 5% of the server's total memory, you might want to down the file server in order to restore this memory to the cache memory pool and increase file server performance. In the example shown in Figure 16-10, approximately 100Kbytes of RAM are allocated to the permanent and alloc memory pools but are not being used. In this case, downing the file server and restarting it will make this memory available to the file cache pool thereby helping to improve performance.

Another concern you need to be aware of, especially on heavily used NetWare v3.11 file servers, is the possibility of exceeding the maximum size of the alloc memory pool. On NetWare v3.12 servers, the maximum size of the alloc memory pool is 8 Mbytes, and it is highly unlikely that this maximum size will ever be needed even on heavily used servers. On v3.11 file servers, however, the default maximum size of the alloc memory pool is only 2 Mbytes, which can be exceeded on servers supporting many users and NLMs. If the alloc memory pool reaches its maximum and the NetWare operating system needs more short term memory, the server can crash, with an error message indicating the alloc memory pool is full. To prevent this problem, monitor the size of the alloc memory pool and use the SET command described later in this chapter to increase the maximum size of the pool.

The Tracked Resources menu can be used to view what NLMs and operating system functions are taking up memory in each of the memory pools. If you want to know, for example, what NLMs and operating system tasks are using up the memory in the alloc memory pool, you can select the Alloc Short Term Memory option on the Tracked Resources menu and then press [Enter] to view all functions that are currently using the alloc memory pool, as shown in Figure 16-11.

Figure 16-11

Alloc memory tagged resources

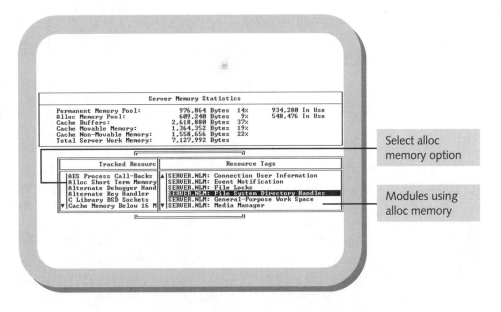

Select alloc memory option

Modules using alloc memory

To view how much of the alloc memory pool is currently used by drive mappings, press the Down Arrow key until you find the SERVER.NLM: File System Directory Handles option in the Resource Tags window. Pressing [Enter] displays the Resource Information window, which shows the amount of memory assigned to the directory handles associated with all the workstation's drive mappings, as shown in Figure 16-12. Use the Esc key to return to the Resource Tags window and either select another resource to monitor or use the Esc key again to return to the Tracked Resources window.

Figure 16-12

Directory Handles Resource Information window

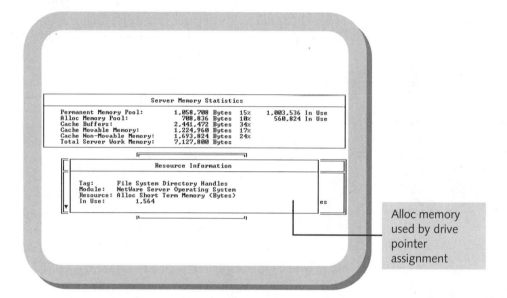

Alloc memory used by drive pointer assignment

System Module Information. If you suspect that a new NLM is allocating an excessive amount of memory, you can use the System Module Information option from Monitor's Available Options menu to select the suspect NLM and then view a list of all memory allocations made by this module. Knowing how much memory is allocated by NLMs can also be used to help you determine an optimum loading sequence (described later in this chapter) in which NLMs requiring the most resource allocations are loaded last.

Suppose, for example, you want to view the amount of resource allocation needed by the PSERVER and MONITOR NLMs in order to help you decide which to load first. You can easily determine the total amount of resource allocation used by both these NLMs. Use the System Module Information option to list all currently loaded modules, as shown in Figure 16-13.

Next, use the Down Arrow key to find the PSERVER module. Press [Enter] to display the module size and resource tag window shown in Figure 16-14. To determine the amount of memory the PSERVER NLM is using in the alloc memory pool, press the Down Arrow key to highlight the "Small memory allocations" field in the Resource Tags window and press [Enter] to display the Resource Information window shown in Figure 16-15.

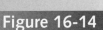

Figure 16-13

System Modules
window

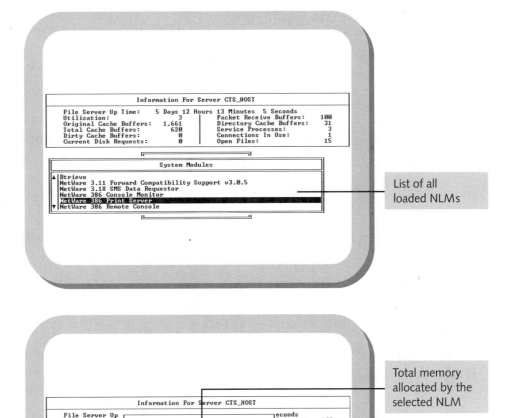

Figure 16-14

PSERVER module
information

Checking the memory resources utilization of a new NLM can help you determine how much memory it is using in each of the memory pools. If the memory use of an NLM seems excessive or is continually increasing, you should unload it and check with the technical support staff of the company supplying the NLM to determine if there are any known problems or new releases.

Figure 16-15

Resource Information
window

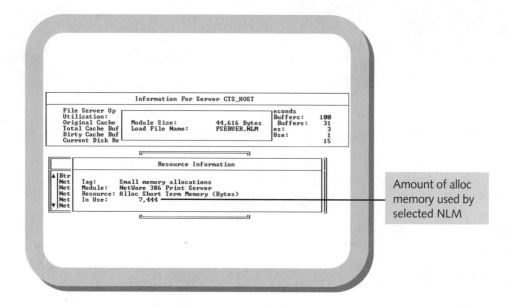

```
                       Information For Server CTS_HOST
┌──────────────────────────────────────────────────────────────────────┐
│  File Server Up                                        econds          │
│  Utilization:        ┌──────────────────────────────┐ Buffers:   100   │
│  Original Cache      │ Module Size:     44,616 Bytes │ Buffers:    31   │
│  Total Cache Buf     │ Load File Name:  PSERVER.NLM   │ es:          3   │
│  Dirty Cache Buf     └──────────────────────────────┘ Use:         1   │
│  Current Disk Re                                                  15   │
└──────────────────────────────────────────────────────────────────────┘
         ┌────────────────────────────────────────────────────┐
         │                  Resource Information               │
┌─┬───┐  ├────────────────────────────────────────────────────┤
│▲│Btr│  │                                                     │
│ │Net│  │  Tag:       Small memory allocations                │
│ │Net│  │  Module:    NetWare 386 Print Server                │
│ │Net│  │  Resource:  Alloc Short Term Memory (Bytes)         │
│ │Net│  │  In Use:        7,444                                │
│▼│Net│  │                                                     │
└─┴───┘  └────────────────────────────────────────────────────┘
```

Amount of alloc
memory used by
selected NLM

Performance factors

There are several interrelated factors that affect a file server's performance and can make the network appear slow to the users. As a CNA, you need to have an understanding of the following performance factors and the basic ways in which they interact to affect server performance:

- Utilization

- Cache memory

- Dirty cache buffers

- Current disk requests

- Packet receive buffers

- Directory cache buffers

- Number of connections

- Permanent memory pool size

With the exception of the permanent memory pool size, all of these statistics are displayed on the main MONITOR window. In this section you will learn more about each of these factors and how they are related to the file server's performance.

Processing workstation requests. In order to better understand the relationship among cache memory, dirty cache buffers, current disk requests, and packet receive buffers you need to understand how a file server processes read and write requests from a workstation. The flowchart in Figure 16-16 shows how a workstation's read request is processed.

Figure 16-16

Path of a
read request

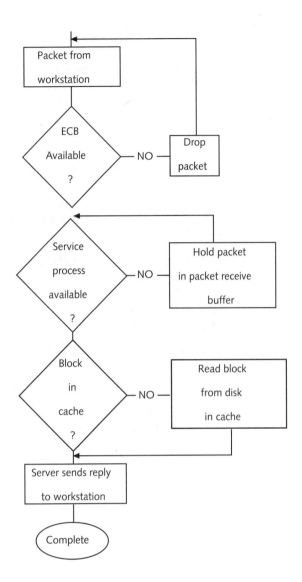

When the request is first received by the file server, the server checks for the availability of packet receive buffers. These are referred to as extended control blocks or ECBs. The No ECB Count for the LAN card is incremented if there are no available packet receive buffers. You can use the LAN Information option of MONITOR to view the number of No ECB Count error messages that have occurred for a network driver.

After the request has been stored in a packet receive buffer (ECB), a determination is made as to where this packet belongs. If the packet belongs to another server, the router function will send the packet out on a different network. If a packet belongs to the current server, it must wait for a file server process to become available before the read request is processed. After checking the FAT table for the correct disk block, the server checks the file cache memory pool for the desired disk block. If the block is stored in a cache buffer, the data is immediately sent to the workstation. If the block is not in the cache memory, the server will issue a read request for the desired block. While this is happening, no other requests can be processed by this service process, causing other requests to be held in the packet receive buffers. As a result, having a large number of blocks in the file server cache memory can really increase the performance of your file server.

A **service process** is a program run by the NetWare operating system that handles a request from a workstation. Because NetWare is a multi-tasking operating system, it can be processing instructions from many programs. By default, a file server can have up to 20 service process events occurring at one time.

As shown in Figure 16-17, write requests are similar to read requests with the exception of dirty cache buffer processing. Like the read request, the write request checks to see if the necessary disk block is in the file cache pool. If it is, it simply updates the data in the buffer and returns an acknowledgment to the workstation. If, within 3.3 seconds, the updated cache buffer has not been written to disk, the server will flag the buffer as "dirty," causing the disk system to write the buffer to a disk block as soon as the disk channel is available.

Utilization.   The utilization percentage displayed on the MONITOR main screen indicates what percent of the time the CPU is actively processing instructions. A utilization percentage of 20 indicates that 80% of the time the CPU is idle or waiting for work. As a rule of thumb, file server utilization should remain under 60% most of the time. If the utilization exceeds 80%, it is an indication that the file server has too many services (NLMs), insufficient memory, or is processing requests from too many users. You can use information from the main MONITOR screen to determine which of these conditions is causing the problem. If the cache memory pool is less than 40% of the server memory, increasing the server's total memory will reduce the server utilization. When cache memory is over 40% but the number of packet receive buffers and number of connections is high, it indicates the server is unable to keep up with the total number of users. As a result, you will probably need to upgrade to a faster server or add another server to the network.

Cache memory.   Having adequate cache memory is perhaps the most important factor affecting file server performance. When cache buffers get too low, the file server is unable to keep frequently accessed blocks in memory, resulting in more disk read requests. This puts more load on the disk channel, which results in a larger number of dirty cache buffers and a backlog of disk requests. Because disk reads are 100 times slower than reading from memory, workstation requests cannot be serviced as quickly, causing an increase in packet receive buffers. More packet receive buffers mean less cache memory, resulting in even more delay. The file server might attempt to correct this problem by allocating more file server processes. This can increase utilization, however, and can possibly result in additional overhead and more memory being allocated from the file cache. The goal is to keep file cache memory above 40% for busy servers by either adding more memory or unloading NLMs.

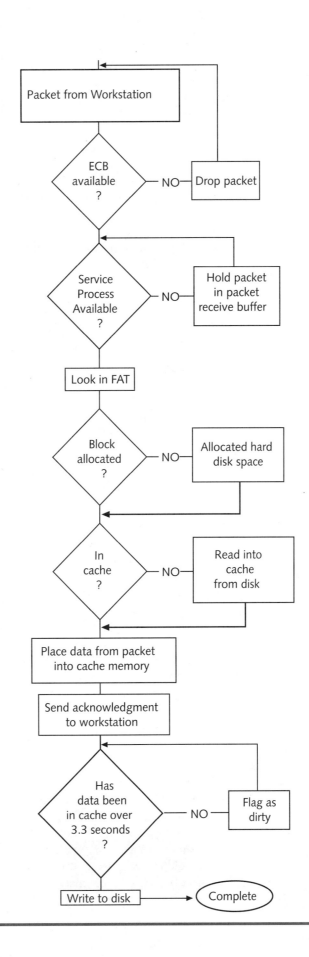

Figure 16-17

Path of a
write request

Dirty cache buffers.   As described previously, when a block is written to the file server from a workstation, it is placed in a file cache buffer. If this buffer is not written to disk within 3.3 seconds, the buffer is flagged dirty and will be written to disk as soon as possible. If the dirty cache buffers exceed 70% of the total cache buffers, or if they consistently show over 50%, it means the disk system is unable to handle the volume of transactions. When utilization is under 60% and the cache memory is over 40% of your file server's total memory, you might be able to relieve this problem by using a SET command to increase the number of concurrent disk writes. In most cases, however, the solution to this problem rests in obtaining a faster disk system—or if you have more than one disk drive on the same controller card, you can add another disk controller card and split the disk drives between the two controllers. This will take some load off any one disk channel, resulting in faster disk access and therefore fewer dirty cache buffers and current disk requests.

 Disk mirroring with two drives on the same controller will increase the number of dirty cache buffers due to the extra time required to write each block twice. Implementing disk duplexing with each drive on a different controller card will decrease the number of dirty cache buffers because a disk write command can be performed simultaneously by both controller cards.

Current disk requests.   The current disk requests statistic shows how many requests for disk reads and writes are currently waiting in the queue. An increase in current disk requests coincides with dirty cache buffers and is normally caused by a slow or overloaded disk system. As described for dirty cache buffers, you might need to add another disk controller to split disk drives or obtain a higher speed disk controller and/or disk drive system.

Packet receive buffers.   By default, a Netware v3.12 server starts with 100 packet receive buffers. When a packet is received from a workstation it is placed in an available packet receive buffer or ECB. If all packet receive buffers are currently being used, the workstation request is dropped, causing the workstation to resubmit the request after the time-out period. If the server continues to lose packets as a result of insufficient packet receive buffers, it will dynamically assign additional buffers up to the default maximum of 400. If you have a large high-speed network with powerful workstations using 80486 or Pentium processors, or if your server does a lot of packet routing between different networks, you might need to consider using the SET command to increase the maximum number of packet receive buffers. (This command is described later in this chapter.) Having an insufficient number of packet receive buffers will greatly reduce the performance of your network by requiring workstations to resubmit packets. The result is an increase in network traffic and the delay time caused by resubmitting the packet.

Another performance factor is the number of the packet receive buffers available when the file server is first started. If your file server consistently needs 300 packet receive buffers, the network will perform more slowly when the file server is first started because of the number of packets lost while the server is determining its optimum number of packet receive buffers. In this situation, you might want to use the SET command to increase the minimum number of packet receive buffers to correspond more closely with your server's normal operating environment. (This command is described later in this chapter.)

Directory cache buffers. To increase the speed of finding the location of a file, the server caches the most commonly used directory buffers. By default, the server initially reserves only 20 cache buffers for the volume directory information. As more requests are made for filenames, the server increases the number, up to a maximum of 500 buffers. If the maximum number of directory cache buffers is reached, additional requests for filenames not in the buffers will require disk reads, resulting in slower performance of the network. This performance reduction is caused by an increase in current disk requests and an overloading of the disk channel, with the corresponding increase in dirty cache buffers and packet receive buffers. On file servers with large-capacity disk drives, a CNA needs to monitor the number of directory cache buffers and use the SET command (described later in this chapter) to increase the maximum number before it reaches the default maximum of 500. In addition if you observe that the server typically needs over 300 directory cache buffers, you can decrease memory fragmentation by using the appropriate SET command to increase the minimum directory cache buffers to correspond more closely to the actual number used in operation.

Number of connections. In addition to informing you how close your file server is to the maximum number of connections your NetWare license will support, the number of connections statistic is important in helping you to interpret other performance factors. For example, if utilization exceeds 70% but there are only 20 connections, you can deduce that file server utilization is mostly consumed by an excess of NLM services. You can unload unnecessary NLMs to improve file server performance.

Building a baseline

In order to recognize potential file server performance problems before they affect network users, you need to determine the normal operating system parameters for a server. You can do this by using the MONITOR utility on a weekly basis to record the file server performance statistics. Figure 16-18 shows sample statistics collected over a four-week period. Record the performance statistics each week for a month. Select a normally busy time period, for example, 10:00 A.M.

To record dirty cache buffers and disk requests, create a directory called TEMP at the root of a volume. If possible, create the TEMP directory on a disk drive other than the one with the SYS: volume. This produces a better indication of your disk system performance by balancing the disk system requests. Next, use the FLAGDIR command to place the Purge attribute on the TEMP directory and then use the COPY command to copy all files from the SYS:PUBLIC directory to TEMP. Placing the Purge attribute on the TEMP directory prevents the files placed in this directory during the test from taking up storage space when they are erased. During the copy process, monitor the dirty cache buffers and disk requests. Record the maximum and mean values. After completing the copy process, delete all the files in the TEMP directory.

After you have recorded the statistics for a month, calculate the average, maximum, and minimum values in each of the performance factors. You can now periodically check the statistics and run the COPY test in order to determine if there are any major changes in file server performance. This method often means a network administrator can make necessary corrections before poor network performance becomes apparent to users.

Figure 16-18

Baseline performance chart

	Date 5 Sept	Date Sept 12	Date Sept 19	Date Sept 26	Date	Ave	Max/Min
Utilization	42	49	53	45		47	53
Cache Buffers	3971	3570	3409	3200			3971/3200
Dirty Cache Buffers	265	170	259	190		221	265/170
Current Disk Requests	25	15	35	30		26	35/15
Packet Receive Buffers	165	200	200	225		197	225/165
Directory Cache Buffers	290	310	305	310		303	310/290
Service Processes	3	4	4	5		4	5/3
Permanent Memory Pool Size	4.1 MB	4.9 MB	5.2 MB	5.5 MB		4.9	5.5/4.1
Permanent Memory Used	3.6 MB	4.2 MB	4.5 MB	4.9 MB		4.3	4.9/3.6
Alloc Memory Pool Size	.8 MB	1.2 MB	1.2 MB	1.2 MB		1.1	1.2/.8
Alloc Memory Used	.7 MB	1.1 MB	.8 MB	.9 MB		.87	1.1/.7

USING SET COMMANDS

As mentioned throughout the chapter, SET commands can be used to help establish maximum and minimum values for variables that affect network performance. In this section you will learn about SET commands that help a CNA maintain efficient file server operations.

Setting maximum packet size

When a workstation is first attached to a file server, the server and workstation negotiate a maximum packet size based on the network or card capacity. By default, NetWare reserves 4202 bytes for each packet receive buffer in order to communicate efficiently on a standard token ring network, which can use up to 4202 byte packets. If, however, a file server is attached to networks that use a smaller packet size, using 4202 bytes per packet receive buffer will unnecessarily use up extra memory on the file server. Suppose, for example, your organization uses an Ethernet network with a packet size of 1514 bytes. By default, the file server will use 4202 bytes for each packet receive buffer. This means that 2688 bytes are wasted in each packet receive buffer. If the file server needs 400 packet receive buffers, the total wasted memory is over 1 Mbyte. To free up the Mbtye of RAM for use by the file cache, you can include the following SET command in the STARTUP.NCF file.

```
SET MAXIMUM PHYSICAL RECEIVE PACKET SIZE=1514
```

If the packet receive buffer size setting is too small for the network, the server will be able to negotiate a packet size only equal to the maximum size of its packet receive buffer. This will result in slower network performance because more packets need to be sent between the server and attached workstations.

Setting packet receive buffers

Packet receive buffers play an important role in file server performance because they provide a holding area for packets that arrive from network workstations. Generally, the more workstations that are communicating with the file server at one time, the more packet receive buffers that need to be assigned. If no packet receive buffer is available for an incoming packet, the packet is rejected and the workstation must retransmit it. The file server is conservative regarding the assignment of new packet receive buffers and only allocates additional packet receive buffers after a number of packets have been rejected. As a result, workstations on a larger network can experience slower network performance when the file server is first booted. Performance should then improve as the file server allocates additional packet receive buffers. If you find that your file server is nearing the default maximum of 400 packet receive buffers, you should place the following SET command in either the STARTUP.NCF or AUTOEXEC.NCF file to increase the number of packet receive buffers by 100:

SET MAXIMUM PACKET RECEIVE BUFFERS=500

The default minimum number of packet receive buffers for NetWare v3.11 is 20. The default packet receive buffers for NetWare v3.12 has been increased to 100. If you find that your file server uses over 100 packet receive buffers during normal operation, you can increase the initial performance of your file server, after it is booted, by including the SET MINIMUM PACKET RECEIVE BUFFERS=n (where n represents the number of packet receive buffers you normally need) in the STARTUP.NCF file. If you use a v3.12 server on a small network with fewer than 20 workstations, you will not need as many packet receive buffers and the default value of 100 on a NetWare v3.12 server can actually be wasting memory. To make more memory available for file caching on a NetWare v3.12 file server, you can include the following statement in the STARTUP.NCF file:

SET MINIMUM PACKET RECEIVE BUFFERS=20

After using the server for several days, you can check the number of packet receive buffers allocated. If a larger number has been allocated, you can increase the minimum to more closely match that number to improve the file server's initial performance.

Setting maximum alloc memory

Because NetWare v3.12 servers allow up to 8 Mbytes of alloc short-term memory, you will rarely, if ever, need to increase the maximum size of the alloc memory pool. If you are using a NetWare v3.11 file server, however, the default maximum of 2 Mbytes might need to be increased on busy servers that have a large amount of RAM. Maximum alloc memory is increased in 1-Mbyte units by placing the following SET command in either the STARTUP.NCF or AUTOEXEC.NCF files:

SET MAXIMUM ALLOC SHORT TERM MEMORY=n

Setting minimum file cache buffers

By default, the minimum file cache buffers with which the server will operate is 20. When the server reaches its minimum number of file cache buffers, it will prevent NLMs from being loaded or the file server from allocating additional memory. Although this can result in the crash of the NLM, it prevents the entire file server from going down. Because most heavily used file servers cannot operate with only 20 cache buffers, you might want to increase this number to equal 5% of the number shown in the Original Cache Buffers field of the MONITOR main window. If the number of original cache buffers is 1661, for example, you can place the following SET command in the AUTOEXEC.NCF file to increase the minimum file cache buffers to 5% of the total:

```
SET MINIMUM FILE CACHE BUFFERS=83
```

Setting concurrent disk writes

Insufficient disk write processes can cause excessive dirty cache buffers when you have a fast disk system because there are not enough disk write processes to keep up with all the requests. By default, NetWare allows up to 50 concurrent disk write processes, but you can use the following SET command to increase the number of disk write processes to 60 in order to decrease the number of dirty cache buffers:

```
SET MAXIMUM CONCURRENT DISK CACHE WRITES=60
```

Setting the immediate purge option

Unless a directory or file is flagged with the Purge attribute, NetWare will keep a deleted file until all file space from previously deleted files has been reused. Even though maintaining salvageable files requires a relatively small amount of processing overhead, it can sometimes slow a server that is short of disk space and has a utilization value of over 50%. If your server's disk space is almost full and performance is slow, you might want to use the following SET command to purge all deleted files immediately. This makes their space available to the server, reducing processing overhead and thereby increasing the server's performance.

```
SET IMMEDIATE PURGE OF DELETED FILES ON
```

Setting directory cache buffers

By default, a NetWare file server starts with only 20 directory cache buffers. As volumes are mounted and new files are opened, additional buffers are added to the directory cache in order to hold the necessary directory information. Storing directory entries in cache memory allows the operating system to find many files without having to read the directory information from the disk. This reduces the number of disk accesses and greatly improves file open speeds. If more than the default 500 directory cache buffers are needed, NetWare will be required to directly read the disk directory table file entries that are not in the directory cache. This can significantly increase file access time and thereby require additional packet receive buffers to store incoming requests. In addition, exceeding the maximum number of directory cache buffers will increase the load on the disk channel, resulting in more dirty cache buffers and current disk requests. Because of this, a CNA should monitor the directory cache buffers and use the following SET command to increase the maximum number if directory cache buffers nears 500:

```
SET MAXIMUM DIRECTORY CACHE BUFFERS=600
```

In addition to increasing the maximum directory cache buffers, increasing the number of buffers allocated to the directory cache when the server is booted can increase performance by reducing the overhead necessary to allocate additional buffers as well as decreasing memory fragmentation. If your server typically needs 300 directory cache buffers, for example, you might want to place the following command in the AUTOEXEC.NCF file to set the minimum number of directory cache buffers to 300:

```
SET MINIMUM DIRECTORY CACHE BUFFERS=300
```

Setting service processes

When a request from a workstation arrives at the file server, it is stored in a packet receive buffer until a service process is available to handle it. When more requests are received than can be processed, NetWare adds additional packet receive buffers. NetWare also increases the number of file server processes, up to a default maximum of 20. As more requests come in, the server attempts to balance the number of packet receive buffers dynamically with the number of service processes to reach an efficient balance. Adding additional service processes is like running more programs concurrently on your workstation. If the processor is powerful enough, it will be able to support running more programs simultaneously, thereby increasing the amount of work it can do.

If you have a heavily loaded network with more than 100 high-speed workstations and a file server that has over 24 Mbytes of RAM with a high-speed processor, such as a 90-MHz Pentium, you might find that the following SET command increases the maximum number of service processes when your current number has reached the maximum and your utilization is under 50%:

```
SET MAXIMUM SERVICE PROCESSES=30
```

Increasing the number of service processes will work in this case because your server computer has the memory and processing speed to support additional service processes without bogging down the system.

Packet signature

By default, the file server uses packet signature level 1, as shown in Figure 16-19, to enable the packet signature only when requested by the client workstation. After the file server is booted, you can use the SET NCP PACKET SIGNATURE OPTION command to increase the packet signature security level but not to decrease it. On a server that contains sensitive information or on a server attached to a large internet, increasing the packet signature level can be desirable to prevent possible unauthorized access from a workstation creating packets that mimic the connection information of another user. If you want to increase the packet signature level to 2 each time the server is started, for example, insert the following SET command in the AUTOEXEC.NCF file:

```
SET NCP PACKET SIGNATURE OPTION=2
```

Figure 16-19

File server packet
signature levels

Signature Level	Description
0	Server does not sign packets (same as v3.11 server).
1	Server signs only if client requests signature.
2	Server signs if client is capable of signing.
3	Server always signs and requires all clients to sign (Workstations running NETX will not be able to log in when level 3 is set.)

University students in Europe performed an experiment showing that an unauthorized workstation could perform Supervisor functions while the supervisor was logged in. They obtained the connection number of the supervisor's workstation and then created packets using the supervisor's workstation connection number. The file server performed the functions because it assumed the packets were from the supervisor's workstation. Although there are no reports that actual intruders have used this technique, the packet signature was designed to close this potential security loophole.

OTHER NETWARE V3.1X CONSIDERATIONS

In response to the rapid growth of the use and size of networks, Novell has included additional features in the NetWare v3.12 operating system and has developed NetWare v4.1 and a DOS VLM requester that can reduce the processing load on file servers as well as reduce traffic on the network. To take advantage of these new features as well as improve compatibility with local workstation operating systems and NetWare v4.1, you should convert workstations that still use the older NETX shell program to the new VLMs as soon as possible. Before converting all your client workstations to the VLM requester, however, make sure to obtain the latest version of the VLM software. Then test the application software you will need to run on a workstation using the VLM environment before committing to the conversion. There are reports of some application software packages that do not run correctly when the VLM requester is used.

The need to integrate servers into larger networks and the ability to administer NetWare servers centrally from a Windows environment will greatly increase the number of NetWare 4.1-based file servers installed on networks.

Properly maintained, NetWare v3.1x servers can continue to provide good performance for small to midsized networks having fewer than 100 users and one or two file servers based on 80386 and 80486 processors. As networks begin to implement more multimedia and image-processing applications that are spread across multiple servers, however, the need for expanded services and more centralized network administration places a strain on the capacity of the NetWare v3.1x architecture. In response, Novell has provided an upgrade path from earlier NetWare environments to the more powerful and flexible NetWare v4.1 operating system.

Although NetWare v4.1 is a more sophisticated network operating system, designed to provide solutions for large networks based on multiple servers that span wide area networks, NetWare v3.1x servers will continue to be an important part of networks. In addition, with NetWare v4.1 it is now easier to integrate NetWare v3.1x servers and NetWare v4.x servers on the same network, making it feasible for organizations to continue to use their existing servers and take advantage of NetWare v4.1 features. As a NetWare CNA, your skills in maintaining and managing the v3.1x file servers will continue to be an important asset in administering NetWare-based networks and in upgrading existing NetWare v3.1x servers to NetWare v4.1.

Chapter Summary

The job security of a network administrator rests more in his or her ability to upgrade and maintain a network than in its initial setup. Due to the rapidly changing nature of computers and the dynamic nature of network technology, the need to continually monitor and upgrade the network hardware and software will make the successful CNA a very valuable asset to any organization.

With continual changes in workstation hardware and application software, one of the challenges a network administrator faces is providing the latest software upgrades and making necessary changes to workstation configurations in order to provide efficient network performance. New software upgrades for both server and client are often obtained through Novell's NetWire forum, available on Compuserve. After the desired software components are downloaded, the WSUPDATE program can be used to copy newer versions of the client software automatically to each workstation that contains older copies of the program files.

In addition to containing the network card driver configuration and VLM modules to be loaded, the NET.CFG file can contain a number of other statements that are used to modify the workstation's network environment. Some of the following common NET.CFG statements are described in this chapter:

- The FRAME statement, which sets the frame types used by the LAN driver of a workstation.

- The CACHE BUFFERS statement, used to cache disk blocks from sequentially accessed disk files in the workstation's memory.

- The CONNECTIONS statement, which can be used if the workstation must be connected to more than eight file servers.

- The FIRST NETWORK DRIVE pointer, which normally makes F the first network drive.

- The LOCAL PRINTERS statement, which can be used to set a local printer to zero. This prevents the workstation from crashing when a Print Scrn key is pressed without a CAPTURE command in use.

- The MAX TASKS statement, used to allow a multitasking operating system, such as Microsoft Windows, to have multiple applications running concurrently.

- The PREFERRED SERVER statement, used to specify a server to which the workstation will connect when it is first booted.

- The PRINT HEADER and PRINT TAIL statements, which can be needed if a printer requires an especially long escape code sequence to set up a printing configuration.

- The SIGNATURE LEVEL statement, which sets the level of packet security in order to prevent other workstations from forging packets.

Once the file server is up and running, the CNA needs to know how to monitor its performance and establish a baseline against which to predict performance bottlenecks and justify additional memory or faster disk systems. In order to monitor server performance, it is necessary to understand how the file server allocates memory using the file cache and permanent memory pools. The file cache memory pool is further divided into the movable cache and nonmovable cache pools. The movable cache pool contains large tables that need to change size dynamically, such as the directory entry table. The nonmovable pool is used to load NLMs. The permanent memory pool is subdivided into the semipermanent pool, for large memory allocations that are likely to be returned to the permanent pool, and the alloc pool, used for small short-term memory allocations needed by NLMs and other operating system tasks such as drive mappings and routing information. Memory pools are necessary because they allow a file server's memory to be allocated for a variety of purposes with a minimum of memory fragmentation.

Fragmentation is the condition of breaking up a large block of memory by inserting a small table in the middle of the block. When this happens, software that needs to allocate large contiguous blocks of memory, such as NLMs, are unable to run, forcing you to down the server in order to free up the needed memory. Proper loading and unloading of NLMs along with using the MONITOR program to monitor the memory pool usage can allow the network administrator to avoid unnecessary downing of a server in order to free up extra memory.

Server operation and performance can sometimes be enhanced by the use of SET commands. With them you can configure a number of different settings, including maximum and minimum packet size, the maximum size of the alloc memory pool, the number of concurrent disk write processes and file server services, and the maximum and minimum size of the directory cache buffers. Although the NetWare file server is designed to perform its own dynamic resource configuration, knowing how to use the MONITOR program to observe the file server's performance and configuration and how to use the SET commands can allow you to increase the performance of the server when it is first booted and reduce the chances of the file server crashing or slowing down because it has exceeded a maximum configuration setting.

Proper management and configuration of NetWare v3.1x file servers and workstations is becoming more important as network applications become more sophisticated and widespread. Although Novell v4.x has provided a powerful and flexible new platform to meet current and future network needs, NetWare v3.1x continues to play an important role in the majority of LANs, making it necessary for CNAs to be proficient in managing and maintaining NetWare v3.1x file servers.

COMMAND SUMMARY

Command	Syntax	Definition
MONITOR	*MONITOR*	A NetWare Loadable Module that is run on the file server and enables the network administrator to monitor the network information. Can be used to monitor CPU and memory utilization, the number of directory and packet receive buffers, and disk system LAN card usage.
SET	*SET [statement]*	A console command that allows configuration of many settings that affect the file server's environment. SET commands include the following: SET MAXIMUM PACKET RECEIVE BUFFERS SET MINIMUM PACKET RECEIVE BUFFERS SET MAXIMUM ALLOC SHORT-TERM MEMORY SET MINIMUM FILE CACHE BUFFERS SET MAXIMUM CONCURRENT DISK CACHE WRITES SET IMMEDIATE PURGE OF DELETED FILES SET MAXIMUM DIRECTORY CACHE BUFFERS SET MAXIMUM PHYSICAL RECEIVE PACKET SIZE SET MAXIMUM SERVICE PROCESSORS SET MINIMUM DIRECTORY CACHE BUFFERS SET NCP PACKET SIGNATURE OPTION
WSUPDATE	*WSUPDATE [source_path\filename] [target_drive:filename] [/options]*	The WSUPDATE program compares the date of the file specified in the source path to the date of the target file. It copies the source file to the target file if the source file has a more recent date.

The *target drive* field can contain only a local drive letter followed by the name of the file. No directory path is allowed in the target field. Options include the following:

/F=[path]filename	Use this option if the commands containing the location of the source and target files to be updated are going to come from the specified filename. The format of each command must be the same as if it were being entered in the WSUPDATE command. An exception is that paths are allowed in the target file specifications.
/C	By default, the WSUPDATE program prompts the operator to select whether an existing file should be overwritten or renamed. Including the /C option in a command statement causes the old file to be overwritten automatically by the newer file.
/R	Including the /R flag in a command statement causes the old file to be renamed with the extension .OLD.
/S	Include the /S option if you want the WSUPDATE program to search all subdirectories of the target drive and update all occurrences of the specified filename.
/L=[path]filename	The /L flag allows you to specify a file to be used to contain a log showing the username, date, and network address of each workstation that has run the WSUPDATE program.
/O	The /O option allows the WSUPDATE program to write over old files even if they are flagged Read Only.

KEY TERMS

alloc short-term memory subpool	**dynamic resource allocation**	**permanent memory pool**
block	**extended control block (ECB)**	**semipermanent subpool**
buffer		
cache movable	**file cache**	**service process**
cache nonmovable	**packet burst protocol**	**sliding window**

REVIEW QUESTIONS

1. The _____ program can be used from either the login script or DOS command line to update files on the client workstation.

2. On the line below, write a login script command that automatically searches the root drive of a workstation's C drive to update all older versions of the file LSL.COM with the latest version of the file stored in the SYS:PUBLIC\NEWFILE directory. The command will automatically replace the older copy of the driver on the workstation even if the current file is flagged Read Only.

   _____

3. On the line below, write a command to update all the programs identified in a text file named NEWVER.DOC located in the SYS:PUBLIC\CLIENT directory and create a log file named UPDATE.LOG containing a list of all workstations that have been updated.

   _____

4. On the lines below, list two sections of the NET.CFG file.

   _____

   _____

5. On the line below, write the NET.CFG section in which you would place the FRAME statement.

   _____

6. On the line below, write a FRAME statement to use an Ethernet frame type that will support TCP/IP packets.

   _____

7. On the line below, write a NET.CFG statement to disable the packet burst feature on a workstation.

   _____

8. Assume you are getting network errors when accessing a file server located on a network separated from your workstation by two intermediate networks. On the line below, write a NET.CFG statement that you could use to be sure your workstation is using a packet size that can be handled by all intermediate networks.

   _____

9. On the line below, write the NET.CFG section in which you would place the statement to use a smaller internet packet size.

   _____

10. The _____ NET.CFG statement can increase performance on workstations that process large nonshared files.

11. Currently certain special print jobs are producing incorrect printer actions. Although many control codes are used, after checking the print functions and modes, you can find nothing wrong with the escape code sequence. On the line below, write the setting in the NET.CFG file that can be used to affect this type of network printing problem.

   _____

12. On the line below, write a NET.CFG statement that will reduce overhead at the workstation by removing the need for the workstation to place a signature on each packet.

_____

13. Data is stored on NetWare volumes in physical storage areas called

_____ .

14. A(n) _____ is a storage location in RAM used to hold disk information.

15. Which of the following is an invalid volume block size.

    a. 4 Kbytes

    b. 8 Kbytes

    c. 12 Kbytes

    d. 16 Kbytes

    e. 64 Kbytes

16. Over _____ percent of a file server's memory should be dedicated to caching data from the disk volumes.

17. The _____ memory pool contains tables, the size of which changes dynamically.

18. The _____ memory pool takes memory from file cache but does not return it.

19. The _____ memory pool is used to store NLMs.

20. The _____ memory pool is used to allocate memory for drive pointers and NLM pop-up screens.

21. Assume you have 60% of your server's memory for file cache buffers and its utilization is only 50%. Network performance seems slow, however, and there are over 300 packet receive buffers and over 50% of the file cache buffers are flagged as dirty cache buffers. In the space below, explain the most likely problem.

22. Your packet receive buffers are normally between 250 and 300. On the line below, write a SET command that will help improve the server's performance when it is first booted.

_____

23. On the line below, write a SET command that might help improve the problem described in question 21.

_____

24. Assume that, when using MONITOR, you discover that the dirty cache buffers on your server are over 70% of the total cache buffers. On the line below, write a command that you can place in your STARTUP.NCF file to improve this condition.

_____

25. Suppose that, when using the MONITOR utility, you notice that the directory cache buffers are normally above 200 on your file server. In addition, when the file server is normally first started on Monday mornings, users often complain about slower network performance. On the line below, write a SET command that you can place in the STARTUP.NCF file to improve file server performance when the server first starts.

EXERCISES

Exercise 16-1: Using NET.CFG

Assume that you are setting up a new workstation that has a hardware configuration that is the same as that of your current computer. You want to create a NET.CFG file that includes your workstation settings in addition to meeting some additional requirements.

Part 1: Documenting your workstation NET.CFG file settings

Refer to the current NET.CFG file on your workstation for the following information:

1. Link driver section heading:

2. Network card I/O port address:

3. Network card interrupt:

4. Current frame type:

5. DOS requester section heading:

6. First network drive:

Part 2: Writing NET.CFG statements

For each of the following requirements, write a NET.CFG statement and identify an advantage of including it in the NET.CFG file:

1. Add a frame type of Ethernet_802.3:

   Advantage:

2. Attach to the server CTI_HOST:

_____

Advantage:

3. Change the first network drive to L:

_____

Advantage:

4. Disable the large internet packet feature:

_____

Advantage:

5. Disable packet burst mode:

_____

Advantage:

6. Double the number of Cache Buffers:

_____

Advantage:

Part 3: Writing a NET.CFG file

Write a NET.CFG file that includes all the statements from Part 1 and Part 2.

Part 4: Testing the NET.CFG file

1. Create a directory on the C drive named TEMP.

2. Copy all the *.HLP files from the SYS:PUBLIC directory to your local C drive TEMP directory.

3. On the line below, record the number of seconds required to perform this operation.

   _____

4. Rename the NET.CFG file on your workstation to NET.OLD.

5. Use the DOS EDIT command to enter the NET.CFG file you developed in Part 3.

6. Boot your workstation and test the NET.CFG file by logging in to the file server.

7. Drive to log in from:

   _____

8. Copy all the *.HLP files from the SYS:PUBLIC directory to your local C drive TEMP directory.

9. On the line below, record the number of seconds required to perform this operation.

   _____

10. Did you notice a performance difference between Step 3 and Step 9?

    Yes or No

11. Which step had the best performance?

    _____

12. Rename your NET.CFG to NET.TST and then rename NET.OLD to NET.CFG.

Exercise 16-2: Using MONITOR

1. Use the MONITOR utility on your classroom file server to record the baseline information in the following chart in Figure 16-20.

Figure 16-20

File Server
Performance
Baseline Chart

File Server

Performance Baseline Chart

Server Name: _____

	Date	Date	Date	Date	Date	Average	Maximum/ Minimum
Utilization							
Cache Buffers							
Dirty Cache Buffers							
Current Disk Requests							
Packet Receive Buffers							
Directory Cache Buffers							
Service Processes							
Permanent Memory Pool Size							
Permanent Memory Used							
Alloc Memory Pool Size							
Alloc Memory Used							

2. Perform the following test to check the performance of the file server disk system. To perform this test you will need to work with another student. One of you will view the monitor screen while the other performs the following steps:

   a. If you do not have a TEMP directory in your ##ADMIN home directory, create one at this time.

   b. Flag the TEMP directory with the Purge attribute.

   c. Change to the TEMP directory.

   d. Station one person at the MONITOR screen to record disk statistics in the second column of the baseline form while the other enters the following commands:

   `NCOPY SYS:PUBLIC\*.HLP`

   `DEL*.*`

   e. Record any observations or unexpected results below.

Exercise 16-3: Memory Pools

Because this exercise requires downing the file server in order to free up the permanent memory pools, you should perform this exercise on the "installation" file server unless your instructor has made other provisions for doing this exercise on the classroom server.

1. In the chart below, record current memory pool statistics.

	Bytes	%	Bytes	
Permanent memory pool:				in use
Alloc memory pool:				in use
Cache buffers:				
Cache movable memory:				
Cache nonmovable memory:				

2. Down the server and restart it.

3. In the chart below, record the current memory pool statistics.

	Bytes	%	Bytes	
Permanent memory pool:				in use
Alloc memory pool:				in use
Cache buffers:				
Cache movable memory:				
Cache nonmovable memory:				

4. Load the BTRIEVE, REMOTE, and RSPX modules.

5. Load the INSTALL Module and open several windows to view volumes, disk partitions, the AUTOEXEC.NCF and STARTUP.NCF files.

6. In the chart below, record the following statistics:

	Bytes	%	Bytes	
Permanent memory pool:				in use
Alloc memory pool:				in use
Cache buffers:				
Cache movable memory:				
Cache nonmovable memory:				

7. In the space below, describe the reason for changes in the memory statistics.

8. In the space below, describe the reason for alloc memory pool size increase.

9. In the space below, describe the reason for cache buffer decrease.

10. In the space below, describe the reason for increase in cache nonmovable memory.

11. Use the appropriate option of MONITOR to determine the amount of memory used by the BTRIEVE, REMOTE, and INSTALL modules. Record the module sizes below.

    BTRIEVE module size: _____

    REMOTE module size: _____

    INSTALL module size: _____

12. On the line below, record the amount of alloc memory in use by the INSTALL NLM.

    _____

13. Unload the modules from Step 4 in reverse order.

14. In the chart below, record the following memory statistics.

	Bytes	%	Bytes	
Permanent memory pool:				in use
Alloc memory pool:				in use
Cache buffers:				
Cache movable memory:				
Cache nonmovable memory:				

15. Describe the reasons for the changes in the following memory usage:

    Unused space in the alloc memory pool:

    _____

    Unused space in the permanent memory pool:

    _____

    Decrease in cache buffers:

    _____

Exercise 16-4: Memory Pool Usage

In this exercise you will need to be able to have access to the MONITOR utility on the classroom file server console to record the following memory statistics.

1. In the chart below, record the following main MONITOR screen information.

Utilization:	Packet Receive Buffers:
Original Cache Buffers:	Directory Cache Buffers:
Total Cache Buffers:	Service Processes:
Dirty Cache Buffers:	Connections in Use:
Current Disk Requests:	Open Files:

2. In the space below, indicate any areas of possible performance weakness.

3. In the chart below, record the following resource utilization information.

	Bytes	%	Bytes	
Permanent memory pool:				in use
Alloc memory pool:				in use
Cache buffers:				
Cache movable memory:				
Cache nonmovable memory:				

4. In the space below, indicate if there are any areas of possible memory usage concern.

5. Use the Resource Tags to determine the amount of alloc memory in use by drive pointers. Record the information below.

6. Use the appropriate options to determine the amount of memory in use by the file allocation table. On the lines below, record the options you use and the size of the server's FAT.

Step 1:

_____

Step 2:

_____

Step 3:

_____

FAT size: _____

EXERCISES

Case 16-1: Workstation Configuration

As a contractor for NASA, Universal Aerospace is involved with designing components for an upcoming space station project. As a part of the engineering team, Stacy Prassas is responsible for developing public relations and advertising material by combining material from the CAD files with the desktop publishing software. Stacy's new workstation needs to support a multitasking operating system performing up to 30 different concurrent processes. This workstation will need to be able to communicate with both a NetWare file server and Unix host over an Ethernet network using both 802.2 and Ethernet_SNAP frame types. Because this workstation will be used for high-resolution graphic files and multimedia software, many of the files accessed will be large graphic documents. The security needs of the workstation are minimal, and its performance should be maximized by reducing unnecessary packet security overhead. The workstation will have no local printer attached and all output will be sent to the networked PostScript laser printer.

1. Write a NET.CFG file based on the network card hardware settings of your current workstation.

2. Print the contents of your current NET.CFG file by first changing to the directory containing the NET.CFG file and then using the command TYPE NET.CFG>PRN to obtain a hardcopy.

3. On the printout obtained from Step 2, record the new statements you plan to add to the NET.CFG file for optimum configuration of Stacy's workstation.

4. Rename the current NET.CFG file NETCFG.BAK.

5. Use a text editor, such as the DOS EDIT command, to create a new NET.CFG file containing the necessary commands from the original file along with the additional statements you recorded in Step 3.

6. Test the new NET.CFG file by booting the workstation and logging in to the classroom file server.

7. Obtain a hardcopy of the revised NET.CFG file on the classroom network printer.

8. Use the ENDCAP command to end the capture of LPT1 to the classroom printer.

9. Try using the Print Scrn key. Record the results in the space below.

10. Keep your finalized NET.CFG printout for your instructor.

Case 16-2: Determining Performance Problems

The Silent Sports company specializes in the sale of nonmotorized sporting equipment such as mountain bikes, windsurfers, diving supplies, and cross-country skiing equipment. The company's business office and all of its checkout stations are attached to a NetWare file server. Recently users have experienced slow performance and have called your service company to see if you can determine the problem. You visit the store and obtain the following MONITOR screen. From the information provided by this screen, identify possible problems and solutions.

Utilization:	60%	Packet Receive Buffers:	400
Original Cache Buffers:	2198	Directory Cache Buffers:	25
Total Cache Buffers:	1200	Service Processes:	5
Dirty Cache Buffers:	800	Connections in Use:	48
Current Disk Requests:	55	Open Files:	90

Problem:

Possible solutions:

Case 16-3: Performance Problems

As the network administrator for Bruce High School, you have recently been approached by several staff members who are concerned about a slowdown in network performance. To help identify the problem, you have obtained the following printouts from the MONITOR program. Using this information, determine possible problems and your recommended solutions.

Utilization:	65%	Packet Receive Buffers:	350
Original Cache Buffers:	3500	Directory Cache Buffers:	50
Total Cache Buffers:	901	Service Processes:	9
Dirty Cache Buffers:	200	Connections in Use:	50
Current Disk Requests:	30	Open Files:	70

	Bytes		Bytes	
Permanent memory pool:	1,698,000		1,700,000	in use
Alloc memory pool:	2,500,000		900,000	in use
Cache buffers:	3,686,000			
Cache movable memory:	2,220,000			
Cache nonmovable memory:	4,200,000			

Problem:

Possible solutions:

Case 16-4: Writing SET Commands

Tom Rizzo, the manager of the Master Builders company, has recently contacted you regarding the performance of the company's new Pentium-based file server. Tom claims that the file server seems sluggish when it is first brought up on Monday morning, not unlike the way he feels. In addition, during the middle of the day, when his sales staff are trying to work with the graphics documents, the server again seems to slow down, as if it is sleeping. Because the server is running on a new, fast computer, Tom would like you to see if you can determine if there are any software or configuration problems.

Part 1: Identifying performance bottlenecks

1. You first use the MONITOR utility to display the main window statistics, recorded in the following chart.

Utilization:	65%	Packet Receive Buffers:	400
Original Cache Buffers:	5000	Directory Cache Buffers:	300
Total Cache Buffers:	3500	Service Processes:	20
Dirty Cache Buffers:	2200	Connections in Use:	100
Current Disk Requests:	50	Open Files:	150

2. Using this information, you decide that the file server's initial performance can be improved by implementing the following SET commands.

_____

_____

3. In addition, by comparing the Dirty Cache Buffers statistic with the percent of file server utilization, you determine that the performance of the disk system can be improved by implementing the following SET command.

_____

4. You also notice a large number of packet receive buffers. You decide to use the following SET command to provide additional packet receive buffers.

_____

5. Finally, you realize that the server's ability to handle more requests can be improved by using the following SET command.

_____

Part 2: Implementing configuration changes

For this part of the case study, your instructor needs to provide you with access to the "installation" file server so that you can update the STARTUP.NCF and AUTOEXEC.NCF files and be able to down and restart the server without affecting other students.

1. Using the "installation" file server, modify the STARTUP.NCF and AUTOEXEC.NCF files to contain the SET commands you identified in Steps 2 through 5 in Part 1.

2. Down the "installation" file server and restart it using the new SET commands.

3. Use the MONITOR utility to verify the results of changing the file server configuration parameters. Record the results you observe below.

SUPERIOR TECHNICAL COLLEGE PROBLEM

Now that school has started and the campus network is operational, your job has settled down to supporting the college's network processing needs, which include managing network performance, working with users to find solutions to problems, installing new hardware and software, and upgrading existing software with new versions.

Project 16-1: Updating Workstation Files

Dave Johnson would like to have you implement a method of updating the minicomputer communication software that he originally installed on all the staff workstations last September. He has recently received new versions of the software and would like you to implement NetWare's WSUPDATE program to check the workstation communication files each time a user logs in and then update the communication software if it is older than the new release. To test the upgrade process, Dave has provided you with old and new versions of the communication software.

Test the upgrade process on your computer by following the steps described below:

1. Create a directory on your workstation named COMMTEST.

2. Copy all files from the OLDCOMM directory of your student work disk into the COMMTEST directory.

3. Flag the files Read Only.

4. Obtain a listing of all the files in the NEWCOMM directory of your student work disk.

5. Create a directory in your Superior Technical College campus structure in which you plan to place new versions of the software.

6. Copy the files from the NEWCOMM directory on your student work disk into the directory you created in Step 5.

7. On the lines below, write the WSUPDATE commands that will automatically replace all the old versions of the communication software files. Remember that some of these files might be flagged Read Only.

    _____

    _____

    _____

    _____

8. Use a text editor or the DOS EDIT command to create a WSUPDATE command file containing the commands you wrote down in Step 7.

9. Test the WSUPDATE program from the DOS prompt. On the line below, enter the command you use.

    _____

10. Obtain a printout of the WSUPDATE command file.

11. Modify the system login script you created in the SCRIPTS directory in Chapter 11 to run the WSUPDATE program automatically when any of your users log in to the file server. Include the option to create a log file in the NEWCOMM directory containing an audit trail of all users who have run the WSUPDATE program.

12. Restore the old files to the COMMTEST directory on your local workstation.

    a. Remove the Read Only attributes from the new files.

    b. Erase all existing files from the COMMTEST directory.

    c. Copy all files from the OLDCOMM directory of your student work disk to TESTCOMM.

13. Obtain a directory listing of the current workstation's COMMTEST directory.

14. Test the WSUPDATE command by logging in as one of your users. The WSUPDATE program should run, updating the old version of the file.

15. Obtain a printout of your COMMTEST directory.

16. Obtain a printout of your COMMTEST directory and updated login script.

17. Place your name on the printouts and organize them so they can be checked by your instructor.

GLOSSARY

10BASE2 A linear-bus implementation of Ethernet using coaxial cable with T-connectors to attach networked computers. A terminator is used at each of the coaxial cable wire segment.

10BASET A popular implementation of Ethernet using twisted-pair wires to connect all stations to a central concentrator.

A

access arm A device used on disk drives to position the recording heads over the desired disk track.

access control A NetWare trustee right that allows a user to assign rights to other users.

access rights Access rights control what disk functions a user can perform in a directory or file. Access rights include: Read, File scan, Write, Create, Erase, Modify, Access control, and Supervisory.

access time The time required for a storage device to locate and transfer a block of data into RAM.

active hub A central hub device used on ARC-NET networks to regenerate signals and send them up to 2,000 feet to another hub or computer.

address A number used to identify the location of data within the computer system.

address bus The number of bits that are sent from the CPU to the memory indicating the memory byte to be accessed. The size of the address bus determines the amount of memory that can be directly accessed. The 20-bit address bus used on the 8088 computer limited it to 1 Mbyte. The 24-bit address bus used on 80286 and 80386SX computers provides for up to 16 Mbytes. The 32-bit address bus used on 80386DX and above computers can access up to 2 Gbytes of memory.

AI Artificial Intelligence. A software program design that is able to make decisions and learn from experience with techniques similar to those used by the human brain.

alloc memory A subdivision of the Permanent memory pool used to store short-term memory allocations from NLMs and operating system tables containing such information-drive mappings and router locations.

analog signals Signals that use a wave form to vary smoothly from one state to another.

ANSI American National Standards Institute

application layer The top software layer of the OSI model that interacts with the user in order to perform a communication process on a network.

application-oriented structure A directory structure that groups directories and subdirectories according to application or use rather than by department or owner.

archive needed A file attribute set by the computer whenever the contents of a file have changed.

ARCnet A star-bus network topology that uses a special packet called a token that is passed from computer to computer allowing only one computer to transmit at any one time.

ASCII American Standard Code for Information Interchange. An American National Standards Institute (ANSI) standard which has a separate 7 bit code for all characters on the keyboard.

asynchronous communication A form of communication where each byte is encapsulated with start and stop bits and then sent separately across the transmission media.

asynchronous link A NetWare remote console environment where the computer acting as the remote console is connected to the file server using a serial port and modem.

attribute options Attributes are used to make files hidden, sharable, and read-only.

attributes Flags that are used by NetWare to determine what type of processing can be performed on files and directories.

File Attributes: Archive Needed, Copy inhibit, Delete inhibit, eXecute only, Purge, Read Only, Read Write, Rename inhibit, Sharable, Hidden, System, and Transactional.

Directory Attributes: Delete inhibit, Rename inhibit, Purge, Rename inhibit, Hidden, and System.

B

backbone network A network cable system that is used to connect file servers and host computer systems. Each file server or host may then contain a separate network card that attaches it to client computers.

bandwidth A measurement of the range of signals that can be sent across a communications system.

baseband A digital signaling system that consists of only two signals representing one and zero.

baud rate A measurement of the number of signal changes per second.

bindery The NetWare files that contain security information such as usenames, passwords, and account restrictions. The bindery files are stored in the SYS:SYSTEM directory and consist of NET$OBJ.SYS, NET$PROP.SYS, and NET$VAL.SYS.

binding The process of attaching a network protocol stack—such as IPX—to a network card.

blind carbon copy A copy of an e-mail message that is sent to another user whose name is not listed on the message's list of users receiving a carbon copy.

block A collection of data records that can be read or written from the computer RAM to a storage device at one time. A block may also refer to a storage location on the physical disk volume consisting of 4K, 8K, 16K, 32K, or 64K

block suballocation A method that allows data from more than one file to be placed in a single data block.

bounded media Media that confines a signal within a cable.

bridge A device used to connect networks of similiar topology. Operates at the data link layer.

broadband A signaling system that uses analog signals to carry data across the media.

buffer A storage location in memory used to hold blocks of data from disk in order to reduce the number of disk accesses needed to process a request.

bus mastering A technique used by certain high-speed adapter cards to transfer data directly into a computer's RAM.

byte A group of eight bits used to store one character of data.

byte stream option A NetWare printing option that sends data directly to a printer without expanding any tab codes.

C

cable system The physical wire system used to connect computers in a local area network.

cache A memory area used to temporarily hold data from lower-speed storage devices in order to provide better access time.

cache movable A subdivision of the File Cache pool used to store tables whose size changes dynamically.

cache non-movable A subdivision of the File Cache pool used to store NetWare Loadable Modules.

carbon copy A copy of an e-mail message that is sent to another user whose name is included on the message's list of users receiving a carbon copy.

carrier sense multiple access with collision detection (CSMA/CD) A channel access control method used on Ethernet networks where a computer waits for the media to have an open carrier signal before attempting to transmit. Collisions occur when two or more devices sense an open carrier and attempt to transmit at the same instant.

centralized processing A processing method where program execution takes place on a central host computer rather than at a user workstation.

CGA Color Graphics Adapter used on early PC-based computers that allowed up to four colors to be displayed using a resolution of 320 x 200 pixels.

channel access method A method of controlling when a device can transmit data over a local area network. Common access methods include token-ring and CSMA/CD.

child Refers to a specific subordinate of a data set such as a file or program.

child VLM A software module used on NetWare client workstations to perform a specific function.

client server A type of network operating system where certain computers are dedicated to performing server functions while other computers called clients run application software for users.

client workstation A networked computer that runs user application software and is able to request data from a file server.

clock A device in the system unit of a computer that sends out a fixed number of pulses or signals per second. The clock pulses are used to synchronize actions in the system unit. The clock speed is measured in millions of cycles per second called megahertz or MHz. The faster the clock speed, the more work a given system unit can do per second.

CMOS memory Complementary Metal Oxide Semiconductor memory that is capable of holding data with very little power requirements. This type of memory is used to store configuration data that is backed up by a battery on the motherboard. The battery prevents CMOS from being erased when power is turned off.

coaxial cable A thick plastic cable containing a center conductor and shield.

collision An event that occurs when two or more nodes attempt to transmit on the network at the same time. After the collision, the nodes wait a random time interval before retrying.

command line utility (CLU) A NetWare utility that performs a specific function from the DOS prompt given specific command line parameters. Examples are NDIR, NCOPY, and MAP.

command queuing A method of storing commands for future processing.

comment character A character used by the NetWare FirstMail system to preceed each line of an original message that has been included in a reply.

compiler A program that converts source commands to a form that is executable by the computer system.

complete directory path Identifies the location of a file or directory by specifying file server name\volume:directory\subdirectory.

computer aided design (CAD) A software application that uses computers to perform complex drafting and design applications.

concentrator A central hub device used to connect 10BASET computers together to form a network.

conditional variables Login script variables that have a value of "True" or "False".

connect time The length of time a user workstation has been logged in to a network file server.

console commands Commands that affect the file server and are issued from the file server console. Examples include CONFIG, LOAD and DOWN.

console operator A username that has been assigned the privilege of running the FCONSOLE program. Console operators are assigned using the Supervisor Options of SYSCON.

control commands Used to tell the NetWare NMENU program how to perform actions such as running a DOS command or starting an application.

controller cards Adapter cards used to control storage devices such as disk drives.

conventional memory The first 640K of memory used by DOS to run application programs.

copy inhibit A NetWare file attribute that prevents Macintosh computers from accessing certain PC file types.

CPU The Central Processing Unit of a computer that controls all activity in a computer system by following instructions in a program.

create A NetWare access right that allows a user to create new files and subdirectories.

cycle The time it takes a signal to return to its starting state.

cyclic redundancy check (CRC) An error checking system that allows a receiving computer to determine if a block of data was received correctly by applying a formula to the data and checking the results against the value supplied by the sending computer.

cylinder The number of disk tracks that can be accessed without moving the access arm of the hard drive mechanism.

D

data bus The "highway" that leads from a device to the CPU. Computers based on 80286 and 80386SX have 16-bit data bus architecture compared to 32 bits on the 80386DX and 80486 computer models.

data link layer The OSI software layer that controls access to the network card.

datagram The name of an information packet at the network layer.

date variables Login script variables that contain date information such as month, name, day of week, and year.

default directory The directory from which data will be accessed when no path is supplied.

default login script The default login script consists of commands stored in the LOGIN.EXE program which are executed when a user does not have a personal user login script file.

delete inhibit A NetWare attribute that prevents a file or directory from being removed.

departmental structure A directory structure that groups directories and subdirectories according to the workgroup or department that uses or controls them.

device driver A software program that controls physical access to an external device such as a network card or storage drive.

differential backup A backup of all files changed since the last "full" backup. When performing a differential backup, the SBACKUP program will backup all files that have the Archive attribute turned on, but will not reset the Archive attribute, making it easier to restore all data after a disaster.

digital signals Signals that can have only a value of zero or one.

direct link A NetWare remote console environment where the computer acting as the remote console is connected to the file server using the LAN cable system.

directory entry table (DET) A table on a storage device that contains the names and locations of all files.

directory hashing A method of improving access time by indexing entries in the directory entry table.

directory path A list which includes the names of directories and subdirectories identifying the location of data on a storage device.

directory trustee A user or group that has been granted access rights to a directory.

disk activity charge A NetWare accounting method used to measure the amount of disk activity by user.

disk duplexing A method of synchronizing data on storage devices attached to different controller cards.

disk storage A storage system that uses magnetic disks to allow direct storage and retrieval of data blocks.

dismounting A method of taking a disk volume off-line in order to perform system functions.

distributed processing A processing method where application software is executed on the client workstations.

distribution list A named group of e-mail users that allows a message to be automatically sent to all users included in the specified distribution list without naming each individual user.

DMA channel A Direct Memory Access device used to transfer data between RAM and an external device without taking time from the processor.

dot pitch A measurement of the spacing between color spots on video monitors. A smaller dot pitch provides sharper images.

downing The process of taking a file server off-line.

DRAM A common form of dynamic memory chip, used in computer RAM, that requires a refresh cycle to retain data contents.

drive pointer A drive pointer is a letter of the alphabet that is used to reference storage areas in the file system.

dynamic resource allocation A method of balancing resource allocation on the file server using AI programming techniques in order to provide maximum performance in a continually changing environment.

E

e-mail address Each user of the MHS system must have a unique address composed of the user's name and workgroup. For example, Mary Read's user address could be "MREAD@PCSOLUTION" where MREAD is Mary's username and "PCSOLUTION" is the organization's workgroup name.

ECB On a NetWare file server, an Extended Control Block is equivalent to a packet receive buffer.

effective rights A subset of the access rights that control which disk processing a user can perform on a specific directory or file. Effective rights consist of a combination of rights the user has as a member of a group along with the trustee rights granted to the username of the user.

EGA Enhanced Graphics Adapters provide up to 16 colors and 640 x 480 resolution.

EISA bus Enhanced Industry Standard Architecture bus that supports both ISA cards along with high-speed 32-bit cards for increased performance.

electromagnetic interference (EMI) An undersirable electronic noise created on a wire cable when it runs close to a strong power source or magnetic field.

elevator seeking A technique used in NetWare file servers to increase disk access performance by smoothly moving an access arm across a hard disk surface to read and write the requested data blocks in the sequence they are encountered rather than in the sequence received.

EMS Memory placed on a separate expansion card that requires special software called an Expanded Memory System to swap information or program instructions stored on this card into page frames located within the upper memory area.

enhanced IDE A disk drive system that improves on the standard IDE system by supporting up to four disk drives, higher-drive capacities, and faster performance.

erase A NetWare access right that allows the user to delete files and remove subdirectories when assigned to a directory.

error checking and correcting (ECC) memory A type of RAM that can automatically recognize and correct memory errors.

ethernet A network system that uses a coaxial bus cable system along with the Carrier Sense Multiple Access with Collision Detection (CSMA/CD) access method to connect networked computers.

execute only A NetWare file attribute that may be used with executable (.COM and .EXE) program files to prevent the files from being copied while still allowing users to run them.

expanded memory Memory located on a separate expansion card that is accessed by dividing it into pages and then swapping the pages in and out of page frames located within the upper-memory area.

expansion bus The connection sockets on a computer's system board that allows adapter cards to be plugged into the computer.

extended memory Memory above one Mbyte. This memory requires special software to access it.

F

fault tolerance A measurement of how well a system can continue to operate despite the failure of certain hardware components.

fetching The process of loading instructions into the CPU from RAM.

fiber optic cable A cable made of light conducting glass fibers which allows high-speed communications.

file allocation table (FAT) A table stored on a disk that is used to link together the storage blocks belonging to each file.

file attribute A flag used by NetWare to determine what type of processing can be performed on the file.

file cache A memory pool used to store the most frequently used disk blocks.

file caching A method used by a NetWare file server to increase performance by storing the most frequently accessed file blocks in RAM.

file scan A NetWare access right that allows the user to view file and directory names.

file server name A unique name assigned to each file server during installation.

file system security A security system that prevents unauthorized users from accessing or modifying file data.

file trustee A user or group that has been granted access rights to a file.

folder In FirstMail, a folder is a file located in the user's mail directory that is used to store messages after they have been read.

frame The name of an information packet at the data link layer.

full backup Causes all files to be copied to the backup media and their Archive attributes to be reset.

G

general-purpose application An application package such as word processing or spreadsheets that is used to perform many different functions.

global search directory A directory in which all users have been given rights to run programs or read files.

global shared directory A directory in which all users in an organization may store and retrieve files.

H

hidden A NetWare file or directory attribute used to prevent a file or directory from appearing on directory listings.

home directory A private directory where a user typically stores personal files and works on projects that are not shared with other users.

hop The transition of a NetWare packet across a router.

host server When using SMS, the host file server is the server that contains the backup tape drive and backs up data from other computers called "target" devices.

hot-swapping A fault tolerant system that allows a disk drive to be replaced without shutting down the computer system.

hub A central connection device in which each cable of a star topology network is connected together.

I

IDE controller cards A disk controller card used to connect up to two Intelligent Drive Electronics disk drives.

identifier variables Login script variables that may be used in login script commands to represent such information as the user login name, date, time, and DOS version.

incremental backup Backs up only files that have been changed (the Archive attribute is on) and then resets the archive attribute on all files that are backed up.

indexed A NetWare file attribute used to provide better performance with large database files by creating an index containing all FAT table entries for the file.

infrared An unbounded media system that uses infrared light to transmit information. Commonly used on television remote control devices and small wireless LANs.

inherited rights Inherited rights are rights that flow down into a directory or file from a higher level directory. For example, if a user is granted the R F W rights to the DATA:SALES directory, they will also inherit the R F W rights into the DATA:SALES\ORDERS and DATA:SALES\USERS subdirectories.

inherited rights mask Each file and directory contains an Inherited Rights Mask that controls what access rights can flow down to the file or subdirectory from the higher-level directory.

input/output (I/O) port An interface used to transfer data and commands to and from external devices.

Institute of Electrical and Electronic Engineers (IEEE) An organization that has established standards for LAN topologies.

instruction set The set of binary command codes a CPU chip can recognize and execute.

internal network number A network address used internally by NetWare to communicate with its software components.

internal router A file server that is also acting as a router by connecting two or more network cable systems.

International Standards Organization (ISO) The group responsible for administering the OSI model.

internet An information highway that is not controlled by any single organization and is used worldwide to connect business, government, education, and private users.

internetwork One or more network cable systems connected together by bridges or routers.

interoperability The ability of computers on different networks to communicate.

interrupt request (IRQ) A signal that is sent from an external device to notify the CPU that it needs attention.

ISA bus Industry Standard Architecture bus that supports 16-bit data and 24-bit address buses at 8MH clock speed. This bus was developed for the IBM AT computer in 1984, and is still popular. However, when using it with high-speed processors, it greatly reduces the performance of expansion cards.

K

KB Kilo Byte or 1024 bytes.

L

landscape Landscape printing is when each line printed on a standard paper sheet can be up to 11 inches wide.

linear bus A LAN topology that consists of a coaxial cable segment that connects computers by running from one machine to the next with a terminating resistor on each end of the cable segment.

local area network (LAN) A high-speed, limited distance communication system designed to support distributed processing.

local bus A high-speed expansion bus that allows adapter cards to operate close to the speed of the interal system board.

local drive pointers Drive pointers (normally A: through E:) that are used to reference local devices on the workstation such as floppy and hard disk drives.

local printer When used in context to network printing, a local printer is used to refer to a network printer that is attached directly to a port of the print server computer. When used in context of a workstation, a local printer is the printer attached directly to a port on the workstation.

local shared directory A directory in which all users of a department or workgroup may store and retrieve files.

login script A set of NetWare commands that are performed each time a user logs into the file server.

login script variable A reserved word that may be used to substitute values into login script statements in order to modify processing.

login security A security system that employs usernames, passwords, and account restrictions to prevent unauthorized users from accessing a file server.

long username The long username is the component of the user's mail address that uniquely identifies a MHS user within a workgroup. The combination of username and workgroup name cannot exceed 253 characters.

M

machine language A program consisting of binary codes that the CPU can directly interpret and execute.

math coprocessor An extension of the CPU that allows it to directly perform mathematical functions and floating point arithmetic.

media The device or material used to record and retrieve data.

megahertz (Mhz) A million cycles per second.

memory buffers Computer memory used to temporarily store data being transferred to and from external devices.

menu utility An interactive NetWare utility that uses menus and windows to prompt users for input and display messages. Examples include FILER, SALVAGE, and SESSION.

message packet A packet containing data that is being sent via the network from one user to another.

MHS The Message Handling Service (MHS) is Novell's standard message delivery system which allows MHS-compatible applications to send messages between users. Basic MHS will only deliver messages to users on one server while Global MHS delivers messages between servers connected by routes or Wide Area Networks.

Micro Channel bus A system board design patented by IBM that allows for 32-bit expansion cards along with automatic card configuration.

microprocessor unit The Central Processing Unit of a microcomputer system.

mirroring A disk fault tolerence system that synchronizes data on two drives that are attached to a single controller card.

mission-critical application An application that is necessary to perform the day-to-day functions of a business or an organization.

modify A NetWare access right that allows a user to change file and directory attributes as well as rename files and subdirectories.

motherboard The main system board that ties together the CPU, memory, and expansion slots.

mounting a volume The process of loading the File Allocation Table and Directory Entry Table of a volume into memory. A volume must be mounted before it can be accessed on a network.

multiple file server network A network with more than one file server attached.

multiple station access unit (MSAU) A central hub device used to connect IBM token ring network systems.

multiplexer VLM A NetWare client module that controls one or more child VLM.

N

nesting A programming technique involving placing one IF statement inside another so that the second IF statement is executed only when the first IF statement is true.

NET$PRN.DAT The printer database stored in the SYS:PUBLIC directory which contains print devices, functions, modes, and forms. The NET$PRN.DAT database is maintained by the PRINTDEF menu utility.

NetBEUI network address A network address used by Microsoft products such as Windows for Workgroups and Windows 95.

NetWare Control File A NetWare Control File is similar to a DOS batch file in that it contains console commands and programs that will be executed by the operating system.

NetWare Loadable Module (NLM) A program that may be loaded and run on the file server. There are four types of NetWare Loadable Modules identified by their three letter extension. The filename extension NLM is used for general purpose programs, DSK for disk drivers, LAN for network card drivers, and NAM for name space support modules.

NetWare Loadable Modules (NLM) Software programs and modules that are run at the file server.

network drive pointers Network drive pointers are letters that are assigned to locations on the file server and controlled by NetWare, normally F: through Z:.

Network Driver Interface Specifications (NDIS) A set of standard specifications developed by Microsoft to allow network card suppliers to interface their network cards with the Microsoft Windows operating system.

network file server A computer dedicated to performing file and print services on a network.

network interface card (NIC) An adapter card that attaches a computer system to the physical network cable system.

network layer An OSI software layer that is responsible for routing packets between different networks.

network layout The physical topology of the network cable system.

network media The method used to carry electronic signals from one computer to another.

network operating system (NOS) The software used to provide services to client workstations.

network topology The physical geometry or layout of the network cable system. Common topologies include ring, bus, and star.

network variables Login script variables that contain the workstation's network and node address information.

non-dedicated A computer that can be used for multiple purposes. A non-dedicated file server can also be used as a client workstation.

NuBus An expansion slot used on Macintosh computers to allow adapter cards to be plugged into the system board.

null modem cable A cable used to directly connect the serial ports of two computers without the use of a modem.

nybble Half of a byte or four bits.

O

open data interface (ODI) A set of standard specifications developed by Novell to allow network card suppliers to interface their network cards with multiple protocols including the IPX protocol used with the NetWare operating system.

open systems inter-connect (OSI) model A model for developing network systems consisting of the following 7 layers: Application, Presentation, Session, Transport, Network, Data link, and Physical.

organizational commands Used in the NetWare NMENU system to establish the content and organ-ization of the menus the user sees on the screen.

P

packet A group of consecutive bits sent from one computer to another over a network.

packet burst mode A packet transmission technique used by the VLM shell to provide faster communication by acknowledging a group of packets from the server rather than acknowledging each packet separately.

packet signature A security technique used by the VLM shell that places a unique packet signature on each packet, making it possible for NetWare to be sure the packet came from an authorized workstation.

parallel port A communications interface that transfers eight or more bits of information at one time.

parent Refers to a data set such as a directory or subdirectory.

partial directory path Identifies the location of a file or directory by specifing all directories and sub-directories starting from the user's current default directory location.

partitioning A method of allocating storage space on a disk drive to an operating system.

passive hub A signal splitting device that is used to connect up to 4 nodes together. The nodes may be workstations or active hubs. Maximum distance between a passive hub and a node is 100 feet.

patch cable A cable segment used to connect a network card to the main cable system.

patch panel A panel that consists of a connector for each cable segment that is used to connect the desired cable segments together using a central hub.

PCI bus A high-speed expansion bus developed by Intel for use in Pentium based computer systems.

peer-to-peer A network system in which each computer can act as both a server and client.

peripherals External devices such as printers, monitors, and disk drives.

permanent memory A memory pool which uses memory from the File Cache to store long-term requests such as the File Allocation Table (FAT) and directory cache buffers.

physical layer The lowest layer of the OSI model consisting of the cable system and connectors.

portrait Portrait printing prints on a standard sheet of paper with each line being a maximum of $8\frac{1}{2}$ inches wide.

presentation layer The OSI layer that is reponsible for the translation and encoding of data to be transferred over a network system.

print job Print jobs are items in a print queue just as files are items in a directory. . Print jobs contain data and printing parameters in a format that can be sent by a print server to a printer.

print queue A holding area where print jobs are kept until the printer is available to print them. In NetWare a print queue is a subdirectory of the SYS:SYSTEM directory. Each print queue subdirectory is assigned a unique eight-digit hexadecimal name that may be obtained from PCONSOLE using the "Print Queue Id" option.

print queue operator A username that has been assigned the privilege of managing print jobs in one or more print queues. Print queue operators are assigned to print queues using the PCONSOLE utility discussed in chapter 10.

print server The software component of the network printing environment that makes printing happen by taking jobs from a print queue and sending them to a printer. In NetWare a print server can support up to 16 printers.

print server operator A username that has been assigned the privilege of managing one or more network printers. Print server operators are assigned to print servers using the PCONSOLE utility.

PRINTCON.DAT The file located in each user's SYS:MAIL\userid subdirectory which contains print job information maintained by the PRINTCON menu utility.

printer definition file (PDF) PDF files contain print device information including functions and modes that can be imported into the NET$PRN.DAT database by the PRINTDEF menu utility.

printer function A specific escape code sequence that causes the printer to perform one specific operation such as setting land-scape mode.

printer mode A printer mode is a configuration setting for a printer that consists of one or more functions.

protected mode The mode used by 80286 and above processor chips that allows access to up to 16 Mbytes of memory and the ability to run multiple programs in memory without one program conflicting with another.

protocol stack The software used to send and receive packets among networked computers.

purge A NetWare file or directory attribute that specifies the storage space of a file that is to be immediately made available for reuse by the server.

R

RAID A Redundant Array of Inexpensive Disks that provides fault tolerance by duplicating data across multiple disk drives.

RAM Random Access Memory. The main work memory of the computer that is used to store program instructions and data currently being processed. The contents of RAM are erased when a computer's power is interrupted or switched off.

RAM shadowing A method of increasing computer system performance by copying instructions from slower ROM to high speed RAM.

read A NetWare access right that allows a user to open and read data from a file or run programs.

read only A NetWare file attribute that prevents data in a file from being erased or changed.

read write A NetWare file attribute that allows data in a file to be modified or appended to.

real mode The processing mode used by 8088 computers.

real time program A program that provides users with data reflecting actual conditions at that moment.

redundant link A NetWare remote console environment where the computer acting as the remote console can be connected to the file server using either the LAN cable system or through a modem attached to the serial port.

register A storage location inside the microprocessor unit.

regular drive pointer A network drive pointer that is normally assigned to a file storage directory on the file server.

remote printer A printer attached to a port of a networked workstation and controlled by the print server. In NetWare, remote printing is done by running the RPRINTER software on each workstation that supports a network printer.

rename inhibit A NetWare file or directory attribute that prevents changing the name of the file or directory.

repeater A network device that allows multiple network cable segments to be connected.

resolution A measurement of the number of bits on a display screen. Higher resolution provides better screen images.

ring topology A topology where the cable runs to each computer and then back to the first, forming a circle.

RISC A Reduced Instruction Set Computer provides high performance for CAD workstations and scientific applications by using a simplified and highly efficient set of instructions that lends itself to parallel processing.

RMF The Remote Management Facility (RMF) is included with NetWare v3.12 and above to provide the ability to access file server consoles from either a workstation attached to the LAN or through an asynchronous communication link.

ROM Read Only Memory. Memory that is set at a computer's factory and cannot be erased. ROM is used to store startup and hardware control instructions for your computer.

root drive pointer A regular drive pointer that appears to DOS and application software as if it were the beginning or "root" of a drive or volume.

rotational delay The time required for a disk sector to make a complete circle and arrive at the disk drive's read/write head.

router A device used to connect more complex networks consisting of different topologies. Router's operate at the Network layer.

router information packet (RIP) A special packet that is sent from a file server and includes the names of each network it has registered along with the number of hops and ticks needed to reach each of the networks.

router tables A table of information kept by each file server that identifies each network that it can access along with information regarding the number of hops and ticks necessary to reach that network.

RS232 A serial communication standard developed by the Electronics Industry Association that specifies which voltage levels and functions to be used with the 24-pin interface.

S

SAP Service Advertising Packets (SAPs) are broadcast from each server on the network and identify the server's name and network location. SAPs are used to create and maintain entries in the router tables.

SCSI The Small Computer System Interface is a general purpose controller card that can be used to attach disk drives, CD-ROMs, tape drives, and other external devices to a computer system.

SCSI-2 An advanced version of the SCSI controller specification that allows for higher speed and more device types.

search drive pointer A network drive pointer that has been added to the DOS path. Search drives are usually assigned to directories containing software to make the software available to run from any other location.

sector A physical recording area on a disk recording track. Each recording track is divided into multiple recording sectors in order to provide direct access to data blocks.

seek time A measurement of the amount of time required to move the recording head to the specified disk track or cylinder.

segment The name of an information packet at the Transport layer.

semi-permanent memory A subdivision of the Permanent pool used to store long-term memory requests from NLMs such as LAN and disk drivers.

serial port A communication port that sends one bit of data per time interval.

service request A packet for a client workstation that requires the file server to perform some task.

session layer The OSI software layer that establishes and maintains a communication session with the host computer.

sharable A NetWare file attribute that allows multiple users to access or update data in a file at the same time.

short username The short username is generated from the long username and is needed to provide compatibility with older MHS-compatible applications. Short usernames are limited to eight characters and can include numbers, letters, hyphens (-), dollar signs ($), and number signs (#).

single in-line memory module (SIMM) A memory circuit that consists of multiple chips and provides the system board with memory expansion capabilities.

SMS The Storage Management System (SMS) consists of several NLMs along with workstation software that enables the host computer to backup data from one or more target devices by using the SBACKUP NLM.

sort options Provides the user with the ability to sequence information in multiple orders.

source menu file A NetWare NMENU component that contains the menu commands in ASCII text format. A source menu file must be compiled before it can be used by the NMENU software.

spanning A technique available with NetWare v3.1x that allows a volume to be expanded by adding space from up to 32 disk drives.

SRAM Static RAM provides high-speed memory that can operate at CPU speeds without the use of wait states. SRAM chips are often used on high-speed computers in order to increase system preformance by storing the most frequently used memory bytes.

star network topology A cable system where the cables radiate out from central hubs or stars.

startup file A file used to initially boot a computer system. Startup files on a NetWare file server include STARTUP.NCF and AUTOEXEC.NCF.

supervisor equivalent A username that has been assigned the same privileges as the user designated as SUPERVISOR.

supervisor utility A command line or menu utility that is normally stored in the SYS:SYSTEM directory and requires supervisor privileges to run.

supervisory A NetWare access right that provides a user with all rights to an entire directory structure. Once assigned, the supervisory right cannot be restricted at lower subdirectory or file levels.

SVGA Super VGA provides higher resolution and additional color combinations if the necessary software drivers have been loaded.

switching power supply A power supply used with most computers that will cut off power in the event of an electrical problem.

synchrononous communication system A serial communication system that sends data in blocks or packets where each packet includes necessary control and error checking bits.

syntax The rules of a programming language.

system board The main motherboard of a computer system that contains the CPU, memory, and expansion bus.

system login script A file that contains login script commands that are executed first by all users when they log in to a file server. System login script commands are stored in the NET$LOG.DAT file located in the SYS:PUBLIC directory.

T

target machine A machine that has data which needs to be backed up by the host computer.

target server A target server is a file server whose data is being backed up by a host server.

TCP/IP TCP/IP stands for Transmission Control Protocol/Internet Protocol, and it is the most common communication protocol used to connect heterogeneous computers over both local and wide area networks. In addition to being used on the Internet, the Unix operating system uses TCP/IP to communicate between host computers and file servers.

text option A printer option that automatically expands tab codes to multiple spaces before sending the text to the printer.

thinnet A Ethernet network system that uses T-connectors to attach networked computers to the RG-58 coaxial cable system.

tick A time measurement representing $\frac{1}{18}$ of a second.

time variables Login script variables that contain system time information such as hour, minute, and A.M./P.M.

token A special packet that is sent from one computer to the next in order to control which computer can transmit when using a token passing channel access method.

token passing method A channel access method that requires a computer to obtain the token packet before transmitting data on the network cable system.

topology The geometry of a network cable system.

tracks Circular recording areas on a disk surface.

Transaction Tracking System (TTS) A NetWare fault tolerence system that returns database records to their original value if a client computer system fails while processing a transaction.

transactional A NetWare file attribute that enables Transaction Tracking on a database file.

transfer time The time required to transfer a block of data to or from a disk sector.

transport layer The OSI layer responsible for reliable delivery of a packet to the receiving computer by requiring some sort of acknowledgement.

TTL A 5-volt transistor-to-transistor logic system used for high-speed transfer of ones and zeros between devices on the computer's system board.

tunneling A technique of placing an IPX packet inside a TCP/IP packet in order to allow the IPX packet to be sent across a wide area TCP/IP-based network.

turn key system A computer system that has been designed to automatically provide the user with prompts and menu choices that allow them to easily do their job.

twisted-pair wire Cable consisting of pairs of wires twisted together to reduce errors.

U

unbounded media Signals that are sent through the air or space.

uninterruptible power system (UPS) A battery backup power system that can continue to supply power to a computer for a limited time in the event of a commercial power failure.

upper memory The memory above 640K used by controller cards as well as by DOS when loading device drivers into high-memory.

user account manager A username that has been assigned one or more user account or group to manage. User account managers are assigned users or groups by using the "Managed users and groups" options of SYSCON's User Information window.

user login script Specialized commands that are executed after the system login script by only a single user. User login script commands are stored in the LOGIN file located in the SYS:MAIL\userid directory.

user templates In the USERDEF utility, a template consists of a set of user standard parameters such as home directory and group membership that may be assigned to each new user that is created.

user variables Login script variables that contain information about the currently logged in user, such as the user's login name, full name, or user id.

V

vertical application A software application that is designed for a specific type of processing. Vertical applications are often unique to a certain type of business such as a dental billing system or an auto parts inventory system.

VGA The variable graphics array is a standard video circuit used in many convential PCs that provides up to 640 x 320 resolution and up to 256 different colors.

virtual memory Allows the computer system to use its disk drive as if it were RAM by swapping between disk and memory.

virtual real mode An instruction mode available in 80386 and above microprocessors that allows access to 2 Gbytes of memory and concurrent DOS programs running at the same time.

volume The major division of the NetWare file system consisting of the physical storage space on one or more hard drive or CD-ROM of a file server. A volume can span up to 32 disk segments with a maximum capacity of 32 terabytes. Up to 64 volumes can exist on a file server.

W

wait state A clock cycle in which the CPU does no processing. This allows the slower DRAM memory chips to respond to requests from the CPU.

word size The number of bits in the microprocessor's registers.

workgroup manager A username that has the privilege of creating new users and groups and being an account manager of the users created. Workgroup managers are assigned by using the Supervisor Options of SYSCON.

workgroup name A component of the e-mail address that identifies the name of the organization or department of a user to which the MHS system belongs. The length of the workgroup name plus the username cannot exceed 253 characters. All users of the Basic MHS system must belong to the same workgroup.

workstation variables Login script variables that contain information about the workstation's environment such as machine type, operating system, operating system version, and station node address.

write A NetWare access right that allows a user to change or add data to a file.

INDEX